The Contemporary

THE SOCIAL

SCIENCES

IN HISTORICAL

PERSPECTIVE

World

THOMAS N. BONNER

University of Omaha

DUANE W. HILL

Montana State College

GEORGE L. WILBER

Mississippi State College

PRENTICE-HALL, INC., ENGLEWOOD CLIFFS, N. J.

1960

Preface

THE CONTEMPORARY WORLD

THE SOCIAL SCIENCES IN HISTORICAL PERSPECTIVE

Bonner, Hill, and Wilber

Library of Congress Catalog Card No.: 60-8504

Printed in the United States of America • 17137 C

Designed by Walter Behnke

Each of us

faces the vexing problem of interpreting the social world around us. There seems to be agreement that we should become more aware of the basic social, economic, and political institutions of our own and other societies, and that we should be introduced to more of the "problems" which confront us as a nation. There is further agreement that we should know something of the formation of personality and how it is affected by our social, cultural, and physical environment. But there is little agreement on how these objectives are best realized or whether there are further topics that might contribute to a better understanding of our contemporary social universe. Should international tensions be included in a book covering the social sciences, for example, and if so how can they be related to other topics? Does history contribute to our understanding of the contemporary social world, and if so, how can historical materials be presented in a study focused on modern society? To raise these questions is to suggest at the same time why high-school and college courses in social science offer such great diversity in organization and content.

The authors believe that a meaningful organization of social science topics will not be achieved by a cafeteria-like piling up of new topics onto a tray that is already overloaded. For this reason they have not been satisfied in their own teaching with books which comprise only a series of readings or a collection of chapters written by specialists. The present book reflects their conviction that social science materials can be made most meaningful when they are organized around central themes which cut across the boundaries between academic disciplines and explore some of the dynamic forces responsible for surface tensions and problems. This has meant sacrificing some topics which are sometimes dealt with in the omnibus-type course in social science, but it has also meant a closer integration of the topics that are included. More important, it has made possible the inclusion of a historical perspective and an analysis of international tensions, both vital to a better understanding of the kind of social world in which we live.

These, then, have been our objectives:

1. *To find integrating themes underlying the tensions and "problems" of the contemporary world.* These we have postulated as: (a) divided personal loyalties, (b) industrialism, (c) urbanism, (d) bureaucratic organization, and (e) international rivalry.

2. *To give an historical perspective to the study of contemporary society.*

3. *To provide the student with maximum aid in "getting" the main ideas of the book.* To this end we have consciously avoided technical jargon, aimed at a simple style and colorful examples, searched for illustrations which really illustrate, and appended lists of general and specific books, novels, plays, and films that bear on the subject of each chapter.

4. *To approach a unified style and organization in our writing.* Every chapter

bears the imprint of the ideas and style of all three authors.

In the following instances, the authors extend special acknowledgment for the use of factual material, ideas, and features of organization: In Chapter 4, G. Mead, *Mind, Self, and Society* (Chicago: University of Chicago Press, 1934); in Chapter 8, J. Bowle, *Western Political Thought* (New York: Oxford University Press, 1948), chaps. 2-8; and R. MacIver, *The Web of Government* (New York: Macmillan, 1947); in Chapter 9, R. Gabriel, *The Course of American Democratic Thought* (New York: Ronald, 1956), chap. 2; in Chapter 11, D. Dillard, *The Economics of John Maynard Keynes* (Englewood Cliffs, N.J.: Prentice-Hall, 1948), pp. 1-12; in Chapter 19, J. Pate, *Local Government and Administration* (New York: American Book, 1954), especially pp. 25-30; and A. Schlesinger, *The Rise of the City* (New York: Macmillan, 1933); in Chapters 20, 22, and 23, P. Blau, *Bureaucracy and Modern Society* (New York: Random House, 1956); C. Mills, *The Power Elite* (New York: Oxford University Press, 1956); and A. Ranney and W. Kendall, *Democracy and the American Party System* (New York: Harcourt, Brace, 1956), chap. 1; in Chapter 24, Table 14 is reprinted by permission of the *Journal of the Franklin Institute* and is taken originally from A. B. Parsons, "Metals and Fuels: The World Has Enough," in the June 1945 issue, pp. 437-444; in Chapter 26,

E. Carr, *Nationalism and After* (New York: Macmillan, 1945), pp. 1-34; in Chapter 27, C. Friedrich and Z. Brzezinski, *Totalitarian Dictatorship and Autocracy* (Cambridge: Harvard University Press, 1956); G. Sabine, *A History of Political Theory* (New York: Holt, 1950), chap. 35; and D. Thompson, "National Socialism: Theory and Practice," *Foreign Affairs*, XIII (July, 1935), pp. 557-573; in Chapter 29, F. Allen, *The Big Change* (New York: Harper, 1952); and V. Van Dyke, *International Politics* (New York: Appleton-Century-Crofts, 1957).

We would be remiss if we did not give warm thanks to our many friends and colleagues who helped us in innumerable ways by reading chapters, criticizing style and organization, offering suggestions, and finding material and illustrations. We hope they will pardon us if we single out for special thanks Dr. Roland Renne of Montana State College, who offered constant encouragement and material aid in completing the work; Dr. Milo Bail of the University of Omaha, who made funds available for typing expenses during the early stages of preparing the manuscript for publication; Dr. Richard Thoman, Dr. Harry Hausser, and Dr. Robert Dunbar, special friends and counsellors; and Mr. Wilbur Mangas of the Project Planning Department of Prentice-Hall, Inc., who often went far beyond the call of his duty as editor.

T. N. B.
D. W. H.
G. L. W.

Contents

PART
SEVEN

TOWARD AN IDEAL WORLD OF JUSTICE
AND COOPERATION   *Page 539*

The Contemporary World

Studying

the Modern World

THEME

The epic of man is a tale of dramatic change. It has been a story of material and physical progress, as well as spiritual and moral challenge.

...YET

The Contemporary World is a place where man's ancient *loyalties*—to self and family, to his social class, to church and state—have been seriously shaken by (1) the impact of modern *industrialism* on his traditional customs, ideas, and patterns of living; (2) the *urban revolution*, which has profoundly affected his family life, criminal problems, educational system, government, and even his personality; and (3) the pressures of *bureaucratic organization* in almost every area of human activity on time-honored beliefs concerning the central importance of the individual. Outside his own nation he sees further *conflict* and *tension* arising from the mixture of age-old struggles between nations for environmental advantage, from clashing racial strains, an explosive nationalism, an aggressive imperialism, and dangerous new political ideologies. Yet, man's past advances, together with the recent progress he has made in achieving social justice at home and international organization abroad, offer him some real grounds for hope that he may one day live in an ideal world of *justice, peace,* and *cooperation.*

CHAPTER ONE

Prologue
to a Voyage of Discovery

Throughout recorded history
man has sought to pierce the unknown,
to find out what is beyond the next hill, to discover
what lies beyond the broad seas—to know.

When the

Englishman George Mallory, a would-be conqueror of Mount Everest, was asked why he had risked so much in trying to reach the summit of the world's highest mountain, he replied, "Because it was *there*." He thus gave memorable expression to man's indomitable will to know, to conquer, to fathom. The unknown is always more challenging than the known, the uncommon more fascinating than the usual, the darkness more mysterious than the light. Throughout recorded history man has sought to throw the narrow beam of his knowledge on the small corner of the dark universe in which he lives.

This urge to discover and to know has inevitably extended to man himself and his social environment. Like the astronomer exploring the black reaches of space, or the physicist probing the tiniest particles of matter, the social scientist seeks to discover, to understand, to explain the mysterious workings of man in society. But what an infinitely complicated work is man! Torn by conflicting emotions, goaded by physical wants, spurred by an unattainable idealism, man lives in a society that demands order, discipline, and agreement as the price of living together. Compared with the astronomer and the physicist, the social scientist faces infinitely more difficult problems in reducing the mass of data on human behavior to the orderly character of a science. In the human brain are as many cells as there are stars in the firmament; in the human will lie motivations more subtle than the forces that stir the most unpredictable atom. And yet the social scientist tries for order and meaning, and he partially succeeds. This book seeks to record for the beginner some of the things social scientists have learned in probing for meaning beneath the erratic and uncertain course of everyday human behavior.

THE IMPRINT OF HISTORY AND GEOGRAPHY

To begin with, the social scientist realizes that the behavior of every individual is related to a group. "No man is an island," said the poet John Donne more than three centuries ago. We are members of family groups, clan groups, religious groups, and social groups. In recent centuries we have come to think of ourselves as members of particular national groups. We are Americans, Germans, Belgians, or Japanese. As such we have a kinship with all other persons, living and dead, who constitute our national group. We are not alone. We have a history.

THE WEB OF HISTORY

Our behavior as a nation and as individuals is affected by the nation's history. Our dress, habits, language, ideals, law, politics, and religion all derive from the past. The past provides the framework and limits the range of possibilities in which individuals and groups work out their destiny. In American society ideas of freedom, individualism, religious liberty, and public education are firmly rooted in our historical past. Our range of religious beliefs, our political processes, our criminal laws, our literature, our

6

school curricula are all traceable to the influence of men now dead. The "dead hand of the past," as Jefferson called it, affects every reader of this book in limiting and directing the choices he will make in life. Whoever despises history despises the source of his most precious ideals and beliefs.

Our Western Civilization, as we shall learn in Chapter 2, rests on the pillars of the Christian religion, the national state, a capitalistic economic system, and the idea of the free individual. All these forces or ideas have had a dynamic, changing history, but their imprint on contemporary America and Western Europe is unmistakable. Christian and Judaic beliefs and practices have left an indelible mark on Western morals, culture, and social philosophy. Fervent allegiance to the national state has been a decisive force in the wars and politics of the past two- or three-hundred years. Modern capitalism has refashioned our concepts of law, property, and social justice. And the Greek-Jewish-Christian belief in the dignity and integrity of the individual human being has exerted an abiding influence on the course of philosophy, literature, and government in Western Civilization. The origin and development of each of these forces as they have affected American life we shall explore in the chapters that follow.

History, then, spins a web that confines and directs our behavior without determining it. The history of any society reflects continuity and gradual change from the past, rather than interruption and sudden innovation. The web may be spun in a new direction, but it is always connected with what went before. Even the Industrial Revolution, as we shall see in a later chapter, came much more slowly than its name suggests. And the Civil War, one of the great dividing lines in Amer-

At all times and in all cultures, man has tried to express himself aesthetically.

ican history, was decades in the making. The web of history may strain but it does not break. It thus teaches us (as another famous web taught the Scottish patriot Robert Bruce) patience, tolerance, and the wisdom of the long view.

If the roots of our contemporary society are covered with the subsoil of history, then why can we not predict how future leaves and branches will grow? A number of recent philosophers of history, especially the German writer Oswald Spengler and the English scholar Arnold Toynbee, have professed to see a pattern in history that may be projected into the future. Both men are pessimistic about the future of our civilization, especially Spengler, and see our Western Civilization sinking into a dangerous "time of troubles." But can man use history to predict coming events? Is there a necessary causal relationship between past, present, and future?

These questions we shall consider at some length in the next chapter, but one word of caution is necessary here. If it is futile to try to understand the contemporary world without a knowledge of history, it is equally futile to attempt it without some knowledge of the other sharp tools of social science. Economics, political science, sociology, anthropology, and social psychology are all interested in the behavior of men in contemporary societies. Each discipline uses special resources, skills, and knowledge that have been painstakingly accumulated over many years. Like history, each has searched for underlying patterns, laws, or similarities that would give meaning to the seemingly random and unplanned activities of men. This book is based on the conviction that history and the social sciences are both vital to any real understanding of the modern world, and that neither alone can provide the range of ideas and perspective needed by the beginning student of contemporary society.

THE ROLE OF GEOGRAPHY

Aside from his cultural conditioning and history, the natural environment does most to set limits to the achievements of an individual and his society. Without a favorable location and climate, abundant resources and fertile soils, adequate space and favorable topography, a people has little opportunity to develop the foundations of a flourishing society. Geographic circumstances may thus limit the growth of a given society. The location of boundaries is especially important in the modern state-system of the world. To possess a "natural boundary," such as a river, ocean, or mountain range, may assure a nation a peaceable growth and protection from envious neighbors. The fact that the United States bordered on two broad oceans goes far to explain the country's peaceful and orderly growth during the nineteenth century. France has had the misfortune to share a common land frontier with an ambitious and aggressive Germany. The Russians have enjoyed an immunity to military conquest thanks to weak neighbors, a severe climate, vast stretches of open land, and a native shrewdness that has been quick to exploit these advantages.

Changing circumstances often affect the importance of particular geographical features. During the age of sail and steam Britain's island location was a great advantage. But in the present era of hydrogen bombs and guided missiles her small size and isolation from the great land stretches of Europe have proved a marked liability. Prior to the Industrial Revolution the possession of huge coal and iron resources had scant strategic or economic meaning. Afterward, no nation could aspire to greatness without them. Before 1898 few Americans were worried about Colombian control of the isthmus across Panama. But after the Spanish-American War it was clear that pos-

session of this route for an interoceanic canal was of vital military significance.

The accident of birth, then, deposits a person in a society that possesses a history and a geography. These factors will go far in determining his standard of living, his occupation, his religion, his pride in country, his prestige among foreigners, and his whole way of life. They are accountable, too, for much of the tension of the modern world. Conflict is bred by historical differences between peoples and by such geographical factors as poor soils, scarce water, critical minerals, or an unfavorable location. Later on we shall take a closer look at this environmental basis of international tension in modern life.

AREAS OF CHOICE: POLITICS AND ECONOMICS

But if historical and geographical factors determine many characteristics of a society, there nevertheless remain important

All men in all cultures have developed methods for obtaining and distributing food. Early man had his organized hunts; modern man has an elaborate distribution and marketing system.

choices that members of a society must make and over which historical and geographical circumstances may exert less influence. Different social institutions may exist in countries whose historical traditions and geographical settings are quite similar.

Certainly few decisions are more important to members of a society than those concerning a form of government and economic system. These decisions will affect every other facet of life in a society. A totalitarian government, to take an extreme example, will leave little untouched in the religious, moral, cultural, and economic life of its people, whereas other governments will leave these facets of life relatively free of control. For government is a pattern of relationships between the many who are governed and the few who do the governing. In a democracy the people retain a veto over the behavior of elected officials, but citizens of a totalitarian state have no effective recourse to the ballot box. They must consent to the arbitrary will of their leaders, who can back up their decrees with force if necessary. To be sure, there is usually some discernible relationship between the interests of the people and the actions of government, even in a dictatorship, but the area of individual freedom and choice will vary widely.

Similarly, the choice of an economic system will exert a profound impact on the whole way of life of a people. For all economic goods exist in short supply; there is not enough of any of them to supply all consumers with all they want. We must therefore decide how and in what proportion goods and services are to be distributed. Likewise, we must determine how farm and industrial resources are to be used in producing finished goods. How shall these decisions be made? Who shall make them? Shall it be the individual members of the society, acting as buyers and sellers in the market place? Or should it be the government? Whichever road we choose, we dare not fail. For failure may mean starvation, want, and social revolution.

What we are saying is that for all the influence which history and geography exert in shaping our destiny, there are moments when individuals and social groups may possess or seize the initiative for change. Certainly the choices which we as individuals make have a great deal to do with the freedom, welfare, and happiness of humankind. Men who blame history or geography for all their ills overlook the role that willful choice and self-discipline have played in history. When told that circumstances determined the fate of nations, Napoleon once retorted, *"Circonstances? Moi, je fais les circonstances!"* (Circumstances? Me, I make the circumstances!)

CONFLICTS OF LOYALTIES AND VALUES

If history and geography provide the grand stage on which the drama of social life is played, it is our freedom to choose that brings tragedy and conflict to the footlights. Our political choices as Americans, for example, have been in the direction of democracy, or popular government. But is it democratic to deprive Negroes and other minority groups of their equal rights as citizens, even if a majority of their neighbors and fellow-citizens demand that their rights be limited? Are there limits to our civil rights as citizens to criticize, protest, and speak freely about what we believe? If so, where is the boundary of free speech to be drawn? And what does democracy mean when applied to education? Does it entail the best education for all who can profit from it, or equal education regardless of ability?

These and other questions we shall consider in later chapters. They are important questions because modern man lives in a world of contradiction and tensions. His personal loyalties range from an inner integrity, which we might call loyalty to self, through loyalties to family, class, church, and government. At each step in this hierarchy of loyalties there are sources of conflict and tension. Should a person follow his church or his state when they take opposing stands on an issue? This is no academic question, at least not for Christians living today under communist rule nor for many Americans who have had to choose between religious scruples and patriotism when called to military service. And frequently we must choose between loyalty to the expectations of our class and loyalty to our private or religious values. We cannot avoid the clash of loyalties, yet in their confrontation lies the possibility of tragedy and insecurity. "To thine own self be true," counseled Shakespeare, but his advice is becoming ever more difficult to follow in this contemporary world of ours.

THE STAMP OF INDUSTRIALIZATION

For one thing, ours is a very different world from the one Shakespeare inhabited. It is infinitely more complex, more organized, more crowded. Probably the single most important feature that distinguishes our world from the world of the Stratford bard is industrialization. The revolution in industry that began in England in the eighteenth century has completely transformed the world. The English peasant working his fields in 1750 had more in common with the peasant of ancient Egypt than with the mechanized farmer of today. A whole new way of life for the farmer and city-dweller, which we call industrialism, had its inception less than two hundred years ago. Its central feature was the application of power-driven machinery to the manufacture and distribution of goods. Its most important results were a dramatic rise in production and levels of living, a vast increase in human population in the industrial centers, the conquest of time and distance by steam and gasoline-powered vehicles that replaced the oxcart and the horse, and the appearance of a disheartening array of new social problems.

For better or worse, readers of this book will live in a society where modern industry plays a dominant role. The second section of the book is therefore devoted to examining the many ways in which the coming of industry has affected the patterns of life in the modern world. The social consequences of the Industrial Revolution; the sharp division of interest between industrial workers, employers, and investors; the resulting stimulus to economic thought; and the newer mechanized ways of life for farmers and city-dwellers are all explored in turn. Later on, we will take a closer look at the connection between the emergence of industrialism and the rise of the modern city and trace the impact of both on the human personality and such institutions as government and education.

Certainly the Industrial Revolution influenced modern economic thought decisively. As we shall see, the theories of both modern capitalism and Marxian socialism were shaped under the pressures generated by the Industrial Revolution. In today's world we find a range of economic systems varying from complete state control over most economic decisions, as in the Soviet Union, to the system of relatively free individual choice in the United States and Western Europe.

Even in the United States, individual choice in economic affairs is frequently tied to membership in organizations that exist to serve group interests. The modern corporation, the business association, the labor union, all have taken unto themselves the

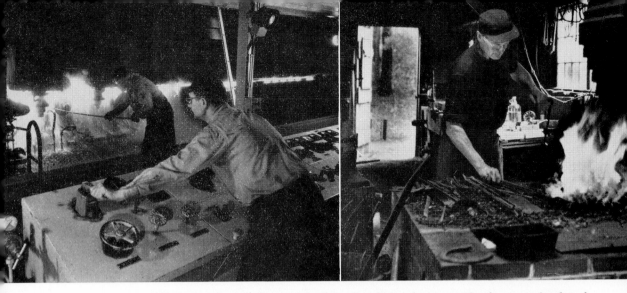

The epic of man also reveals that all cultures have a technology, or developed methods for utilizing resources and manufacturing goods. A most striking feature of some cultures is man's capacity for technological change. Whereas just a few years ago a blacksmith was confined to his bellows, today a single man can oversee the manufacture of a far greater quantity of material.

power of deciding vital questions that affect the nation's economy. In the resulting clash of business, farm, labor, and consumer interests, the power of one group often tends to counterbalance the power of another. Where this clash results in an equilibrium of power, we say that a "check-and-balance system" exists. Increasingly, however, the national government has been forced to play a greater role in maintaining an equilibrium of power among the many group interests.

THE SURGE TO THE CITIES

Hand in hand with the spread of industrialization has come the rush to the cities. Although cities existed long ago in ancient Egypt and Mesopotamia, they were the exception rather than the rule until the Industrial Revolution occurred. Then the weight and cost of modern machinery made it impossible for workers to continue to buy the necessary tools of production and keep them in their cramped cottages. Instead, the workers had to be brought to the machines. Factories, slums, and cities sprang up across the continents, and all kept pace with the

growth of industry in Britain, Germany, America, and the other industrial nations of the world.

The rise of the modern city had important social consequences. Life in the city, by its very nature, was more organized, disciplined, and impersonal than it was in the countryside or village. Problems of housing and transportation, sanitation and public health, became more acute in the city. The urban family became smaller, less stable, and more democratic. The congestion, ready money, and anonymity found in the modern city added to the seriousness of crime and delinquency. And American schools, too, were profoundly influenced, especially by the larger numbers of children and the more generous financial support, which made specialization and grading more possible. School curricula were also changed to meet the needs of an urban-industrial environment.

As the urban population mounted during the nineteenth century, cities were confronted with ever more pressing problems. New services had to be provided, new functions assumed. Even today, city governments still struggle to overcome the burdens of inadequate finances, public apathy, political corruption, and haphazard and unplanned expansion. And, finally, what of the effect of urban living and the machine on the human personality? Is there a real danger that we may become a generation of neurotic robots? These and other related questions we shall consider in Part 3, "Our Urban World."

THE BUREAUCRATIC LEVIATHAN

It is clear that modern industrial society has inspired us with a tendency to do everything in a big way. We produce more goods, live in bigger cities, expect more from our governments, and organize our lives on a scale undreamed of in the past. Order and stability in our affairs rest on organization. In governments, military services, labor unions, businesses, and even professions the same pattern exists. The sheer weight of numbers and of complex human problems forces all organizations in the Big Society toward bigness, impersonality, and a set routine—in brief, toward bureaucracy. The bureaucratic fabric is thus woven from the strands of population and industrial growth, reinforced by demands for more government services, more experts, and greater efficiency in everything we do.

A bureaucracy is thus made up of individuals who have thrown in their lot with a particular business, union, or government department. Like the individuals that constitute them, bureaucratic groups are interested in growth, efficiency, and self-preservation. Yet at the same time, bureaucratic groups may resist change, inhibit new choices, stifle initiative, or outlive their usefulness. They may challenge basic values and raise serious problems for democracy. Yet, this condition may be the necessary price we pay for order and growth in the Big Society, as we shall see in Part 4.

INTERNATIONAL TENSIONS AND CONFLICTS

Here, then, is the kind of world in which today's student of social science will live. It is a world industrialized and urbanized, fraught with competing loyalties, and characterized by bigness and impersonality. Beyond this world, however, is another larger world of international pressures and tensions that will at times also affect his life. Indeed, the future of the human race may well depend on how these external conflicts are resolved in the next quarter-century.

The forces behind these international tensions are related to the same forces that have shaped our domestic world. Industrialism has shrunk the size of the stage on which the drama of international relations is played. Through modern transportation it has made neighbors of people who did not dream of one another's existence a few centuries ago. It has also raised the stakes in the game of international diplomacy. For a boundary dispute today may involve the possession of mineral resources representing incomparable riches. And it has made the game infinitely more dangerous. For the first time, weapons of ultimate destruction have been put in the hands of statesmen by the masters of modern science and industry.

At the very time when some common core of principles and values is needed to offset the destructive forces afoot, we have witnessed a decline of international unity. The French Revolution destroyed the earlier idea of an international community based on the fraternity of brother monarchs. And World War I destroyed the economic unity among nations that had been based on Britain's leadership in the worlds of banking and trade during the nineteenth century. In the place of international unity, there has risen the phenomenon of nationalism, a single-minded loyalty to one's own nation and people. Nationalism has spawned the fanatical hatreds, the unreasoning pride in nation, the "we or they" feeling that pervades the present international scene. Out of the ashes of the old community of nations arose the specter of totalitarianism, demanding unquestioning obedience, promising to fulfill the needs of the masses, catering to every emotion and prejudice, and defying Western democratic ideals. Fascism, Nazism, and now Soviet Communism have in turn tested the resoluteness, the faith, the strength of the Western democracies in defending the principles that gave them birth.

In the 1960's the American people stand at one of the two poles of significant international power in the world. Abroad they face the menace of growing Soviet strength, the threat of an awakened and aroused Red China, and the necessity to meet the problems of the world's uncommitted nations who have sought to remain aloof from the strains and tensions of the Cold War. In their diplomacy Americans depend heavily on their armed might, their allies in Europe and the rest of the free world, and the United Nations. At home they continue their quest for social justice, seeking to strike a balance between freedom and security, private enterprise and public welfare, strong government and popular liberties. They have accepted the principle of governmental responsibility to aid the underprivileged and discipline the forces of free capitalism. But they continue to cherish traditional ideals of personal freedom in movement and thought and private judgment in the market place. Upon them has been thrust the leadership of the democratic world in opposing by force and example a new barbarism that threatens another dark age for Western Civilization. Never before have Americans faced such a challenge. Never again may they have so magnificent an opportunity to prove the mettle of their values and their civilization.

SOME WORDS OF SUMMARY

As the book begins, let the reader imagine himself at the center of a series of concentric circles, of which the innermost is his circle of personal loyalties—to self, family, class, religion, and government. Let him then picture this ring enclosed by a second ring and a third one, representing the industrial and urban forces that impinge on his way of life and his loyalties. Then comes a fourth ring, representing the growing bureaucracy that surrounds, pervades, and sometimes threatens to strangle him. Finally, there is an outer ring that stands for the world of international tension and conflict. Now imagine the rings all revolving and occasionally shifting their planes of rotation so that they sometimes intersect and deflect one another. All this is a figurative way of saying that in our immensely complicated world we can introduce the social sciences as a whole only by selecting arbitrarily a few such pervasive forces as loyalty, industrialism, and bureaucracy and then measuring their impact on our lives and institutions. This method does not make for completeness of coverage (what method does?), but it does insure clarity, simplicity, and a unified viewpoint. Most important of all, it enables the beginner to grasp the interrelatedness of the social sciences in a series of case studies. These, then, are our motives—to introduce the reader to his social universe, to encourage him to explore it further, and to demonstrate the essential unity of the social sciences.

History
and the Contemporary World

From ancient Athens to modern Athens
is but a short distance, but more than 2,000 years in time.

In our introductory chapter we spoke of the "web of history," which confines without determining the fate of individuals and civilizations. But what is history? Of what value is the study of the past? What does it have to do with the pressing problems of contemporary civilization? What good is history anyway? How often these disturbing questions are asked of the unfortunate teacher of history! Even if people are considerate enough not to ask them directly, they nevertheless think about them. What, indeed, are the uses of history, and why are we devoting so much space to it in a book on social science? Let us have a further look at this important question.

THE USES OF HISTORY

HISTORY AS A SOURCE OF PIETY

All of us have a sense of history even if we are not history scholars. We feel a kinship with the past, an identity with peoples and eras now vanished, a nostalgia to see in actuality what our imaginations create. This attitude is what the Oxford scholar, A. L. Rowse, had in mind when he wrote:

The past is not something dead, shut away like a series of damp catacombs, which you enter by a difficult and uncongenial mode of ingress (in other words, an examination course on unappetising textbooks)—it is alive and about you. History is about life and has the appeal of life itself; the feeling for history is a nostalgia for life, subtly transmuted. That is the answer to the question of one of the most academic—and at the same time poetic—of present-day historians, F. M. Powicke: "Shepherds have kept their sheep in all ages: why am I stirred so deeply because I can trace the very sheep-walks of the monks of Furness?" *

Who among us has not likewise stood on some historic spot and felt a surge of emotion for the memory of some statesman long dead, some battle long ended? We find history appealing and useful, for it is the cement that binds together the past and the present, the dead and the living, in a community beyond time and space. Written history, however fragmentary, seeks to recapture the struggles, the aspirations, and dreams of millions of our fellow human beings who since the dawn of time have built and suffered and prayed and fought and wept. Rightly conceived, the study of history is as broad as man's interests, as deep as his struggle to fathom order and meaning out of an unpredictable existence. History has no greater use than the tolerance and perspective it brings to a person as he realizes that unnumbered human beings have passed his way, have faced the same problems he faces, have had the same doubts he has, and yet have found the courage and the faith to struggle on, to fight for what they cherished and believed to be just.

HISTORY AS A SOURCE OF TOLERANCE

A remarkable Frenchman once observed that "to know all is to forgive all." He meant that a great deal of the hatred,

* A. L. Rowse, *The Use of History* (London: Hodder and Stoughton, 1946), pp. 44-45.

prejudice, and conflict in human affairs stems from gaps in our knowledge. If we understood all the circumstances and background of human activities, we should find it hard to bear malice or spite. A knowledge of history promotes tolerance and understanding. History is like a mountaintop from which we can see the trail we have blazed, as well as the terrain around our campsite. The citizen versed in history will know that contemporary social problems are rooted deep in the past, that economic depressions tend to recur in cycles, and that wars begin long before the first shot is fired. He will study the record of human intolerance toward opposing religions, nationalities, and races. And from that knowledge he will recognize the danger signs for the present. An Irish-American, for example, who looks back to the anti-Catholic movement of the 1830's and 1840's, is more likely to understand and respect the minority groups that are fighting for status and recognition today.

History deepens our understanding of human beings. It acquaints us with the sublime creative powers of a Shakespeare, the egotistical genius of a Napoleon, the towering wisdom of a Socrates, the warm humanity of a St. Francis, and the satanic character of a Hitler. All were human beings. In their infinite variety they exemplify the awesome range of human capabilities. The study of history, by adding the dimension of the past to our present observations of man, helps us to understand and to tolerate him in all his bewildering diversity. To paraphrase a modern historian, history has value because we can learn what man is while we are learning what man has done.

HISTORY
AS A TOOL OF UNDERSTANDING

Historical-mindedness, then, is conducive to patience, tolerance, and the wisdom of the long view. What alarms us today may reassure us tomorrow; what is forgotten today may rise to plague us tomorrow. A mind tempered by historical study is likely to recognize this truth. It is apt to value calm, rational judgment and deliberate action. But a knowledge of the past has other important uses. In Francis Bacon's memorable words, "knowledge is power"; that is, knowledge offers us greater possibility for new discoveries, alternative courses of action, methods for controlling our environment, and greater ability to understand our fellow man and adjust to his needs. Like any other segment of knowledge, history adds to these possibilities and thus strengthens our effectiveness as individuals.

We all know how annoying it is to have a conversation interrupted by a newcomer who knows nothing at all about the topic under discussion, yet insists on being filled in at every step of the way. To the student of history many of the problems and decisions of life are like such a conversation. For all life may be viewed as a great conversation about life's goals, purposes, and values. The newcomer to this great conversation is the man who is ignorant of history, who reasons and argues as if the world had been created only yesterday and every problem we face today were glaringly new. The man who knows history has an advantage over such a person in knowing that neither problems nor their solutions spring full-blown out of any given moment in time. He has a sense of the interrelatedness of past and present, of the dynamic, continuous wholeness of the human story, of the seamlessness of the historical web. He will be less likely than others to believe that a particular opinion is altogether right, that any purpose is altogether altruistic. And he will be able to assess the slanted appeals to the past of the demagogue who would use history to buttress his own opinion. How often have we heard the claim that "History teaches" or "History proves," only to hear the phrase

it often tells us what *not* to do and thus narrows our range of choice. It is significant that Winston Churchill, historian, virtually alone among English political leaders read correctly the meaning of Hitler's revolution in Germany. And several of our strong presidents during the twentieth century—Theodore Roosevelt, Woodrow Wilson, Franklin D. Roosevelt—have been keen students and even teachers or writers of history.

THE MODERN LEGACY

History, then, has many uses. It should promote within us a spirit of tolerance and train us to meet opposing opinions and new ideas with dispassion. It should provide us with advantages unavailable to those ignorant of history. It should give us a critical spirit and a discriminating taste. It should help us formulate a philosophy of life, be it pragmatic, fatalistic, optimistic, or any other. It should quicken our appreciation of the wonderful adventure that is life. And it should serve as a practical guide to the flow of great events at home and abroad. Above all, it should deepen our understanding of the heritage that is ours as a people.

In recent years Americans have turned almost instinctively to that heritage as nation after nation has been torn from the democratic fold. Threatened by bullying dictators, their ideals under fire, confused by strident new ideologies, Americans have sought certainty and strength by searching their past for the values that nourished their national growth. This "search for roots" has stimulated a new interest in history that is reflected in book-club choices, histories written for popular consumption, and new historical magazines.

WESTWARD THE COURSE OF EMPIRE

Where do we look for these roots, the landmarks that have marked the rise of Western Civilization? What are the enduring characteristics of this Western way of life? Where do we in the West stand today in the light of history and contemporary events?

As the American historian Henry Steele Commager has stated with characteristic brilliance, we of this generation stand at one of the great watersheds of history. During all of recorded history we in the West have supposed that the course of civilization flowed from East to West—from the Tigris and Euphrates valleys to the Fertile Crescent, from Egypt and Palestine to Greece and Rome, from Western Europe to Britain and then westward across the ocean to America. All the great institutions of our way of life followed a similar course. Christianity spread from Palestine to Rome to Western Europe, and thence to America and the Far East. Our ideas of democracy and personal freedom took root in ancient Greece, spread to Britain and France, and were carried by settlers to the New World. The path of industrialism led from Western Europe to America to Japan and thence around the world. It was always to the West that civilization seemed to be moving.

Now, for the first time in the memory of Western man, the familiar pattern no longer holds. The founts of creativity and innovation no longer emanate almost exclusively from Europe. A powerful industry and technology have sprung up in Russia at the eastern borders of our Western Civilization and are exerting a powerful influence on our Asian neighbors. The borders of Western society are everywhere circumscribed by hostile or neutral powers. Europeanized peoples are fighting to throw off the last vestiges of European control. All Europe now looks beyond the Continent for its protection and security. America, once the rimland of Europe, has become the central pivot of an Atlantic civilization.

THE SIXTEENTH-CENTURY WATERSHED

Four hundred years ago the Western world stood astride another great watershed. On the one side was the world of the Middle Ages—feudal, agrarian, otherworldly, symbolized by the fortified castles of the nobility and the great cathedrals dedicated to God; on the other, the emerging modern world—dynamic, secular, increasingly urban, symbolized by the sensuous art of the post-Renaissance and the full sails of the explorer's ship. America was only the far outpost of a Europe

The sensuous art of the post-Renaissance symbolizes the emergence of the modern world.

caught up in a throbbing, unceasing activity. In the space of barely a century (1450-1550), a score of cataclysmic events tore and pulled at the remaining strands of medieval unity. The capitalistic impulse, issuing in a great burst of trade and banking, overcame the restraints imposed by the self-contained manorial economy of the Middle Ages. National states emerged out of the fragmented duchies, baronies, and estates of the medieval age. Within a scant fifty years, Columbus discovered a New World across the great sea barrier that had been raised by medieval geographers, Machiavelli urged the rulers of rising national states to forget medieval conventions and morals and pursue their own national interests, Luther split the religious unity of Western Christendom, Erasmus waged war on blind superstition and reliance on authority, and Copernicus substituted observation for tradition in the study of the heavenly bodies. How much, to redirect a modern eulogy, was owed by so many to so few!

Modern Europe was on the move. The voyage of Columbus was repeated by dozens, scores, and finally hundreds of bold seafarers. England, France, Spain, Holland, and ultimately all the states of Europe found a new sense of unity behind the strong national leaders who took Machiavelli's advice. The unity of Western Christendom was forever broken by Luther's Protestant revolt; the nation-state now became the repository of man's highest loyalties. A new culture—secular, individualistic, materialistic—followed in the wake of the Renaissance across the face of Europe. And science, by the seventeenth century, was forging a vision of a new heaven and a new earth simply by disregarding authority and following the evidence of the human senses.

For the next three hundred years, and more, Europeans planted their outposts, their peoples, and their ideas in every corner of the world. Supremely confident in their superior culture and technology, they peopled the great empty stretches of the New World, sent their traders and missionaries to faraway Asia, and extended their hegemony over vast areas of the globe. Helpless before the machines, skills, and guns of the white man, Filipinos, Hottentots, and Bushmen acquiesced in the rule of Europeans. In their supreme egotism, the Westerners boasted of "discovering" new lands and territories, though as one Filipino put it many years later, "We knew we were there already!" Today we are finding that he was correct.

THE NINETEENTH CENTURY —AN AGE OF HOPE

The Industrial Revolution of the eighteenth and nineteenth centuries widened the technological gap between Europeans (and Americans) and non-Europeans. The steamship, the railroad, the factory, and the rifle intensified the natural assumption of superiority that the white man carried to distant and underdeveloped lands. They also contributed to the white man's comfortable feeling of ease and authority, which was reinforced by the conviction that further progress was certain and inevitable. In the warm afternoon of nineteenth-century Victorian civilization, the European could congratulate himself not only on his marvelous achievements in technology but also on his towering feats of mind and spirit. His ideas of freedom, law, and democracy inspired men from Oslo to Capetown; his God was worshipped from Hong Kong to Moscow; his music and philosophy had become the property of all civilized men.

He took no greater pride than in the belief that his was the freest, most democratic, and doubtless the happiest civilization that humankind had ever known. The rule of law protected his person, his property, and his human dignity in every area administered by Europeans. The ideal of abstract justice impartially administered to all he considered the greatest invention of the human mind. And he took it to be inevitable that Western legal processes would conquer the world and put an end to disorder, conflict, and even war itself. Nor did he wish to confine the benefits of freedom under law to those of his own kind. In colony after colony, Western statesmen introduced by formal act or by inadvertence the powerful ideas of liberty, self-government, and human dignity, which would explode like time-bombs in the present century. Sometimes, as in the case of America's acquisition of the Philippines, they were imperialists with an uneasy conscience, recognizing the incongruity between democratic ideals and imperialistic practice, and promising early self-government and independence to the people they engulfed. All in all, the nineteenth was the most hopeful of all modern centuries. The Victorians were convinced that science would banish hunger and want, that progress was written into the very movement of history, that freedom would ring across every battlement of resistance, and that a triumphant democracy would put an end to the foolishness of war. Tennyson spoke for a generation and a century when he wrote:

> For I dipt into the future, far as human eye could see,
> Saw the vision of the world, and all the wonders that would be;
> Saw the heavens fill with commerce, argosies of magic sails,
> Pilots of the purple twilight, dropping down with costly bales;
> Heard the heavens fill with shouting, and there rain'd a ghastly dew
> From the nations' airy navies grappling in the central blue;
> Far along the world-wide whisper of the south-wind rushing warm,
> With the standards of the peoples plunging thro' the thunder-storm;
> Till the war-drum throbb'd no longer, and the battle-flags were furl'd
> In the Parliament of man, the Federation of the world.

SERPENTS IN THE GARDEN

Out of that confident age came the men who were to lead the movements during the first half of the twentieth century for freedom, democracy, law, and peace. At Blenheim Castle, young Winston Churchill, growing up in the peaceful 1880's, learned the simple Victorian lessons of fair play, resistance to evil, social progress, and human dignity. At Hyde Park, Franklin D. Roosevelt was being likewise instructed to trust in human decency, to believe in democracy, to have faith in God and his purposes in this world. By the time these men had reached middle age, their generation had been shocked by the explosive emotions aroused during the Great War of 1914, discouraged by the violent nationalism spreading across Europe, disillusioned by the failure of democracy to capture the globe, and horrified by the rise of totalitarian government in Soviet Russia. In their maturity, these two statesmen from a Victorian world were to lead the greatest armies in all human history against the cruelest, most savage dictatorship in modern time.

What had gone wrong? Why had the world of the Victorians been turned upside down? Was it possible that there were human beings who did not want freedom, who despised Western ideas of law and democracy? How strong were the roots of Western Civilization anyway?

Every force that disrupted the smooth course of civilization in the twentieth century was present in the nineteenth. Out of that same peaceful Victorian age came the new biology of Charles Darwin, the first well-organized communist parties, the conquest of Africa and Asia by the imperialist nations, the modern nationalistic spirit, and the triumph of the machine and modern technology. Each development has had devastating consequences for the twentieth century. Darwinism unloosed the modern skeptical temper—doubting, uncertain, scientific, and reasonable. Communism seized on the injustice and inequality of early industrial societies and scorned Victorian ideas of law and fair play as representing merely the ethics of the strong against the weak. Imperialism, however rationalized, brought the West by force into the non-Western world and provoked a resentment that has sparked riot, war, and revolution in the present century. The prideful and exclusive love of nation to which Germans and others appealed a century ago has become a blind, fanatical force of destruction in the twentieth century. And the triumph of modern industry has contributed to man's insecurities, even as it gave him the physical power to avenge ancient hatreds and wrongs.

These are the forces that have destroyed

Charles Darwin, the man who shook history itself.

Victorian complacency and shaped the civilization which we are about to study in detail. Their influence will be manifest in the chapter-by-chapter analysis of our modern social life that follows.

THE ENDURING ROOTS

What the future may hold is not given us to see. In the three score of years since 1900, we have learned to temper confidence with fear and to salvage hope from despair. We now know that the world does not revolve about Europe, that technology is not the genius of Westerners alone, that other civilizations are capable of achieving a high culture, and that the Western monopoly on military strength is ended. The game is once more open, with the highest stakes in history; and victory is likely to go to the side with the greatest resolution, courage, diligence, and self-discipline. In the world struggle against communism, Western Civilization confronts a monolithic power resting on a technology and a philosophy that are Western in origin. Some of the West's strongest weapons, however, are still the compelling appeal of freedom, a contagious faith in the worth and dignity of the human personality, and the proven strength of popular government. Even behind the Iron Curtain, as events in East Germany, Poland, Hungary, and other places have eloquently testified, the flame of freedom has not yet been extinguished.

The roots of human liberty strike deep in our Western way of life—back through Gettysburg, Lexington, Plymouth Rock, and Runnymede, through the medieval age of authority, to imperial Rome, ancient Greece, and even beyond. In their growth they have become entangled with ideas of self-government, individual worth, and equality before God. They have been nourished by opposition to despotic authority and the example of brave men and enlightened statesmen.

They have been strained by military defeat, indifference, and the ethical relativism of the modern age, which deprives all absolutes, including freedom, of force. Yet there is no stronger barrier between our world and the communists' than this insistence of ours that men must be permitted to know, to think, to speak, to believe, and to act as conscience and personal conviction direct. No one has yet been able to improve on Pericles' famous twenty-four-hundred-year-old description of what a free and democratic community is like.

Our institutions are not borrowed from those around us; they are our own, the creation of Athenian statesmen; an example, and not a copy. In the political language of the day we are called a democracy; and the name is true and not true. It is true, because the administration of our city is in the hands of the people; and there is one law for rich and poor; it is not true, because, above all states, we recognize the claims of excellence. In this sense we are an aristocracy; not of birth, for among us there is no privilege; not of wealth, for poverty is a bar to none; but of merit; a state in which every one who *can* benefit the city *may* do so without let or hindrance.

Such is the freedom of our political life, and in society we are equally without constraint. Everyone does what he pleases, without suspicion or offence. There is nothing modish, nor exclusive, in our habits; we do not banish a man from our company because his ways are different from our own. But along with this unconstrained liberty there goes a spirit of reverence, which pervades every act of our public life; authority is maintained; the laws are obeyed, not from fear of punishment, but from principle; and of all ordinances the most sacred in our eyes are those which protect the injured, who cannot retaliate; and the unwritten laws, which, though enforced by no legal penalty, bring reproach to the transgressor.

Here is the ideal, deeply rooted in the past, which gives meaning to our struggles for freedom and democracy. In the long perspective of history, certainly, the future of freedom seems brighter than in the pale light of contemporary events. Even if freedom should yet be crushed, it may arise once more as it has in ages past. With Cicero we may believe that "freedom suppressed and again regained bites with keener fangs than freedom never endangered." In our loyalty to the ideal of personal freedom, in any case, lies all that really matters in our fight against totalitarianism.

THE MEANING OF HISTORY

Looking back across the centuries at the unfolding drama of human life, what meaning or purpose can we discern in history? Does history have a purpose? A goal? A pattern? Will study of the past enable us to discover the direction in which we are going and the goal we must reach? Can man find ultimate truth in history?

THE RELIGIOUS INTERPRETATION

Medieval man had no doubts. History had a beginning, an end, and a purpose. All life was part of a divine plan in which no squirrel was lost, no tree fell without God's knowledge. There was purpose and intelligence written into the very design of nature, which any man might see for himself. Created in God's own image, man lived in the center of the universe on a planet designed and intended for his use. Furthermore, God had revealed his intentions and purposes to man through His Holy Scriptures and His Holy Church. History began in the Garden of Eden; it would end with God's final judgment. Its grand theme was the triumph of man over his sinful and corrupt nature through the gratuitous mercy of God and the sacrifice of His beloved Son.

This religious interpretation of history,

still vigorous among churchmen and many Christians, has been forced on the defensive by five hundred years of skeptical and scientific thought. Copernicus and his followers moved man from the center of the universe; Hutton and Lyell advanced an evolutionary explanation of the development of the earth; Darwin questioned the uniqueness of man; Freud challenged man's rationality; and Einstein painted an awesome universe in constant motion with no apparent plan or purpose. What resulted was a view of the cosmos as "a blindly running flux of disintegrating energy," in Carl Becker's telling phrase. For modern man there was seemingly no beginning in history, no end, no way station. There was movement, but no direction or goal. The historian has tried to view the whole sweep of history in the light of this preconception of our age and to give meaning to it. But the meaning he can give to human experience is severely circumscribed. Historians, who once believed that life was a divinely inspired, meaningful drama, now accepted life without question and described it without understanding it.

HISTORY A SCIENCE?

Does history then have no meaning? Scarcely. There is much in human life that has great meaning for us as individuals, even when human life itself is not considered a part of a cosmic plan. Love and freedom, suffering and evil, are all as real as if the very stars in their courses shouted their meaning. In history, likewise, we can recognize old struggles and causes, past triumphs and tragedies that give meaning and purpose to our life as human beings. Because there is no one purpose in history, it does not mean that there are no purposes. Because there is no single pattern, it does not follow that there are no patterns at all. Just as the scientist seeks to measure and manipulate the natural world without necessarily finding any ulti-

mate purpose behind nature, so the historian tries to understand the evolution of the social world without postulating any final end in history.

Indeed, so impressed were some nineteenth-century historians with the methods of science that they were convinced that history itself was well on the way to becoming an exact science. Why should history not be as objective, detached, and impartial as the study of inorganic chemistry? If the historian would only rid himself of his biases, analyze the historical data as impersonally as a laboratory technician, and set down his results as rigorously and fairly as a chemist, we should have a record of what actually happened in the past rather than a historian's personal view of things. History should forsake literature for the exact sciences. It should seek only to find the truth and nothing more. It should begin with a careful amassing of all the relevant facts about, let us say, the formation of the American Constitution. Out of this accumulation of facts there would emerge slowly, painfully, but accurately, an interpretation that was not mapped out in advance. The facts, in other words, would speak for themselves.

But later historians did not believe that the facts spoke for themselves. If this were so, the historians argued, why was it that they always spoke the language of the investigating historian? Why did no two historians ever select precisely the same facts and give them the same stress in their written works? In the writing of even the most objective of the "scientific" historians there were signs of temperamental, national, or social biases.

The critics argued that complete objectivity would mean no interpretation at all, which would reduce history to a mere chronicle of events. For every historian is influenced by the time and circumstances of his life. The historical facts themselves have no meaning apart from the historian's "frame of reference." As the historians Carl Becker and Charles Beard have stressed, each historian must begin with some theory or hypothesis to guide him in his search through the vast jungles of historical fact. A historian without a hypothesis, in the words of one modern scholar, is like a woodsman at night without a lantern.

Furthermore, it has been argued that history differs from the exact sciences because historians are unable to test their results. What is the ultimate authority when two historians using the same facts come up with differing interpretations? The physicist can retire to his laboratory and check his findings. But a historian cannot summon Abraham Lincoln to the bar of history to ask him whether he freed the slaves in 1863 because of Radical Republican pressures, because of military considerations, or because of strong moral convictions against slavery. Even if Lincoln could be recalled, it is doubtful whether historians, being human, would all accept Lincoln's account of his motives!

History, then, is both art and science. It uses the methods of science to establish the reliability of documents, to test tentative theories, and to ascertain statistical probabilities. But in interpreting findings and presenting them to others, the historian becomes a creative artist seeking to convey through words a true picture of what happened and why it happened. His imagination tries to break through the thin barrier of fragmentary records left to him in order to catch a glimpse of truth. He struggles with the problem of complex human motivation, often a puzzle to us in our friends, but a stark enigma when clouded by the passage of time. As a scientist, he is interested in facts, witnesses, confirming evidence, authority for his findings; as an artist, he cultivates imagination, insight, and creativity. History, then, belongs as much to the imaginative studies as to the domain of science.

HISTORY A CYCLE?

Imagination, logic, reasonableness, painstaking care—these are the qualities of the best historical writing. But some scholars are not content to find only limited meaning and partial patterns in the flow of historical events. Their imaginations, inspired by long study and a bent toward philosophy, point to a larger order and meaning in the story of humankind. Since the time of the Greeks the idea has recurred that all of history is an endless cycle. The author of Ecclesiastes expressed it well when he wrote, "The thing that hath been, it is that which shall be; and that which is done is that which shall be done; and there is no new thing under the sun." In our own time the German philosopher Oswald Spengler has given the idea its most systematic analysis in his massive *Decline of the West* (1918). For Spengler, history was the "collective biography" of a number of cultures which "arise, ripen, decay, and never return." In the life cycle of every culture, including our own Western Civilization, there was a springtime of rapid growth, a summer of high promise and achievement, an autumnal season of mellow decay, and a frozen winter of decline and death. We in the West, according to Spengler's gloomy formulation, were in the winter season of our civilization and in rapid decline. All civilizations, wrote Spengler, must pass through these consecutive stages to oblivion unless wiped out earlier by some catastrophe.

Among those markedly influenced by Spengler's theory of civilizations was Arnold J. Toynbee, whose A *Study of History* has sold more copies than any comparable work in size and historical erudition. Toynbee identifies twenty-six civilizations in the world's history, most of them now extinct. These civilizations grew and prospered as long as they were inspired by creative individuals or by creative minorities. At the point in their cycle of growth when the creative minority was no longer able to inspire the majority and was forced to resort to coercion, the forward thrust ended. Social disunity set in, an aimlessness of purpose became apparent, and disintegration followed. This process is not inexorable in Toynbee's view, and he sees some hope for Western Civilization, providing that some overarching purpose is restored to our lives, especially in the spiritual sphere.

At bottom, all such theories are speculative and unprovable. There is, indeed, evidence to show that all the great civilizations of the past have foundered and perished and that this corresponds to the natural processes of birth, growth, decay, and death. But no one has proved that this process is necessary and inevitable. We can no longer accept Spengler's simple analogy to the biological world. Furthermore, the cyclical view of history has always been strongest in times of trial and crisis when men have feared that their own society was in process of disintegrating. Our times are no different from other times in this respect. If we are headed for the bottom of the cycle, this attitude seems to say, let us take comfort in the knowledge that all other societies have followed the same path and that we are helpless in the grip of destiny.

THE OPEN SOCIETY

But even if, as the philosopher George Santayana suggests, the only enduring result of man's works is that the earth may cast a slightly different shadow on the moon, there is something in our personalities that rejects simple fatalism. Whatever meaning there is in human history, we ourselves have helped create it. To surrender our freedom, our hopes, our struggles to some vague determinism, fatalism, or cyclical view of history is to bear part of the responsibility for whatever cataclysm may follow. No one has said better than Herbert J. Muller what the final meaning of history is:

History has no meaning, in the sense of a clear pattern or determinate plot; but it is not simply meaningless or pointless. It has no certain meaning because man is free to give it various possible meanings. His freedom is sharply limited, of course. Man has to choose within the conditions imposed by his biological structure, his natural environment, and his cultural heritage. He cannot do whatever he has a mind to, and at that his mind has been largely made up by his ancestors. For such reasons he is always prone to believe that history somehow makes itself, in spite of his efforts, by the automatic operation of natural laws or God's will. Still, at any moment, he has a wide range of choices and is willy-nilly making more history, discovering the meanings of his past and determining the meanings of his future. . . . This insistence on human freedom is not simply cheering. It means that we have to keep making history, instead of leaning on it, and that we can never count on a final solution. It means the constant possibility of foolish or even fatal choices. Yet the dignity of man lies precisely in this power to choose his destiny. We may therefore welcome the conclusion that we cannot foretell the future, even apart from the possibility that it may not bear knowing. Uncertainty is not only the plainest condition of human life but the necessary condition of freedom, of aspiration, of conscience—of all human idealism.*

* H. J. Muller, *The Uses of the Past* (New York: Mentor Books, 1954), p. 73.

SOME WORDS OF SUMMARY

In this chapter we have discussed the uses of history, traced our modern heritage, and speculated on the meaning of history. History, we have said, promotes piety and tolerance, gives us a tool of understanding, provides adventure, and acts as the protector of liberty and a guide for the present.

In our own time we stand astride a great historical watershed just as our ancestors did four hundred years ago. On the one side is a powerful Europe, expansive, dynamic, and creative; on the other is the misty future with Russia and non-Western peoples perhaps wielding the balance of power in the world. The revolution in world outlook that occurred during the fifteenth and sixteenth centuries was equally dramatic. In a single generation powerful forces turned the interest of Europeans toward secular affairs, the world of science, and the new lands discovered by Columbus. There followed three hundred years of overseas expansion, industrial development, and democratic growth until the nineteenth-century European basked in the superiority of his civilization. But in the same peaceful age of the Victorians there emerged a modern skeptical temper, a dangerous reliance on nationalism, a nihilistic communism, an overbearing imperialism, and doubts about the blessings of industrialism. In the twentieth century we have been forced to defend Western ideas of liberty and democracy against combinations of power rooted in these developments.

To find meaning in a history marred by so much recent catastrophe is increasingly difficult. The religious interpretation of history has lost support in face of the skeptical and scientific attitudes of modern man. Some have sought to make of history itself a science by eradicating all subjective elements in the writing of history. But this attempt has been sharply challenged by modern critics who are impressed by the influence that each historian's environment exerts on his selection and arrangement of historical facts. They point, too, to the historian's inability to test his hypotheses in any kind of controlled experiment. Still other historians have seen a pattern or cycle in man's development and have likened the cycles of civilization to the natural processes of birth, growth, decay, and extinction. Both Oswald Spengler and Arnold Toynbee find such patterns in history, though Toynbee's system is much less rigid and deterministic than Spengler's earlier one.

There is a great deal of speculation and unproven surmise in the great philosophies of history. We, the authors, are convinced that no cyclical view of history and no determinism can excuse man from the weighty responsibility he bears as he makes his own history. Whatever the end result of human history, human beings are free to choose between alternatives and are thus in a measure at least the masters of their own destiny.

FURTHER ROADS TO LEARNING

GENERAL ACCOUNTS

C. Brinton, J. Christopher, and R. Wolff, A *History of Civilization*, 2nd ed. (Englewood Cliffs, N. J.: Prentice-Hall, 1960). Two volumes. An outstanding and delightful textbook in this field.

C. Gustavson, A *Preface to History* (New York: McGraw-Hill, 1955). For the beginning student seeking the "whys and wherefores" of history.

H. Muller, *The Uses of the Past* (New York: Mentor Books, 1954). A brilliant and exciting inquiry into the meaning of history.

A. Nevins, *The Gateway to History* (Boston: Heath, 1938). Still an excellent introduction to the study of history.

A. Rowse, *The Use of History* (London: Hodder and Stoughton, 1946). A chatty, informal discussion of the uses and pleasures of historical study.

SPECIAL STUDIES

C. Becker, *Everyman His Own Historian* (New York: Crofts, 1935). Superbly written essays on history and politics by a leader of the revolt against scientific history.

H. Commager, *et al., Contemporary Civilization* (Chicago: Scott, Foresman, 1959). A unique publishing venture that seeks to summarize and interpret the significant events and trends of our own time.

L. Snyder, *The World in the Twentieth Century* (New York: Van Nostrand, Anvil Books, 1955). A handy summary of the important events and documents of our century.

Social Science Research Council, Committee on Historiography, *The Social Sciences in Historical Study* (New York: Social Science Research Council, *Bulletin 64*, 1954). An important statement of the relations between history and the other social sciences, but hard going for beginning students.

O. Spengler, *The Decline of the West* (New York: Knopf, 1926-28). Two volumes. A translation of Spengler's famous theory of civilization.

A. Toynbee, *A Study of History* (New York: Oxford University Press, 1946-57). This is the two-volume abridgement of Toynbee's great work, done with perception and skill by D. C. Somervell.

H. G. Wells, *The Outline of History* (Garden City, N. Y.: Garden City Publishing Company, 1930). An ambitious attempt to catalogue all of history from the birth of the sun to our own century in a single volume.

FICTION AND DRAMA

G. Orwell, *1984* (New York: Signet Books, 1959). An arresting novel of life in a fictional totalitarian society, which alerts us to the abuses of history and their consequences.

FILMS

American Heritage (National Educational Television, 1955, 29 min., sound, black and white). A televised review of the American political heritage with stress on the legacy of freedom.

Our Inheritance from the Past (Coronet Films, 1951, 11 min., sound, black and white or color). How past civilizations and their accomplishments have contributed to modern life and better understanding.

Winston Churchill: Man of the Century (Association Films, 1957, 58 min., sound, black and white). One of the great documentary films of our times on the life of a man whose career has spanned all the major developments of the twentieth century.

CHAPTER THREE

Social Science
and the Contemporary World

*Social scientists mold research tools
and techniques, carry them into society, and attempt
to measure actual behavior,
attitudes, and other human phenomena.*

The school

of social science has many classrooms. If we have lingered overlong in the room assigned to history, it is because we believe that history can make an important contribution to the social sciences. In many ways history and the other social sciences are one in their attempt to understand human behavior and to find meaningful patterns in man's life in society. Each discipline depends on the other for fresh materials and new perspectives. Each seeks to substitute logic, order, and rational analysis for offhand impressions and unchecked opinions. Most social scientists make some use of history, and all historians analyze past human behavior in terms of their knowledge, however imprecise, of the behavioral sciences. An eminent philosopher, John Herman Randall, Jr., has aptly summed up the kinship between history and social science in these words:

Nothing in the social sciences can be understood in terms of its history alone, though nothing can be understood without reference to that history. . . . History cannot do its job without the social sciences, and the social sciences cannot do theirs without history. Each needs the other but neither is to be confused with the other, or absorbed in or reduced to the other. Here are all the makings of a perfect marriage. What God hath joined together, let no man put asunder! *

Many an irate intruder, however, has sought to stay these happy nuptials. To many social scientists the historian seems a being set apart from his fellows by his addiction to unproven theories, his lack of scientific discipline, and his quaint musings about human motivations. On the other hand, to the disciples of Clio—the muse of history—the social scientist frequently seems unimaginative, obsessed with his scientific objectivity, and given to using jargon and meaningless phrases in place of good English words. As a result, many textbooks in social science manage to avoid any mention of history, while historians in their texts give a wide berth to studies in human behavior. In many a beginning course, despite Randall's warning, either history or social science has in fact been "absorbed in or reduced to the other."

HISTORY AND SOCIAL SCIENCE: THE PARTING OF THE WAYS

Where does the root of this mutual suspicion and antagonism lie? In large part it is to be found in the historical past. A half-century ago, historians, like sociologists and other students of human society, were convinced that the study of human behavior was being rapidly reduced to an objective science. Darwin's great works on biology and evolution impressed many American scholars with the similarity between animal and human development. Would not the study of human society likewise yield to patient scientific investigation? Were there not laws to be found governing human society, like the law

* J. H. Randall, Jr., "History and the Social Sciences," in Salo W. Baron, *et al.*, eds., *Freedom and Reason* (Glencoe, Ill.: The Free Press, 1951), reproduced in A. W. Thompson, ed., *Gateway to the Social Sciences* (New York: Holt, 1955), p. 369.

of evolution governing animal development? Did not the unscientific character of history and the other social studies stem from their failure to apply the exact techniques of study used in biology and physics? Would not some Darwin or Newton inevitably appear to reduce the chaos of social science to order, as these great men had done in the natural sciences? Was not social science potentially as scientific as physics itself?

Historians were as diligent as economists and sociologists in seeking the laws that governed human development. Social scientists and historians moved easily back and forth from one field to the other in their studies. Perhaps the most influential social scientist of the World War I period was a historian, Charles Beard, who was so highly respected by one branch of social science—political science—that he became president of their national association. And historians were mightily impressed with the work of such sociologists as Lester Ward and William Graham Sumner, as well as with the brilliant economist Thorstein Veblen.

But as we saw in Chapter 2, historians soon grew tired hunting for law and meaning in history. They despaired of making history an objective science and were content to use science only to test the reliability of their documents and materials. The "historical laws" discovered by some researchers toward the end of the nineteenth century proved on closer inspection to be no more than convenient generalizations to fit the historian's purpose. More and more, the historian began to move away from his former associates in sociology, economics, and political science back toward the humanities from where he had come.

Meanwhile, his colleagues in social science, far from abandoning the quest for scientific status, were becoming more confident that an objective science of society was possible. They grew impatient with historians and others who questioned their contentions,

and they insisted that a full-fledged body of scientific data on human behavior was already being accumulated. For them it was only a matter of time until social scientists would possess all the laws and generalizations that would permit them to predict accurately the behavior of social groups. "It is the business of social scientists," announced a leading sociologist later in the century, "to be able to predict with high probability the social weather, just as meteorologists predict sunshine and storm."

The parting of the ways between history and social science can be traced back to that generation of scholars which flourished around World War I. In the writings of two leading representatives of that group can be found the basic conflict in outlook between historians and social scientists that has persisted until relatively recent times. Both John Dewey, an eminent philosopher and psychologist, and Charles Beard, the outstanding historian of his generation, agreed on a great many things. They both saw history as a keen tool for understanding the present, agreed on the importance of economic forces in society, and saw eye-to-eye on the need for social scientists to work for the betterment of human society. But they differed sharply over whether the study of society would ever be finally scientific. Dewey believed that all matters affecting human society, including questions of morals and values, were reducible to scientific categories. To determine what was best for society, an investigator need only trace the consequences of alternative lines of action, and the policy that was best for society would emerge clear and unmistakable. The job might be extremely difficult, but it was feasible and realizable in most instances. A scientific study of society divorced from personal preferences or biases was therefore a real possibility. There was such a thing as social *science*.

Charles Beard thought otherwise. Every scholar, he believed, brought a point of view and a set of values to his study of human society. However great his passion for truth, however determined his effort to be objective, the student of society showed by his selection of problems for study and the arrangement of his materials and conclusions that he was human in his preferences. If science meant that all scholars should agree publicly on particular research projects, then the study of society would never be scientific. If it meant the ability to predict future behavior, no social law could ever be as exact or as universal as the physical law of gravitation. For there was a qualitative difference, Beard believed, in the data of the physical and social worlds which sprang from the fact that man, in observing social phenomena, was observing something in which he had a vital, personal stake. Scientific study was essentially neutral and could never tell society what to do, as Dewey believed, because man could never be indifferent to what happened to himself. The great achievements in social science, according to Beard, were works such

as the *Federalist* papers, which asserted human values. Broadly conceived, the social sciences were really *ethical*, not neutral. For Beard there was really no such thing in the strict sense as social *science*.

This sharp difference in outlook, clearly apparent by 1915, has had enormous consequences for the study of society in the twentieth century. Not the least important result has been the parting of the ways between historians and social scientists. Though there were other important factors, it is probably safe to say that few men have had greater influence on the spirit and methods of social science research in this century than John Dewey, while the stamp that Charles Beard left on the study of history is still clear today in any textbook on historical method. It would be assigning far too much importance to these two men to make them personally responsible for the rift that developed among American scholars of human behavior in the twentieth century, but their views clearly illustrate the divergence that has taken place.

SOCIAL SCIENCE AS SCIENCE AND AS ART

IS SCIENCE A SPIRIT OR A METHOD?

Actually, the roots of the conflict were not so deep as they seemed. For the basic quarrel between historians and social scientists was not so much a question of whether social science was truly a science as it was a matter of defining what science actually was. It was difficult, if not impossible, for the two camps to agree on whether sociology or economics was a science until they agreed on what science itself was. In America the criterion for a science was that it be precise and objective in the manner of the physical sciences. To be scientific, a discipline had to lend itself to impersonal investigation and precise description, provide a basis for prediction, reveal the existence of basic laws,

and be capable of experimental proof. Both physics and chemistry met these conditions. But what of sociology and anthropology? Did biology and astronomy qualify? There was a real question, for example, whether a biologist could discover laws that would make possible the prediction of future species. And the astronomer had no bottle-crammed laboratory where he might check experimentally the hypotheses that his mind invented. Were biology and astronomy less "scientific," therefore, than physics or chemistry?

What did the word "science" mean? The Germans, whose scientific achievements during the nineteenth century numbered among the most significant, had only one word for the logical and systematic investigation of any subject—*wissenschaft*. History and sociology were as much *wissenschaft* as astronomy and chemistry, since the word meant only *a system of organized knowledge*. Its meaning embraced both what Americans meant when they spoke of *science* and what they intended when they spoke of *scholarship*. There was no fundamental cleavage between scholarship devoted to the study of chemistry and that devoted to sociology or history. This definition of science demanded only that the scholar be precise and thorough, that he keep his mind open and change it when confronted with new evidence, and that he be humble in the face of enormous and complex problems. The essence of science was its spirit rather than its method.

Was there, then, no scientific method that began with a hypothesis to be tested and proceeded surely through observation, classification, and generalization to some final conclusion? There was indeed, but were there not other equally scientific avenues to truth? Could a person not begin with observations, before he had a hypothesis to test? Were there not scientific *methods* rather than a single scientific *method*? Was it not possible that the particular methods suitable to attacking problems in physics were inapplicable to zoology or to economics? One of the great theoretical physicists of this century, Percy Bridgman, remarked that he was "not one of those who hold that there is a scientific method as such. The scientific method, so far as it is a method, is nothing more than doing one's damnedest with one's mind, no holds barred."

We could include all the social sciences within such a definition. But many people insisted that science was something more than *wissenschaft* and that it must take its cue from those sciences that had been most successful in unlocking the secrets of nature. These were the physical sciences or, as they are sometimes called, the exact, or mathematical, sciences. According to this school

of thought, all scientific scholarship must aim for the high degree of certainty and precision that characterizes chemistry and physics. Here the human element was reduced to a minimum. Here objectivity and mathematics worked hand in hand to determine the exact relationships existing in the natural world. Science was exact, precise, impersonal, and mathematical. It sought to discover basic laws of matter and motion; it enabled its master to predict accurately the behavior of atoms, gases, and planets; it harnessed the pressure of steam and the power of electricity to do the work of man. What praises awaited the scholar who would apply this method to the science of man!

THE SCIENTIFIC METHOD

What was this scientific method which had served physical scientists so well in their work? It consisted, according to its adherents, of four basic steps.

1. *The Tentative Hypothesis.* The scientist begins his work with a hypothesis, which is an informed hunch or guess. This hypothesis he sets down as clearly and explicitly as possible. It is not something he must defend but rather something he must test by experiment.

2. *Gathering Data.* Once he has carefully formulated his hypothesis, the scientist is ready to go to work in earnest. He now makes repeated, careful observations or measurements bearing on his problem. He gathers sufficient data to prove or disprove the hypothesis he is testing. His observations or measurements must be rigorous, dispassionate, and stated as far as possible in precise terms. He must set them down in such a way that they can be repeated and confirmed by other researchers.

3. *Organizing Data.* Having gathered all the evidence necessary to confirm or deny his hypothesis, the scientist then thoroughly

studies and classifies his data. He looks especially for patterns or uniformities that will point to some underlying relationship among the data. He organizes his results in a precise, methodical way so that other scientists will understand and respect them.

4. *Generalizing.* The scientist finally must describe his results in such a fashion that they will apply to all similar phenomena studied under the same conditions. Preferably, he will express them in a convenient mathematical formula or a clearly stated proposition. If other researchers confirm his results, they become a *scientific law.*

IS THE SAME METHOD APPLICABLE
TO THE SOCIAL AND NATURAL SCIENCES?

Can this method be applied to the study of man? Can scientists find uniform patterns of behavior in people as well as in electrons? Does the study of the social sciences on the one hand and the natural sciences on the other involve any basic differences in technique? Is social science simply the use of the scientific method to answer questions about human behavior?

These questions are easier to raise than to answer. A quarter-century ago almost all social scientists agreed (as historians had earlier) that the method used so effectively by natural scientists would yield as fruitful results in the study of human behavior. Numerous sociologists were certain that their techniques need be no different from those of the physicist, and that with them they would discover laws of human behavior that all reasonable men would accept.

Many social scientists still hold this view. Man, they argue, has up to now made only feeble attempts to apply the scientific method to his social problems. Though facing great difficulties, he will yet arrive at the day when the scientific method will achieve results in the social world comparable to what it has wrought in the physical world.

The problems facing social scientists, this view holds, are imposed by human frailty and stubbornness and by the newness of the subject rather than by any real difference between them and the natural sciences. Man is a part of nature, and the laws of nature, whether physical, chemical, or biological, must apply to him as to all matter and energy.

Skeptics, on the other hand, assert that the differences between the social sciences and the natural sciences are differences of kind rather than merely of degree. They harken back to Beard's warning that everyone who studies human behavior begins with certain preferences or values that prevent complete objectivity. Man has a personal emotional stake in problems of depression, crime, sexual behavior, and democracy, which he does not have in studying the behavior of electrons or gases. This emotional stake affects the kinds of subject he chooses to study and the data he selects in the process of formulating his final conclusions. The basic problem of the social scientist, according to this view, is that he must deal much of the time not with observable behavior but with the internal, hidden workings of the human mind, which cannot be measured or directly observed. Some psychologists have tried to avoid this problem by disregarding "mind" altogether and studying only the observable, measurable behavior of man.

But what of those uniformities of nature that we call "scientific laws"? Are there similar all-embracing laws to be found in the social world? A number of sociologists, although certainly far from all, have followed the historians in recent years and given up the search for universal laws of human behavior. This is not to say that they have found no uniformities in human behavior. They have. But they have discovered no comprehensive, unvarying laws of human behavior that correspond to the sweeping character of physical laws. Every uniformity discovered to date is limited in time and space and admits of numerous exceptions, even under ideal conditions of observation.

Does this mean that social scientists are divided over whether sociology, economics, and the other social sciences are actually sciences? No, it means only that they are divided, as we saw earlier, over what science actually is. If we define science as organized knowledge, then all will agree that the social sciences are true sciences; but if we regard science as a precise, exact, and unvarying method for arriving at truth, then some would say that the social sciences can never be truly scientific. Listen, for example, to Arnold Rose, a sociologist of the skeptical type we described earlier:

> While the sociologist and many cultural anthropologists have recognized the limited scope of their propositions, they have not fully faced the implications of the fact. To do so would mean that they would have to acknowledge that it is impossible to find universal laws respecting many phases of human action. To admit this seems to them an acknowledgment that social science can never be completely a science. If science is to be defined as the derivation of universal laws by empirical observation, then there can be no social science except perhaps in limited fields. . . . But if science is defined as the accumulation of knowledge that can be used for predictions more accurate than chance alone would allow, it is already a science. It is maintained that this is the only sense in which it can be a science. . . .*

THE THORNY QUESTION OF VALUES

If social scientists have disagreed for several decades about the meaning of science, they have argued even more vigorously over the influence and place of human values in the study of social science. *Values are the ideas, sentiments, beliefs, or preferences*

---

* A. M. Rose, *Theory and Method in the Social Sciences* (Minneapolis: University of Minnesota Press, 1954), pp. 161-62.

cherished by an individual or a whole society. They express people's judgments about the relative worth or importance of things. Some values, such as the preference for a beautiful car, are materialistic; others are non-materialistic or spiritual. In the United States, for example, we characteristically value such non-materialistic things as individual initiative, democracy, freedom, and education.

How do these values relate to the study of social science? Few questions have been more vexing and more earnestly debated in the past quarter-century. Basically, the question has boiled down to this: Are these human values which we hold (a) external to, (b) a part of, or (c) basic to the central concern of the social scientist? Can we divorce ourselves from our human values when we don laboratory coats and become social scientists? Ought we to try? Are not values themselves a vital part of the society which the social scientist studies? Are they not a proper object of investigation?

a. *Values Are Extraneous.* Social scientists who endorse the first position maintain that the student of society must place his human values to one side when he becomes a scientist. He must look at human society and its problems through non-human eyes. As a scientist, he must emulate the physicist and the zoologist and not permit his own stake in human existence, his own attitudes and opinions, to color his observations or conclusions. His ideal is to study the movement of peoples as dispassionately as the chemist studies the movement of ions, to observe the sexual behavior of humans as disinterestedly as the biologist probes the mating habits of gallwasps. He is a scientist, and no matter what his private preferences may be, he must report what is, not what ought to be. Man is an animal living in the natural world. To forget this fact is to lapse into poetry and fantasy.

This compelling point of view is firmly

supported by many social scientists who be-lieve their methods can be as exact and dis-interested as the methods of the botanist or inorganic chemist. Indeed, those who sub-scribe to this approach are for the most part the same scholars who would make science something more than *wissenschaft* and would model social science after the exact sciences. They believe that science by its very nature is nonethical and should be concerned neither with the scientists' values nor with the practical application of their work. Sci-ence must be value-free. The scholar who permits his studies to be used in support of particular programs or objectives, in the words of one leader of this school, "must be regarded as one of the most dangerous enemies of science."

b. *Values Are Part of the Social Scene.* The view that social science should be value-free, objective, and, if possible, quantitative, reached the peak of its influence about a quarter-century ago. It has since faded imper-ceptibly into a second viewpoint, which has become a widely accepted explanation of the relationship between values and the study of society today. This second school believes that the scholar cannot escape the problem of values. For better or for worse, values are part of the social scene. Although the ideal of a value-free social science re-mains, the individual social scientist works in fact in a climate of values that inevitably affects him. If this is so, then why not make the study of values themselves a primary aim of the social sciences? By doing so, the social scientist may recognize and correct the errors in his own judgment caused by value assumptions. By frankly recognizing his own biases, members of this school of thought contend, the scholar will approach one step closer to that objectivity which is his ultimate concern. But since he doubts his ability ever to be completely value-free in his own thinking, the social scientist should also refrain from telling his fellow

men what the best society is or how they should solve their social problems. Such ad-vice would inevitably involve the personal values of the social scientist. According to this view, the social sciences are like a car and chauffeur—they stand ready to take us where we want to go, but they cannot tell us where to go.

c. *Values Are the Heart of Social Science.* Still a third provocative view on the place of values in social science would have the social scientist openly champion his values in his society. Because he is better informed than the average citizen about social problems, and because he shares the same basic values as his fellow citizens, the social scientist *ought* to battle in the market place for what he believes to be true. Failure to do so means that the most important social decisions will be made by people who know least about them. No one attacks the value judgments of the biochemist, who investigates the causes of cancer, polio, or heart disease, because he values health over disease. Few would challenge either the many economists who study such social ills as unemployment and depression simply because they desire to rid society of these problems. Why should not the sociologist likewise declare war on racial discrimination, crime, or divorce?

For champions of this point of view, there is no such thing as a value-free social science. Every selection of a research problem, every choice of a fact to be included or excluded from a study, involves some kind of prefer-ence or value judgment, whether hidden or acknowledged. As the sociologist Jessie Ber-nard has stated: "The scientific problems which men attack do not impose themselves on men. Men choose them. And men reveal their values in the kinds of problems that they choose, as artists do. The personality of the scientist is as clearly revealed in the prob-lems he selects, the questions he asks, the choice of methods he makes, and the inter-pretation of his results as is the personality of the artist in his design." * The yardstick for measuring whether a particular subject should be investigated, or a particular fact included, is most often its relevance to contemporary life. This is precisely the conclusion that Charles Beard reached in his thinking about history a half-century ago when he stated that all history is seen through the eyes of a historian rooted in a particular society and a particular time. Like Beard, the proponents of this third school insist that social scientists should be avowedly on the side of such values as freedom, individual rights, and social welfare.

SCIENCE AS A SOCIAL PRODUCT

One important by-product of the debate over the place of values in social science has been a stimulation of interest in the scientific process itself. To many social scientists a quarter-century or more ago, science was a kind of neutral, impersonal standard against which to measure the subjectivity and bias of human values. Science was one instrument for measuring society that did not repeat the man-centered errors of former methods of investigation. Yet, science itself, observers came slowly to realize, was not totally disinterested, or value-free. Historians of science have demonstrated that the scientific method was not something just stumbled on by Francis Bacon or Galileo. Rather, it grew out of certain values that had become important in our Western Civilization, such as the beliefs in rationality, progress, and the division of labor. Western man invented and improved the techniques of science because they were useful to him. They helped him to understand and control the world through rational thought and activity. Because he believed in progress and the possibility of changing his environment, the European was intrigued by the possibilities that science

* J. Bernard, "The Art of Science: a Reply to Redfield," *American Journal of Sociology*, LV (July, 1949), p. 5.

At issue among social scientists is whether they should be dispassionate and confine themselves to reporting what is, or whether they should describe and recommend what ought to be and try to correct such social eyesores as these.

opened to him. And the rise of industrialism enabled him to probe many of the possibilities and create a scientific revolution. For it was not until Western Europe had reached a stage of economic development where specialization and the division of labor permitted a Newton or Leibnitz to devote most of his time to scientific activity that a scientific revolution was possible.

Science itself can be viewed and studied

as a particular kind of social activity. It has its own values—honesty, accuracy, objectivity —yet must assume that the natural universe is as indifferent to them as to other human purposes and motives. But the values of science are clearly of vital importance even to the most zealous social scientists who would rid science of its cargo of human values. Listen to Stuart Chase, a champion of exact, scientific techniques in social science, as he describes the scientific method as the most *moral* discipline:

To judge an experiment, to slant a conclusion, to report anything but the whole truth as one knows it alone in the night, brings ignominy and oblivion. There can be no secret processes, no patent medicines, no private understandings or payoffs on the side. The calculations must be laid on the table, face up, for all the world to see. In this sense, science is perhaps the most *moral* of all man's disciplines. It will be corrupted and debased if ever its direction falls permanently into the hands of national governments and ideologists. It is as international as the north wind.*

THE ART OF SOCIAL SCIENCE

In the preceding chapter we said that history was both art and science. And we have said enough in this chapter to indicate that the other social sciences also straddle the boundary line between art and science at times. Here, at least, is ground on which historians and social scientists might ultimately meet. Basically, there is little difference in outlook and approach between those historians and sociologists, for example, who conclude that value premises are implicit in all social science study. Both seek greater objectivity by frankly avowing the difficulties that their own values pose. Both are forced to be more humble than their predecessors because final explanations in the field of human behavior frequently have been so elusive. Both now study, too, the social milieu out of

which scientific activity has developed, and both recognize their common commitment to uphold the values of the society in which they live and work. Finally, both can find plenty of room for their activity within the ample folds of science.

If historians still feel more comfortable on the artistic side of the boundary line between art and science, their colleagues in social science feel more at home on the scientific side. But both now recognize that they have friends across the line and that the boundary is less well fortified than it used to be. An occasional historian will venture into the land of the social scientists and return unscathed to the delight of his brethren, while not a few social scientists have dared to speak of the need for more contacts with history and the humanities generally.

The anthropologist Robert Redfield, for example, went so far as to suggest that there is an "art of social science." He contends that the most enduring books dealing with the American social scene—De Tocqueville's *Democracy in America*, Sumner's *Folkways*, and Veblen's *Theory of the Leisure Class*, for example—are those whose methods and style resemble those of the creative artist. Despite important differences between the humanities and the social sciences, writes Redfield, they are very similar in many respects. "The subject matter of both is, centrally, man as a human being. Human beings are not the subject matter of physics and chemistry. So it would be error to build a social science upon the image of physics or chemistry." Sympathy, insight, creative imagination—these are qualities of the great social scientist and novelist alike. In a passage that Charles Beard would have applauded, Redfield charges his colleagues with becoming better social scientists by becoming better versed in history and the arts:

Social science is also an art. It is an art in that the social scientist creates imaginatively out of his own human qualities brought into

---

* S. Chase, *The Proper Study of Mankind*, rev. ed. (New York: Harper, 1956), p. 7.

connection with the facts before him. It is an art in degree much greater than that in which physics and chemistry are arts, for the student of the atom or of the element is not required, when he confronts his subject matter, to become a person among persons, a creature of tradition and attitude in a community that exists in tradition and in attitude. With half his being the social scientist approaches his subject matter with a detachment he shares with the physicist. With the other half he approaches it with a human sympathy which he shares with the novelist. And it is an art to a greater degree than is physics or chemistry for the further reason that the relationships among the parts of a person or of a society are, as compared with physical relationships, much less susceptible of definitions, clear and machine precise. In spite of the great advances in formal method in social science, much of the understanding of persisting and general relationships depends upon a grasp that is intuitive and that is independent of or not fully dependent on some formal method. In advancing social science, we invent and practice techniques, and we also cultivate a humanistic art.*

THE BRANCHES OF SOCIAL SCIENCE

We have been talking of social science in the preceding pages as if it were a single branch of study presenting a united front to history and the humanities at one end of the spectrum of knowledge and aping the methods of natural science at the other. This approach, however, is only a convenient fiction, for actually the study of society embraces more than a half-dozen disciplines, ranging in interest and age from political science, older than Aristotle, to anthropology, a mere infant among the social sciences. Most observers would also include economics, sociology, social psychology, and human geography as partners in this joint enterprise. Some would include such disciplines as general psychology. A growing cooperation and similarity of method among students of society in recent decades has made it easier to generalize about the methods, problems, and trends in social science; but each of the individual branches of social science has its own special interests and techniques, and to these we must now turn.

DEFINING THE SOCIAL SCIENCES

The common bond drawing social scientists together is an attempt to develop and refine techniques for studying man and his society. *Indeed, we may define the social sciences as those studies that seek systematically to apply the spirit and techniques of modern science to man in his relation with others.* Each branch of social science has staked a claim to special segments of man's social relations. Thus, political scientists long ago claimed the political and governmental processes as their locus of interest; economists have studied the ways in which men apportion their resources, goods, and services to satisfy needs and demands; sociologists have been interested in social interaction and man's institutional patterns; anthropologists have studied his origins and cultures; social psychologists have explored the human personality; while geographers, with one foot in the natural sciences and the other in the social sciences, have studied man in his natural setting and stressed man-land relationships.

But in recent years it has become increasingly apparent that the traditional boundary lines between the branches of social science are shifting and, in some cases, disappearing, because of new concepts and changing points of view. The subject of human personality, for example, is being explored by psychologists, sociologists, and anthropologists, as well as by social psychologists and psychoanalysts.

* R. Redfield, "The Art of Social Science," *The American Journal of Sociology,* LIV (Nov., 1948), p. 188.

Political behavior interests the sociologist, anthropologist, and psychologist, as well as the political scientist and the historian. Indeed, there is a growing tendency among many social scientists to define their own branch in such a fashion that it excludes nothing in the entire range of the social sciences. Thus, some anthropologists define their interest as "man and his works," while many historians describe history as "all that man has thought and done." No more modest, some sociologists have, on occasion, likened themselves to cowhands exercising "an oversight over the social science rancho as a whole."

This tendency toward "academic imperialism," together with the vagueness of the boundary lines between the branches of social science, makes it very difficult to define the individual social sciences with any sharpness. In the interest of clarity, let us avoid simple or misleading definitions and think

Automation has placed new tools in the hands of social scientists and has opened up new areas of study and investigation to them.

instead of the branches of social science as representing a *division of labor.* Each branch investigates those things that it is peculiarly able to attack and follows them wherever they lead. Boundary lines are disregarded; the neighboring branches of social science stand ready to help; and the results are shared by all the social sciences. More and more, this process characterizes the best of social science research. Like all divisions of labor, this one must be judged by its results. If such cooperation and interdisciplinary study and research yield a greater fund of reliable information and knowledge than would a more rigid division and assignment of tasks, then it will be continued.

Within this division of labor, each of the branches of social science has tended to employ certain intellectual tools that have proven especially fruitful. These tools include concepts and methods that have become hallmarks of the activity within the particular branches. To understand what each of the social sciences is doing today, let us ask of each branch: (1) What is one of the more useful tools or concepts employed by specialists in your area of learning, and (2) What kinds of question are you seeking to answer? Such an inquiry ought to make clear the special interests and emphases of each branch of social science, and yet not obliterate the very real interrelatedness that exists among the various social sciences today.

SOCIOLOGY
AND THE CONCEPT OF GROUP

Like historians and anthropologists, sociologists have had a strong historical tendency to maintain an interest that is coterminous with all human society. And rightly so! For whether sociology is defined in the older and more traditional sense as *the scientific study of human society* or in the more modern sense as *the science of human interaction,* very few phases of human activity or human society—economic, political, or intellectual—are foreign to it. We need only glance through the chapter headings in standard books on sociology to notice how wide are the sociologist's interests—in institutional behavior (such as family, church, and school), social disorganization (such as juvenile delinquency, crime and divorce), population growth and movements, crowd behavior, personality, public opinion and propaganda, to name just a few. At every turn, he shares his interest with specialists from other branches of social science. With political scientists he studies crowd behavior, public opinion, and mass communications (some would go so far as to say that political science is a segment of sociology); with social psychologists he turns to the factors shaping human personality; with anthropologists he studies how different cultures affect man's ways of life; with historians he shares an interest in the social organization and behavior in ancient Athens or medieval France.

How, then, can sociology be considered a separate field of social science in its own right? It is because sociology, like all social sciences, is also distinguished by its conceptual tools and methods. Perhaps one of the most useful tools devised by sociologists and now used by other social scientists is the concept of *group*. *A group is two or more persons who are interacting. Interaction occurs whenever two or more people stimulate, influence, or modify each other's behavior by verbal or non-verbal communication.* Talking, making faces, pushing, and similar types of stimulation are examples. Take a situation in which you are relating some personal experience of yours to a friend. If he becomes bored and twists in his chair, you will probably change the subject. His response to your story has modified your behavior.

This mutual stimulation and response (social interaction) is common to all groups. Before social interaction can occur, however,

group members must be in contact, either directly or indirectly, and mutually aware of one another. Finally, members interact within a framework of mutual expectations. A church member, for instance, is expected to respond in accordance with the behavioral expectations of the other members around him. If a member suddenly begins singing a popular song when the congregation is chanting the creed, or if he stands while they are kneeling, he may stimulate other members to respond—they may look at him with disapproval or forget to continue chanting. But his behavior and much of their response is outside the religious group's behavior patterns and its expectations. Group interaction is therefore channeled by mutual expectations and social standards, or norms, that define rights and obligations of group members.

A group is thus more than an aggregate of persons or a number of individuals who may have qualities in common, such as age, sex, or occupation. All college students do not interact, but members of a college class do. All New York Yankee fans are not a group, but a local Yankee booster club is. Among sociologists today, few problems receive more attention than how groups are formed, how group members interact, how the group reaches decisions, acts, maintains itself, and disintegrates.

Sociologists have made considerable progress in analyzing group behavior. They have studied, for example, how *primary groups*, such as family and close friends, affect personality development, especially the way they influence our ideas and attitudes about ourselves (see Chapter 4). They have also investigated the way in which members of the same group regard each other as opposed to outsiders. This *in-group* versus *out-group* distinction is an important key to all intergroup relations. It affects strongly a person's attitudes, opinions, and scale of values. What is wrong for someone not a member of our group may be permissible or even welcome in one of our own. If we know how judgments are formed about people both within and outside our own groups, we will be in a much better position to understand and evaluate all types of human action, including peaceful cooperation and conflicts between neighborhood gangs, racial groups, and even nations.

Now what are some of the questions the sociologist seeks to answer? The following is a sample, which in its brevity can only be suggestive:

1. How do groups form, function, and disintegrate?
2. How does interaction in a small, informal group differ from interaction in a large, formally organized group?
3. What are the consequences of various types of human behavior?
4. How does participation in various types of groups affect our personalities?
5. What are the causes of social disorganization?
6. How do traditions and social values affect our behavior?

ANTHROPOLOGY
AND THE CONCEPT OF CULTURE

Anthropologists, too, according to Robert Redfield, are united in their efforts, as indicated by their objective "to see all man, animal and human, as a whole." This objective has been sought along two major lines of interest, one followed by the physical anthropologists and the other by the cultural and social anthropologists. Physical anthropologists seek to "unravel the course of human evolution." They deal primarily with the distribution and sequences of physical types of men and, among other things, seek the origins of man and races.

Cultural and social anthropologists, on the other hand, are like sociologists in their concern with the way human beings act in persisting social groups or societies. Unlike sociologists, however, cultural anthropologists have spent a great deal of their time studying man in his primitive habitat in order to learn something of the *comparative* ways in which human societies have developed. To their research has been added the studies of a more recent group, the social anthropologists, who concentrate on modern literate communities. To most anthropologists, however, both the literate and existing nonliterate societies are a kind of world-wide laboratory in which they seek answers to such questions as:

1. How did human society evolve?
2. How much of the pattern of human behavior is world-wide and how much is rooted in particular societies or cultures?
3. How does a particular society's way of life affect the growing-up process in that society?
4. What happens when two different ways of life come into contact?

Doubtless, the most important contribution that anthropologists have made to social science in general is the concept of *culture*. *A culture consists of the behavior patterns that are transmitted from generation to generation.* It is the sum total of everything human in origin in a particular people's way of life and includes customs, beliefs, morals, language, art, government, family life, and ways of making a living. Anthropologist Melville Herskovits, in seeking a definition of culture stripped to its essentials, declared that "a society is composed of people; the way they behave is their culture." Culture thus is the man-made part of the environment.

At the most elementary level, culture consists of specific traits or activities, such as ways of dressing or staging a hunt or conducting a religious ceremony. The study of anthropology developed largely as a great cataloguing process based on the extensive data early anthropologists had collected on the specific habits and traits of each tribe or primitive society they studied. But gradually it dawned on anthropologists that a deeper meaning to culture lay in the way in which cultures were *organized.* Underlying every culture was a pattern or configuration that gave meaning and purpose to the individual characteristics or traits they had already studied. Cultures, it was widely believed, could be best understood *as a whole* rather than as isolated segments consisting of bits of random information about dress or religious ceremonies. To be sure, the people of a particular society might be totally unaware that any unifying pattern underlay their way of life, but a pattern, most of it implicit, is nevertheless present behind the way of life of each persisting society. In our Western Civilization, for example, the importance of the individual is the unifying theme on which many of our legal, political, and social customs rest. To the contemporary anthropologist, nothing is more exciting than the study of these fascinating "patterns of culture."

SOCIAL PSYCHOLOGY
AND THE STUDY OF PERSONALITY

In recent years social anthropologists have turned more and more to contemporary Western society to answer questions about the effect of culture on personality. In doing so, their work has become almost indistinguishable from sociology at many points. And as if this were not enough, these two groups of scholars have been joined by social psychologists, who also are investigating the same area.

Psychology is often not included in the social sciences because of its concern with man's physical and psychological make-up. But since men are social creatures and are inevitably influenced by their social environment, psychology has a foot in social science. In the area of *social psychology,* then, the interests of psychologists, sociologists, and anthropologists meet.

Despite a good deal of debate among social psychologists about the meaning of the term, they agree that the concept of *personality* is one of the most useful tools invented by social scientists in the present century. *Personality is the total organization of an individual's habits, attitudes, values, ambitions, and all those things that make a person distinctive or different from others.* In the words of a popular song, "It's what makes you you." Social psychologists are vitally concerned with the relationship between personality and culture, with how we learn, and what motivates us to act the way we do. They are especially interested in the role that child-rearing practices and family environment play in shaping attitudes and motives. They have studied our own society in an attempt to learn how such ideas as success, competition, and class consciousness influence us during our development, and, along with sociologists, they examine public opinion patterns and propaganda techniques, advertising practices and effects, and the roots and results of prejudice. Their inquiries center around such questions as these:

1. Must adolescence be a time of stress and strain, as it is in American society?

2. Through what stages does an infant pass on the way to adulthood?

3. Can an entire society share the same personality characteristic—for example, moodiness, hostility, or cheerfulness? How could this development come about?

4. How important is the small, intimate group in molding fundamental habits or attitudes toward life?

5. What are the respective roles that heredity and environment play in determining a child's chances for success in his society?

POLITICAL SCIENCE
AND THE CONCEPT OF POWER

No branch of social science has undergone so extensive a change in its orientation and techniques in recent decades as political science. Among the oldest of the social science disciplines, political science has been transformed in the twentieth century from a study of forms and theories of government to a study of the actual operations of government and the political behavior of individuals. For more than a quarter-century, political scientists have been slowly absorbing viewpoints and techniques from anthropology, sociology, social psychology, and even the natural sciences. Once closely linked with history, today it is growing much closer in its research techniques and central concepts to sociology. Today's political scientists are asking less about constitutional structure and more about how government actually works, less about the "division of powers" than the power relationships among human beings.

Indeed, today's political scientist cannot avoid being concerned with *power relationships*. He needs to know how power relationships between individuals and groups are established and maintained. A *power relationship involves a situation in which one or more individuals direct, control, influence, limit, alter, or otherwise affect the decisions or actions of other persons.* To put it another way, in a power relationship someone is acting or can be made to act according to the intent and policy of another. These relationships exist in all groups and at every level of society. When persons use their position in a power relationship to influence or control some action or decision of others, they are usually involved in social interaction. In fact, where no interaction occurs, it is extremely difficult to prove that a power relationship exists. Anyone desiring to know how power relationships are established and maintained, therefore, must give considerable attention to social interaction. Otherwise, he will have difficulty in determining who makes the decisions, how decisions are reached, and how they are carried into effect or enforced.

A long-standing interest of political scientists in public policy (by policy we mean *intended action*) leads them naturally to ask how policy is formulated, declared, and enforced. To answer these questions, they must know a great deal about political behavior. To understand political behavior, an investigator must know something about social interaction and human behavior in general—hence, the parenthetical observation we made earlier that political science is a behavioral science and related to sociology.

Thus, political science now bears in new directions, although it still retains a great deal of its older orientation toward the detailed description and study of the forms, structures, institutions, and processes of government. These new directions are apparent in the growing interest of political scientists in public opinion and propaganda, administrative behavior, voting behavior, personnel problems, interest group activity, bureaucracy, and the role of elite groups in government. The contrast between this approach and the older view is apparent, too, in the way in which the Constitution of the United States is now studied. Sociologist George Simpson writes:

In the older method there would be intricate, detailed internal analysis of the clauses of the Constitution with accompanying history on the interpretation of these clauses by the judiciary; discussion of the legal pros and cons of various important judicial decisions, the relations of the states to the national government, the internal meaning of separation of powers, checks and balances, and the legal interpretation of the freedoms guaranteed in the Bill of Rights. In the newer politics the clauses of the Constitution are shown to have definite functions in the larger society of which the state is only a part. . . . There is investigation of the social reasons why the Supreme Court has reversed itself over the years, the meaning of the statement that the Supreme Court follows the elections, the continuing struggle between the Congress and the President of the United States . . . the fact that like any other law or set of laws the Constitution is a scrap of paper unless it lives in the habits, customs, and traditions of the governed. In short, the Constitution today is studied as political behavior evinced in the actions of judges, citizens, legislators, state governments.*

You should now realize that many of the questions posed by the contemporary political scientist are somewhat similar to those asked by the sociologist and the social psychologist. For example, he may ask:

1. Can behavior within the context of a power relationship be predicted?

2. How do loyalty and value conflicts affect government decisions and policies?

3. What has been the impact of modern industrialism and urbanism on government and political methods?

4. How is political behavior related to the rest of human behavior, and how do people differ from one culture to another in their political techniques?

5. How does modern bureaucracy reflect the social and psychological conditions of our contemporary society?

6. How do personality differences affect political relationships?

ECONOMICS
AND THE PROBLEM OF VALUE

At one time, the study of economics was a part of political science, and nineteenth-century authorities devoted many im-

_____
* G. Simpson, *Man in Society: A Preface to Sociology and the Social Sciences* (New York: Random House, paperback, 1955), pp. 22-23.

portant volumes to what they described as *political economy*. This was in frank recognition on their part of the important role government attitudes and policies played in determining the economic future of any society. Nevertheless, not all of them agreed that this influence was healthy. For more than a century the trend in economic thought was in another direction. The so-called classical economists of the nineteenth century assumed that a free market, free trade, and free competition were the necessary and desirable conditions of a well-functioning economic system. They argued, in brief, that economic systems should be free from government influence and control. Today, however, the trend seems to be in the other direction. With half the world's population living under state-managed economic systems and the other half surrendering more and more responsibilities to government, we are less prone to think of a close relationship between government and economics as quaint and old-fashioned.

But only gradually did the economists, influenced in part by the other social sciences, begin to think of economic behavior as a special kind of human behavior. The older assumptions about human psychology used by the classical economists first had to be modified in the light of new findings and information. Economic activity, it soon became clear, did not occur in a vacuum, but was sharply affected by the social, political, and intellectual currents of the age. Studies of the economic organization of nonliterate societies by anthropologists shed considerable light on how culture influences economic activity. Like political scientists, the economists became less concerned with forms and institutions and more concerned with human behavior and the actualities of life. In the words of one observer, the new economists, "instead of imagining a realm that never was on land or sea prefer when-

The trading floor of the New York Stock Exchange—a center of changing economic values.

ever possible to look directly at Main Street and see what they can make of the behavior of the crowd." Thus did psychology, sociology, and anthropology gradually influence economists to convert their discipline into more of a behavioral and *social* science.

Today, economists deal essentially with human behavior, with the way people divide scarce resources for their own use. One of their more useful concepts is *value, which involves choosing among the competing demands of different individuals and groups for scarce resources in order to allocate them in some rational way.* (Values in general we defined elsewhere as choices or preferences or ideals cherished by a person or a society.) This problem of choosing is most difficult. What value should we assign to the claims of the capitalist who supplies the money, to the claims of the worker who has given his labor, to the claims of the engineer

48

who furnishes the "know-how," and to the claims of the landlord who owns the land on which the factory stands? What role should a government play in the economic process? There are other vital questions to which the economist addresses himself:

1. How do businessmen decide about wages, expansion, and investment?
2. How do they decide what to produce and in what quantity?
3. Does the individual consumer receive his share of the nation's output of goods and services on the basis of his needs or on the basis of his contribution as measured by earnings? (Notice the contrast in answers given by a capitalist and a communist or socialist to this question.)
4. What causes the ups and downs of the business cycle?
5. What proportion of the national income is paid out in wages, dividends, interest, and rent?
6. What is the effect of a decline in the national income?

GEOGRAPHY
AND THE CONCEPT OF THE REGION

A survey of the branches of social science would be incomplete if it neglected to include geography, or at least that part of the subject called *human geography.* It is curious that so many introductory books in social science fail to mention geography, despite the fact that next to history it is probably the branch of social science with which graduates of elementary and secondary schools are most familiar. Perhaps the omission stems from the fact that geographers in the past were largely concerned with the physical features of the natural environment. But for some time now, many younger geographers (and a few older ones, too) have been redefining the locus of interest of their subject, striving to make it a genuine social science without sacrificing its connection with the physical sciences.

A recent definition of geography describes it as the study of spatial associations among human, cultural, and natural features. Man and culture are studied in relation to the natural setting and environment. The focus of interest is man; the natural features of the environment take on importance as they relate to man's needs or problems. Modern geographers have assembled reliable atlases depicting the economic and cultural as well as the natural features of various regions of the world. They have developed the important concept of the *region,* or *an area of the world that by virtue of its combination of natural features and human adaptations to them may be considered and studied as a whole.* The human geographer today may divide the globe into the following regions: Europe, the Soviet Union, the Middle East, Africa, the Orient, the Pacific area, Latin America, and Anglo-America. In each of these regions, he looks for combinations of cultural and physiographic features that produce common interests, common objectives, and common problems. In Europe, for example, the mild, moist, and accessible character of the region, coupled with a common cultural background, creates a similarity of interest in the areas of defense, trade, and agriculture. In studying a particular region, the contemporary geographer asks such questions as:

1. How does the climate of a region affect the character of its cultures?

2. What is the relationship between population and the natural resources of a particular region?

3. How may the potentialities of a given region be evaluated?

4. What are the common problems of a particular region under study?

5. How does the environment affect the character of political and economic institutions and behavior?

The regions we listed a few sentences back are made up of single nations or groups of nations. But geographic regions may have other boundaries—outer limits of city-trading areas, divides between river drainage basins, edges of mountains, or the lines marking transitions between different types of land use—depending on the purpose of study.

In addition, some geographic work is *systematic* rather than regional. Here the viewpoint is world-wide rather than compartmentalized into regions, and the subject matter is limited to a single aspect of geographic interest such as urbanization, economies, countries, soils, or climates. The ultimate objective in both regional and systematic geography, however, is global interpretation of interrelationships among human, cultural, and natural features.

The branches of social science, we may say in summary, are as intertwined as worms in a can. The geographer who stops his investigation short of the boundary of economics, the sociologist who refuses to pass over the border to anthropology, is certain, like the blind man touching the elephant, to mistake the tail for the whole of the animal. *The division of labor among social scientists today should not be mistaken for a division of subject matter.* For the vital concepts of social science research—group, culture, personality, power, value, region, and others not mentioned here—are the common tools of all the branches of social science. One branch may characteristically use one tool more than another, may investigate certain questions more than others, but basically social scientists are united in seeking to push back the boundaries of ignorance concerning the social behavior of man. And this is a task worthy of anyone who has the knowledge and patience to pursue it!

WHAT OF THE FUTURE?

What does the future hold for the study of social science? Hopefully, there will be still more cooperation among students of society, less bickering, and more public understanding. There will always be obstacles, of course. Let us admit that the emotional stake which all of us have in the areas that social scientists investigate is not likely to decrease. Very probably we shall always be more concerned about queries directed at our private lives than about questions aimed at the impersonal world of nature. The attitude reflected by a congressman from Ohio who questioned the wisdom of appropriating congressional funds for social science research is apt to be always with us, however deplorable. "The average American," the congressman protested, "does not want some expert running around prying into his life and his personal affairs and deciding for him how he should live ... (nor) a lot of short-haired women and long-haired men messing into everybody's personal affairs and lives, inquiring whether they love their wives or do not love them and so forth." *

The congressman was simply airing a prejudice against social science investigation that many people privately share. By its very nature, according to Robert Redfield, social science will continue to be ambiguous, precarious, and yet critically important. It is ambiguous because people do not know what it is; precarious because people, when alarmed, move reflexively to hamper the objective study of human affairs; and critical because only social science can supply answers, however inadequate, to the most pressing problems confronting humankind today. It is not science, but the uses of science, which pose the biggest headaches for the wielders of power in modern society.

It is not military weapons, but the way we play the diplomatic cards based on these weapons, which will determine our survival as a free people.

We should not be discouraged about the progress we have made. In a scant fifty years there have been startling innovations in our social lives as a result of ideas and investigations emanating from social science fields. Listen to the sociologist Louis Wirth as he summarizes what the past fifty years have brought:

One could scarcely imagine such innovations as we have made in the last fifty years as the Juvenile Court; our social security system; the TVA; our methods of marketing, of dealing with industrial disputes, of selecting personnel for government, the armed forces, or business; our ways of educating and rearing the young, of dealing with crime, slums, poverty, old age, race prejudice, unemployment, and personal maladjustment, of conducting political campaigns, of planning cities and improving the life of the farmer, of waging wars and making peace, of managing the complex problems of self-government in our democracy and promoting the general welfare—all these would be hard to imagine without the stimulation and contribution of the social sciences.*

For better or for worse, social science may represent the last, best chance we have to construct a social order more rational and meaningful than the one we now possess. However imperfect, it is our only source of verified information about how human beings actually behave in their social universe. To diagnose, even to grasp, the meaning of our social existence today, we must begin with the work of men and women who have come to the study of society in a spirit of humility, skepticism, and truth. To understand the status of current thinking about

---

* Bernard Barber, *Science and the Social Order* (Glencoe, Ill.: The Free Press, 1952), pp. 248-249.

* L. Wirth, "The Social Sciences," in M. Curti, ed., *American Scholarship in the Twentieth Century* (Cambridge: Harvard University Press, 1953), p. 69.

man in society, we must try to look at society as a whole, not as historians, economists, or social psychologists but as investigators looking for patterns of behavior that embrace information from many subject areas. As teachers, we have found a number of such patterns or integrating concepts that cut across the usual boundaries of academic departments and lay bare the interrelatedness of social science. To the first of these conceptions—loyalty—we now turn in Chapter 4.

SOME WORDS OF SUMMARY

All branches of social science, including history, seek to substitute rational analysis and verified knowledge for prejudice, opinion, and so-called "common sense." In the past, however, historians came to a parting of the ways with other social scientists when historians failed to find laws or sweeping generalizations that could be applied to the human past. Many other social scientists, taking the physical sciences as their model, sought the same kind of exactness, predictability, and measurability in the social world that prevailed in the physical realm.

The ambiguity of the meaning of science was responsible for much of the debate among social scientists. Some wanted to follow the German example and make science only a system of organized knowledge. Others, however, saw a single, unvarying scientific method as the true measure of a subject's scientific character. This method, embracing a series of steps beginning with a hypothesis and proceeding through observation and classification to generalization, was especially successful in the exact, or mathematical, sciences. Some people questioned its applicability to some of the branches of social science, claiming that the private emotional stake of the investigator in his work and the fact that he dealt with things that he could not measure or directly observe made it imperative that he use different techniques.

Social scientists have also differed sharply on the place of *values*, or human preferences or commitments, in the study of social science. Some of them contended that the social scientist was obligated to keep values from affecting his work, making it mandatory that he look at his data as coolly and indifferently as any other natural fact. Still others, who believed the value-free ideal was impossible, sought to make values a part of social science investigation. This second group agreed with the first, however, that students of society should refrain from telling society what is best or which social problems it should solve next. A final group of social scientists placed values at the core of social research and made social science investigations revolve openly about them. A by-product of this debate over values has been the recognition that science is based on such obviously man-centered concerns as truth, honesty, and objectivity. Some have even spoken of social science as an "art" because of the high dividends that human sympathy and creative imagination have yielded in arriving at some of the lasting social insights.

Social science research today is typically team-work based on a *division of labor*. Each scholar pursues that part of the task best suited to his personal capabilities and interests and pools his results with his colleagues. The individual branches of social science, to be sure, have greater interest in some questions than others, and each has devised certain intellectual tools for explaining social behavior. Some examples are: the concept of the *group* in sociology, *culture* in anthropology, *personality* in social psychology, *power* in political science, *value* in economics, and *region* in geography.

What the future may hold for social science, as for all man's aspirations, is uncertain. It is highly unlikely that the emotional stake we have in questions affecting our private lives will be less of an obstacle than in the past. Yet no area of investigation is more critically important in a civilization teetering on the brink of an atomic catastrophe than human behavior in all its baffling complexity.

FURTHER ROADS TO LEARNING

GENERAL ACCOUNTS

C. A. Beard, *The Nature of the Social Sciences* (New York: Scribner, 1934). A clear though somewhat outdated statement of the nature and branches of social science.

S. Chase, *The Proper Study of Mankind*, rev. ed. (New York: Harper, 1956). A spirited, popular account of social science techniques and recent advances.

G. Lundberg, *Social Research*, 2nd ed. (New York: Longmans, Green, 1942). A thorough treatment of techniques and problems of social research by a champion of the scientific, value-free school of social science.

J. Madge, *The Tools of Social Science* (New York: Longmans, Green, 1953). A difficult but rewarding discussion of social science methods and limitations by an English social scientist.

A. Rose, *Theory and Method in the Social Sciences* (Minneapolis: University of Minnesota Press, 1954). Perhaps the best statement of the view that science cannot be considered solely as the product of the experimental and quantitative method.

G. Simpson, *Man in Society: A Preface to Sociology and the Social Sciences* (New York: Random House, paperback, 1955). A succinct coverage of a number of the problems and topics dealt with in this chapter.

L. Wirth, "The Social Sciences," in M. Curti, *American Scholarship in the Twentieth Century* (Cambridge: Harvard University Press, 1953). An admirably lucid treatment of the historical development of the social sciences during the past half-century or so.

SPECIAL STUDIES

B. Barber, *Science and the Social Order* (Glencoe, Ill.: The Free Press, 1952). Perhaps the best brief treatment of the "sociology of science."

J. Bernard, "The Art of Science: a Reply to Redfield," *American Journal of Sociology*, LV (July, 1949), pp. 1-9. An interesting exchange with Robert Redfield, whose article is included below.

F. Hayek, *The Counter-Revolution of Science* (Glencoe, Ill.: The Free Press, 1952). A difficult, in many ways an exasperating, book but immensely suggestive on the differences between investigation in the social and the natural sciences.

G. Lundberg, *Can Science Save Us?* (New York: Longmans, Green, 1947). A popular appeal for more science in our human relations.

J. Randall, Jr., "History and the Social Sciences," in S. W. Baron, *et al.*, *Freedom and Reason* (Glencoe, Ill.: The Free Press, 1951). An important brief statement on the relations between history and social science.

R. Redfield, "The Art of Social Science," *American Journal of Sociology*, LIV (Nov., 1948), pp. 181-190. A stimulating short essay on the non-scientific aspects of social science.

————, "Social Science in Our Society," in T. L. Smith and C. A. McMahan, eds., *The Sociology of Urban Life* (New York: Dryden, 1951). An excellent brief statement.

Social Science Research Council, *The Social Sciences in Historical Study* (New York: Social Science Research Council, 1954). The famous *Bulletin 64*, which outlines the uses of social science from the vantage point of the modern historian.

A. Standen, *Science is a Sacred Cow* (New York: Dutton, 1950). A humorous, iconoclastic attack on the pretensions of modern science, including social science.

FICTION AND DRAMA

R. Bradbury, *Martian Chronicles* (New York: Doubleday, 1958). A series of short stories with a scientific theme.

A. Huxley, *Brave New World* (New York: Bantam Books, 1957). What a test tube world might be like!

O. LaFarge, *Laughing Boy* (New York: Houghton Mifflin, 1929). A moving novel by an anthropologist, which treats maladjustments of the Navajo Indians in a social science perspective.

S. Lewis, *Arrowsmith* (New York: Harcourt, Brace, 1925). A famous novel that relates the struggles of a physician who is empirically oriented.

FILMS

How Philosophy Differs from Science and Religion (National Educational Television, 1954, 28 min., sound, black and white). Portrays differing methods and objectives of three major branches of human experience.

Nature of Government (National Educational Television, 1954, 29 min., sound, black and white). Discusses fundamental ideas of government and the necessity for government to command power in order to function.

Scientific Method (Encyclopaedia Britannica Films, 1953, 12 min., sound, black and white). Outlines the principles of thought and describes the steps in scientific procedure.

Scientist Examines Life (National Educational Television, 1955, 29 min., sound, black and white). Shows the major steps in scientific procedure from the recognition of a problem to the formation of laws and principles.

The World
of Personal Loyalties

T H E M E

The contemporary world is a place where man's ancient loyalties— to self and family, to his social class, to church and state—have been seriously shaken. . . .

CHAPTER FOUR

Loyalty and Self

Youngsters first become aware of themselves
as separate persons by "taking the role of the other."

If the

major objectives of social scientists are to understand, describe, analyze, and predict human behavior, then there is probably no better place to begin than with the individual person himself. We need to know more about our "selves," or as one wit has said, "Men need to be introduced to themselves." They need to know who they are and what makes them think and act as they do. But despite the huge quantity of fruitful research in the social and biological sciences, as well as two thousands years of speculation and study given over by philosophers and theologians to questions about the nature of man, a great deal still remains to be discovered about the complexities of the human personality. We have not yet been adequately introduced to ourselves! Why? No doubt, it is partly because the human being is so complex. As Professors Clyde Kluckhohn and Henry A. Murray have pointed out, each of us is in many respects: (a) like all other men, (b) like some other men, (c) like no other man. A great deal of our inability to discover more about ourselves, and our conflicts and troubles, too, stems from a lack of information about these complexities. Man is, to use the words of another writer, Nicolas Berdyaev, "a riddle in the world, and (he) may be, the greatest riddle." Working to solve this riddle will no doubt help us meet the problems of everyday life, resolve the conflicts that arise, and carve out a better life for ourselves. Indeed, it already has! Most of all, however, each of us needs the information to understand and live with himself, adjust socially, and maintain his self-respect.

To live with ourselves, we must first learn to get along with others. This requires us to make compromises. And the compromises we make begin almost at birth and continue throughout our lifetime. We must choose whether we will do what *we* want to do, possibly at the risk of incurring the disapproval of others, or whether we will do what others expect of us, with the accompanying reward of getting along easily with them. Occasionally, of course, we can convince or force others to accept what we want or get them to act as we do, but this is not easy. More often we must act somewhat in accordance with the expectations of others, thus compromising our wants and needs with theirs. So, even though our personality and behavior characteristics are well-established by adulthood, each day brings new experiences, changing relations with other people, and additional problems to solve that necessitate compromise and challenge our self-respect. Take the case of an ordinarily self-respecting man desperately in need of money. He decides to sell his automobile, knowing it has a cracked engine block. Should he reveal the car's true condition to an unsuspecting buyer? If he believes in being honest, he may not sell the car to obtain the needed money. If he sells the car to an uninformed buyer, he may deceive the buyer, but not himself. Thus, his self-respect may be damaged. The ever-present compromises necessary to daily living challenge our loyalties to others and jeopardize our self-respect.

Although oversimplified, our illustration suggests one kind of problem we often face in everyday life, one that seems to defy a completely satisfactory solution. It is frequently difficult to maintain self-respect and still satisfy our personal desires and needs.

Depending on the severity of the conflict, our souls may be torn when personal gratification and self-respect are inconsistent. In such cases of inconsistency, either we must act in ways contrary to what we believe is right and proper and risk losing our self-respect or else we must fail to accomplish our objective.

THE SELF AND THE TOTAL PERSONALITY

So, even though we can learn a great deal about the intricacies and complexities of man and his behavior from both the social and the biological sciences, the problems of maintaining self-respect and social adjustment are sometimes as confusing as gravitational forces were to people a thousand years ago. It may be that we will never fully understand ourselves! Nevertheless, for the moment let us examine part of what has been learned about the broad aspects of personality development, self-respect, and social adjustment.

The word "personality" is derived from the Latin *persona*, which refers to the masks once worn by Roman actors to indicate to their audiences the different roles they played. The derivation is particularly apt for each of us plays a number of roles in daily life and may change our "masks" to meet different situations or reflect different attitudes. Although variously defined, personality, as we saw in Chapter 3, generally refers to habits, attitudes, motivations, aspirations, temperament, character, and even physical traits that result from a combination of hereditary and environmental influences. Although the relative importance of heredity and environment has long been debated, most authorities now concede that both influence personality development profoundly.

Authorities agree also that attitudes are an important aspect of personality. *Attitudes are the socially acquired predispositions or tendencies that cause people to behave in certain ways under certain circumstances.* For example, if your attitude is very favorable toward education, you are likely to work hard as a student or to support increased revenues for schools as a citizen. Or, if you come to regard international warfare as despicable, you probably will oppose any action you fear will endanger peace. Some attitudes are habits in the sense that they are consistent and repeatedly demonstrated in our behavior. Attitudes also reflect our motives, ambitions, temperament, and character. Some are directed to external things—to other people, objects, and abstract things such as ideas—while others are directed inward, toward ourselves. A set pattern of attitudes that is consistent and integrated helps balance the personality and keeps it socially adjusted.

The inner-directed, or self-regarding, attitudes constitute the self. Since the term "self" is an abstraction, no one ever "sees" a self. Yet most of us understand the general meaning of the term as a result of such commonly used words as "I," "me," "mine," and "myself." These words indicate an awareness of self-regarding attitudes and the fact that we "see" ourselves as separate and distinct from other persons. A man who builds a house, for example, may say "I have done this," and after it is paid for, "This is mine." In countless and simple ways, we show that we are aware of ourselves. But our reactions to our selves vary from one experience to another. Sometimes we feel a sense of pride for an individual accomplishment, sometimes failure. Sometimes what we have done contributes to our self-respect, and at other times to our self-disrespect. But whatever the particular attitude toward one's self, this fascinating aspect of personality begins to take shape early in life and remains a permanent part of personality.

THE DEVELOPMENT
OF SELF-CONSCIOUSNESS

Understanding how a person develops self-awareness helps us gain an insight into the total personality. George Herbert Mead, a famous psychologist, described the process most colorfully. According to Mead, a youngster first becomes aware of himself as a separate entity by *taking the role of the other*. The child imagines that he is someone else and in a make-believe fashion either thinks through or acts out a situation the way he believes the other person would. The four-year-old girl who plays "mother" to her doll is taking the role of the other. In the process of play-acting, the doll may misbehave and be spanked, which reflects the way

the little girl thinks her mother would treat her if she misbehaved, a reaction probably based on painful experience. Therefore, by repeatedly taking the role of the other, the child sooner or later comes to think of himself not only as a separate entity but also in the same way that he feels others regard him. His conception of himself becomes geared to his judgment of how others evaluate him. To a very great extent, then, self-consciousness is socially conditioned.

In addition to taking the role of a specific other, the individual gradually comes to *take the role of the generalized other*. He reacts to the world as a whole, or at least to his conception of that world. He incorporates into his self-consciousness the behavior standards of the society in which he lives and moves. In doing this, of course, the person tends to judge himself by the standards which he believes exist in the world at large.

Working diligently to acquire shop skills, these boys are learning—a primary process in personality development.

He may misjudge those standards, or for some reason may disagree with and not abide by them. He is likely to know what his society deems ethical and moral, and may even recognize that some of the standards are inconsistent and conflicting. At the same time, there are probably certain situations in which the individual lacks the knowledge that would permit him to take successfully the role of the generalized other, as in the case of an illiterate in a highly literate society or a pampered or isolated child who suddenly is forced to face the outside world.

Mead's explanation of the way in which self-consciousness originates and develops is extremely helpful to our understanding of personality. As we seek social approval by attempting to meet the standards of acceptable behavior, our "self" motivates us to conform and the threat of social disapproval inhibits us from doing things that are socially unacceptable. Most of us, of course, will rebel occasionally against what is traditional or proper, even though our actions may expose us to ridicule or disgrace. The rebel or the innovator is likely to have a difficult time adjusting in a tradition-bound society, and in a society which itself is plagued by conflicting or inconsistent behavior standards, a person's self-regarding attitudes are likely to reflect tension, anxiety, and uncertainty.

Self-consciousness and self-respect are thus vital parts of a balanced and adjusted total personality. Before we can fully understand these terms, however, we must consider them in relation to the process of socialization.

THE PROCESS OF SOCIALIZATION

Personalities differ from one society to another. An Egyptian acts, thinks, and responds quite differently from a Peruvian, just as an Englishman's attitudes, beliefs, and motives are quite unlike a Samoan's. It is also true that identical twins reared separately and under quite different circumstances develop different personalities. This kind of evidence, in addition to the preceding remarks we made about the way social factors influence the self, suggests that social experiences are very important in shaping our personalities.

But first, of course, there must be the raw materials. Most obvious are the glands, muscles, nerves, and internal organs that provide the foundation for personality development. Then there are unlearned behavior tendencies that we inherit, such as reflexes, drives, temperament, and capacities. We do not learn *reflex* responses; we are born with them. All it takes is a certain stimulus to activate a reflex response. We all know, for example, that a quick flick of the hand close to a person's eyes will make him blink. Many of our *drives*, sometimes called instincts, also are present at birth. There is little doubt that drives such as hunger are biologically inborn. On the other hand, it is very difficult to relate basic drives such as hunger to complex motivations that lead us to acquire wealth. It is sometimes useful to distinguish between the primary, or biological, drives and the secondary, or socially acquired, drives, but we can't always be certain which is which. The same kind of problem pervades the concept of temperament. *Temperament*, a typical or prevailing emotional pattern, is presumably inborn and therefore not learned. Investigators have found, however, that quick-tempered persons may learn to control their anger, which indicates an environmental influence at work. *Capacities* are inborn flexibilities in the central nervous system that enable us to develop our *abilities*. We are able to add 2 and 2, for example, only because we possess the necessary underlying capacities.

Our personalities develop out of these raw materials in two ways: by *maturation* and by *learning*. Maturation is a biological process through which certain raw materials are modified as we grow. A child's ability to walk, for example, will develop as his muscular control increases. Learning, on the other hand, is the way we acquire our attitudes, habits, ideas, and social values, whereas *conditioning* is a special kind of learning that modifies our behavior. Even our innate characteristics may be altered by conditioning, and many classic experiments have been concerned with the effect of conditioning on reflex responses. Pavlov, a Russian scientist, demonstrated years ago that reflex tendencies can be conditioned. He first placed meat before a dog and noticed that saliva flowed freely from the dog's mouth, a reflex response. Then he rang a bell as he gave the meat to the dog and observed that saliva still flowed. Finally, Pavlov rang the bell but did not give the dog the meat. Saliva still flowed freely. What had happened was that the reflex response of salivation had been conditioned to a stimulus different from the meat, in this case the ringing bell. Many other conditioned-response experiments have been conducted over the years to bolster Pavlov's initial evidence. Some authorities now conclude that regardless of our innate reflexes, drives, temperament, and capacities, we are so thoroughly conditioned by adulthood that we bear little relationship to the hereditary equipment we had at birth.

We learn or are conditioned, then, because we receive or expect a *reward*. Without the promise of a reward, we would be unlikely to continue to act in certain ways or to acquire new characteristics. As a matter of fact, there is a kind of learning that results from a negative reward, or punishment. When we are punished, we try to avoid repeating the behavior for which we are punished, just as we tend to repeat behavior for which we are rewarded. The reward does not have to be something tangible. A sense of satisfaction may be enough. A student, for example, may spend long hours studying simply because he feels that knowledge will be rewarding in and of itself. Another may

work hard in order to make high grades, whereas others will work to win the approval of their teachers, or to become eligible for scholarships. All of these students work in the expectation of some reward. But some other student may neglect his school work completely. He may think his friends will look down on him as a "bookworm" if he spends too much time on his lessons. His incentive to study is negative. The anticipation of reward or punishment is crucial to learning, in the situations we have just mentioned and in many others as well. But rewards by themselves are not enough to assure learning. A person must have the capacity and opportunity to learn, as well as incentive and rewards.

How do we learn? Actually, we learn in a number of ways, two of the more basic being *imitation* and *suggestion*. Imitation involves copying from a model and requires drive and ability as well as something to imitate. Physical activity is especially easy to imitate, and many of us learn to ride a bicycle, play golf, or use a typewriter by imitating the way other people ride or swing a club or type. *Suggestion*, on the other hand, involves the uncritical response to a stimulus (the suggestion). We are all more or less suggestible and able to learn a number of things fairly easily. The danger in being highly suggestible lies in learning things of questionable value. The highly suggestible person is susceptible to all sorts of suggestions, worth while or not.

Imitation and suggestion thus are both important processes that influence learning. In taking the role of the other, for example, we naturally imitate what we believe we are expected to do or say. We are normally suggestible to those things that are currently popular. We also have a strong desire generally to conform to traditions and thereby help perpetuate the customs of our society. An easy way to get along is to learn the traditional, customary, and usually popular ways of doing things. Nonconformity is the exception, not the rule. The nonconformist, as we have already indicated, is therefore likely to develop serious social adjustment problems. Yet, he may be the person who is contributing most to social change.

THE CONSTANT NEED TO ADJUST

But things never remain static, not even in the most stagnant societies. Societies themselves constantly change, however imperceptibly. Many innovations become permanent and traditional, whereas some traditions grow obsolete and are discarded. As it is with society, so it is with our personalities. We must constantly adjust to our maturing bodies and to changing social relationships; our needs and desires change with the passage of time. At thirty years of age our needs and desires will be quite different from what they were when we were five or ten. Our personalities are never completely crystallized because socialization is a process that never quite ends.

SOCIAL POSITION
AND PERSONALITY REQUIREMENTS

As a person becomes socialized, he acquires social positions that help channel his behavior and structure his personality. A person's qualities and his relationships with other people define his social position. In terms of age, we are either young or old, and the usual sex dichotomy separates us into males and females. Age and sex, then, are simply characteristics that help define our position. To be a forty-year-old male or a twenty-year-old female obviously requires no special effort or ability on our part. On the other hand, a business executive, a scientist, a priest, a politician, and a student all occupy particular positions through some effort, and normally as a result of some ability.

We are always encountering demands in the form of duties and obligations, as well as receiving rewards in the form of rights and privileges, regardless of our particular position at any given time. A physician, for instance, is expected to care for the health of his patients. This is his duty, and as a private practitioner he has the right to charge a fee for his services. Society grants a doctor the unique privilege of investigating the most intimate details relating to health and disease. Other positions also have their unique privileges, but the same basic principle holds true—namely, that social expectations tend to establish behavioral requirements for any given position.

The social expectations that go with a position not only condition the personalities of those holding a particular position but also help to select those with the most suitable personality traits for the position. A good business or political leader, for example, must be decisive and able to assume responsibility. Therefore, a person with authoritarian personality traits is a potential executive as well as a person who will very possibly emphasize his authoritarian traits after he becomes an executive. A clergyman, on the other hand, may be much more concerned with moral behavior, whereas a public relations officer will strive to be genial and even-tempered. As we shall presently see, such personality traits and the expectations attached to social positions help define loyalty.

SOCIAL POSITION AND LOYALTY

In essence, loyalty involves being faithful, true, enthusiastic, or deferential to one's self, another person, a duty, a cause, or a principle. Loyalty is something we are generally expected to have, but demands imposed by different social positions we occupy make it no simple matter. A man may become so embroiled in politics or business that he loses sight of the loyalties he owes to himself and his family. Or he may become so attached to his family that he neglects his business or civic responsibilities. It is quite apparent, then, that there are varying degrees as well as different kinds of loyalty in the contemporary world.

A *loyalty system* is essential to the welfare of a culture or society. A society can successfully incorporate a number of inconsistencies and conflicting elements so long as its members agree on certain ultimate values. These ultimate values, or *core loyalties*, cut across differences that otherwise might disunite us. Core loyalties are based on *common interests*, *beliefs*, and *ideals* that are related to ultimate social values. Our religious, political, and family loyalties are core loyalties because they involve what we believe to be the really fundamental things in life. Loyalties to particular organizations or groups, however, are of secondary importance to core loyalties. Our feelings about institutions such as the church or family, nevertheless, often run high simply because of the core loyalties they represent.

Fringe, or alternative, loyalties are based on *like interests* and are concerned with more immediate and personal gratification than are core loyalties. Although less likely to promote strong unity, they do not necessarily disrupt or disintegrate a society when general consensus is absent. Loyalty to a business firm, a social club, or a college may be very important to certain people but relatively unimportant to others or to society as a whole. We frequently disagree among ourselves about fringe loyalties but rarely about core loyalties. In fact, when we disagree about core loyalties they tend to become fringe loyalties. We generally accept core loyalties without questioning them, and over a period of time they receive additional force through the sanction of tradition.

WHY ARE WE LOYAL?

Why are we loyal? From the many possible reasons, we may summarize some of the more basic.* The strongest and socially most important reason is our sense of moral obligation. Our religious ideals and our convictions about family life are powerful and longstanding, and most of us are so thoroughly convinced of their fundamental importance that we bristle at any challenge or threat to them and are prepared to defend them if necessary. We need no "pep talks" or admonitions to convince ourselves of their importance.

Second, we are loyal because we find in common loyalties an opportunity to pursue common interests. Loyalty to the United States permits us to participate together as citizens. Loyalty to our family helps us to satisfy our interests through close personal contacts. Religious loyalty, as we shall see in Chapter 7, also provides common interests and binds people together.

Third, we may be loyal to a dominant person. In this case, allegiance is akin to obedience and is much less likely to endure than a loyalty founded on moral obligation or enlightened self-interest. Political and business leaders, for example, may enjoy a sense of power from the loyalty or deference shown them by others, but changing political and economic conditions may easily upset their control.

Finally, we may be loyal because we fear the consequences of being disloyal. To avoid ostracism, expulsion, or annihilation, we may act as if we were genuinely loyal. Anti-Nazis in Germany who feigned loyalty to Hitler in fear of reprisals illustrate this attitude very nicely, as does the anti-communist in Russia today. A loyalty system based on fear

* The following discussion is based on Robert C. Angell, *The Integration of American Society* (New York: McGraw-Hill, 1941), Chapters 1-3.

alone may be superficially powerful, but is often unstable.

"RULES OF THE GAME"

From general considerations of loyalty we turn now to the question of why we are loyal in particular situations. One way to understand loyalty in specific situations is to consider it in terms of the social positions we occupy. This approach is particularly promising in attempting to analyze systems of loyalties in a society, for only as a system are loyalties important in integrating a society as a whole. A position, by definition, is a part of a social system, since it has meaning only in relation to all other positions in the system. What one person does must be appraised in light of what others do. A positional system is based on interdependence. A job, like all other positions in society, carries a socially prescribed set of rules that governs the behavior of the people who occupy the job by defining their duties, responsibilities, rights, and privileges. Sometimes these rules are set down formally, as in a company rule book; at other times they are merely understood. We are able to hold particular jobs in part because we conform to the rules. Our behavior, therefore, demonstrates our loyalty or at least our outward expression of loyalty to the rules.

These "rules of the game" indicate what is permissible and what is mandatory. They tell us how loyal we are expected to be. By general consensus, a wife, for example, is expected to be loyal to her husband, to be faithful and true, although there is no agreement on how enthusiastic or deferential she must be. Likewise, the president of a bank must be loyal to the rules governing the behavior of bank presidents, which means, among other things, not absconding with the depositors' money. A Christian must be loyal to his religion, which often entails not marrying non-Christians or embracing non-Christian beliefs. And a student is expected to observe the rules of his school. The same principle is true for most positions we occupy.

"We behave the way we do because of loyalty to the position we occupy." This statement would seem to be true. Our actual behavior and the decisions underlying it, however, are not nearly so simple. We may be dissatisfied with our particular position, may resent some of the rules, or dislike our superiors. We may not fully understand what is expected of us. For these and other reasons, then, we may not demonstrate a high degree of loyalty, or, if we do, our behavior may not really reflect our true sentiment. As we shall now see, one of the problems involved in this situation lies within the system of loyalties itself.

CONTRADICTION AND CONFLICT IN LOYALTIES

CONFLICTS IN CORE LOYALTIES

We often are uncertain and anxious about decisions we make and actions we undertake. Of course, a certain amount of tension may be normal and justified, but insecurities and fears sometimes take on extreme proportions. A system of loyalties that is harmonious and compatible contributes a great deal toward minimizing these fears, insecurities, and personal tensions. People know what to do, when to do it, and how to do it. In other words, from past experience and knowledge of the society's loyalty system, they know what is expected of them and what is acceptable. A system of compatible loyalties reflects the dominance of core loyalties and, therefore, provides certainty and security.

But in a society where core loyalties are

weak and where fringe loyalties predominate, people are more likely to experience strain, tension, and conflict. The American loyalty system is probably not extreme in either direction. It has a rather substantial core but is weakened at many points by contradictory or inconsistent loyalty demands. Two Americans may be intensely loyal to their country and yet divided over whether American interests are best served by permitting persons accused of communist subversion to refuse to testify on the constitutional ground that they might incriminate themselves. We are generally loyal to Judaic-Christian concepts of morality, including brotherhood, but for some of us this loyalty conflicts with our allegiance to a state or sectional heritage that forbids close relations between whites and Negroes. Similarly, the loyalty many Americans feel for their traditional ideals of freedom and individualism runs counter to rising demands that government intervene more actively in the social and economic life of the people.

Dilemmas arise when a system contains inconsistent and incompatible loyalties. In a free society, where differences in belief are encouraged, or at least tolerated, conflicting ideals develop. Then, too, organizations representing persuasive fringe loyalties may compete for a person's loyalty. Individuals who desire personal stability, and societies that are socially stable, both must have a set of standards that is internally consistent. Otherwise, loyalty dilemmas are inevitable, and in reality this is frequently the case.

Often it is difficult to make an immediate choice between two conflicting standards of loyalty, especially if we are inclined to favor an unpopular belief that threatens our own social acceptability. A person may be genuinely concerned about the denial of civil rights to a minority group in his community, but may be unable to decide whether to speak out or remain silent because his friends or associates are passive about the matter or disagree with them. In localities or groups where a definite stand has been taken, it may be easy to succumb to suggestion and agree with neighbors and friends. But less suggestible people will realize that few intelligent decisions can be made without carefully considering all the opposing arguments and pressures surrounding the issue. Our predispositions, of course, may determine how we decide. We may, for example, believe that the civil rights issue is so vital that we will not hesitate to take a stand against all instances of legal or social discrimination.

MORALITY AND LEGALITY

Many conflicts between loyalties involve moral issues, or moral and legal issues. What is just or ethically correct depends on standards of judgment. Efficiency and the dollar sign have become increasingly popular standards of judgment. A factory-owner who gives his shiftless son a responsible position in his plant may be demonstrating loyalty to his son and family at the expense of efficiency within his organization. What should a father do in such a case? The answer is difficult because conflicting standards and loyalties are involved. If he refuses his son a job, he will be accused of disloyalty to his own kin. If he does take him into the company, he may be disloyal to other people who have an interest in the business.

Should society assume complete responsibility for a person who is unable to provide for himself, or should he be left to care for his own welfare? This issue is typical of conflicting standards that disturb so many of us. A man's loyalty to traditional laissez-faire economic concepts may clash with his Christian concern for the needy and underprivileged. The social security system in the United States, for instance, is based on the view that society should provide for the minimum financial needs of the unemployed, the retired, and the widowed. Many people subscribe to the humanitarian principle the program embodies but at the same time are troubled by government's growing tendency to intervene in social and economic matters.

In many instances morality and legality may be in conflict. A shady businessman or shyster lawyer may stay within the law but still violate its spirit and intent. A man's actions may be legal yet immoral. In letting contracts, purchasing equipment, hiring employees, and "padding" expense accounts, employers or administrators may not violate any laws or regulations but still may be "taking advantage" of their positions. Basically, the question is one of loyalty or faithfulness to what laws and rules represent as well as loyalty to rules themselves. Actions may be perfectly legal and according to the rule book yet, in reality, be dishonest, disloyal, or even immoral. What is legal may have no relation to what is moral.

DUAL LOYALTIES

The person who is encouraged or compelled to maintain dual loyalties rather than to choose from among alternatives is in a troublesome situation. The immigrant in the United States is a classic illustration. Initially, he remains loyal to his homeland and to old familiar customs and ways of doing things. He may retain this allegiance indefinitely, but sooner or later he develops an attachment to his adopted land as well and to new ways of life. In which direction should he channel and concentrate his main loyalty? Many immigrants have solved this problem by abandoning loyalty to the homeland, though only after much soul-searching and torment. For the immigrant's son and daughter born in the new land, the dilemma is not easily resolved either. Their ties to the old country are more tenuous than their parents'. But conflicts and maladjustment beset them, nevertheless. They are immersed in their parents' culture while at home, yet move in totally different surroundings at school or during their leisure time. During World War II the Nisei, or native Americans of Japanese parentage and ancestry, had to decide whether to cast their allegiance with the land of their parents or remain loyal to the land of their birth. The overwhelming majority chose the latter course.

Another type of person who is confronted with dual loyalties is the "marginal man." He is called marginal because he is influ-

The foreman, the marginal man in industry, is compelled to maintain dual loyalties—to management, the people who employ him; to the workers under him, from whose ranks he has risen and whom he is expected to represent.

enced by two or more cultures or groups but does not participate fully in either, does not accept either completely, and is not fully accepted by either. A foreman in industry is an example of such a person. On the one hand, he is expected to be loyal to his company and the people who employ him. On the other hand, he is expected to represent the workers under him, from whose ranks he has risen. Which loyalty should predominate when these interests clash?

PROBLEMS OF MEANS AND ENDS

Another aspect of opposing loyalties involves the different ways in which prevailing means and ends are accepted, which may be illustrated by the following diagram. Such a scheme yields four basic combinations, ranging from the highly loyal to the highly disloyal.

| | | MEANS | |
		Loyal	Disloyal
ENDS	Loyal	(1) Conformist	(2) Inventor
	Disloyal	(3) Follower	(4) Noncon-formist

Type 1, who is loyal to both the means and ends of behavior that are generally accepted in society, is a *conformist*. His route is customary, his goals the popular and acceptable ones. He is staunchly loyal to basic social values in his social system. The conformist encounters no difficulty insofar as allegiance to core loyalties is concerned. When it comes to fringe loyalties, however, he may have as much trouble as anyone in choosing from among many alternatives. As a conformist, an American husband, for example, may champion the core values of family life. He may believe that families are best when there are several children scampering around home. This same husband, when confronted with a loyalty on the fringe of family life, may act in an apparently inconsistent or

"disloyal" manner. He may constantly berate his energetic children and bemoan their noisy presence. Despite inconsistencies of this kind, the conformist as a type nevertheless remains a strong supporter of the loyalty system of a society.

Type 2, the *inventor*, accepts the standards of his society more or less completely, but tends to substitute new and different approaches for traditional ways of doing things. He is not necessarily disloyal to things as they are; he simply feels that there are better ways. Henry Ford was a classic illustration in the field of business. Thoroughly convinced of the merits of the free-enterprise system, he introduced the techniques of mass production to the automobile industry because he was positive that the old, tailor-made, hand-production system was inefficient. He was able to demonstrate the greater efficiency of mass-production techniques, but in so doing engendered conflict and opposition. His "disloyalty" to the old system resulted in new means of maintaining the free-enterprise system of production.

The case of General Billy Mitchell is similar to Ford's, though Mitchell was severely condemned for his efforts at innovation. The way to maintain military dominance, Mitchell argued, was through air power, at the time a novel and revolutionary suggestion. In the face of strong opposition from those reluctant to depart from traditional military strategy, General Mitchell steadfastly held to his argument. His immediate reward came in the form of a court-martial, but the subsequent development of air power vindicated Mitchell's position.

Many of the great contributions to mankind have come from men like Pasteur, Rickover, Ford, and Mitchell. Men of this type accept the values and goals of their society but seek better ways of achieving or realizing them. Often, as in the case of Mitchell, such men are condemned and their ideas or innovations are ignored or violently opposed,

Inventors such as Lee DeForest, shown here with one of his early contributions, an audion tube, generally accept the standards of the society in which they live but tend to substitute new and different approaches for traditional ways of doing things.

With the passage of time, however, at least some of them gain the recognition warranted by their contribution.

Type 3, called a *follower*, accepts and emphasizes the proper ways of behavior but is "disloyal" to the ends. Actually, the follower is more disinterested than disloyal. He is a follower in the sense that he adheres rigorously to the standards of his group and society but cares little for their purposes and goals. His main concern is to behave appropriately and legally, to uphold custom and tradition. The stereotype of "the timid soul," who is extremely cautious about doing anything improper, is a somewhat exaggerated version of the follower. He resembles the conformist but is less aggressive and rarely takes the initiative. Yet, for all his reticence and hesitancy, the follower supports and helps perpetuate the loyalty system of his society through his strong adherence to traditional ways.

Type 4, the *nonconformist*, is "perfectly disloyal," rejects both the traditional means and ends of behavior. The nonconformist is likely to be unpopular or may even be a complete misfit, though he may have good reasons for being a nonconformist. If he is very articulate, he may undermine the existing loyalty system by constantly challenging it. If, however, peaceful persuasion and oratory fail, he may seek to gain his ends by different means, by force or revolution. A successful revolution will change the standards of loyalty in a society, and its leader will become the focus of a new loyalty. George Washington was disloyal to his British king, led a successful revolution, and became the father of a new loyalty and conformity. Needless to say, not all nonconformists are as fortunate as Washington was.

In considering the problems of conflicting loyalties, we must discuss one final point. It makes a real difference whether means or ends are at issue. A lack of agreement about the ends of behavior may be the more fundamental question. For we have just seen that followers and nonconformists—those who reject, disagree with, or are disloyal to the ends —do not provide strength and stability in a

69

society as do conformists and inventors. But conflicting means are also extremely troublesome for the individual and the society. Consider the national education problem. Most Americans agree that education is good for everyone and that we ought to provide greater opportunities for education. There is consensus, in other words, about the objective—namely, to educate each person to the limits of his capacity. When it comes to the question of means, however, of how to provide ideal learning conditions, there is very little agreement. Some people feel that a "tough," rigid curriculum in the classics is best. Make the student work hard and learn to think for himself! Others feel that the student should move only as rapidly and as far as his interests permit. Let the student learn whatever his interests dictate! There also are people who favor private over public education. Only a select few should receive higher education, according to some, whereas others favor college educations for all. In short, loyalty conflicts may arise from the disagreements among us about the means we use to achieve our ends.

CAUSES OF STABILITY AND INSTABILITY

We are thus confronted constantly with a great variety of fundamental, deep-seated conflicts. The more violent kinds— wars, riots, gang fights, and murders—are familiar to all of us. Less apparent, but no less pervasive, are the stresses, strains, pressures, and counterpressures we encounter in our jobs, in school, in our family and community life, and in all kinds of interpersonal relationships. On every side, we face the problem of getting along with people. Virtually every day we are confronted with problems of morality and ethics, with the constant need to adjust and readjust as we grow to maturity. In the face of all this, how can a person develop and maintain self-respect or any semblance of balance and unity in his personality? Before we can answer this question, we must first examine factors that lead to instability in personality.

SOURCES OF DISTURBANCE

Disturbances in our personalities originate from at least three basic sources: *physical, personal,* and *social.* The person who suffers from some physical defect or disease *may* experience grave personality problems. Often he is unable to do the things a healthier person does with ease. The amputee or cripple, for example, left out of many activities, may tend to withdraw further and further from all social contacts. He may worry about being a burden to his family and to others and become increasingly distraught and irritable.

Personal difficulties stem mainly from defects or imbalances in the emotions or the intellect, or from a lack of balance between emotions and the intellect. To refer to these problems as "personal" does not mean that they are unrelated to the physical or social circumstances. It is just that the primary problem for some people is to control their emotions—whether fear, hate, love, or something else. Some highly intelligent persons, the stereotyped "neurotic genius," for example, are unable to control their emotions. A moron, on the other hand, may rarely become excited. Persons with the most extreme personal difficulties, however, are often the ones least aware and concerned about their problems.

This lack of awareness may be either an asset or a liability. A moron, unaware of his condition or the reasons for it, may adjust very well socially. His lack of critical and perceptive powers prevents him from worrying or complaining. His lack of awareness is an asset. On the other hand, a person not knowing his own personal shortcomings is unlikely to help himself by seeking or effecting a cure. A neurotic is frequently unable to help himself until he recognizes the nature of his trouble.

Social causes of instability may be even more important and are certainly more elusive than physical or personal factors. We Americans live in a highly industrial, materialistic, competitive, and success-oriented type of society that has obvious advantages but also imposes strains on the personality. Our emphasis on competition offers a good illustration of how social factors affect the personality. In politics, business, education, courtship, and many other areas of behavior, Americans compete constantly. More significant, the "winner" gets the recognition and reward. We put a high premium on "winning the game." But only one person can win; many are defeated. Despite our occasional admonitions about "playing the game for its own sake," we accord the losers everything from indifference to scorn. Most people take occasional defeats in good grace, but repeated failures sooner or later begin to disturb all but the most "hard-shelled" of us.

There are many other potentially disruptive influences in American society. Among them, congestion, noise, and the tempo of living in cities; our virtual obsession with materialistic and monetary rewards; and all our moral dilemmas, dual loyalties, and group conflicts are disturbing to the personality. At first glance, it would seem virtually impossible for any of us to maintain balanced personalities in the face of such problems. Fortunately, however, there are various devices and conditions that exert a stabilizing influence. To these we now turn our attention.

SOURCES OF BALANCE

Just as there are *physical, personal* and *social* sources of instability, so there are stabilizing influences that stem from each of these areas. There is a kind of stability, for example, in the fact that our personalities are "attached" to our bodies; and since our bodies last for the duration of our lives, so, too, do our personalities. Our ability to remember is an additional source of stability, as is our ability to forget, particularly unpleasant experiences. Good health, or at least the belief that we are in good health, likewise contributes to the over-all stability of the personality.

The personal sources of stability are primarily a set of psychological devices that we all use more or less commonly. *Goal substitution* is one of the more common. When we are prevented from reaching certain goals, we substitute another that we think will be easier to attain. Sometimes the substitute goal is just as important to us as the original one. But at other times it may be less significant, and in pursuing it we are forced to lower our sights. The important thing for the well-being of the individual is that he regard the substitute goal as satisfactory, otherwise his frustration may not be reduced at all.

Projection and *identification* are other ways in which we maintain balanced personalities. Through *projection* we tend to transfer our weaknesses to others. The *part* of our personality we do not want or are ashamed of we shift to someone else. A person who boasts incessantly of his accomplishments projects when he says to a friend, "You brag too much!" Through *identification*, we transfer briefly our *total* personality to someone else. Some people identify themselves completely with performers they see or hear on television, on stage, or in the movies. In effect, they take the role of the performer, for whatever satisfaction it may bring them. Seemingly, some people receive great satisfaction from identifying themselves with a handsome actor or glamorous actress.

Still another way of protecting our integrity is the technique called *rationalization*.

When we rationalize, or alibi, we offer an excuse rather than the real reason for our failures and inabilities. The golfer who blames his clubs for his poor score or the student who claims he did not have time to read his assignments after he has failed his exams may be rationalizing his shortcomings. As long as the alibi convinces the alibier, it has the effect of protecting his ego. Whether the alibi convinces anyone else is not so important.

Goal substitution, projection, identification, and rationalization are some of the more common devices people resort to in an effort to stabilize their personalities. The social environment and individual reactions to it are also important to personality stability. Generally speaking, a person who is well-adjusted socially is likely to have a rather stable personality. If he takes pride in what he is doing, feels that his efforts are worth while, and believes that he is accomplishing in life what he set out to do, he is unlikely to become socially maladjusted, particularly if his associates and friends accept him readily. Likewise, the person who has a sense of security about his health, his family, his job, and things in general is likely to feel well-adjusted. Conditions in the community and in the society in which he lives and moves are important, of course. People who live in a society that itself is highly disorganized will find it difficult to maintain their own personal integrity. But when people have many shared values, they also have the makings of a healthy personality.

SOME WORDS OF SUMMARY

The central theme of this chapter has been *loyalty*—primarily a person's loyalty to himself. But since loyalty to self cannot be viewed in a vacuum, we have considered loyalty to others, the loyalty system in a society, and some of the problems of maintaining loyalty as well.

To understand self-loyalty, we must first understand the human personality and its relation to our roles in the loyalty system of society. Although personality requires certain raw materials that are biologically inherited, it develops primarily through a process of socialization. Learning is one of the most important aspects of this socialization process that influences personality in general. It is especially important in acquiring self-consciousness and self-respect. In the imaginative process of taking the role of the other, the individual learns to define his own personality as he thinks others see him and is thereby able to comprehend his position in society.

A person's social position is, in fact, the connecting link between individual personality and the system of loyalties in a society because each position a person occupies carries with it certain duties, rights, responsibilities, privileges, and rewards that are defined for it by people in general. Therefore, the way in which a person comes to regard himself, both as an individual and in relation to those about him, is governed by his social position. Norms, or standards of expected behavior, moreover, "tell him how to behave," teach him the rules of the game. A system of loyalty, or the loyalties of many individuals in combination, is based on socially defined rules that regulate the behavior of people in particular positions.

Problems of maintaining a cohesive loyalty system in a rapidly changing society such as our own stem from fringe rather than core loyalties. When the alternatives provided by the less stable fringe loyalties begin to outnumber and overshadow the core loyalties, the cohesiveness of the loyalty system is threatened. For the hesitancy and uncertainty caused by the increased number and frequency of choices threaten the smoothness and stability of the loyalty system. And if many people come to disagree over choices, social cohesiveness suffers both from conflicts in allegiance and from questions of legality and morality.

By distinguishing between loyalty toward means and loyalty toward ends, we gain a further understanding of the relation between the individual and the cohesiveness of the loyalty system. Conformists are the real stalwarts of a loyalty system by virtue of their acceptance of both the customary means and ends of behavior. Nonconformists, on the other hand, may threaten the solidarity of the system by rejecting those means and ends that are normally accepted. But at the same time, they perform a valuable service by constantly challenging and, in effect, requiring conformists to justify their position. Although followers meekly uphold customary and popular ways of behavior wherever they may lead them, inventors forever challenge the old ways of doing things without intending to upset society's major objectives.

Finally, self-loyalty may be disturbed by disruptions of the personality itself. Basic sources of personality instability stem from physical, personal, and social factors, such as a crippling disease, a neurosis, or failure to compete successfully. From these same general sources, however, come counterbalancing, stabilizing influences, so stability is always relative and depends on the interaction of both stabilizing and disrupting influences. Self-loyalty in all its aspects is built on the combined influences of the socialized personality, the social heritage, and present-day social conditions.

FURTHER ROADS TO LEARNING

GENERAL ACCOUNTS

R. Faris, *Social Psychology* (New York: Ronald, 1952). A most instructive text.

C. Kluckhohn, H. Murray, and D. Schneider, eds., *Personality in Nature, Society and Culture* (New York: Knopf, 1953). A veritable gold mine of information on social influences and personality.

A. Lindesmith and A. Strauss, *Social Psychology* (New York: Dryden, 1949). Communication among people is the theme of this highly regarded text.

S. K. Weinberg, *Society and Personality Disorders* (Englewood Cliffs, N. J.: Prentice-Hall, 1952). Another excellent slant on sociological aspects of personality problems.

R. Williams, Jr., *American Society: A Sociological Interpretation* (New York: Knopf, 1951). Contains one of the finest presentations of the social norms in contemporary American society.

SPECIAL STUDIES

R. Angell, *The Integration of American Society* (New York: McGraw-Hill, 1941). A penetrating analysis of values and institutions by a leading sociologist.

H. Blumer, "Attitudes and the Social Act," *Social Problems*, III (October, 1955), pp. 59-65. Probably the best, brief analysis of the human act.

E. Fromm, *The Sane Society* (New York: Rinehart, 1955). A distinguished social psychiatrist presents the thesis that societies themselves may be the root of our personal problems.

A. Gesell, *et al.*, *The First Five Years of Life* (New York: Harper, 1940). A scientific study often consulted by bewildered parents.

E. Hoebel, *The Law of Primitive Man* (Cambridge: Harvard University Press, 1954). A thoroughgoing analysis of the rules of behavior in nonliterate society by a distinguished anthropologist.

K. Horney, *The Neurotic Personality of Our Time* (New York: Norton, 1937). One of the most provocative books of our age with a thesis that inconsistencies and conflicts in society are the bases of neurosis.

E. Katz and P. Lazarsfeld, *Personal Influence: The Part Played by People in the Flow of Mass Communications* (Glencoe, Ill.: The Free Press, 1955). Very scholarly examination of the way small groups reinforce rules of behavior; mass media and their influence is the major concern.

R. Linton, *The Cultural Background of Personality* (New York: Appleton-Century-Crofts, 1945). One of the outstanding anthropologists of this century traces the social and cultural influences on personality.

K. Mannheim, *Ideology and Utopia* (New York: Harcourt Brace, Harvest Books, 1955). The struggle for ultimate values cast in a solid but readable style by a noted European scholar.

M. Mead, *Growing Up In New Guinea* (New York: Mentor Books, 1953). Here is convincing evidence that people can grow to adulthood with a minimum of stress and strain.

————, *Sex and Temperament in Three Primitive Societies* (New York: Mentor Books, 1950). A brilliant anthropological exposition of cultural influences on temperament.

———— and M. Wolfenstein, eds., *Childhood in Contemporary Cultures* (Chicago: The University of Chicago Press, 1955). Socialization under different behavior rules.

A. Rose, ed., *Mental Health and Mental Disorder: A Sociological Approach* (New York: Norton, 1955). Treats a great many aspects of mental health within a social setting.

F. Shaw and R. Ort, *Personal Adjustment in the American Culture* (New York: Harper, 1953). An excellent discussion of adjustment problems in twentieth-century America.

A. Stanton and M. Schwartz, *The Mental Hospital* (New York: Basic Books, 1954). A careful study of a women's ward in a mental hospital, which includes accounts of unplanned events.

A. Strauss, ed., *The Social Psychology of George Herbert Mead* (Chicago: The University of Chicago Press, Phoenix Books, 1955). A collection of Mead's best works.

W. Sumner, *Folkways* (Boston: Ginn, 1906). A truly great classic on behavioral norms by one of the "fathers" of modern sociology.

W. F. Whyte, *Street Corner Society* (Chicago: The University of Chicago Press, 1955). This study, which shows that youth gangs have their own rules, is fast becoming a classic.

W. Whyte, Jr., *The Organization Man* (New York: Doubleday, Anchor Books, 1956). Rules and formalities dictate loyalties to groups in which we participate.

FICTION AND DRAMA

S. Anderson, *Poor White* (New York: Huebsch, 1920). A poor white turned inventor finds that he is not fitted to his new world.

————, *Winesburg, Ohio* (New York: Huebsch, 1919). A number of sentimental and bitter short stories illustrating how small-town hypocrisies and traditions distort personality.

B. De Voto, *We Accept with Pleasure* (Boston: Little, Brown, 1934). A history teacher who was shell-shocked in war lets his pride destroy his chances to adjust and find happiness.

J. Farrell, *Ellen Rogers* (New York: Vanguard, 1941). A cunning and deceitful cheat preys on others to get ahead.

R. Hughes, *The Innocent Voyage* (New York: Harper, 1929). The effects of a series of horrible experiences on the lives and minds of seven young children.

H. Ibsen, *An Enemy of the People* (London: S. French, 1939). Doctor Stockman suffered ridicule and persecution from those he served because he opposed established social institutions.

T. Mann, *Doctor Faustus* (New York: Knopf, 1948). A beautifully written and profoundly serious novel that tells the story of conflict between an artist's love of beauty and his responsibilities to the outer world.

A. Miller, *Death of a Salesman* (New York: Bantam Books, 1957). A successful salesman is forced to reassess his roles in society.

I. Turgenev, *Fathers and Sons* (New York: Modern Library, 1959). A young man steadfastly refuses to conform to traditional social standards and ideals.

T. Wolfe, *Look Homeward Angel* (New York: Scribner, 1947). Small-town influences on personality development are presented in one of the most powerful novels of this century.

FILMS

Belonging to the Group (Encyclopaedia Britannica Films, 1953, 15 min., sound, black and white). The idea of respect and its essential relation to living in a democratic society are examined.

Child Development: Heredity and Prenatal Development (McGraw-Hill, 1950, 20 min., sound, black and white). Demonstrates how physical and mental characteristics are determined by heredity and modified by training and environment.

Child Development: Principles of Development (McGraw-Hill, 1950, 20 min., sound, black and white). Demonstrates that patterns of human development are orderly and predictable.

Child Development: Social Development (McGraw-Hill, 1950, 20 min., sound, black and white). Stresses the processes in the development of social behavior.

Children Learning by Experience (British Ministry of Education, 1947, 32 min., sound, black and white). A number of unrehearsed glimpses of how children learn.

Conflict (McGraw-Hill, 1956, 18 min., sound, black and white). Conflict is an inescapable aspect of life and has an important influence on behavior.

The Meaning of Adolescence (McGraw-Hill, 1952, 16 min., sound, black and white). The unsure adolescent is neither adult nor child.

Out of Darkness (McGraw-Hill, 55 min., sound, black and white). An account of an actual case study in which psychiatric treatment rescues a woman from the throes of mental disturbance.

Principles of Development (McGraw-Hill, 1950, 17 min., sound, black and white). Development proceeds from the general to the specific; there is a right time for learning everything.

Role Playing in Human Relations Training (National Education Association, 1949, 25 min., sound, black and white). A demonstration of how to get groups and individuals to play roles.

Unconscious Motivation (Association Films, 1950, 38 min., sound, black and white). How behavior is influenced by unconscious motivation.

CHAPTER FIVE

Kinship Loyalties

The family tie—intimate and affectionate,
the foundation of our loyalties and entire mode of life.

From the world

of personal loyalties to the realm of family loyalties is only a short step, for family life is the most intimate of all group associations. Few social bonds are as close or as firm as those between mother and child or husband and wife. Breaking them nearly always brings anguish and sorrow. Intimacy, affection, and privacy, all hallmarks of the home, make it a refuge from the storms and stress of life. In the home, we can momentarily shut out the pressures, cares, and troubles of the world around us and be our true selves. In no other place is the individual's unshackled personality more apt to express itself than in the family.

We cannot, however, detach society completely from the home, for society and family exert a deep and profound influence on one another. From the family, youngsters learn what society at large expects from them, and from society they learn the value of family life and how to act toward other family members. Society actually depends on the family for survival, for it is through the family that society is reproduced and perpetuated. Here the child is first delivered into society; here he develops his sense of "self," is socialized, protected, and taught to live with others.

Indeed, the family is basic to all human societies and is found wherever human society exists. The family actually contains many features of society itself. Within the family we find the origin of many of our governing processes, economic activities, religious beliefs, recreation, and other institutional patterns. Certainly the family is a source of many of our loyalties and influences our entire loyalty system profoundly. Brothers and sisters may fight among themselves, but let a neighborhood child attack one of them and they will unite to repel the "outsider." When American soldiers were asked during the last war what they were fighting for, they frequently replied, "To get home." Letters from home and family were important factors to their morale. Home is more than just a house where we eat and sleep, more than a mere base of operations. It includes our hopes, our loved ones, and our friends. It is here that we first learn our religion, our politics, and our work and play habits. The family institution provides a foundation for our loyalties and our way of life in its entirety. It has long been considered the backbone of society.

In this chapter we shall consider first the historical background of the family and then some of the major characteristics of family life in the United States. We shall be concerned, too, with the family as a focal point of loyalty. In Chapter 16 we shall treat the family in the midst of modern urban conditions.

HERITAGE FROM THE PAST

The roots of the family are lost in the mists of far-distant time. Family life may even be related, as some authorities contend, to pre-human life; and certainly some traits of other animals, particularly their mating practices and care of their offspring, remind us of ourselves. Here, however, we are more interested in the social and anthropological roots of the family than in its biological connections with lower animals.

TRIBAL SOCIETIES *

A century of anthropological investigation into the sources of family life has brought forth a number of different and contradictory theories. Two diametrically opposed concepts were advanced in 1861. Sir Henry Maine, a British legal scholar, maintained vigorously that the oldest male, or *patriarch*, had always ruled the family with virtually unlimited authority. This theory was very old, having been held by both Plato and Aristotle in classical times. Johann Bachofen, a German scholar, challenged it with an evolutionary theory of family development. The family, according to Bachofen, had evolved by stages from a time when men lived in hordes, were largely unregulated, and had no families. In this original condition, Bachofen contended, relations between the sexes were largely promiscuous and children took the names of their mothers since fathers were often difficult to identify. The mother-child bond was thus the only trace of a family condition. But women soon wearied of this condition, Bachofen believed, and established families. He claimed that a woman, or *matriarch*, became the center of authority in the prehistoric family and that the patriarchal family, so prevalent in modern times, had evolved from these earlier matriarchies. Men simply rebelled against their female overlords, taking advantage of their superior strength to assert their own dominance.

Bachofen's theory soon found many disciples, especially among those anthropologists who were deeply influenced by the evolutionary theory of Charles Darwin. Be-

* This discussion is based on Meyer F. Nimkoff, *The Family* (New York: Houghton Mifflin, 1934).

fore the nineteenth century had ended, many anthropologists agreed that the family had developed through a long, slow process of evolution. But as sociologist George Lundberg has pointed out, evidence was scarce and conclusions were based largely on sheer speculation.

It remained for a renowned Finnish anthropologist, Edvard Westermarck, to blaze the trail for modern students. After studying the life of ancient societies, Westermarck concluded early in the twentieth century that pair marriages, or *monogamy* (one man to one woman), had existed from the earliest times. Secondly, he observed that the family has always been the basic social unit. These two major conclusions challenged Bachofen's theory that men were originally promiscuous, without families, and that monogamy was the product of evolution.

In checking Westermarck's theory, students began to rely more heavily on evidence drawn from existing tribal societies. They have found, interestingly enough, that the family is universal among nonliterate peoples, although the form of family organization may vary from society to society. They have also found that monogamy is the most prevalent form of marriage relationship and that it frequently exists in those societies that sanction other forms of marriage. Contrary, however, to Westermarck's conclusion that plural forms of marriage, or *polygamy*, are merely temporary deviations from the established pattern of monogamy, plural marriage patterns are quite common. Although polygamy is illegal in the United States and in many parts of the world, a number of societies have sanctioned *polygyny* (marriage of one man to more than one woman at the same time), and a few have recognized *polyandry* (marriage of one woman to more than one man at the same time).

Further study of family life in nonliterate

societies has revealed that social control, or the regulation of human behavior, is a universal function of the family. The family, for example, exerts considerable control over the sex relations of its members. Anthropologists have found that all societies invoke an *incest taboo*, which forbids sexual relations or marriage between close relatives. But since societies vary in their definition of a close relative, the taboo is applied differently from one society to another. In the United States, for instance, this taboo applies primarily to the immediate family group of parents and their children. Cousins may marry, but usually not first or second cousins. In other societies the rules governing marriage of cousins vary considerably from prohibition to compulsion.

Societies, in fact, vary widely in their rules concerning acceptable marriage partners. Most societies enforce the rule of *exogamy*, which obligates people to marry someone outside a specific group, such as their clan, tribe, or fraternal order. In effect, this reinforces compliance with the incest taboo, since both designate those persons not considered suitable as marriage partners. The Murngin tribe in Australia, for instance, has developed the rule so meticulously that suitors must select marriage partners from a specific group. The tribe is divided into two groups, and a young man must pick a girl from the opposite group, which also insures that she will belong to a different clan. Societies may also require individuals to marry *within* their own group, tribe, clan, or religious order. This practice is called *endogamy*. Whatever requirements are established in a given society, loyalty to the system is expected and is often backed up by punitive measures that range from death to social ostracism.

Societies differ in still other aspects of their kinship organization. *Kinship organization* refers to the ways in which people related by blood, marriage, or adoption are grouped together, and to the conception of family life that is implied in a particular kind of grouping. A *nuclear* family, for example, consists of husband, wife and children living together in a household. In societies where nuclear families predominate, kinship loyalties are strongest within the immediate family. An *extended* family, in contrast, contains several generations and possibly many cousins, aunts, and uncles, within the same household, and loyalties are extended beyond nuclear kin to encompass many kinfolk.

Nearly every society recognizes both units. But in some societies, such as the American, nuclear relations take precedence, whereas in others, especially some nonliterate societies, extended relationships are considered more important. Other differences in kinship relations will become more apparent in the discussions that follow on the ancient Chinese family, the European family, and the American family.

THE ANCIENT CHINESE FAMILY

A peasant society displays many characteristics of a tribal society, including intimate local groups and strong kinship ties. Kinship or family loyalties were so dominant in ancient China that some authorities use the term "familistic" to describe the system. *A familistic system is one in which all behavior, standards, and values originate from, focus on, and aim at the welfare of the family.* The family is thus the point of reference for all personal judgments and actions.

The early Chinese family was an extended one with as many as five generations living together as a household unit. Family solidarity was strengthened by the custom of ancestor worship and loyalty to the patriarch. Ancestors were venerated, and the older living members of the family were accorded great respect and devotion because of their age, which the Chinese equated with wisdom and knowledge. The family in ancient

China, therefore, was patriarchal, with the oldest living male member acting as patriarch. Other men were ranked after him according to their ages, and women were always subservient to the men.

The Chinese wife's supreme duty was to her husband and his family. When she married, she went to live with her husband and his family and was expected to serve and obey them. Typically, she went through a period of training and instruction in order that she might be a dutiful wife and render proper service.

Filial piety was carried to an extreme, and the Chinese child was expected to show great devotion and respect for his parents. He was given no voice whatsoever in the decisions they made concerning him; nor could he ignore their commands or go against their wishes. Likewise, younger brothers were expected to be devoted and obedient to the eldest brother. To be otherwise was to be worse than a thief.

The Chinese family was a highly stable social unit in which family loyalties were clearly delineated and understood by all. Deference and obedience to the family "ruler" were central to a system in which the family itself was a pillar of society. In moving now to the European family system, you will see that behavior and loyalty patterns vary greatly from one society to another.

THE EUROPEAN FAMILY

Family life in Europe underwent many changes over the centuries, and at no time was it identical all over the Continent. It is, however, possible to identify several of the more outstanding features of European family life that have so profoundly affected the American family.

For one thing, the patriarchal heritage of the American family may be traced to Europe and back even further to the ancient Hebrews. European immigrants brought this heritage with them to America, a heritage

The extended family tradition still persists among some modern Chinese, spanning a number of generations and including close relatives.

that, as we have seen, stresses the dominant position of the father and husband and the legal headship of the male. In Roman Europe, the patriarch enjoyed exceptionally wide powers, limited only by the requirement that he consult the male relatives before carrying out a death sentence on his wife. The Hebrew husband, on the other hand, held the power of life and death over his wife only if she committed adultery.

With the rise of Christianity in Europe came disparagement of sex, stress on monogamy as the ideal marriage relationship, and identification of marriage as a sacrament. The Church Fathers praised virginity and celibacy. Sexual relations were proper only within marriage, and then solely for the procreation of children. Marriage thus became a useful means of avoiding sin, for as St. Paul aptly said, ". . . it is better to marry than to burn." Christianity has always favored monogamy and condemned pre- and extra-marital relations, just as it has opposed divorce. In the thirteenth century, marriage was made a sacrament, and only ceremonies conducted by a priest were held to be valid.

Under feudalism an interesting paradox developed. Women were accorded low social and economic rank, yet at the same time they were glorified as persons. Knights fought to win the favor of fair ladies; chivalry to the fair sex became the order of the day. The ideal of romantic love was thus revived and has remained very much a part of modern life, as any observer of the current scene will verify.

Another European influence on American family life involved a greater measure of civil and political control over marriage. This developed as a part of the more general conflict that marked the relations between the civil authority and the Church during the Protestant Reformation. Led by Martin Luther, many Protestants came to recognize the right of the government to make laws controlling marriage, whereas Catholics fought to keep control of marriage in the hands of the Church and perpetuate its sacramental character. Today, all American marriages are either licensed by a state government or recognized by it under common or civil law. All Catholics are also obliged to marry in the Church if they want their marriage to be sanctioned by the Church. Many Protestants, too, feel obliged to be married under both religious rites and civil law. The conflict between state and church is developed further in Chapter 7.

FAMILY LIFE IN AMERICA

Brief as the preceding discussion has been, it nevertheless permits the reader to distinguish some of the European developments that have influenced the American family: the patriarchal tendency, monogamy, romantic love, and a greater degree of civil control over marriage. Some of these developments, as we shall see later, have caused strains and tensions within present-day American families.

The typical American family today is a small, monogamous, and equalitarian unit that lives in a middle-class district of a city. It is smaller than it was, with perhaps two or three children today as compared with six, eight, or more a few generations ago. The decrease stems partly from the shift in America from a predominantly rural to a largely urban type of society. City folks find that children cost money. They do not help to support the family as they once did on the farm.

THE RULE OF MONOGAMY

Allegiance to the rule of monogamy is one of the strongest loyalties on the American scene. Almost everyone believes firmly

The American family is a conjugal unit that stresses the father-mother-children bonds and de-emphasizes close ties with other relatives.

in the principle of pair-marriage, and it is very doubtful if a serious proposal to abandon this custom would receive much of a hearing in this country. Our strictly monogamous system has been weakened a trifle in recent years by the increase in divorce and remarriage, or "serial monogamy," as it has been called. But no serious inroads on the monogamous system appear to have been made as yet.

URBAN AND MIDDLE-CLASS FEATURES

We shall discuss urban and middle-class features of the American family in greater detail later. For now, just a brief observation. American family life has been caught up in the general trend toward urbanization. As a result, a whole new way of life, with new attitudes, values, and behavior patterns unknown to the rural society of two or three generations ago, has made its appearance. Middle-class values and attitudes have placed a premium on appearances, on the drive for recognition and conspicuous success, and on comforts and material values. Life in the city has thus become more than a matter of mere location.

EMPHASIS ON THE IMMEDIATE CONJUGAL FAMILY UNIT

One of the most distinctive and important developments on the American fam-

ily scene is a new pattern of relations that has appeared within the immediate, or *conjugal*, family. Briefly, *conjugal relations stress mutual husband-wife duties and obligations within the immediate family unit, rather than relations within the entire kinship group.* Kinship relationships are still apparent in family reunions and in the procession of visiting aunts, uncles, cousins, and grandparents. But the young husband and wife in modern America not only establish their own residence away from their parents but also tend to detach themselves from their former families. It is becoming increasingly rare for married couples to involve themselves economically, socially, or psychologically with their former families or other kin. Many people today do not know the names of all their aunts, uncles, and cousins, let alone have much to do with them. Americans stress the immediate conjugal family unit to the exclusion of in-laws.

American consensus on the marriage pair as the basic family unit has led to a pattern of isolated families. Each family, according to popular belief, should be independent and free of interference from the in-laws. It is considered extremely unfortunate when a newly married pair must move in with in-laws. Only under extreme circumstances is it considered proper for parents to interfere with the families of their children. Ameri-

83

In America the emphasis is on romance and being in love.

cepting financial or material assistance from relatives. Although dowries are virtually nonexistent, receiving "gifts" is common practice.

American families have become more democratic. In this respect they reflect the equalitarian trend in American politics and social thought. Although patriarchal tendencies still persist, husbands and fathers no longer rule the roost as they once did. Now it is fairly commonplace to find all family members, including children, having some voice in family affairs. Several foreign observers have remarked skeptically that democracy in the American family now has reached the point where children dictate family decisions. Actually, with respect to authority and decision-making, the American family is in transition. It is no longer patriarchal, but neither is it completely equalitarian.

The trend toward equality extends to a wide number of family relationships. Unlike many societies in which sons are favored over daughters or where the oldest son receives special preferences, Americans expect fathers and mothers to treat their children impartially and equally. Age and sex cannot be used to justify unequal treatment. All children are recognized under American law as equal heirs to family property, and popular opinion holds that all are entitled to equal affection.

Likewise, the principle of equality determines many kinfolk relations. Both in-law families of a marriage pair are on an equal footing. A husband's family is given no special preference over the wife's. Parents are expected to treat their childrens' marriage partners equally. A father's brother has a position and role similar to the mother's brother. Kinship loyalty in America thus has departed drastically from the old Chinese system of ancestor worship and the extended

cans believe that the immediate "father-mother-children" group should be free to make its own decisions and determine its own destiny. About the only major exception to this rule of "noninterference" is in ac-

84

family pattern, as well as from the European patriarchal system.

EMPHASIS ON ROMANCE

Romance, with its emphasis on being "in love," is one of the most highly publicized traits of American society. Democratic and equalitarian tendencies in the American family leave children relatively free to choose their marriage partners without parental interference. Indeed, it is considered improper in America for parents to select formally a child's spouse, as has often been the practice in Europe, Asia, and elsewhere. A marriage, after all, brings a new family unit into being, which is quite independent of the families of both partners and devoid of the strong and perpetual kinship ties found in other societies. The new marriage need not meet the interests and needs of an extended family, as was true in ancient China. In the Chinese and European family systems, husbands and wives were expected to perform certain prescribed duties such as cooking, washing, child-rearing, and supporting the family. In America these traditional duties have become more or less incidental; the most important requirement is to be in love. With kinship ties weakened, the marriage pair is heavily dependent on one another for security and affection and for the satisfaction of emotional needs. Neither marriage partner can easily retreat to the solidarity of an extended family group of kinsmen for the comfort, solace, or assurance he may be craving. Severance of kinship ties and free choice of mates thus place a premium on personal attraction, mutual affection, and mutual dependence. Romance—love and affection—bulks large in America.

Romance can be exciting and exotic, but it is also unstable, since it is based on emotion. Few people are blessed with the ability to maintain effervescent amour over a period of years. Some claim romance is far too unstable a factor on which to establish something as basic as a family.

BREAKDOWN AND READJUSTMENT

DESERTION AND DIVORCE

The rapid changes in family life that have occurred during the twentieth century and the stresses and strains accompanying these changes have resulted in a widespread feeling that something is drastically wrong with the American family. Most obvious, and to some, most dangerous, is the casual dissolution of marriage by separation, desertion, or the more formal and final act of divorce. Belief in marriage as a permanent, indissoluble, sacred bond lasting "till death do us part" still persists. But along with this belief has come a newer attitude that under certain intolerable conditions the dissolution of the marriage contract may be a wise and even happy choice for a couple to make.

The hard fact is that marriage does not work for some people. Whether such people should stay together, maintain the marriage at all costs, or recognize that a real marriage does not, in fact, exist, is not an easy question to answer. Decisions of this kind will be influenced by moral and religious considerations, educational and social backgrounds, the presence or absence of children, and still other factors. Serious loyalty conflicts—to self, to family, to religion—inevitably arise when a marriage begins to crumble.

At mid-century there were 2 million divorced persons in the United States, a sharp increase over the figure for 90 years ago (see Table 1). There are no reliable figures on the extent of desertion, or unofficial separations of husbands and wives, but some observers believe the number is substantial. Desertion probably reached a peak during the depression of the 1930's, when it was known as "the poor man's divorce." Many husbands who could not afford the costs of divorce simply deserted their wives and children. The number of divorces declined after reaching a peak just after World War II, but the number is still substantial and indicates, of course, that the practice is becoming more socially acceptable.

TABLE **I**   DIVORCE RATE IN THE UNITED STATES, 1870-1950

Year	Divorces per 1,000 Marriages
1870	3.1
1880	4.3
1890	5.8
1900	7.9
1910	8.8
1920	13.4
1930	17.4
1940	16.5
1950	23.1

Source: Federal Security Agency, *Vital Statistics, Special Reports.*

AFTER DIVORCE

A critical question for Americans is whether the rising tide of divorce, desertion, and marital discord will ultimately destroy the institutions of marriage and family life as we have come to know them. Authorities disagree. At one extreme are those who warn of the inevitable collapse of the family; while at the other pole are those who feel that there is and will be no breakdown. This latter group maintains that such a venerable institution as the family, whatever the storms and changes that bear on it, will survive as long as humankind. Furthermore, they argue, divorce and separation may be only a healthy release from the marriage bond for men and women who are emotionally or psychologically unfit for marriage.

What happens after a divorce? The answer to this question may help us to speculate more fruitfully on the future of the American family. First of all, disintegration of marriage usually begins well in advance of divorce or separation. The most dangerous period for marriages is during the first five years, for that is when the divorce rate is the highest. This, of course, is the period when husbands and wives are learning to adjust to the new situation and the frequently unexpected and strange ways of their partners. Friction and disagreement may stem from any number of sources—from how to bring up the children, from how to spend leisure time or money, from religious differences, from in-law troubles. If the particular point or points at issue cannot be resolved, a divorce may be the only logical way out. Divorce is a recognition at law that a marriage has failed, something often recognized far earlier by the marriage partners themselves. It is the last stage in the disintegration of a marriage and the first step in readjusting to new conditions for the former partners.

The divorced person must redefine his role in society. His loyalty obligations to his former spouse have ended; no longer is he obliged to love, honor, and cherish her. Aside from the question of alimony, a husband is freed from all financial obligation to his former wife. The wife, in turn, is freed from all responsibility toward her former husband.

Investigation shows, however, that not all divorced persons are happy with their new freedom. Some, in fact, are so unhappy that they consider remarrying their former spouses. Many feel personally inadequate. Divorce, for whatever reason, signifies failure, and those who have failed in marriage are rarely applauded in American society. For this important reason, the divorcee finds it difficult to explain his action to himself and others and to refashion a new pattern of relationships.

Considerable readjustments face a man

and woman after they are divorced. A financial settlement is often a part of the divorce arrangement; a change of residence, a different social life, and changed relationships with the opposite sex are to be expected. Children of divorced parents present a special problem. Often the mother is granted custody, but the youngsters are deprived of a normal home life.

Divorce, though it may produce profound changes in the individual and leave perma-nent scars, is not necessarily the end of married life. Remarriage is common. A Bureau of the Census survey in the 1950's showed that three out of every four divorced persons remarried within five years. Whether remarriage is a real and satisfactory solution to a divorcee's problems is debatable. Contrary to popular belief, limited evidence does indicate that those who remarry are relatively better adjusted than those who remain single.

FUNCTIONS OF THE FAMILY IN A CHANGING SOCIETY

Of the traditional family functions, three remain virtually intact despite the changes that have recast modern American society: affection (in the broad sense), procreation, and child-rearing. Other functions —educational, religious, and economic—have been drastically altered or taken over by other groups and organizations. But the very intimate understanding we call affection is unattainable, at least for long, outside the family. The bearing and rearing of children outside the family, although possible, has never been very successful historically. That a vast majority of all births continue to take place within the family suggests the existence of strong allegiance to this ancient institution. The family system remains the focal point of some of our strongest ties and loyalties.

The number and rate of births tend to fluctuate over periods of time. Births hit an all-time low during the depression of the 1930's. Thereafter the birth rate rose steadily through World War II, reaching a spectacularly high level in the late 1940's and maintaining a relatively high level throughout the 1950's. These shifts reflect changing social, economic, and political conditions as well as changing enthusiasm, or even fashions, respecting the desirability of large families.

Child-bearing thus remains a vital function of family life despite the impact of the urban-industrial revolution.

Although home and family are still highly important, especially to the very young, the task of upbringing has been shifted partly to nurseries, schools, churches, playgrounds, television, and other agencies. Responsibility, nevertheless, remains largely with the parents, though many observers fear that parents have relinquished entirely too much control over their children, even to the point of shirking their duties. But the child-rearing function seems destined to remain a central obligation of the family, based as it is on custom, parentage, and affection.

MORALITY, RELIGION, CITIZENSHIP

Parents are still responsible to a considerable degree for the training and guidance of their children in morality, religion, and citizenship. We have already seen that churches, schools, and other community groups have assumed many of these responsibilities; but it is still the home environment that molds the young child's basic attitudes about life, morals, citizenship, and religion. What he learns there may conflict with what impresses him in the outside world, where he spends more and more of his growing hours. The growing child—indeed, the adult, too—faces a conflict in loyalties in a world where materialistic success is accorded great prestige, where the biggest, fastest, most expensive things are the most desired, and where people are encouraged, at least mildly, to "win at any price." Never to betray a confidence or a trust, to play fair at all times, often contradicts our emphasis on "success" and "winning at any price." Children and their parents encounter an endless round of conflicts in a society where standards of behavior are constantly changing or clashing.

The family has supported religious and political institutions for many generations by teaching children socially accepted standards of behavior, inculcating in them moral standards and religious beliefs, and giving them a deeper understanding of their religious and political heritage. The American child learns about God and is taught to pray by his parents. And in the home he is taught right from wrong. The American youngster, likewise, receives his first impressions about legal requirements and political standards from the family.

Changes wrought by the industrial-urban way of life have altered the family's role in the religious and political training of the child. Not that the family has ceased to perform these functions, but the gradual separation of these functions from the family has proceeded at a rapid pace in recent decades. Religious devotion and training, once so central a family and church activity, now is becoming more exclusively a church function. Families in rural areas of the coun-

Trends have changed in the ways that Americans care for the aged.

try still gather to sing hymns and spirituals, a rare event in our cities. Professional pallbearers sometimes serve at funerals, a function once reserved to none but relatives and close friends.

With the impending demise of the patriarchal family and with the rise of strong governmental and police agencies, the family has lost some of its political significance. In tribal societies, family or clan groups were sometimes indistinguishable from the tribe as a political unit. Today legislatures enact laws to be administered and enforced by executive agencies and the police and interpreted by the courts. The family as such has very little to do with the operation of modern government, but it still is instrumental in influencing attitudes toward government and politics. This situation helps explain why so many Americans follow the same political party as their parents.

PRODUCTION AND CONSUMPTION

One of the greatest differences between the modern and the earlier family lies in changed economic functions. No longer is the family a producing unit. Only in a few cases, among sharecroppers in some southern states, for example, does the entire family pool its labor and work together in producing crops. Industrial and urban development has all but eliminated this once important aspect of family life. Individual members of urban families are, of course, still employed in productive labor but usually not as a family unit.

Consumption remains a family function, but it too has changed considerably under the impact of urban-industrial changes. In extreme cases, family members may share no more than the same house. More commonly, they share at least some meals, an occasional movie or television program, and probably a vacation. The net result is that the modern American family, although still a consumption unit in a substantial way, has departed greatly from the unitary production and consumption patterns of the past.

CARE OF THE AGED AND INFIRM

Traditionally, the aged and infirm were cared for by their families at home. Poorhouses and county farms were for those unfortunates who had no family, or at least no relatives able to support them. There was a social stigma attached to poorhouses, and no self-respecting son or daughter would see his parents sent there if he could possibly prevent it. Now, however, private and public homes for the aged have become more acceptable. Better-trained staffs, improved facilities, and active recreational and guidance programs have removed much of the old-time stigma. An old-folks home is no longer an unattractive place where oldsters sit out their declining years alone and forgotten.

Other and important factors contribute to this present trend in institutionalized care of the aged. City-living, small homes, and more active lives have made many married couples reluctant to take aging parents into their homes. The number of persons aged 65 and over in this country has increased by about half since 1900 and is bound to become larger. Awareness of this trend, together with the disinclination or inability of children to care for their parents, should lead to expanded facilities for the care of the aged in the future. Already, movements in this direction represent a drastic departure in the traditional loyalty pattern of children to parents.

SOME WORDS OF SUMMARY

The heritage of the American family goes far back into history and has roots in many places. Patriarchy, monogamy, exogamy, endogamy, familism, state and religious control of the family, the concept of romantic love, and specific family roles and obligations have all existed among various family systems. In at least a modified form, all these features of family life have been incorporated into the American family system.

The American family today is small, urban, middle-class, monogamous, and equalitarian. Loyalty to this pattern has not fully crystallized. Strong traces of the old heritage remain, but where traditions are inconsistent with changing social conditions—as with patriarchy and democracy—traditions are gradually giving way to new loyalties. Social change in a jet-age society is so rapid that changes in loyalty may never quite catch up to changes in behavior.

Some authorities believe that the increase in desertion and divorce rates endangers the very existence of the family as a social institution. Others, however, simply view such developments as an attempt on the part of the family to adjust to changing social conditions. In any case, loyalty to the permanency of marriage has weakened somewhat. Divorce is becoming increasingly more acceptable, and there is evidence which indicates that the divorced person is likely to remarry and readjust satisfactorily to a new environment.

Major functions of the family also have changed, reflecting changing patterns of loyalties. Child-rearing, along with affection and procreation, continues to constitute the core of family life, but it, too, is undergoing modification. Training in morality, religion, and citizenship suffers from confusion over which institution—family, school, or church—properly should be responsible for it. Production, consumption, and care of the aged have changed greatly in relation to family functions.

Loyalties centering on and embodied in the institution of family life have changed a great deal, but a hard core of traditional loyalties persists. The family will no doubt survive, although considerable guessing is required to foresee its future shape.

FURTHER ROADS TO LEARNING

GENERAL ACCOUNTS

R. Baber, *Marriage and the Family,* 2nd ed. (New York: McGraw-Hill, 1953). A standard textbook on the family.

E. Burgess and H. Locke, *The Family,* 2nd ed. (New York: American Book, 1953). Two leading sociologists survey the family as a social institution and how it now places greater emphasis on companionship among the members.

R. Cavan, *The American Family* (New York: Crowell, 1953). Very good on problems of marriage adjustment.

C. Kirkpatrick, *The Family* (New York: Ronald, 1955). An institutional approach to the family.

M. Nimkoff, *Marriage and the Family* (Boston: Houghton Mifflin, 1947). Another good institutional treatment of the background of the American family system.

SPECIAL STUDIES

C. Arensberg and S. Kimball, *Family and Community in Ireland* (Cambridge: Harvard University Press, 1940). This vivid description of the Irish family provides an invaluable basis for assessing the American family.

H. Becker and R. Hill, eds., *Family, Marriage and Parenthood* (Boston: Heath, 1955). An excellent collection of readings.

E. Burgess and P. Wallin, *Engagement and Marriage* (Philadelphia: Lippincott, 1953). An inquiry into how marital adjustment is related to engagement.

E. F. Frazier, *The Negro Family in the United States* (Chicago: The University of Chicago Press, 1939). The best account of a minority group family system thus far.

P. Glick, *American Families* (New York: Wiley, 1957). One of a series of census monographs that abounds in information on the family.

W. Goode, *After Divorce* (Glencoe, Ill.: The Free Press, 1956). Some heretofore unknown aspects about the lives of divorced women are illuminated.

W. Goodsell, *A History of Marriage and the Family* (New York: Macmillan, 1934). Notable history and source book on the European family system.

N. Himes and D. Taylor, *Your Marriage* (New York: Rinehart, 1955). Things you should know and appreciate in preparing for marriage—on housing, personal finance, home management, child care, and marital adjustment.

J. Landis and M. Landis, *Readings in Marriage and the Family* (Englewood Cliffs, N. J.: Prentice-Hall, 1952). A stimulating and readable volume that is most helpful on matters of marriage adjustment.

H. Locke, *Predicting Adjustment in Marriage* (New York: Holt, 1951). A landmark in attempts to forecast successful marriages.

B. Malinowski, *The Sexual Life of Savages in Northwestern Melanesia* (New York: Halcyon House, 1929). A complete picture of the family life of the Trobriand Islanders.

G. Murdock, *Social Structure* (New York: Macmillan, 1949). Comprehensive survey of family systems of various societies showing the relativity of family styles of living.

W. Ogburn and M. Nimkoff, *Technology and the Changing Family* (Boston: Houghton Mifflin, 1955). How technological factors have wrought changes in the American family.

H. Pilpel and T. Zavin, *Your Marriage and the Law* (New York: Rinehart, 1952). A layman's guide to the legal and contractual obligations involved in man-wife relations, property, children, separation, and divorce.

J. Thomas, *The American Catholic Family* (Englewood Cliffs, N. J.: Prentice-Hall, 1956). An exhaustive treatment of the Catholic family.

E. Westermarck, *The History of Human Marriage* (New York: Macmillan, 1921). Two volumes. A classic study of marriage among nonliterates and the origins of modern family patterns.

FICTION AND DRAMA

L. Alcott, *Little Women* (Boston: Little, Brown, 1934, and other editions). A touching and somewhat idyllic family story that provides a good glimpse of American family life in the nineteenth century.

F. Colby, *The Black Winds Blow* (New York: Harrison-Hilton, 1940). The marriage of an Irish girl to a New England lad results in severe conflicts between two family traditions.

J. Galsworthy, *The Forsyte Saga* (New York: Scribner, 1934). A history of a typical English family from mid-Victorian times to the close of World War I by a great master in storytelling.

T. Mann, *Buddenbrooks* (New York: Knopf, 1931). A superb piece of art that pictures the decline of a German middle-class family.

J. Marquand, *The Late George Apley* (Boston: Little, Brown, 1937). A Pulitzer Prize-winning novel centering around the head of an old Boston family, which leaves an unforgettable impression of a locality, a class, and an age.

FILMS

Hindu Family (Encyclopaedia Britannica Films, 1952, 10 min., sound, black and white). This film reflects Hindu family relations in a wedding of a village herdsman's daughter.

Japanese Family (International Film Foundation, 1950, 23 min., sound, black and white). The everyday life of a middle-class Japanese family.

Marriage and Divorce (McGraw-Hill, 1949, 15 min., sound, black and white). Covers the problems surrounding divorce and broken homes in the United States.

Peiping Family (International Film Foundation, 1949, 21 min., sound, black and white). The daily life of a Chinese family during the present century.

The Watusi of Africa (an Advanced Native Culture) (Erpi Classroom Films, 1939, 11 min., sound, black and white). A good demonstration of family and tribal life in an African culture.

Class and Caste Loyalties

On a luxury liner, as elsewhere,
rank has its privileges,
even in an open-class system such as the American.

Each of us

is born into a particular social position, usually with the same social rank as his parents. For every society has a *stratification system,* or a *hierarchy of differently valued ranks,* and people are ranked by their social positions according to birth, income, property, or some other standard of evaluation. But whether a person remains in the position to which he has fallen heir depends primarily on the kind of stratification system he happens to have been born into. In a caste system of ranking, as we shall presently see, a person has no opportunity to change his position, whereas in an open-class system a person may not only move up when opportunities come along but he is generally encouraged to seek a higher social position and is applauded when he succeeds. In the broadest terms, then, our opportunities and incentives for mobility are determined by the kind of stratification system in which we live.

No matter how slight or great the opportunity to change our status, however, we are expected to play our role according to the rules for our particular status. We must, in other words, remain loyal to the system under which we live. But along with the differences in opportunity to change one's status, stratification systems also vary considerably in the loyalty demands they impose on the people who occupy particular statuses. Class loyalties in America, for example, differ sharply from Hindu caste loyalties in India, as they differ from class obligations in Great Britain. And even within a stratification system, socially imposed loyalties vary at different levels of the social hierarchy.

Basic beliefs and social values provide primary support for loyalties in a social hierarchy. A caste man, for example, firmly believes he was destined to his station in life before he was born and therefore tries to make the best of his hereditary status. In a class system, on the other hand, a man feels obliged to improve his lot and climb the social ladder. In either case a person's loyalty may well depend on his rank in his system, the strength of his beliefs and social traditions, and the opportunities he has for improving his rank.

CASTES, ESTATES, AND CLASSES

THE HINDU CASTE SYSTEM

In India, an agrarian society where economic and social change has been extremely slow, a very rigid type of stratification called a *caste system* existed for more than three thousand years. The structure of this caste system was based on four major castes or strata: (1) the Brahmans, or priests; (2) the Kshatriya, or soldiers; (3) the Vaisya, or farmers, herdsmen, and merchants; and (4) the Sudra, or menials. The "untouchables," still another group, was at the bottom of the whole social hierarchy, and the members were "outcasts" in the sense that they did not belong to any caste. Personal contact between castes was limited by restrictions on touching, associating with, dining with, or eating food cooked by outsiders. If so much as the shadow of a low-

In a caste system, a person is born into his caste, remains there for his entire life, and carries out his caste obligations faithfully.

caste person fell on a high-caste person, the latter became "polluted" and had to bathe to purify himself. Special types of dress, such as a colored turban, often identified particular castes so that a person could be readily and visually identified with his caste in the eyes of his community.

Loyalty to a single caste and to the entire caste system was sanctioned by the Hindu religion. Each caste was accorded a different degree of holiness, and caste purity was protected by taboos against intercaste mobility and intercaste marriage. Born into a particular caste group, a person remained there for as long as he lived. His chief hope of rising to a higher caste depended on carrying out his caste obligations so effectively that he would be born into a higher caste when he was reincarnated, or when he was "reborn to live another life."

Caste inequalities were therefore justified and accepted generally. As a matter of fact, down through the centuries, not caste inequalities but obligations to fulfill caste objectives were the most important con-siderations. The best caste men were those who showed loyalty to their caste by upholding its purity and honor. Among the Sudra, for example, the most diligent and efficient workers who avoided contaminating other castes were considered good caste men. The same was true for priests, soldiers, and all other caste members. By fulfilling one's caste obligations, a person might gain greater esteem from his fellow caste members, but his position in the caste system would remain the same.

THE ESTATE SYSTEM
IN FEUDAL SOCIETIES

The *estate system*, which existed in medieval Europe, contained features of both caste and class stratification. Based primarily on birth, the estate system assigned distinctive rights, obligations, and duties to each of three major groups, or estates: the nobility, the clergy, and the so-called "third estate," which included workers, merchants, and peasants. According to a common saying of the times, it was the duty of the nobles to fight, of the priests to pray, and of the rest of the populace to work. Marriage and social contacts between the estates were extremely rare, although some social climbing within each estate and later between them was possible. The estate system represented a kind of intermediate stage between the caste system and the more mobile class system that we know today.

The European estate system emerged after the downfall of the Roman Empire, when local lords became powerful enough to acquire ownership rights to land. To protect these rights, the lords maintained their own military forces, which were soon used to assure workers and peasants of protection in return for their labor, and to bind them to the lords. As the power of the lords increased, their position became more aristocratic and hereditary. When the Church became a landowner, members of the clergy also served as feudal landlords, and thus the Church and its clergy became a part of the estate system. The structure of the system was then complete, with recognition extending downward from the nobility and the clergy to the members of the "third estate."

Unlike the caste system, which keeps a person from changing his inherited social status, the estate system is much more flexible and permits some social mobility. The upper nobility in feudal Europe usually inherited its position, but a few less fortunate in their choice of parents were able to spring from a lowly social perch to a loftier one. This mobility became more common with

the rise of wealthy merchants whose daughters (with their dowries) often were coveted by impecunious noblemen. And the estate of the clergy and the cloistered and scholarly life lay open to gifted young men. Talent was not subdued completely by rules of status inheritance.

THE EMERGENCE OF CLASS SOCIETIES

Ultimately, the rise of towns and cities and the growth of trade and commerce sounded the death knell of the estate system in Europe. Businessman in the cities, the "bourgeoisie" as they came to be called, grew wealthy and powerful, thereby weakening the control of feudal lords, who became more and more dependent on the bourgeoisie for money and support. Frequently the king would line up with the new business class against the old nobility. As a result of these developments, the old privileged order gradually crumbled, and new social groupings began to crystallize. The final collapse of the system came in dramatic fashion with the French Revolution in 1789.

Out of the ruins emerged the modern, fluid class system of Europe and America. In America social mobility was nourished by the existence of cheap land, a scarcity of labor, and the growing ideals of human equality and dignity. The emergence of a capitalistic economy provided men with many new avenues to power, advantage, and prestige. And to the west the raw unsettled frontier offered opportunity and certain advantages to resourceful, versatile men, no matter what their birth and breeding.

THE NATURE OF AN OPEN-CLASS SYSTEM

A class system, or, as it is sometimes called, an open-class system, is as distinctive as a caste system. In broad terms, it is characterized by vertical mobility, seeking after status, competition, intermarriage between people of different class levels, and a philoso-

phy that stresses individual success. It is "open" because theoretically, at least, everyone is free to find his own level. The successful competitor is rewarded both with material possessions and increased prestige. No birthright confines anyone to a lowly status or necessarily protects a person born to wealth. There is no landed aristocracy and there are few well-guarded legal privileges to benefit a select minority. A social class in an open-class system is not rigid or binding. It consists simply of those individuals who happen to be occupying the same social status at the same time. Interestingly enough, the Hindu religion supports and justifies the Indian caste system, whereas Christianity and Judaism tend to encourage mobility in the American class system by emphasizing human equality and individualism.

SOCIAL AND TECHNOLOGICAL CHANGE

An open-class system usually emerges in a social and economic environment that is undergoing rapid and drastic changes. In America the frontier, with its promise of free or cheap land, provided the initial spark. Waves of European immigrants fleeing from poverty and oppression in the Old World came sweeping into this new "land of freedom and opportunity." Some headed west; others crowded into the new seaboard cities to become the backbone of the labor force that was needed to man the new factories. They were making new lives for themselves, and, in the process, a new society. More and more factories began to darken the landscape; the gospel of free enterprise went hand in hand with progress. "Log cabin to White House" became a national myth, Horatio Alger a national model. Standards of living, measured in terms of material possessions, soared. Cookstove supplanted fireplace and was itself soon superseded by gas and electric ranges. Tin cans and refrigeration replaced ancient methods of preserving food, and improvements in transportation and new production techniques made many luxuries as staple as salt and placed them within the reach of nearly everyone. Soon many a family had a radio, then a car, and now a TV and two cars. In short, social and

technological change enriched and brought a quickening tempo to life, the ramifications of which today challenge even the most astute observers.

THE PRINCIPLE OF MOBILITY

Such rapid social and technological change is conducive to social mobility, which is an intrinsic aspect of a class system. Without upward or downward mobility, the various social strata would harden permanently. Americans have always believed in vertical mobility. We expect it, even demand it. In contrast to an estate or caste system, there are few barriers to movement between classes in an open-class system. Underlying the open-class society is a common faith in ability and achievement as yardsticks of social status.

ACHIEVEMENT

Achievement of status is the primary means whereby a person changes his class position. Status tends to be ascribed at birth according to the standing of the parents, as in a caste system. A hod-carrier's son is obviously born to a lower status than the son of a bank president but may end up with much more prestige than the banker's son.

From birth on, any change in social rank or status is theoretically achieved. But in practice this is not always true. Achievement normally signifies some effort on the part of a person to reach his goal, but common observation indicates that many people succeed in improving their status or position with little in the way of genuine achievement. Some gadget salesmen, for example, may gather a fortune and thereby reach a higher status simply because a teen-age craze suddenly brings on a huge sale of their product.

Ordinarily, we connect the idea of achievement of status with ideals such as equality of opportunity and rewards based on merit and competition. Most Americans realize that these ideals do not always square with reality, but we still remain loyal to them and they often motivate us to strike out against discrimination, inequality, and injustice. Scholarships and other financial aids to education, for example, are designed to provide equal educational opportunity for all. Fair employment practice programs aim to guarantee equal job opportunities to those people who might otherwise suffer discrimination. Wage and other differential rewards presumably signify differences in ability. Given a fair chance, however, the rest is up to the individual in an open-class society.

COMMUNICATION AND EDUCATION

One further essential to the maintenance of a class system involves the unob-structed communication of information and a broadly based general system of education. Communication is vital if people are to be kept informed of opportunities for jobs, schooling, housing, and other avenues to higher status. The mass media of communication—newspapers, radio, and television—contribute most to the process, but personal contacts are often significant, too. Learning experiences, both in and out of school, are obviously very important for the individual's prospects of mobility. Through learning, we acquire new skills and broaden our horizon of opportunity, thus giving the educated man an edge over the less educated.

So far, we have been considering social status and social class in very general terms. To get a clearer idea, we now turn to some of the more specific aspects of the class system in the United States.

AMERICA'S CLASS STRUCTURE

THE ABSENCE OF ORGANIZED CLASSES

We have nothing in the United States quite comparable to Hindu castes or the estate system that existed in feudal Europe. An occasional writer or commentator may point to the caste-like status of Negroes or the social etiquette governing relationships between races. But such features of our national life, even if we accept them as caste characteristics, are not universal enough to prove the existence of a caste system.

Nowhere in the United States, moreover, can there be found any social class organized as a group, despite occasional practices that approximate the characteristics of a caste system. The lower class, the upper class, or any other class is simply not organized as such, whereas castes are more or less organized locality groups. What we do find, however, is that certain organizations seem to represent class interests or include only persons from the same class level. A church, a lodge, a country club, a businessman's association, a labor union, and other kinds of organization may confine their membership to people from certain status levels and represent certain class biases, but this tendency is not the same as organization along class lines. Neither does the frequent claim by individuals that they are members of a particular class mean that there are organized classes in America.

STATUS AGGREGATES:
INCOME, OCCUPATION, AND EDUCATION

If social classes are not organized groups, what are they? Social scientists have come up with several definitions. Some regard a class as comprising all persons who possess similar social or economic characteristics. Income, occupation, and education are commonly regarded as indicators of social class. For example, all persons whose annual income is between $5,000 and $6,000, all white-collar workers, or all college graduates might belong to the same social class. From this standpoint a social class is a *status aggregate*, which means *a number of people with similar status characteristics such as similar income, level of education, living conditions, or occupation.* Members of a status aggregate are unorganized, do not necessarily know one another, and do not share common goals as an organized group might. They do not interact with one another as they would if they were members of a social group. All American bankers and all people who make between $3,000 and $5,000 a year are two different status aggregates and must be distinguished from a *social group*—the local lodge or church congregation—*wherein the members interact face to face, share common goals, and behave according to accepted standards.* Although members of the same social group (a school, a church, a local club, a family, or a citizens' reform league) will probably feel some allegiance to the group and its members, individuals as a status aggregate will not. Therefore, when social scientists speak of social classes as status aggregates, they are using the term as pure abstraction solely for statistical and investigative purposes.

The usefulness of employing the concept of social class as a status aggregate is shown in Table 2, which reveals a generally close relationship between occupation, income, and education. The same pattern has existed for several decades. With the exception of craftsmen, incomes of manual workers range below the national average. The white-collar, business, and professional occupations rank above the national average. The correlation between education and occupation is equally clear. The manual worker averages about three years less schooling than the non-manual worker. Farmers and farm laborers rank low in both education and income, but data must be evaluated carefully because figures for agricultural and non-agricultural incomes are not directly comparable.

The concept of status aggregates is most

The plight of migratory workers indicates that American society, though it may be fluid, continues to have clear class distinctions. If for no other reason, our incomes and job opportunities make a difference.

useful for investigating social classes. Richard Centers, for example, in his *Psychology of Social Classes*, shows that persons with a higher income tend to be more "conservative" and those with a lower income more "radical" in their politics. Other studies have revealed that socio-economic status is related to a person's "life chances," such as life expectancy, family size, type of medical care he receives, and the type of justice he can expect under the law. A person's socio-economic status will even affect his dating, marriage, and child-rearing practices, according to authorities. Status certainly influences his attitudes and behavior.

TABLE **2**   MEDIAN INCOME AND MEDIAN YEARS OF SCHOOLING FOR MALES BY OCCUPATION, UNITED STATES, 1950

Occupation	Income	Years of Schooling
All occupations	$2,668	9.7
Professional	3,958	16.0
Managerial	3,944	12.2
Craftsmen	3,125	9.5
Sales	3,028	12.2
Clerical	3,010	12.2
Operatives	2,607	8.9
Service Workers	2,195	8.8
Laborers	1,961	8.2
Private household	1,176	8.2
Farmers and farm managers	1,455	8.3
Farm laborers	863	8.0

Source: U. S. Bureau of the Census.

OCCUPATIONAL PRESTIGE

Social scientists also try to identify social classes according to the way that people evaluate and rank certain occupations as somewhat better or more desirable than others. This process is called the identification of social classes according to *occupational prestige*. Although there is no perfect consensus about the importance of a given occupation, a number of studies have shown an amazing consistency in the way people

rank occupations. The National Opinion Research Center interviewed a cross section of Americans in the late 1940's and asked them to rate ninety different occupations. In general, government officials ranked at the top, followed by professional and semi-professional occupations, with laborers and service workers bringing up the bottom (Table 3). White-collar and skilled occupations were bunched somewhere near the middle of the prestige scale.

TABLE **3**   PRESTIGE RANKING OF MAJOR OCCUPATION GROUPS

Rank	Occupation Group
1	Government officials
2	Professional and semi-professional workers
3	Proprietors, managers and officials (except farm)
4	Clerical and sales workers
5	Craftsmen and foremen
6	Farmers and farm managers
7	Protective service workers
8	Operatives
9	Farm laborers
10	Service workers (except domestic and protective)
11	Laborers (except farm)

Source: *Opinion News*, IX (Sept. 1, 1947).

ORGANIZATIONAL AND COMMUNITY AFFILIATIONS

Still another approach to America's class structure involves the kinds of group to which people belong. In a study of Newburyport, Massachusetts, W. L. Warner and his associates found that various organizations in the community could be class-typed; that is, many organizations—social and business clubs, country clubs, and even schools—drew their members from the same social class. And people living in the same neighborhood usually belonged to the same social class. Some organizations, such as the American Legion, were classless in the sense that all class levels were represented in the membership.

CLASS LOYALTIES:
CONSCIOUSNESS AND IDENTIFICATION

Quite different from the preceding approaches to the concept of social class is the view that a class consists of all those people who *identify* themselves with the same social class. Several opinion surveys have shown that the vast majority of Americans claim to be members of the middle class, whereas relatively few say they are either upper or lower class. In a nationwide survey in 1945, Richard Centers found, however, that when people were given the choice of "working class" along with upper, middle, and lower class, about as many chose working class as middle class to represent their status. Irrespective of what class they identify themselves with, people will tend to behave as they think a person of that class ought to behave. Someone who regards himself as a member of the middle class, for example, will adopt the customs, habits, and attitudes of that class. In his book, *The Organization Man*, William H. Whyte amusingly describes how the residents of "suburbia" readily take to the yard-tending, train-catching, coffee-klatsching activities of their neighbors.

A person's own evaluation of his social position, then, becomes the basis for his class identification. This class identification, in turn, is important for his entire pattern of behavior and his feelings of class loyalty. One group of authorities holds that the behavior standards a person sets for himself are those of the group or class toward which he is oriented. Thus, if a person thinks of himself as upper class or aspires to upper-class status, he will likely reject the obligations imposed by his actual socio-economic standing and try to act according to what he conceives upper-class standards to be. On the other hand, if his aspiration coincides with his actual socio-economic status, his class loyalty will likely be very strong. If his ambition outruns his money and his milieu, he may be regarded as "uppity," a snob, disloyal, or a traitor to his class. Such a person may become a social hermit, cutting himself off from his old contacts and yet not winning acceptance from those with whom he wishes to identify.

Class loyalties appear strongest when most members of society are content with their present class rank. Glaring discrepancies between a person's actual status and his ambitions to crash a higher status not only may be frustrating for the individual personally but may also present a serious challenge to the whole loyalty system. We Americans display a general middle-class orientation and a consuming aspiration for "better things." Thus, the "American Dream" of ever-mounting opportunity and abundance serves both to create loyalty to its essentially middle-class ideals and to impose strains on those who never realize its promise. We will discuss some of the consequences of these strains in Chapter 9.

CLASS LOYALTIES
AND STANDARDS OF BEHAVIOR

Most Americans tend to be loyal to those ideals of their class system that set requirements for class status and define and encourage mobility. But within each class, interpretation of the ideals varies. The truly aristocratic upper class, for instance, frequently feels that family background is very important to one's social standing, even more important than wealth and education. Men must have breeding, which explains why the newly rich may not be accepted in upper-class circles despite their wealth. A person tends to marry within the aristocratic layers of his own class; it is "disloyal" to marry beneath one's level. Social niceties also reflect upper-class standards. One must have the proper "social know-how" to really belong; he must know how to dine, wine, and entertain. Old, established, upper-class families feel less strongly than others about the desirability of upward mobility for all people.

Middle-class people regard income, occupation, education, clothes, home, car, and neighborhood as important. Taken for granted by the upper class, these things are marks of distinction for the middle class. Often great sacrifices are made to buy a home in a nice neighborhood or to send children to college. Participation in church affairs, civic activities, and community improvement campaigns are middle-class rather than either upper- or lower-class activities. It is the middle class, too, that stands for strict morals; and opposition to drinking, crime, and loose sex behavior tends to be strongest at this level.

Lower-class people generally receive low incomes, work at unskilled jobs, rent quarters in deteriorated areas, and lack education. From a middle- or upper-class viewpoint, these people frequently lack ability and initiative and often seem to violate standards of middle-class morality. Crime, unemployment, and divorce are highest at this level, and a sense of social and community responsibility may also be very weak. It is a mistake, however, to assume that lower-class people have no standards of behavior or loyalties to their class. Quite the contrary. William Foote Whyte, in his *Street Corner Society*, demonstrates that the lower class imposes a strict code of behavior on its members, and violators may be dealt with severely by their own people. He shows, for example, that sex behavior—which might be considered very loose by middle-class standards—actually may conform to quite rigid patterns when set against the lower-class context in which it prevails. And lower-class loyalties become powerful and even clannish in a great many instances.

CLIMBING THE SOCIAL LADDER

AVENUES OF SOCIAL MOBILITY

Americans long have boasted proudly that theirs is the "land of opportunity" where "everyone has a chance to get ahead." This claim has been very pervasive and has convinced many people that with a modicum of luck and some diligent effort any person might get ahead. Reinforcing this attitude are the dominant middle-class values we have just examined. Some sociologists have declared that we Americans are imbued with a culturally created desire for upward social mobility, sanctioned by the traditions of the American class system and rewarded by the attainment of higher position.

Not everyone, however, is able to move

upward. Some move downward; still others remain where they are. What are the qualities or conditions that determine whether a person moves up, down, or stays in a rut in this ruthlessly competitive modern world?

First of all, if you would succeed, according to the experts, try to be born into a good family. For the social position of the family, as we have already seen, establishes the social position of the child. Family influences persist even after a person reaches maturity. They have already determined his attitude toward mobility and will, by affecting his education and social contacts, exert a strong influence on his climb along the social ladder.

If your family background isn't of much

A good education—one of the dreams of middle-class America.

help, the next best thing is a good education. From Table 2 you will recall the close
correlation between schooling on the one
hand and occupation and income on the
other. A great deal of research has verified
that education is of prime importance in self-
improvement. The middle-class belief that
an education is the best way to get a better
job and more money pervades most American homes. The belief is so strong that many
adults re-enter school or continue their formal schooling for years after they have passed
"school age."

Today's children receive more education
than their parents and grandparents did.
This means that each generation must get
more education than the last just to remain
on the same rung of the social ladder. Competition weeds out the unambitious and the
unable. So education, traditionally an important boost to the status-seeker, becomes
more and more universal as its social value

becomes more and more evident. And by its
universality it also tends to level class differences.

Wealth is a third "booster" on the road
to higher social position. Indeed, many people feel it is the chief prerequisite for social
advancement. Americans tend to regard poverty in material things as a sign of poverty
in initiative and ability. This is especially
true of the middle-class viewpoint. Wealth
is a visible symbol of status and achievement.
The length of a man's car, the square feet of
space in his house, the number of days he
spends vacationing, all help locate him on
the social scale. More directly, wealth may
be used for such prestige-advancing purposes
as philanthropy, acquiring higher class associates, or enticing a marriage partner from a
higher class.

Migration is a fourth route to social advancement. Though our information is
scanty, it appears that people who migrate

usually move upward socially. Workers, for example, migrate from one city to another to obtain better jobs. Negroes who move north tend to improve their lot. A change of residence in and of itself does not guarantee upward social mobility, of course, but in practice, migration and mobility often go together.

Several political scientists have pointed out that politics also is a means of rapid social advancement. Many talented sons from immigrant backgrounds, men like former mayors Anton J. Cermak of Chicago and Fiorello LaGuardia of New York, entered politics and improved their social positions. Whereas sons of the upper and middle classes frequently ignored the political world in favor of business and professional careers, these clever and ambitious young men turned from the blight and squalor of their early years to politics and soon found themselves in a different social whirl with many new doors of opportunity opening up before them.

These five avenues—family, education, wealth, migration, and politics—are among the more obvious means by which people improve their social positions. Ascending the social ladder, however, is not quite so simple as our brief discussion might indicate.

HOW MANY CLIMB?

Are chances for mobility increasing or decreasing? For one thing, students of the problem do not agree on how much upward movement is taking place. Yet the vast majority of Americans still believe the chances are good. The Horatio Alger tradition and the heritage of the frontier are still strong. And many people still make it to the top. But, as some authorities argue, if there is little increase or even a decrease in upward mobility, then the American class system is not as open as we would like to believe. One of the reasons for the disagreement

among authorities, of course, is that the evidence in not convincing on either side. Bernard Barber, in his *Social Stratification*, points out that studies of social mobility in the United States show considerable movement in every generation, possibly as much as two-thirds of the population moving either up or down the social scale in every generation while the remainder stay in the same place. Movement, either up or down, is slight and gradual. A few people have always climbed or plunged spectacularly, but not so many as the "rags to riches" tradition would suggest. A careful conclusion would be that there has been no consistent trend in the amount of mobility in this country over the past several generations. But the fact that mobility has taken place at all helps to justify faith in the open-class society and, for many people, keeps their hopes alive.

LOYALTIES THAT ENCOURAGE MOBILITY

Loyalties that encourage mobility are embodied in the middle-class ideology that permeates American society. Americans believe in social change or, as they prefer to call it, social progress. They have faith in social justice, in reward for hard work, and in individual opportunity. They have an unswerving confidence in their ability to solve the problems that change and mobility bring. In their own work they are rewarded by promotions and advances in pay. They are inspired to succeed and to acquire the "good things of life." The very principles, ideals, and attitudes to which most Americans are loyal spur them on to climb the next rung in the social ladder.

The drive to get ahead, which at times amounts to an obsession, pervades our entire society. Reaching a higher class level is almost an imperative. Disappointments are sharp for those who fail. Yet, disappointment and failure are inescapable for many. In some industries seniority rules governing promotion, for example, definitely discourage the drive toward mobility. Mass communication and mass-produced commodities, too, are levelers of class distinctions and consequently blunt the desire for upward mobility. Failure to compete successfully is not only frustrating to the individual but may also bring him humiliation or degradation. Middle-class values decree shame or disgrace for failure. The also-rans are ignored and quickly forgotten.

MERITS
OF THE AMERICAN CLASS SYSTEM

Yet, few Americans are willing to abandon their open-class society. Even those who fail to move upward or who drop down the social scale tend to support it. Possibly this is because many hope that eventually their chance will come. Certainly the American system has many merits. For one thing, individuals are rewarded competitively according to their abilities and contributions. And it is the entire society rather than any single individual that imposes standards of merit and judges the value of a person's contribution. The nobleman, the priest, and the warrior, highly valued and rewarded for their abilities and contributions in medieval Europe, have been devalued in twentieth-

century America and their material rewards reduced accordingly. In contrast, businessmen, movie stars, public relations experts, and sports heroes have been accorded increased status and importance in the social hierarchy.

The class system also operates to allocate personnel. When a shortage of workers develops in a given occupation, the rewards (usually monetary) for this particular kind of work are increased, which tends to overcome the shortage. Similarly, an oversupply of workers in a given occupation will reduce the rewards. Each person, if compensated accordingly, gravitates toward his position of maximum usefulness, and the monetary reward he receives provides a rough index of the value that society attaches to each position.

Finally, any status system will protect the integrity of its members. Low-status persons, such as janitors, are not expected to comply with the same behavior standards as high-status persons. A janitor is exempt from decision- and policy-making obligations. By the same token, a business executive usually is not obliged to sweep floors. The occupant of each position is protected by the definition of his duties and obligations. His loyalty to his social position is in part a reflection of the security it affords him.

SOME WORDS OF SUMMARY

Loyalty to social class is a primary kind of loyalty, along with loyalty to self, family, community, state, and God. Loyalty to a class system such as exists in the United States means that people commonly aspire to a higher social position with some reasonable hope of success, an aspiration that is also an obligation.

Although castes and estates are rigidly stratified and inflexible, American social classes are quite flexible, less easily distinguished, and are not organized groups as such. But the American class structure exerts a powerful influence on the behavior of individuals, even though it is best "seen" through such intangibles as status aggregates, occupational prestige, group affiliations, and class consciousness. Analysis of the class structure in terms of these intangibles reveals that class loyalties tend to be directed toward principles such as mobility rather than toward particular groups.

The drive for status is virtually a national pastime in America, but not everyone reaches his goal. Wealth, education, and family background, along with migration and politics, are major ways to climb the social ladder. Authorities are divided on the extent of mobility in America's class system, but they agree that the class system rests on a foundation of loyalties that generally encourages upward mobility.

Members of an open-class system are constantly faced with the problem of whether they should be loyal to the standards of their actual status group or to the group to which they aspire. For loyalties directed away from a person's actual position, by definition, make him disloyal to that position. But the American class system really encourages this type of disloyalty by inculcating in people the desire to "get ahead." Perhaps the universality of this desire will provide the class system with enough stability to offset whatever strains it might otherwise engender.

FURTHER ROADS TO LEARNING

GENERAL ACCOUNTS

B. Barber, *Social Stratification* (New York: Harcourt, Brace, 1957). A general text on an increasingly popular topic.

R. Bendix and S. Lipset, *Class, Status and Power* (Glencoe, Ill.: The Free Press, 1953). A comprehensive collection of readings on the subject.

J. Bennett and M. Tumin, *Social Life* (New York: Knopf, 1948). An introductory text that contains several superb chapters on caste, class, and the American stratification system.

J. Cuber and W. Kenkel, *Social Stratification in the United States* (New York: Appleton-Century-Crofts, 1954). Synoptic treatments of several community studies.

J. Kahl, *The American Class Structure* (New York: Rinehart, 1957). A recent text that does an excellent job of sifting the mass of important information collected during the past twenty years.

K. Mayer, *Class and Society* (Garden City, New York: Doubleday, 1955). Concise summary of the sociology of classes.

P. Sorokin, *Social Mobility* (New York: Harper, 1927). The comprehensive, pioneer study on which most of our later analysis of mobility is based.

SPECIAL STUDIES

E. Baltzell, *Philadelphia Gentlemen* (Glencoe, Ill.: The Free Press, 1958). By depicting gentlemen of a quietly powerful elite from colonial times to the twentieth century, the author raises the question of a national, metropolitan ruling class.

R. Centers, *The Psychology of Social Classes* (Princeton: Princeton University Press, 1949). Analysis of a nation-wide survey on social class identification and the relation between class consciousness and social position.

J. Dollard, *Caste and Class in a Southern Town*, 3rd ed. (New York: Doubleday, Anchor Books, 1949). Reprint of one of the earliest community studies revealing the caste-like position of southern whites and Negroes.

D. V. Glass, ed., *Social Mobility in Britain* (London: Routledge and Kegan Paul, 1954). One of the most important studies to date on mobility, with cases taken from England, Scotland, and Wales.

E. Havemann and P. West, *They Went to College* (New York: Harcourt, Brace, 1952). Are colleges class conscious? Do employers favor graduates of ivy-league colleges? Do working students make as much money after graduation as students whose parents paid their way through college? This national survey provides some clues for answering questions of this kind.

A. Hollingshead, *Elmtown's Youth* (New York: Wiley, 1949). A popular and readable study of social class among high-school students in a midwestern town.

F. Hunter, *Community Power Structure* (Chapel Hill, N. C.: University of North Carolina Press, 1953). A careful study of influential, policy-making citizens in a southern city.

J. Hutton, *Caste in India: Its Nature, Function and Origins* (Cambridge: Cambridge University Press, 1946). One of the very best descriptions of the Hindu caste system.

A. Jaffe and R. Carleton, *Occupational Mobility in the United States, 1930-1960* (New York: King's Crown Press, 1954). Compilation and projection of data on one of the important kinds of social mobility.

R. Lynd and H. Lynd, *Middletown* (New York: Harcourt, Brace, Harvest Books, 1959). This study, first published in 1929, established a tradition for community studies in this country. Together with its companion volume, *Middletown in Transition* (New York: Harcourt, Brace, 1937), it presents a vivid portrayal of the changes in community class structure.

C. Mills, *The Power Elite* (New York: Oxford University Press, 1956). Sets forth in penetrating fashion a critique of influence groups in America.

————, *White Collar: The American Middle Classes* (New York: Oxford University Press, Galaxy Books, 1956). An equally penetrating analysis of how America's millions are fast becoming "the masses."

V. Packard, *The Status Seekers* (New York: McKay, 1959). A best-seller that treats the American class structure comprehensively.

B. Ryan, *Caste in Modern Ceylon: The Sinhalese System in Transition* (New Brunswick, N. J.: Rutgers University Press, 1953). Provides an interesting contrast to the Hindu caste system and describes processes of change.

W. Sumner, *What Social Classes Owe to Each Other* (Caldwell, Idaho: The Caxton Printers, Ltd., 1952). Reprint of a fascinating essay by a famous sociologist, which focuses on the obligations of classes to one another.

T. Veblen, *The Theory of the Leisure Class* (New York: Mentor Books, 1953). A classic and incisive volume presenting "conspicuous consumption" as the chief characteristic of America's upper elite at the turn of the century.

W. Warner, *Big Business Leaders in America* (New York: Harper, 1955). Compares three generations of business executives and finds slight change in mobility.

————, *et al.*, *Democracy in Jonesville* (New York: Harper, 1949). A superb description of the class system in Hollingshead's "Elmtown."

W. Whyte, *Street Corner Society* (Chicago: The University of Chicago Press, 1955). This study shows youth gangs are not without rules.

FICTION AND DRAMA

E. Caldwell, *Tobacco Road* (New York: Random House, 1947). The story of a degraded sharecropper family existing in deplorable conditions at the bottom of the social ladder.

G. Flaubert, *Madame Bovary* (New York: Random House, 1950). A truly great classic that provides brilliant insights into the attitudes and false illusions of social climbers.

S. Lewis, *Babbitt* (New York: Bantam Books, 1946). An extremely popular novel that depicts an "average businessman" who struggles against his class requirements and finally succumbs to its dictates.

J. Marquand, *Point of No Return* (Boston: Little, Brown, 1949). This fascinating novel doubtlessly presents one of the very best pictures of American social classes and some of their effects on character.

J. Steinbeck, *The Grapes of Wrath* (New York: Viking, 1939). A striking portrayal of the poverty-stricken and degraded migratory farm workers of the 1930's.

S. Wilson, *Man in the Gray Flannel Suit* (New York: Pocket Books, 1956). A delightful novel depicting the attitudes and struggles of the rising executive class.

FILMS

Boundary Lines (International Film Foundation, 1948, 10 min., sound, color). A description of the lines we draw to divide ourselves from one another.

A Family Affair (Teaching Film Custodians, 1946, 19 min., sound, black and white). Pictures a crisis in a judge's middle-class family after he issues an unpopular restraining order that damages his children's social relationships.

India (March of Time Forum Films, 1944, 15 min., sound, black and white). Treats the Indian caste system and shows the extremes of poverty and luxury.

Social Class in America (McGraw-Hill, 1957, 16 min., sound, black and white). Describes how social class influence affects three boys.

CHAPTER SEVEN

Religious Loyalties

*A common acceptance of sacred objects
and religious beliefs
is a prime integrating and unifying force in a society.*

In the best

of all possible worlds a man's loyalties would arrange themselves in a neat and untroubled hierarchical order ranging from an inner loyalty to self (call it personal integrity, if you like) through loyalties to family, community, and state, and culminating in loyalty to his God. There would be no conflict, either within or between these concentric rings of commitment. Each man would feel himself complete and whole. But we have discovered already that modern man is beset by contradictions and conflicts that make it difficult for him to maintain his personal integrity. The inevitable tensions afflicting the modern family are deepened by a fast-changing social environment; climbing the social ladder means frustration and tension as well as opportunity; and, as we shall see in the next chapter, a man's loyalty (or disloyalty) to his state may cost him his life.

Religious loyalties, too, sometimes collide and conflict with other loyalties. The early Christians were forced to choose between paying homage to the Roman emperor or honoring no other than their Christian God.

Nor, from their side, could the Roman rulers themselves escape choosing between their traditional policy of religious toleration or putting down a movement regarded as a subversive threat to the state. Today a young girl may have to decide whether to follow the dictates of her heart and marry the man of her choice or reject him because her family disapproves of his religion. Or perhaps some of you may be finding it increasingly difficult to choose between religious beliefs you have held since childhood and new, challenging attitudes you are encountering in the laboratory, dormitory, or classroom.

None of us is ever completely free of such conflict, and we all strive for some measure of integrity and a set of standards to help us resolve conflicting claims on our loyalties. To find out what claims religion makes on us, we must now turn to an examination of (1) the origins of religion in nonliterate societies, (2) the expansion of tribal religions into world religions, (3) the social value of religion, (4) the crisis in religion caused by the rise of modern science, and (5) the condition of religion in twentieth-century America.

PRIMITIVE MAN AND PRIMITIVE RELIGION

Imagine a hill in ancient Britain. Long shadows are falling in familiar but fearful patterns across a grove of oak trees nestled on its side, the steady, ominous drone of a religious incantation fills the late afternoon air, and a Druid priest kneels before what looks like a funeral pyre. In a huge wicker image is imprisoned a human sacrifice, a prisoner of war in this case, and presently

a few wisps of smoke begin to climb above the summit of the hill. The chant of the celebrants of the sacrifice mounts in volume and tempo. A few loud shrieks, a murmured prayer, and the holocaust is done.

Is this religion? The modern mind starts at such a suggestion. Religion for the civilized man of the mid-twentieth century conjures up comfortable visions of majestic churches, rich, sensuous music, well-remembered creeds, and a reassuring, if sometimes stern, voice from the pulpit. But what is religion? Does its essence lie in belief and creeds, in a faith in God, in religious ritual, in the existence of churches? Which came first, doctrine (i.e., formalized beliefs) or ritual?

CAN RELIGION BE DEFINED?

The question is not easily answered. The scholarly English anthropologist, Sir James Frazer, took the common-sense view that religion involves belief in superhuman beings who rule the world and man's attempts to please and worship them. This view, of course, was true of Christianity and the other Western religions as he understood them. First came belief since, in Frazer's words, "we must believe in the existence of a divine being before we can attempt to please him." But faith alone is not enough to define religion, said Frazer. Religion must affect man's behavior; it must "make a difference." No man is religious, Frazer concluded, "who does not govern his conduct in some measure by the fear and love of God." By taking his bearings from the way religion was practiced in his own society, Frazer was doing what might be expected, just as many of us would invariably find it difficult to conceive of a religion that had neither creed nor church. That crusty Englishman Samuel Johnson spoke for all such skeptics when he rebuked a man about to spend three years living with natives in New Zealand with the rhetorical question: "And what account of their religion can you suppose to be learnt from savages?"

But this common-sense approach to religion raised serious problems for later anthropologists who were intent on discovering the essential character of religious behavior. Some popular faiths, such as Buddhism, for example, have no God in the Christian or Judaic sense. Many peoples have worshipped nature itself. Some nonliterate peoples, furthermore, have believed in supernatural spirits that they did not necessarily "fear and love." Others have recognized a "trickster" god, one who was mischievous and erratic and was not "worshipped" in the Western sense at all. Still others have erected complicated systems of polytheism (belief in many gods), which only added to the difficulties of the investigators.

At bottom, the scholars' problem was even more serious than they realized. For if religion was to be defined solely as what a man believed, how could the investigator ever be certain that he had correctly interpreted the beliefs of a people he was studying? Religious beliefs involve what a man holds to be true about the big (ultimate) questions of life. Very often beliefs become sacred. They generally include answers to such questions as: What is the source of life? What is man's place in the universe? What is the purpose and meaning of life? Quite obviously, what a man says he believes to be the answers to these ultimate questions may be quite different from what he actually believes, or at least from what he is willing to act on. Evidence based on what men said they believed was therefore unreliable. And a researcher, of course, could never thrust himself inside another man's mind to determine his basic beliefs, and even if he could have, his very presence would have affected the interviewed man's reactions. Then, too, the barriers of language and culture intensified the problem.

Many modern researchers have therefore adopted a more practical or functional approach to the study of religion. Instead of trying to state formally what people believe (or say they believe) about the big questions of life, they spend more time analyzing religious behavior. Going back to Frazer's definition, they are much more concerned with whether religion "makes a difference," what kind of difference it makes, and how much.

This approach permits them to study freely those religions that have no fully developed set of beliefs, religions that may be based solely on rituals and myths (of which more later).

If pressed for a definition, a modern social scientist might define religion, then, as the way people behave in seeking answers to the ultimate questions posed in life. In this definition it is what men do regarding their beliefs that is important rather than what they say. In the next chapter we shall see that it is likewise possible to define government in terms of what men do politically rather than what they say or write in constitutions or state papers.

RELIGIOUS BEHAVIOR IN NONLITERATE SOCIETIES

What, then, were the characteristic patterns that early men followed in seeking answers to the big questions? In searching for these patterns, anthropologists have discovered the widespread, perhaps universal, existence of religious rituals. A *religious ritual is any repeated, solemn, and deliberate action that has symbolic significance for a people.* It involves acting out something significant in the life of the group that cannot be expressed in words alone. Thus, rituals may celebrate the mysterious cycle of the seasons, which is echoed in the irreversible cycle of birth, life, and death in all living things. They may hail the generative principle of life, expressed in phallic symbols, or the achievement of puberty by a son of the tribe. Through dances, sacrifices (like the ceremonies of the Druids), processions, or ordeals, rituals reflect the deep, emotional, universal feelings of man for nature and for his fellow man. Rituals reinforce beliefs. They antedate all modern religion and represent the early strivings of human beings to give, if not meaning in our sense, then continuity and expression to the yearnings in

the human heart for stability, order, and purpose in life.

Myths, which are *beliefs with symbolic significance*, play an equally important role in the religions of mankind. A good example of a myth is the old Icelandic belief that the earth was created of a strange mixture of fire and ice. This idea reflected the symbolic truth of a life lived against a landscape rugged and forbidding, lashed by cold Arctic winds during the long, dark winter and brightened for all too short a spell by the brief summer sunshine. Cold and ice were the manifestations of evil spirits whereas heat and light were accorded a special place in the Icelanders' pantheon of beneficent spirits. The great Northern god, Odin, when he sat on his mighty throne at the top of the world, fixed his gaze toward the south and west, the directions of hope and warmth for the northern peoples.

Neither rituals nor myths are confined to the religions of nonliterate and ancient peoples. Indeed, both theologians and social scientists find them in all religions, Christianity included. Our Western religions, for example, reflect such ancient rituals as the Jewish *Brit Milah*, which through circumcision of the new-born male symbolizes the Hebrew covenant with God. And among many Christians, rituals are often used to symbolize man's reverence for God.

Religious behavior, then, is universally characterized by rituals and myths, and a great deal of study has been devoted to the roles of both, especially their roles in the development of Christianity. What then are their roles? Not everyone is agreed, but in any case we should not, as apprentice social scientists, fall into the error of passing judgment on any man's religious practices and beliefs while we are attempting to make an objective analysis of his religious behavior. It is the scholar's duty to observe and report on religious behavior as he finds it, or at most to seek some explanation for it. To attempt more is to encroach on the domain of the churchman and the theologian.

First of all, we should not regard myths as a kind of naive, pre-scientific way of explaining the origin of the universe and man's place in it, as too many literal-minded students have done. Myths, after all, need not be taken literally. A much more common fallacy, however, has been to equate myths with something untrue, although they often contain a great deal of symbolic truth. Many modern scholars have maintained, for example, that the story of Adam's fall symbolizes and helps explain the evil many people find in human nature, even for those who question the historical authenticity of the account in Genesis. We shall see in the next chapter, moreover, that the *state* can be defined as "an *idea* or *myth* characterized by symbols filled with hoary tradition and lore."

The test of a myth, then, is not its historical or empirical verification but the meaning and symbolic significance it has for those who make it a part of their religion. Myths, and rituals, too, give symbolic meaning to the three-fold relation among man, nature, and society. In those religions that honor one god or several gods, myths and rituals also help make the divine an active reality. According to the sociologist and scholar Joachim Wach, myths and rituals provide something over and beyond mere feeling, willing, rationalizing, or thinking. With philosopher William James we must conclude that they contain "that element or quality in them which we can meet nowhere else."

A drawing by George Catlin, nineteenth-century American artist, depicting the Mandan Indians observing a religious ritual of sacred and symbolic significance.

THE ORIGINS OF RELIGION

As we have just seen, religious behavior is not easily explained. Nor are the origins and causes of religious behavior. Social scientists recognize that the institution of the family is rooted in man's need for affection, companionship, and an efficient way to care for the young, and our educational system clearly reflects man's concern to pass on his culture from one generation to the next. But what of religion? What basic needs and concerns does religion satisfy?

This question is not so easily answered. Let us begin by saying that we know very little about the origins of religion and that a great deal of what we do know is speculative. Imagination tells us that ancient man moved in a world of dark mystery and traumatic change. Most overpowering probably was the phenomenon of death. As one authority has put it, "of every ten persons born, ten die. For man, mortality represents a fundamental and unavoidable frustration of deep desires and wishes." * Early man, like modern man, could scarcely have avoided the question: Why? Death awed him as did the great unknown that enveloped him: the flashes of lightning that interrupted the dark

---

* R. Williams, Jr., *American Society: A Sociological Interpretation* (New York: Knopf, 1951), p. 307.

night, the storms that beat on his makeshift shelter, the eerie fires that danced in the night, the "different" tribe across the river. Doubtless he speculated on the meaning of sleep and dreams and their similarity to death. Did not death, too, have its dreams, and did not the spirit return to the body one day, just as the dream-spirit returned to the sleeping body?

What more natural, then, that man should believe himself possessed of a spirit or soul? And if a spirit was encased in human flesh, why should there not be spirits that caused the lightning to flash, the thunder to roar, or the earth to flower? And from here it was but a brief step to the belief that animals and plants, even rocks and mountains, likewise possessed a spirit that was separate from their visible forms. Indeed, was not all nature inhabited by what that vigorous old Puritan leader and theologian Cotton Mather as late as 1693 called "the wonders of the invisible world"?

That awe of the unknown and of nature should take the form of worship should not surprise us. If spirits controlled storms, floods, droughts, pestilence, and other catastrophes that plagued the life of man, they held in fact the power of life and death over him. Their favor should be courted and their anger appeased. And so sacrifices, prayers, and fasting—all self-denying—were offered to

Magnificent houses of worship that dot the entire globe testify to man's religious experiences.

please the gods. Soon these practices had hardened into ritual.

Thus did man come to worship nature, or rather the spirits that lived in nature. One authority on the origins of religion, Professor E. Washburn Hopkins, writes in these words of the remarkable range of objects that have commanded man's reverence and veneration from time immemorial:

Man has worshipped everything on earth including himself, stones, flowers, hills, trees, streams, wells, oceans, and animals. He has worshipped everything he could think of beneath the earth, metals, caves, serpents, and under-world ghosts. Finally, he has worshipped everything between earth and heaven and everything in the heavens above, mist, wind, cloud, rainbow, stars, moon, sun, the sky itself, though only in part has he worshipped the spirits of all these objects. Yet with all this bewildering jumble to his discredit, man to his credit has never really worshipped anything save what he imagined behind these phenomena, the thing he sought and feared, power.*

Anthropologists and other scholars have devised special names to describe theories of how religion began and developed. One such theory, that religion had its origin in the early belief that every object in nature had a spiritual counterpart, or double, is called the animistic theory. *Animism is the belief that spirits reside in all objects of nature, animate and inanimate.* What was active must be alive, according to many nonliterate peoples, and volcanoes that belched forth lava must be as "alive" as the dead man who moved about and talked in his friends' dreams. It was a belief in animism that prompted the ancient Egyptians and many other early peoples to bury food and weapons for use by the dead in the afterlife. Some early scholars, such as Sir Edward Tylor and Herbert Spencer, believed that animism was the first primitive stage in the development of all religion. Modern scholars, however, are more

---

* E. Hopkins, *Origin and Evolution of Religion* (New Haven: Yale University Press, 1924), p. 13.

likely to regard animism as merely one of several possible origins of religion, which may overlap and are by no means mutually exclusive.

Another theory, called *naturalism* or *nature-worship*, stresses the *fear and reverence of nonliterate peoples for the powerful forces of nature,* which themselves emerge as objects of worship in the form of a sun god, perhaps a thunder bird, or a moon goddess. Where water was scarce, as in Egypt, the river god of the Nile became an object of worship and veneration. Something of this awe and respect for the force of the river in the lives of modern human beings survives in stories such as *Huckleberry Finn,* in which the Mississippi seems to possess a spirit that exerts a force for good and evil in the life of Huck and his friends.

Still a third hypothesis about the origin of religion was championed by the great French sociologist Émile Durkheim, who maintained that the widespread practice of totemism was the crucial key to early religion. *Totemism embraces the view that the ancestors of a particular clan are derived from a plant, an animal, or some other natural object* ("totem"). Totemism is therefore a religion of the clan and not of the individual, and thus Durkheim postulated a social origin for religion. Since the clan has a common, venerated ancestor in some animal, let us say, it is held together by this common belief and by public ceremonies. This earliest form of religion has its *taboos,* or forbidden behavior, especially relative to the totem itself. Normally, no member of the clan is allowed to touch or eat the tabooed object. Indeed, according to another student of early religions, "the forbidden totem animal, incestuous or forbidden intercourse, the tabooed action or force, are directly abhorrent to him. I have seen and felt savages shrink from an illicit action with the same horror and disgust with which the religious Christian will shrink from the committing of what he considers sin." * The clan of the deer, by way of example, would shrink from eating the flesh of the deer since they believed it to be the flesh of their own ancestors.

Fetishism, one of the most elementary forms of religious behavior, has also been considered the source of religion. Since prehistoric times men have been given to beliefs *that certain objects possess mysterious powers.* Fetishism differs from totemism in that a fetish is believed to have specific powers for a single individual only, whereas a totem is believed to have the same kind of power for an entire tribe or group. Charms, rabbit's feet, images, and lucky coins are all modern examples of fetishes.

Although the origins of fetishism are debatable, one of them no doubt lies in the simple assumption that because two events occur simultaneously, or in sequence, there must be a cause-and-effect relationship between them. A football coach may wear the same necktie to game after game simply because he had it on when his team won a stunning victory. He believes that the tie has some magical power over his team's fortunes. The presence or absence of some object—a weapon, a garment, or some charm—may be associated with good or bad luck in life. When something fortunate or unfortunate occurs, not only the individual himself but his family and friends as well may attribute special powers to the object. And all persons sharing the belief may begin searching for all instances and evidence that help confirm the belief. A mere coincidence or accident can thus result in a fetish that may endure for decades, even centuries.*

UNIVERSAL RELIGIONS

FROM POLYTHEISM TO MONOTHEISM

We have now reviewed some of the characteristics of early religions together with several theories concerning the origin of religious behavior. The invisible world in which early man lived was inhabited, as we have seen, by many spirits, some of them resident in the familiar animals and physical objects of his neighborhood, others lodged in the firmament above his head, where they controlled the forces of nature that shaped his life. Some of these spirits were more important than others, of course. Those that were most significant in his life were most likely to be feared or worshipped and to assume the character of deities: the sun god, the river god, or perhaps the god of the sea. Gradually, in some tribes or nonliterate societies, some one god came to be recognized as superior to the others, such as the famous Zeus of Greek mythology who ruled over the great pantheon of deities atop Mount Olympus.

From the *polytheism* (belief in many gods) of the Greeks and other early peoples there developed very slowly in several tribes the concept of *monotheism* (belief in one god). The ancient Hebrews were probably the first to worship a single god who created and sustained the universe, but even they lapsed occasionally into polytheism, as the Old Testament tells us. From the sacred books of the Old Testament and the Talmud (an encyclopedic account of the teachings and experiences of the Jews for over 1,000 years), the Jews developed the idea of a stern, majestic, but merciful God who had created man in his own image. Christianity and Islam, the two other great religions that

---

* B. Malinowski, "Social and Individual Sources of Primitive Religion," in J. M. Yinger, *Religion, Society and the Individual* (New York: Macmillan, 1957), pp. 352-53.

* G. Lundberg, *et al.*, *Sociology* (New York: Harper, 1954), pp. 555-557.

have profoundly influenced Western Civilization, owe a very great debt to Judaism. The idea of the fatherhood of a single God, the theory of divine purpose in history, the ethical duty of the religious man, and the divine origin of the soul, which has been so basic to the idea of individual worth and dignity, have all been derived from Hebrew sources.

THE DIFFUSION OF RELIGIONS

Even Judaism, however, was conceived as a tribal rather than as a universal religion, and the Hebrews regarded themselves as the chosen people of God. Monotheism was limited at first to a single tribe or nation, and only much later did men begin to think of their god as the universal god of all mankind. The spread of religion beyond tribal or national boundaries depended on conquest or (later) on conversion. In the case of military conquest, the god or gods of the conqueror might be forced on the vanquished or else blended with the local deities. The Moslems, as an example of the first, forcibly converted all of North Africa to Islam in the seventh and eighth centuries. The Spanish conquest of Mexico, on the other hand, resulted in a partial blending of Aztec and Spanish Christian culture. On the site of an Aztec temple in Guadalupe, where the goddess of the earth and of corn had been worshipped, a shrine to the Virgin Mary was later erected. F. S. C. Northrup has described the significance of this development in his interesting book on *The Meeting of East and West:*

There is something unique about this Madonna, something typical of Mexican Catholicism, and of far-reaching consequences. She is dark of skin and an Indian. When the Indian Juan Diego first met her in 1531 on the hill of Tepeyac, behind the present basilica, she said to him, according to the official account, "I am the Virgin Mary, Mother of the true God." That the Virgin Mary in Mexico should be an Indian is significant . . . the churchmen in their

artistry did not dare to tamper with the spontaneous movement of the Indians' spirit by even attempting to insure the orthodoxy of the Virgin by placing a Christ-child in her arms. She appeared in the shrine of the basilica of Guadalupe alone and in her own right.*

A universal religion is, by definition, neither tribal nor national. The god of the tribe or nation is regarded as the god of all mankind, and men are linked together across territorial boundaries by ties of allegiance to a common faith. By their nature, universal religions tend to be dynamic and evangelistic, since implicit in their creeds is the idea that they represent the one true faith to which all mankind should aspire. Sometimes this dynamism may breed conflict. The religious wars we know as the Crusades stemmed from Christian efforts to recover the Holy Land from the Moslems, who had extended their sway from India in the East through the Middle East and North Africa to distant France in the West. Contacts between the great religions of the East—Buddhism, Confucianism, Taoism—and those of the West have come only comparatively recently with the dawn of Asia as a force in European and world politics. What the eventual results of these contacts may be it is yet too early to say.

RELIGION AND THE STATE

Universal religions not only may clash with other dynamic religions but also may find themselves at odds with the state. We have mentioned already the fierce struggle for men's minds that raged in ancient Rome between the Roman government and the Christian leaders. Nor did this struggle end when Christianity became the official religion of the Roman Empire. Throughout the Middle Ages, conflict arose over papal claims that loyalty to the Church and to

---

* F. S. C. Northrup, *The Meeting of East and West* (New York: Macmillan, 1946), pp. 26-27.

Rome transcended all secular obligations, including allegiance to the German emperors, who claimed to be the successors of the great Roman rulers. The uneasy truce known as the "doctrine of the two swords," whereby the Pope was recognized as supreme in spiritual matters, the emperor in worldly or secular affairs, did not really solve the problem of loyalties, especially when specific issues, such as the right to select an important bishop, were at stake. With the rise of national states in England and France and other West European countries, the conflict of loyalties became acute. The new, confident, aggressive rulers of these states (though they were, of course, Catholics) would brook no allegiance stronger than that owed the crown. At bottom, the loyalty issue represented a struggle for power, with the national rulers holding the higher cards. The Protestant Reformation and the splitting of the religious unity of Western Christendom were probably as much politically as theologically inspired. The rulers who sheltered Protestantism in its infancy (such as Frederic of Saxony, who protected Luther) were as much concerned with political as they were with religious independence from Rome.

Even Protestants, however, or at least most of them, were unwilling at first to effect a complete separation of church and state. Most political authorities, whether Protestant or Catholic, sought to overturn church control of the state and make the state dominant over the church. The results were disastrous for national unity in most Protes-

tant countries, and many of the religious dissenters who eventually made their way to America did so because Protestant rulers had attempted to control the form and content of religious services. These monarchs and their clerical servants, or "watchdogs," believed that religious conformity was necessary for national unity and that the state should lend its mighty support to a particular church, be it Catholic, Lutheran, Calvinist, or Anglican. The alternative, they feared, would be a disunited nation of brawling religious sects that could not unite for any national purpose.

Against this view and with the horrors and tortures of two hundred years of religious wars and conflict in mind, Thomas Jefferson argued persuasively in 1784 for the doctrines of religious freedom and the separation of church and state:

It is error alone which needs the support of government. Truth can stand by itself. Subject opinion to coercion: whom will you make your inquisitors? Fallible men; men governed by bad passions, by private as well as public reasons. And why subject it to coercion? To produce uniformity.... Is uniformity attainable? Millions of innocent men, women, and children, since the introduction of Christianity have been burnt, tortured, fined, imprisoned; yet we have not advanced one inch towards uniformity.*

And so through the efforts of Jefferson and others, state support for particular churches in America was removed, and Congress was forbidden in the First Amendment to make any law abridging freedom of religion.

RELIGION AND SOCIAL CONTROL

What the Protestant monarchs had seen, of course, as Catholic rulers had realized earlier, was that religion was useful for controlling human behavior or, as the sociologists say, for exerting social control. Religion does "make a difference" in the way people

behave. The religious teachings and beliefs that help a child to adjust to his world profoundly influence his attitudes toward justice and injustice, right and wrong, fair and foul

---

* T. Jefferson, *Democracy*, selected and edited by S. Padover (New York: Appleton-Century, 1939), pp. 169-70.

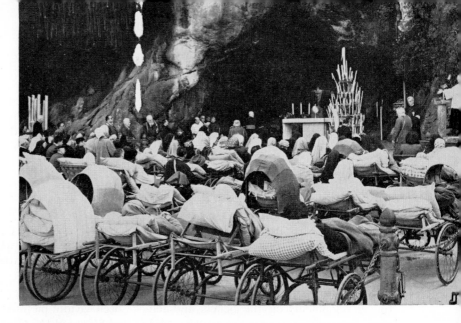

Pilgrims throng the grotto at Lourdes seeking divine intercession to heal their afflictions and bring them comfort.

play. Christian and Jewish children in our culture are warned firmly against stealing, lying, and adultery and are told to honor their parents. But religion affects not only popular attitudes toward ethics and moral behavior but also the views we hold toward political and social authority and even economic behavior. Two famous scholars who studied the question of the influence of religious attitudes on economic behavior, Max Weber and R. H. Tawney, came to the conclusion that Protestant (especially Calvinist) emphasis on the dignity of labor ("The devil has work for idle hands."), worldly success as a sign of God's favor, and Spartan austerity in daily living helped to create a climate of opinion favorable to the development of modern capitalism with its similar stress on thrift, hard work, and individual enterprise.

The churches have normally taught obedience to legally constituted political authority. The doctrine of the two swords, which we mentioned earlier, clearly implied that the things of Caesar should be rendered unto Caesar. Like governments, churches prefer order to disorder, organization to anarchy. Within their own sphere, the churches have likewise sought historically to maintain some measure of social discipline. The medieval church (and the modern Roman Catholic Church) used the weapon of excommunica-

tion to enforce social control. Denying them the holy sacraments is a very effective way to control people who believe that the road to eternal life leads only through the church. The Amish sect in America affords us another example of a group that has established a very strict set of social controls to preserve a religious society against the encroachments of a modern, secular civilization. Many of you have seen pictures of the austerely dressed Amish or have read about their bans on radios, television sets, automobiles, cameras, and other modern inventions that might threaten the isolation and solidarity of their society.

Churches as social institutions must be interested in their own self-preservation, so they must naturally concern themselves with the stability of the family and with the training and sexual mores that affect that stability. This has been true of most religions, ancient and modern. Churches must also be concerned with war and social ills that may disrupt the religious as well as the social community. Great religious figures from the Hebrew prophets and the Apostle Paul to the present Pope and leaders of world Protestantism have grappled long and hard with such socially disruptive evils as poverty, slavery, and war.

Religion has served a most useful social

function, too, in affording emotional release for a person faced with crisis and doubt. To the family of a departed parent, a soldier facing death in battle, to the persecuted and op-pressed of this world, religion has often brought peace of mind and consolation, comfort and hope, and a restoration of confidence and assurance.

SCIENCE AND THE CONTINUING CRISIS IN WESTERN RELIGION

Religion's effectiveness as an agency of social control in Western Civilization has been considerably weakened in the past century or so by the cumulative impact of scientific developments on the beliefs and religious behavior of modern man. The crisis that came was two centuries in the making before the findings of Charles Darwin dramatized its impact for the churchman as for the average man. Before Darwin, scientists had believed that each species of life on earth was the product of a special, independent creation with man, of course, having been created in God's own image. For this ancient idea Darwin substituted a theory which stated that present forms of life on earth were the culmination of an incalculably slow, evolutionary process from simple to complex forms. Changes had occurred as a result of accident, by mere chance variation. Nature herself had selected those variations most fit to survive (e.g., a slightly longer neck in a giraffe) by destroying in the fierce competition for existence those specimens least able to hold their own. Man himself, Darwin and his followers held, had also developed from simpler forms of life.

One of the dramatic moments in the history of modern science occurred at the meeting of the British Association for the Advancement of Science in 1860, just after the publication of Darwin's theory. Bishop Samuel Wilberforce of Oxford rose in the crowded university library to denounce Darwin's theory as atheistic and incompatible with religion. He queried Darwin's supporter and friend, Thomas Huxley, whether it was through his grandfather or grandmother that he claimed to be descended from a monkey. The scene as Huxley rose to answer him has been vividly pictured by Homer W. Smith in *Man and His Gods:*

> He rose to the scattered applause of a few friends, his face pale with anger under his wild, thick hair: "I am here only in the interests of science," he said, "and have not heard anything which can prejudice the case of my august client [Darwin]." He went on quietly to review the facts, to indicate the Bishop's essential incompetence to treat of such matters as geology and the mutability of species, and ended by saying in effect—there was no transcript of the speakers' remarks and the excitement was such that these were variously recalled by the audience—that he would rather have an ape for an ancestor than . . . Bishop Samuel Wilberforce. Laymen applauded, the massed clergy raised their voices in offended dignity, and a Lady Brewster achieved immortality by fainting and having to be carried out.*

The battle was on and it has not ended, despite occasional truces and a growing indifference, to our own day. It was not the theory of evolution alone that brought the issue to a head but the accumulated fears and frustrations of a world that in a little over three hundred years had seen the earth moved from the center of the universe to an insignificant point lost in the vastness of the skies and the age of the earth pushed back from a few thousand to hundreds of millions

---

* H. W. Smith, *Man and His Gods* (Boston: Little, Brown, 1952), p. 370.

of years. And now man himself was held to be only one small part of the animal kingdom, derived from common ancestors with the ape and the baboon! Small wonder that some were driven to vehement defense of the old orthodoxies while others were driven to equally vehement attacks on the old beliefs.

What man wanted most was consistency and certainty, but they were becoming increasingly more difficult to achieve. Some simply gave up. The sharp-tongued H. L. Mencken summed up the view of a generation of American skeptics when he wrote that "The cosmos is a gigantic flywheel . . . Man is a sick fly taking a dizzy ride on it. Religion is the theory that the wheel was designed and set spinning to give him the ride." * But others, more numerous, were certain that the needs that traditional religion had served still remained and that the task of modern man was to find stability in the midst of change, to come to terms in some way with the new science.

MODERNISM AND FUNDAMENTALISM

Those religious leaders and their followers who were convinced that the conflict between science and religion was irresolvable and chose the pathway of religion came to be known as *fundamentalists*. The fundamentalists continued to believe in the authority and infallibility of the Scriptures as sacred documents; they accepted the miraculous events described in the New Testament as well as the divinity of Christ, his atonement for man's sins, his resurrection, and his second coming to earth as definite historical facts. Largely a Protestant movement, since the doctrines of the Catholic Church had remained relatively unaffected by modern science, fundamentalism was initially a counterattack on the ideas held by another group of

* H. L. Mencken, *Prejudices: Third Series* (New York: Knopf, 1922), p. 132.

Protestants known as *modernists*. The modernists sought to reconcile their Christian beliefs with science and with history by appealing to allegory in the Bible and deemphasizing theology in favor of ethics in religion. Modernism was not so much a creed, then, as a method for accommodating Christian thought to the findings of modern scholarship. The modernists, or religious liberals, as they are sometimes called, stressed the right of the individual to decide the question of religious truth for himself. They accepted the scientific view of a universe of natural laws, which left no room for Biblical miracles or a physical resurrection of the body. The Bible they regarded as a remarkable human document but subject to the same errors and contradictions as any other human document; Jesus was the supreme religious teacher, but in the eyes of some of the modernists, not necessarily divine. Out of liberalism sprang the concept of the *Social Gospel*, or the belief that Christianity had to deal more effectively with the social injustices of this world, such as war, poverty, inequality, and discrimination, if it was to remain a vital, active force in the world. Modernism had its counterparts in the Catholic and Jewish churches as well as among more orthodox Protestants.

Essentially, modernism was an optimistic faith that stressed the application of Christian teachings as the best way to improve human society. Echoing Frazer, the modernists felt that religion must "make a difference," not only in the life of the individual but of society as well. But after the wars and depressions of the twentieth century and the revelations of Nazi barbarism and atrocities at Buchenwald, Auschwitz, and other concentration camps, some Protestant thinkers became convinced that modernism had committed the ancient sin of pride in holding man's own puny efforts enough to remake the world and its morals.

Modernism, admitted one of its former champions, had "left souls standing like the ancient Athenians, before an altar to an unknown God."

That man had forgotten God was the essential message of a new group of Protestant thinkers, chiefly seminarians and other intellectuals. *Neo-orthodoxy*, as their views were called, was a reaffirmation of historic Christian doctrine with such changes as modern scholarship seemed to require. Theologians such as Reinhold Niebuhr argued that man was incapable of finding salvation through his own efforts and sharply questioned the scientific method as a tool for comprehending ultimate values and purpose in life. The Book of Genesis, while not to be taken as literal history, was nonetheless true, said Niebuhr, in the sense that God had created the universe and man and that man was estranged from God because of his sinful nature. The fall of Adam, the followers of neo-orthodoxy believed, was symbolically true, for how else could we explain the great resurgence of evil and human bestiality in a century that had placed great stress on social reform and human betterment? So ran the argument of the neo-orthodoxists.

THE RELIGION OF THE STATE

Not all Western thinkers, however, have reacted to the rise of modern science in the fashion of the fundamentalists, the modernists, or the neo-orthodoxists, all of whom were seeking in their own way to preserve the vitality of Christian belief in an age of shifting values. Some others have sought to secularize religion completely, or to put it somewhat differently, they have sought to spiritualize secular ideas or institutions. They have tried to channel the emotional fervor and loyalties formerly felt for Christian beliefs into other secular channels. In eighteenth-century France, for example, a religion of progress was partially substituted for traditional Christian beliefs. The idea of inevitable human progress in history replaced for some French intellectuals at least the belief in a hereafter where all wrongs would be righted. Heaven on earth would come through the reform of human institutions in accordance with man's reason. The nineteenth century witnessed the development of a kind of religion of science in which all knowledge and superstitions not derived by the scientific method were to be discarded for the certain and final truths of science.

The twentieth century has seen the rise of new religions of the state—fascism and communism—both of which are political movements with religious overtones. Certainly these movements have inspired fanatical loyalty with their promise of heaven on earth and belief that man is nothing outside the state. As a result, new forms and objects of public worship have been created. But is it correct to speak of them as religions? Perhaps not. But if we return to our definition of religion as primarily a matter of behavior with respect to the big questions of life and what is held to be sacred, they come close to meeting the requirements. Both fascist and communist states (and indeed all modern states, in some measure) have their rituals (such as the communist May Day parade), their myths (the Nazi theory of Aryan superiority), their infallible gods (Karl Marx), and their tension-free heavens (the eventual withering away of the communist state). Listen to André Gide, the famous French writer, as he wrote of his acceptance of communism in 1932:

> My conversion is like a faith. My whole being is bent towards one single goal, all my thoughts —even involuntary—lead me back to it. In the deplorable state of distress of the modern world, the plan of the Soviet Union seems to me to point to salvation. . . . And if my life were necessary to assure the success of the Soviet Union, I would gladly give it immediately.*

* R. Crossman, ed., *The God That Failed* (New York: Harper, 1949), p. 173.

RELIGION IN MODERN AMERICA

The faith that André Gide found so compelling during the 1930's is the faith that sustains millions of fanatical communists today both inside and outside the Soviet Union. In the continuing world struggle between communistic and democratic systems, between the Soviet Union and the United States as the leaders of these two camps, what have we to oppose the militant communist faith?

Let us admit that the communist has a faith that welds religious and political loyalty into one simple, attractive force. In Western Europe and the United States, religious and political loyalties have been historically separate and (as we have seen) not infrequently in conflict. We still see the symptoms of divided loyalties in America, such as Jehovah's Witnesses refusing to salute the flag, Amish parents refusing to send their children to public schools, or Catholic leaders asking that federal aid to education be extended to parochial schools. On the whole, however, such instances of divided loyalty are becoming increasingly less common and certainly less bitter than they were a century or more ago.

DISTINCTIVE HISTORICAL FEATURES OF AMERICAN RELIGION

For one thing, the distinctive features of American religious practices have been in harmony with American political ideals. There has been no sharp conflict in theory between the goals of American Christianity (or Judaism) and the goals of American democracy. What are some of these distinctive features? Perhaps most important have been the separation of church and state, the lack of an established (state-supported) church, and the immense variety and diversification of religious sects that have been most sensitive to any encroachments on religious freedom and toleration. Like America's political leaders, her religious leaders have stressed an optimistic approach to life and have been more often believers in human progress and perfectibility than in human depravity. Democratic, too, has been the tendency toward local or congregational control of church affairs and the greater role given to lay leadership than in Europe. The lack of an established church has also prevented a divisive, militant, anti-clerical movement from developing in this country.

This religious heritage has kept America free from the deep-seated and bitter conflicts and tensions that have marred church-state relations in Europe. Even the sharp religious differences between major denominations and churches have been greatly softened in the wake of the gradual secularization of much of American life during the twentieth century. There has been a marked decline in religious prejudice, particularly between Protestants and Catholics. There has been no resurgence of the malice and hate, no resurrection of the defamatory journals and convent-burning, that flared up throughout the nineteenth century. That Al Smith, a Catholic, could run for president in a country three-fourths Protestant in 1928 and receive 15 million votes (against 21 million for Hoover) was a sign of waning rather than waxing prejudice. Smith's answer to questions about possible conflict between his religious and national loyalties was a thoroughly American statement:

I summarize my creed as an American Catholic. I believe in the worship of God according to the faith and practice of the Roman Catholic Church. I recognize no power in the institutions of my Church to interfere with the operations of the Constitution of the United States or the enforcement of the law of the land. I believe in the absolute freedom of conscience for all men and in equality of all churches, all sects, and all beliefs before the law as a matter of right and not as a matter of favor. I believe in the absolute separation of Church and State.... I believe in the right of every parent to choose whether his child shall be educated in a public school or in a religious school supported by those of his own faith.*

AMERICAN PARADOX:
MORE RELIGION AND MORE IRRELIGION

To say that American life has become gradually more secularized in the twentieth century, as we did a few lines above, is to point to a most interesting paradox, for many observers are agreed that a genuine revival of religion has been taking place in this country, at least since World War II. How can we explain this contradiction? Is it only a sham revival, without deep emotional significance? Or does the outward prosperity of religion reflect a real shift of inner loyalty and sentiment?

Will Herberg, a long-time student of American religious trends, has put forward a very suggestive explanation of this interesting American paradox. In America, he says, there are three "religious communities"— Protestant, Catholic, and Jewish—with common, underlying, spiritual values: the father-

* H. W. Schneider, *Religion in 20th Century America* (Cambridge: Harvard University Press, 1952), pp. 93-94.

hood of God, the brotherhood of man, the dignity of the individual. Each value is authentically American. The American has thus been free to give expression to the religious loyalties of his family and ethnic heritage and still uphold the basic American values. Indeed, the immigrant did just that. Whether Catholic, Jewish, or Protestant, he usually clung to his faith, even when trying to lose his ethnic identity. With the end of mass immigration in the late 1920's, a third generation, descended from immigrants who had arrived in this country during the 1880's and 1890's, began coming to maturity. The ethnic background their fathers wanted to forget, the grandchildren, born in America of American parents, wanted to remember. They searched for roots, something that would give them a sense of community and identity, and they found it in the old family religion.

According to Herberg's theory, then, the religious revival of recent years reflects a social necessity, a yearning to belong in this nation of immigrant stocks. It is not external pressure—the need to conform and to be like one's neighbors—but inner necessity that explains the flocking to the churches. To "belong" in America, says Herberg, means to belong to one of the three great religious com-

Even in busy industrial America religion has been on the upsurge.

munities found in this country. "American-ness today entails religious identification as Protestant, Catholic, or Jew in a way and to a degree quite unprecedented in our history. To be a Protestant, a Catholic, or a Jew are today the alternative ways of being an American." *

Underlying the three religious communities of America and forming a common base of politico-religious loyalties is an American counterpart to the union of religious and political values in communism: the American Way of Life. This ideal, concludes Herberg, is the operative faith that joins the three communities. It is the symbol by which a nation of immigrants defines itself and establishes a unified loyalty. This American Way of Life is based on the common political and religious beliefs we discussed earlier: the dignity and worth of the individual, the stress on freedom, the gospel of hard work

---

* W. Herberg, *Protestant-Catholic-Jew* (Garden City, N. Y.: Doubleday, 1955), p. 274.

and worldly success, opposition to unchecked authority, the perfectibility of man, and the inevitability of progress. It is humane, optimistic, and democratic. It is committed to action, to improving the here and now. Of necessity it preaches self-improvement, education, and idealism.

Herberg concludes that it is meaningless to be opposed to this kind of patriotic religion and that the old-time atheist seems to have disappeared without his absence being noticed. Religion is now so completely a part of American life that anti-religion is all but impossible. In the old sense, of course, this new "American Religion" is not a religion at all and lacks any specific doctrine and content. It can be and is perfectly compatible with the growth of secularism in the traditional sense. Thus, an explanation of how America in the twentieth century can seemingly head in two opposite directions—toward religion and away from religion—at the same time.

SOME WORDS OF SUMMARY

We have been concerned in this chapter with the place of religion in society and only incidentally with specific religious beliefs. The social scientist studies human behavior—political, economic, social, religious—and by the nature of his profession cannot (and should not) be concerned *as a scientist* with the truth or falsity of particular beliefs. (His personal beliefs are another matter.) In a functional sense we defined religion as the manner in which a group of people behave in answering the big questions of life. Rituals are a form of religious behavior widespread in place and time. The role of rituals and myths (beliefs with symbolic significance) in the life of early man were extremely important in defining the three-fold relation between man, nature, and society.

Various investigators have attributed the origin of religious behavior to a belief in spirits resident in animate and inanimate objects (animism), to early man's awe and reverence for the forces of nature (naturalism), to the widespread belief of early man that he was descended from a plant, animal, or other natural object (totemism), and to the individual person's penchant to ascribe special powers to objects (fetishism). From belief in many gods (polytheism) there developed gradually a belief in a supreme, then a solitary deity (monotheism). The diffusion of religion beyond tribal and national boundaries culminated in the appearance of universal religions whose deities were held to rule over all people. It was probably inevitable that religion with claims to universal loyalty should conflict with the secular state for the loyalty of men, as in medieval Europe. In America the conflict between church and state was settled by separating them completely through state government action (begun in Jefferson's Virginia) and in our federal Constitution.

As a means of social control, religion has always exerted an important influence on human behavior through its ethical teachings and attitudes toward authority, business, and institutions such as the family. The effectiveness of religion as a means of social control in the West has been influenced by the impact of modern science on traditional beliefs. The conflict between science and religion was dramatized, though not originated, by the evolutionary theory of Charles Darwin and the violent reaction it touched off in church circles. Those seeking to harmonize modern science with religion came to be known as modernists, and those who clung to religious teachings and Biblical infallibility in the face of scientific findings were called fundamentalists. Wars and social problems have tempered some of the modernist's optimism in the twentieth century, and among seminarians and other intellectuals, a countermovement known as neo-orthodoxy has developed, which reaffirms, symbolically in some cases, the historic Christian doctrines.

Religion in modern America presents a paradox of religious revival coupled with a decline in religious belief. This development has been explained by Will Herberg as a need to "belong," to identify one's self with one of the three great religious communities—Protestant, Catholic, Jewish—which together with the American Way of Life command the loyalties of Americans today.

FURTHER ROADS TO LEARNING

GENERAL ACCOUNTS

W. James, *The Varieties of Religious Experience* (New York: Longmans, Green, 1902). A classic, psychological interpretation, a bit tough-going for beginners, by one of America's most gifted philosophers.

W. King, *Introduction to Religion* (New York: Harper, 1954). A very useful, general study.

H. Smith, *Man and His Gods* (New York: Grosset and Dunlap, Universal Library, 1956). Takes a naturalistic view of religion; some will not like its "debunking" tone.

W. Sweet, *The Story of Religions in America* (New York: Harper, 1930). Still the best general history of religion in the United States.

J. Wach, *Sociology of Religion* (Chicago: The University of Chicago Press, Phoenix Books, 1958). A scholarly sociologist speaks on religion.

SPECIAL STUDIES

Annals of the American Academy of Political and Social Science, Vol. 256. The entire issue for March, 1948, is devoted to "Organized Religion in the United States."

R. Crossman, ed., *The God That Failed* (New York: Bantam Books, 1952). How such intellectuals as Gide, Silone, and Richard Wright were attracted to communism.

É. Durkheim, *The Elementary Forms of the Religious Life* (Glencoe, Ill.: The Free Press, 1947). The most important statement on the subject by this French master; perhaps a little difficult for some beginning students.

J. Ellis, *American Catholicism* (Chicago: The University of Chicago Press, 1955). A brief, authoritative history written in pleasing style by a monsignor of the Catholic church.

J. Frazer, *The Golden Bough* (New York: Macmillan, 1958). An abridgement of probably the most famous account of primitive religious practices ever written.

R. Green, ed., *Protestantism and Capitalism* (Boston: Heath, 1959). A most useful collection of materials bearing on the historic connection between the rise of Protestantism and the growth of capitalism.

W. Herberg, *Protestant—Catholic—Jew* (New York: Doubleday, 1955). A suggestive treatment of contemporary religion in America.

E. Hopkins, *Origin and Evolution of Religion* (New Haven: Yale University Press, 1924). An old but still useful account.

R. Lowie, *Primitive Religion* (New York: Liveright, 1924). One of the best brief treatments of this subject to be found anywhere.

H. Schneider, *Religion in 20th Century America* (Cambridge: Harvard University Press, 1952). Surprisingly comprehensive coverage of the main religious trends of the century told in brief compass.

A. White, *A History of the Warfare of Science with Theology* (New York: Braziller, 1955). A reissue of a famous and important book first published in 1894.

J. Williams, *What Americans Believe and How They Worship* (New York: Harper, 1952). Popular and easily read survey on the beliefs and practices of the major religious groups in America.

FICTION AND DRAMA

W. Cather, *Death Comes for the Archbishop* (New York: Knopf, 1927). A sympathetic novel of the triumph of faith of a French priest in the New World who becomes the archbishop of Santa Fé.

J. Cozzens, *Men and Brethren* (New York: Harcourt, 1936). A somewhat cynical novel centering around a modern, liberal clergyman in New York.

F. Dostoyevsky, *The Brothers Karamazov* (New York: New American Library, 1959). No writer has ever surpassed the passages in this book dealing with the religious conscience in an age of turmoil and shifting values.

A. Koestler, *Darkness at Noon* (New York: New American Library, 1958). Portrays vividly the hold which the new "religion" of Communism can exert on men's minds.

J. Lawrence and R. E. Lee, *Inherit the Wind* (New York: Random House, 1955). A dramatized version of the famous "monkey trial" in Tennessee in 1925 where evolution was debated by William Jennings Bryan and Clarence Darrow.

G. Shaw, *Saint Joan* (Baltimore: Penguin Books, 1951). Vivid dramatic picture of the conflict between nationalism and the medieval church at the trial of Joan of Arc.

C. Sheldon, *In His Steps* (Chicago: Advance Publishing Company, 1897). A widely sold book that deals with a minister who imitated Christ's life in his daily living. Good expression of the "Social Gospel" idea.

T. Wilder, *Heaven's My Destination* (New York: Harper, 1934). How a salesman finds it impossible to follow his religious principles in a world filled with materialistic values.

FILMS

Major Religions of the World: Development and Rituals (Encyclopaedia Britannica Films, 1953, 20 min., sound). Survey of a half-dozen of the world's more important religions, their origins, rituals, and symbols.

Martin Luther (Lutheran Church Productions, 1953, 105 min., sound, black and white). A much talked about film of feature length on the life of the Protestant reformer.

Religions of Man (National Educational Television, 1956, 30 min., sound, black and white). An overview of a sixteen-film series of television lectures on the universal religions, their origins, and their importance.

World's Great Religions (*Life* Corporation, 1956, color, captions, and title frames). A series of filmstrips based on the *Life* magazine series of the same title.

Political Loyalties

*Supporting hands of political loyalty
are an essential element in any political system.*

Some two

thousand years ago, the little Greek state of Athens put Socrates to death on the charge that he had corrupted the youth of his tiny city state and had, thereby, been disloyal. Although the Athenians missed the wise old man after he was gone, this was of no avail to Socrates then. Some people have since argued that Socrates was killed unjustly; but he nevertheless died a traitor, supposedly a threat to the community he loved. Athenian political authorities had defined his actions as treasonous and acted accordingly. Most significantly, a majority of Socrates' friends and contemporaries accepted the verdict and went quietly on with their daily chores.

A little reflection will reveal that few institutions can invoke the death penalty for disloyalty. The Church and other institutions have been able to on occasion, but only political authorities have been consistently successful in obtaining general acceptance of such a prerogative. The governors of communities and national states have not only been able to threaten the disloyal with death but have convinced large numbers of people that they should give their lives, if necessary,

Socrates drinks the hemlock by order of the Athenian authorities. Very few institutions besides government can invoke the death penalty for disloyalty.

for what is affectionately called the "homeland" or the "fatherland." More extreme demands on a person's loyalty are difficult to imagine, yet we accept them almost without question. Indeed, to question them is to invite suspicion of disloyalty and treason.

Why? we ask. Why should such extreme demands be made on a person's loyalties, and why do we accept them so readily? What do political authorities use as a legitimate basis for these demands? Have people always been obliged to render such loyalty? What is the origin and character of the agencies that make the demands? Are there any limits to the obligations an individual owes his state or community, and what does he receive in return for his loyalty? These are a few of the many questions that arise and that we shall attempt to answer in the remainder of this chapter.

GOVERNMENT AS AN AGENCY OF SOCIAL CONTROL

THE ROLE OF GOVERNMENT

Who makes the demands on us? In the last analysis, it is the whole community. But the agency through which the demands are articulated is something we rather loosely call *government*. Some may prefer to call it the *state*, but whatever we call it, every person is affected by its decisions and actions. Each of us is subject to a welter of institutions or behavior patterns that speak for the community at large. In the name of the "general welfare" or the "public good," governments regulate human conduct. Political authorities order us not to steal and punish us if we do; they regulate the public health and public morals; they require a teacher to have a certificate before he can teach, or a physician a license before he can practice medicine. Governing bodies, then, lay down rules and codes of behavior. They provide means of informing people how to live in accordance with these rules and they enforce conduct that conforms to the rules.

Government is thus an agency of social control similar to the church, the school, or the family. Like them, it is concerned with maintaining a well-ordered society. But the power of government to shape an individual's life, as Socrates must have understood, is frequently far greater than the church's, the school's, or the family's. Indeed, government often sits in judgment on the rights and limitations of these other institutions. Despite their religious tenets, for example, the Dukhobors are forbidden by the Canadian government to appear publicly in the nude. Likewise, the government has outlawed the practice of polygamy in the United States.

We can say, then, that the political organization called government is a primary institution in the maintenance of social control. Its ultimate objective is normally public order. Consequently, we may define political government as a pattern of human behavior *for maintaining order throughout a society.* Socrates was forced to drink the hemlock because the political authorities in Athens felt that he was destroying order in Athenian society. The question of whether he was actually undermining order, however, is not so significant for us as the power of the ruling authorities to condemn him as subversive.

One of the primary roles of a governing group, then, is to define and enforce the limits of legitimate activity for the community at large. By telling us what is correct and legitimate, what we may and may not do, and then enforcing compliance to these dictates, government rules on the fitness of human activity. Even when it fails to act, it may claim the right to do so. Much of what we do is thought legitimate merely because the government has taken no action in that particular area of behavior or has simply ignored it. In many instances governments have begun acting in areas where they have not acted before because the community itself or its political authorities believed that social and political needs required it to act.

Who would deny the great significance of government in the life of the individual? Its manifold activities and decisions reach down into the lives of each of us, defining our opportunities, our freedoms, and our obligations. Most important, it demands from us the ultimate in loyalty—allegiance. It can demand our most precious possession, our very lives. And that is a great deal to ask. No doubt, Socrates thought so.

THE TAPROOTS OF GOVERNMENT

Government has two origins and no ending, says Professor Alfred de Grazia. One root extends far back into the reaches of human history, and yet another is found in each individual person. Where is the end? Apparently it is with the end of man himself, for we know of no historical instance where two or more persons have lived together completely devoid of a governing process. There is an old adage that says, "Governments may change and particular governments may disappear altogether, but the governing of mankind endures." *

The origins of government are partially within man himself. Government is what man has made it. It is not a logical exercise or the result of a magic formula. All laws and demands for loyalty are ultimately stated and enforced by men. Government is human activity. As an eminent British statesman, Benjamin Disraeli, expressed it, "England is

---

* A. de Grazia, *The American Way of Government* (New York: Wiley, 1957), p. 3.

governed by Parliament, and not by logic." We can conclude that the major source of government is human experience and human behavior. It reflects man's needs and problems, his genius and his limitations.

THE FAMILY
AS A SOURCE OF GOVERNMENT

Many historians, sociologists, and anthropologists have sought for the sources of government in mankind's earliest institutional arrangements. One of the more important of these institutions is the family, since it appears that the family not only preceded government historically but also is where a person first learns to react to a governing authority. It is in the family that the child is first civilized by being initiated into a disciplined way of life. The family, as we saw in Chapter 4, helps to mold the conscious "self." It inculcates attitudes, habits, and customs. Within the family circle a child learns the meaning of a rule and how to respond to the governing authority that enforces it. He will jump when Daddy speaks, or suffer the consequences. As a member of the family, then, a person learns something very basic to the governing process— how to function in terms of primary responsibilities and obligations. The family is an elementary school for citizenship. The connection between child and father or brother and brother is, after all, much more fundamental than the relationship of citizen to citizen. As sociologist Robert MacIver concludes, "Wherever the family exists—and it exists everywhere in human society—government already exists."

A child learns extensive rules and codes of conduct as a family member. These familial codes, which anthropologists have encountered in every family system ever studied, have been adapted and administered by political authorities as interfamily relations gradually increased. Codes governing economic and property relations, for example, first originated in the family, were later taken over by the tribe, and finally became a matter for government to decide and interpret. Rules governing inheritance and alimony passed through similar stages.

Codes governing extra-marital sexual behavior provide another example. Originally, and especially among many nonliterate peoples, these rules were defined and rigorously enforced by the family. But as populations multiplied and interfamily relations grew more complex, illegitimacy became an ever greater social menace. For illegitimate children may be deprived of the necessary care and attention that is so vital during infancy and early childhood. Moreover, widespread illegitimacy often places a heavy burden on the society-at-large, for many of the children will have to be housed and cared for by persons other than their parents or in special institutions that the society provides for such purposes. Therefore, some standards for extra-marital sexual behavior have been devised for society as a whole and left to a centralized political authority to enforce. Today, governments speak in many of these areas that were once administered by the family hierarchy. Fathers of children born out of wedlock, for example, not only risk social and family ostracism but are apt to run afoul of the law and even be fined or jailed unless they comply with rules and regulations of ancient origin.

THE ECONOMIC BASIS OF GOVERNMENT

These family rules and codes, as we have just seen, extend into the economic sphere. Very often we are inclined to overlook the fact that in the family circle a person acquires his initial appreciation of some very fundamental economic and property relations. It is here that he first learns to distinguish among "mine," "thine," and "ours," one of the most important political

distinctions he makes during his entire lifetime. In the family setting he acquires an appreciation for mutual possessions—those things that are "ours," such as the house, the yard, or the shop. He thus develops a ready basis for understanding actions which are taken by the government for the common good. A great many government actions are certainly taken in a context of common possessions, rights, obligations, and functions. Probably the most important knowledge a person gains, however, is an appreciation of the deep and abiding connection between government and property relations.

Indeed, some renowned writers and thinkers have believed that the sole source of government, as well as the justification for its existence, lay in the protection of private property. James Harrington, an English political philosopher, felt that government had emerged to protect private property. And economist Adam Smith declared, "Where there is no property, or at least no more than exceeds the value of two or three days' labour, civil government is not so necessary." Although both Harrington's and Smith's positions were extreme, they help make clear that the protection of property has long been considered an important obligation of government. We all have some stake, however small, in personal property we would like protected. At the very least, everyone wants his own bed and toothbrush!

There is, then, a fundamental connection between government and property. To be sure, the possession of wealth or property very often carries with it a prerogative to influence the decisions of government. On occasion it has meant actual control of the engines of government. Briefly, economic power tends to translate itself into political power. "Money talks," we say.

No matter what the character of the family, in all societies—literate and nonliterate—the family has wielded a profound influence on both political and economic institutions. Just as most of us obtain our religious convictions from our family backgrounds, so, too, most of our economic and political views can be traced to the family. If your father voted for more Democrats than Republicans, you probably will too. Upwards to 75 per cent of all American voters in fact lean toward the political party their parents supported. Most American housewives sooner or later tend to adopt their husband's political and economic views and vote the same way as their husbands.

It is no accident either that great political leaders are often regarded as fathers by their subjects. Russians, for example, called their Czars "Little Fathers," and the American Indian spoke with respect of the "Great White Father" in Washington. Nor should we be surprised to find governments treating their citizens as if they were wards or children. Paternalism is a common characteristic of many governments. It is furthermore reasonable to expect the individual to respond to governmental decisions as he would to paternal or family ones, for his reactions are conditioned by the expectations he develops as a result of his early family experiences.

GOVERNMENT AS A FUNCTION OF HUMAN NEEDS AND DEMANDS

Political institutions, as we have seen, evidently emerge in response to individual needs. These needs give rise to special demands that a government must satisfy if it hopes to survive. Governments exist to answer demands for order in human relations, and indeed, a great deal of government activity is justified on the grounds that such demands are being met. Apparently this demand issues from a deep-felt human need for order. Men certainly seem to face death courageously when their orderly existences are threatened.

Moreover, as more and more people are brought closer and closer together, they tend

to get in one another's way. Think about the traffic jams in our cities or the bargain basement of a department store on a sale day. To ease such situations, some agency must define the limits of a person's prerogatives and actions. "My nose ends where your's begins," Justice Holmes once remarked. Someone must define the line between noses. In short, growing population concentrations produce an accompanying need for restrictions, or life would be menaced indeed. Without the police and public health ordinances, crime and disease would run rampant. In a wilderness, people can build barns and burn them to the ground if they like, but in the modern city such freedom would seriously jeopardize the freedom and property of others. It makes a difference in a great city when someone dumps his garbage in the river that supplies the metropolis with its water.

Furthermore, a concentration of population brings with it an accompanying need for services. As people begin living more and more closely together, some common enterprise must provide for sewage disposal, police protection, and public schools. The number of such services, like the number of restrictions on the individual, increases with the growth of population. For instance, in 1842 the city of Detroit was providing 23 services of this type; but by 1940 the number of such municipal services had skyrocketed to 349.

Just as government restricts, so too it must serve. Our political institutions function positively as well as negatively. They satisfy our needs for goods and services and safeguard our right to individual opportunity. In the words of Lincoln, "The legitimate object of government is to do for the community of people whatever they need to have done, but cannot do so well for themselves in their separate and individual capacities." Thus, men err when they view government as an institution created by the strong to subordinate the weak. Political institutions are not merely regulatory; government is not something that acts only against individuals. It exists to satisfy human needs. Its functions are also the functions of effective demands, and these demands are one of the sources of its being. They are also the foundation of allegiance. Let us have a look.

THE WELLSPRINGS OF POLITICAL ALLEGIANCE

ALLEGIANCE VERSUS OBEDIENCE

A government must command the allegiance of members of a community in order to meet the needs of that community. Mere obedience is not enough. Coercion and fear techniques may be effective, but a government cannot always follow a majority of its citizens around with bayonets. In World War II, during the German occupation, French farmers sat passively by while their crops rotted, harvesting them for their oppressors only when they were threatened and prodded. Obedience may secure compliance, but allegiance yields the best results. For loyalty or allegiance implies acceptance, and, more important, a willingness to defend and preserve. That is why governments strive for *legitimacy*, a publicly recognized and accepted status. It explains why they go to such pains to justify what they do. Governments need allegiance!

Any analysis of political loyalties, then, begins with a recognition that rulers must enlist the allegiance of those they rule. A clear understanding of this fact depends on our capacity to distinguish the rulers from the ruled. Every society is so divided, despite the difficulty of locating where the division falls in some cases. In a democracy or representative system such as ours, we often speak recklessly about rule by all the people. Yet most of us do not "rule" in the sense of making and enforcing political decisions. Rather, we (the ruled) elect those who rule us and hold them accountable for what they do. If we feel that the rulers are not defending our interests, we can refuse to vote for them or try to have them removed. Here, as in most systems, the ability of the rulers to remain "in the saddle" depends to a large extent on the willingness of the people to accept their leadership.

THE NEED TO IDENTIFY INDIVIDUAL WITH GROUP AIMS

This necessity to inspire allegiance brings us back to the individual, whose needs and wants are reflected in political organization. The basis of government is thus deeply psychological, a fact no government can afford to ignore. Political leaders normally try to identify themselves and their actions with the needs and desires of their people. If a great majority of the people are convinced, for instance, that preservation of the capitalistic system is in their interest, then the government will either have to protect the system, engage in a propaganda campaign to convince them it is not in their interest, or else risk loss of allegiance. If the ruling group is expected to preserve and defend the Church, it may be disastrous for it to refuse. A number of like failures may lose a government the loyalty of its citizens, provoke widespread disobedience, or bring on a revolution.

Not even the powerful group in the Kremlin can afford to thwart or ignore the convictions, aspirations, and needs of its subjects. The Orthodox Church still functions in Russia despite the party's opposition. The Russian people, furthermore, demand more consumer goods, and get them. Hitler was extremely powerful, but his regime was not built on guns alone. He identified himself with the aspirations and goals of the German people by initiating programs for rebuilding the German economy, providing work for the jobless, and seeking revenge for the harsh treatment Germany had received at the hands of the Allies following World War I.

To stay in power, then, political leaders must give expression to what their subjects value and desire to preserve. In practice, this means that a government must appear essential to the preservation of those things the individual regards as fundamental and central to his everyday existence. Most men are, after all, primarily interested in basic, immediate, and rather simple wants and needs. They seem most concerned with the preservation of their lives, homes, families, jobs, property, the soil they till, and a host of other familiar things. A leader will be assured of the allegiance of his subjects when he is able to convince them that the fate of these most cherished possessions, hopes, and aspirations rests with him.

It is hardly surprising, then, that political leaders are judged not so much by their legislative, administrative, or judicial talents as by their ability to symbolize the hopes, values, and aspirations of their subjects. This statement is especially true of executive leadership. Men like Lincoln, Franklin D. Roosevelt, and Churchill symbolized something deeply cherished by their people. The rise of Fiorello LaGuardia to mayor of New York City, and later to national prominence, symbolized the hopes and aspirations of many immigrants and their sons. Fiorello was one of *them*. He presumably knew what was good for them and would protect them. The successful leader must convince those he leads that he has their best interests and welfare at heart. He must appear essential.

The actual process of giving expression to the desires and needs of men, however, is often very subtle and involved. Governments must be ever on guard to make sure that their actions agree with the manner in which a person interprets his own needs. A manufacturer, for example, may believe that a protective tariff is his best insurance against the competition of cheap foreign goods. Whether the tariff actually does help him is not the question. The point is that he believes it does. If enough people agree with him, the government will probably enact a tariff, even if such a policy does not actually benefit everyone concerned. The alternative would be a loss of popular support.

Finally, governments must be careful to abide by accepted procedures and ways of doing things. Men are loyal to a system as well as to the people within the system. We may believe, for instance, that it is the system, rather than the people in it, that protects our interests. Many Americans disliked the New Deal passionately, yet never entertained the notion of changing the American political system. Presumably, they would have been satisfied with a change in administration. Most governments, therefore, are obliged to follow accepted and customary standards of procedure as they conduct their business, lest they incur the wrath of their people. Many governments, in fact, go to extreme lengths to give the appearance that they are meeting all the required standards. Witness the instances in which condemned prisoners have been given blood transfusions or surgical treatment to keep them alive until their appointed times of execution. Not only must the condemned man be killed, but society demands that all the formalities be satisfied. Governments expend a great deal of time and effort keeping up appearances, complying with formalities, and making their subjects feel secure. By complying with standards and upholding a "system of rule," a government can acquire some of the allegiance that citizens accord the system itself. In sum, political loyalty must be identified with the ruler; it must be inspired; it must be won. A government cannot rule by force alone,

THE DEMAND FOR SECURITY

It appears, then, that political allegiance depends heavily on securing men in their lives, property, and all else they hold dear. As we saw in Chapter 4, the demand for security is universal among human beings. Life would be unbearable for all of us without some semblance of security. When tomorrow comes, we want to be here to enjoy it. "Life must go on!" Most of us express concern for a great many things, but life and property we hold to be especially vital. This is why life insurance companies flourish in America. How better might government secure allegiance than to pose as the primary agency for the protection of life, limb, and property?

Most living things, of course, are concerned about survival. But the human concern for self-preservation and security goes far beyond the mere satisfaction of animal needs and protection from physical harm. Men work profound changes on nature in an effort to extend their life span. Salk vaccine, chest X-rays, more hospitals, improved diets, and better housing are but a few of the many examples. But we want more than a longer life. We are historical beings; we see life in terms of a beginning and end, a past and a future. Such a perspective begets uncertainty, apprehension, and anxiety about what lies ahead. It impels us to search for security in terms of years rather than the moment. It makes planning animals of us and directs our allegiance toward those institutions that secure our plans and our future. And government is certainly one of the more important of these institutions. For it provides security beyond the momentary perils of nature, against crimes and all manner of transgressions. Governments establish and maintain our rights to property. We all depend heavily on government for our future security.

A deep concern for security also tends to bind men together. Since human beings cannot destroy or control all that threatens them individually, they seek strength by cooperating with others. And government, of course, offers them a very important medium through which they can cooperate and plan together.

Conversely, our concern for security can make us potential enemies of one another. We have a strong tendency to view persons outside our own group as threats. Strangers in nonliterate societies are frequently feared as "outsiders" or regarded as portents of disaster. Even the most advanced and civilized peoples are suspicious of "newcomers." This ancient human trait is often used by political leaders to consolidate a group or win its support. Demagogues try to evoke allegiance by focusing attention on a common enemy. Hitler united the German people behind him by making the Jew and the Russian symbols of a mortal threat to the welfare of Germany. Survival and security are thus important factors in dividing political loyalties as well as in uniting them.

THE DEMAND FOR ORDER

The demand for security expands into a demand for stability. Security requires order. A person must know where he stands and what he can reasonably expect. Stability and security derived through *order* (regularized processes) relieve a person's apprehensions about the future, leave him free to follow his daily endeavors without fear if he follows the regularized and orderly processes. And the presence of a superior group such as government to ensure order further relieves his apprehension. It is an orderly life that government seeks to nurture; order must be a part and parcel of every government's objectives. Inability to maintain it generally spells death to a political organization. No ruler can expect to command allegiance without it. Without order, all is chaos.

SOME HISTORICAL ROOTS

Successful political leadership, then, requires skill in obtaining allegiance as well as obedience. The political leader must identify himself with his subjects and satisfy their demands for security. This is not easy! Nor is it the whole picture. The maintenance of order requires a government, as we shall presently see, to organize and control the major means of force and violence. A government must provide orderly and just procedures for settling social differences, and this necessitates the maintenance of a system of written or unwritten legal standards, no matter how crude. And as Professor Harold Lasswell points out, governments must manipulate symbols (words, objects, and myths), allocate certain goods and services, and preserve social values.

But all these things can be carried out in different ways and have different effects under differing times and conditions. If we could call back to life people from bygone ages and ask them what they owed their political authorities or why they were loyal to them, the differences would be more apparent. Some would speak solely in terms of a small city-state, others of great empires. Still others would hardly acknowledge the need for loyalty to political authorities. A number of them would refer to the *actual* loyalty the people tendered, whereas others would speak only of those loyalties people *ought to* tender.

The ancient Mesopotamian would tell us that he was obliged to obey and give loyalty to his prince, or *patesi*, because the prince in his time was literally the "tenant farmer of the civic god." The material achievements of his civilization were made possible through the *patesi*. Under the *patesi's* strong social discipline, swamps and thickets had been tamed, canals built, floods controlled, and the desert made habitable. Moreover, the prince was a god king, the representative of the community and mediator between god and man. The palace in which the *patesi* lived was called "The House of Man" and symbolized security and plenty.

Likewise, the Egyptian would speak respectfully of his pharaoh as "He of the Great House," the one who insured his future. "The king gave me rewards above those of the ancestors, because I did righteous unto the king," said one ancient Egyptian. To this was added terror techniques. "The people regard him who terrorizes them," Pharaoh Amenhemet counseled his son. Many of the ancients believed that their god or gods were the ultimate political authorities, and, therefore, those who occupied the positions of government received their authority directly from the gods.

In Greece the Pythagoreans believed that the individual was obliged to subordinate himself to the greater whole (the group). Political loyalty involved respect for authority, the laws, and the well-administered state. And Democritus added the following as the basic reason for political loyalty: "When the state is healthy, all things prosper." The Sophists, on the other hand, argued that laws were merely inventions of the weak to enslave the strong. Gorgias claimed that the great men of history were the disloyal and the disobedient.

If we were to ask Plato, he would remind us that governing is the highest form of human endeavor. It is a "kingly science," which includes the whole art of living and seeks the "Good Life." We ought, therefore, to give government our unquestioned loyalty. Aristotle's answer would have been similar but much more practical. Since the solitary man is "either a beast or a god," all men live in groups or communities. They are social animals. As moral beings they aim at the highest good. The highest good, according to Aristotle, would be achieved through the highest form of community—the state. The state was an organic whole that was as natural to man as the family or clan. Separated from it, men were worse than beasts. He went so far as to say that if the state is bad, the man who is a good citizen in it must certainly be bad. If man is a beast outside the state—ceases to be man—there is no choice other than to be loyal to the state; and from a practical point of view, the state insures us of those things that are logically, morally, materially, and intellectually satisfying.

Both Plato and Aristotle confined their analysis to local and small city-states, but the soldier in Alexander's armies most probably would not have done so. With Alexander came the ideas of "world rule" and "empire" that dwarfed the idea of city states. Lines of loyalty now extended over great distances. No longer did most persons live a few miles from their superior political authority. Governments had to find broader and vaguer symbols for evoking loyalty. Their answer was found in universal concepts and appeals that were common to all men. Men during the Hellenistic age became citizens of the world. The Stoic philosophers, for example, developed universal concepts of Natural Law and natural reason that were believed common to all men, which transcended and undermined the early, more virile local political loyalties of civic patriotism that had flourished in Greece.

The Roman and the early Church thinkers also employed the idea of a universal world society. Cicero combined the ideal of a universal law for all men with efficient and just bureaucratic administration. The Roman took pride in his citizenship, which was extended to non-Romans and included nearly 5 million persons during the second century A.D. He was also duly proud of the practical and legal achievements that he attributed to the empire.

The early Churchmen rooted their universal society in the belief that God is the Father of all men and that all men are thereby brothers. Governments, like other institutions, derived their powers from God, and so men could be loyal to political authorities only when the rulers obeyed the laws of God. The great mass of people during the Middle Ages, however, with the Roman Empire crumbling and its civilization destroyed by barbarian invasions, were forced to accept reality and give loyalty to local lords and princes who could protect them and their land in return for their labor and produce. The all-consuming loyalty question of the Middle Ages, then, was how a man's loyalties should be divided between the Church and the temporal monarchs. According to St. Thomas Aquinas, a man's loyalties had to be divided. He had to be loyal to God's laws to gain salvation, and he had to be loyal to human law, since Aquinas, like Aristotle, held that a government's supreme purpose was the good of the group. But a man's superior loyalty was to the Church. Even the monarch had to be loyal to the ruler of the Church. Political authority was thus divinely established and disloyalty to it was disloyalty to God.

The emergence of the modern national state led to the formulation of new and challenging concepts of loyalty. Machiavelli was quite lucid. Political obligation, he said, is owed those who can gain power, unite the people and the territory into an independent national state, and provide the people with the benefits accruing from such a union. Royal monarchs, however, bid for loyalty on the old basis that they were authorized by God to rule, but this no longer meant that the Church and its ruler were supreme. Royalty waged a furious battle to win loyalty away from the Church in temporal matters. Kings' courts began to challenge the right of Church courts. Separate national churches, such as the Church of England, were established. Monarchs identified themselves with their lands, their peoples, and national symbols. They amassed great armies and posed as the principal protectors and administrators of true justice.

As a result, answers to questions about political obligation were becoming more practical and devoid of religious ties. Hobbes was clear. Men are brutes without government, he argued. Their basic drive for self-preservation dictates that they agree to be governed. Their agreement or contract to be governed makes it incumbent on them to obey and be loyal to political authority or live a life of terror in a state of nature. We must be loyal to a tyrant, says Hobbes, since even his regime would be better than bestial conditions.

John Locke, on the other hand, although he agreed that loyalty stemmed from a contract situation, argued that the contract imposed obligations on the government to preserve the group, to protect human rights and freedoms, and to follow defined procedures. In return, the people owed the government their loyalty. This, of course, gives loyalty a constitutional basis similar to the one found in the American Constitution. Ultimate power resides with the people, and the government is obliged to follow constitutional rules in return for its people's loyalty.

Both Hobbes and Locke viewed government as a mechanism that men contrived for their own needs and purposes. Although both agreed that some sort of government was necessary, any government was separate from the people themselves and could therefore be changed, destroyed, or replaced by another government. But organic theorists, such as Herbert Spencer, have likened the state to a living organism in which the people are but parts of the organism, having much the same relation to the state as cells have to the human body. Thus, without the state we die, for we are a part of it. We must be loyal to our state and its authorities, for we cannot live outside of it. Disloyal persons are cancers in the social organism. This theory naturally appeals to authoritarians.

A complete history of political obligation is yet to be written, but our brief sketch here indicates that political loyalty is not easily attained. Governments must bid for it, and a successful bid requires a government to act and to justify its actions in ways that the people can understand and accept. Justification, especially, must be couched in terms and symbols that make the people feel that their welfare is being protected and that order is being preserved.

THE BASIS OF ORDER AND JUSTICE

Order is not something we come by easily. It took countless centuries for men to emerge from their caves, and we are constantly in danger of slipping back. Order, therefore, must be guarded zealously if governments are to endure. And if a government is to have the primary responsibility for maintaining order, it must have the tools to do the job. It must have the power to coerce those who threaten the existing order. Thus, every government seeks a monopoly of violence within its territory.

THE ORGANIZATION OF VIOLENCE

To be unchallenged in its function of maintaining order, a government will seek to be the sole possessor of the most effective coercive techniques. Governments do not shrink from violence; they organize it and seek to monopolize it. They arm some to disarm others. They assume the authority to determine who can possess and use weapons and other instruments of violence.

Actually, no government dares to re-

nounce violence. Police officers, state mili-
tiamen, national guardsmen, all use their
weapons when danger threatens. Every government worthy of the name makes a conscious, deliberate effort to monopolize and
organize violence to maintain domestic
tranquility. If a government failed to monopolize violence, it would be signaling its
imminent capitulation. It would cease to
be the prime protector, and it would hardly
command the allegiance of its subjects.

On the other hand, wherever force and
violence are available to associations or
groups other than government, the embryo
of a new government already exists within
the association or group. As the pirate said
to Alexander the Great: "How darest thou
molest the whole world? But because I do it
with a little ship only, I am called a thief;
thou doing it with a great navy, art called
an Emperor." Criminals appear antisocial
since they prey on the larger community.
Some criminals, however, have turned themselves into rulers by acquiring the most
effective techniques of coercion. Both Hitler
and Stalin spent time in jail as common
criminals before seizing the reins of power.

This says neither that might makes right
nor that government necessarily represents
the will of the strong. But it helps to be
strong. Through a monopoly of violence,
governments are at least given a means for
keeping the peace.

THE NEED FOR JUSTICE

The mere monopoly of violence, however, is not enough. Men seek "justice."
They want to be treated fairly. When your
car is stolen, you want to get it back; if it
is damaged, you will want to be compensated.
Certainly you do not expect to pay a large
sum for its return. Nor could you easily re-
trieve it without help. Hence, you expect the
government to help you and also to apprehend the offender, possibly prosecute him,

and provide courts to which you can apply
for damages. "That is only just," you say.
In sum, governments must maintain a type
of order that makes a citizen feel he is being
treated fairly. To ensure protection and ignore justice may gain a person's obedience
but hardly his allegiance.

Definitions of justice vary greatly from
society to society and from individual to
individual. Most Americans agree, for example, that it is unjust for a public official to
search a man's home without a warrant. But
many Orientals do not feel this way. Most
assuredly, what is just to a Russian differs
markedly from what is just to an American.
No doubt, *justice* is best left loosely defined;
namely, whatever strikes the human breast
as fair within a particular society.

Methods of justice, then, relate to fair

*A government cannot shrink from vio-
lence; it must organize and display the
major coercive techniques.*

play. People want to know where they stand. They want to be sure of a fair break in their dealings with other people. They want to be sure that the government will protect their interests according to standards and procedures that the society regards as fair. Without forms of established justice, governments are but great frauds and find it difficult to maintain their power.

THE NEED FOR LAW

"Law and order," we say. We speak of the two as if they were inseparable. Law generally accompanies order; many people regard it as a guide for achieving and maintaining order. As such, it is often considered the basis of a political system. Law is not merely the command of rulers, as some writers have mistakenly contended. It is that and more. Repeal all laws ever passed by legislatures and all decrees ever issued by executives and there still would be law. Persons would still be jailed and fines would still be collected. The courts would continue to exist and function.

Some authorities define law as the product of the community. They contend that it is as much a product of custom and convention as it is a product of a lawgiver or lawmaker. Law is actually a great body of knowledge that issues from past practices and tradition as well as from lawmakers. It is something that has durability and on which men can depend. If you quarrel with your neighbor over the use of a driveway, for example, you can appeal to law to have the issue righted. Law thus can be used to defend your rights and your opponent's as well. The standards and precedents are there to guide you before you get into the fracas. Where law exists, men are assured that principles, rules, and guides exist that can be employed for their own defense against those who may jeopardize not only their security but the security of society as well. Law is thus a guide for

action and an instrument for protection. It defines rights and obligations of individuals and groups within a society and provides the government a justification for action when violations occur.

Law, then, is basic to an orderly society. Under it the individual is made reasonably secure that his daily existence will not be subject to the arbitrary whim of others. Further, a system of law relieves government of its arbitrary appearance since the judgments of today accord with the judgments of the past. Rule by decree or whim makes a fraud of government. Certainly many governments have been just that, but rule of this sort depends far too much on obedience and far too little on allegiance. The life of tyranny is usually short, for allegiance depends heavily on an orderly process for settling social differences among individuals and groups. Unsatisfactory or arbitrary settlements breed disorder and contempt. Government without firm roots in the legal traditions of the past is not just government by whim; it is government by chaos. And no one can endure chaos for very long.

Orderly processes for composing social differences, therefore, must function through tribunals that inspire public confidence, and the decisions and procedures must be fair. Decisions that courts render, like those of other government bodies, must appear less irritating than the situations created by their absence. Otherwise, government runs the risk of inviting revolution and disorder.

THE CEMENT OF TRADITION AND CUSTOM

It is now clear that communities, like the individuals in them, depend heavily on established custom, tradition, and morals. Conformity to the expectations of the community or group makes a person's behavior both meaningful and acceptable. Essentially, men want today to be rather like yesterday.

Strong roots of tradition and custom make life more stable and acceptable. This is not to say that complete conformity is the rule, or that it is desirable. Nevertheless, but for the few radical nonconformists we discussed in Chapter 4, most of us honor tradition and adhere to customary practice; we adhere to both the traditional ends and means of the society into which we are born. The cake of custom is difficult to cut, which is why most governments usually defer to established customs and traditions.

Certainly men will depart from established paths when convinced that it is in their interest to do so. But for a government to attempt a sudden change in basic objectives or ends of a society is to risk losing its subjects' allegiance. No sultan of the great Muslim Empire, no matter how absolute, could have risked outlawing the Mohammedan religion without placing his throne in serious jeopardy. Those governments that have enjoyed the longest and most successful tenure have therefore found it wise to strengthen the time-honored traditions and practices. Radical departures from established patterns hinder effective law enforcement, breed disorder, and undermine people's confidence in the system. Man is clearly a creature of habit.

The more the law is violated, the greater the indication that order is lacking. When society jails a criminal, it is tacitly admitting its failure to maintain order. This statement applies to all types of institutional control. The child is spanked and the church member is excommunicated because the family or church has failed to uphold standards and maintain order. More serious, however, is the fact that a failure to maintain a standard breeds contempt for the standard, and also for the agency that failed to enforce it. One of the main arguments against prohibition was the government's inability to enforce it. This lack of enforcement, critics said, bred contempt for all law, even for the Constitu-

tion itself. Order depends on the maintenance of standards. The maintenance of standards depends on the subjects' willingness to follow and respect them. They do this best when standards complement traditional and familiar patterns.

THE WONDERS OF SYMBOLS

Everyone loves a parade. At least nearly everyone does. The pulse quickens at the sight of a colorful pageant, the unfurling of the national colors, or the strains of military music. A galaxy of hallowed symbols evokes a warm response in the human breast. Our behavior is to a large degree symbolic, and we spend long hours supporting, justifying, and embellishing symbols. The preservation of symbols, it often seems, matters a great deal more than their truth or validity. We tend to dislike people who criticize or scorn our symbolic behavior.

Government, like other institutions, makes extensive use of symbols to evoke support and allegiance. American life, political and

From the time we are youngsters, our government impresses us with its symbols to invoke our allegiance and support.

otherwise, is full of symbolic significance that is readily recognized but seldom appreciated for the function it serves. We honor the "unknown soldier" on Memorial Day. "It is as American as apple pie," we say. "Uncle Sam" and even some of our large buildings represent something of our national pride.

We visualize, too, the symbolic image of a whole *state*. We speak of an American or a German state in a particular way. Yet when we are forced to define what acted, we then must admit that a government did the acting and its actions were merely taken in the name of something called the state. This state was actually nothing more or less than a symbol for a complex of land, people, boundaries, and common tradition. *The state is an idea or myth characterized by symbols filled with hoary tradition and lore.* The government acts in its name. Although the state symbolizes objects that are real and tangible, it is itself neither of these. It certainly does not think, feel, and act as would a person, animal, or other living organism. Its main purpose is to inspire allegiance and cloak the actions of government in respectability.

Symbols that represent the state evoke a very real response in a person. The tears that come to the Frenchman's eyes as the first strains of the *Marseillaise* fill the air are evidence of a common bond among Frenchmen. Such symbols are powerful weapons for uniting a people and producing allegiance to a political system. All political leaders exploit them. Through them men are able to identify themselves with untold millions they will never know and with ground they may never traverse.

This identification begets *nationalism*. "Nation," of course, is a much-abused term. *Historically, it refers to a kindred people who share a common birthplace and a common group allegiance.* This definition has been expanded in recent years. *The word "nation"*

now frequently refers to a group of people who feel a common attachment, bond, and enthusiasm, resulting from a shared historical experience, common cultural patterns and institutions, a common language, and often common residence in the same territory. Any one or several of these factors produces an "in-group" feeling, a tendency for one group to separate itself from others. Such groups often aspire to political independence. *This aspiration for national independence from others, whether political, economic, or otherwise, is called nationalism.* When the Hungarians attempted to free themselves of Russian domination in 1956 and set up a government of their own, they were political nationalists. When the Egyptians attempted to throw off the yoke of British and French economic influence during the Suez crisis, they were economic nationalists.

Political leaders in modern times have attempted to implant and foster the feeling of nationalism in their subjects by manipulating symbols of state. The process is not always easy, however, since some national states are composed of many different national groups. Prior to World War I, for example, Austria-Hungary was composed of a number of national groups—Germans, Magyars, Croats, Serbs, and others. National feelings are persistent and difficult to root out. Poland was divided for centuries among other national states, but Polish nationalism endured. It persists even today under Russian domination. And the Jews have been scattered to the far ends of the earth since ancient times, but they remained united under the Star of David and the vision of eventually establishing their own homeland. We shall investigate the consequences of nationalism later. For now, however, suffice it to say that such feelings owe a great deal of their intensity to symbols, and the symbols—words, objects, myths—can be readily exploited by political leaders.

THE NEED FOR A ROAD TO POWER *

We have already seen how necessary it is for governments to appear legitimate in the eyes of their subjects, since legitimacy inspires confidence in the rulers. Rulers must

A former president is greeted at one of America's most festive and important political events—a national convention. The road to power in America is through the people or through delegates such as these on the convention floor who act in the name of the people they represent.

not only justify what they do but must also appear to have the right to do it. They must appear as rightful possessors of the seats of the mighty. American politicians, for instance, clothe themselves with legitimacy by coming to power through an orderly election process, or by being appointed by someone

---

* The following material is based on L. Lipson, *The Great Issues of Politics*, 2nd ed. (Englewood Cliffs, New Jersey: Prentice-Hall, 1960), pp. 220-253.

who has been elected. This routine presumably makes their voice the voice of the people.

Justifications for the exercise of political power are disarmingly simple and primitive. The one that seems to die the hardest holds that the right to direct the destinies of others issues from God. God anoints the rulers. Political authorities who can make this claim are in a rather enviable position since deity is rather formidable. To question the acts of the ruler is to question God. Treason is therefore not just treason; it is heresy. Indeed, the slightest criticism is apt to be considered sinful. These claims are usually reinforced by magic and religious rites. It is hardly surprising that medicine men and priests were so influential in nonliterate societies.

A second justification lies in heredity rather than heaven. Men succeed to the helm of government because they were born into the proper family, class, or caste. The right to rule over others is a matter of status, ancestry, and hereditary rights, usually devolving on the eldest son. History and heredity select the man. This method makes discovery of the proper ruling authority very simple and assures continuity in government since the procedure for transferring power is sure and direct. Very probably this is why hereditary monarchies have survived long after the belief in the principle of hereditary rule declined.

A third justification appeals to force and the instruments of coercion. It is all very simple. The right to rule goes to those who can grasp and hold on to the instruments of power. According to this view, *might makes right*. Justice represents the interest of the strongest.

A fourth justification embodies Plato's principle that only the most talented or the best qualified should rule. This principle sounds very wise and practical, but those who base their right to rule on this theory are usually self-selected and often try to vindicate their position by invoking wealth, experience, age, or some supposed genius. Plato felt that only properly educated philosophers should rule since they presumably had a special insight into truth, whereas Alexander Hamilton felt that only the rich, the well-born, and the able should have the right to make political decisions. More important than the principle itself is the fact that it has been used to uphold dictatorships and tyrannies. The men in the Kremlin, for instance, justify their authority by claiming to have a unique ability to interpret the laws governing class conflict. Not content with the mere claim of being anointed by God, Hitler claimed he was born with superhuman talents and turned himself into a god. Rulers of this stripe may ultimately be required to rely on force to maintain themselves in power.

God, grandpa, guns, and greatness have all been used as grounds for justifying political rule. To these claims must be added still another justification that is familiar to all of us—election by the people or some segment of the people. The road to power here is through approval by the people; the exercise of power is made legitimate because the people have sanctioned it. Government is based on the consent of the governed. To put it another way, the voice of the people is the voice of God.

Nearly all rulers appeal to one or more of these justifications. The simplicity and primitive character of some of their arguments should not detract from the important fact that rulers must justify what they do and that order requires a rather well-defined and accepted means for attaining power as well as using it.

ORGANIZING FOR ORDER

When we speak of governing, we are talking about actions taken by a few on be-

half of the whole population of a society. For it is a characteristic of a politically organized society that the reins of government are given to a few persons who are recognized as public officials acting in the name of the state for the community at large. Rulers are separated from the ruled and are organized to do the job. What is public is distinguished from what is private.

Organizing such an enterprise generally divides itself into three major areas of endeavor: (1) Someone must be responsible for changes in the ruling formula and in the law; (2) there must be a superior agency of interpretation; and (3) there must be someone to enforce and administer the decisions. Without the latter, the first two functions are meaningless.

Without an executive arm, government ceases to exist in a realistic sense, for all governments depend on the executive function to enforce and carry out their policies. Since decisions are of little avail without someone to enforce them, executives appeared long before legislatures and courts. Many executives have performed all three functions of government, of course, but this does not deny that the executive is basic to all governments. The executive is the axle around which the wheel of government turns.

As society changes, so must the law, and the more rapidly society changes, the more rapid must be the change in law. Therefore, as contacts among people increased and became more complex, courts and legislatures put in their appearance. The first need was for some political arm to interpret the law to fit new circumstances. As a result, the number of courts increased. But, as we have already seen, men not only demand change in the law but also demand that the law be kept true to tried principles so that a person may know where he stands. It is, then, the difficult task of judicial bodies to find a balance between certainty and flexibility in the law. Courts are thus the primary agency

The Italian House of Deputies, the lower house of one of the many policy-determining legislatures throughout the modern world.

in the administration of justice, adjusting the law to social change while they attempt to afford satisfactory remedy and restitution to the injured. A more important function in society is difficult to imagine.

But judicial functions are almost entirely remedial in nature. Men go to court after the injury is done; court action comes after the fact. As society grows more complex, as social relations increase and change becomes the order of the hour rather than the order of years and centuries, the need for preventive justice arises. To fill this need legislatures have arisen. Our buzzing modern world has, in fact, been filled with them. The legislator attempts to provide men with guides to conduct that will help them avoid conflict and strife. We call him a *lawmaker*, and he should be distinguished from the *lawgiver* and *lawfinder* of earlier times.

All three functions—legislative, executive, and judicial—are complementary. All three could conceivably be performed by a single agency, although such an arrangement is quite unlikely in our modern world setting. Governments today could not function effectively if they were unable to perform any of these three functions.

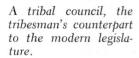

A tribal council, the tribesman's counterpart to the modern legislature.

SOME WORDS OF SUMMARY

We have seen in this chapter that government is an agency of social control as is the church, the school, and the family and that like them it seeks to maintain a well-ordered society. Its taproots lie within man himself, in his desire for regularity and stability, and in the family, which is a kind of government in miniature. The growth of human society has spawned complicated social problems and created a need for community protections and services that neither family nor tribal organizations could meet. Government arose in response to this need.

A government commands political allegiance through its ability to identify itself with the common needs and desires of its subjects, most of which are immediate and rather simple. People will usually support a government so long as it protects them in their lives and property and makes them secure. To make their subjects feel secure, governments engage in pageantry, display their strength, propagandize their people, and resort to many other devices. Security also requires order, and to maintain order governments must monopolize the major means of violence within the society. More than this, successful governments must convince their subjects that they will provide justice and protect their interests by standards and procedures generally recognized as fair. And in obtaining justice, law is basic to an orderly society. It makes the individual reasonably safe against arbitrary and unreasonable interference with his private life and relieves government of its arbitrary appearance. Allegiance, finally, depends to a considerable extent on the successful manipulation of symbols that evoke support and sentimental identification with the national state and the governing group that acts in its name.

To appear legitimate in the eyes of the governed, a government must justify the method by which it acquires and holds power. Down through the years governments have buttressed their right to rule by appealing to divine sanction, history and heredity, force, superior talent, and the concept of government by consent of the governed. Most governments, moreover, generally find it necessary to maintain three institutional processes—legislative, executive, and judicial—although, at times, the three have been combined in various ways.

FURTHER ROADS TO LEARNING

GENERAL ACCOUNTS

The reader's attention is called to the following great classics on politics and government, all of which are available in reasonably priced paperbound or other editions: Plato's *The Republic;* Aristotle's *Politics;* Cicero's *On the Commonwealth;* Marcus Aurelius' *Meditations;* St. Augustine's *City of God;* St. Thomas Aquinas' *Summa Theologica;* Dante's *Monarchia;* Machiavelli's *The Prince* and his *Discourses;* Bodin's *Republic;* J. Harrington's *Oceana;* T. Hobbes' *Leviathan;* J. Locke's *Two Treaties on Civil Government;* J. Rousseau's *The Social Contract;* T. More's *Utopia;* J. Milton's *Areopagetica;* D. Hume's *Essays;* G. Hegel's *Philosophy of Right;* and E. Burke's *Selected Works.*

E. Barker, *Principles of Social and Political Theory* (London: Oxford University Press, 1951). A volume inquiring into the principles underlying government action, which contains a brilliant analysis of the grounds and limits of political obligation in Book V.

A. Bentley, *The Process of Government* (Chicago: The University of Chicago Press, 1908). A celebrated behavioral study of the political processes that marked out new directions for students of politics.

R. Brewster, *Government in Modern Society* (Boston: Houghton Mifflin, 1958). A brief, readable survey of many of the subjects covered in this chapter.

D. Easton, *The Political System* (New York: Knopf, 1953). What political science is all about.

W. Ebenstein, *Political Thought in Perspective* (New York: McGraw-Hill, 1957). A sturdy and brief account that provides accurate descriptions of the grounds men have used for political obligation.

H. Lasswell, *Politics: Who Gets What, When, How* (New York: McGraw-Hill, 1936). A penetrating examination of the character and composition of political elites, the techniques they use, and the conditions necessary for their existence.

L. Lipson, *The Great Issues of Politics*, 2nd ed. (Englewood Cliffs, N. J.: Prentice-Hall, 1960). An admirable attempt to assess the timeless and still unanswered political questions.

R. MacIver, *The Web of Government* (New York: Macmillan, 1947). A distinguished sociologist seeks to discover the roots of political authority and behavior.

G. Sabine, *A History of Political Theory*, rev. ed. (New York: Holt, 1950). This is not only the best general text on the subject, but is also an excellent source for a variety of theories of political obligation.

G. Wallas, *Human Nature in Politics* (New York: Crofts, 1921). A brilliant, early attempt to analyze political behavior from a psychological basis.

SPECIAL STUDIES

A. Barth, *The Loyalty of Free Men* (New York: Viking, 1951). A survey of the administrative loyalty programs of the national government.

B. Cardozo, *The Nature of the Judicial Process* (New Haven: Yale University Press, 1925). This little volume contains a clear statement of the basis on which courts and law function.

H. Commager, *Freedom, Loyalty, Dissent* (New York: Oxford University Press, 1954). How the American concepts of freedom, loyalty, and tolerance have been faring during the present century.

C. Friedrich, ed., *Authority* (Cambridge: Harvard University Press, 1958). A series of essays, two of which deal with the history of authority, and all of which cover the subject in a comprehensive fashion.

O. Holmes, Jr., *The Common Law* (Boston: Little, Brown, 1951). One of America's greatest jurists says forthrightly that law exists to settle social differences and serve society.

H. Lasswell, C. Merriam, and T. Smith, *A Study of Power* (Glencoe, Ill.: The Free Press, 1950). Three of America's most distinguished political scientists direct their attention to a fundamental concept underlying all political action.

J. Maritain, *Man and the State* (Chicago: The University of Chicago Press, 1951). Government exists to serve men!

J. Mill, *Utilitarianism, Liberty, and Representative Government* (New York: Dutton, 1950). These three treatises, which are fast becoming great classics, probably should be read by everyone who is loyal to the ideals of political freedom.

R. Nettleship, *Works of Thomas Hill Green*, Vol. II (London: Longmans, Green, 1886). Contains Green's celebrated classic on political obligation.

B. Russell, *Authority and the Individual* (New York: Simon & Schuster, 1949). A series of lectures concerned with reconciling public order with private initiative.

T. Smith, *The Legislative Way of Life* (Chicago: The University of Chicago Press, 1940). A legislator-poet-political scientist gives some insights into the role of legislative processes in society.

H. Spiro, *Government by Constitution* (New York: Random House, 1959). By employing a simple style and the comparative method of analysis, Spiro seeks to raise new questions about politics.

D. Spitz, *Democracy and the Challenge of Power* (New York: Columbia University Press, 1958). Spitz says that the question of loyalty is entangled in our endless quest for solutions to specific abuses of power.

D. Truman, *The Governmental Process* (New York: Knopf, 1951). This study builds on Bentley's approach to discover the truth about political behavior.

FICTION AND DRAMA

J. Dos Passos, *Adventures of a Young Man* (New York: Harcourt, Brace, 1939). An American lad who embraces communism is betrayed by those to whom he was loyal.

G. Hicks, *Only One Storm* (New York: Macmillan, 1942). A loyalty struggle between communist and democratic ideals within a young man.

A. Saxton, *Grand Crossing* (New York: Harper, 1943). This novel contains good discussions of democracy, unionism, pacifism, and politics.

J. Steinbeck, *The Moon is Down* (New York: Viking, 1942). Persons loyal to democratic ideals cannot be conquered!

FILMS

Death of Socrates (McGraw-Hill, 1955, 27 min., sound, black and white). A "You Are There" program in which Socrates defies ignorance and prejudice rather than renounce his convictions.

General Election (British Information Service, 1946, 20 min., sound, black and white). See an actual British election in progress.

How to Vote (Teaching Films Custodians, 1936, 10 min., sound, black and white). Wonderful satire by Robert Benchley of a political meeting.

Social Process (Encyclopaedia Britannica Films, 1952, 20 min., sound, black and white). A well-known political scientist, Harold D. Lasswell, conducts a seminar on patterns of human behavior common to all cultures.

Loyalties under Stress

Cultural values clash.
Leaders of one culture are tried and condemned
by leaders of other cultures
at Nuremburg in 1946. Showing contempt
for the whole proceeding, the Nazi leaders Admiral Doenitz
and Admiral Raeder (behind blanket),
Goering, and Hess greet one another jovially.

Civilized

or savage, men are a rather quarrelsome and inconsistent lot. They vary widely in their beliefs and values, their loves and hates, their weaknesses and their loyalties. They bubble with contradictions, attacking certain types of behavior on one occasion and defending them on another. Speakers deplore the morals of our youth, pound with clenched fist, yet fail to detect signs of similar trouble in their own children and defend them as different from the rest. The very same man who recites on Sunday that the meek shall inherit the earth will berate the meek at his sales meeting on Monday. The girl down the street must be at once the symbol of motherhood and also of sex. Many of us are like the proverbial Kansan who staggered perversely to the polls to vote against legalizing liquor. Some of us are amused by these human contradictions; the cynic may sneer; the parson may pound; but our behavior persists. Life is shot through with nearly every type of contradiction imaginable.

Many illustrations might be drawn from the past few chapters to show how our loyalties, too, conflict and contradict each other. In the chapter on religion, we saw that the girl entering college faced a conflict in loyalties between the behavior she was taught in Sunday school and what was expected of her by her school chums. Likewise, boys may be urged by the church and their parents to be "good," only to find that society winks at the promiscuous chap and says, "Boys will be boys!" Other examples abound. Society, for instance, expects all of us to succeed, which is manifestly impossible. "Nothing succeeds like success," we chirp.

We teach it and we preach it. But many who succeed, those agile enough to climb the social ladder, do so only by violating their moral and religious standards. The shyster lawyer who wins his cases by legal trickery is successful. The shady businessman who cheats his way to the top commands the respect of his fellows. In such cases, success has won out in the conflict of loyalties. Some people, of course, perhaps a majority, try to be moral, ambitious, and successful at the same time, but the way is difficult. And many, it need not be said, never seem to succeed at all.

Such contradictions make life difficult. Many a lad has patterned his life after someone he respects, very often his father (taking the role of "the other"), only to be disillusioned by learning that his hero achieved success by questionable means. Yet the father, let us say, may have done no more than what others expected of him. He was assuming the role of the "generalized other." He was supposed to succeed, was he not? Wracked by the contradictions within himself and his surroundings, the lad may resort to those psychological mechanisms we mentioned in Chapter 4—substitution, projection, identification, or rationalization. He may rationalize his actions so ably that he no longer recognizes the existence of any conflict. He may become an outward conformist or a complete nonconformist. He may even become neurotic and require skilled professional attention. Under certain conditions he might desert organized society for the criminal world or creep off to become a hermit. Whatever the resolution of his problems, his loyalties are certain to undergo profound strain.

THE SOURCES OF CONTRADICTION

THE SIMPLE EXAMPLE

Why the prevalence of contradiction? Since the time of Plato and even earlier, men have searched for answers. On the popular level we have always had ready answers. "That's life!" we quip. A great many of us blame the "cussedness of human nature." Or we blame Adam for having eaten the apple and thus despoiling our human nature. Sometimes we blame ourselves.

"I'm the victim of sosh-shiety, hiccup!"

But these simple common-sense generalizations do little more than satisfy us temporarily. Throughout human history men have sought more precise and accurate explanations. Yet even the very best explanations are based largely on guesswork or, at best, are hypotheses that still must be verified. Let us examine a few of the explanations that have won widespread attention.

BLAME IT ON SOCIETY

When asked to repent his sins, the old drunk may retort, "I am just a victim of sosh-shiety." He is simply using the psychological device of projection to avoid responsibility for his weakness. Nevertheless, there are many authorities who insist that our contradictory behavior and social difficulties stem from the difference between individual and group behavior. Reinhold Niebuhr, a famous American theologian, points out that men as individuals act quite differently from men in groups. Gustav Le Bon, in his important work, *The Crowd*, indicates that men tend to lose their individual identities when they enter the group or act in the name of a society or group. They become one among many, and thus, capable of behavior they would never dream of outside the group. Otherwise mannerly co-eds, for example, will throw vegetables and hurl insults at the opposition in the name of their team. People who abhor killing willingly slaughter their fellow human beings in the name of their national state. The group thus becomes a medium through which we express ourselves in ways that would be unacceptable, and in some cases even criminal, were we to do it solely as individuals. There is safety in numbers. You are not alone in a crowd. If someone points to you, just point to all those others who are there with you! If damage results from the group's action, you can claim that the group did it, not you certainly! As George Orwell points out in *England Your England*, the group can absolve us of responsibility for how we act.

Niebuhr maintains that the group affords men a great opportunity to revert to their animal behavior and uses this contention to reinforce his neo-orthodox religious views that we discussed in the chapter on religion (see p. 122). What is important for us here, however, is his suggestion that our personal behavior within groups differs from group to group and that group behavior differs from individual action. These differences between individual and group behavior frequently produce conflicts and subject a person's loyalties to severe strain. A pacifist, for example, may find it difficult to conform to group loyalty requirements in a national state that erects statues to the memory of experts in homicide.

BLAME IT ON CULTURE

Niebuhr's group analysis is suggestive of another school of thought, which holds that *culture* is at least partly responsible for our conflicting loyalties. To understand the position of this group, however, we must first explain clearly and precisely what we mean by "culture." In Chapter 3, we referred to culture as the sum total of a group's cumulative experience, or the learned patterns of behavior that are transmitted from generation to generation. As a product of man's experience, culture is man-made. For better or for worse, it is the result of man's own doing. Such institutions as the family may have appeared originally to answer human needs, but we have made them what they are through generations of living together.

Culture is our own invention, but we are also deeply influenced by it. From birth, culture provides us with blueprints or patterns that guide our behavior and attitudes toward situations we will most likely face in life. It provides us with a position in society and furnishes the means and training that enable us to assume that position. American culture, for example, establishes patterns for the good student, good mechanic, good housewife, and good businessman. Culture also provides us with tailor-made definitions and explanations of our origin, our nature, or even our relation to the rest of the universe. It tells us what is acceptable and unaccept-

able, normal and abnormal, permitted and prohibited, natural and unnatural, sacred and profane. Our cultural patterns establish standards of right and wrong that become a part of our personalities. Through culture, for example, we acquire a conscience, which floods us with guilt feelings when we violate group standards.

Likewise, culture provides patterns for satisfying biological and psychic needs. From birth, we learn culturally approved ways to satisfy our hunger pangs, quench our thirst, and fulfill our sexual needs. As culture satisfies needs, so, too, it often creates needs. A person's desire for a college degree, for example, may be stronger than his drive for food and recreation.

Culture, then, is transmitted; it is learned; it is our own doing. It establishes patterns; it standardizes behavior. Eminent social scientists such as Ruth Benedict and Émile Durkheim have maintained that we are what we are largely because our cultural influences are so telling. Although culture changes, sometimes swiftly, the average person is so saturated with it at maturity that he often fails to recognize the profound effect it has had on him, let alone free himself from its influences.

So even though culture does not totally determine our lives, it does furnish a framework within which our behavior is limited and directed. We are partly the products of that framework. Hence, when our cultural patterns conflict, we are apt to find that our behavior and loyalties conflict. For instance, there is one cultural pattern for the able businessman in America, another for the able politician. We expect the businessman to be aggressive, highly competitive, and capable of driving a hard bargain, while the politician is supposed to be public-spirited, selfless, and willing to sacrifice his own welfare for the public good. Then we insist that "government should be businesslike," and proceed to draw our governing officials from the business world, only to complain bitterly when they act like businessmen. Cultural patterns of the business world conflict with those of the political world.

Such conflicts abound within a culture. Persons who have been taught by their family and church that it is improper to drink alcoholic beverages often find it difficult to conform to job requirements that obligate them to take an occasional social drink. Children likewise find it difficult to follow one standard that advises them to stand up for their rights when at the same time they are asked to refrain from fighting and to treat other children with kindness and respect. Thus, if human contradiction and conflict bother us, we should look to culture to find out why. So say those who stress cultural factors as major determinants of human behavior.

The position of this school of thought is made even stronger by those studies that go beyond conflicts and differences within a culture to the conflicts between cultures. A comparison of two cultures will soon convince us that culture sometimes does astonishing things to people. For example, one of the authors had a chum in college who was born in the United States to Americans of Norwegian descent. He was taken to China as an infant. When he returned to the United States to enter college, he trotted everywhere he went, waved his arms wildly when excited, consumed large quantities of rice, and complained about American dishes and clothing. Except for physical features, he was Chinese. As a result, most Americans resented his behavior, especially because his physical characteristics led them to expect a different type of behavior. Consequently, many would purposely disagree with him, others would tease him, and a few were always trying to anger him in hopes that he would fight with them. The differences in cultural patterns made life miserable for him and were full of possibilities for conflict.

Margaret Mead makes essentially the same point by comparing the nonliterate cultures of two New Guinea tribes. Among the hostile Mundugumor, men are cannibalistic, fierce, dominating, and compete vigorously for women. Yet just a short distance away live the Tchambuli, whose men are effeminate, gossipy, curl their hair, and simply love to shop. Take a small child from the Mundugumor and place him in the Tchambuli tribe and he would soon take on the manner and characteristics of his new cultural environment. Return him to the Mundugumor after fifteen or twenty years, and he would very likely not be accepted. His own kin might even kill him. And even if they did not, he would probably find adjustment difficult and life miserable.

The influences of culture may be difficult to measure accurately, but they are unmistakably deep. Within a single culture, varied experiences and different learning processes produce varied attitudes, values, and behavior. These variations are even greater between cultures. The differences and conflicts in the cultural patterns will be reflected in the human behavior. Therefore, the members of this school of thought are certain that any attempt to discover the sources of conflict and contradiction in behavioral and loyalty patterns must account for cultural differences.

BLAME IT ON CULTURAL LAG

Among those who stress the cultural basis of human conflict and contradiction are a number of social scientists who place particular emphasis on *cultural lag* as a causative factor. As they see it, some cultural patterns change more rapidly than others, and hence, one type of behavior will lag behind the other and cause conflict. The renowned sociologist William F. Ogburn has suggested, for example, that many of our dilemmas are caused by a rapidly changing technology, which outstrips our morals and our traditional ways of doing things. We work profound and rapid changes on the physical world, then appear unable to adjust rapidly to those changes. Moth-eaten traditions and custom, tired slogans and catchwords, linger on to frustrate our ability to adapt. We invent automobiles, airplanes, and television; we isolate the atom and generate phenomenal physical power; we fire rockets into outer space. Yet no one tells us why or for what purpose. Science tells us how to do it, but not what to do with it. This was the substance of General Omar Bradley's complaint when he referred to America as a nation of nuclear giants and moral infants.

New types of aircraft become obsolete while still on the drafting board, yet we seem unable to develop adequate means for regulating air traffic. We are preparing to go to the moon—maybe Mars—yet we continue to think in terms of political boundaries set centuries ago by methods as old as the Sphinx. Ogburn and the philosopher John Dewey were convinced that this reluctance to depart from established ways of doing things, especially in the social sphere, cripples us in meeting the challenges produced by advancing technology. Our ability to cope with change thus lags behind change itself. This is another way of saying that humanity adjusts too slowly to the dynamic changes it produces. One weakness in this analysis, however, is its inability to account for the contradictions found in those situations where change is slowed to a snail's pace.

BLAME IT ON THE INDIVIDUAL

Another group of observers puts the basic reasons for contradiction and conflict back at the door of the individual. Many of these theorists have drawn their inspiration from Dr. Sigmund Freud, who, in his theories of psychoanalysis, contended that men had innate drives of love and hate. Freud was convinced that "... civilised society is perpetually menaced with disintegration through this primary hostility of men towards one another." In brief, an aggressive, cruel, and destructive instinct is basic to all human problems. Several members of the Freudian psychoanalytic school have attributed aggression to a neurotic tendency in many individuals to seek superiority and dominance over others, to idealize themselves into heroes, geniuses, and gods, or to strive for perfection. Others have claimed that aggressive behavior stemmed from a deep-seated longing to avoid isolation, loneliness, or a feeling of insignificance.

Many Freudians base their contentions on the proposition that human behavior is largely irrational. Arthur Koestler, the European novelist, is convinced, for instance, that men are far more irrational than we would care to believe. Most of our behavior, he avers, is based on emotion and not rational choice. Full of fears, hates, loves, desires, and even madness, men will often reject sound evidence and rely on inner feelings and whim. Accordingly, men are at best mere animals covered by a thin veneer of sophistication and civilized behavior. A person can be convinced that the use of tobacco is harmful—all scientific evidence and rational assessments may dictate that it will eventually kill him—yet he is not apt to stop smoking. Moreover, we laugh at the Eskimo who burns his totem after a bad day's fishing. But supposedly "rational" and "civilized" Americans do not laugh at their irrational tendency to burn in effigy their Secretary of State after the country has suffered some setback in foreign relations. Most students are often aware that more study would mean better marks, and that better marks might mean better jobs when they graduate; yet many refuse the rational choice in favor of entertainment or something else that suits their whims at the moment. We are far from being as rational as we believe ourselves to be, and this irrational tendency creates conflict.

Still other members of this school of thought see us as complex organisms full of *drives or states of restlessness that stimulate us to action.* Bodily tensions arising from glandular and muscular activity seek release; hungry men seek food; aggressive people search for ways to assert themselves. According to this view, culture is a human invention by which men are afforded an orderly means for satisfying basic drives and desires. It teaches us, for example, how to secure and prepare food to satisfy our hunger drive. In short, culture is more a result or product than a cause. A great deal of what we call culture, this group contends, is a framework in which our behavior is limited and directed. But both the behavior and the framework of culture in which it occurs have their primary sources in the individual human being himself. Knives and forks followed hunger pangs.

This group, then, admits that culture affects us profoundly. But since biological and psychic drives are basic to human behavior and hence, to human contradiction, they believe that we must first study the drives to discover the elemental sources of conflict. Modern scientific psychologists are not so bold in their assertions, however. They will concede that both culture and the physical structure of human beings are important, but they are reluctant to make dogmatic assertions until they know more about the problem. They know, for example, that a group of persons with large adrenal glands is inclined to be more aggressive than a group with small adrenals. But we must know a great deal more about human beings before we dare to make broad generalizations and attribute causes to behavior.

BLAME IT ON WHOM?

If we heed the counsel of the modern psychologist, then, we must postpone an attempt to assign causation until the time arrives when we have sufficient information to make valid generalizations. It is worth noticing, however, that intelligent men have made sincere and, in many cases, fruitful attempts to explore the wilderness of human relations and have held up to our gaze several prisms of varying hue and refraction through which we can view the baffling problems of human contradiction and conflict. We have mentioned but a few of these approaches, and many of the scholars we have alluded to have, of course, used more than one approach in their studies.

LOYALTY AND VALUES

At the beginning of this section of the book, we defined loyalty as faithfulness to one's self, another person, a duty, a cause, a principle, or a goal. And we also said that people tender their loyalty from a sense of moral obligation, a feeling of common interest, a recognition that others are in control, or out of fear of the consequences. We value the things to which we are steadfast or loyal. We are loyal to our parents, for example, because we have been taught to honor them, because we identify our happiness and best interests with them, because we respect their authority, or because we are afraid of them. Loyalties, then, are anchored to values.

WHAT ARE VALUES?

Values, as we have already seen, are the ideas, beliefs, principles, or preferences

In modern Bombay, ancient core values continue to invest cows with a sacred and privileged status.

that we prize. They include objects, principles, and goals to which we aspire. They provide us with something to *live by* and to *live for*. If a man values the esteem of his fellow Americans, he will seek position and wealth and display conspicuously the fruits of his wealth, such as a luxury car, a country house, or a wife with the proper social standing. He will value and tender loyalty to these things and the institutions that gave him a chance to obtain them: the free enterprise system that permitted him to pile up his wealth; the political system that protects it; his family and friends who helped him on the way up. His loyalties are thus likely to be a function of his values.

What such a person values and is loyal to will depend heavily, in turn, on what he believes will best accomplish his goals. Although one person believes that his political system is protecting his opportunity to acquire wealth, another person may feel that it is preventing him from making money. The latter may feel that those at the top of the political order are killing his chances by heavily taxing or severely regulating his business. Thus, values, loyalties, and beliefs not only are always closely related but may become serious sources of conflict between

persons harboring two opposing loyalty patterns, such as the two above.

CORE VALUES

We have been talking about values in terms of individuals. But as social scientists have told us, a great number of such values are common to an entire society. They are a part of our cultural baggage. A large segment of the population of India, for example, believes in reincarnation, or the return of man's soul to earth after death, perhaps in the form of a cow or some other animal. As a result, a unique system of principles and values is attached to cows in India. Unlike her sisters in other parts of the world, she is not milked or butchered but instead is a privileged creature to be respected and even worshiped. Thus, belief in reincarnation in India has given rise to a set of values that greatly affect an entire way of life. If the Indian government wants to retain the loyalty of its people, it had better treat cows with respect as long as its citizens cling to these values.

Values common to a national group or to a wide segment of the population, as in the above case, can be called *core values*. Sometimes these core values cut across national boundaries to encompass a large portion of the world's population. We saw earlier the shock that Darwin gave our forebears a century ago when he challenged some deeply cherished religious values of the Western world. His suggestion that men were akin to apes and not divinely created reverberated from Moscow to San Francisco and stirred protest from Oslo to Naples. He had contradicted Scripture, and thus had called into question certain fundamental moral, legal, and philosophical precepts of the Western world. Little wonder that there was such a commotion.

Every culture contains core values that are closely allied to its core loyalties, and when a culture experiences a conflict in values, a corresponding conflict in loyalties is apt to accompany it. What, then, are the core values in our American culture, and what are some of the conflicts that arise within our loyalty and value pattern? In short, what underlies our national character and from what sources do many of our conflicts and frustrations stem?

AMERICAN TRAITS AND VALUE ORIENTATIONS

Some people find it is fun to talk about themselves; others find it difficult. It is even more difficult to talk about a whole people. What is the American character? the American mind? No one has ever seen either. Actually, there is no "thinking mind" apart from the individual nervous systems of the people who make up a community. To think of a national state as a moving, thinking, and living organism is to indulge in utter nonsense.

Yet a national character there surely is. There are traits of a whole people that distinguish them rather sharply as a group from other peoples. Germans are extremely thorough and precise; Englishmen are sensitive about their privacy; Chinese are noticeably respectful to their elders; and Spaniards love a siesta. Not everyone in a national group may share a particular cultural trait, but the behavior of the great majority adds up to some distinguishing characteristics. We have a tendency, in fact, to acquire the habits and actions of those around us. We tend to act like them, think in their idiom, and even look like them. An American is easily spotted in England, if for nothing other than his loud necktie. The little things often give us away.

AN AMERICAN PORTRAIT *

Although largely the sons of immigrants (30 million Americans in 1860, many of immigrant stock, had absorbed another 30 million immigrants by 1930), American soldiers during two world wars struck Europeans as being a distinct type. Geoffrey Gorer gave a live indication of our distinctive national character when he dedicated his book, *The American People*, to "Erling C. Olson, Jr., half Norwegian, half Czech, good American." We are an amalgam of nationalities forged into a distinct type.

And what is this type? The American is friendly, optimistic, self-confident, practical-minded. He is genial and self-satisfied. He believes progress is inevitable if men work at it. For him, this is the best of all possible worlds. He thinks that he has the best of all governments, the most virtuous of all societies, and the best-managed of all economies. Direct contact with good plumbing in

---

* For this portrait the authors are indebted to G. Gorer, *The American People* (New York: Norton, 1948); H. Commager, "Portrait of an American," in *Years of the Modern* (New York: Longmans, Green, 1949); H. Laski, *The American Democracy* (New York: Viking, 1948); and G. Myrdal, *An American Dilemma* (New York: Harper, 1944).

Germany during two great wars did not disturb his conviction that he enjoys the best plumbing in the world. And when bigger and better plumbing is devised, Americans will devise it.

The American likes things to be efficient, businesslike, and big. He distrusts theory and admires experience. When two Americans meet, they usually exchange experiences. The man with experience normally gets the job. For the American, a life of contemplation is wasteful, even slothful, and those who think and dream are suspect. Restless and anxious, he prefers doing to being. He has no fixed social station in life and seldom entertains the idea of ending life where he started it. The American is mobile, moving from job to job, town to town, frontier to frontier. His is a life of acting and doing. He is more apt to ask little Johnny what he *did* in school than what he *learned*. Action, he feels, is the heart of life.

American culture is a materialistic culture. We are quantitative. Our taxi drivers proudly point out to their passengers the longest street or the highest building in the world. We have a tendency to compute everything in terms of numbers, even our churches and art. Things must be *big* in America. Inventive, ingenious, and experimental, we revel in our machinery and gadgets, especially the new ones. Wherever a new building is going up, sidewalk superintendents abound.

Casual, informal, careless, the American seeks the quick route, admires speed, is "lawless in small matters," anxious to avoid "red tape," slurs his speech, wastes his resources, piles up a huge public debt, and is little perturbed about public litter or noise. His is a luxury of carelessness.

It is utterly naive to suggest that any list of traits would completely describe us or our culture. The one we have just run through is merely suggestive. It is derived, however, from the reports of many observers of the American scene, both domestic and foreign.

THE AMERICAN DEMOCRATIC FAITH

Probably no American belief is more deep-seated than the belief in "democracy." We hammer at it and are hammered by it. Professors teach it; parsons preach it; we all pay homage to it. What is democracy anyway? Practically every American gives it his own unique definition. For most of us, the things that are American are also democratic. The way we do things is the democratic way to do them. If we like something, we are apt to believe it is democratic; if we dislike it, then we may consider it undemocratic. Democracy is part of our ideology.

One of our finest historians, Ralph Gabriel, calls this democratic ideology an American "faith." Agreeing with him, Gunnar Myrdal, a Swedish sociologist, calls it a creed. This faith, which seems to saturate our history, is based on an historic belief that dates back to the eighteenth-century American, who was confident that God had created us and provided us with laws to live by. For this early American, and for many Americans since, these laws were unchangeable and everlasting. It was man's duty to use his intelligence to discover these laws and live by them. All men, all governments, all human action should be subject to this higher law of God (or of Nature and Nature's God, according to some). In brief, there was presumably a *law above law*, and ours was a government guided by a law higher than the dictates of any ruler or any human law. Government was limited by a Constitution that defined governmental powers rigidly. This Constitution conformed as nearly as possible to the higher, or moral, law descended from God or written in Nature. When a government flouted or ignored this higher law, men had a right to change the government; if thwarted in their attempt to change it, they had a right to revolt.

This ideology placed Americans historically on the side against government. It followed quite naturally that government was a necessary evil that encroached on our freedoms unless it was kept in check. Actions of the government were thus suspect, and men had to be protected from them as much as possible. Our constitutions (both state and national) have consequently become instruments through which we limit governmental powers and keep governments from interfering with our rightful freedoms that issue from the higher moral law. .

According to this higher moral law, men are *free* and endowed with inalienable rights, which Gabriel describes as the second doctrine of the democratic faith. Since most Americans have historically believed that man was created in God's own image, each individual person must be respected for his own dignity and worth.

Accordingly, every individual is entitled to freedom of speech, association, religion, and press. Further, all men must be assured of equality of opportunity, equal standing before the law, and a right to have governments conduct their processes according to known, fair, accepted, and time-honored methods. Governments must not be arbitrary, for we in America have historically affirmed the central value and importance of the individual. All institutions exist to serve him; he does not exist to serve them. *The individual is primary.*

Gabriel claims that this historic principle of the "free individual" is written indelibly on the American conscience. Nearly all Americans have long believed that progress is inevitable where men are free. Progress depends on freedom. It follows that each man should be afforded the opportunity to realize his potentialities and to carve out his own destiny. In economic affairs this attitude implies that there should be as little government interference as possible. The business of government is to keep out of business and leave men free to struggle for the bounty of nature. Even today the average American fears the regimentation of government more than the regimentation of industry or labor unions.

As we shall see later on, even the most ardent advocates of governmental regulation have believed that government should take no more than the minimum action necessary to do the job. Many New Dealers, for example, thought that the government should concern itself with social and economic matters only in great national emergencies. The American's world has been a free world from his standpoint. It has been a world in which men could flex their muscles and be masters of their own destinies.

Consequently, Americans have traditionally been highly sensitive to the exercise of political power and have seized almost every possible means to shackle government. They have divided and dispersed political power as widely as possible in hopes that it will not become concentrated in the hands of a few. From the Frenchman Montesquieu, they borrowed the idea of "separation of powers" and proceeded to isolate the legislative function from the executive, and both from the judicial. In all except one instance, national and state legislatures presently are divided into two equal houses. Finally, Americans have appropriated the idea of *federalism*. In their written Constitution, they have methodically divided powers between two levels of government. The national government has been given those powers that the Constitution delegates to it specifically or by implication (e.g., power to coin money, regulate interstate commerce, and conduct foreign affairs); the states exercise all the rest (e.g., power to establish and maintain schools, roads, and public-welfare institutions and to guard public health, morals, and safety). Concerted efforts are made to keep the domain of each level of government separate. Grants of money by the national government to the states for the construction of roads or the support of education are viewed with alarm in many quarters. Invariably the cry goes up that such efforts constitute an invasion by the national government of the *reserved powers* of the states. The national government, the attitude runs, must be kept within the limits of its *delegated* powers.

The federal principle and the idea of a separation of powers are so firmly established as part of the democratic faith that it is difficult for Americans to believe that any government could be democratic without them. In short, democracy is considered a matter of keeping all political power from settling in one place. Americans believe, with Lord Acton, that "power corrupts and absolute power corrupts absolutely."

A further check on government comes from the cherished principle of *popular sovereignty*—one man, one vote. Government derives its power from the consent of the governed; otherwise it is illegitimate. Those who rule are chosen by the vote of the people or appointed by someone who is elected. Throughout our history we have gradually broadened the number of qualified voters to include practically all our citizens, both male and female, who have reached their majority. To deny the ballot to anyone qualified to vote is considered undemocratic. For a great many Americans, voting and democracy are synonymous. We have been so zealous in this belief in the past that some states even enfranchised aliens. Americans have seen few crusades more exciting than the one that granted women the privilege of voting. Americans are convinced that a person who cannot vote cannot be free.

The third doctrine of the American democratic faith is what Gabriel calls the "mission of America." Not only must we be democratic, but it is our mission in life, our duty, to carry the message of democracy to the rest of the world. Gabriel contends that Americans throughout their history have been

confident that such was their destiny. Having left Europe behind them, Americans were certain that they were carving out of the wilderness, a citadel of democracy which would serve as a beacon for all mankind. Our citadel would be the model for future democracies everywhere. America had a destiny! Longfellow had no doubts:

> Thou, too, sail on, O ship of State!
> Sail on, O Union, strong and great!
> Humanity with all its fears,
> With all the hopes of future years,
> Is hanging breathless on thy fate!

Longfellow was by no means alone. Nearly every writer in the nineteenth century, except Melville, joined him. The historian George Bancroft was absolutely certain that God had made it a part of his grand design to have America become a democratic laboratory for the entire world. Supreme Court Justice Joseph Story was convinced as early as 1826 that the rest of the world was catching the spirit of our institutions. Poets such as Emerson and Whitman captured America's imagination in their hymns to our future greatness. We were a lamp on the hill; we would teach by example; we would invite the world to come and be like us. We preferred, however, to push our cause by means other than force of arms.

Yet the depth of this faith is shown by our willingness even to go to war on its account. Before the nineteenth century had run its course, Admiral Dewey had taken "democracy" to Manila on a battleship. Three bloody years of war followed before the Filipinos accepted our idea of "democracy." Since 1900 we have entered two world wars to "save the world for democracy." Even today one of our severest disappointments is the knowledge that there are people in the world who do not want to be like us. We are apt to sulk and be unfriendly toward those who will have nothing to do with our kind of democracy.

Thus, ours has been a history of promise

and hope, one in which men envisioned a bright, glorious future not just for themselves but for all mankind. President Lincoln spoke for all Americans, living and dead, when he affirmed that the Declaration of Independence meant happiness and freedom "not alone to the people of this country, but hope for the world for all future time." Here a beloved leader expressed a supreme value for all Americans, a confidence in history and in themselves, a faith to live by. It was a dream, a beautiful dream, the American dream.

BELIEF IN PROGRESS AND SUCCESS

Sturdily anchored to this hope and promise of the American dream is a belief in *progress* and *success*. Both words represent ultimate values for Americans. To progress and be successful is to be virtuous. Historically, we have kept a firm grip on Jefferson's abounding confidence in the "perfectibility of man." Given freedom, Americans have believed that men were capable of improving themselves and the world around them. How often have we heard, "All things work together for the good," or "God helps those who help themselves." We think progress is inevitable when we work at it. It is nearly always better to live today than yesterday.

Progress has meant success in America, and the successful people have been considered progressive. The successful boy in school is often the one who shows the most progress. If he jumps from an F to a B level in his work, his teachers will probably praise him more for his efforts than they will the steady B performer. What mother fails to admonish her child to show progress and be successful? It sometimes matters very little how someone succeeds, as long as he does. America insists that every person "get ahead," and most of us run fast to make sure that we do.

MATERIALISM

Certainly Americans attach great value to what they believe to be the symbols of progress and success. Most obvious and easily understood, of course, are the things we see, touch, and hear, such as a tall building, a huge bulldozer, a shiny new car, a

"I want it because it's a symbol of success, prestige, acceptance . . . and to make my neighbor insanely jealous."

piano, or a fur coat. These things are tangible and easily appreciated. Every new design, every invention, and every change in our material universe symbolizes progress and success. Hence, prestige goes with the acquisition of material goods and benefits. We honor those persons among us who pile up material goods and comforts, and those who work wonders on our physical world to provide us with these things. Sometimes we even collect objects we do not need or want so that others will know we can do it and admire us for it. We conspicuously and wastefully consume our material wealth so others will look up to us. The economist Thorstein Veblen, called this tendency "conspicuous consumption."

Ours is a material and quantitative existence. We revere the big, the best, the newest, the most. We tend to believe that knowledge is valuable only when it can produce new wonders for us to consume or display. We are so quantitative, in fact, that we sometimes heap praise and admiration on those students who can grind out the most facts on their examinations. It matters not whether the facts are a clutter, or whether the person has a junkyard for a mind. We honor the accumulation, not the ability to use it. When bigger and better minds are developed, Americans will develop them.

BELIEF IN CAPITALISM

Normally we attribute our great material wealth to the workings of capitalism.

We are quite certain that capitalism has made America what it is. We are equally certain that the doctrine of the "free individual" and the lack of government interference in economic affairs also have contributed to our success and progress. Beliefs in the virtue of a "free market," the law of supply and demand, and the protection of private property all add up to capitalism, which seems to go hand in hand with democracy. For many Americans, democracy is capitalism and capitalism is democracy. We even speak freely about a capitalistic form of government. Whatever else capitalism represents, it is certainly part and parcel of the American democratic faith.

From the concept of moral law to the doctrine of the free individual, the mission of America, and the theory of capitalism, the American has a creed, an ideology, which may or may not conform with reality. It does, however, shape his goals in life and help him explain the world in which he moves.

DOUBTS AND FISSURES

Our historic democratic faith may seem firm, yet there are many cracks in it. One serious fissure appeared in the 1930's when many Americans, disillusioned by the depression, joined communist and fascist movements. The deplorable economic conditions at the time may have been an underlying cause of their action. But many people have since questioned the strength of our ideals because so many persons criticized and strayed from the democratic creed. Was the American dream weakening? It may have been, as some have suggested, that those who defected believed so strongly in progress and other American ideals that they could not endure the conditions and were therefore seeking new routes to realize their ideals. The reeling national income, the soup lines,

and the widespread unemployment at the time certainly left the impression that America was going backward economically rather than forward. We were not progressing! But America had endured depressions before without such widespread defection to foreign political and social philosophies, had it not? The question weighed heavily on the American conscience.

Following World War II the fissure widened. Faced with the responsibilities of world leadership and the need to stay Russian aggression, Americans became more security-conscious and more concerned about internal threats to their way of life. A number of Americans, led by Senator Joseph McCarthy of Wisconsin, demanded the removal from government positions of all persons who had ever been affiliated in any way with communist-dominated and communist-front organizations. It sometimes mattered little what the person's connections with a totalitarian movement had been, or whether he had long since left the movement. Any connection, past or present, cast suspicion on him unless he had turned into

"... and if the people don't want to be free, by Judas, we'll force 'em to be free."

an informer. A wave of sensational congressional investigations followed, security tests were imposed, and loyalty oaths were required both inside and out of the government. The Smith Act, passed just prior to the war to deal with subversives, was vigorously enforced. The past and present activities of countless persons from all walks of life—government, business, education, and religion—were scrutinized.

The fissure penetrated to the very core of the American value system, calling the Constitution itself into question when it was contended that no one should be allowed to

invoke the constitutional protection that grants a person immunity from testifying against himself. Extremists argued that constitutional protections should not be extended to those who sought to destroy the Constitution. Their opponents retorted that protections had always been granted the accused, even to the Nazi saboteurs during World War II. After all, a man is entitled to have the government prove its case against him. But others felt that the threat to our security was so great we could not take any chances, even with free speech and free association. A number advocated labeling fringe groups and denying certain kinds of employment to those who joined such movements. Nor would some brook radical and seemingly dangerous ideas. For example, in some cases communist literature and books considered un-American were weeded from libraries to protect children and unsuspecting adults. One opinion survey indicated that many Americans would not buy the products of a company sponsoring a radio or television artist suspected of being "leftist."

An upshot of all this was a growing concern about the attitudes, values, and behavior of American youth. Coming almost as a revelation to some people was the discovery that a large segment of our youth grows to adulthood without ever understanding, knowing, or often caring about its religious or political values. As a result, liberals and conservatives alike advocated reforms for the schoolroom, church, and the family. Some state legislatures, for example, passed laws requiring students to take more courses in civics and politics, not necessarily to teach them more about the realities of political behavior, but to make absolutely certain that America's children would be steeped in democratic values.

One major controversy raged over civil rights, however—especially the rights of free speech, thought, and association. To challenge these was to challenge the very cornerstone of the democratic faith, for as Justice Holmes had pointed out, a free society must brook opposition and even the most threatening ideas to be called free. The reaction to those who would deny civil rights was sharp indeed. A more liberal-minded camp charged that by their denial of civil rights they were stifling freedom and that they were using totalitarian tactics to defeat totalitarian ideas. They also pointed out that many innocent Americans were having their reputations damaged and even their pocketbooks threatened by wild accusations and "witch hunts." Such activity, the argument ran, destroyed rather than preserved the Constitution and the democratic faith.

While both of the above camps were concerned over how to preserve the American dream, other persons withdrew from the cultural pattern or rebelled against it. One such group—the "beat generation"—has attracted a great deal of attention. Beatniks, as they are called, are not necessarily dope addicts, and they are certainly not criminals, ordinary juvenile delinquents, or even juvenile in many cases. Many are adults with families and jobs, and although they defy many social standards, most of them do not steal, fight, murder, or engage in other

forms of behavior typical of criminals. They are in open rebellion against social standards, especially some of the standards that surround the democratic faith. For example, they bitterly oppose the businessman's standards of success. They hate the business-man—"the fount from whence all blessings flow, enterpriser *par excellence*, organizer of progress, job-maker, charity-giver, endower of churches and universities and patron of the arts, who has given us the highest standard of living. . . ." * They will have no truck with Rotarians, Elks, Masons, Babbitts, precinct workers, reformers, and "joiners," and they forswear all materialistic values. They want no mortgage, nice home, or other symbol of prestige and success. In their personal appearance they symbolize their rejection of the American's obsession with cleanliness and standards of health. Probably the clearest indicator of the nature of their rebellion is found in the answer one beatnik gave to a business executive who wanted to hire her at a substantial salary. The beatnik's reply was forthright: "I will sweep your floors, clean your shoes, or empty your garbage, but I will not lie for you, cheat for you, or wear

* L. Lipton, *The Holy Barbarians* (New York: Messner, 1959), p. 147.

In the sequestered surroundings of their "pads," coffee houses, and other reclusive establishments, the beatniks reject American core values as hypocrisies and build a new life and value system, complete with music, art, and poetry.

a false smile to get ahead." This voice speaks from conviction. It is the voice of someone who rejects certain behavioral standards and social graces as monstrous hypocrisies and therefore refuses to uphold them. The beat generation's refusal to conform to social standards often appears barbaric, but if beatniks are barbarians, they are what Lawrence Lipton calls them, "holy barbarians," who cast certain doubts on our loyalty system.

Nothing produces more sudden, searing heat than a threat to our loyalty structure. Countless agitated persons have given countless agitated reasons for our loyalty crises. One group charges that American religious foundations have crumbled in the face of an advancing science. Certainly our religious convictions have been seriously challenged by the findings of science, and this challenge, many people believe, has forced religion to retreat and has seriously threatened those aspects of our democratic faith that are rooted in religious belief. Today we are called a religious nation without religious convictions. More and more people, it is said, go to church, not because they believe but because it is proper, or in order to "belong" in their society, or simply to be seen there. Without belief in the religious doctrines on which our democratic faith was founded, it is contended that democracy itself will become a hollow formula and our loyalty structure will be shaken to its very foundation.

Others contend that our loyalty problems can be traced to the disillusionment occasioned by two world wars that did not save the world for democracy. For some, it is difficult to believe that we ever fought to preserve democracy. So proponents of this view stoutly maintain that the resulting disillusionment over our inability to defend and spread democracy, some believe, shatters the American dream, deprives us of our mission in the world, and kills our enthusiasm for the democratic faith.

Still others tend to blame our loyalty dilemmas on family weaknesses. They decry the loss of parental discipline, the working mother who leaves her child to the care of others, and the high divorce rate. These people maintain that the family, most basic of all social institutions, has crumbled, and with it have crumbled the institutions and loyalties it maintains.

Another interesting contention finds us no longer striving for democracy. Rather, to these observers, democracy is already fully developed and mature. Whereas democracy was once something that all Americans were perfecting, to some it is now an accomplished fact, and these people claim that our loyalty problems arise from efforts by radicals and liberals who want to change things. It follows that those who criticize or seek to change institutions are subversive or un-American.

A fruitful line of attack might involve an investigation into inherent conflicts in the democratic faith itself. The moral law, after all, commits us to the doctrine of the free individual, which places us on the side against government. Public officials must be feared and watched. Yet the same moral law also commits us to the principle that democratic government is the best government on earth since it is a "government of the people, by the people, and for the people." We thus hold government to be suspect and a threat, our politics to be "dirty" and "corrupt," yet present both as a model for all men to adopt. It is, in fact, our mission to carry the message of democracy to the rest of the world. There is something very contradictory in this posture—something quite disturbing to our loyalties.

The whole concept of "freedom," furthermore, is filled with contradiction. If a person is to be free, he must in some way be protected from those who would deny his freedom. Each man's freedom must be restricted to keep him from infringing on the freedom of others. In the words of the great English statesman Edmund Burke, "Liberty, too, must be limited in order to be possessed." Or as the venerable Justice Holmes remarked, our freedom of speech does not entitle us to cry "fire!" in a crowded theater. Paradoxically, we look to a superior agency to secure our freedom and, at the same time, we view this agency as the greatest threat to our freedoms. This attitude, too, is contradictory.

ARE WE HYPOCRITES?

Continuing our analysis, we find contradictions in the democratic faith that make us appear hypocritical. No belief is more deeply imbedded in the American dream, for instance, than the belief in human equality. Men stand before their Maker, and before American law as well, in equal relation and dignity. We boast of the equality of opportunity and the fact that every man can rise from office boy to company president. Every mother dreams of having a son who might become president of the United States. Yet our legal procedures are very often too expensive to afford equal justice to the poor, and we are all quite aware that the boy born in a little West Virginia coal-mining town does not have the same opportunity as the chap reared on Sheridan Road in Chicago. No matter how we try to explain the fact away, it still comes home to haunt us and makes us feel a bit hypocritical.

The equality we applaud and believe in is not always a fact of life. Certainly we know that the Negro is not on an equal plane with his Caucasian brethren. The second-class citizenship of the Negro, says Gunnar Myrdal, is perhaps the heaviest weight on the American conscience. It certainly challenges our democratic faith. Long segregated in his schools and on streetcars and buses, zoned into poorer sections of our cities (in both the North and South), denied the ballot in many areas and required to be content with inferior services and accommodations, the Negro's position makes a mockery of our belief in equality and our democratic faith.

We cherish, too, the idea of political equality—one man, one vote—only to see the halls of government invaded by powerful interests and lobbies who obtain (even buy) the protection of government for their own selfish ends. Businessmen are quick to complain when government invades their domain, but think nothing of trying to use government to further their own selfish interests. They seek to advance their own ends at the public expense by supporting candidates favorable to them and bringing influence to bear on those people already in office. American belief does not always conform to American practice.

Finally, there is an apparent hypocrisy (or lack of conformity between belief and practice) in our federal system. As we have seen, governmental powers are divided constitutionally between the national and state governments. This arrangement divides our political obligation and loyalties. We are obligated to the states in some instances and to the national government in others. But what about our loyalties to the states? What Kansan would die for Kansas? Americans are barely conscious of their states, state boundaries, or state officials; many do not recognize their state flag, flower, or other symbols; and very few take a live interest in state government. Yet we complain bitterly about the condition of state government, bemoan its ineffectiveness and the loss of state functions to the national government.

No one need infer, of course, that loyalty to a state should involve a willingness to die for it. But Robert E. Lee had no doubts about whether Virginia or the Union came first. Certainly, citizens must feel more loyalty to their states than they do now if states' rights and federalism are to continue to have meaning. In the past, states have been little more than tools of special interests who ran them for their own private benefit (e.g., railroads in many states, cattlemen's groups in others, and dairy associations and farm groups in still others). To ask that powers be returned to the states and the people, only to have those powers fall back into the hands of special interests, would also make a mockery of democratic ideals.

"We the people" did ordain and evolve a democratic faith. So say the historians and the social scientists. Fraught with contradiction and inconsistency, this faith nevertheless has served as a rallying point for our loyalties and values. It has helped us explain the buzzing, confused world around us; it has helped give meaning and purpose to our existence. It has served South Carolinian and New Yorker, businessman and laborer, Christian and Jew, immigrant and native born, rich and poor, in war and in peace, in bad times and good. To serve so many purposes, to adapt to each person's requirements, where each has a different background and experience, to mean all things to all men, it would have to be very flexible—even contradictory. Very possibly, the contradictory character of our democratic faith is its greatest virtue, and inconsistency the source of its great vitality.

SOME WORDS OF SUMMARY

The inconsistencies and contradictions in our personal and institutional loyalties and ways of life have been the source of a great deal of frustration and the object of intensive investigation. Some authorities explain the dilemma in terms of human nature, others attribute it to the fall of man, many point to cultural lag, still others to the difference between individual behavior and group behavior, to a maladjustment between the cultural and environmental heritage, or to the individual himself. All these approaches help us understand our social problems and the confusing array of cultural and personal conflicts in loyalties and values that threaten our unity.

American culture, like any culture, has certain distinguishing traits. Among the more pronounced is the American democratic faith, which is rooted in a deep-seated belief in God, the existence of a higher moral law, and the essential dignity of the individual. Doctrines of this faith include the idea of a moral law, the principle of the free individual, and the mission of America. Securely anchored to the moral law, the principle of limited government or constitutionalism, together with the doctrine of the free individual, establishes safeguards or rights against governmental interference with individual liberty. Through the medium of a written Constitution we guarantee these fundamental rights to the individual, disperse and limit the powers of government through the principles of separation of powers, federalism, and popular sovereignty. The final doctrine of this faith, the mission of America, involves the conviction that Americans are destined to carry the message of democracy to all mankind. Securely fastened to these doctrines of the democratic faith are beliefs in progress and success, a materialistic outlook, and a capitalistic frame of reference.

Those American experiences indicating a weakening in our loyalty structure, such as the civil rights-national security controversy and the outright rejection of American values and standards by some groups, have called forth a wide variety of diagnoses. One of the more persistent is the charge that science has destroyed the religious foundations of the democratic faith.

Another approach stresses American disillusionment over the apparent impossibility of making the world democratic. Three other approaches stress the supposed collapse of the family structure, the desire to change our present way of life, and the inherent conflicts within the democratic faith itself. Certainly, the conflicts between American action and American belief leave all Americans open to the charge of hypocrisy. We endorse but do not uphold the principle of equality, and we applaud states' rights but tender little loyalty to the states themselves. But perhaps we should expect our ideals to be contradictory, for they must appeal to many people with a variety of backgrounds. They must be all things to all men!

FURTHER ROADS TO LEARNING

GENERAL ACCOUNTS

R. Benedict, *Patterns of Culture* (New York: Mentor Books, 1950). This valuable book stresses that men are products of their cultures.

J. Cuber and R. Harper, *Problems in American Society* (New York: Holt, 1951). A sociological treatment of values in conflict.

J. Dewey, *The Public and Its Problems* (New York: Holt, 1927), and his *A Common Faith* (New Haven: Yale University Press, 1934). A leading philosopher pins his faith to shared experience, democratic methods, and a scientific approach.

F. Sheen, *Peace of Soul* (New York: McGraw-Hill, 1949). An American Catholic statement on personality integration.

B. Skinner, *Walden Two* (New York: Macmillan, 1948). A psychologist would resolve our difficulties by scientifically conditioning and psychologically adjusting the individual.

A. Toynbee, *Civilization on Trial* (New York: Oxford University Press, 1949). A study of the careers of cultures.

R. Weaver, *Ideas Have Consequences* (Chicago: The University of Chicago Press, 1948). Are civilized men moral idiots?

L. Whyte, *The Next Development in Man* (New York: Mentor Books, 1950). This man pins his hopes on our ability to live in harmony with nature, to develop community consciousness, and to slough off our guilt feelings.

SPECIAL STUDIES

The reader's attention is called to a number of delightful works depicting the "American character": D. Brogan, *The American Character* (New York: Knopf, 1944); J. Chase, *Years of the Modern* (New York: Longmans, Green, 1949); L. Coleman, "What Is American: A Study of Alleged American Traits," *Social Forces*, Vol. 19 (May, 1941); G. Gorer, *The American People* (New York: Norton, 1948); B. Perry, *Characteristically American* (New York: Knopf, 1949).

T. Arnold, *Symbols of Government* (New Haven: Yale University Press, 1935). A biting statement on American values and institutions.

E. Barker, *The Character of England* (Oxford: Clarendon Press, 1947). A good characterization of a foreign people.

H. Cantril, "Don't Blame It on Human Nature," *The New York Times Magazine*, June 6, 1947. An article about our tendency to blame human nature for our woes.

M. Curti, *The Roots of American Loyalty* (New York: Columbia University Press, 1946). A sound treatment of historical background of some of our loyalty patterns.

S. Freud, *Civilization and its Discontents* (London: Hogarth, 1930). Our sense of guilt and drive for self-destruction prevent progress and happiness.

R. Gabriel, *The Course of American Democratic Thought*, 2nd ed. (New York: Ronald, 1956). The classic statement on the American democratic faith.

G. Le Bon, *The Crowd* (London: Macmillan, 1925). On crowd psychology.

L. Lipton, *The Holy Barbarians* (New York: Messner, 1959). All about the beatniks.

M. Mead, *And Keep Your Powder Dry* (New York: Morrow, 1942). Provides some excellent descriptions of American value conflicts.

H. Meyers, *Are Men Equal?* (Ithaca, New York: Cornell University Press, 1955). A very challenging statement on equalitarian values.

G. Myrdal, *An American Dilemma* (New York: Harper, 1944). The finest work ever done on the American Negro problem. Written by an eminent Swedish sociologist, this book includes an analysis of the "American dream."

R. Niebuhr, *Moral Man and Immoral Society* (New York: Scribner, 1936). Niebuhr's thesis on the difference between the individual's behavior inside the group and outside it.

W. Ogburn, *Social Change* (New York: Viking, 1950). The authoritative statement on "cultural lag."

D. Potter, *People of Plenty* (Chicago: The University of Chicago Press, 1954). This book tells how historians have dealt with the American character.

S. Stouffer, *et al.*, *The American Soldier*, 2 vols. (Princeton: Princeton University Press, 1949). An analysis of American soldiers' attitudes during World War II.

R. Williams, Jr., *American Society: A Sociological Interpretation* (New York: Knopf, 1951). A readable and scholarly analysis of American values.

FICTION AND DRAMA

J. Cooper, *The Deerslayer* (New York: Harper, 1926). An idealistic story of the blending of democratic values and the noble qualities of early American Indian society.

E. Forster, *A Passage to India* (New York: Random House, 1940). Completely explosive story involving value conflicts of the British in India.

E. O'Neill, *The Iceman Cometh*, 2nd ed. (New York: Random House, 1946). Our troubles result from our refusal to forego comforting illusions and face reality.

M. Twain, *A Connecticut Yankee in King Arthur's Court* (New York: Random House, 1949). An uproariously funny skit dramatizing the cultural differences between nineteenth-century America and the Old World.

FILMS

Brainwashing (Prudential Insurance Company of America, 1958, 60 min., sound, black and white). How the communists change attitudes, beliefs, and loyalties.

Devil Is a Sissy (Teaching Film Custodians, 1936, 9 min., sound, black and white). The son of a man who is about to be electrocuted faces a serious loyalty dilemma.

Guilty or Not Guilty—The Nuremberg Trials (Film Forum Foundation, 1948, 29½ min., sound, black and white). Treats incidentally the loyalty conflict faced by the German political and military leaders who served the Nazi regime.

National Security Versus Individual Rights (McGraw-Hill, 1955, 27 min., sound, black and white). The news commentator Edward R. Murrow uses an actual case study to demonstrate differences between a loyalty and a security risk.

Our

Industrial World

THEME

*The contemporary world is a place where man's ancient loyalties . . .
have been seriously shaken by the impact of modern* industrialism
on his traditional customs, ideas, and patterns of living. . . .

The Industrial Revolution
and the Modern World

Modern industrialism, majestic
and dynamic, has played a vital role
in creating our modern world. Such factors
as prosperity and political
and military superiority are obviously
related to industrial strength.

In the preceding section, we say that modern man moves in a world of personal loyalties—to self, family, class, religion, government, and country. Now we shall explore another world, one that cuts across our patterns of personal and institutional loyalties and vitally affects every facet of our personal lives—the world of the machine. Consider how closely our way of life is attuned to that whole complex of machines, factories, mines, and railroads that we loosely call *industry*. No modern country would long exist without machines; no city could survive one week without modern roads and rails; no person from an industrial civilization would long feel at home in a pre-industrial community. One of the very best descriptions of *industrialism*, or the way of life associated with power-driven machinery and modern transportation, has been set down by the well-known British economist and Oxford scholar G. D. H. Cole:

Industrialism is fundamentally an affair of productive technique. It is based upon the discovery and exploitation of improved methods of producing wealth, primarily in the processes of manufacture but also to an increasing extent in agriculture and in the extractive industries yielding primary products. It is closely associated with an increase in the scale of production, with the development of capitalistic methods in both manufacture and marketing and with the employment of wage labor. Its secondary effects have included hitherto a concentration of the population in densely inhabited urban areas, a very rapid increase in the volume of international trade, much lending of capital for development by the more advanced countries to those less advanced and a very rapid increase in the number and social importance of the middle classes, including those engaged in the professions as well as in the administration and supervision of industry and commerce.[*]

What we are dealing with here, then, is a whole new world based on machinery—industrialism. None of the components of this new way of life—the machine, factories, production for profit—is as new as industrialism itself, as we shall see later. It is impossible to determine exactly when modern industrialism began, for its origins reach back over the past two centuries to the time when machines driven from a central source of power began to replace hand labor in many manufacturing and distributing processes. Its characteristics will be the subject of other chapters in this section, but first we will trace the historic roots from which it came.

BRITAIN LEADS THE WORLD, 1750-1900

"A revolution is in the making," wrote Arthur Young, the well-known eighteenth-century traveler, in 1788. He was commenting on how far machinery had replaced hand labor in the English cotton and woolen industries—and he was right. Far back in English history the roots of the dynamic development Young was witnessing had taken hold: England's isolation from the rest of Europe, her achievement of national unity and political stability, the discovery of rich coal deposits, and, more

[*] *Encyclopaedia of the Social Sciences,* 14 vols. (New York: Macmillan, 1931-34), VIII, p. 19.

176

recently, her mighty naval and commercial triumphs, which had left her mistress of the seas and of an empire spread over four continents. To these developments were added a large population, a climate conducive to textile manufacturing, and a geographical compactness that made shipment from mine and field to factory and customer easy and inexpensive.

By Young's time these factors had quickened the tempo of change in farming, textiles, manufacturing, transportation, and coal and iron production. As a result, Britain pushed still further ahead of the rest of the world in the race for international supremacy. By 1850 British inventions were known and used throughout the world, British manufacturers sold their wares in places as distant as Port Said and Hong Kong, British sailors took leave in every world port, British writers were read across a half-dozen continents, and British statesmen were acquiring an empire on which the sun would not soon set. The *Pax Brittanica*, or "British Peace," of the nineteenth century owed a great deal to the harnessing of the machine.

WAS THERE
AN INDUSTRIAL REVOLUTION?

So important were these changes in industrial production and transportation in the century after 1750 that for several generations historians and other scholars described them as an "Industrial Revolution." As used by a number of nineteenth-century scholars, the term implied a contrast with the *political* revolution that shook France and the Continent after 1789. It seemed clear to many of these observers that the peaceable, orderly *economic* revolution in Britain had far greater significance to the world.

Some later historians, however, were less certain that a revolution, with all the conno-

tations of violence and suddenness which that word evokes, had actually taken place. They found evidence which indicated that factories, machinery, and improvements in transportation had developed gradually since the sixteenth century, not suddenly in the eighteenth, and that these changes had far from run their course by 1850, the date suggested by some earlier historians for the close of the Industrial Revolution. These later writers, therefore, preferred the term "Industrial Evolution" rather than "Revolution;" but the force of tradition, along with the actual evidence that Western economic life was changing at a phenomenal rate, prevented the term "Industrial Revolution" from falling into disuse. Much of the historians' quarrel may be attributed to the scholar's disdain for easy explanations and for painting history only in bright and somber hues. But in this case the continued use of the name "Industrial Revolution," with the qualifications we have already mentioned (and some others that we shall take up in the next chapter), seems fully warranted.

THE BRITISH FARMER
PREPARES THE WAY

A newcomer to the field of history is likely to assume that the Industrial Revolution had its end and its beginning wholly in the manufacturing centers of Great Britain. Actually, the Industrial Revolution, even in the beginning, was never confined to England, nor was the first act of the drama of industrialism played out in the city. As one clever writer, Eric Lampard, has put it, industrialism "was born in the country and only moved to town when well-advanced in years." It took a revolution in agriculture to enable English farmers to supply the great quantities of produce needed to feed both the new machines and an English population that jumped incredibly

Until the farmer had machines to replace harvesting methods such as these, indus-trialization was not possible.

from 9 million in 1800 to 32 million in 1900.

One of the first farmer-revolutionists was a quiet, retiring English country gentleman by the name of Charles Townshend, who lived in Norfolk. Townshend was one of the first to discover that the lowly turnip could be fed profitably to cattle. So great was his enthusiasm over this discovery that his countrymen promptly nicknamed him "Turnip Townshend." This imaginative gentleman-farmer also demonstrated how soil could be improved by planting clover, using marl as fertilizer, and employing new methods of crop rotation. One of Town-shend's contemporaries, Jethro Tull, devised a crude mechanical planter, which he called a "drill," and also invented a new kind of plow that would cut roots and weeds as well as loosen the topsoil. The inventive genius that was to re-make English manufacturing was already apparent in the silent agricul-tural revolution that was transforming the farms of England.

Certainly this revolution in agriculture made farming far more profitable. It high-lighted the inefficiency of surviving medieval methods of tilling the soil and the long-standing practice of dividing estates into three fields, which in turn were subdivided into individual peasant holdings with sepa-rate strips reserved for the use of the lord of the manor. These individual holdings that were held in common by the peasants under ancient deeds, together with the pasture-lands, were now combined into single-unit farms that were managed and cultivated ac-cording to the new methods. Since these common lands were now to be "enclosed," the new arrangement became known as the *Enclosure Movement*. The practice of enclosure had begun as early as the fifteenth century, but not until the last half of the eighteenth did the movement finally threaten to destroy the medieval manorial system in England. Unhappily, the gains in efficiency and productivity that wealthy farmers realized through enclosure were off-set by the misery the movement inflicted on the peasants, many of whom were dispossessed or found it difficult to adjust to the new system. Thousands of them found a way out by seeking employment in the factories and towns that were growing simultaneously with enclosure. From the viewpoint of the factory-owners, these landless peasants afforded a ready and inexpensive supply of needed labor. The close connection between the two eighteenth-century English revolutions—one on the farm, the other in the towns—is further illustrated by this absorption of the peasants into the factories.

Arthur Young was right. A revolution was in the making. By 1890, the inventions of Kay, Hargreaves, Arkwright, and Cartwright had transformed textile manufacturing into a gigantic industry.

COTTON IS KING

The revolution in the towns is what normally comes to mind when we think of *the* Industrial Revolution. More narrowly, we think of the transformation of the textile industry and the great work of that quartette of inventors known to every schoolboy: Kay, Hargreaves, Arkwright, and Cartwright. For it was in textile manufacturing, specifically in the making of cotton cloth, that machinery was applied most rapidly and spectacularly.

The introduction of new machinery in the textile mills can be regarded as a race between the spinners and the weavers. Up to 1733 the spinners were far in the lead, since they could manufacture considerably more yarn than the weavers could work into cloth. Then, in 1733, came the crucial invention by John Kay, a Lancashire loom-builder, of the flying shuttle, which doubled the weavers' output. The spinners now fell behind and a thirty-year search began for some method of speeding up the spinning wheel. In 1767 James Hargreaves, a carpenter and weaver, produced a machine that he called a "spinning jenny," consisting of a crude wooden frame with eight spindles mounted upright and rotated by a crank. Legend has it that the idea came to him after his wife had upset her spinning wheel and the spindle continued to revolve. When outraged spinners, fearful of losing their jobs, threatened Hargreaves and his machine with violence, the inventor was forced to move to another town. Mob outbursts of this nature were, of course, quite common during these times.

Now spinners could handle eight, sixteen, and later a hundred threads of yarn at once with the new machine, which even children could (and did) operate. The weavers were behind! The gap was widened by the work of Richard Arkwright, a destitute barber, described as "a plain, almost gross, bag-cheeked, pot-bellied Lancashire man," who patented the water frame, a horse-driven machine that by means of rollers produced a strong, coarse yarn that was superior to the thread turned out by the spinning jenny. The secrecy surrounding Arkwright's work led his suspicious neighbors to believe that the inventor was dabbling in witchcraft, especially when two elderly ladies heard strange humming noises emanating from his secluded cottage. But secrecy was necessary in the highly competitive textile industry at a time when inventions received only uncertain protection from governments and the law.

In 1779 Samuel Crompton, a shy, retiring spinner made irritable by the imperfections of the spinning jenny, completed the cycle of spinning inventions with his famous hybrid "mule," which combined Arkwright's rollers with Hargreaves' jenny and added a spindle-carriage that removed the strain on the yarn and made possible a finer and stronger thread. Like most of the great inventors of this age, Crompton never won wealth or fame. Driven to distraction by spying competitors and unprotected by patents, he was reduced, he said, to the "necessity of making it [his machine] public or destroying it, as it was not in my power to keep it and work it, and to destroy it was too painful a task. . . ." * So he made a present of it to the public.

The balance between spinners and weavers was restored once more by Edmund Cartwright, a clergyman, who patented a power loom in 1785 for harnessing the power of steam to the weaving process. It was several decades, however, before the power loom became a serious threat to the hand loom in the cotton and woolen industries. Numerous other inventions, including Eli Whitney's cotton gin, completed the mechanization of the textile industry. By 1850 more than fifty thousand power looms were in operation in Britain and cotton goods made up one-half of all British exports. Machines and technology had seized the imagination of Britain and the world, and the revolution in textiles (if we can call it that) was duplicated in scores of other industries.

---

* P. Mantoux, *The Industrial Revolution in the Eighteenth Century*, rev. ed. (New York: Harcourt, Brace, 1929), p. 241.

THE BLACK BLOOD OF INDUSTRIALISM

For one, the iron industry also underwent a dramatic transformation. The introduction of machinery on so vast a scale in textiles triggered an increased demand for iron. But the iron industry had been on the decline during the early years of the eighteenth century because of a shortage of charcoal, which was used to smelt out the impurities in the native ore. English forests had been virtually denuded to supply the demand for charcoal; and in a mercantilist-minded age, imports were not the answer. So the search began for a substitute fuel. It was Abraham Darby in 1709 who first devised a method of smelting iron with coal and later discovered a way of turning coal into coke for smelting purposes. The quality of British iron was further improved by a process known as "puddling," which burned more impurities out of the ore than had earlier techniques. Iron production reached 68,000 tons in 1788, and then expanded even more rapidly to a million and a half tons by 1839.

Steel was being manufactured as early as the 1800's, but the process was slow and very expensive. Not until Henry Bessemer hit on a way of extracting still more carbon impurities from iron ore did steel become a serious competitor of iron. In 1856 Bessemer invented his egg-shaped converter with holes at the bottom through which compressed air was forced into the molten metal. The oxygen combined with the carbon and silicon, thus removing them from the metal. The Age of Steel had begun.

The black blood that coursed through the industrial veins of England was coal. England, one wit has remarked, is "built on coal and surrounded by fish." Coal not only was basic to iron and steel production but was the source of the steam power that James Watt and others harnessed to the engines, railways, and ships on which Britain rode to industrial supremacy. There were, of course, other older sources of power, notably wind and water; but steam released industry from its dependence on rainfall and river-bank locations and also freed vessels from the fickle and unpredictable winds. Since electricity would not become a competitor of coal for many years, because of high production costs, coal became the life-blood of industrialism.

BY STEAM OVER LAND AND SEA

It was a Watt steam engine that powered Robert Fulton's famous *Clermont* up the Hudson River in 1807. Fulton wrote to a friend after the event that

The power of propelling boats by steam is now fully proved. The morning I left New York there were not perhaps thirty persons in the city who believed that the boat would ever move one mile an hour or be of the least utility; and, while we were putting off from the wharf, which was crowded with spectators, I heard a number of sarcastic remarks. This is the way in which ignorant men compliment what they call philosophers and projectors.*

Steamboats soon were plying the inland waters of America and Europe, but they were uneconomical for ocean crossings. Samuel Cunard's first transatlantic steamers in 1840 needed about half of their storage capacity for coal. It was the heyday of the famous Yankee Clippers, perhaps the most beautiful sailing ships ever built, and not until the 1860's was their dominion over freight shipment between America and the rest of the world successfully challenged by the steamboat.

If ships could be propelled by steam, as Fulton had proved, why not put the steam engine on wheels to move machines overland? As a matter of fact, the first locomotive had already been built in England by Richard Trevithick. It ran over wooden rails at a speed slightly in excess of 5 miles per

* E. Bogart and C. Thompson, eds., *Readings in the Economic History of the United States* (New York: Longmans, Green, 1916, and later editions), p. 251.

The railroad, a product of the Industrial Revolution, was soon binding continents together and shortening distances.

hour, which was no improvement over the horse and certainly more expensive. But in 1829 George Stephenson won a prize of $2,500 over several competitors for his *Rocket*, which traveled at speeds varying from 12 to 29 miles per hour. The Liverpool and Manchester Railway, binding these two great port and manufacturing centers together, was opened with great ceremony in 1830 with the Duke of Wellington and several members of Parliament riding in the jolting cars. The celebration was marred by the accidental death of William Huskisson, one of England's prominent politicians and a champion of free trade, who became an early martyr to modern speeds. The following colorful account of the accident from a contemporary newspaper gives some of the flavor of novelty that surrounded the early railroads:

... the Rocket was perceived to be on the advance, and a general move took place to get out of its way, several persons calling out, "Get in! get in!" Some followed this advice, scrambling up as they best might in the absence of steps—others made their way round the end of the car, and Mr. Huskisson appeared to be acting under the idea of crossing the Rocket's railway before the engine came up.... [Mr. Holmes] had time to perceive the irresolution of the right hon. gentlemen, and he called out to him, "For God's sake, be firm, Mr. Huskisson." *

Despite accidents and hostility, the new "iron horse" made rapid strides, and by 1848 the main railroads of modern Britain had already been built.

There were, of course, other improvements in transportation and communication aside from those that issued from the harnessing of steam. Highway construction was greatly improved by the work of "Blind Jack" Metcalfe who, despite his infirmity, designed many of the important roads in

---

* W. Bowden, *The Industrial Revolution* (New York: Crofts, 1928), p. 45.

northern England; and of Jack Macadam, whose "macadamized" roads of coarse stones covered with finer stones and a top layer of crushed rock became models for road-builders in Europe and America.

The period from 1790 to 1830 was also the great era of canal-building, and by its close England was covered with a network of the man-made water arteries that stretched out over the countryside for hundreds of miles. Americans are most familiar with the Erie Canal that was built during this period to bind the expanding northwestern frontier in New York and beyond to the port of New York via the Hudson River. Inexpensive, fast communication was also made possible by the inauguration of the "penny post" in Great Britain in 1840 and by telegraph service, which was perfected by the American Samuel Morse in 1844.

THE MAGNITUDE OF THE BRITISH ACHIEVEMENT

Britons could well be proud of the achievements they displayed to the world in the first great industrial fair opened by Queen Victoria in the famous Crystal Palace in 1851. It was evident to everyone who visited the exposition that Britain had indeed become the workshop of the world. British furnaces were supplying one-half of the world's finished iron, her mills were producing more finished cloth than the rest of the world combined, her ships carried the lion's share of the world's trade, and her banks handled the financial transactions of six continents. When Napoleon's troops marched into battle against the English at Waterloo, they wore coats cut from English cloth; when Americans started later to span their continent with railroads, they used rails forged in British mills.

At home the Industrial Revolution had made great changes in the face of Britain. The English countryside had finally been

Main hall of the Crystal Palace Exposition in London in 1851. The Palace was an engineering marvel of iron and glass designed to display the new mechanical feats of the Industrial Age.

enclosed in the patterns familiar to modern visitors, new cities sprang up in the industrial Midlands, and old cities grew black with smoke and grime. Some towns experienced an extraordinary growth, as the following population estimates reveal at a glance:

TABLE 4   POPULATION GROWTH OF SELECTED
BRITISH CITIES, 1685-1881

	1685	1760	1881
Liverpool	4,000	35,000	552,000
Manchester	6,000	35,000	394,000
Birmingham	4,000	29,000	401,000
Sheffield	4,000	25,000	284,000
Nottingham	8,000	17,000	112,000

Source: A. Toynbee, *Lectures on the Industrial Revolution* (London: Longmans, Green, 1928), p. 11.

Such rapid change had a tremendous impact on centuries-old towns and cities. A popular song about the growth of Birmingham during the 1820's and 1830's went something like this:

> Full twenty years, and more, are past,
>   Since I left Brummagem [Birmingham];
> But I set out for home at last,
>   To good old Brummagem.
> But every place is altered so,
> There's hardly a single place I know;
> And it fills my heart with grief and woe,
>   For I can't find Brummagem. . . .

> I remember one John Growse,
>   A buckle-maker in Brummagem:
> He built himself a country house,
>   To be out of the smoke of Brummagem:
> But though John's country house stands still,
> The town itself has walked up hill,
> Now he lives beside of a smoky mill,
>   In the middle of the streets of Brummagem.*

* Bowden, *Industrial Revolution*, pp. 71-73.

183

The rapid growth of towns and cities, like the rapid advance of industrialization generally, had important social and political consequences, as we shall see in the next chapter. Certainly self-sufficiency in the old sense, particularly in foodstuffs, was no longer possible for an island crowded with factories. Britain began to import her daily bread from agricultural countries and from her colonial possessions in exchange for the products of her industries. The conditions for the "export or die" economic philosophy of modern Britain were thus set during the eighteenth and nineteenth centuries.

THE DIFFUSION OF INDUSTRIALISM, 1850-2000

It was not too long, however, before the consumers of British goods wanted to import industrialism itself and end their dependence on the "workshop of the world." In the eyes of some countries, it was humiliating to depend on a foreign country for goods that could be made at home. Furthermore, British prosperity as well as her political and military superiority were obviously related to her industrial strength. The economic historian Herbert Heaton has summed up the motives behind the worldwide expansion of industrialism in one brilliant sentence:

If China, Japan, and India were to count in the eyes of the western world they must westernize their industrial equipment as well as their judicial and educational systems; if Canada, Australia and even the United States were to emerge from colonial status or stature they must cut the ties that bound them to the factories of Lancashire, Yorkshire and the Black Country; if new or reborn nations, such as Germany or Italy, were to make their unity or freedom real they must translate nationalism into factories, mines, banks and statistics of industrial output; and if Russian communists wished to justify their faith and place in a hostile capitalistic world they must teach a nation of peasants how to make electricity, tractors, cloth, electric lamps and cheap matches.*

Until about the year 1870, however, the future rivals of Britain were concerned with far-reaching internal problems—Germany with political unification, the United States with a civil war and its aftermath, Japan

* *Encyclopaedia of the Social Sciences*, VIII, p. 8.

with domestic ferment against its medieval political and social order. After 1870 the tempo of industrialization in non-British areas increased rapidly, making use of new sources of power, notably electricity and oil, and benefiting from the mistakes Britain had made earlier. By 1900 Germany and the United States were challenging British industrial superiority, and Japan was making tremendous advances. And just fifty years later, a new industrial giant, the Soviet Union, had stepped on the stage, while India and China were waiting in the wings.

CONTINENTAL INDUSTRIALIZATION

The first threat to British supremacy came from Germany. France, it is true, was the first continental nation to become industrialized, but it lagged far behind England because of the prosperity of French farming and the survival of medieval restrictions on initiative and industry. Germany, on the other hand, had made rapid strides toward industrialization even before the country was finally unified politically in 1871. Textile machinery had been brought from England, German coal mines were being worked extensively, and there were already signs of the German genius in metallurgy, chemistry, and dye-making. After 1871 the pace was stepped up by a central German government that gave every encouragement to industrial expansion. Farm production mounted steadily, the rich Ruhr Valley became the nucleus of the German steel industry, and

German dyes, chemicals, fertilizers, and electrical apparatus became known all over the world. The following table shows the vigor of the race Germany ran by 1913.

TABLE 5   COMPARATIVE COAL AND STEEL
PRODUCTION, 1875-1913

Country	Coal (in millions of tons)		Iron and Steel (in millions of tons)	
	1875	1913	1875	1913
England	99	287	6	8
France	11	40	1	2
Germany	28	273	2	14

Source: T. Wallbank and A. Taylor, *Civilization Past and Present* (Chicago: Scott, Foresman, 1956), p. 333.

THE METEORIC RISE
OF AMERICAN INDUSTRY

Meanwhile, another and even more formidable rival to Britain had appeared across the Atlantic Ocean. The beginnings of the factory system in the United States date back to the first decade of the nineteenth century, when textile machinery designed from British models was first introduced. But at least until the 1850's, most manufacturing in America was done on a small scale and carried out in a small shop or cottage. The Civil War, with the demand it created for shoes, uniforms, munitions, and transportation, gave a great boost to American manufacturing. There followed in the late 1860's and for the next few decades a titanic expansion of the American industrial plant that almost beggars description. No other country, with the possible exception of the Soviet Union, has industrialized so completely in so short a time. American manufacturers enjoyed the benefit of the British experience as well as British capital; abundant natural resources of good coking coal and high-grade iron ore combined with a never-failing supply of immigrant labor to make their task easier. A huge domestic market without tariff barriers encouraged risk, initiative, and investment. And the American's practicality and ingenuity, which we noted in the last chapter, were of real benefit. Nor did America lack imaginative business leaders, such as the great steel-maker Andrew Carnegie, who envisioned steel's future role in the American economy: John D. Rockefeller, who expedited the flow of crude oil to an oil-hungry nation; and the railroad-builders such as Jim Hill and Jay Cooke, who pushed 200,000 miles of track across the continent in only fifty years. By World War I the United States had clearly emerged as the foremost industrial nation in the world.

Between 1800 and the Civil War, American manufacturing developed slowly. Plants were modest and resembled this early cotton mill in Pawtucket, Rhode Island.

THE INDUSTRIAL REVOLUTION
AND THE NON-WESTERN WORLD

The diffusion of industrialism beyond Western Europe did not end in the United States. To some extent, however limited, the machines and techniques of industrialism have made inroads all over the world. But the most impressive new development of industrialism thus far in the twentieth century has occurred in the Soviet Union. In 1928 the Russians launched a vast, concerted campaign to exploit their abundant resources of crucial industrial minerals. The first Five-Year Plan called for a rapid expansion of all phases of the Soviet economy, especially the production of industrial goods, farm output, and the transportation network. The number of machines, farm implements (especially tractors), and electrical goods turned out far exceeded the ambitious goal of a 20 per cent increase per year, but some aspects of industrial growth lagged, especially the manufacture of iron, steel, and chemicals. By 1940, however, Russian steel production had drawn abreast of Germany's, and machine tools and motor vehicles were being produced on a large scale for the first time. During and after World War II, Soviet industrial production mounted still more spectacularly, until only the United States stood between her and the pinnacle of world industrial leadership. This dramatic rise was accomplished only through tremendous sacrifice on the part of the Russian people and at the expense of a standard of living still considerably below the average in Western Europe. But for the nonindustrialized nations of the world, the Soviet example, however great the costs to Russian citizens, held

Following the Civil War, industries grew at a phenomenal rate and many cities, such as Pittsburgh, were growing and changing with them.

In the non-European countries, Japan has become the industrial pace-setter.

out promise of a day not too far distant when they, too, might enjoy the fruits of industrialism.

The nonindustrialized countries, in fact, have rightly attributed their inferior power status in the world to the industrial advantage long enjoyed by Europeans. The great wave of nineteenth-century imperialism stemmed not only from the Europeans' need for markets and raw materials but also from the weakness of the non-European countries who lacked the weapons and the industrial know-how to wage a modern war. Japan was the only non-Western nation in the nineteenth century to protect itself against the West by imitating the West's industrialization. A large supply of cheap labor, government subsidies to railroads and steamships, and the exploitation of native coal made Japan, once started on the road to industrialism, the most respected nation in Asia. Before 1880 there were no cotton mills in the entire country, but by 1914 Japanese textiles were rivaling those from Manchester and Birmingham.

The recent example of the Soviet Union and the older one of Japan have stirred the other nations of Asia and now Africa to strive for parity with the West. They are determined to share in the fruits of industrial development. China and India, in particular, have embarked on far-reaching programs of economic expansion designed to lift those countries out of their traditional poverty and weakness. They face tremendous problems: illiteracy, a population expanding more swiftly than the food supply, inadequate raw materials, and the competition of well-developed industrial systems in the West. But though their way be difficult, what student of modern history would dare predict their failure? The cost will certainly be high—but then so was the cost to the West, as we shall see in the next chapter.

SOME WORDS OF SUMMARY

Industrialism has played a vital role in creating our modern world. In the three chapters that follow we shall trace the impact of industrialism on social life and institutions, economic thought, and the relations between social groups, while in Chapter 20 we shall see how modern industrialism and urbanization have affected man's personality development. In this chapter we have been concerned with the historical timetable of industrialization. The first nation to be transformed by the application of machines to the production and delivery of goods was Great Britain. Between 1700 and 1850 British agriculture, manufacturing, transportation, and her distribution system were deeply affected by a series of inventions—the mechanical sower, flying shuttle, spinning jenny, power loom, steam engine, and macadamized roads—which made Britain the workshop of the world. At home the English countryside was enclosed to promote large-scale farming and the application of advanced agricultural methods, and many towns and cities experienced an extraordinary growth.

After 1850 other countries, especially Germany and the United States, began to compete seriously with Britain and both had surpassed her in iron and steel production by World War I. Between the two world wars the Soviet Union made great gains, overtaking Germany in steel production by 1940. Since World War II, Soviet industrial growth has been even more spectacular. The non-Western world, which with the exception of Japan trailed far behind the West in industrialization during the nineteenth and early twentieth centuries, has been impressed with the examples of Japan and Russia. In the second half of the twentieth century the further diffusion of industrialism on a major scale to Africa, and especially to such Asian nations as India and China, looms as the next stage in the historical timetable.

FURTHER ROADS TO LEARNING

GENERAL ACCOUNTS

T. Ashton, *The Industrial Revolution* (New York: Oxford University Press, 1948). Probably the best comprehensive one-volume treatment of the subject.

F. Dietz, *The Industrial Revolution* (New York: Holt, 1927). A brief but clear book centering on Britain and Europe.

J. and B. Hammond, *The Rise of Modern Industry* (New York: Harcourt, Brace, 1926). Still worth reading for its vigorous style and clarity, despite a strong emphasis on the social consequences of modern industry.

H. Heaton, *Economic History of Europe* (New York: Harper, 1936, and later editions). Contains a number of interesting chapters on the course of modern industrialism.

L. Mumford, *Technics and Civilization* (New York: Harcourt, Brace, 1934). Nowhere is the impact of technology on modern life as a whole treated with such sweep and imagination.

SPECIAL STUDIES

E. Bogart and C. Thompson, eds., *Readings in the Economic History of the United States* (New York: Longmans, Green, 1916, and later editions). A number of interesting documents, arranged chronologically, which illustrate phases of American economic growth.

W. Bowden, ed., *The Industrial Revolution* (New York: Crofts, 1928). A brief but excellent collection of source material bearing on the early Industrial Revolution and its results.

J. Clapham, *The Economic Development of France and Germany 1815-1914* (Cambridge: Cambridge University Press, 1921, and later editions). The best book on this topic in English.

V. Dean, *The Nature of the Non-Western World* (New York: Mentor Books, 1957). One of the clearest explanations of the role of industry in the awakening of Asia and the Middle East.

H. Faulkner, *American Economic History* (New York: Harper, 1924, and later editions). Perhaps the best textbook in this field.

A. Usher, *A History of Mechanical Inventions* (New York: McGraw-Hill, 1929). A classic work in a difficult field.

P. Taylor, ed., *The Industrial Revolution in Britain: Triumph or Disaster?* (Boston: Heath, 1958). A most useful compilation of conflicting views on the Industrial Revolution in Britain and its social significance.

A. Toynbee, *The Industrial Revolution* (Boston: Beacon, 1956). The beginner can still learn a great deal from these famous lectures, first delivered at Oxford in 1881.

P. Mantoux, *The Industrial Revolution in the Eighteenth Century*, rev. ed. (New York: Harcourt, Brace, 1929). A standard work on the beginnings of the modern factory system in England.

FICTION AND DRAMA

P. Bentley, *Inheritance* (New York: Macmillan, 1932). A family chronicle depicting the rise and decline of the weaving industry in Yorkshire, England.

W. Churchill, *The Dwelling Place of Light* (New York: Macmillan, 1917). A sordid story of the lives of women caught up in the clutches of the Industrial Revolution.

G. Gaskill, *North and South* (New York: Dutton, 1914). By using the English Industrial Revolution of the 1850's as a setting, the author contrasts the industrial north of England with the agricultural south.

G. Hauptmann, *The Weavers* (New York: Huebsch, 1911, and in many collections). A drama of life and struggles among German weavers in the middle of the nineteenth century.

J. Hergesheimer, *The Three Black Pennies* (New York: Knopf, 1917). The background of this novel is the development of the iron and steel industry in the United States.

FILMS

Goddess of Merchants (British Information Service, 1950, 21 min., sound, black and white). A comprehensive pictorial history of the British wool trade from medieval times to the present.

Industrial Revolution (Encyclopaedia Britannica Films, 1942, 10 min., sound, black and white). Contrasts the amazing technological and production changes of the present century with the slower changes of the nineteenth, and shows how the Industrial Revolution raised the level of living.

Machine: Master or Slave? (New York University, 1941, 20 min., sound, black and white). Deals with this provocative question through a discussion of industrial organization and its accompanying problems.

Productivity: Key to Plenty (Encyclopaedia Britannica Films, 1949, 21 min., sound, black and white). Here we are shown how the technological revolution has increased production and raised the level of living.

CHAPTER ELEVEN

The Social
and Economic Consequences
of Industrialism

*But for all its dynamism,
for all the progress and the comforts it brings,
industrialism has its seamy side, too.*

The Industrial

Revolution ushered in a new way of life for the world's peoples, for industrialism, as G. D. H. Cole's definition in the preceding chapter made sharply clear, is more than a way of producing goods. It brings with it an increase and concentration in population, a vastly expanded trade, and a rise in importance of the middle classes, who engage in business, industry, and commerce. These changes, in turn, produce abundance and want, comfort and misery, pride and jealousy among the different peoples of the world. At home, industrialism may bring in its wake a train of new social tensions and strains, as well as an improvement in the standard of living and increased leisure time for the average industrial worker and his family. Abroad, industrialism may create tensions between nations by setting off a race for markets, capital, and raw materials, at the same time that it binds nations closer together through swifter transportation and communication.

THE PARADOX OF INDUSTRIALISM

In measuring the impact of industrialism on society, we are continually confronted with this paradox: at one and the same time industrialism has created sharper contrasts and greater similarities among peoples, more want and more abundance among workers, and bloodier wars and broader understanding among nations. Some scholars and critics have blamed industrialism itself for all the evils of modern times, and they delight in detailing the unrelieved horrors of working conditions in the early factories of Britain or Germany. Still others see industrialism as the golden age of man's achievements, in which toil, want, and poverty are on their way to extinction.

Essentially, industrialism is neither good nor bad but is simply what men make of it. When men surrender to the machine their ability to choose or judge or decide, they invite the very tyranny they often denounce. Then, indeed, as Emerson wrote, "things are in the saddle and ride mankind." But the supposed evils of a mass industrialized society—standardization, lack of imagination, neglect of the arts—are found in many pre-industrial societies as well. And history has not yet demonstrated that industrial societies cannot protect individualism or foster the imaginative arts. This is not to deny that the machine can become and often has become the master rather than the servant of men. It means only that such a development is by no means inevitable.

THE IMPACT OF INDUSTRIALISM ON ENGLAND AND EUROPE

Why should such a pessimistic view of industrialism and its effects have arisen in the first place? Primarily because the early phases of the Industrial Revolution, whether in England or America, India or the Soviet Union, revealed a host of shocking abuses. Working conditions in the early English factories left witnesses shocked and appalled. One such witness, a Prussian-born emigrant to England named Karl Marx, constructed a whole new social order as a theoretical alternative to what he saw in England.

ABUSES IN EARLY ENGLISH INDUSTRY

What were these conditions like? First of all, there were the long hours of labor, ranging from 14 to 16 hours each day except Sunday. Wages were poor, discipline was severe, and union organization strictly forbidden. Factories were poorly lighted and ventilated and were grossly unsanitary. From these oppressive surroundings, the worker retired at night to a dismal slum dwelling, where he and his family were crowded together with many other families in equally unhygienic and depressing quarters. Recreation and leisure were confined to the few hours on Sunday when the local public house, or saloon, was open. Disease and mortality rates were fearfully high in the new factory towns, and crippling and maiming from the unguarded machinery all too common. In France one statistical study revealed that the death rate among infants in certain industrial towns was three times what it was in the country.

Worst of all, perhaps, was the widespread employment of women and children. Boys of seven, eight, or nine years were taken into the coal mines to labor 14 or more hours daily in cramped, stifling surroundings. One official report disclosed that boys as young as four, still attired in nightgowns, were found in some of the smaller mines in the hills. Normally, the men worked completely naked, assisted, according to this same report, "by females of all ages, from girls of six years old to women of twenty-one, these females being themselves quite naked down to the waist."

What a shattering effect such experiences must have had on the lives of the young can only be imagined. We do have records, however, of the testimony of some of these children before parliamentary investigating committees. No stronger evidence has been found to support the pessimistic view of industrialism's impact on Western life:

[*Joseph Hebergam examined.*] What particular department of the mill had you to attend to?—I attended what are called the throstle machines. . . .

Were there many children in that mill?—Yes, I believe there were about fifty, of about the same age that I was.

State to the Committee how this excessive labour agreed with the health of these children so employed?—They were often sick and poorly; there were always, perhaps, half a dozen regularly that were ill.

From excessive labour?—Yes. . . .

Did you not become very drowsy and sleepy towards the end of the day, and feel much fatigued?—Yes; that began about 3 o'clock, and grew worse and worse, and it came to be very bad towards 6 and 7.

And still you had to labour on?—Yes.

What means were taken to keep you at your work so long?—There were three overlookers; there was a head overlooker, and then there was one man kept to grease the machines, and then there was one kept on purpose to strap.

Was the main business of one of the overlookers that of strapping the children up to this excessive labour?—Yes, the same as strapping an old restive horse that has fallen down and will not get up.

Was that the constant practice?—Yes, day by day. . . .

Do you think the children could be kept so long to labour as you have stated, if they were not so treated?—No, they could not; they are obliged to do it. . . .

Did you meet with frequent accidents?—Yes.

So that you were not capable of performing the labour that was exacted from you without this perpetual cruelty?—No.

Had you any brothers or sisters similarly occupied?—I had at that time a brother and a sister; they called him John, and my sister Charlotte.

What ages were they when they began working at the mills?—I cannot say how old my sister Charlotte was, but my brother John was 7.

How did it suit their health?—It did not suit it at all; they were often sick.

Where is your brother John working now?—He died three years ago. . . .

To what was his death attributed by your mother and the medical attendants?—It was attributed to this, that he died from working such long hours, and that it had been brought on by the factory.*

THE OPTIMISTIC VIEW

Without denying the truth of many of these charges, some historians have insisted that they give a false picture of early industrialism as a whole. For one thing, the everyday life that the factory worker left behind was far from a pastoral idyll. In the country and in the "cottage industries" of earlier centuries, there had also been poverty, exploitation, misery, and disease. Desperate though life was in the factory towns, it was scarcely better in the rural slums of the English countryside. Furthermore, the crowding of a rising population into towns was bound to create slums and health problems at a time when there was little capital or cheap building materials to accommodate the newcomers.

According to Herbert Heaton, what was new and revolutionary was not the "evils" of the new factory life but the discovery that they were evils. For this realization, says Heaton, we have to thank the generation that brought the Industrial Revolution to England. It was employers, legislators, reformers, and humanitarians who, together, began to redress the very real grievances of the early factory workers. Finally, the great material benefits bestowed by the Industrial Revolution were certain in time to raise the standard of living of the great mass of workers. By the end of the nineteenth century, the real wages (that is, the value of wages in terms of what they will buy) of workers in England and other industrial pioneering countries were far in advance of what they had been at the time of the textile revolution of the eighteenth century. In Germany, to take one example, the annual per capita consumption of meat jumped from 38 pounds in 1816 to 115 in 1912. Similar figures for meat and other commodities are available for England and the United States. Beyond the abuses of the factory system lay a better and more comfortable life for everyone in which industrial workers would be better housed, better clothed, and better fed than even the well-to-do in some African or Asian countries.

AMERICA AND THE INDUSTRIAL REVOLUTION

Now what of the social consequences of the Industrial Revolution in the United States? Industrialism played a most vital role in the emergence of modern America. Changes were swift, overwhelming, and enduring. Almost overnight, America was transformed from a rural, agricultural, decentralized nation into a dynamic industrial

world power. Factories sprang up, cities mushroomed, and a whole way of life began to change. With America's industrial revolution came new social problems, new attitudes toward the family, church, and other social institutions, as well as a bounteous prosperity that filtered down to many of the farmers and wage-workers of the nation. Industrialism acted, too, as a kind of cement in fastening together a nation torn apart by civil war. For industrialism brought Americans closer together, speeded up transporta-

---

* G. H. Knoles and R. K. Snyder, eds., *Readings in Western Civilization*, rev. ed. (Philadelphia: Lippincott, 1954), p. 572.

Throughout North America and South America, indeed, wherever it intrudes, the machine forges a new and different environment and brings industrialism into our backyards.

tion and communication, and created a similar culture across the continent. Industrialism and the factory system tended to make cities look alike. Problems of American communities were becoming more alike, more national in scope. Deep-rooted cultural contrasts between North and South began fading. A large factory town in Alabama resembled a factory town in New England more than it did the nearby county seat, which cherished memories of the heyday of the plantation system. Industry, confined to New England before the Civil War, now spread through the Middle West and into the South. The machine was forging a common environment for Americans, which weakened the sectional forces that had plagued American politics and plunged the nation into civil war.

THE NEW RICH AND THE NEW POOR

Before the Civil War there had been few extremes of wealth and poverty in the United States. Cheap land and scarcity of labor had combined to provide plentiful opportunity for most Americans and to permit them to avoid extreme poverty and deprivation, while the provincial prewar economy prevented the amassing of great wealth. But the industrial revolution of the 1860's and 1870's changed all this. Fabulous fortunes were won in oil, steel, railroads, and a dozen other enterprises. Andrew Carnegie and John D. Rockefeller accumulated fortunes on a scale hitherto unknown in the world's history. Over three thousand millionaires had been created by 1900, of whom at least twenty-five were multimillionaires. They lived in a manner that generally accompanies great wealth, and their spectacular social doings were a sensation at the turn of the century. Sometimes they used their great fortunes to establish worthy philanthropic enterprises—museums, libraries, galleries, universities—but their disproportionate share of the national income could not but cause others to envy or resent their wealth. By 1900 seven-eighths of America's wealth was owned by one-eighth of her citizens, and the upper 1 per cent owned more than the remaining 99 per cent. Many Americans began to question the rules of a game that made possible such inequality.

At the opposite extreme of the social scale, the workers in the new and expanding industries found themselves in the same plight into which their English cousins had fallen a few decades earlier. Here, too, hours were long, wages were low, and working conditions were miserable and unsafe. America also had its share of slums, unsanitary conditions, child labor, and poor health. As in England, the early unions in the United States were opposed or stymied by unfriendly employers, neutral governments, or tradition-minded courts. But here, too, we would hardly be justified in blaming industrialism or the industrialists for all these evils. In America, as in England and Germany, and later in Russia and Asia, the coming of industrialism wrought havoc with established customs as well as with legal, political, and economic traditions. Only slowly and incompletely did social institutions adjust to the throbbing, restless, ever-changing climate of industrial society. To take only one example, labor organizations in Western Europe and America did not gain acceptance in law and custom for several generations because legal tradition, surviving from an earlier age of small independent producers, stipulated that unions were "conspiracies in restraint of trade."

THE IMPACT OF INDUSTRIALISM ON SOVIET SOCIETY

In the Soviet Union industrialism has arisen as much in response to political calculation as to economic motives. For the Soviets, industry has meant security—modern weapons and a modern, efficient transportation system. Stalin was certain that communism would triumph over capitalism only if the Soviet Union were able to compete with, and even excel, the West in industrial production. Historically, Russia has envied and imitated, feared and resented the West, just as do many underdeveloped nations of Asia and the Middle East today.

To the factory workers of Russia, sunk in a slough of misery worse than anything known in England, Lenin and Trotsky addressed their revolutionary appeal in 1917. No measures of social reform lightened the Russian workers' grievances as they did for workers in Western industrial countries. Seemingly, they had everything to gain by supporting Lenin and his associates.

Once in power, the Soviet leaders were faced with the choice that now confronts officials in every underdeveloped country. Should their peoples' hopes for a higher standard of living come first, or should every effort be made to create a strong industrial bastion from which to exert political and military influence? A contented population or a place in the sun: which was more important? The Soviets unhesitatingly chose to develop their heavy industries, suppress all criticism and resistance, and enforce by dictatorial means a sharp austerity in consumer goods. Japan had likewise surrendered the comfort of its people to rapid industrialization a half-century before. Now all Asia is watching the example of democratic India, which seeks to ensure its citizens a modicum of consumer goods while contending for Asian leadership with Communist China, which is following the Russian example of austerity enforced by tyranny.

By Western standards, the Soviets have paid a high price for their industrial progress —tyranny, loss of individual freedoms, and stifling of initiative. But in the light of recent Soviet achievements in science and military weapons, as contrasted with Soviet capabilities only four decades or so ago, some Asians find the Russian formula an appealing one, whatever the cost. Certainly the next great phase in the world's history will be shaped in large part by whether the uncommitted countries of the world choose the Soviet or the Western pathway to industrialism.

THE NEW SPECTRUM OF ECONOMIC AND SOCIAL THOUGHT

Industrialism, as should now seem clear, profoundly influenced the way of life of nineteenth-century Europeans and Americans. It was inevitable that so widespread and shattering a change also should influence and alter men's views about economics, law, politics, and social justice. The triumphant middle classes, who profited greatly from the surge of industrial and business activity, sought to justify their stake in this new way of life. In their eyes private property became virtually sacred; poverty, they believed, was the result of laziness and incompetence. Every man had been supposedly endowed by nature with the right to do what he would with the things that were his. For the poor, poverty was considered a good thing since it taught them to be humble and grateful for the favors that were conferred on them. For the rich, wealth was their natural reward for aggressiveness and superior business sense and ability. The new business aristocracy in Europe sometimes imitated the older landed aristocracy by seeking titles, building town and country estates, or marrying into the titled upper classes. In America, of course, there was no titled aristocracy to imitate, but this deficiency did not prevent industrial tycoons from "collecting" art and refinement in Europe and bringing it back with them to their town houses. The results, as the famous historian Charles Beard once pointed out, were sometimes ludicrous:

The armor of medieval knights soon stood in the halls of captains of industry whose boldest strokes were courageous strokes on the stock market or the employment of Pinkerton detectives against striking workingmen; while Mandarin coats from Peking sprawled on the pianos of magnates who knew not Ming or Manchu and perhaps could not tell whether their hired musicians were grinding out Wagner or Chopin. Grand ladies, who remembered with a blush the days when they laundered the family clothes, shone idly resplendent in jewels garnered by a search of two hemispheres. European tutors were imported to teach the "new people" and their offspring "parlor and table etiquette," music and "appreciation," as Greek preceptors had served Roman families in the time of Cicero. European artists were brought over to design and decorate for them as the artists of Athens were summoned to beautify the homes of Trimalchio's contemporaries. Private libraries of the "sets," rare editions, and rich bindings were quickly assembled in job lots to give tone to establishments—a diversion that afforded gratifying appearances of culture with none of its laborious penalties.*

THE FIVE COMMANDMENTS OF LIBERALISM

The views of the middle class with respect to law, economics, and politics can perhaps best be summarized in the form of five commandments that made up the creed of the nineteenth-century English and American liberal. Together they constituted the essence, it was believed, of a well-regulated nation's economic life.

1. *Thou shalt not interfere with the rights of the individual.* This commandment meant

---

* C. A. and M. R. Beard, *The Rise of American Civilization* (New York: Macmillan, 1927), Vol. 2, pp. 386-87.

that a person had the right to hold, use, or dispose of his property as he saw fit. Property was understood to include every variety of personal holding, whether house or garden, business or industrial plant. No community or government could know better than the individual himself what was best for him. By permitting each individual to follow the dictates of his own reason and selfish interests, the community as a whole would prosper and maximum happiness for all would result.

2. *Thou shalt not permit government to interfere with the economic life of the individual.* A strong government was an enemy of the rights of the people. Governments should properly restrict themselves to the preservation of law and order. They were the courts of last resort in event of disagreements. They should protect property but never intervene in economic matters. In Thomas Jefferson's famous words, "that government governs best which governs least."

3. *Thou shalt obey the natural law.* As we saw in Chapter 9, the average nineteenth-century American (and Englishman) believed in a universe of natural laws. These laws governed economic as well as other kinds of activity. The law of supply and demand, for example, was believed to be rooted in the very processes of nature and always operated to produce the fairest price. To go against a law of nature by attempting to control prices, or wages, or the conditions of production, was to invite disaster.

4. *Thou shalt not limit freedom of contract.* All types of negotiations between individual parties should be free of outside restraint or pressure. No laborer should expect aid from the government or from unions in contracting for wages with his employer. Once established, however, a contract should receive the protection of law and the government.

5. *Thou shalt not limit the freedom to compete and trade.* The very nature of economic processes assumed a competitive striving for sales, jobs, and markets. No government should limit this competition by fixing prices, granting monopolies, or protecting native industry through tariffs.

ADAM SMITH AND LAISSEZ FAIRE

Certainly the most influential of all the liberal economists who advanced with varying qualifications the ideas we have just recounted was the Scotsman Adam Smith. Smith was probably the first modern economist, if his systematic and comprehensive analysis of economic ideas is any indication. His most famous book—almost the Bible of the middle classes in the nineteenth century —was called *An Inquiry into the Nature and Causes of the Wealth of Nations.* In this book, Smith held that labor was the source of a country's wealth. Efficient use of labor distinguished the good from the bad industry. Labor was used most efficiently where each man was permitted to perform the single task for which he was best fitted. This *division of labor*, in Smith's view, marked English industry off from its competitors. In a famous example, Smith showed what this principle had meant to the lowly trade of pin-making:

. . . a workman not educated to this business . . . nor acquainted with the use of the machinery employed in it, could scarce, perhaps, with his utmost industry, make one pin in a day, and certainly could not make twenty. But in the way in which this business is now carried on, not only the whole is a peculiar trade, but it is divided into a number of branches, of which the greater part are likewise peculiar trades. One man draws out the wire; another straights it; a third cuts it; a fourth points it; a fifth grinds it at the top for receiving the head; to make the head requires two or three distinct operations; to put it on is a peculiar business; to whiten the pins is another, it is even a trade by itself to put them into the paper; and the important business of making a pin is, in this manner, divided into about eighteen distinct operations, which, in some manufactories, are all performed by distinct hands, though in others the same man will sometimes perform two or three of them. I have seen a small manufactory of this kind, where ten men only . . . could make among them upwards of forty-eight thousand pins in a day.*

But the economic philosophy for which Smith is best remembered can be reduced to the French phrase, *laissez faire*, meaning "let it go," or "hands off!" As applied to the realm of economics, laissez faire meant simply that government should keep hands off domestic business and foreign trade (our Commandment Number 2). Free enterprise and free trade were the twin goals of a country seeking the most efficient use of its energies and its resources. Smith looked askance at all protective tariffs, wage- and price-fixing, or other governmental controls as dangerous to a country's economic health. Finally, he believed firmly that all economic operations were governed by fixed laws with which men might tamper only at their peril. By permitting people to buy and sell according to their own inclinations, a country could achieve complete harmony in production and demand. In the inscrutable bosom of nature, all the whims and caprices of people canceled each other out in a symphony of agreement.

---

* Knoles and Snyder, eds., *Readings in Western Civilization*, p. 596.

The individual person could presumably feel happy in the knowledge that his selfish impulses triggered a mechanism that was set unerringly in the direction of social progress.

THOMAS MALTHUS AND AN EXPANDING POPULATION

Of all the so-called classical economists who explained and justified the new economic and social order produced by industrialism, none attracted more attention than Thomas Malthus, an English clergyman. In 1798 Malthus published his widely-known *Essay on Population*, which advanced the dismal theory that mankind might possibly breed itself into starvation. A country's food supply, wrote Malthus, tends to increase in steady arithmetical proportion (1-2-3-4) as new techniques are developed and more land is constantly brought under cultivation. But unless population growth is checked by natural causes or moral restraint, the human species increases in a relentless geometric proportion (1-2-4-8), since parents tend to produce at least four children for the next generation. Thus, in the very process of nature, Malthus found an iron law that decreed misery for the vast lot of mankind. The population, according to this perverse impulse in humankind, always outran the

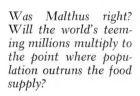

Was Malthus right? Will the world's teeming millions multiply to the point where population outruns the food supply?

food supply. In preceding centuries excess population had been checked by famine, war, and disease, but humanitarians and reformers were now seeking to check these salutary natural forces. More prosperity would only mean more children, who, in turn, would devour the fruits of prosperity and invite a new struggle for the inadequate means of sustaining life. Small wonder that Malthus was dubbed the "gloomy prophet" and economics the "dismal science." The predictions of Malthus proved unfounded as far as Western Europe and America were concerned, but a new Malthusian specter lies today over much of Asia, where the birth rate in fact is rapidly outdistancing gains in agricultural production.

DAVID RICARDO
AND THE IRON LAW OF WAGES

Another early economic thinker who fastened the reputation of "dismal science" on economics was David Ricardo, a wealthy English landowner and member of Parliament. He, too, was a prophet of gloom. Where Malthus had seen the mass of laborers doomed to misery and starvation in a capitalist economic system, Ricardo saw their income locked in an iron law of wages. Workers could never earn more than a bare subsistence wage because of the natural law of supply and demand. Here is why: if wages rose in an era of prosperity, then the labor supply would increase (as Malthus taught) since more people would seek to take advantage of this abundance, and thus wages would be forced back down to a subsistence level. Conversely, if wages sank below the subsistence level, starvation and want would reduce the labor supply, thus forcing wages back up to a subsistence level. Although Ricardo qualified his pessimism somewhat, he constantly maintained that wages should be left to the fair and free competition of the market. Interference by reform-

ers, humanitarians, or legislators would only do harm by impeding or reversing the logical processes of nature. Thus, Smith, Malthus, and Ricardo held very similar convictions respecting laissez faire, free competition, and a free-market economy. Their position is called "classical economics."

JOHN STUART MILL
AND DEMOCRATIC SOCIALISM

Not all nineteenth-century Englishmen took so pessimistic a view of the possibility of arresting or reversing these supposed laws of nature. The cold, gloomy, statistical studies of Malthus and Ricardo left little room for hope, for optimism, for progress. Yet the nineteenth century was supremely a time of optimism and faith in the future. Through men like John Stuart Mill, compassion and warmth reasserted themselves and sought a pathway out of the dark maze that the gloomy economists had constructed. And of those who blazed this new path, none wrote more brilliantly or exposed the weakness of the arguments of the prophets of doom with greater skill than Mill himself.

Mill found a middle road between the pessimism of the classical economists and the prophetic revelations of the later socialists. A child prodigy, he had grown up in a circle of brilliant thinkers that included his father, James Mill, and the reformer Jeremy Bentham. From them he learned to distrust all sweeping theories and laissez-faire economics in particular. He went beyond them to reject completely the "dismal science" of Malthus and Ricardo. "Can political economy do nothing," he queried, "but only object to everything, and demonstrate that nothing can be done?" Mill thought something could be done. Instead of lamenting the inevitability of overpopulation, why not encourage emigration to the colonies and sparsely populated regions of the globe? Instead of mourning about the iron law of wages, why not encourage workers to form trade unions, start cooperatives, and strive for more education? Furthermore, there were some instances where direct governmental intervention might be desirable. Certainly the conditions in the mines and factories of England, especially where children were employed, called for stringent legislative action. Mill thus advocated more radical departures from laissez faire than his predecessors. Although he distrusted strong government, he recognized that government action might be the only recourse to social injustice and popular grievances. Freedom was doubtless the greatest boon that a free society might confer on its citizens, but there were times when the government must interfere with one man's freedom to protect the freedom of others. Here was liberalism with a heart, foreshadowing the vast social reforms that would be carried out by democratic governments in the twentieth century.

THE UTOPIAN SOCIALISTS

There were still other nineteenth-century economists and philosophers who rejected both the strict laissez faire of the classical economists and the middle way of John Stuart Mill. Some of them found in the misery and poverty of the industrial workers a reflection of the injustice of capitalism itself. They denounced private property, the profit motive, and the free-enterprise system as foreign to man's nature and the laws of history. They charged that capitalism had failed to distribute fairly the fruits of industry and had opened a gulf between employers and employees. Many of them believed that capitalism must be replaced by a socialist system in which private property would be converted to collective ownership.

The "Utopian socialists" anticipated a peaceful, gradual transformation of society. Inspired by a burning sense of injustice, their programs took the form of visionary schemes, demands for wholesale reform, or experiments in communal socialism. One of the first and most impractical of these early socialists was a French noble, Henri, Count of Saint-Simon. From early youth he had a passion for reform and self-improvement. According to one story, Saint-Simon had his valet awake him each morning with the words: "Arise, monsieur le comte, for you have great things to do." At age 17 he embarked for America where he served under General Washington in the American Revolution. Romantic, adventurous, impetuous, Saint-Simon was convinced that he had found the answer to the social malcontent of his age. It was all absurdly simple: just establish an industrial state based on science and justice. Each man should be employed according to his abilities and paid according to his contribution. The right of inheritance should be abolished, for it transmitted the social privileges of one generation to the next. Everyone should start equal in the game of life and competition should be eliminated. Competition was an economic evil. Saint-Simon's plans were vague, unsystematic, and infinitely Utopian. He never came to grips with the insuperable obstacles that stood in the way of such a grandiose plan and contented himself by addressing constant futile appeals to King Louis XVIII and others to act on his suggestions. More crank than reformer, his ideas appealed to a small group of equally visionary intellectuals. His only importance in history lies in the impact his ideas have had on others.

Less impractical but still Utopian was another French socialist, Louis Blanc. An active politician, a journalist and author, he had more experience than Saint-Simon with the hard realities of life. In 1840 he published his *Organization of Labor*, in which he denounced the capitalistic system as harsh and inhumane. In its place he demanded a system of national workshops, which would step by step replace private ownership of factories,

farms, and shops. The government should inaugurate them, but once begun, the workers would themselves take over their management. A half-hearted attempt to try Blanc's scheme was actually made during the French Revolution of 1848 but failed.

Most practical of all the Utopian socialists was the English industrialist, Robert Owen. Owen is known as the father of the cooperative movement and the patron saint of British socialism. He was also a pioneer in his demands for factory legislation and universal education. When he took over the cotton mills at New Lanark, Scotland, he was deeply shocked at the condition of the workers. For the mills were full of orphan children from six to eight years old, dwarfed in mind and body, and of adult laborers, sunk in degeneracy and drunkenness. Owen embarked on a revolutionary plan to prove that he could raise profits and workers' morale at the same time. Within five years he successfully transformed New Lanark from a city of dirty hovels and streets filled with filth, squalor, wild children, and broken adults into a model industrial community. Beautiful gardens soon stood adjacent to comfortable dwellings, which were rented to workers at cost. The best known methods in garbage disposal and health protection were employed. Company shops sold food and provisions at wholesale prices. Workshops were (for that day) models of well-lighted and ventilated efficiency. Hours of work were cut to ten, and no child under ten was employed. Nurseries and schools were provided for workers' children. And children were to be taught by example rather than by punishment and fear. In fact, except for a few incorrigibles who had to be expelled, no one was punished.

Within just ten years New Lanark had become world-famous and was attracting scores of visitors, many of whom were impressed, others of whom found conditions unbelievable. Perhaps the most unbelievable, New Lanark was profitable, immensely profitable. Here was Owen's answer to the skeptics who believed that benevolence and profit were incompatible. Here, too, was his answer to the callousness and indifference of British industrialists. To the champions of laissez faire, Owen answered that man was the measure of economic systems, not the reverse. As Owen saw it, each man was the product of his environment. If the people of New Lanark had once been shiftless, drunken, and degraded, it was their surroundings that had made them so. Change the environment, Owen preached to the stream of visitors to New Lanark, and you change man.

But Owen soon tired of the excuses and indifference of his fellow employers who failed to follow his example. He was disgusted, too, with Parliament, which failed to carry out the far-reaching industrial reforms he advocated. He felt driven to the conclusion that his fellow capitalists would never change voluntarily—capitalism itself must be abolished. He advocated model social communities in which the profit motive would be absent and men's characters might be trained in cooperation and goodness. Some of his proposals, however, such as his suggestion that conventional ties of marriage and family be abandoned, were far too radical to win much support.

Nevertheless, at New Harmony, Indiana, far from his native soil, Owen financed one of his proposed model communities. But the experiment failed and placed a heavy drain on his financial resources. The rest of his long life was expended in the cause of various social reforms, including the formation of cooperatives to reduce the workers' cost of living. Throughout his career, Owen unfortunately offended many of his countrymen by his views on marriage, his savage attacks on the churches, and his advocacy of spiritualism.

KARL MARX
AND "SCIENTIFIC" SOCIALISM

By 1848 the schemes of the Utopian reformers were nearing bankruptcy. The work of Saint-Simon, Blanc, Owen, and others like them, had, with a few slight exceptions, come to naught. The Industrial Revolution had by now swept across France and Germany and was invading other portions of the Continent. With it came a repetition of the misery and suffering, the abuses and the injustice, which had incited the early reformers. In 1848 Karl Marx and Friedrich Engels issued a manifesto to workingmen everywhere to throw off the chains of capital-

ism and adopt their new, militant brand of socialism. For voluntary cooperation and visionary schemes, Marx substituted class war. "The history of all hitherto existing society," reads the famous opening line of Part I in the *Manifesto of the Communist Party*, "is the history of class struggles."

Socialism entered a new and radical phase with the publication of this *Manifesto*. The term "communist" was deliberately chosen by Marx and Engels for the title of the *Manifesto* since "socialism" had been used by the Utopian reformers. The Utopian socialists were despised as no more effective, in Marx's words, than "members of societies for the prevention of cruelty to animals." Utopian protests did nothing to relieve the horrible conditions of laborers and the poor. What would Marx do? For Utopian "vagueness" he would substitute precision; in place of pleas for reform there must be strength and violence; but most of all, Marx insisted, there must be *action*. Unlike earlier philosophers, who sought to explain the world, Marx would change it! He would incite men to act, and this he certainly did!

No more controversial figure has crossed the stage of modern history than Karl Marx, prophet of revolutionary communism. Born in Prussia in 1818, son of a Jewish lawyer turned Protestant, Marx studied philosophy, history, and law at the University of Berlin. His early plans to teach philosophy ended with his discovery of radical ideas and the sufferings of the workers. He turned to journalism, only to have his paper suppressed. Removal to Paris brought him in contact with early socialists and their theories. Here, also, he met Friedrich Engels, son of a wealthy German manufacturer, who shared Marx's revulsion from the conditions created by the Industrial Revolution. Together they sought to unify the working class and make it into an instrument for overthrowing the capitalistic state, which they believed responsible for the tyrannies and injustices of the new industrial order. Both men became interested in the Communist League, a small radical group of workers. It was for the League that they drew up the *Communist Manifesto* in 1848.

In the *Manifesto* and in his later analysis of capitalism, *Das Kapital*, Marx advanced three revolutionary ideas that have profoundly influenced the modern world. The first was the theory of *economic determinism*. In Marx's view, all society and government, all religion and art, as well as all thought and action, were ultimately expressions of economic conditions. Law, for example, reflected the will of the ruling classes. It was an expression of their economic relations, brought into being to protect their interests and their property. Government, too, existed to serve the interests of the rulers. And, likewise, the family had been reduced by modern capitalism to a debased economic partnership. According to Marx, each man thinks and acts as he does because of the economic circumstances in which he finds himself.

Secondly, Marx taught the *labor theory of value*. This idea was by no means new with Marx. Both Adam Smith and Ricardo had espoused it, but Marx drew some very revolutionary implications from it. All value in manufactured goods, according to his theory, was derived from the labor expended to produce it. In brief, labor was the common denominator of all commodities and gave them their precise value. Contributions of the capitalist Marx either depreciated or completely ignored. Since labor created the value of a commodity, Marx concluded that the worker had just claim to the finished product. But did he receive full value for his labor under a capitalist system? "No!" said Marx. He could not obtain his just return because the capitalist withheld a portion of it, called "surplus value," or profit, for his own enrichment. Capitalism, therefore, was nothing short of an unscrupulous arrangement for defrauding

the worker of what was rightfully his. The worker was justified, it followed, in seizing control of the instruments of production and distribution and erecting a new society.

Finally, Marx preached the *historical inevitability* of this whole process. All history,

Karl Marx, whose theories were to rock the economic, social, and political world as fully as Darwin's ideas rocked the scientific and religious.

the *Communist Manifesto* had said, was a record of class struggles. In ancient Rome patrician and plebeian had fought for control of the Empire's wealth. During the Middle Ages a titled nobility struggled against the onslaught of the serfs and a rising middle class. Now the middle class (bourgeoisie) had won control of industry, the new source of wealth, and was defending it against a growing army of workers.

In each period (historical stage of class

conflict) the dominant and privileged class controls the major means of production and its technology (systematic "know-how"), while a new and emerging class is identified with a new and emerging technology. Eventually the two classes do battle, and out of the conflict comes a combination of the best elements of the two. This whole process culminates in a new set of economic conditions, and hence, a new society and class structure. Then it starts over once more. This condition of class against class and the changes that emerge as a result of the conflict continues until the communist society is reached. Then the process stops, Marx asserts. Society becomes classless and there is no basis for further class conflict. This is history's pattern, which Marx called *dialectical materialism.* The dialectical method of reasoning and analysis Marx borrowed from the famous German philosopher Hegel. It runs like this. Every affirmative has in it a contradiction (opposite), which will express itself and ultimately destroy the affirmative. In applying this method of logic, Marx reasoned that each class and its technology (affirmation or thesis) contained within itself an opposite class technology (antithesis). The two eventually struggled and out of the struggle arose a new set of social conditions and class structure (synthesis). The forces that moved the pattern along the road of history were a changing technology and the economic relations among men, not the men themselves, not their ideas, not their political or social institutions. Thus, not only is all life and thought ultimately "determined" by the productive forces, but history proves it. Marx, for example, said that the bourgeoisie, armed to the teeth, controlling the productive means, the state, and the law, faced an inevitable final showdown with the expropriated workers. In this struggle the emerging class of workers (proletariat) was bound to win, for the whole pattern of history was on its side. The bourgeoisie would naturally defend its privileged position. Doing so meant greater exploitation of those who were not members of the bourgeoisie. The poor became poorer as well as more numerous, while the rich became richer. The selfishness that lay at the root of the capitalist (profit) system permitted no other course. Exploited workers and others not identified with control of the major means of production would follow the pattern of history and engage the bourgeoisie in a struggle.

For Marx, history was the key to the secrets of human relations. History proved that progress was inevitable. Each historical period moved toward an ideal society. For out of the class struggles would come ideal economic conditions, ideal human relations, better people, and a classless society. History proved, moreover, that economic relations and a changing technology were the major ("ultimate") determinants of human action, ideas, and events. The proof was all revealed in a regular and dialectical pattern of economic and social change. The pattern itself moved along a road that led to proletarian victory and the classless society. History thus had a goal, a destiny. It was going somewhere. And history was also rational and scientific. In summary, the changes in technology, the constant interplay (dialectic) between class and class, oppressor and oppressed, and the resulting changes in economic conditions were the stuff of history. For Marx, history was economically determined, patterned, dialectical, full of destiny, rational, and scientific. In history, Marx believed he had found the dynamic force that moved and explained events. It was a secret that had eluded the historians.

THE "ACHILLES HEEL" OF MARXISM

That Marx's ideas have had a profound effect on the course of the past century only a fool would deny. A militant communism spread halfway around the globe is thought by many to be the supreme threat of our generation. Although modern communism has changed, even corrupted, Marxian ideas, it is nevertheless built on Marx. Yet the very success of Marx's ideas and their effect on events belie the economic determinism Marx taught. For if Marx's ideas have affected so profoundly historical events of recent years, why cannot other ideas be equally effective? Is it not likely that many events are shaped as much or more by ideas as by productive forces? Further, there is a glaring contradiction at the very core of Marxism. For if the dialectical pattern of history and class conflict are inevitable, why should classes disappear when the communists take over? And why should conflict disappear? If cooperation and classless harmony are to prevail in the classless society, then class conflict is not inevitable at all. This logical inconsistency, so basic to communist ideology, is an "Achilles heel" of Marxism.

Other obvious weaknesses in the Marxist position are equally apparent. Marx finds that we are all products of our productive forces. If men are corrupt, if they are evil, selfish, and unjust, Marx says it is because their economic conditions have made them so. Change these economic conditions and man changes. Correct the economic conditions and you correct the condition of man. In the classless society, where conditions are supposedly ideal, men suddenly become different creatures. There is something terribly naive about this. People do behave differently in different environments. They do change, sometimes profoundly, when their social, economic, or physical environment changes. But there is no conclusive evidence or proof anywhere that men will behave as Marx says they will in the classless society.

A most serious shortcoming in Marx arises from his historical methods and what he assumes about history. He uses history to support the contentions we have just criticized. History is the tool for demonstrating

that men will reach the classless society and live harmoniously without strife, selfishness, and evil. Marx had a purpose. He would change men by changing the world and show that the process of change was historically scientific. He started with a goal, knowing exactly what he wished to prove, then searched out those factors in history that appeared to prove it. He did not let all the facts speak for themselves, as his disciples would have us believe he did. He does muster a wealth of evidence to prove his point. Yet he fails to produce any more evidence or to argue more convincingly than some historians who contend that great men, great ideas, or God are the moving forces in history, rather than productive forces. In many ways, Marxism is just one among many other historical interpretations. It is one that has had a profound impact, but that hardly proves its validity.

Finally, the rich did not necessarily become richer and the poor become poorer during the past century. The status and economic well-being of workers in Britain and America has actually been improving, not deteriorating. Besides, the ownership of the major means of production has not been concentrating into fewer and fewer hands in the way that Marx predicted it would. And in many instances ownership is becoming more rather than less diffused. Marx's apostle, Nikolai Lenin, recognized these facts and, of course, supplied explanations. He contended that these developments stemmed from the exploitation of underdeveloped areas (e.g., China, India, Africa) by industrially developed countries (e.g., Great Britain, Germany, and the United States).

Capitalism, says Lenin, inevitably breeds monopoly, and monopoly shuts off possibilities for the investment of "surplus capital." The upshot of this is an enormous accumulation of capital that seeks investment abroad. Lenin contends that "surplus capital will never be utilised for the purpose of raising the standard of living of the masses in a given country, for this would mean a decline in profits for the capitalists." Surplus capital will therefore be exported, into the "backward countries" especially, in order to raise profits. "In these backward countries," Lenin says, "profits are usually high, for capital is scarce, the price of land is relatively low, wages are low, raw materials are cheap." The "backward" (or underdeveloped) countries are thus exploited for the benefit of capitalist countries. Workers and the poor in the capitalist countries, of course, share in some of the benefits and profits accruing from exploitation. This, Lenin asserts, is why the worker's lot in some capitalist countries has been improving rather than deteriorating. They have benefited at the expense of the workers and the poor elsewhere.

It follows from Lenin's argument that the effects of capitalism are felt in the underdeveloped countries first, and therefore it is perfectly natural, Lenin thought, for communist revolutions to occur in the underdeveloped areas of the world first. Hence, Lenin was convinced that Marx was not wrong in his predictions. Rather, Marx had merely neglected to account for the world-wide effects of capitalist exploitation of the proletariat.*

We should notice, however, that Lenin discounted the effects of strong labor unions that were able to wrest advantages for the workers from their employers. Nor did he foresee what a benevolent government interested in social justice could do for the poor and underprivileged. Many of the reforms that Marx, Engels, and Lenin championed —free education, greater equalization of income, inheritance taxes, and greater control of transportation and communication—are now established in democratic countries. Asians and East Europeans have not been

so successful as we in obtaining reforms by free and democratic methods. This may be why communism appeals in the East to a greater extent than in the West. Certainly it is absurd to ignore this important fact and maintain that the American high standard of living is based on the exploitation of foreign populations. The communists ignore far too many facts that weaken their historical argument. To recognize only supporting factors and to discount the opposing ones is to be either intellectually dishonest or a poor analyst.

JOHN MAYNARD KEYNES AND "MODIFIED CAPITALISM"

Neither was it fair for Lenin to assume that capitalistic theory would remain any more fixed and immutable than the capitalistic processes that the classical economists had described. Lenin's quarrel, like Marx's, was with the doctrines of Smith, Malthus, Ricardo, and Mill. He paid no heed to non-socialist economists who also attacked the validity or justice of the Five Commandments of liberalism. He simply agreed with Marx that capitalism was unjust, contradictory, and doomed to destruction by the unbending laws of history.

Many in the capitalistic world had been arguing almost as forcefully as Marx that laissez faire, the iron law of wages, and the sanctity of private property added up to economic injustice. Reformers in Europe and America had long crusaded for governmental intervention to aid the working classes and discipline the forces of economic greed. A host of economists on both sides of the Atlantic sought to provide theoretical justification for what the reformers were after. By the end of the nineteenth century, the extent of the revolution that capitalistic theory had undergone since Ricardo's day was apparent in the writings of Britain's foremost economist, Alfred Marshall.

---

* The material in the three previous paragraphs is based on V. I. Lenin, *Imperialism* (New York: International Publishers, 1939), pp. 15-128.

From his quiet academic surroundings at Cambridge, Marshall sent forth a stream of technical publications that affected profoundly the economic thought of his day. Through his writings there shone a warm concern for human beings and a desire to improve society. Moderation was the hallmark of all his work. Although he praised competition, Marshall admitted that it had its bad features as well as its good ones. He saw the necessity for private wealth, yet hated the extremes of poverty that had moved him to pity while a young man at Cambridge. With John Stuart Mill he agreed that the state must play a larger role in economic affairs, but at the same time he thought that the free-enterprise system must be preserved. For Ricardo's iron law of wages Marshall substituted the more humane concept of a "standard of comfort" that would make workers more efficient and thereby pay for the increased outlay in wages. He unhesitatingly accepted labor unions and their right to bargain with employers. He insisted that workers should have a larger share of the national income. And although he disliked reformers, he welcomed the idea of reform. His was a typically British performance.

One of Marshall's favorite students was John Maynard Keynes, a brilliant, urbane young man from one of Britain's oldest families.* By coincidence, he was born in 1883, the year of Karl Marx's death. While still in his thirties, he sat as an adviser to the British delegation at the Paris Peace Conference in 1919 and condemned the final treaty as lacking in economic realism. The Big Four, he wrote in his famous book, *The Economic Consequences of the Peace*, "paid no attention to these [economic] issues, being preoccupied with others,—Clemenceau to crush the economic life of his enemy, Lloyd George to do a deal and bring home some-

thing that would pass muster for a week, the President to do nothing that was not just and right. It is an extraordinary fact that the fundamental problems of a Europe, starving and disintegrating before their eyes, was the one question in which it was impossible to arouse the interest of the Four."

Keynes predicted failure for the Versailles Treaty in keeping the peace—and he was right. His prediction and other writings had already made him famous by the time he wrote to George Bernard Shaw in 1935 about the work he was doing on his most important book, *The General Theory of Employment, Interest, and Money*. "I believe myself," he told Shaw, "to be writing a book on economic theory which will largely revolutionize—not, I suppose at once, but in the course of the next ten years—the way the world thinks about economic problems." Once more, Keynes was right—and the world listened to this scholar-professor-diplomat, who had incidentally demonstrated his financial acumen by making a fortune in international exchange.

There were five principal ideas in Keynes' *General Theory:*

1. *Full employment is not a natural condition of capitalism.* The classical economists from Adam Smith on had assumed that the capitalistic system had a built-in regulator that tended to keep employment at a maximum. Yet it was an obvious fact to Keynes, writing in the midst of the Great Depression of the 1930's, that unemployment was chronic as well as widespread in many parts of Britain. Was not classical theory then only a *special* case, applicable only in the realm of pure theory and largely irrelevant to a world in acute economic distress? Keynes' *general* theory held that less than full employment might be the normal condition of a society and that economists must learn to look at economic activity in *aggregate* (total) terms rather than through the books of an individ-

---

* The following discussion is based heavily on Dudley Dillard's *The Economics of John Maynard Keynes* (Englewood Cliffs, N. J.: Prentice-Hall, 1948), pp. 1-12.

ual business firm or industry. The aggregate, or over-all, concepts of employment, national income, consumption, and so forth, should be studied along with such traditional subjects as how individual prices are determined in the market place.

2. *Money is a barometer of people's confidence in the economy.* The subject of money played an important part in Keynes' thinking. If you have a surplus of money, you may hoard it, lend it, or invest it. If many people hoard it, however, there is a severe shortage of money for the other two purposes, and the entire economy suffers from an inability to expand. Normally, there is a preference for lending or investing one's money since these operations yield a return in the form of interest or profit. If this is not the case, and money for investment or loans is in short supply, then this can be taken as a sign of popular uncertainty about the economic future.

3. *Interest is paid for not hoarding money.* The wish to keep one's money secure and close at hand, however, is not an unqualified one. We may be induced to lend or invest our money if the *rate* of return is sufficiently high to offset the risk. The rate of interest that is paid on loans or investments at any given moment is thus a reflection of how deep our desire to hoard money actually is. Looked at from the point of view of the economy as a whole, if there is widespread confidence in the future, businessmen will seek to borrow money to expand their operations; but, since the amount of money available for borrowing is always limited, a higher price must be paid for the money that is needed. Those who want money must pay a higher premium to those who part with their money. But the rise of interest rates discourages new businesses that might be willing and able to borrow if lower rates of interest prevailed. This means, Keynes concluded, that a rise in interest rates tends to reduce the demand for certain things, which,

in turn, at least in normal times, tends to cause unemployment.

4. *Employment depends on the amount of investment.* Every capitalistic society can produce more than it can immediately consume. The well-to-do soon reach a point of satiety and the poorer members of society are stopped from consuming more by their limited incomes. There is, therefore, a potential surplus of productive power that must be devoted to making things not immediately wanted, such as railroads, buildings, or factories. Keynes called this production of goods over and above immediate want *investment*. Whether there is anything approaching full employment at any given moment, he argued, will depend on the amount of investment in a society. If investment stops, unemployment begins. Production for immediate wants alone will not keep all able-bodied men at work. Control investment and you control employment. But how can this be done? What causes investment to fluctuate?

5. *Investment depends on irrational factors.* In the last analysis, investment fluctuates because of the precarious state of knowledge on which all economic decisions are based. The future is not known; yet investment involves a confidence in the future. The investor deals in guesses and expectations; they can never be more than this because factors affecting the future can be neither fully known nor controlled. Yet decisions must be made. So the investor tends to rely on "expert" knowledge, which in reality is no more than the pooling of a number of informed guesses or expectations. This "expert" knowledge Keynes calls the "conventional judgment" of the market place. It is subject to sweeping and sudden change in response to new developments. This is in marked contrast to the classical view of the market place, which assumed that strong-minded individual opinions would cancel each other out, leaving a consensus of rational judgment.

The significance of this "Keynesian Revolution" against classical economics may perhaps now be clear. Its practical consequences in the area of governmental policy were simply tremendous. For if you assume, as the classical economists did, that the natural state of economic equilibrium is one of full employment and that any loss of equilibrium stems from interference with competitive business enterprise, then you are likely to agree that governmental action is as harmful as any other kind of unnatural interference with business. Government should never spend to keep up employment, never fix minimum wages, never compete with private enterprise. But if you assume, as Keynes did, that economic equilibrium may be reached while there is considerable unemployment, you will probably insist with Keynes that government should do all in its power to bridge the gap left by private enterprise.

Keynes and his followers came to believe that the ups and downs of prosperity known as the "business cycle" were subject to a large measure of control by governments. If the tax power were used to reduce private spending in boom times, demand, and hence prices, could be kept down, while in times of depression government could use its revenues for public-works programs, thereby keeping demand and prices up. There was thus a middle way between unregulated capitalism with its extremes of boom and bust on the one hand, and socialistic remedies on the other. An unregulated competitive market was no longer believed by the Keynesians and their political allies, notably the New Dealers of the 1930's, to be necessarily the best thing for the nation as a whole. In a time of severe national crisis, the older capitalistic views seemed to be discredited and outmoded. Their newer doctrines of "modified capitalism," without completely abandoning free enterprise by any means, seemed to place major responsibility on the government to guide the nation's economy and protect the material welfare of the individual.

To evaluate Keynes and his work is still a difficult matter. Few questions are likely to stir so much debate among contemporary economists as one inquiring into the status of Keynes' thought today. For one thing, he died in 1946, much too recently for economists and historians to see his work in the proper perspective of time. He wrote, too, in a time of near economic collapse, and it is always easier to find fault with the surgeon once the illness is passed. Yet it is probably fair to say that a considerable majority of today's economists regard him as the most original economic thinker of the twentieth century—stimulating, thoughtful, and always provocative. Most would agree further that the main body of current theory in economics borrows heavily from Keynes' analysis in the *General Theory*. Some will argue that there are erroneous ideas in Keynes' work, others that his central thesis is entirely mistaken, and still others that his followers, by their excesses, have destroyed whatever validity his argument contained. But few will deny his influence. Not only in his native Britain but throughout the Commonwealth, the Continent of Europe, and here in America, Keynes' ideas have markedly influenced politics, legislation, and social thought, as well as the teaching and study of economics. Our own chapter 29 is devoted to a discussion of America's quest for social justice in this century—a movement in which Keynes' influence has been and still remains unmistakably strong.

SOME WORDS OF SUMMARY

In measuring the consequences of industrialism, we are confronted with a paradox. On the one hand, industrialism created more wealth, a higher standard of living, and a world in which people are closely linked together. On the other, it brought abuses and misery to some industrial workers, sharpened the antagonism between employers and employees, and tended on occasion to stifle the creativity of men. A pessimistic view of the consequences of industrialism drew heavily on the evidence of abuses in early English factories, especially the brutality and ill-treatment of children.

Outside England, the Industrial Revolution produced the same train of grievances and social tensions that shocked English reformers. In America, industrialism widened the gulf between rich and poor and weakened the American faith in individualism and unregulated economic enterprise. In Russia, the misery of the factory workers made them susceptible to the Bolshevik appeal of Lenin and Trotsky. Following the Russian Revolution, the Soviets chose to give priority to industrial strength before satisfying consumer demands and needs. This system of forced austerity is today being copied by Communist China, while India travels a road of greater freedom.

The impact of the industrial way of life on Western Europe upset old ways of thinking and produced a new spectrum of social and economic thought. Defenders of the wealth and status of the middle class stressed individual rights, natural economic laws, freedom of contract, free trade, and competition as the lifeblood of a thriving social system. Certain economic theorists made important contributions to the growing body of classical economic doctrine. Adam Smith argued the need for laissez faire and a natural division of labor; Malthus gloomily compared statistics on population and food supply; and Ricardo held that wages were forced by an iron law to a subsistence level.

Others held out the possibility of reforming the social situation. John Stuart Mill urged that strict laissez-faire ideas be tempered by a concern for human suffering. Some Utopian socialists went further in urging the abandonment of capitalism and the repudiation of competition, private property, and profits. Saint-Simon urged a new start with a society constructed on principles of science and justice. Louis Blanc proposed that national workshops be substituted for profit-making enterprises. Robert Owen campaigned for model social and industrial communities.

Disgusted by the weakness of the Utopian socialist movements, Karl Marx constructed a new design for a social revolution. Basing his theory on ideas of class struggle, the labor theory of value, and economic determinism, Marx taught that revolution was intrinsically a part of historical design. Each oppressed class of the past had struggled against the dominant class. This would also be true of the proletariat, or exploited workingmen, who would one day seize control of the state and usher in a new era of peace and abundance. Deep in the logic of Marxism lies the contradiction that the dynamic thrust of class warfare, uncontrollable by human effort through all history, will blunt itself when the worker's paradise, the classless society, is reached.

While Lenin and others were revising Marxian theory to fit the needs of modern communism, Alfred Marshall and John Maynard Keynes were adapting capitalistic theory to the problems of a twentieth-century civilization. Keynes, in particular, exerted great influence on modern economic thought by his questioning of the classical idea that economic equilibrium meant full employment and by championing governmental intervention as a means of sustaining demand and hence employment. The status of Keynes' thought among contemporary economists is perhaps debatable, but few would deny its impact on the central body of capitalistic theory and fewer still its influence on public policy in times of economic crisis.

FURTHER ROADS TO LEARNING

GENERAL ACCOUNTS

The works of T. S. Ashton, J. L. and B. Hammond, H. Heaton, and L. Mumford, cited in the last chapter, continue to be useful for the theme of the present chapter.

E. Roll, A *History of Economic Thought*, 2nd ed. (Englewood Cliffs, N. J.: Prentice-Hall, 1956). Thorough presentation of economic theory from its origins in antiquity to the present.

SPECIAL STUDIES

See the volumes by W. Bowden, V. M. Dean, H. U. Faulkner, P. A. M. Taylor, A. Toynbee, and P. Mantoux cited at the end of the last chapter.

I. Berlin, *Karl Marx* (New York: Oxford University Press, 1948). Probably the best biography of this controversial figure.

M. Buer, *Health, Wealth, and Population in the Early Days of the Industrial Revolution* (London: Routledge, 1926). A sane, balanced account of certain social features of the early Industrial Revolution.

D. Dillard, *The Economics of John Maynard Keynes* (Englewood Cliffs, N. J.: Prentice-Hall, 1948). A simple account of a very difficult subject.

F. Dulles, *Labor in America* (New York: Crowell, 1949). A good, popular treatment of the history of the American labor movement.

W. Ebenstein, *Today's Isms*, 2nd ed. (Englewood Cliffs, N. J.: Prentice-Hall, 1958). A brief, accurate summary of some of the economic theories discussed in this chapter.

R. Heilbroner, *The Worldly Philosophers* (New York: Simon & Schuster, 1953). A sparkling popular account of such economic thinkers as Smith, Malthus, Ricardo, Mill, Owen, and Marx.

H. Laski, *The Rise of Liberalism* (New York: Harper, 1936). A critical historical examination of liberal ideas by a well-known British scholar and Labor Party leader.

V. Lenin, *Imperialism* (New York: International Publishers, 1939). One of the classic communist analyses of capitalism and its effects, by the leader of the Russian revolution.

K. Marx and F. Engels, *The Manifesto of the Communist Party* (many editions). The charge delivered to the working classes in 1848 by these two communist leaders.

W. E. Moore, *Industrialization and Labor* (Ithaca, N. Y.: Cornell University Press, 1951). Provides some stimulating ideas and novel perspectives on industrialization.

R. Owen, *The Life of Robert Owen, by Himself* (New York: Knopf, 1920). A full autobiography of this pioneering Utopian socialist.

T. Parsons and N. Smelser, *Economy and Society* (London: Routledge and Kegan Paul, 1956). A thoughtful, wide-ranging treatment of the interrelatedness of economy and society.

K. Polanyi, *The Great Transformation* (Boston: Beacon, 1957). A refreshingly different interpretation of the social implications of the market economy.

J. Schapiro, *Liberalism and the Challenge of Fascism* (New York: McGraw-Hill, 1949). Contains several good essays that treat the liberal thinkers discussed in this chapter.

A. Schlesinger, Jr., *The Age of Jackson* (Boston: Little, Brown, 1945). A Pulitzer-Prize winning account of the intellectual, economic, political, and social currents of a transitional period in the development of American social ideas.

G. Soule, *Ideas of the Great Economists* (New York: Mentor Books, 1955). A remarkably thorough and easy presentation of the thoughts of the major economists.

N. Thomas, *A Socialist's Faith* (New York: Norton, 1951). A most incisive statement on the nature of socialism by a leading American journalist and socialist.

P. Viereck, *Conservatism Revisited* (New York: Scribners, 1949). A retrospective criticism of the main body of ideas associated with nineteenth-century liberalism and radicalism.

E. Wilson, *To the Finland Station* (Garden City, N. Y.: Doubleday, Anchor Books, 1953). A justifiably well-known survey of modern socialistic thought.

E. Woodward, *The Age of Reform, 1815-1870* (Oxford: Clarendon Press, 1938). A broad treatment of these crucial years in Great Britain.

FICTION AND DRAMA

E. Bellamy, *Looking Backward* (New York: Modern Library, 1951). Good example of a Utopian outlook in an American setting.

C. Dickens, *Hard Times* (New York: Dutton, 1907). One of Dickens' best treatments of social problems resulting from industrialism.

J. Galsworthy, *Strife*, in J. Galsworthy, *Plays* (New York: Scribner, 1928, and other editions). Story of labor violence by a famous dramatist.

M. Gorki, *The Lower Depths* (New Haven: Yale University Press, 1945). Depressing drama of outcasts and derelicts in the lower stratum of Russian society.

W. Howells, *A Hazard of New Fortunes* (New York: Harper, 1890). About the strife between industrial classes played against the background of metropolitan New York.

A. Monkhouse, *First Blood*, rev. ed. (in M. J. Moses, *Representative British Drama*, Boston: Little, Brown, 1931). Struggles of labor and capital in the cotton trade of Lancashire.

E. Zola, *Germinal* (New York: Knopf, 1925). The greatest of French naturalistic writers tells about the lives of unhappy French miners caught in the industrial vise.

FILMS

Backfire (Princeton Film Center, 1952, 15 min., sound, black and white). Poses the question whether men should be rewarded in proportion to their investment or according to the Marxian formula—"to each according to his needs."

Look at Capitalism (National Education Program, 1955, 12½ min., sound, black and white). Defines capitalism and its workings, primarily from the American point of view.

Two Views of Socialism (Coronet Films, 1950, 15 min., sound, color). A presentation designed to stimulate discussion about the differences between capitalism and socialism.

Checks and Balances
in American Industrial Life

*Today the government plays an important role
in balancing the conflicting pressures of the various
interest groups in American society.*

Powerful

and active organizations of businessmen, workers, farmers, and others have sought to enlarge their stake in our increasingly industrialized society, the roots of which we have just traced. These special-interest groups seem to feel that they have unique contributions to make to society, and each one develops its special line of charges and countercharges, complaints against encroachments, and pleas for protection, propaganda and lobbying, organized resistance, and positive action campaigns. At one time it is a labor union acting as though businessmen are out to crush unions and exploit workers; another time it is a business organization complaining loudly of monopolistic labor unions, a group of doctors fighting socialized medicine, or a group of farmers demanding crop insurance. Sometimes the maneuvering is frank and open; at other times it is covert and behind the scenes. Behind it all we find an interesting story about the organization and growth of many special-interest groups and how each tends to hold the others in check.

Organization became almost a fetish in America as industrial growth jumped ahead by leaps and bounds. Thousands of people, vast stores of materials, and many machines were welded into efficient productive units. With this massive organization came domination and control. And organization begat organization. Individual workers were rapidly dwarfed and swallowed up by the giant organizations that employed them. Indeed, the worker needed help if he hoped to defend his interests in a world that was becoming increasingly complex. He, too, was forced to organize. As a result, labor unions appeared and were soon affording the individual a more effective means of bargaining with employers than could individual effort. Industrialists also banded together into employer organizations, and even farmers sought strength through the unity of organization. The appearance of one organization tended to bring others into being to challenge it and attempt to balance its power. Without the countervailing power of labor against management or consumers (as represented in legislatures) against labor, any one of these interests alone might have clamped a monopolistic hold over large areas of the economy.

What helped prevent the rise of a "ruling class" was a system of *checks and balances*. Protected by the principles of freedom of assembly and free speech, men banded together in common cause to prevent others from encroaching on their interests. Each group was restrained from realizing complete domination by a combination of power on the part of other interest groups. Since some organizations and interests were more powerful than others, several weaker ones might have to unite to check and balance the power of a strong one. The system of checks and balances in America is thus very elaborate and involved.

THE NATURE OF A CHECK-AND-BALANCE SYSTEM

In political life, our national government provides one of the very best illustrations of the ancient principle of checks and balances. As every schoolboy knows, there are three branches of our national government—executive, legislative, and judicial. In the Constitution the duties and responsibilities of each are made clear. Each is supposedly held in check by the other two. The president of the United States, for example, has the power to veto legislation enacted by the Congress. Conversely, the Congress may pass a bill over the president's veto, as well as enact legislation that lays the foundation for executive action. And the Supreme Court may check the actions of both Congress and the president through its right to declare actions of both unconstitutional. But the Supreme Court, too, may find its field of influence narrowed by the action of a hostile Congress. Thus, in this fashion the framers of the Constitution sought to prevent the concentration of political power in the hands of either a select minority or a selfish and transient majority.

Outside of politics, the system of checks and balances in our national life operates less obviously. Yet the American economy, for example, operates under the restraints of a system of checks and balances as surely as our political system does. Businessmen, farmers, and industrial workers all seek to advance themselves through organizations that reflect the economic, political, and so-cial interests of their members. Businessmen seek to maintain trade and production at a high level of profit and to turn aside interference from the government. Workers are interested in higher wages, shorter hours, and better working conditions. Farmers want the best possible price for their products and protection against crop failures. These diverse interests are certain to come into conflict, as when workers strike for higher wages, or businessmen combine to force down the price of raw materials. *These organized interest groups serve to check and balance one another.* Sometimes two of these interest groups may square off against the third. Labor unions and farmers might line up against a business monopoly or an industry that is reaping unreasonably high profits. Or farmers may side with employers against compulsory union membership. So long as all three groups are strongly organized, however, the public need not fear that any one interest will completely dominate the others and, hence, the economy. But how has the system actually worked in the past and what is the situation today?

CORPORATIONS AND BUSINESS ASSOCIATIONS

The modern business corporation is the most important form of commercial enterprise in the world today. It is more than an agency for producing and marketing goods and services, although this is its historic and primary function. Today's corporation has interests that transcend the realm of economics and carry over into the political, the social, and even the intellectual worlds. It is, in fact, a world of its own with its own rules, traditions, and system of loyalties.

RISE OF THE MODERN BUSINESS CORPORATION

Most simply defined, *a business corporation is a productive enterprise owned by many persons and authorized by law to act as a single person.* Each of the owners is protected from losing more money than he has invested, which specifically *limits his liability,* a sharp contrast with the liability of a business partner, who stands to lose far more than his investment. Also, in contrast with sole ownerships and business partnerships, a corporation may continue in existence for an indefinitely long period of time. Following this principle of *perpetuity,* stockholders may come and go but the organization continues, whereas retirement or death of a sole owner or partner may dissolve their businesses. Our interest lies primarily with the growth of the business corporation as a device for representing special interests. We will ask what interests a corporation serves, and on whose behalf the organization operates. We shall also see that business corporations have introduced a drastically changed conception of property rights.

As early as the fifteenth century there were mining corporations in Germany, while great overseas trading corporations, such as the East India Company, began to emerge in England during the seventeenth and eighteenth centuries. In America, however, the corporate form of business organization was not common until after the Revolutionary War, and it was many years after that before it played an important role in American life.

The first great modern corporations in America appeared toward the close of the nineteenth century. Among these early leaders were the Standard Oil Company, the Carnegie Steel Corporation (later incorporated as the United States Steel Corporation), and the E. I. duPont de Nemours Company. By 1904 a well-known business analyst, John Moody, commenting on the strength of these big corporations, estimated that twenty-six of them controlled at least 80 per cent of production in their fields. This sensational growth provoked a controversy that has raged to the present time. Should any business be permitted to control so large a share of the production in any field? Is bigness in itself an evil? What should be done about it? Critics of the modern corporation have come from labor unions, the small-business class, and from other groups and individuals who often fear so much power being wielded by so few persons.

SENTIMENT AGAINST CORPORATIONS

Why should corporations be the object of so much suspicion? Two of the major reasons are the size of the modern corporation and uncertainty about how large corporations will use their power.

A relatively small number of business corporations have dominated vast areas of our economy throughout the twentieth century. In 1948, for example, one-third of all employment was attributable to 3,100 organizations, or only one-tenth of 1 per cent of all American firms.[*] And the 361 largest corporations, those with assets of at least $50 million, were responsible for about a third of the total assets of the more than 3.5 million business enterprises in the United States. A large share of production and sales in particular markets, such as automobiles, is often concentrated in a few big corporations. Some corporations have become so large, so complex, and so important in their influence in society that they antagonize considerable numbers of people.

Uncertainty about whose interests the corporations represent, however, is an even more common cause of resentment than sheer size. If bigness is difficult to appreciate fully or to portray accurately, representation of interests is even more so. Who has the legal right to control a corporation, either for his own or other interests? Who actually controls a corporation? What groups can and have laid claim to having corporations run in their interest? Such questions suggest part of the turmoil over whose interests ought to be represented by the corporation.

First, let's look at the question of the legal right to control. Traditionally, owners have had the right to control and to use their property as they saw fit. And legally we still uphold the principle that control follows ownership. Nevertheless, in recent decades ownership has become divorced from management of corporations. Individual stockholders, the true owners of corporations, have become so numerous that very few of them can individually influence the affairs of a corporation. Because stockholders have

---

[*] *Survey of Current Business*, May, 1950.

not exercised their right to control the corporation completely and effectively, professional managers have assumed the function. The lawful right to control has thus become inactive for many stockholders. They no longer make the important decisions.

So for the second question of who actually controls a corporation, the answer is mainly a group of professional managers. And whose interests do they represent? Critics, including many stockholders, often feel that the managerial class is concerned primarily with its own interests. A stockholder may compare his small dividend with the large bonus received by a manager and be irrevocably convinced that he is not getting his fair share. Some critics feel also that professional managers are primarily concerned with their own careers at the expense of profits and the general welfare of the corporation. Executives of a corporation, of course, stoutly maintain that their efforts are directed toward the best interests of the organization, its owners, and at times, even the entire United States.

But it is not just stockholders who have demanded that corporations—indeed all business organizations—be run in their interest. In addition to owners who are mainly after profits from a prosperous business, workers and consumers assert their claims. Workers have a very vital stake in corporations as a means of earning a livelihood, and they want the best wages and working conditions possible. The consuming public is interested in prices, quality of goods and services, and in safety, styling, taxation and other matters involving corporate activities.

BUSINESSMEN ORGANIZE

Although corporations have become larger and more prominent in the business world, they represent only a part of a variety of business interests. Businessmen in general have organized themselves to help protect and promote their interests. Hundreds of associations have come into being, some of them national in scope, others more localized. Some represent rather general interests of businessmen, others more specific interests. The National Association of Manufacturers, probably the best-known business organization, has enlisted the support and active participation of thousands of employers for more than half a century. In countless ways the N. A. M. serves the interests of business by supplying businessmen with information, arranging business contacts, promoting good public relations, and fighting hostile legislation. At times in its history, particularly during its early days, the N. A. M., like other business organizations, seemed to take the position that what was good for business was good for all Americans. For many years employers reflected this attitude by openly opposing labor organizations and

The stock is the thing. Stockholders come and stockholders go, but the corporation goes on forever.

resorting on occasions to violence and other methods designed to bar unions from their shops. Now, however, all but the most ardent anti-labor employer associations have adopted a "live and let live" policy toward unionism.

Employer opposition has become much more subtle and enlightened than it used to be and, in contrast with the anti-labor emphasis of a half-century ago, employers' associations are today far more concerned with business trends, foreign trade, and government policies. Through such agencies as the National Industrial Conference Board, employers and people in general receive basic facts and information on population, economic conditions, legislation, and public opinion. A person would find it difficult to argue that such information is of interest solely to businessmen. A further illustration of the broadness of business associations is found in the local chambers of commerce across the nation. Though traditionally composed of business and professional people, and often regarded as businessmen's organizations, local chambers have sought to make their membership more representative by opening their rolls to labor leaders and appointing wage-workers to various committees. Their programs, too, are not confined solely to narrowly defined business interests; they seek to promote both community and business growth.

Both businessmen's associations and labor unions have similar goals: each seeks to act as spokesman for its members and to defend them against pirating of privileges by others; and each in its own way serves a larger purpose by promoting community projects and by taking an active role in national and international affairs. We have already seen how businessmen's associations serve business people, and we now turn to the labor movement to see how labor unions have come forward to defend the interests of wage-workers.

A stockholder speaks her mind. Actually, however, stockholders no longer make important corporate decisions.

ORGANIZED LABOR

THE RISE OF ORGANIZED LABOR

American labor organizations emerged from the carpentry, shoemaking, and printing crafts as early as the 1790's, but it was a great many years before labor unions reached a position of power and influence. As long as business markets remained local, labor unions, too, remained local. But as the market area expanded to take in national and even international customers, labor likewise began to see that its problem embraced more than merely local wages and working conditions.

Not until the latter half of the nineteenth century did American business and labor organizations break out of their local confines. City or even state-wide unions were no longer able to speak for a working force that cut across state and regional boundaries. Employers operating firms and hiring labor in a half-dozen states could ignore the puny protests of locally based unions. After several experiments at organizing a national labor movement, a number of craft unions combined to organize the American Federation of Labor in 1881.

Under the leadership of its able first president, Samuel Gompers, the A. F. L. grew steadily from a membership of less than 150,000 at its birth to about 4 million in 1920. The mission of the A. F. L., as Gompers and his lieutenants saw it, was to see that labor shared generously in the profits of American industrial enterprise. He fought hard for limited goals, including the eight-hour day, a shorter work week, and the outlawing of child labor, adopting the simple motto of "more." Determined to avoid the mistakes of earlier labor leaders, Gompers steered the A. F. L. away from outright involvement in politics, preferring, as he put it, to "reward the friends of labor and punish its enemies."

He did, however, rely heavily on the strike and the boycott, which he used frequently against employers to advance the interests of the skilled workmen in his organization. Thus, the American labor movement under the guidance of Gompers became wedded to the ideals of business unionism, seeking a larger share in the profits of industry rather than advocating radical economic and social changes.

The A. F. L. was as much interested in protecting its skilled craft workers against unskilled laborers as against the oppression of employers. By the early 1930's a rift was beginning to appear between the champions of *craft unionism* and the defenders of *industrial unionism*. Believers in craft unionism, such as Gompers and William Green, his successor, thought that the labor movement should be based on craft unions, whose members shared a common skill, such as cigarmaking or tool-and-die-making. These skilled workers need not be in the pay of the same employer or even work in the same industry. But champions of industrial unionism argued that an effective labor movement must be founded on industrial unions, whose members worked in the same industry, irrespective of their particular skills. Automobile-workers, steel-workers, or rubber-workers, regardless of their specific jobs, should all belong to the same industry-wide union.

In the middle 1930's the American labor movement split wide open over this issue. John L. Lewis, leader of the United Mine Workers, insisted on organizing the largely unskilled mass-production workers in spite of the opposition of other A. F. L. leaders. Out of the deadlock that ensued, came the Congress of Industrial Organizations (C. I. O.), which set out to organize industry's rank- and file-workers. After a series of violent strikes, the C. I. O. successfully organized workers in the steel, automobile, rubber, and other heavy industries.

While the A. F. L. and C. I. O. federations of unions grew in membership, overtures were made from time to time by both organizations to reunite the house of labor. But A. F. L. chieftains, who considered themselves aristocrats of labor, regarded the C. I. O. leaders as "young upstarts." C. I. O. leaders, on the other hand, were fearful of being absorbed by the older federation. Personalities clashed, and leaders on both sides were frequently involved in open, bitter arguments. But in time, the feeling that organized labor needed to present a unified front eventually overcame the many differences. So, in 1956, after more than twenty years of feuding, the A. F. L. and C. I. O. joined hands in a remarriage. And today the ranks of this mammoth organization number more than sixteen million workers as members.

Aside from this rift in basic labor philosophy and split in organization, now apparently healed, the house of organized labor has been plagued by a number of other troublesome problems. There have been disputes over union jurisdiction in industries where more than one union has claimed the right to represent the same workers. Communist infiltration has been a source of concern to union leaders and the public alike ever since the Great Depression of the early 1930's. More recently, instances of labor racketeering have seriously shaken public confidence in several labor leaders. In addition, there are personal feuds between union chiefs, and disagreements over labor strategy and tactics. On occasion, too, the state and federal legislatures, and also the courts, have taken actions unfavorable to the interests of labor unions. Yet, despite all these problems, the American labor movement today holds a position of great national influence and acts as a powerful check on the power of big business and employer groups.

AIMS AND STRATEGY

And what have American labor unions tried to achieve? Put most simply, unions have aimed at higher wages, shorter hours, and better working conditions. Modern unions have been interested, too, in health protection, insurance, pensions, and other welfare benefits. As an individual, a worker was at a great disadvantage in trying to bargain with his employer. He might have threatened to quit or refused to work, but such threats rarely had much effect on an employer. Combinations of workers, however, have been able to win important concessions from management. With the *strike* as a major tool, unions have obtained wage increases and other concessions from employers. Thus, the chief reason for the existence of a labor union is its ability to apply pressure on business and industry to improve the lot of its members.

From the employer's standpoint, the counterpart of the strike is the *lockout*. If an employer decides such an action is necessary, he literally locks the doors of the plant and prevents his employees from working. On occasion, both strikes and lockouts have been violent. Early labor disputes were frequently long and bloody affairs with casualties on both sides. In recent years, however, many work stoppages have become remarkably peaceful. In one instance the strikers, after carefully notifying the employer of their plans and helping him close the plant, set up an orderly picket line. While they marched, they were comforted by hot coffee and television sets provided by their employer.

Today the strategy and technique of both parties are remarkably similar. Both plead their cause through the mass media in an effort to win the public to their side. Both employ lobbyists to work for favorable legislative action in the state and national capitals. Both hire outstanding counsel and seek to redress their grievances through the courts. And both recognize quickly where the power and the advantage in the struggle lie and tend to make the best bargain possible. The major differences between labor and management today, therefore, lie in the objectives they seek rather than in the techniques they follow.

Modern unions are concerned with many specific objectives as they aim to advance workers' interests. For one thing, a union seeks first to be recognized by the employer as a bargaining agent in order to protect the workers' interest effectively. Once this recognition is granted, the union aims at obtaining a contract with the employer, which usually includes provisions governing hiring, firing, promotion, transfer, wages, hours, leaves of absence, and grievance procedures. Once recognition and a contract have been attained, the aim is to administer and improve contract provisions.

Unions have also encouraged their members to form political action and education committees and have provided workers with social, recreational, and welfare programs. They have, in fact, sought increasingly to represent the workers' interests in the very broadest sense. It is not at all unusual today for an ambitious union to sponsor a sickness and accident program, run a bowling league,

Although once accompanied by considerable violence, most strikes tend to be rather peaceful affairs these days.

offer free concerts, and provide educational lectures for its members, in addition to caring for their economic interests.

A major outcome of the growth of organized labor, however, is that workers now have an effective means of protecting their interests. Employers in turn are no longer able to exercise unilateral control over workers to the extent they did before workers became organized.

ORGANIZED FARMERS

Like businessmen and workers, farmers have also organized to protect themselves and to correct maladjustments in the economy. But unlike worker and employer groups, farmers' organizations seldom directly oppose an easily identified opponent. Workers may protest to their employer against low wages or lack of old-age security, but to whom can the farmer protest? Who or what is responsible for low farm prices or high interest rates? Sometimes the American farmer has blamed Wall Street, the gold standard, or the middleman for his assorted economic woes, but never consistently or unanimously or at the same time. Farm protest movements have therefore necessarily been more diffuse and less sharply focused on objectives and programs than have labor or business organizations.

THE GRANGE

Most venerable among America's farm organizations is the Grange, organized in 1867. Initially a purely social organization, it soon plunged into economic and political affairs. In the flickering light of a thousand prairie schoolhouses after the Civil War, farmers aired their grievances: low farm prices and high tariffs, inflated railroad charges and deflated currency. If their grievances were chiefly economic, the remedies they sought were chiefly political. From the beginning the Grangers aimed at control of markets and prices. They quickly learned that it was wiser to support independent political activity rather than the established political parties. Like the A. F. L., they sought to reward their friends and punish their enemies at the polls. At the peak of its influence the Grange was a formidable force in American life. As one author puts it:

At its height the Grange was running stores, maintaining state purchasing agents, selling raw farm commodities co-operatively, and operating some buying clubs, some manufacturing plants, and even a bank. In a few states the Grangers elected legislators, governors, and other officers, and in half a dozen states they were the dominant influence in many political parties. In all these activities they were striking directly or indirectly at price, market, and credit adjustments.*

THE FARMERS' UNION

More militant than the Grange was the Farmers' Educational and Cooperative Union, which appeared in Texas in 1902. Like the Grange, the Farmers' Union was originally a fraternal organization that turned to the operation of farm cooperatives in such fields as grain and cotton storage, meat processing, and the manufacture of cheese and other dairy products. Particularly did the Farmers' Union champion the cause of the low-income farmer. Though opposed to involvement in partisan politics, the Union

nevertheless gained considerable influence over political affairs in a number of states. The Union was also instrumental in securing legislation providing for rural free delivery, parcel post, and rural credit. It has even operated insurance companies, sponsored cooperative medical societies, and sought ties with organized labor.

THE FARM BUREAU FEDERATION

A third major farm organization, which represents the larger and more prosperous farmers, is the American Farm Bureau Federation. Local farm bureaus existed as early as 1911, but not until 1919 did the national federation emerge. Although the family is the unit of membership, the Bureau has become largely a male organization with a strong focus on economic matters. The size of the membership has fluctuated with the condition of the economy, increasing during periods of prosperity and falling off in slack times. The Bureau claims to represent every aspect of rural society and exerts a considerable influence on state and national politics and on economic matters. It has supported such institutions as the extension service and the experiment station in land-grant colleges, favored farm research and rural electrification, and backed international agreements and the work of the United Nations Food and Agriculture Organization. Like the Grange and the Farmers' Union, the Farm Bureau has sponsored cooperatives in a number of states, and in recent years has promoted 4-H clubs and other youth programs.

THE FARM MOVEMENT

These three organizations have played an important role in the life of the American farmer. Significantly, all of them have sooner or later come to regard price, market, and credit problems as among their major con-

---

* Carl C. Taylor, *et al.*, *Rural Life In The United States* (New York: Knopf, 1949), p. 513.

cerns. Each organization has encouraged common marketing, emphasizing cooperative buying during its early years and endorsing cooperative selling later on. Farmers' cooperatives may rate few headlines, but they are one of the permanent achievements of the farm movement in the United States.

The organization of farmers has proceeded step by step with the growth of commercial agriculture. As long as farming remained a local family affair, there seemed to be little need for farm organization. But with the growth of crop specialization and the spread of markets beyond the local community, farmers found themselves in an increasingly difficult situation. For now they faced, individually and alone, the economic might of big railroads, powerful meat-packers, and ambitious food-processors. Like the laborer, helpless before the corporate might of his employer, the farmer found himself at a distinct disadvantage in his dealings with carriers, processors, and distributors.

The farmer's main aim in organizing was to better his bargaining position relative to the industrialists, merchants, and railroaders on whom he depended. His was no peasants' revolt aimed at overthrowing an autocratic or feudal system. Organization, not revolution, was his method. Although there has never been a real "farm party" in American politics, some of our third-party movements have received strong support from the farmers. Mainly, farmer and rancher have sought redress for their grievances through cooperation, economic pressure, and lobbying. In fact, farmers have often been accused of having the most effective lobbying machinery in the country. Whether they have or not, certainly the agricultural lobbies have been among the more effective organizations in Washington and the various state capitals.

Yet, despite the effectiveness of the farmer's organization, the farm economy still suffers economic disabilities. The agricultural industry has long been plagued with the dilemma of declining income in the face of rising costs. As a result, a huge exodus from the farm has been underway for some time, but especially during the late 1950's. Various specialists have offered many reasons for the farmer's plight, among them overproduction, inefficient farm operation, too much marginal land in production, a continuing poor bargaining position, and farm programs that are only temporary, provide little more than limited relief, and actually encourage greater overproduction. Although there is a great deal of truth in each of these explanations, all ignore many other important factors that compound the farmer's problem.

First of all, agriculture as an industry has been losing its struggle to compete successfully with other sectors of the economy. On the marketing side, the farmer sells to processors rather than to consumers. As a result, he cannot take advantage of the mammoth advertising industry in marketing his produce, as can the processor, wholesaler, and retailer. Any industry that can make use of this important medium for distribution gains an immediate advantage over those that cannot. Second, the farmer has no organized method of controlling his commodity output, as has the automobile industry, for example. He has little or no available means for limiting production and no way to invoke an effective economic boycott. Third, and too often ignored, farm organization and management are inefficient and outdated. Farmers cannot take advantage of modern streamlined administration methods, advanced accounting techniques, personnel practices, greater specialization, and division of labor. Finally, the industry depends on government and processors for research programs and on other outsiders for the development and marketing of new products.

On the production side, the farmer is plagued by an inability to make maximum use of his machinery. A great deal of his machinery, which involves a large capital risk, can be used only at certain times of the year. Whereas other industries can use their machines 24 hours a day 365 days a year, the farmer must leave much of his expensive equipment idle for many months. Although surrounded by machinery, farmers are not fully mechanized. They are in no position to compete with those industries that can make maximum use of their machinery and can take full advantage of modern methods of mass production and automation.

Today the farm problem still persists, in spite of powerful organizations and a lobbying set-up that is one of the most effective in the country. Farmers still must depend mainly on government aid programs to stay afloat in an otherwise rapidly expanding and prosperous economy.

TECHNIQUES AND OBJECTIVES

Farmers, workers, and businessmen thus pursue objectives that are largely economic by means that are primarily political. Prosperity and material well-being are the primary goals of each group, though each sees the total situation in the light of its own special interests. Profits never seem high enough for the businessman, wages are never adequate for the worker, nor prices high enough for the farmer. These attitudes, of course, are natural, since materialistic success is a major goal in an acquisitive society. As levels of living rise and profits soar, everyone wants more. Each of the special interest groups, furthermore, seeks to secure itself against any threat to its material well-being. Business has succeeded in winning "protection" against the importation of certain commodities that compete with goods produced domestically. Labor fights hard to gain wage increases even in times of industrial peace and prosperity. Farmers have favored support programs in good times as well as bad.

NON-ECONOMIC FACTORS

This is not to say, of course, that individual workers, farmers, or businessmen are motivated by material impulses only. Many industrialists and merchants are as much concerned with the quality of the goods and services they provide as with profits. Indeed, the two things cannot be wholly separated. Likewise, farmers and workers may take great pride in their skill or craftsmanship. Research in industrial relations has shown, in fact, that workers are frequently more concerned with job prestige and social recognition than with higher wages. But despite such evidence, the objectives of the chief business, farm, and labor organizations tend to be heavily economic.

LOBBYING AND PROPAGANDA

If the objectives are still largely economic, the means used by organizations to achieve them are political in the broadest sense. Outright involvement by business, farm, or labor groups in partisan politics has been rare in our history. Most have preferred to follow Gompers' philosophy of supporting those who supported them. But many organizations have become very adept at using propaganda, at lobbying, and otherwise pressuring elective officials. Rare is the interest group that makes no direct use of lobbying and propaganda or, to employ the more genteel term, "public relations." Certainly none of the large interest groups is without its paid writers and lobbyists. So great has the influence of these lobbyists become in shaping particular legislation that some critics have even questioned whether legislators or lobbyists do the legislating. But in a system of checks and balances, the influence of lobbyists for one interest group is frequently offset by the influence of another. Each congressman who is contacted by a labor spokesman in Washington regarding pending legislation may expect an early call from an employer's representative dealing with the same legislation. It is therefore important to the special-interest groups that they be represented by equally skillful and powerful lobbyists who will communicate to congressmen as much information as possible before the lawmakers decide how they will vote on particular legislation.

Advertising is the most obvious kind of propaganda. We know who the advertiser is and we can evaluate his message. When a voice comes over the air waves entreating us to "Go Buy Sudsy Soap," we know at once who is making the appeal and what his objective is. But many appeals on behalf of a special interest are difficult to recognize as propaganda. A skilled public-relations man often can create a demand for almost anything within reason, or beyond, for that matter. Joseph Goebbels, propaganda chief for Adolf Hitler, once boasted that he could make the German people believe anything he wanted them to within two weeks. Although he was exaggerating, Goebbels' claim reflects the confidence many people have in propaganda as a major determinant of human behavior. By maintaining "public-relations" programs, the major interest groups of American society show that they are not disposed to let the public choose by chance.

VIOLENCE AND COERCION

Though publicly condemned as immoral and uncivilized, violence is still a weapon in the arsenal of special-interest groups. As recently as the 1930's the efforts of the C. I. O. to organize the mass-production industries touched off a wave of violence and strife. Hundreds of strikers and company representatives, together with many law officers and innocent bystanders, were killed or injured. Since World War II, labor disputes have brought violence often enough to make work stoppages lively and sometimes brutal. Even farmers, on occasion, have resorted to violence to achieve their ends. In the depths of the Great Depression, many farmers defended their property against foreclosure with pitchforks, clubs, and shotguns. Today violence is much less frequent in industrial relations and very rare among farmers, but it remains nevertheless an unspoken threat wherever special-interest groups collide.

Coercion may range from open, direct, and unmistakable terrorism to threats and intimidation. A labor union may intimidate a nonunion worker into joining the union or supporting a strike. Businessmen may try to forestall union demands by threatening to relocate their plants. Farm organizations, for the most part, have relied on the gentler techniques of lobbying and political pressure.

TREATY-MAKING

Business and labor organizations also seek to protect their interests through labor-management contracts or agreements and through the process of collective bargaining, or, more properly, *contract bargaining, the process by which points of agreement are selected for inclusion in labor-management contracts.* "Collective bargaining" in the more general sense includes not only the negotiations to reach a labor-management contract but also labor-management sessions to settle problems of administration and interpretation of contract provisions, and negotiations for the settlement of grievances that arise under the contract, called grievance bargaining. The labor-management contract is like a treaty between nations in that it reflects the relative strength of the parties that sign it, and as with any contract, it defines the "rights and duties" of the respective parties. Labor and management representatives negotiate a contract on the basis of their strength and the public support they command. As at any peace conference, concessions and compromises are vital. If both sides are approximately equal in bargaining power, the kind of contract signed will depend on the skill of the bargainers and will probably represent some compromise. During the long history of labor-management relations in the United States, organized labor has steadily increased its strength to the point where many labor unions are at least as successful as management in protecting their rights. Thirty or forty years ago, before there were many strong unions, employers were able to claim exclusively many prerogatives that they now share with labor, such as hiring and firing, setting wage and production rates, and controlling apprenticeship programs. Today, however, most employers can no longer hire and fire with impunity because of concessions they have yielded at the bargaining table.

THE ROLE OF THE GOVERNMENT

Up to this point we have not said very much about the role of government in our system of checks and balances. Fifty years ago we wouldn't have had to say very much. Today, however, the government plays an important role in balancing the conflicting pressures of the various interest groups in American society. Men have always disagreed over how far the government should intervene in economic affairs. Should the government be umpire, moderator, or balance wheel? All these views have found their supporters at various times in our history.

Jefferson's ideal government would have confined itself to the maintenance of law and order, acting as an umpire but not intruding into the private lives of its citizens. Franklin D. Roosevelt regarded government as a tool for redressing the balance of power in American life in the direction of the underprivileged. Still other spokesmen have believed that government should play the role of moderator among competing economic forces in our society, intervening only temporarily in the interests of order, security, or justice.

Throughout the nineteenth century, government exercised only a slight control over the lives of American businessmen, workers, or farmers. What controls there were dealt with distribution of the public land; the regulation of money, banking, and trade; and the protection of American industries against foreign competition. But the Industrial Revolution of the post-Civil War years created a new and unprecedented situation. Entrepreneurs in oil, steel, and railroads battled savagely for control of natural resources, markets, and trade. It became increasingly more difficult for small firms to compete in those fields where a few giants had won out over their competitors. Monopoly and consolidation were strangling competition. Industrialism was spawning a whole host of serious social problems—harsh working conditions, child labor, slums, and periodic unemployment. What should be done? Should the national government step in? The answer came in a wave of trust-busting activity, the establishment of controls over business corporations, and the passage of legislation to aid the farmer, the worker, and the unemployed. Eventually the national government would reach out to control crop acreage, the licensing of radio, television, and airline routes, and the sale of stocks and bonds. It would also protect the aged and the unemployed.

With the decline of laissez faire and the

ideal of the umpire state, the argument narrowed to whether government should be a moderator or a balance wheel between competing economic interests. But whatever the ideal or theory, in practice government tends to play both roles. When the major interest groups are equally powerful, the government tends toward the role of moderator, and when one or another of the competing interests seems to be gaining the upper hand, the government moves, however slowly, to redress the balance. In the 1930's, for instance, the national government moved to strengthen labor in its quest for self-organization, collective-bargaining rights, minimum wages, and protection against court interference with picketing and other labor weapons. Farmers likewise were aided when the government helped limit farm production to raise prices and protect farmers against foreclosure. Since the Great Depression, however, government has moved back toward its role of moderator. In reality, government plays several roles simultaneously as a result of the existence of numerous specialized agencies and branches, each serving more or less different purposes. One government agency may be acting as a balance wheel while at the same time another is umpiring. And at any given moment agencies of our multifaceted government may be caught in a cross fire of pressures, with different special-interest groups applying pressure at various levels of government, and even on the same agency.

CONTROLS OVER BUSINESS

Some people, particularly those whose activities already have been restricted, feel that the national government has already intervened too much in economic affairs. The sting of the early antitrust laws, notably the Sherman Antitrust Act of 1890, produced such a reaction. That act forbade "combinations in restraint of trade" and was aimed at the great monopolies and trusts that had arisen in oil, steel, railroading, and many other fields. There were loopholes in the law, of course, and neither the administration nor the courts were disposed at first to apply the law vigorously. Even after Theodore Roosevelt began his colorful campaign of trust-busting, some firms were able to evade the intent of the law by entering into trade agreements that set prices and limited output. Another evasive device was the holding company, which, though independent of its constituent firms, owned enough stock in each to exercise effective control over the whole corporate pyramid.

A second antitrust law, the Clayton Act, passed in 1914, was designed to plug some of the gaps left by the earlier Sherman law. The Clayton Act outlawed price discrimination that was intended to lessen competition, agreements that prevented purchasers from buying from competitors, the acquisition of stock in competing corporations, and interlocking boards of directors in corporations and banks. But the Clayton Act, too, was sporadically enforced, and the courts were reluctant to convict business firms that had been charged with violating its provisions.

Although no one would claim today that American business is entirely competitive, the antitrust movement helped to preserve a large measure of free competition in our increasingly complex economy. It is significant that the West German government since World War II has adopted a number of antitrust ordinances modeled after American law and experience.

Antitrust legislation demonstrates one way the national government can make its influence felt in a system of checks and balances. Most of this legislation was enacted at a time when organized workers and farmers were powerless to protect themselves against the monopolistic practices of American business. The government simply stepped in.

The wage and price controls that were imposed during World War II provide a further example of decisive governmental intervention in the economy. Business firms might have reaped a financial harvest simply by charging all the traffic would bear for consumer goods that were in short supply. Further, the shortage of labor could have touched off an epidemic of cut-throat competition among employers for available workers and sent wage rates skyrocketing. But Congress inaugurated wage and price controls for the mutual protection of both businessmen and consumers. Although imperfectly drafted, these controls helped check inflation and bolster civilian morale while the war was in progress.

LABOR LEGISLATION

By the time wage controls were enacted in World War II, American labor had come far in its quest for security and recognition. Prior to the 1930's workers and unions not only had operated at a disadvantage in their dealings with employers but also had encountered opposition from hostile courts and indifferent national administrations. A flurry of new labor laws during the New Deal era, however, gave labor a shot in the arm and made it an effective weight in the American system of checks and balances.

In 1932 Congress passed the Norris-LaGuardia Act, barring employers from obtaining injunctions in federal courts against strikers without proof of damages in open hearings that gave labor an opportunity to present evidence. This act was a major milestone in labor's march to power, since the court injunction had been one of the employer's most effective weapons against organized labor. Three years later the first national social-security act was pushed through Congress. This measure sought to relieve the economic insecurity of workers, which the depression had brought into sharp

relief, by providing retirement insurance, unemployment compensation, aid to the blind and to dependent children, and many other benefits, to be financed by contributions from employees, employers, and the national government. Coverage and benefits have gradually been extended in subsequent laws. Social-security legislation represented our first comprehensive attempt to deal with the problems that confront unemployed or retired workers in an industrial society.

Still other legislation followed that buttressed the position of labor. In 1938 workers employed in firms engaged in interstate commerce were brought under the protection of laws establishing minimum wages and maximum hours. And Congress also moved to redress the balance between labor and management with the National Labor Relations Act (Wagner Act). This measure assured labor the right to organize and bargain collectively, as well as to strike on behalf of its demands. Employers were now prevented from discriminating against unions and were compelled to bargain with accredited representatives chosen by the workers. Under the protective cloak of this law, unions grew strong and employers were soon complaining that the law discriminated against them. In response to these complaints and a growing public feeling that a new imbalance in favor of labor actually had been created, Congress passed the Taft-Hartley Act in 1947, which made unions liable for damages and breach of contract, outlawed the closed shop, and provided for a 60-day "cooling-off" period before calling a strike if the government requested and received a court order.

Employers remained dissatisfied, however, since the provisions against the closed shop and the secondary boycott were not strictly enforced. A secondary boycott, or a refusal by a union to have normal relations with or to handle the products of an employer whose workers are out on strike, was a weapon labor wished to keep. But late in the 1950's, employers won more public support when several congressional investigations uncovered a number of labor scandals. After a number of attempts to pass labor reform bills, Congress agreed to accept the Landrum-Griffin bill in September of 1959. This act required unions to file regular financial reports and disclose their administrative procedures. Former convicts were barred from holding union offices, unions were required to hold periodic elections, and further restrictions were placed on secondary boycotts and "recognition picketing." Thus has the national government shifted its position to reflect new estimates of the relative power relationship between labor and management.

FARM LEGISLATION

Like the early industrial worker, the farmer until quite recently was unable to gain support for legislation that he felt was vital to his own interests. To be sure, in many states farmers were represented in their legislatures out of all proportion to their actual numbers because of failure to redistrict the legislative seats as population grew and shifted to urban centers. But farm problems extended beyond state borders to the national level, where the achievement of favorable legislation depended on the growth of strong farm organizations and the work of congressmen from agricultural states.

Farmers have long sought federal aid in attacking their major problems—credit, prices, and markets. To help farmers get long-term loans at moderate rates of interest, Congress in 1916 passed the Farm Loan Act, which created regional banks empowered to loan money to farmers and ranchers. Subsequent legislation during the 1930's enlarged farm credit facilities. In 1929 came the Agricultural Marketing Act, which was designed to promote cooperative marketing among farmers. And later in the 1930's a whole host of new farm legislation affecting

farm prices, surpluses, and credit was passed by Congress. Most important was the Agricultural Adjustment Act of 1933, which authorized a new farm agency, the Agricultural Adjustment Administration, to enter into agreements with farmers who were willing to reduce their acreage of such basic crops as cotton, wheat, and corn in order to raise prices. The Supreme Court declared this law unconstitutional because it placed an accompanying tax on food processors to pay the farmer his subsidy. Congress then authorized benefit payments to farmers who retired their worn-out land and practiced crop rotation in the interest of soil conservation. Then, in 1938, Congress passed a new agricultural act empowering the Secretary of Agriculture to fix the acreage of basic crops each year and establish "marketing quotas" to restrict the sale of surpluses. In poor crop years, the government would grant farmers "parity payments" sufficient to offset the difference between the low price they were then receiving and the equivalent price their produce would have commanded before World War I. This concept, known as *parity*, has become the basis of most subsequent farm legislation as well as the center of a great deal of controversy.

In the 1950's the Eisenhower administration contributed the idea of the soil bank as a means for solving the farmer's plight. Farmers were permitted to convert cultivated acres to forest and grass in exchange for cash payments based on the potential returns of the acres banked. The theory was that this plan would take land out of production, prevent crop diversion, and most important, reduce agricultural surpluses that were depressing the farmer's market. But this program, too, has been the center of much controversy. It certainly points up a central question that has long plagued both politicians and economists: Is the goal acreage reduction or providing a minimum income for farmers?

PROTECTION FOR THE UNORGANIZED

In the midst of the vast organizational movement to protect special interests we have so far described, one important group remains relatively unorganized—namely, the *consumer*. Businessmen, farmers, laborers, doctors, lawyers, and veterans have their own organizations. Women, too, have their Woman's Christian Temperance Union, Daughters of the American Revolution, and League of Women Voters. But the consumer as a general rule is without organizational protection in our system of checks and bal-

ances. Relatively few Americans participate in consumer cooperatives, enterprises operated on a non-profit basis that aim to sell consumer goods at low prices. The consumer co-op movement, therefore, has never flourished in the United States as it has in the Scandanavian countries. Nor have consumer buying guides been utilized enough to be of much help, despite the fact that they report the results of tests on a great variety of products, from can openers and vitamin pills to vacuum cleaners and automobiles. Consum-

Buyer beware! The one person in our economy that receives little protection is the consumer.

ers' Union, one of the major organizations offering this test and evaluation service, has but few members out of the entire population.

Consumers are not without some protection, even though, organizationally speaking, the consumer is a "forgotten man." Individually, consumers protect their interests by resisting price increases and refusing to buy inferior goods, just as the individual laborer may bargain with his employer. But when confronted by a heavy barrage of clever advertising and shrewd salesmanship, consumer resistance is usually nullified. Ours is a society that relies as much on advertising as on quality to sell the goods it produces. Even the most intelligent buyer soon discovers that it is almost impossible to make a rational choice among products when he is being constantly bombarded with a mass of equally colorful and equally persuasive information about all of them. Time alone would bar most consumers from investigating carefully each product they buy. Buyer resistance and efforts to discriminate skillfully are therefore relatively ineffective protective devices for consumers as a whole.

What effective recourse, then, do consumers have? As in other areas, government has come forward to provide at least a modicum of protection. Such laws as the Pure Food and Drug Act remove the most dangerous commodities from retailers' shelves and thereby relieve consumers of the burden of investigating carefully many of the things they buy. On the grounds of protecting the "public interest," legislative controls have been extended to misleading advertising, inspection of weights and measures, and unsanitary meat. Butchers can be prosecuted if they are caught adding the weight of their thumbs to the price of meat. Low-grade milk cannot be sold as "Grade A." Fountain pens cannot be guaranteed "forever." This legislation is not intended to restrict the consumer's choice but only to protect him from harmful or misleading tactics.

There are many consumer goods and services that still lack adequate regulation. Firm controls over navigable airspace, for example, are a pressing twentieth-century need. And many spurious medical products and services, some of which may even be harmful, are loudly hawked over radio and television. But considerable progress has been made in protecting consumer interests despite the lack of agreement over what should be regulated and how.

SOME WORDS OF SUMMARY

Business, labor, and farm organizations represent the most influential special-interest groups in the United States. Serving interests that are often at cross purposes, these organizations tend to hold each other in check. This condition of equilibrium among pressures exerted by special interests we call a system of "checks and balances."

Big corporations and business associations have effectively protected their own interests against outsiders. But within the business world itself there are many tensions and conflicts. Relations between small and big businesses, between business and government, and among the conflicting interests represented in any corporation itself are frequently far from smooth. The separation of ownership from control in a large corporation and the divergent interests of stockholders, managers, and workers raise a troublesome question: In whose interests should the corporation be run?

To equalize the imbalance in their bargaining power with employers, workers formed labor unions. Unions have won the right to represent workers in bargaining with employers over hours, wages, and working conditions. The most effective weapon in the labor arsenal has been the strike. Farm organizations, on the other hand, have centered their interest on rural pricing, marketing, and credit problems. Less militant than labor, they have relied on lobbying, cooperatives, and political influence to further their interests.

As these special-interest groups have matured, violence has become less common. Lobbying, propaganda, and "public relations" have now become the indispensable tools for winning an advantage over opponents. Today the differences between special-interest groups lie primarily in the goals they seek rather than in the means they employ to reach them.

The role of government in this system of checks and balances is a changing one. A half-century ago the national government, in particular, played a very modest role in the economic life of the United States. Now government plays an active part, serving, as one writer put it, as a "countervailing power" to big business and big labor. Whether government should act as a moderator or a balance wheel in our system of checks and balances, however, is still a moot question. Certainly government is destined to become increasingly important in protecting the rights of the unorganized, especially those of the consumer.

FURTHER ROADS TO LEARNING

GENERAL ACCOUNTS

A. Berle, Jr., *The Twentieth Century Capitalist Revolution* (New York: Harcourt, Brace, 1954). A provocative analysis of our changing economic system.

J. Galbraith, *American Capitalism: The Concept of Countervailing Power* (Boston: Houghton Mifflin, 1952). The classic exposition of the checks-and-balance thesis. Bigness is accepted as a constructive factor in our economy.

W. Moore, *Industrial Relations and the Social Order* (New York: Macmillan, 1951). A second edition of an early textbook in industrial sociology that contains a good analysis of the industrial system.

M. Stewart, *The American Way: Business Freedom or Government Control?* (New York: Public Affairs Pamphlet No. 90, 1944). A discussion of the relation of free enterprise to administrative and legislative controls.

D. Truman, *The Governmental Process: Political Interests and Public Opinion* (New York: Knopf, 1951). A brilliant sociological analysis of the role of interest groups in American politics.

SPECIAL STUDIES

A. Berle, Jr. and G. Means, *The Modern Corporation and Private Property* (New York: Macmillan, 1933). A classic discussion of the separation of ownership and management and the emergence of a management control group.

R. Brady, *Business as a System of Power* (New York: Columbia University Press, 1943). A good account of business organizations' ability to protect their interests.

T. Cochran, *A Basic History of American Business* (Princeton, N. J.: Van Nostrand, Anvil Books, 1959). Just what the title says, a good basic history.

J. Hicks, *The Populist Revolt* (Minneapolis: University of Minnesota Press, 1931). Historical account of how a farmers' party misfired.

D. Lindstrom, *American Rural Life* (New York: Ronald, 1948). Contains a summary of the growth of farm organizations in Chapter 11.

C. Loomis and J. Beegle, *Rural Social Systems* (Englewood Cliffs, N. J.: Prentice-Hall, 1950). A sound sociological analysis of rural society.

W. McCune, *The Farm Bloc* (New York: Doubleday, Doran, 1943). Revealing description of the organization and influence of farm-state congressmen.

C. Mills, *The New Men of Power* (New York: Harcourt, Brace, 1948). Contrasts the new generation of labor leaders with the old.

J. Rayback, *A History of American Labor* (New York: Macmillan, 1959). The fascinating story of the long and continuous development of organized workers from colonial times to the present.

F. Shannon, *American Farmers' Movements* (Princeton, N. J.: Van Nostrand, Anvil Books, 1957). An authoritative history by a noted historian.

C. Taylor, *et al.*, *Rural Life in the United States* (New York: Knopf, 1949). In Chapter 29 of this book there is a reliable statement on the farmers' movement.

T. Veblen, *The Theory of Business Enterprise* (New York: Mentor Books, 1958). A reprint of Veblen's famous analysis of the influence of business practices on American life.

FICTION AND DRAMA

H. Garland, *A Spoil of Office* (New York: D. Appleton, 1897). The story of the rise of the Farmers' Alliance and the Grange as opposition political party movements.

T. Mann, *Joseph in Egypt* (New York: Knopf, 1938). A truly great novel that gives a foreigner's assessment of American business values.

J. McIntyre, *Ferment* (New York: Farrar and Rinehart, 1937). A story of labor violence, racketeers, strikebreakers, and labor spies.

R. McKenney, *Industrial Valley* (New York: Harcourt, Brace, 1939). This novel is very pro-labor, but it does an excellent job of portraying the growth of the C. I. O. and the use of the sit-down strike.

D. Meyersburg, *Seventh Avenue* (New York: Dutton, 1941). A clothing manufacturer fights labor unions and eventually becomes a "runaway industrialist."

O. Rølvaag, *Giants in the Earth* (New York: Harper, 1927). Widely considered by many critics to be the finest novel ever written about pioneer life and problems on the Great Plains.

U. Sinclair, *Co-op* (New York: Farrar & Rinehart, 1936). The story of the establishment of a cooperative community in California.

E. Ward, *The Silent Partner* (Boston: Houghton Mifflin, 1871). The oldest significant American labor novel.

FILMS

Livestock Cooperatives in Action (United States Department of Agriculture, 1950, 15 min., sound, color). The history of livestock producers' marketing cooperatives and what they do for the farmer.

Local 100 (McGraw-Hill, 1951, 30 min., sound, black and white). A highly instructive account of a labor union that shows how democratic industrial relations culminate in compromise and thereby avoid a strike.

What Is A Corporation? (Coronet, 1949, 11 min., sound, color). Advantages and disadvantages of business corporations are compared with partnerships and sole ownerships.

Working Together: A Case History of Labor-Management Cooperation (Encyclopaedia Britannica Films, 1951, 24 min., sound, black and white). Industrial relations in an American plant change from bitterness to mutual understanding through collective bargaining.

You Are There at the Bargaining Table (American Management Association, 1955, 50 min., sound, black and white). Via a TV camera, you sit in at an actual unrehearsed session of contract negotiations between the Rogers Corporation and the A. F. L. International Brotherhood of Paper Makers.

Some New
Patterns of Life

*Industrial patterns of our own creation
have dwarfed us and changed our environment, our method
of work, and our entire way of life.*

All facets

of our social, economic, and political life have felt the impact of a multitude of inventions over the past two centuries, as we have seen in the last three chapters. We shall narrow our perspective a bit in this chapter to see how the new technology has brought about a drastic alteration in agriculture and industry, how levels of living and employment have soared to unprecedented heights in the wake of record-shattering production of goods and services, what dangers mechanization poses for the individual person and for society, and how the Industrial Revolution has influenced our social values.

TECHNOLOGY AND THE MECHANIZED FARM

A firm, highly productive agricultural base is a prerequisite to a large-scale, urban-industrial society. Until farmers could produce enough to provide for people other than themselves, industrial growth was limited. For many centuries agricultural production could free only relatively few persons for other kinds of enterprise. The agricultural revolution lagged behind the parallel revolution in industry until the beginning of the twentieth century, but gradually larger and larger numbers of people were released from agricultural production to turn their hands to manufacturing. The internal combustion engine, the discovery of new chemical fertilizers, and the application of electricity to farm machinery and processes sparked the agricultural revolution that, once launched, has become almost as extensive as its industrial counterpart.

Agricultural yield has almost kept pace with industrial output. In the period from 1910 to 1945, production per worker in American agriculture almost doubled, while production per worker in industry increased only slightly more. These gains in agricultural production become all the more remarkable when we consider that many farms are small-scale operations that cannot take advantage of division of labor, assembly-line techniques, and other efficient productive processes.

There is one important difference, however. Although both industrial production and employment continue to rise, on the farm only production, not employment, is on the increase. In 1820 the farm labor force constituted nearly three-fourths of the total labor force in America and almost one-fourth of the entire population. Yet, as Table 6 indicates, by 1954 the farm labor force had declined to less than one-tenth of the total labor force and total population. A great deal more than increased farm output is involved in this drastic shift in the employment picture in the United States. A first requirement was a broad expansion in industrial employment opportunities. Industry has generally absorbed many workers who might otherwise still be following a plow.

The decline in farm population has been accompanied by a decline in the number of farms. More farm machinery has meant that fewer farmers can produce more food per acre. The owner of a small, family-size farm has found it increasingly difficult to compete with the operator of a large com-

TABLE **6** RELATION OF FARM LABOR FORCE *
TO TOTAL LABOR FORCE AND TOTAL
POPULATION, U. S., 1820 TO 1954

Year	Farm labor force as a percentage of total labor force	Farm labor force as a percentage of total population
1820	72	22
1830	70	22
1840	69	22
1850	64	21
1860	59	20
1870	53	17
1880	49	17
1890	43	16
1900	38	14
1910	31	13
1920	27	11
1930	21	8
1940	17	7
1950	12	4
1954	9	4

* Prior to 1930, persons 10 years of age or older were in-cluded, and since 1930, persons 14 years of age or older.
Source: U. S. Bureau of the Census, *1954 Census of Agriculture.*

mercial farm. From Table 7 we see that there were over 1 million fewer farms in 1950 than in 1920. Farms in 1900 averaged less than 150 acres; in 1950, over 200 acres. The farm population, which remained fairly stable from 1900 to 1933, declined rapidly in the depression years of the 1930's. More than a third of the 30 million people who were living on farms during the first third of this century have left the land in recent years.

How can we account for these changes? Five main factors seem to be responsible:

TABLE **7** NUMBER OF FARMS AND AVERAGE NUMBER OF ACRES PER FARM, U. S., 1900-1950

Year	Number of farms (in thousands)	Average acreage per farm
1900	5,737	146
1910	6,362	138
1920	6,448	148
1930	6,289	157
1940	6,097	174
1950	5,382	216

Source: U. S. Bureau of the Census, *1954 Census of Agriculture.*

(1) increased use of power-driven machinery; (2) improvements in plant and animal breeding; (3) more effective control of insects, pests, and animal and crop diseases; (4) wiser utilization of the soil; and (5) improvements in managerial and marketing techniques.*

Until about 1900 the farmer did most of his work by hand, aided only by some simple tools and a limited amount of animal power. To be sure, the mechanical reaper had been invented in 1833 and the threshing machine in 1850, but farmers were slow to adopt

TABLE **8** TRACTORS AND MOTOR TRUCKS ON FARMS IN THE UNITED STATES IN 1920 AND 1954

	1920	1954
Number of tractors per 1,000 acres of cropland harvested	0.7	13.0
Number of farms with tractors (in thousands)	229	2,877
Percentage of farms with tractors	3.6	60.1
Number of farms with motor trucks (in thousands)	132	2,213
Percentage of farms with motor trucks	2.0	46.0

Source: U. S. Bureau of the Census, *1954 Census of Agriculture.*

them. One by one the March harvester, twine-binder, corn-binder, corn-husker, cotton-seed planter, fertilizer-distributor, and improved plows and harrows made their appearance. Then came the power revolution. Not long after the gasoline tractor was introduced in 1903, the farm truck came into use. Both have largely displaced horses, mules, and men as sources of power. As late as 1920 there were only 229,000 American farms with tractors, but by 1954 the figure had jumped to nearly 3 million. Table 8 shows that in 1920 there was less than one tractor for every 1,000 acres of crop land har-

* *Cf.* D. Miller, "Impact of Technology on Agriculture," in F. Allen, *et al., Technology and Social Change* (New York: Appleton-Century-Crofts, 1957), pp. 326-340.

The farmer and his team represent an important but passing phase of the agricultural revolution. The rapid replacement of horsepower by machine power during the first half of this century made large-scale, urban-industrial growth possible. Machines such as the potato-digger enabled farmers to produce more food for urban-industrial workers.

vested in the United States. A generation later there were 13 tractors per 1,000 acres. Only 2 per cent of all farmers owned motor trucks in 1920 whereas almost half of the farms were equipped with trucks by 1954. From these figures it would appear that "horsepower" has become an outmoded expression.

THE FACTORY SYSTEM

The modern factory, along with the mechanized farm, has created new patterns of life in the industrialized nations. As owner, manager, worker, or consumer, modern man has been profoundly influenced by the factory. Based on an elaborate division of labor, a factory system brings men, raw materials, and tools together in order to produce large quantities of standardized goods. Work in the factory system is organized through a hierarchy of positions, ranging from the chief executive to common laborers. Output of work is tied to the machine, the assembly line, and the production schedule. Ownership tends to be divorced from management, and the consumer is the target for a barrage of standardized, mass-produced goods that provide him with a way of life unimagined a few decades ago.

FROM GUILDS TO FACTORIES

Modern factory employment is a far cry from the simple tasks that were carried out in ancient nomadic and pastoral societies, where a "worker" was almost completely independent and self-sufficient. With handmade tools, he produced for himself and his family, rather than for the market as we know it today. Work relationships were sim-

240

ple and informal, and there were no such distinctions as "labor" and "management."

As early as the eleventh century, independent artisans living in European towns began producing for the market. They soon banded together in organizations known as *guilds.* Craft guilds were organizations of workers who possessed common skills or who worked with the same materials, and public authority protected their right to the exclusive practice of their craft in a local area. Tradesmen were also organized in merchant guilds, and soon they were as successful in monopolizing trade as the craft guilds were in monopolizing production. Specialization, except for a few finishing touches, was unknown. These guilds sought to control production at every stage from raw materials to marketing, and they were largely successful. For many years the quality, quantity, and prices of finished goods were rigidly determined by these monopolistic organizations.

After the thirteenth century, the guild system went into a decline. Pressures from within and without combined to force its demise. Journeymen and masters frequently quarreled and town authorities were obliged to intervene. Public reaction grew hostile to the guilds' strength and their monopolistic powers. At least a few masters piled up fortunes by hiring work that was performed outside the guild system and thereby undermined the guilds. Merchant capitalists encouraged manufacturing in non-guild towns. Finally, the market for manufactured goods gradually widened until guilds became dependent on export merchants. Under these circumstances the guilds were doomed to disappear.

Out of these changing conditions emerged a new type of business figure, the merchant-capitalist. Gradually he gained control over guild organizations but found the system too inefficient for his purposes. Rather than convert craftsmen into wage-workers, capitalists sought workers outside the guild system. As

a consequence, a new method of production arose, known as the *putting-out system,* or sometimes as the *domestic system.* Under the putting-out system, the merchant-capitalist supplied the materials and took the finished product. Workers usually owned their own tools, and theoretically, at least, were their own bosses. They could work at their own speeds in their own homes or shops and were no longer bound to a master by guild regulations. Gradually, almost imperceptibly, guild characteristics disappeared. Ultimately, workers no longer bought materials, sold the finished product, or owned their own tools. Neither did they determine the quantity, quality, or kind of goods they produced. Thus, a new concept of the worker emerged. Wage-workers had little but their labor to offer and virtually no control over their work situation.

By the eighteenth century the *factory system* was replacing the putting-out system and opening the door for the development of "modern" industry. Under the factory system work was separated from the worker's home and performed under a single roof—the factory. Although shop production had been carried on in ancient Rome and in ancient Egypt, this new variety added *free labor* and *fixed capital* to the system. Shop production had always required that production be unified and coordinated within a single organization, but not necessarily under the same roof. But the introduction of fixed capital made it necessary to move production out of individual workers' homes into one factory. "Fixed capital" includes those instruments of production, such as heavy machinery, which cannot be moved easily from one location to another or subdivided into smaller units. Free labor, as an alternative to slave labor, may not have been an absolute requisite to the factory system, but European industrialists found ready an abundant supply of cheap labor and therefore had no need for slaves.

SPECIALIZATION
AND DIVISION OF LABOR

Development of the factory system brought with it a very refined *specialization* of work and extensive *division of labor*. In handicraft production a worker was likely to fashion the entire finished product from raw material. A shoemaker produced a shoe from raw leather, a tailor made an entire suit or dress, and so on. With the advent of specialization, however, a worker in a shoe factory began to perform one more or less minute operation, perhaps on the sole or the upper. As one wag put it, specialization has now reached the point where we have not only eye specialists, but some who specialize on the right eye and some on the left. There seems to be no end to specialization.

Were it not for the division of labor, specialization would be chaotic indeed. The term "division of labor" is not a misnomer, even though it refers to the coordination of interdependent parts. This coordination of specialized activities is central to our production system. In the manufacture of an automobile, for example, one plant may produce bodies, another engines, another wheels, and so on, each being coordinated in the over-all production of a finished automobile.

AUTOMATION

A more recent development in industry is a process called *automation*. In an automated factory one man may oversee a machine or group of machines that takes a piece of raw material and converts it into a finished product "untouched" by human hands. With automation we appear to be

With the factory system came the assembly line, an extensive division of labor, and a high degree of specialization, all of which has meant greater efficiency, mass production, and a wider variety of more products for everyone.

well on the way toward a push-button society. Authorities, however, disagree: Have we merely coined a new term or does "automation" signify the dawn of a new industrial revolution? Certainly automation bids fair to reduce the demand for labor and vastly speed up the production process. Thousands of workers in the past have been displaced by the machine, but eventually the very machines that replaced them created new jobs and new opportunities. Whether this pattern will be repeated under automation remains to be seen. In the short run, workers may be thrown out of work, but ultimately they may be absorbed in a new wave of industrial expansion.

PRODUCTION AND LEVELS OF LIVING

INCREASED OUTPUT

Automation is likely to boost still further the phenomenal increases in production of the past two centuries. Levels of living are likely to continue to rise. In the United States alone, as Table 9 indicates,

TABLE **9** INDEX OF TOTAL MANUFACTURING PRODUCTION, UNITED STATES, 1899-1939 (1899 = 100)

Year	Index
1939	374
1929	364
1919	222
1909	158
1899	100

Source: U. S. Bureau of the Census, *Historical Statistics of the United States, 1789-1945* (Washington, D. C., 1949), p. 179.

the output of manufacturing industries quadrupled between 1899 and 1939. World-wide industrial production, shown in Table 10, doubled between 1929 and 1950. During this same period American production was also

TABLE **10** WORLD INDEX OF INDUSTRIAL PRODUCTION, SELECTED AREAS, 1929 AND 1950 (1948 = 100)

Area	1929	1950
World	64	118
Europe	89	129
United States	57	104
U.S.S.R.	16	147

Source: United Nations, *Statistical Yearbook*, 1952. (New York, 1952), Table 33.

doubling, whereas Russian output jumped more than ninefold. European industries were increasing their production at a much slower rate, although they had been in the forefront for a long time.

Production has increased in rapid spurts in industry after industry. Three to three and a half times more automobiles were produced annually in America during the 1950's than the 1920's. Aluminum production went up by more than ten times over the same period. Output of electric energy increased more than sixfold in the quarter-century after 1930. Consumption of coal jumped threefold, oil, eightfold, and gas by tenfold. Over the same period many new products were placed on the market—television, transistor radios, tape-recorders, microfilms, air-conditioned cars and buildings, electric skillets, nylon tires, and Dacron suits. Almost as quickly as such a list of new products is compiled, it becomes obsolete.

STANDARDIZATION

What does mass production mean for the average citizen? For one thing, it means the standardization of most consumer goods from underclothes to overcoats, from household furnishings to the houses themselves, and from breakfast cereals to cuts of meat. More goods are available to more people, but in less variety. Whether the consumer seeks a car, house, or suit of clothes, he is typically confronted with mass-produced merchandise that varies only slightly in regard to color, style, size, and quality. Individuality of choice is sacrificed for lowered costs of mass-produced goods. There are advantages for consumers, of course, besides those resulting from lower costs. Mass-produced merchandise usually means that parts are standardized and interchangeable. A damaged refrigerator or furnace, for example, can be repaired fairly easily, especially where a nation-wide network of parts-distributors stands ready to satisfy consumer needs.

HIGHER LEVELS OF LIVING

More important than standardization for practical-minded consumers is the ever-rising level of living in the industrialized nations. If we define "level of living" in terms of the possession of material goods, Americans outrank all other peoples in the world. Food consumption in the United States, measured by calorie intake per capita, is half again as high as the average level of consumption in India and generally higher than the average for other nations. Even low-income Americans enjoy more material comforts and possessions than most of the inhabitants of the less industrialized areas of the globe. And middle-income groups today can take advantage of many luxuries unavailable to upper-class people a century ago. Mass production has led to a mass uplift in levels of living.

EMPLOYMENT AND UNEMPLOYMENT

Another major effect of industrialization has been the heightened economic and psychological tension accompanying recurring cycles of boom and bust, prosperity and depression, employment and unemployment. Throughout the country employment has risen spectacularly. During World War II some politicians predicted that the economy would soon be supporting "60 millions jobs," but their forecasts were dismissed as utopian and unrealistic. Yet this mark was passed a few years after the war had ended. Seventy million jobs will exist in the 1960's, and the figure will undoubtedly go still higher.

But there is another side to the story. Successive waves of business depression, alternating with prosperity, threaten jobs and incomes of millions of workers. Historians have recorded the onset of "panics" every few years, and recessions and depressions are an ever-present threat. The difference between panic, recession, and depression is largely one of duration and intensity. Depressions are more severe than recessions and panics are more fear-ridden and sudden than either of the other two. A depression sometimes begins with a panic.

The worst period of depression ever recorded followed in the wake of the devastating crash of the stock market in 1929. Production fell off drastically, especially in the manufacturing and construction industries. Millions of dollars were lost by investors as the market declined. Unemployment reached an all-time high of 15 million by 1932. Professionals, executives, and office workers stood with hand laborers in bread lines and welfare offices. Poverty and starvation haunted tens of millions of people around the world, for the depression was not confined to America alone.

What happened to bring on such a depression? Students of the problem point to overproduction during the 1920's, speculation on the stock market, displacement of workers by machines, and the slowing of international trade, among other causes. It may be that for some unexplained reason an industrial society must go through such periodic downturns in its economy. Older

Periodic panics and depressions have created special problems in an industrial era. One of the severest depressions in modern times followed the panic of 1929. Many Americans, some of them former millionaires, were reduced to poverty and forced to stand in bread lines in order to survive.

generations, who recall vividly their own bouts with unemployment, remain ever fearful of a recurrence, sometimes arguing that prosperity and depression go in cycles. Economists strive valiantly to explain the past and predict future business conditions, but economic storms are less predictable than meteorological ones.

Since the beginning of World War II a high level of employment has prevailed in the United States. But to speak of full employment would be misleading. Like most things, full employment is only relative. Even in 1943, at a time of very severe wartime labor shortage, a half-million workers were still unemployed. During the late 1950's, 4 and 5 million workers without jobs could scoff at "full employment." Experience suggests that Keynes was right when he concluded that some unemployment always exists in an industrial society.

In the aftermath of the Great Depression a number of measures were taken to alleviate the distress of jobless workers and stricken business concerns. Public works programs and unemployment compensation were inaugurated in the 1930's. Lending, tariff, and tax programs to aid floundering businesses have been devised. Further, many businesses have themselves taken steps to stabilize their employment and production. These efforts range from extensive research programs on new materials, processing, and marketing to restyling and rescheduling of production to compensate for seasonal variations in demand.

HAZARDS OF MECHANIZATION

To the specter of ruinous business depressions and haunting unemployment must be added the great dangers to life and limb that have accompanied mechanization of industry and agriculture. Greater numbers of machines have exposed both industrial workers and farmers to new and greater accident hazards. New industrial processing techniques and more widespread use of potent and sometimes unfamiliar insecticides have exposed workers and farmers to fumes, dusts, and sprays from dangerous chemical substances. Each year during the 1950's about 2 million Americans on the farm and in the shop were accidentally injured. Permanent disability resulted from about 4 per cent of these injuries. Ten to fifteen thousand workers were killed each year as a result of on-the-job accidents.

Efforts to reduce farm accidents are spearheaded by county agents, farm organizations, and agricultural colleges. Farm implement and insecticide producers, too, have backed safety campaigns against a number of hazards. Vocational training programs include instruction on safe practices in handling tractors, combines, and other machines. But despite all these efforts, greater mechanization has led to a steady increase in accidents. Consequently, farmers, as well as industrial workers, need protection against loss of earning power stemming from accident or injury on the job. In contrast to industrial workers who are protected by state laws, the farmer's only protection is to carry a private insurance policy.

Industry also has taken steps to control on-the-job hazards, sometimes on its own initiative, sometimes after prodding by unions. One of the lasting contributions of John L. Lewis as chief of the United Mine Workers was his success in getting mine operators to introduce safety measures in the mines. With explosions and cave-ins and the danger of inhaling disease-producing dusts always threatening, coal-mining has long been one of the most dangerous occupations. Safety experts in the automobile factories set up a ventilation system that would help prevent workers from inhaling poisonous lead fumes. Operators of huge presses for stamping the sheet metal for automobile bodies face a constant threat of losing a finger or an entire hand if the press comes down while they are inserting a sheet of metal. An electric eye was introduced to prevent the press from descending until the worker backed away a safe distance. Employers carry on continuous safety campaigns to instruct and alert workers to the dangers in the shops.

As a result of the dangers inherent in mechanization, legislation has been enacted to ease the financial burdens of people suffering from industrial injury or disease. Workmen's compensation laws, pioneered by New York State back in 1910, guarantee payments for job-related injuries or diseases. The more a particular injury reduces a person's earning power, the higher the rate of compensation. The person who loses an arm or a leg, for example, receives greater compensation than a person who loses a finger or a toe. If a worker is killed on the job, his family is entitled to relatively large payments under compensation laws.

LOYALTIES IN AN INDUSTRIAL WORLD

Under the impact of rapid and far-reaching advances in agriculture and industry, our loyalties have undergone extensive modification. For many years prior to the onset of the Industrial Revolution, men lived in a slow-moving, close-contact, hand-production world where material possessions were meager. In contrast, the twentieth-century world is one of high speed, rapid communication, mass production, and high levels of living. Dependent as we are on such environmental conditions, our personal and social loyalties are intricately woven into a highly complex loyalty pattern. To afford some notion of what has happened, let us consider a few of the primary loyalties of an industrial society—efficiency, quantity, and group loyalty.

EFFICIENCY

Efficiency is one of the watchwords in an industrial society. The farmer who still uses a mule to cultivate, the department store without an escalator, the large factory without an assembly line or conveyor belt are all "inefficient," for they involve a waste of time, energy, or resources. Airplanes are more efficient than bicycles for long-distance travel, formal schooling more efficient than informal learning, and well-organized play activities more efficient than unorganized. Our belief in efficiency becomes a standard that tends to channel our behavior and influence our choices.

QUANTITY

Admiration of efficiency is part of our general commitment to *quantitative* rather than *qualitative* production. We reward the salesman who sells the most brushes and point with pride to the factory that produces the most goods, the train that carries the most passengers, the university that graduates the most students, or the church with the largest congregation. Some may dissent, but the champions of quality carry less weight than the champions of quantity.

GROUP LOYALTIES

Belief in the concepts of efficiency and quantity have altered the nature and kinds of groups to which a person is loyal. Some personal loyalties, such as those we tender to family and friends, still remain warm and intimate, whereas loyalties to other groups that stem from our urban-industrial milieu are more impersonal in nature. Size has made for impersonality, whether in the great corporation, the bustling city, or the huge department store. In many instances the cold anonymity of urban-industrial life has weakened our concern for our fellow men. Organized charity has become efficient, but impersonal, and often lacks the humanitarian aspect that characterized its origin. Administration of large bureaucratic organizations is immensely complicated by difficulties of getting people to generate enthusiasm for organizational rules and doing things for the good of the whole group. Nevertheless, without the cohesive force of these group loyalties, any society would soon disintegrate.

An industrial worker in one of our giant manufacturing concerns may have close personal friends among his co-workers for whom he may feel a very intense feeling of interpersonal loyalty. Additionally, he is expected to demonstrate a certain amount of loyalty to his company. As a union member, he is expected to be loyal to his union by supporting its decisions and by not crossing its picket lines or the picket lines of other unions.

Professional people are loyal to their professions and to their colleagues. The growing number of professional men—doctors, lawyers, engineers, architects—is itself a result of an industrial system of production. For abundant professional services are not available in a society where most people must be producers. Mass production enables some members of a society to turn their attention to enterprises rendering services rather than goods. As the various professions have grown in numbers and prestige, however, their members have formed their own special-interest groups. As a result, loyalty to a profession grows strong and loyalty to other groups is submerged. A doctor, for example, may be more loyal to his colleagues and his profession than to the hospital that happens to employ him. Professors likewise are sometimes more loyal to their special discipline than to any college or university. Such a situation need not necessarily breed conflict so long as administrative policies and practices do not threaten professional codes and principles.

Like professionals, craftsmen are loyal to their trade and to their fellow craftsmen. Skilled workers take great pride in their special abilities and are quick to defend their interests. Unlike professional people, however, craftsmen have had to stand by while more and more of their special skills have been rendered obsolete by machine methods of production. Cigar-makers, for instance, are no longer in much demand; neither are carriage-makers nor hand book-binders. The demand for professional services, on the other hand, increases by leaps and bounds. This situation reveals why skilled workers may tender more loyalty to their craft than to their employer.

SOME WORDS OF SUMMARY

The full story of the many and complex consequences of the Industrial Revolution remains for future historians and social scientists to compile. For the present, we can trace only a few of the more obvious implications.

Mechanization of agriculture, less publicized than the great revolution in industry, has vastly increased agricultural output, reduced the number of farms and farmers, and raised farmers' levels of living. Accompanying the revolution in farm machinery and "horsepower" has been a whole series of changes in production, distribution, and marketing techniques. If these trends in agricultural production and way of life continue, the traditional rural-urban, "hayseed-city slicker" distinctions may eventually disappear.

The factory system has also brought great changes in economic and social life. By bringing workers and heavy machinery together, the factory made possible an extensive specialization and division of labor. The earlier guild and putting-out systems of production were ill-adapted to large-scale business operations. As free labor and fixed capital came into use, work was permanently separated from the home.

Employment, wages, and levels of living have all moved upward under the impetus of the new technology. But against these quantitative and materialistic gains are the consequences of industrialization that are more difficult to evaluate. Mass production yields standardized and mediocre commodities. "Better living" becomes a matter of more and more material possessions, which critics interpret as a narrow kind of hedonism. Unemployment and industrial accidents, injuries, and deaths have become by-products of large-scale production.

Important loyalties are adapted to meet requirements of an industrial world. In the present stage of industrialization we place a high value on efficiency, quantity, and group loyalty.

FURTHER ROADS TO LEARNING

GENERAL ACCOUNTS

F. Allen, *et al.*, *Technology and Social Change* (New York: Appleton-Century-Crofts, 1957). A provocative series of essays by noted authorities relating social and technological change to the institutions of society.

T. Caplow, *The Sociology of Work* (Minneapolis: University of Minnesota Press, 1954). A scholarly study of the implications of work in an industrial society.

J. Dewhurst and associates, *America's Needs and Resources: A New Survey* (New York: Twentieth Century Fund, 1955). An elaborate review of the physical and human resources of America in relation to industrial conditions.

SPECIAL STUDIES

E. Durkheim, *The Division of Labor in Society*, translated by George Simpson (Glencoe, Ill.: The Free Press, 1947). The famous French sociologist's classic analysis.

L. Mumford, *Technics and Civilization* (New York: Harcourt, Brace, 1934). An absorbing study of the implications of some early and important inventions.

See references in Chapter 12 for additional special studies.

FICTION AND DRAMA

M. Gellhorn, *The Trouble I've Seen* (New York: William Morrow, 1936). How several different types of people, all from widely different backgrounds, ended up on relief rolls.

E. Nichols, *Danger! Keep Out* (Boston: Houghton Mifflin, 1943). A fascinating novel about a midwestern oil industry that gives a lucid picture of the problems of technological unemployment, personnel policy, and labor relations.

U. Sinclair, *Little Steel* (New York: Farrar and Rinehart, 1938). A steel executive fights valiantly to keep new ideas and methods in industry from displacing the old.

W. Smitter, *F. O. B., Detroit* (New York: Harper, 1938). What the machine does to men.

J. Sprague, *The Making of a Merchant* (New York: William Morrow, 1928). The evolution of a large department store.

FILMS

The Agriculture Story (United States Department of Agriculture, 1956, 14 min., sound, color). How American agriculture became so highly efficient.

Atomic Power (March of Time, 1947, 19 min., sound, black and white). Outstanding scientists are portrayed in this living history of atomic power. A look at future industrial and business applications provides an interesting basis for speculation.

Automatic Machines (Columbia Broadcasting System, 1955, 25 min., sound, black and white). A tour of a pioneering laboratory in the field of automation.

Man in the Twentieth Century (McGraw-Hill, 1950, 17 min., sound, black and white). Technological progress accompanying the Industrial Revolution has led to a variety of social, economic, and political problems, as portrayed in this film.

Pageant of Progress (J. I. Case, 1948, 20 min., sound, color). How things have changed on the farm in the last 5,000 years.

For other films on the Industrial Revolution, see references in Chapter 10.

Our Urban World

THEME

The contemporary world is a place where man's ancient loyalties have been seriously shaken by . . . the urban revolution, *which has profoundly affected his family life,* criminal problems, educational system, government, *and even his personality. . . .*

CHAPTER FOURTEEN

The Rise
of the Modern City

*The late nineteenth-century American city was
already a turbulent and bustling center—full of people, trams,
carriages, and a variety of businesses.*

To understand

the contemporary world in all its kaleidoscopic variations, we have explored first our circle of personal loyalties and then the impact of the Industrial Revolution, a historical phenomenon that has cut across and deeply affected our personal lives, our loyalties, and our institutions. While discussing these integrating themes of loyalty and industrialism, we have stressed their interrelatedness, many of the conflicts and tensions they seemingly produce, and the possibilities for a richer life accruing from them. To these themes we now add another, *urbanism*, a second historical phenomenon that cuts across the usual divisions of modern life and affects us

profoundly affects each of us in a wide variety of ways.

For modern man lives in cities. Although more characteristic of some parts of the world than others, the rush to the city is a continuing phenomenon of world-wide extent. Further, as with industrialism, *urbanism—which is the characteristic way of life in cities*—is more than an isolated feature of modern life. It exerts a powerful influence on the family, education, government, criminal behavior, and human personality, as we shall see from the chapters that follow in this section. If we would understand today's world, we must first study the complex of historical, social, and economic pulsations that throb in the heart of the modern city.

THE CITY IN HISTORY

From industrialism as a major feature or theme of the contemporary world to urbanism as another is an easy and natural step. For not until the Industrial Revolution began changing the face of the world in the eighteenth and nineteenth centuries did the modern city in all its diversity and influence, splendor and squalor, begin to take shape. Without modern industry and especially modern transport, the vast crowds of humanity huddled in scores of major cities today could not be kept alive for a single week. The railroad, the steamship, and the motor car are the indispensable media for transferring the produce of the farmer to the dinner table of the city-dweller. Only once in modern history has a metropolitan center been fed in any other way. That was in 1948 when

the world witnessed the spectacle of a city of 2 million people—Berlin—being supplied solely by aircraft (another mechanized means of transport).

ANCIENT CITIES

But we must not be led to suppose that there were no great cities prior to the coming of modern industry. Along the rivers of the Ancient World, Memphis and Thebes, Nineveh and Babylon grew strong behind their fortress walls. Rivers were the natural avenues of trade and cities the entrepôts for the transaction of business. Cities served, too, as social and religious centers where public affairs and religious observances were carried out. Whether these early cities were

In the Western World and elsewhere, cities have been the cradles of civilized life. High in the Andes, the ruins of this ancient Incan city include a magnificent temple and beautifully terraced gardens.

primarily founded as places of defense, seats of government, or sites of religious fetes is a question on which historians and others have not yet agreed.

From Egypt and Mesopotamia the cities of the Ancient World spread along the indented shores of the Mediterranean and Aegean seas. In Phoenicia, Tyre and Sidon prospered during the halcyon era of sea-borne trade prior to the rise of Rome. Carthage, a Phoenician colony in Africa, rose to wealth and power on the strength of a powerful navy and her control of the rich trade of the western Mediterranean. Then came the Greek city-states, centers of commerce, culture, and advanced political development,

and finally Rome, master of the Mediterranean world. From a pastoral village astride the Tiber, Rome grew to a great metropolis of perhaps a million people. Crowded yet well-governed, dynamic yet sophisticated, Rome was the most modern of ancient cities. Paved streets, good sewers, and public baths all anticipated the sanitary awakening of the nineteenth century. Her corruption in the midst of reform, crime side by side with a great legal tradition, all have a distinctly modern ring.

Cities were thus the cradles of civilization. The very word "civilization" is derived from the Latin *civis*, or citizen, which meant city-dweller in much of the Ancient World. For it was in cities that art and politics, sculpture and literature, all the bench marks of civilization, were fostered and stimulated. When cities fell before the barbarians during the early Middle Ages, so did civilization. For at least seven hundred years city life was in eclipse in Europe. Populations declined, commerce almost disappeared, and the arts languished. Not until the eleventh century, with the renewal of commerce, especially between Italy and the Middle East, did town life revive. It was no accident that the great burst of energy in the creative arts which we call the Renaissance coincided with the dynamic growth of such cities as Florence, Venice, Genoa, and Rome.

CULTURAL ADVANTAGES OF CITIES

Why should this be so? What is there about city life that spurs the imagination and the creative impulse? In the first place, cities are pre-eminently the home of a new and different type of individualism from that found in rural societies. "Neighborliness" in the rural sense is replaced by anonymity and a dependence on one's self for employment, recreation, and diversion. Organizations are far more numerous, but much less intimate than they are in the country. Cities, too, permit (in fact, demand) a division of labor unknown to rural areas, so that talents that would go unused in the country now find employment. Painters, sculptors, and writers are able to find a market for their work, something they could never find in the country. "Art bakes no bread" is likely to reflect the attitude of the village rustic rather than the city-dweller toward the aspirations of creative artists. The city, further, permits like to meet like. No matter how strange or abstract a man's interests, he can always locate others of like mind in a great metropolis. The uncommon enterprise will always find mutual encouragement and stimulation. Organizations, meetings, professional socie-

ties in every sphere of life abound in great cities. Cities, to cite one further source of their cultural pre-eminence, are the seats of government. As such they register the pulse of a nation. They are full of movement and throbbing activity, of drama and great events —apt stimulation for the sluggish pen of any writer. The mere fact that cities attract great numbers of people insures patronage for the theater, ballet, newspapers, orchestras, and other cultural institutions. Cities, finally, are likely to be centers of wealth. Here the country boy comes to seek fame and riches. Here fortunes made in trade and business

To many a country boy cities were places of fame and riches, ". . . the spires that were gleaming."

may be used to sponsor a Leonardo da Vinci or to endow great universities, museums, and libraries. Cities, by their very nature, are thus centers of wealth, talent, cooperation, dynamic activity, and individualism. Cities are symbols of civilization.

INDUSTRIALISM AND THE MODERN CITY

Two striking differences distinguish modern cities from their ancient or medieval predecessors: their size and number. The few great cities of the Ancient World were exceptions in a rural, decentralized period of history. Land was, in fact, the chief source of the world's wealth until the nineteenth century. Man depended on it for a living; it shaped his views of life, society, and politics. Not until the Industrial Revolution did cities become the *typical* dwelling-places of large segments of the world's population.

The relationship of industrialization to urbanization is clear. The harnessing of steam put an end to the semi-rural cottage system of manufacture. It was patently impossible to put steam engines and the machines they powered in the cottages of thousands of workers. The workers and the raw materials had to be brought to the machines. Here was the dynamic force behind the factory system that drew thousands of English, German, American, and other workers from the villages and farms to the cities. New towns and cities mushroomed across the face of England, Europe, and North America. Existing cities grew at a fantastic pace. Between 1850 and 1890, both London and Paris doubled in size, while Berlin quadrupled in population. New cities, unknown to the Europe of 1800, numbered 100,000 people or more a century later. With characteristic penetration and wit, Lewis Mumford has described this process in his rewarding book *The Culture of Cities*:

It took the better part of a century before all the agents of agglomeration were developed in equal degree: before the advantages offered industry in the towns counterbalanced the lure of independent organization in separate factory villages, sufficient to make the former the prevailing mode. Once these agents played into each other's hands, the attractive power of the city became irresistible; and the cities came to absorb an ever larger share of the natural increase in population.

By the end of the eighteenth century most of the necessary conditions were satisfied in London, Paris, and Berlin: hence the ability to pile people into these throbbing centers was limited now only by the human tolerance for an obnoxious environment. Unfortunately, on this score, human beings show qualities that remarkably resemble those of the pig: give swine a clean sty on hard ground with plenty of sunlight, and they will keep it remarkably clean: put them in the midst of muck and putrescence underground, and they will accommodate themselves to these conditions. When starvation and homelessness are the alternatives, there is apparently no horror to which defeated men and women will not adapt themselves and endure.*

THE MECHANIZATION OF AGRICULTURE AND TRANSPORTATION

But the crowding of human beings into cities depended not only on the factories, which lured them from the farm, but also on the application of mechanical power to agriculture and transportation. For every farm boy who went to the city, those who remained behind on the farm had to produce that much more food with one less pair of hands. To take up the slack the stay-at-homes, as we have already seen, turned to crop rotation, chemical fertilizers, and such new inventions as the reaper and mechanical plow. The average American farmer in 1890

* L. Mumford, *The Culture of Cities* (New York: Harcourt, Brace, 1938), p. 157.

planted 26 acres, compared with only 17 in 1870, just 20 years before. Today a dwindling farm population produces a surplus of food in the United States. What this revolution in agricultural production has meant for life on the farm we know from our reading of Chapter 13.

Once in the city the farm boy relied mainly on mechanized transport to take him to and from his job. The years of the rush to the city were also the heyday of the street railway and the trolley car. Many great American fortunes were made in city transportation in the last quarter of the nineteenth century. In addition to internal transportation, the city-dweller, as we mentioned earlier, was also very much dependent on the railroad, which brought him his food and other necessities. Throwing iron rails across the American continent, in fact, had a great deal to do with the location of cities in the West. Many a midwestern prairie or plains city today owes its origins to a railroader's decision to run his line in a particular direction. Likewise, the laying of hard-surface roads exerted a decisive influence on the location and growth of many American cities and towns.

CITY GROWTH IN THE UNITED STATES

Many of these new cities and towns grew at a phenomenal rate. In a single generation, America was transformed from a static, agrarian society into a dynamic, urban one. Rural America, in the historian Arthur Schlesinger's picturesque phrase, was like a stag at bay, making its last desperate stand against the domination of the urban Northeast. But the fight it fought, while it had its heroes and colorful moments, was doomed to failure. Inexorably the lure of city jobs and city attractions drew the young, the hopeful, and the adventurous, as well as the newcomers from Europe. According to census figures, there were only 141 cities of 8,000 persons or more in the United States in 1860, compared with 547 in 1900. Five of every six Americans lived in a community with fewer than 2,500 people in 1860, but by 1890 one of these persons had gone to the city and by 1910 still another had turned his back on rural life. Small cities grew large and the large cities became even larger. New York leaped from 1,500,000 population in 1860 to 2,500,000 in 1890 and to about 5,000,000 in 1915. Chicago grew even faster. Numbering only 100,000 inhabitants in 1860, this sprawling midwestern giant increased tenfold to 1,000,000 in 1890 and twenty-five times to 2,500,000 in 1915.

THE CITY IN AMERICAN HISTORY

Here was a movement of peoples to rival the barbarian hordes that overran the Roman Empire. In terms of numbers involved, the movement to the cities surpassed even the great westward march of Americans during the nineteenth century. Arthur Schlesinger and other scholars have suggested that perhaps the city, rather than the frontier, was the vital factor in molding the American character. Where earlier historians (particularly Frederick Jackson Turner) had stressed the westward movement as the creator of American traits—individualism, democracy, national loyalty—Schlesinger defended the view that the city had fathered many of these American characteristics. Were not cities the home of most of the fathers of the American Revolution? Would America have achieved independence without Boston and Philadelphia? In the cities, too, were born many of the democratic reforms of the nineteenth century: free public education, women's rights, more humane

One of the most hateful and demoralizing results of rapid urban growth was the appearance of horrid pest holes, death traps, and slums in many cities.

treatment of the insane. And who would deny the role of the city as a melting pot in forging millions of European immigrants into an American nationality?

Before the Civil War, the urban influence in America was stronger than the number of cities warranted. New York, Boston, Philadelphia, Baltimore, Charleston, and New Orleans had all played significant roles in American economic, social, political, and cultural life during the ante-bellum period. Prior to the coming of the railroad, it was a virtual necessity for an aspiring city to front the ocean, preferably at the mouth of a great river. In these few cities were congregated most of America's writers, painters, and journalists. The whole story of that great flowering of American arts and letters in the 1840's and 1850's can be told almost exclusively against a background of Boston and New York and their environs. In the words of Professor H. J. Muller, "Without London and Boston Thoreau could have had no Walden." Here, too, was amassed much of the capital and labor that were vital to the first stage of America's industrial revolution.

But to the masses of Americans, the city was evil incarnate, a place of idleness, sin, and crime. Country ministers never tired of warning their flocks against big cities, cursed, as one of them put it, "with immense accumulations of ignorance and error, vice and crime." Editors of farm journals urged young men seeking their fortunes not to sacrifice their independence in the city where they must "cringe and flatter, and . . . attend upon the wishes of every painted and padded form of humanity." From the printing presses, too, came such lurid books as *Vampires of New York*, *Tricks and Traps of Chicago*, and a host of others. Cities were sinks of iniquity.

As industrialism began to flourish and the surge to the cities continued, this hostility began to break down, though suspicion remained. Cities were becoming national and could no longer be identified with a distant and suspect East. Middlewestern as well as East and West coast cities felt the stimulus of industrialism. Of fifty principal American cities in 1890, twelve were in the Middle West. Urbanization was becoming a controlling force in American history. A new way of life for Americans was taking shape. Walt Whitman, poet of the new urban democracy, could write of the "splendor, picturesqueness, and oceanic amplitude and rush of these great cities." About him he saw the achievement and the promise of "these hurrying, feverish, electric crowds of men."

THE URBAN IMPACT ON RURAL LIFE

Never were the drawbacks of rural life felt so keenly. Not only the drudgery and monotony of farm life but now also the comparison with the lot of the city-dweller made the farmer discontented. Further, the farming frontier was now passing over the Great Plains, a region of low rainfall, sprawling, scattered farms, and consequent isolation and loneliness. Farm women, in particular, contrasted their lot with the photographs and stories of city women appearing in the new ladies' magazines. Some historians feel that this social frustration played as important a role in the farmers' protest movements of the 1880's and 1890's as their economic grievances over low prices, railroad abuses, and high interest rates. Certainly many farmers, for whatever reason, enlisted in the ranks of the Greenbackers, Farmers' Alliance, Populists, and other rural reform movements. In William Jennings Bryan of Nebraska they found a dynamic spokesman for their cause, one who could frame in words their anger and frustration, their self-esteem and pride in the land. "Burn down your cities and leave your farms," he cried, "and your cities will spring up again as if by magic; but destroy our farms and the grass will grow in the streets of every city in the country." But Bryan, like Robert E. Lee, had drawn his sword in a lost cause. The great cities of America buried him in an avalanche of votes for William McKinley, spokesman for the new industrialism and urbanism, which were remolding American politics as well as American life generally.

CITY TENSIONS

For the city-dweller this new way of life brought discord and tension as well as opportunity and advancement. Habituated to a rural environment, the newcomer to the city found it difficult to adjust to the frantic tempo of urban life. Cases of acute nervousness and mental breakdown multiplied. Noise, distraction, competition, and impersonality, as well as speed, were all greater in the city than in the country. Some doctors were diagnosing a form of urban neurosis and calling it "neurasthenia." One called it "the national disease of America." Problems of lighting, water supply, housing, transportation, and police and fire protection cried out for attention. By the end of the century, many prominent men and women were voicing their concern over the future effect of the city on American life. Lyman Abbott, a famous Congregationalist clergyman, voiced the alarm of many when he said:

What shall we do with our great cities? What will our great cities do with us? These are the two problems which confront every thoughtful American. For the question involved in these two questions does not concern the city alone. The whole country is affected, if indeed its character and history are not determined, by the condition of its great cities. . . . The city is not all bad nor all good. It is humanity compressed, the best and the worst combined, in a strangely composite community.*

HERITAGE FOR THE FUTURE: GOOD OR BAD?

For better or worse the nineteenth century left the United States and the world well embarked on the way to an urban civilization. The next century would see urbanism follow industrialism into eastern Europe, Asia, and Africa. Was this heritage of urbanism a blessing or a menace? For those in the underdeveloped nations, who saw in the Western city only wealth, opportunity, leisure, and the sinews of industrial strength, there could be only one answer. Yet there were others, especially in the West, who saw the city as an abnormal, even cancerous, excrescence on the body of civilization. The city, they argued, robbed mankind of its individuality, security, and dignity. It uprooted man from the soil, took away the flowers, sunshine, and open spaces natural to his habitat. It substituted the artificial environment of the machine, the skyscraper, and the tenement for the natural environment of man. Furthermore, there seemed to be no end to the degrading process. More and more human beings were being stuffed into the hothouse atmosphere of the city and its environs. Nowhere did the process

seem to be arrested or even to falter; rather, the reverse was true in large areas of the globe. In an age of atomic warfare this crowding and centralization seemed to critics even more suicidal than it had been before. Where would it all end? The great problem of today, writes sociologist E. Gordon Ericksen,

. . . would seem to be neither divorce, immorality, disease, nor poverty, but something much deeper and more subtle, specifically: Do we want to live as city people with all that city life implies—human indifference, tension, monotony, often a negative birth rate, a world, ironically, in which men travel everyday from institutions where they prefer not to work to residential districts where they prefer not to live, yet a setting where the greatest riches in art, music, and literature have been accumulated, where reside the greater institutions of education and medical skill, plus museums and exhilarating forms of recreation? In this surging masslike society, the ordinary little man does not seem to count for much and is constantly being reduced to smaller proportions. He is made to feel that he does not count any more; he complains of being out of touch with his spokesmen, of being in a poor position to obtain the complete answers to current problems which intimately concern him.*

Others, however, although concerned with these same problems, find more cause for optimism. They point to the fact that although city populations in Western industrial countries continue to increase, the *rate of increase* has slowed considerably. The areas of most rapid industrialization today embrace those countries that are passing through the early stages of industrialism and not those that are already heavily industrialized. Furthermore, there has been a pronounced tendency for the residents of our industrial centers to push to the periphery or suburbs of cities in order to regain at least a measure of the space and sunshine whose loss is lamented by critics of cities.

* A. M. Schlesinger, *The Rise of the City 1878-1898* (New York: Macmillan, 1933), p. iii.

* E. G. Ericksen, *Urban Behavior* (New York: Macmillan, 1954), pp. 5-6.

Then, too, cities are undeniably the centers of learning, culture, and recreation in all industrial countries. However strong the urge to "return to nature," few persons today will remove themselves very far from the advantages of a city. Finally, no matter how much cities shrink the spiritual horizons of modern man, they are indispensable for that concentration and specialization that are the *sine qua non* of material progress. We may regret the excessive concern of our fellow men for material benefits, but to limit our industrial growth for the sake of greater spirituality would be to lop off our noses to spite our faces. In all ages of history the great cultures of man have rested on a base both material and spiritual. Ideally, spiritual and material growth are partners rather than antagonists. Cities, in any case, are here to stay.

SOME WORDS OF SUMMARY

Like industry, cities have made a deep impression on modern man's way of life. Family life, politics, education, and the human personality have all felt the impact of urbanism. The modern city in all its size and diversity reflects the growth of industrialism, particularly in Western nations. But there were many cities, some of them large and influential, before the emergence of modern industry. Indeed, cities were the cradles of civilization, for it was in Memphis, Thebes, Nineveh, Babylon, Carthage, Athens, and Rome that much of the greatness of ancient civilizations was concentrated and nourished. In cities, political power and cultural talent were gathered behind one set of protective walls. Following the fall of Rome, cities went into eclipse during the early Middle Ages, then stirred to new life again as commerce began to flourish during the eleventh century. To the wealth and leisure concentrated in cities the Renaissance owed much of its grandeur.

Modern industry gave a powerful stimulus to the growth of cities. With industry came the factories, mills, railroad terminals, banks, and warehouses that make up the complex organization of an industrial city. On the farms, too, mechanical power made lighter the farmers' burdens and sent their output soaring. Mechanical power also revolutionized transportation, linking the mushrooming cities with their food supply and providing fast and efficient transit for industrial workers who manned the factories and the machines.

City growth transformed the face of America. From a rural, decentralized nation America was converted into a dynamic, urbanized society within a single generation. This transformation had deep significance for American democracy, reform movements, and the assimilation of immigrants. Earlier suspicion of the city gave way in the wholesale rush from the farms and rural areas. In parts of New England and the states along the eastern coast, rural decline began to set in. Compared with the fortunes of the city-dweller, the farmer, particularly if he lived in lonely isolation on the Great Plains frontier, often felt frustrated and unequal. In the cities themselves serious problems of noise, smoke, lighting, sewage, crime, and fire had to be met or endured.

It is difficult to evaluate the historical significance of the rise of the city because the urbanization process is far from complete. Critics are concerned with man's loss of individuality, dignity, and security in the artificial surroundings of our cities. But others defend the city as the home of wealth, culture, leisure, and social and material progress. Hopefully, the "urban crisis" of modern civilization can be overcome without great loss either of spiritual values or material well-being.

FURTHER ROADS TO LEARNING

GENERAL ACCOUNTS

E. Ericksen, *Urban Behavior* (New York: Macmillan, 1954). A good general account of historical, ecological, and psychological factors affecting city life.

R. Lee, *The City: Urbanism and Urbanization in Major World Regions* (Philadelphia: Lippincott, 1955). World-wide perspective on the growth of cities and their relation to social institutions and problems.

L. Mumford, *The Culture of Cities* (New York: Harcourt, Brace, 1938). Though opinionated, an invaluable historical, sociological, and cultural analysis of cities that defies classification.

L. Wirth, "Urbanism as a Way of Life," *American Journal of Sociology*, XLIV (July, 1938), pp. 2-24. One of the best brief statements of what a city is, together with a suggestive theory of urbanism.

SPECIAL STUDIES

L. Atherton, *Main Street on the Middle Border* (Bloomington: Indiana University Press, 1954). A charming account of midwestern country towns in America from 1865 to 1950.

R. Dickinson, *The West European City* (London: Routledge & Kegan, 1951). A comprehensive survey by a geographer.

R. Fisher, ed., *The Metropolis in Modern Life* (Garden City, N. Y.: Doubleday, 1955). Suggestive essays on the historical, political, economic, legal, technological, and spiritual aspects of big city life.

E. Peterson, ed., *Cities Are Abnormal* (Norman: University of Oklahoma Press, 1946). A series of essays revolving about the theme that the modern city has become a kind of Frankenstein monster.

S. Queen and D. Carpenter, *The American City* (New York: McGraw-Hill, 1953). Probably the best general sociological account of the American city.

A. Schlesinger, "The City in American History," *Mississippi Valley Historical Review*, XXVII (June, 1940), pp. 43-66. The best brief statement anywhere of the role of the city in American history.

———, *The Rise of the City 1878-1898* (New York: Macmillan, 1933). A social history emphasizing the emergence of the city as the dominant theme in American history during the period 1878-1898.

F. Vigman, *Crisis of the Cities* (Washington, D. C.: Public Affairs Press, 1955). A pessimistic book that finds American cities facing inevitable disaster.

FICTION AND DRAMA

P. Claudel, *The City* (New Haven: Yale University Press, 1920). A three-act play centering on city life.

V. Fisher, *City of Illusion* (New York: Harper, 1941). A novel of the wild mining community of Virginia City, Nevada, created by the discovery of the Comstock Lode in 1859.

H. Goodman and B. Carpenter, eds., *Stories of the City* (New York: Ronald, 1931). A collection of short stories.

T. Hardy, *The Return of the Native* (New York: Pocket Books, 1950). A tragedy provoked in part by a leading character's longing to escape to Paris, a symbol of glamorous metropolitan life.

S. Lewis, *Main Street* (New York: Harcourt, Brace, 1920). The tragic-comic story of Gopher Prairie, Minnesota, as it appeared to the author.

U. Sinclair, *The Jungle* (New York: Viking, 1946). Reprint of a dramatic novel picturing the abuse and oppression of an immigrant family by Chicago and its stock yards.

G. Stewart, *Years of the City* (Boston: Houghton Mifflin, 1955). The story of the rise, flowering, and decay of an ancient Greek city as reflected in the lives of its citizens.

FILMS

Cities—How They Grow (Encyclopaedia Britannica Films, revised, 1952, 11 min., sound, black and white). Good pictorial summary of factors that determine the location and growth of cities, especially in the United States.

Cities—Why They Grow (Coronet, 1949, 11 min., sound, black and white). Concentrates on human activity, especially of urban workers, to depict the "why" of urban growth.

Growth of London (United World Films—Educational, 1952, 23 min., sound, black and white). British film showing principal historical events, including the Industrial Revolution, which have shaped modern London.

Urban Ways (National Educational Television, 1956, 30 min., sound, black and white). Discussion of the interdependence in urban life from old New Amsterdam to modern New York.

The
Twentieth-Century City

Mighty Gotham bursts from the earth.

If cities

grew rapidly in the nineteenth century, they exploded during the twentieth. Not only in Europe and America but across the face of the globe, mankind joined in a great rush to the cities. In 1900 there were fewer than 150 cities in the world with populations of 100,000 or more, but by 1940 there were more than 700. They grew in size as well as in number. By 1950, five cities in the United States alone had passed the 1-million mark.

The city-dwellers far outnumbered their country cousins in industrial states. Over half of all Americans were living in urban communities of 8,000 or more inhabitants by 1930. And the number living in urban areas, places of 2,500 or more as defined by the Census Bureau, tripled between 1900 and 1950, as shown in Table 11. The figures in Table 12, which compare the growth of the urban and rural populations between 1900 and 1950, clearly reveal the scope of the cityward trend.

TABLE 11 NUMBER OF URBAN PLACES, UNITED STATES, 1900 TO 1950

| | | Urban Population | |
Year	Number of Places, 2,500 Or More	Number in Millions	Percentage of Total Population
1950 (new) *	4,741	96.5	64.0
1950 (old) *	4,023	88.9	59.0
1940	3,464	74.4	56.5
1930	3,165	69.0	56.2
1920	2,722	54.2	51.2
1910	2,262	42.0	45.7
1900	1,737	30.2	39.7

* Definition of urban areas changed in 1950, allocating over 7 million more people to urban areas under the new definition.
Source: U. S. Census of Population.

TABLE 12 PERCENTAGE INCREASE OF THE POPULATION, URBAN AND RURAL, UNITED STATES, 1900 TO 1950

| | Percentage Increase Over Previous Decade | | |
Year	Total	Urban	Rural
1950 (old) *	14.5	19.5	7.9
1940	7.2	7.9	6.4
1930	16.1	27.3	4.4
1920	14.9	29.0	3.2
1910	21.0	39.3	9.0
1900	20.7	36.4	12.2

* Definition of urban areas changed in 1950, allocating over 7 million more people to urban areas under the new definition.
Source: U. S. Census of Population.

WHY THE EXPLOSION?

We have already given part of the explanation for this stampede to the cities in the preceding chapter. Over the past century or so, technological and scientific improvements have vastly increased farm production and created a surplus of farm workers, who have turned to the shops, offices, mills, and factories of the cities for employment. Thus far, no one has been very concerned about the continuing ability of urban employers to absorb the flood of rural migrants. Fortunately, throughout our history American workers have benefited from a shortage of labor. Indeed, our economy has absorbed millions of European immigrant workers, in addition to the native-born. With the advent of automation and atomic power, there seems to be no immediate end in sight to industry's potential for growth.

The great migration to the cities has been

266

facilitated by our modern transportation system. A century ago, waterways were the major thoroughfares for hauling goods and people. But railroads, and later, trucks and automobiles, gave a new lease on life to those cities that were not accessible by water. The automobile also made it possible for large retail stores to attract customers from ten, twenty, and even fifty miles around. This development in turn meant a greater volume of business, and hence, created a demand for more employees in the urban centers. Trucks have an advantage over railroads in not being confined to particular roadbeds, and they can also make doorstep deliveries. Where speed is unimportant, water transportation continues to offer the cheapest means of moving goods, which explains why cities lo-

cated on water routes continue to thrive. Even great railroad centers such as Omaha and Kansas City grew up on river banks. But those cities that have prospered and grown the most have been located at a break in the transportation system. New York, Detroit, Chicago, and other great cities are points where goods are transferred from land to water transportation. It is quite possible that air transportation will change this pattern as improvements in equipment and facilities make possible lower air-carrier costs.

Still another source of urban growth in the twentieth century has been the tremendous expansion of government services. Our seats of government have become the homes of extensive bureaucracies, which serve the growing needs and wants of many people.

The cities that prospered most, such as New York and Philadelphia, were located at a break in the transportation system where goods had to be transferred from rails to boat, or vice versa.

The Ginza district of downtown Tokyo. Throughout the world great cities beckon and enchant us with their flickering lights and gaiety, their bustle and vigor.

State and national capitals, in particular, have grown amazingly. The great port city of London might well be a metropolis even if it were not the capital of a world-wide commonwealth. But Washington, on the other hand, might still be a rather crude, dismal little village had it not been chosen to house our national government. A number of state capitals in the United States also owe a great deal of their phenomenal growth to the fact that they are nerve centers of growing government bureaucracies. The growth in government services certainly cannot be neglected as a source of rapidly increasing urbanization.

Nor can the social attractions of the city, made more alluring by new and exciting recreational advantages, be overlooked as a cause of urban growth. To the timid as well as the adventurous, great cities are places of perennial excitement. They are centers of flickering lights and gaiety. Here the would-be adventurer finds escape from the prying eyes of the small community. Here few people care or know what you do. The hurry and scurry, the hustle and bustle, the ebb and flow of opportunity appeal to the daring and bold, to those anxious to break with tradition. In the pulsating metropolis things happen and happen fast. Things change. The vigor and enchantment excite the imagination and kindle the human spirit. Cities were not built for the timid.

Many and varied are the social and recreational outlets of the city. Here are dance halls, bars, movies, amusement parks, and sport spectacles that have a powerful attraction for some people. Here, too, are theaters, museums, art galleries, concerts, and fine restaurants that appeal to others. As a social capital, the city sets styles, patterns, vogues, modes, and even moods. It is a school of etiquette, grace, manners, urbanity, and taste. Although a city may be a spiritual wasteland for some, it can be loved for its charm, and is. Full of noise, ugliness, and vulgarity, cities nevertheless abound in attractions that cater to every taste.

Industrial growth, important though it was in the rise of the modern city, is thus not the only cause of rapid urban growth. Moreover, its relative importance has declined. Some twentieth-century cities have never been noted for their industries. Miami, Florida, for example, has prospered as a resort town; Ann Arbor, Michigan, is a university city; and Great Falls, Montana, is a "cow town." Though such cities are not the largest by any means, they do bear witness to the role that nonindustrial factors play in the development of cities.

CONSEQUENCES OF URBAN GROWTH

Our twentieth-century cities, then, have continued to grow, and at a constantly faster rate. The impact of this development on modern life has been tremendous, though largely unmeasured. Here we can only suggest some of the consequences.

DEMOGRAPHIC CONSEQUENCES

For one thing, the American city has become pre-eminently the home of the Negro, the foreign-born, and the American woman. Cities number considerably more women than men, despite the fact that the fairer sex is only slightly more numerous in the whole population. The disparity stems from the fact that there are more employment opportunities for women in cities than in rural areas. In Washington, D.C., for example, thousands of young women from all parts of the country are drawn each year into clerical positions in the United States government. Similarly, the Negro finds opportunities in the city that are inaccessible to him in his native habitat in the rural South. For almost a half-century there has been a steady

The urban explosion created a pressing need for more and better housing. One of the solutions to this problem was the modern apartment house in which people can be literally stacked together yet still live comfortably.

drift of American Negroes to northern cities. During World Wars I and II, in particular, the demand for unskilled labor drew tens of thousands of Negroes northward and city-ward. And much the same attraction has existed for the American immigrant, who has settled predominantly in our larger cities.

City-dwellers are generally younger and better educated than their rural cousins. There is an old adage which tells us that the farm youngster moves to the city during his productive years but returns to the farm or small town to retire. Although not wholly accurate, there is more than a grain of truth in the saying. For there are proportionately more children on farms and more young adults in cities than you might normally expect. And certainly many people move out of the city and back toward the farm and village when they retire.

HOUSING

The accelerated movement to the cities has placed a great strain on housing facilities in urban areas, which is reflected in high rents, crowded apartment and tenement living, and a growing public concern. It is doubtful if urban housing has ever been really adequate. In many of the industrial boomtowns early in the century, workers were coming in faster than houses could be built. In Flint, Michigan, automobile workers were even living in tents. For some people, a crowded tenement existence with all its attendant miseries has come to symbolize city life. But nevertheless, as measured by the amount of electricity, inside plumbing, and central heating, urban housing has generally been more advanced than rural housing. In recent decades, housing projects sponsored by public and private agencies have gone far to alleviate the shortage of living quarters in the larger cities. And people who could afford it have abandoned the congested atmosphere of the urban centers for suburban retreats

beyond the city limits. A considerable proportion of America's middle class, including many industrial workers, has joined the ranks of the daily commuters to the heart of the metropolis.

TRANSPORTATION

This move to the suburbs would have been impossible were it not for the train, the subway, the bus, and especially the automobile. All these developments, with the exception of the first, have come largely in the twentieth century. Earlier, the horse-car and the street-railway had made mass transportation within the city feasible. Today the survival of the entire metropolitan area, suburbs included, depends on continued, fast, efficient transportation.

The life of the commuter has one great disadvantage—the time and often the inconvenience of traveling back and forth each day to work. The suburbanite may spend as many as two or three hours each day riding between his home and his place of work. He justifies this loss of time by weighing it against the fresh air, out-of-doors recreation, and play space his children enjoy in the suburbs. More and more Americans are thus seeking to enjoy the advantages of city life while suffering as few of its disadvantages as possible. How long this trend can continue, with proportionately fewer people bearing the taxes for increasing municipal services, is at best a moot question.

RECREATION

The typical suburbanite continues to look to the city for recreation. With so many people congregated in the metropolitan area, almost any form of recreation will find its devotees. A great deal of this activity will be heavily commercialized. It costs the metropolitanite something to enjoy his theater, golf, dancing, boxing, ice-skating, or bowling. Commercialized recreation has become one of our biggest businesses. But the quality of the recreation will generally be high. Whether an opera or a taxi-dance hall, the city-dweller can expect the best of its kind.

This immense variety of attractive recreation leads to the individualization of recreational taste. More specifically, city folk tend to enjoy their recreation apart from their families. Each family member goes his own way. The father may go golfing, mother to church, brother to the movies, and sister to a dance. Students of the subject have placed some of the blame for the breakdown of the urban family on this tendency. For a while they hoped that television might restore some of the family-type recreation common in rural areas. But for the most part, there is very little interaction between members of a family sitting with their eyes glued on a TV set.

This "spectatoritis," or tendency toward passive recreation, has become a national disease. We have become a nation of viewers and listeners, mere spectators at huge recreational extravaganzas staged for profit. Aside

from millions of television viewers and radio listeners, millions more on a given Saturday afternoon in autumn simply watch football games from the sidelines. No one would seriously suggest that all these people should play sandlot football instead of going to the game. But without much doubt, most of their recreation is of this type, passive and vicarious rather than active and personal. We miss the very real benefits—physical, emotional, mental—that come from active participation in some kind of recreation. The National Recreation Association has long advocated that every person have some sport, hobby, or outdoor activity that will fully engage his energies and "re-create" his mental and physical well-being.

EMPLOYMENT

The need for active, individual recreation is more pressing in cities than in rural areas. Farmers often work in isolation, their main contacts being with members of their own families. But in the modern city, most people work in one place and associate with many other people. Although contacts

A handful of participants and thousands of fans at a 1959 World Series game. A vast number of Americans spend their leisure hours as passive spectators.

among people who work elbow-to-elbow may be intimate and informal, their dealings with management are likely to be formal and bureaucratic. A worker's life is apt to be highly routinized, whether he tends an impersonal machine or regulates the massive flow of paperwork that characterizes most urban industries. Even his labor union is apt to be so large and highly organized that he will feel powerless before it. Everywhere he must sacrifice his personal inclinations to the urban need for order, discipline, and routine.

On the other hand, he will find job opportunities abundant and rewarding in the city. Although these things are difficult to measure, his pay probably will be higher, his hours of work shorter, and his job steadier than would be the case in rural areas. Urban employment also offers a worker many twentieth-century "fringe benefits," such as paid vacations, rest periods, unemployment benefits, accident insurance, and retirement plans. Job opportunities, moreover, are more varied in the city than in the country. This wide diversity in occupations tends to sharpen social distinctions among urbanites. There is a wider social chasm in the city, for example, between the manual laborer and his boss than in the rural community. These social distinctions we shall consider later in the chapters on the urban family, crime and delinquency, modern education, local government, and the urban personality.

CHURCHES

Certainly the urban movement has left an indelible mark on all the basic institutions of human society. In the case of the church, for example, its influence has been profound. In rural areas many churches have been forced to close their doors because their congregations have moved to the city. In the cities, on the other hand, churches have grown and prospered. City churches are larger, more costly, and more attractive. Ministers tend to seek pastorates in the cities, where they can command greater prestige, larger salaries, and more opportunity for service.

But all is not well in the city churches either. In a bustling urban center a church must compete for support and membership with hundreds of secular activities. Here, too, religious skepticism and indifference reach their peaks. Many people announce that they are "too tired" to attend Sunday services after a Saturday evening round of entertainment. Others prefer a round of golf or a picnic on their day of recreation. As a result, churches find themselves in a dilemma. Should they compete with secular attractions at the expense of religious fundamentals? Should they bring dancing, card parties, and bingo into the church? Most churches have made gestures in this direction, but they are uneasy about such innovations.

Churches located near the heart of the city also have special problems. As population spreads outward from the business area at each city's center, newer churches arise in the outlying areas to meet the need. Older churches are left stranded and badly in need of members and financial support. Although some have had to close their doors, others have struggled on. Those that do remain open experience a considerable change in the character of their congregations. In fact, a few have become little more than mission houses for the "floating population" found in the center of every large city.

Yet despite these problems, the churches of America, as we saw in Chapter 7, have prospered in recent years. Church membership and interest in religion have been at an all-time high. True, many churches have had to undergo a drastic change in character, placing far less stress on traditional theology and more on social services and goals, but as an institution the church continues to show amazing vitality and adaptability.

THE FUTURE OF CITIES

Now what of the future? Can cities solve all their technological and human problems and continue to grow? Will the city of the future look very much like today's city? Is it possible that eventually urban industries will move to the suburbs and that urban dwellers will disperse to the countryside from whence many of them came? Are very many metropolitan problems likely to be solved in the near future?

No one knows the answers to these questions, but it is interesting to speculate about them. If the past is any guide, we can expect American cities to grow larger and larger. In time, virtually everyone may live in an urban area if the present trend continues. Theoretically, then, there are no limits to the expansion of urban populations.

According to one interesting prophecy, a few big "strip cities" are apt to develop.* In the northeastern part of the United States, for example, we might one day have a continuous city extending from Boston to Washington along the Atlantic Coast, or we might see the same kind of area extending from New York through Pittsburgh, Cleveland, and Detroit to Chicago and St. Louis. A person might be able to travel hundreds of miles without ever leaving such a city. Areas between existing cities in a strip of this kind might be transformed into commercial and residential zones. Workers would live within short driving distances of their jobs. Superhighways would connect them with their work and with convenient shopping centers. Industry and commerce would relocate along the strip. The prophecy is not in the least bit fantastic, for this sort of pattern is already taking shape on the eastern seaboard and in the Chicago and Los Angeles areas and other parts of the country.

Certainly a pattern of this type promises to solve many of the present problems of urban growth, especially those relating to congestion and inaccessibility.

Other observers foresee a future decentralization of industries and population, prompted in part by civil defense requirements in the event of an atomic attack. In some respects, decentralization is already in process in a slow and informal way. Despite this gradual tendency, however, metropolitan areas continue to grow at a faster rate than nonmetropolitan areas. It may require a severe crisis, perhaps an actual atomic attack, to promote a substantial degree of decentralization.

Actually, many authorities no longer see any real economic need for so much centralization. The reasons for the original explosion of the cities no longer exist. One student of the problem, W. S. Thompson, points out, for example, that it was the inability to transport high-pressure steam over long distances that started the initial rush to the city.* For steam, together with running water, was the great source of power in the early Industrial Revolution. Machinery powered by steam or water was essential to all basic industries in nineteenth-century England. The factories of a generation ago, therefore, clustered about the central steam plants, or near the best sources of water power, and the workers clustered around the factories. Until the advent of electric power, factory owners and workers had no other alternative but to congregate in the vicinity of the factory.

With the development of railway and other transportation facilities, business executives began locating their offices at some distance from their factories. But before the spread of telephone communication,

* See *U. S. News & World Report*, April 5, 1957 and November 28, 1958.

* W. S. Thompson, *Population Problems* (New York: McGraw-Hill, 1953), Chapter 19.

they found it advantageous to be near one another in order to keep abreast of current happenings in manufacturing, banking, and the stock market. As a result, offices sprouted in downtown districts, a movement that was encouraged by the advent of the skyscraper. All the attendant operations of industrial economy—distribution, retail sales, advertising—required more and more offices. New York, Boston, Chicago, and Philadelphia soon became great commercial as well as manufacturing centers.

But steam power has all but moved off-stage as electricity and the combustion engine have moved into the fields of industrial power, transportation, and communication. Since electricity can be carried cheaply over long distances, it does not have to be used close to its point of production. Telephone, telegraph, and closed-circuit television permit swift communication. Automobiles, diesel locomotives, and airplanes move businessmen quickly. Thus, factories and workers, offices and bosses, no longer need to be clustered together. And in the future, nuclear power, which is developing at a very rapid rate, may permit even further decentralization. But even now, when conditions seem to favor decentralization, our human

and material resources continue to be concentrated in our large cities. Whether this tendency will still exist fifty or even twenty-five years from now, however, is conjectural.

PLANNED AND ORDERLY DEVELOPMENT

Another factor that looms large in the future of American cities is the city-planning movement. Early American cities just grew. Whenever someone decided to build a store, a factory, or a home, he built it. City growth was a random development. There were few if any controls, and the result, more often than not, was disorder. The only discernible pattern was the location of the business district at or near the center of the city, surrounded by a residential zone and an outer layer of light industries, truck gardens, and eventually suburban housing.

Random growth produced a host of severe problems for today's city: traffic congestion, slum housing, inadequate space for parks, schools, and playgrounds. Starting several decades ago, a movement toward urban redevelopment has grown up in a score of major cities. With urban renewal came a comprehensive attempt to weed out slum areas, restore and beautify public buildings,

"Palace of the Dawn," the President's residence in Brasília, the new capital city of Brazil, an example of conscious planning to provide for future urban growth and development.

provide more parking space, and encourage new businesses to come downtown. Essentially, it sought to correct the mistakes of the past and to plan for orderly growth in the future. It was, and still is, a part of the more general city-planning movement, which attempts to substitute blueprints and a philosophy of planned growth for the catch-as-catch-can methods of the past. All large American cities today practice some type of city-planning and employ staffs of specialists to coordinate and run the various programs.

Despite the promise the city-planning movement holds for the future, many difficult hurdles must be cleared before urban redevelopment can be successful. Certainly our "horse and buggy" system of local government is ill-adapted to the needs of the large metropolis of the 1960's. How can a city plan an orderly development when its jurisdiction ends at the city limits? Half its working population may live beyond those artificial boundaries. Or, how can a city plan and grow when it is bounded on all sides by a dozen or more small towns and villages that successfully resist both annexation and regulation? And how can growth be coordinated in a community that has separate tax systems for roads, bridges, schools, fire protection, and other facilities? Finally, how can planning be coordinated in a city that is cut up into separate units of government, each with its own powers and taxing authority right within the city limits? In Peoria, Illinois, for example, the Park Board had its own police force and taxing authority, both separate from the city government.

Furthermore, the term "planning" frequently connotes socialism and an undesirable interference by "big government " in the affairs of individuals. The modern planner thus faces a myriad of problems. Yet he perseveres in the face of odds. For many believe that city-planning is the only possible way out of our present urban crisis. Planning undoubtedly will be vitally important to the future of the American city, providing the planners themselves show the skill, imagination, and persuasive powers necessary to convince urban residents and officials of the vital importance of orderly urban development. We shall look into this important matter again in the chapter on urban government.

SOME WORDS OF SUMMARY

Twentieth-century urban growth has reached the point where specialists speak of an "explosion" taking place in our cities. In America and around the world, the number and size of cities dwarf anything seen in the past. Much of the explanation for this unparalleled expansion lies in the natural acceleration of trends that already were underway before 1900. Advances in scientific agriculture, improvements in transportation, and the continuing centralization of industrial resources account for the lion's share of this new growth. But there are still other causes. The tremendous expansion of governmental services, itself a function in part of urban growth, has brought more and more people to the cities to fill the ranks of the governing bureaucracies. Social attractions have also become giant magnets pulling our population cityward. Some cities with little or no industry have become important as social, cultural, and resort centers.

The meaning of this vast growth in the number of city-dwellers can only be suggested. In the American city there are proportionately more women, more foreign-born, and more Negroes than anywhere else. The attractions of the city—

employment opportunities, anonymity, greater freedom, and excitement—have a special appeal, not only to these groups but to many others. Youth, too, is attracted, for the average city resident tends to be younger than his rural counterpart.

But the march to the cities has taxed the resources and ingenuity of even the most astute officials. Housing and transportation, as well as public health, fire and police protection, and many other services have become infinitely more difficult for the modern city to provide. Virtually every social institution, moreover, has felt the impact. Urban churches, for example, despite a growing membership, must compete with secular activities on a scale undreamed of in the rural areas. And many downtown churches have been stripped of members and financial support as urban blight has pushed the middle classes and their churches into the outlying areas.

What the future holds for the teeming metropolis is a matter of uncertainty and debate. The trek to the cities shows no signs of slackening, although city problems are already immense. Some experts believe that the "line cities" connecting already existing urban areas will dominate future patterns of urban development; others expect to see a general decentralization of industry and population set in, especially while the threat of atomic warfare hangs over us. Some students of the urban scene feel that the need which prompted the early growth of cities no longer exists, and that cheap, efficient communications and electrical power have made great urban clusters obsolete. Still others who have investigated urban problems pin their hopes on the city-planning movement, which proposes to substitute a controlled, orderly pattern of development for the haphazard growth that cities experienced in the past.

FURTHER ROADS TO LEARNING

GENERAL STUDIES

N. Gist and L. Halbert, *Urban Society* (New York: Crowell, 1956). A broad sociological treatment covering the theme of this chapter.

S. Riemer, *The Modern City* (Englewood Cliffs, N. J.: Prentice-Hall, 1952). A sound, basic, sociological text on the city.

For other general studies on the city, see references in Chapter 14.

SPECIAL STUDIES

R. Angell, *The Moral Integration of American Cities* (Chicago: The University of Chicago Press, 1951). An excellent treatment of the problem of social solidarity in the city.

D. Bogue, *Metropolitan Decentralization* (Oxford, Ohio: Scripps Foundation Studies, 1950). A technical but enlightening analysis of patterns of city growth.

———, "Urbanism in the United States, 1950," *American Journal of Sociology*, LX (March, 1955), pp. 471-486. Discusses the trend toward large urban centers and compares urban and rural populations.

G. Breese, *The Daytime Population of the Central Business District of Chicago* (Chicago: The University of Chicago Press, 1949). An interesting study of the commuter and the big city.

O. Duncan and A. Reiss, *Social Characteristics of Urban and Rural Communities, 1950* (New York: Wiley, 1956). A masterful examination of what has happened as a result of our transition to an urban society.

A. Gallion and S. Eisner, *The Urban Pattern: City Planning and Design* (Princeton, N. J.: Van Nostrand, 1950). A good introduction to city-planning as a solution to urban problems.

The Editors of Fortune, *The Exploding Metropolis* (Garden City, New York: Doubleday Anchor Books, 1958). The blight of rapidly growing cities has dehumanized and smothered the joys that both urbanite and suburbanite might have had.

A. Hawley, *Human Ecology* (New York: Ronald, 1950). An elaborate argument for the idea of continuity in community life and organization.

————, *The Changing Shape of Metropolitan America* (Glencoe, Ill.: The Free Press, 1956). A skillful sketching of the forces that brought about our great metropolitan growth.

H. Pirenne, *Medieval Cities* (Garden City, New York: Doubleday, 1956). In chapters 19 and 20 there is a penetrating discussion of the reasons for city growth and the prospects for the future.

U. S. News & World Report, "A Billion People in the U. S.?" November 28, 1958, pp. 72-84. An interview with Dr. Philip M. Hauser, leading population authority, in which he forecasts rapid population growth and "strip cities."

M. Weber, *The City* (Glencoe, Ill.: The Free Press, 1958). An astute German sociologist dissects the urban organism as methodically as a physician performing an autopsy.

FICTION AND DRAMA

J. Dos Passos, *Manhattan Transfer* (New York: Harper, 1925). One of the best novels ever written on what happens to a variety of diverse persons who are thrown together in a growing city and forced to mold a new life out of unplanned confusion.

J. Farrell, *Studs Lonigan* (New York: Vanguard, 1935). A combination of three novels detailing the squalid and sordid life led by a growing boy in the streets of Chicago.

H. Fuller, *The Cliff Dwellers* (New York: Harper, 1893). The first significant novel on American city life.

C. Hawley, *Executive Suite* (Boston: Houghton Mifflin, 1952). A well-informed novel on life in the higher levels of the urban financial world.

D. Runyan, *Guys and Dolls* (New York: Stokes, 1931). Tales of New York told in the light-hearted, entertaining, Runyan fashion.

M. Sandoz, *Capital City* (Boston: Little, Brown, 1939). A picturesque story of life in the capital of a Great Plains state.

B. Tarkington, *Growth* (Garden City, N. Y.: Doubleday, 1927). A trilogy devoted almost exclusively to the story of the growth of a middlewestern city.

The Baltimore Plan (Encyclopaedia Britannica Films, 1953, 20 min., sound, black and white). How a great city tackled urban redevelopment and succeeded in rehabilitating slum areas to provide better living conditions for its citizens.

The City (Museum of Modern Art, 1939, 30 min., sound, black and white). An excellent contrast between the unplanned city and the planned community.

Growth of Cities (Encyclopaedia Britannica Films, 1942, 20 min., sound, black and white). A vivid portrayal of the many factors contributing to the location, growth, and prosperity of our cities.

The Living City (Encyclopaedia Britannica Films, 1953, 25 min., sound, black and white). How our cities grow and decay, and how civic and community loyalty provide a firm foundation for urban renewal.

Search for Happiness (McGraw-Hill, 1948, 17 min., sound, black and white). Gadgets, blaring radios, and traffic jams, all the machines that were supposed to make life easier, seem to make it more frustrating and complicated.

The Urban Family

*The American family is urban-centered,
small, democratic, conjugal, and impregnated
with middle-class values.*

Urban life

has left its mark on all human institutions, particularly on the family. Our entire pattern of living has also been modified by changes in the family, such as the changes in its pattern of organization and its loyalty focus that we noted in an earlier chapter. What has happened to family life in an urban-industrial society grown large and complex? Is the family of today smaller by accident or by design than the family in rural America of a century ago? How has the march to the cities and the suburbs affected the ties that traditionally held families together? How does the urban-industrial custom of employing more and more women affect marriage and family life? Do democratic, middle-class, and urban influences strengthen or weaken the family? We turn now to examine these and other questions raised by the convergence of changes in family life with the continuing changes being wrought by urbanization.

THE URBAN SETTING

We have seen in preceding chapters what the movement to cities has done to our modern patterns of living. A rapidly expanding population has crowded into our urban and metropolitan areas. Many different occupations in factories and offices have come into being. Relationships between people in the city are less intimate and more formally structured than in a rural society. Urbanites are highly mobile, both in their daily routines and in their frequent change of residence. Cities depict the most extreme contrasts. Luxury exists side by side with poverty, the Gold Coast alongside the slum. Conditions in cities are generally unfavorable for the extended family of several generations living under one roof. Youngsters are no longer an economic asset and oldsters, too, are less welcome in the urban family. A new individualism expressed in a "what is good for me" philosophy now permeates a good part of our behavior. Urban women seek release from household drudgery in office, store, or factory. This is the broad background against which the drama of modern family life in the American city is played.

The centrifugal growth pattern of American cities has fostered a wide diversity of family life. This tendency for cities to fan outward has left distinctive subcenters of family life. As cities have grown in size, a larger number of families have settled in the suburbs. By 1950, 32 per cent of all Americans lived in cities of at least 50,000 or more people, and another 14 per cent resided in the urban fringe areas. The rise of suburbia has in fact been one of the most significant American social developments in the first half of the twentieth century.

Fringe-area families have become a distinctive type. They come primarily from an urban background, although a few have moved directly from rural environments. On the whole, these suburban families seek to enjoy the city's cultural and economic benefits while avoiding its congestion. They are overwhelmingly middle-class in origin and aspiration; and they are looking for a way of life more leisurely, more out-of-doors, and more private than the city can afford. There are differences among suburban families, of course. Only well-to-do families can afford to live in the luxurious and expensive residential areas. Style and price of "model houses" in the mass-produced, standardized housing developments, on the other hand, attract young middle-class families. At the bottom of suburbia's housing scale are the trailer courts and suburban slums.

Living styles follow social class lines as well as the cultural and racial dictinctions that are found in the older, more central areas of the city. Family life thus varies considerably from one neighborhood to another in our urban centers. On the bottom rung of the city's social ladder is the tenement-house family, whose chief breadwinner is an unskilled worker with an income too low to permit middle-class comforts but whose children number six or eight, maybe a dozen. Young middle-class families normally gravitate toward modest, centrally located apartment houses where couples are on the road to establishing themselves financially and maritally and both husband and wife have jobs. Older middle-class families include professional workers, small-business owners, office and sales workers, and higher-paid skilled workers. These people are likely to live in modest homes located away from business and industrial areas. Mothers in these older middle-class families are consumed with household duties and raising their children but since World War II have shown an increasing tendency to work outside the home, especially after their children have grown up. Upper-class families of long standing often reside in the family mansion located close to the downtown section where the mother oversees the children and the home while the father is responsible for the family's financial affairs, a family-life pattern not unlike the suburban middle-class one.

Various cultural and racial groups within the city also portray distinctive family patterns. Recent immigrants from Europe, southern Negroes, and others such as Puerto Ricans in New York City tend to reside in those residential areas of the city where their old family customs can be perpetuated. Among first-generation European immigrants, there is a strong tendency toward the paternalistic type family. Newly arrived immigrants, especially those who came in large numbers from southeastern Europe before World War I, have clustered in older, less expensive quarters, and frequently in the tenement-house districts that contain a large number of metropolitan lower-class families. Puerto Ricans, who come from a patriarchal background, have arrived mainly since World War II and have settled overwhelmingly in the Harlem area of New York City. Unlike European immigrants and Puerto Ricans, American Jews are more widely dispersed throughout a city and are almost entirely urban in their background. Negro families that have recently migrated from the rural South to northern and western cities bring with them a family pattern in which the mother is dominant, and they also

Unlike its urban counterpart, the rural family has tended to be an economic unit in which the children share the father's occupation and are considered an economic asset.

tend to locate in those areas that reinforce this matriarchal family pattern. But whether their family pattern is mainly patriarchal or matriarchal, families in all these groups move toward a more equalitarian pattern under the impact of the strong urban middle-class influence that permeates American society.

URBAN-INDUSTRIAL INFLUENCES ON THE FAMILY

FAMILY SIZE

Families today are generally smaller than they were a century ago since the urban birth rate declined steadily from 1800 to 1940. City families showed no signs of averaging as many children as their rural brethren until after World War II, when nation-wide births jumped to record highs of 3 to 4 million each year. In fact, if the present urban birth rate continues, the long-time trend toward small-sized urban families may be reversed.

The city-dweller not only tends to have fewer children than his rural counterpart but the size of his family is related also to his occupation, income, and education. Professional men and white-collar workers generally have smaller families than skilled or unskilled workers, particularly unskilled workers; the higher we ascend the income scale, the fewer children per family we find; and the greater the parents' education, the smaller their family.

The wide range of wealth, occupations, and educational experience found in the modern industrial city is far greater than in a rural society. Differences in family size thus result from a combination of urban and industrial influences.

THE DEMOCRATIC FAMILY

Another important change in urban family life follows the shift from the patriarchal family pattern to a more democratic family, as we described in Chapter 5. For more than a century a number of social forces, including urbanization, have been forging a larger role for wives and children in deciding family matters.

One of these forces, the oldest from the standpoint of historical perspective, was the *feminist movement*, formally organized in 1848 at a Women's Rights Convention at Seneca Falls, New York. Here the embattled ladies took a firm stand against the disfranchisement of women, unequal divorce laws, different moral standards for men and women, and limited occupational and educational opportunities. The ladies said:

"When in the course of human events it becomes necessary for one portion of the family of man to assume among the people of the earth a position different from that which they have hitherto occupied, but one to which the laws of nature and of nature's God entitle them, a decent respect to the opinions of mankind requires that they should declare the causes that impel them to such a course. We hold these truths to be self-evident; that all men and women are created equal. . . ."

And so the ladies continued their passionate plea in the form as well as the spirit of '76.*

Women finally gained the right to vote under the Nineteenth Amendment to the Constitution in 1920, certainly the greatest monument to the feminist revolt. Many other accomplishments have converged in the general emancipation of American women, as shown in Table 13.

---

* R. Billington, B. Loewenberg, and S. Brockunier, *The Making of American Democracy: Readings and Documents*, Vol. II (New York: Rinehart, 1950), p. 266.

TABLE **13**   A CENTURY OF LEGISLATIVE PROGRESS FOR WOMEN IN THE UNITED STATES

1848	1948
1. Voting denied women.	1. Voting privileges universally available.
2. No share in lawmaking.	2. Participate actively in lawmaking.
3. No share in jury duty.	3. Eligible for jury duty in most states.
4. Not eligible to public office.	4. Eligible to all major elective and appointive positions, including civil-service jobs.
5. Marriage destroyed woman's legal personality for various business functions.	5. Marriage has little effect on woman's legal capacity.
6. Marriage stripped wife of valuable property rights, including her personal earnings.	6. Wife generally has full property rights; her personal earnings belong to her.
7. Wife's criminal acts were chargeable to her husband if committed in his presence.	7. Wife is generally responsible for her own wrongdoing.
8. Wife was subject to her husband; he could restrain her personal freedom and punish her for disobedience to his commands.	8. Wife is a free person, not subject to her husband's forcible restraint or punishment.
9. Divorce laws favored husbands.	9. Divorce laws generally recognize rights of both husband and wife.
10. Guardianship laws favored fathers.	10. Guardianship laws mainly recognize rights of both husband and wife.
11. Women's property was taxed without representation from her sex in legislatures.	11. Women help choose the legislators who write the tax laws, and may be elected as lawmakers themselves.
12. Profitable employment generally closed to women.	12. Women have the legal right to enter professions, and practically all profitable occupations and trades.

Source: U. S. Department of Labor, Women's Bureau, *The Legal Status of Women in the United States of America as of January 1, 1948*. Bulletin No. 157 (Washington, U. S. Government Printing Office, 1951), p. IV.

Women's gains in education and employment are two of the outstanding features of emancipation that are especially important in shaping a more equalitarian family life. Since 1900 the enrollment of women in colleges and universities has increased steadily, until today women account for a third of the entire college population. Most professional and graduate schools now admit women, though informally administered "quotas" may limit their enrollment in a few instances. A continuation of the present trend toward more equal educational opportunities for women may lead to the disappearance of traditional discrimination within another fifty years.

Greatly improved chances for employment paralleled women's increased educational opportunities. Wartime labor shortages provided a golden work opportunity for urban women. Demands of the city's "cash economy" coupled with the desire to ascend the social ladder gave women the incentive to seek employment. Automatic dishwashers and a vast array of household gadgets have helped free the urban housewife's time so that she can work.

The educated urban housewife who brings home her own paycheck is now in a position to command a voice in family affairs. She is no longer the unpaid chattel of the husband as she was in feudal Europe. With both the freedoms and the protections granted her by law, with her greater educational experience and her new financial and job status, she now rates an "equal" voice in family decision-making. All these developments have taken place outside the

The American family has become more democratic. Even children share in such important decisions as planning a new home.

family, but all have influenced women's family role very drastically.

Children, too, have been caught up in the increasing democratization of the American family. Beginning with the White House Conference on the Care of Dependent Children in 1909, various programs have stressed the importance of home life for children. A few years later came the Federal Children's Bureau, which is charged with the responsibility of looking after children's welfare in all classes of our society. Additional White House conferences through the years have repeatedly emphasized the importance of the child's individuality. States have contributed to the educational growth of children by providing free public schools, making school attendance compulsory, and prohibiting child labor. Other specialized programs, such as reform and rehabilitation programs for juvenile delinquents, organized youth recreation, and aid to dependent children, have aimed at protecting the rights and individuality of children. As a result of these and other developments external to the family,

284

children have risen to a position where they influence family decisions to a marked degree. No longer does the old admonition, "Children should be seen and not heard," hold true.

THE WORKING WOMAN

Employment has opened up an entirely new role for women in our urban-industrial society. Not that she didn't have enough to do already! The *wife-mother* role, oldest and most traditional for women, provided economic security in return for home-making and child-rearing duties. Traditionally, the wife-mother role made women economically dependent on husbands and generally subordinate to men. More recently, within the past two or three centuries, women have become *companions* to their husbands, sharing in their interests and activities. Over the years many women undoubtedly were both confidante and companion to their husbands, but today wives are not only permitted but expected to play these roles. In addition, the modern wife must be *glamorous*. She must keep her beauty, be entertaining and charming, and a source of pride to her spouse. But if she becomes too obsessed with glamour, she may turn out to be an expensive luxury to her husband. Some wives take on a fourth role—that of a *working wife*—which permits them to contribute to the support of their home and family and thereby achieve a measure of economic independence. In pre-industrial societies, wives necessarily depended on their husbands. Now, as employed workers in their own right, they have invaded the traditionally masculine business world and threaten to upset the long-standing balance of family life.

Although this feminine invasion of the employment arena has made women and men "more equal," it has spawned more male-female conflicts. The multiple roles now open to a married woman present her with a dilemma and force her to make a choice. Theoretically, a wife may play all four of the major roles open to her. But as a practical matter, few women have the ability and desire to spread their efforts so thin. Most women settle for one or two roles, or else move from role to role. Inevitably the situation leads to tensions and conflicts. In a society that stresses masculinity, women are conditioned to wear slacks, smoke, go to school, take a job, and assume many

other formerly masculine traits. To many people, such behavior is inconsistent with a woman's traditional wife-mother role. Many men, especially the conformists, resent and resist competition from women, particularly in the business world. And many men protest when women demand equal privileges and, at the same time, special considerations. Though women now work side by side with men, the "weaker sex" still claims alimony. On the city bus or subway, men are still expected to give up their seats to their female co-workers.

At least part of the disagreement over the proper role for women centers on the difference between *equivalent* and *identical* rights. The assumption that women are equal to but different from men forms the basis for the feminist idea of equivalent rights. This attitude stresses the economic and legal equality of men and women yet emphasizes differences in physical strength and assigned roles that supposedly work to a woman's disadvantage and entitle her to special privileges. Laws designed to protect the unique position of women are founded on this assumption. The theory of identical rights, on the other hand, works from the assumption that men and women should be treated with complete equality, as if no sex differences existed. Special protective legislation for women, this school of thought

The urban explosion has created new roles and opportunities for American women.

holds, actually discriminates in favor of women and represents, therefore, a confession of inequality.

Urbanism, industrialism, and the feminist movement—these are the factors that are drawing women away from the home and helping them break the shackles that have accompanied the wife-mother role for centuries. But this new-found freedom has its price. The trials that confront a woman who assumes a variety of roles create serious tensions for her and her family. Women who decide to concentrate on a career sacrifice the satisfactions inherent in the wife-mother role. The glamour role, though promising and exciting, can only provide fleeting satisfaction, for inevitably the years will begin to take their toll. A combination of employment and other roles seems consistent with the realities of twentieth-century conditions, if traditional resentments and oppositions do not interfere too much.

The point of no return has probably already been passed. The curve of female employment probably will continue to rise, which means that husbands and children as well as wives will be forced to adjust to a new pattern of family life. Clinging to tradi-tional attitudes and ways may only make the adjustment difficult or impossible. Husbands must face up to the fact that their wives may some day decide to take a job. Women, if they are to fulfill their several roles, must cultivate a variety of talents. Youngsters, too, have important adjustments to make, especially those who are too young to fathom the changes taking place in our society. Care must be taken to see that they do not feel neglected, an ideal more difficult to attain when both parents are away at work.

Until the day when women achieve full and complete equality, however, they will continue to suffer lingering discrimination. They will have to learn that special protections and concessions are scarcely compatible with full equality. Certainly the most burdensome consequences of this urban-industrial transformation of the family fall on the shoulders of women.

THE MIDDLE-CLASS IDEAL

There is an urban upper class and an urban lower class, but middle-class characteristics predominate in cities. In favoring change, small families, upward mobility,

A common complaint about working mothers is that children are sometimes neglected and left to shift for themselves.

independence from kinfolk, and material success, our urban communities reflect a typically middle-class viewpoint.

Absorbed with earning a living and obsessed with climbing the social ladder, urban families live in the present and look to the future. They have no past. They scarcely remember their grandparents or great-grandparents and place very little store in faded portraits and heirlooms. The family moving up the social ladder prefers to sever its connection with the past, unless some ancestral tie links it to the upper classes, in which case the family genealogy is hurriedly traced to provide some reflected glory and prestige. But by ignoring the past, the urban family forsakes the unity that consciousness of background often provides. The religious, national, and traditional ties that bound the immigrant family together have been diluted in the swift-moving currents of American life.

A middle-class flavor also permeates urban patterns of employment. The employment of middle-class women, for example, rare in rural districts and small towns, is common in the city. Middle-class standards discourage child labor by their insistence that young children go to school, not to work. Older children may take week-end or summer jobs as a means of nurturing middle-class ideals of independence and individualism. Although a variety of jobs is available in the city, middle-class employment preferences run to business and the professions.

Middle-class patterns and urban-industrial conditions thus go hand in hand. In cities families are small, broad educational and cultural opportunities serve middle-class aspirations of upward mobility, and social and recreational facilities fit individualistic middle-class tendencies. The city offers virtually ideal conditions for realizing the goals of middle-class life.

CONJUGAL RELATIONSHIPS

City life also strengthens *conjugal* rather than *consanguine* family relationships. A consanguine family, as we saw in Chapter 5, is bound together by a strong sense of obligation among kinfolk. Blood relatives, so-called, are more important than husband or wife. Kinship is everything; the spouse, secondary. During ceremonial celebrations, social events, and times of crisis, a person's obligations are defined for him by rules that govern his particular kinship position. A conjugal family, on the other hand, stresses the tie between husband and wife. In this type of family, husbands and wives may observe their own birthdays but not their relatives'. Their social life is likely to be their own and rarely if ever involves family reunions, once so common in rural America. In times of crisis husband and wife turn to one another for consolation and support, not to their kin.

In the city consanguine tendencies in family life have virtually disappeared. Marriages are no longer arranged by families; young couples do their own mate-choosing. From the first date to the marriage ceremony the principle of free courtship prevails. Companionship between husband and wife has replaced the consanguine tie that characterizes the patriarchal type family. Having children is no longer so important because people have grown less concerned about carrying on the family name and perpetuating a large kinship group. Today the city family that houses several generations under the same roof is a rare exception.

PROSPECTS FOR THE NEW TYPE OF FAMILY

THE "NEW FAMILY"

You should now have a clear picture of the type of family that is emerging in America today. *It is essentially urban, small, democratic, middle class, and conjugal.* In large part the modern family reflects urban-industrial conditions, democratic ideals of liberty and equality, and middle-class aspirations that have found unique expression in the great modern city.

THE QUESTION OF SURVIVAL

There can be no question that the urban family of today and the rural family of yesterday are decidedly different. But there can be and is a question about how desirable the changes have been. Critics bemoan the fact that the family "ain't what it used to be," that it has lost its stability and strength. The modern family, they claim, is in danger of decaying and disintegrating. High divorce rates, juvenile delinquency, and neglect of the aged, they believe, all point to the modern family's eventual demise. With the father no longer a patriarch, authority has been fractured. Children do as they please and rebel at the slightest hint of parental discipline or control. Wives no longer obey their husbands. Instead they assert their independence by getting a job or, thanks to modern labor-saving devices, by following a heavy social schedule. Countless investigations and court reports and surveys tell of an increase in extra-marital sex relations. Small wonder, say the critics, that the family is doomed. What might replace the family, however, they do not say. Constructive criticism has been scant.

The opposite view, that the family is here to stay, has always been popular. Proof of the family's toughness lies in its long existence, longer, in fact, than recorded history. Its defenders today argue that its current problems and disruptions are only an indication of its continuing adaptation to modern industrial and urban life. The pessimists, say these defenders, are just old-fashioned and unrealistic. Even current high divorce rates may be no more destructive than the double standard of morality that prevailed during the Victorian age, which permitted considerable sexual freedom to men and imposed rigid controls over women. Indeed, according to some moderns, it may be far more realistic for a couple to separate and go their own ways when their marriage is clearly unworkable than to remain unhappily together and contribute to the maladjustment of their children.

ADJUSTMENT AND ADAPTATION

But the question of whether or not the family will survive is not the immediate issue, and perhaps not a real issue at all. Any pronouncement on what is happening to the family today might better be viewed in terms of adjustment and adaptation. How well are husbands, wives, and children responding to these changes in family life? How well is the new family adapting to changed social conditions? What will be the consequences of these adjustments and adaptations? These are the dynamic questions that press closely on the real issues.

To judge how well family members are adjusting and adapting, we must first establish criteria stated in terms of *social values, the ideals and standards of behavior about which people generally agree.* Values, as we saw in an earlier chapter, are the things cherished and sought by almost everyone in a society. The extent to which changes in family life are "good," therefore, depends on how closely they coincide with existing values.

But we encounter an immediate difficulty in using social values as the criteria for assessing changes in family life because the values themselves are changing. Values may be either traditional or current. And whether we conclude that changing family patterns are desirable or undesirable hinges on what kind of values we use in our appraisal. According to traditional values, for example, a woman's place is in the home. But a more recent standard recognizes that women have a right to express themselves and to participate more fully in all the activities of a society. Hence, if we use traditional values as a basis for judging, we may conclude that the modern family is "maladjusted," losing its vitality, or disintegrating. But if we use modern or current values for our standards of judgment, we may conclude that the changes in the family have been important, positive, and even necessary.

When family life embodies and mirrors the most basic and recent values in our current national life, then adaptation is keeping pace with changing social conditions. Democracy, free enterprise, individualism, success, and equality of opportunity are among the fundamental values (or "core values," as we called them in an earlier chapter) in American society. These are also the very qualities that make today's family distinctive.

We can also use social values as a yardstick in evaluating the present and future effects of changes in the family. If traditional values should disappear and current values predominate, then the family would become ever more adjusted to its environment. Current standards, of course, may in turn become traditional and be displaced at some time in the future by still newer values. So the question of family adjustment is a relative one, subject always to the dynamic conditions of a changing society. The fact that families and individuals have confronted changing conditions for centuries and somehow pulled through and ultimately adjusted is a hopeful sign. Only when social conditions change as rapidly as they have in twentieth-century America is the question of the future of the family very prominent. Basically, then, the real task confronting the family, as well as other social institutions, is to keep up with social change. We may derive some sort of negative consolation from the fact that the church, the school, local government, and other institutions have been experiencing the same kind of adjustment difficulties as the family with no appreciably greater degree of success.

SOME WORDS OF SUMMARY

We must view family life in the twentieth century largely within the framework of an urban society. Two-thirds of America's citizens lived in cities at midcentury, and many of the remaining third fell within the orbital influence of one or another of the nation's main metropolitan centers. Urban families are smaller than farm families and those of earlier generations. From 1800 to 1940 the birth rate in the United States declined, yet cities grew larger and larger. Urban families, however, differ considerably in size. The professional, better educated, and high-income persons tend to have fewer children than those farther down the social ladder.

The old-style paternalistic family has gradually given way before democratic and equalitarian influences. By working against double standards for men and women, the feminist movement has contributed a great deal to improving women's position vis-à-vis men's. In politics, schools, and the job market women have achieved major breakthroughs. Having acquired the right to vote, hold a job, and secure an education, women were in a better position to claim an equal voice in family matters. Emancipation has not been confined to women. Children, too, have felt the effects of these liberalizing influences.

Urban job opportunities have contributed to a troublesome dilemma for American women. To their traditional wife-mother duties, many women have added the roles of glamorous companion to their husbands and supplemental breadwinner. But such a situation breeds conflicts. Each additional role the modern woman plays brings accompanying tensions and difficulties, and few women can play all the parts demanded of them equally well.

The middle-class ideal of life, which we have elsewhere called the American Dream, and which emphasizes success, individualism, and upward mobility, centers largely in the modern city and casts its spell over the entire population, rural and urban. Typically, the middle-class urbanite has no concern for the past, lives in the present, and dreams of the future. Urban employment patterns reflect the outlook of this middle class and its penchant for a disciplined, orderly, materialistic way of living.

The modern American family is thus urban-centered, small, democratic, conjugal, and impregnated with the middle-class outlook. Some prophets of doom point to the rising divorce rate, decline in the number of children, and general family instability as signs that the future of the American family is in grave danger. More realistically, it appears that today's family is simply undergoing a transition through which it seeks to maintain a balance between changing social conditions and traditional family ways and customs. As in the past, the direction of future changes will be guided largely by forces external to the family.

FURTHER ROADS TO LEARNING

GENERAL ACCOUNTS

J. Bossard, *Parent and Child* (Philadelphia: University of Pennsylvania Press, 1953). A comprehensive account of American family behavior ranging over such matters as the influence of family size, family income, interclass marriage, and the effects of the father's income.

S. Queen and J. Adams, *The Family in Various Cultures* (Philadelphia: Lippincott, 1952). A comparative study of family systems in eleven cultures that provides some excellent historical background.

J. Sirjamaki, *The American Family in the Twentieth Century* (Cambridge: Harvard University Press, 1953). A part of the Library of Congress Series in American Civilization that covers everything from the influence of European cultures on the American family to patterns of modern family development.

A. Truxal and F. Merrill, *Marriage and the Family in American Culture* (Englewood Cliffs, N. J.: Prentice-Hall, 1953). A good textual reference on the American family.

For additional general accounts on the American Family, see "Further Roads to Learning" in Chapter 5.

SPECIAL STUDIES

Editors of *Look*, *The Decline of the American Male* (New York: Random House, 1958). A provocative statement on the effects of "petticoat rule."

R. Winch, *The Modern Family* (New York: Holt, 1952). A sociological study of all types of family life that contains one of the best analyses of romantic love.

G. Winter, *Love and Conflict* (Garden City, N. Y.: Doubleday, 1958). This volume analyzes the family of today's "organization man."

For further special studies on the American family, see "Further Roads to Learning" in Chapter 5.

FICTION AND DRAMA

S. Anderson, *Many Marriages* (New York: Viking, 1923). An excellent overview of changing American attitudes toward marriage.

T. Bell, *Till I Come to You* (Boston: Little, Brown, 1943). Using the "plains of Brooklyn" as a background, this novel presents typical attitudes of the twentieth-century, urban family.

W. Churchill, *A Modern Chronicle* (New York: Macmillan, 1910). Illustrates the changing patterns and attitudes involved in marriage and divorce.

F. Dell, *Souvenir* (Garden City, N. Y.: Doubleday, 1929). The story of a divorced man's relationships with his former wife and their son.

J. Lawrence, *There Is Today* (Boston: Little, Brown, 1942). What are the issues involved in a war marriage? This novel covers them.

FILMS

Courtship to Courthouse (McGraw-Hill, 1946, 15 min., sound, black and white). Depicts conditions contributing to the increasing divorce rate.

Families First (New York, State Youth Commission, 1949, 17 min., sound, black and white). Emphasizes family responsibility for filling the child's need for security, affection and recognition.

Family Affair (National Health Film Board, 1955, 31 min., sound, black and white). The Cooper family suffers from a number of strains—resentful children, a runaway son, a mother who cannot understand her husband or children, and a father who leaves home.

Future in Hand (McGraw-Hill, 1953, filmstrip, 35 frames, black and white). How good family relationships produce a person who is more able to adjust and get along in society.

Marriage Is a Partnership (Coronet, 1951, 15 min., sound, black and white). Flashbacks show adjustments necessary to marriage, such as budgeting and in-law problems.

Marriage Today (McGraw-Hill, 1950, 22 min., sound, black and white). Most marriages can be made to work if allowances for shortcomings are made.

This Charming Couple (McGraw-Hill, 1950, 19 min., sound, black and white). About the courtship of Winnie and Ken, who are "in love with love" and refuse to evaluate each other realistically.

Who's Right (McGraw-Hill, 1954, 18 min., sound, black and white). Conflict between patriarchal and equalitarian qualities in an American family centers on who's boss.

CHAPTER SEVENTEEN

Crime and Delinquency in an Urban World

Seeds of crime. Crowded neighborhoods,
inadequate play facilities,
and greater opportunity for bad companionship
turn the heart of a city into a fertile seedbed of crime.

The current

high incidence of crime in American cities is widely publicized and just as widely condemned. Gruesome reports of murder, assault, and rape overshadow less spectacular news of burglary, robbery, and embezzlement. The more brutal and scandalous the crime, the more avid the public is to know about it. Obliging news agencies have frequently catered to desires for sensational reports and have thereby served as unwitting "press agents" for the underworld. Everybody is against crime, at least publicly, but everyone likes to read or hear about it. Both the fascination with crime and its association with the urban milieu are widespread.

More indignant than fascinated, many reformers and ordinary citizens view crime as a real and serious threat to themselves and to society. Clergymen and other moralists decry our moral degeneracy and enter a plea for parents, educators, and citizen groups to take action against crime-inducing personal habits and social conditions. Educators admonish parents to keep their children out of trouble and guide them toward a healthy social life. Community and youth organizations across the nation maintain programs aimed at preventing delinquency, while law-enforcement officers are beseeched by citizens to protect people in their homes and on the streets.

Actually crime has always been with us, and, from all present indications, will probably continue to be. Not that this justifies crime or means that we should sit back and simply observe it. Quite the contrary. Popular opinion supports the contention that something needs to be done, but the line of attack is blurred because no one really knows what causes crime. Control of crime, not elimination of it, is the most realistic hope.

Trying to control crime without knowing the precipitating factors is like trying to cure a disease when its cause is unknown. Paralytic polio epidemics, for instance, for a long time foiled all efforts to control them. Then Dr. Jonas Salk developed a vaccine that drastically reduced the danger of infection, even though the exact cause of polio was still unknown. The prospect for control of crime in our society today is at about the same stage as efforts to control polio epidemics in the days before vaccine. To make matters worse, we are still plagued with problems of defining crime in such a way that causes may be discovered and cures administered.

DEFINITIONS OF CRIME AND DELINQUENCY

WHAT IS CRIME?

The average person's understanding of criminal behavior and criminals is typically vague and ambiguous. He frequently uses the word "crime" to designate any behavior that is unpopular and is apt to hang the "criminal" label on business or labor leaders, communists, capitalists, or on anyone else whose beliefs or actions he finds disdainful. Such name-calling is inadequate for purposes of scientifically analyzing either crime or criminals. More objective observers demand criteria by which crime can be identified and analyzed more consistently and impartially.

Legal conceptions of crime provide such impersonal standards of judgment. Responsibility for one's acts and the ability to distinguish right from wrong are basic in the legal approach to crime. Usually children under the age of seven are not legally responsible for their actions. The law likewise presumes that insane persons are unable to distinguish right from wrong, and are therefore excused from the consequences of their acts. In general terms, *behavior is criminal when it violates a law that requires punishment by death, imprisonment, or a heavy fine, after being judged guilty by a court of law.* A man is presumed innocent under American law until he has been found guilty in court by an impartial tribunal of his peers.

WHAT IS DELINQUENCY?

Delinquent behavior, on the other hand, involves the illegal acts of persons who are defined by law as juveniles. State laws vary, but the juvenile age limit usually runs between seven and eighteen years. In addition to everything that constitutes adult criminal behavior, such offenses as truancy, running away from home, being incorrigible, and consorting with bad companions are applied exclusively to juveniles.

TRENDS IN CRIME

Although other classifications exist, an especially useful one is employed by the Federal Bureau of Investigation to tabulate figures on the frequency of different kinds of crime.* The F. B. I. scheme includes two major types: crimes against the *person*, which include murder, assault, rape, and robbery; and crimes against *property*, such as burglary, larceny, and auto theft.

Generally speaking, the number of crimes of all types has increased in the last several decades, and proportionately more crimes are reported in urban than in rural areas. Such increases are often attributed to the disorganizing effects of urban industrialism, which has shaped the lives of more and more Americans in recent decades. Other factors, however, are also part of the explanation.

For one thing, the increased number of crimes may be due in part to the great increase in the size of our population, which is continuing to grow. But there are also indications that the number of reported crimes is rising more steeply than the population.

* See *Uniform Crime Reports*, U. S. Department of Justice, Federal Bureau of Investigation.

From 1940 to 1952, offenses reported to police jumped from 1.5 million to 2 million a year; and between 1950 and 1956 the number of reported offenses climbed by 43 per cent, while the population increased by only 11 per cent. It is clear that population increase alone cannot account for the rising number of offenses.

Since 1900, too, jail and penitentiary facilities have been greatly expanded, thus making it possible to detain a greater number of criminals. This growth in "housing" facilities is reflected in figures on inmates. The number of prisoners in state and federal prisons alone rose from 173,000 in 1940 to 185,000 by 1955.

Also, better reporting of crimes may be part of the explanation for the increase. Not until the 1930's was a nationwide system of reporting criminal offenses instituted—under the auspices of the F. B. I.—and reporting has become gradually more complete since then. Increased police efficiency, too, in the laboratory as well as on the beat, has undoubtedly helped in apprehending and convicting criminals.

The urban crime rate may stem in part from better reporting of offenses and more thorough police coverage in cities than in rural areas. Also, it is obvious that the opportunity for committing both personal and property crimes is greater in the city.

Despite the growing efficiency in reporting, apprehending, and convicting criminals, it shocks some people to learn that arrests are made in only 26 per cent of all crimes reported to police, with convictions obtained only once in every twenty reported cases, and prison sentences handed down in only one of every thirty. In 1958, for example, *Uniform Crime Reports* showed that police had made arrests in less than 27 per cent of all known offenses, while convictions were obtained in 21 per cent of these cases. And crimes committed but not reported are unnumbered. In the face of such evidence, the old adage that "crime does not pay" seems untrue. Although questions about the actual amount of crime remain open, a new angle, raised twenty years ago in very succinct fashion, promises to open new vistas to the ultimate causation of crime.

WHITE-COLLAR CRIME

The late criminologist E. H. Sutherland was the first investigator to focus on a "new" kind of crime, white-collar crime. His analysis was legalistic and formal. He defined *white-collar crime* as a violation of trust and of law by a person in the upper socio-economic groups in the course of his occupation or by corporate groups. Like other types of crimes against property, white-collar crime is punishable by an impartial tribunal after a finding of guilt. Business organizations, for example, have been found guilty of violating antitrust, advertising, and labor-relations laws by such agencies as the National Labor Relations Board and the Federal Communications Commission. These agencies act as impartial tribunals, conduct hearings similar to a court of law, and impose penalties on a finding of guilt. Strangely enough, public censure against white-collar crime is much weaker than in other criminal cases, even though the number of people affected, as in a case of fraudulent advertising, for example, may be much greater than in a private criminal act. Conviction for criminal corporate acts is even rarer than conviction for other crimes.

CRIME AND DELINQUENCY IN THE CITY

The larger cities of America have recently experienced an alarming increase in arrests, especially for auto theft, assault, and homicide committed by teen-agers and young adults. Since smaller cities and towns lag in this respect, it seems that big cities somehow encourage crime. Danger of bodily assault is so great in certain sections of several cities that many persons will not venture forth after dark. Muggings, rape, and brutal murders have come to characterize our big cities as much as bright lights, factories, and tall buildings; and policemen often must patrol their beats in pairs for their own protection. Teachers, too, are threatened and sometimes attacked in the "blackboard jungle" of the urban school systems. Locked doors offer uncertain protection and may even invite prowlers. Motorists dare not lock their parked cars for fear their windows will be smashed. Grade-school children are endangered by maniacal sex perverts. Gambling spots, narcotics dens, and brothels flourish. Teen-age gangs have their "rumbles," affairs sometimes as brutal as the gang wars of prohibition days.

ORGANIZED CRIME

Cities have long been meccas for criminals of various and sundry description, and invariably the most effective organizations of criminals base their operations in the city. Since prohibition days, syndicated crime has become the fashion for clever and ambitious criminals in the United States. "Scarface" Al Capone elevated crime to the level of "big business." Reports have it that he grossed as much as $6 million a week from his illegal liquor business. During the Capone era, gang wars were frequent, reaching their climax in the bloody St. Valentine's Day massacre of 1929, which consolidated Capone's underworld power. Through his own private hoodlum army and his control over numerous politicians, he was able to prosper and extend his influence and operations before the law finally caught up with him on an income-tax evasion charge. Organized rough-house gangs on the Capone model still operate by stealing automobiles, robbing warehouses, hijacking trucks, and selling "protection" to business houses.

The latter-day syndicates, however, avoid violence as much as possible. Syndicate leaders today outdo even Al Capone as they pursue gentlemanly lives, mingle with socialites, business tycoons, and political leaders. Commercialized vice, the narcotics trade, the confidence game, black-market profiteering, large-scale embezzlements, and bookie rackets—all have caught the interest of big-time syndicates.

During the Kefauver Committee investigations in 1950, witness after witness documented the bizarre attempts of big-time criminals to present themselves as legitimate businessmen. Some bought run-down breweries and forced barroom operators to buy their beer. Many criminals had invested in resorts, race tracks, dance halls, taprooms, or hotels. And in 1957-58, the McClellan Committee hearings divulged a shocking number of connections between the criminal world and some segments of organized labor.

CRIMINALS AND DELINQUENTS

What kinds of people become delinquents and criminals? "Only the ones who get caught," is the answer we sometimes hear, which implies that there is little real difference between criminals and law-abiding citizens. There is at least a germ of truth in the remark because most people violate some law almost daily. But many of the laws we break involve either trivial or archaic matters and are no longer applicable or enforced. Since both white-collar and "blue-collar" crimes so often go unpunished, almost the only information we have on the characteristics of criminals comes from lawbreakers who have been arrested and convicted. Convicts are not only "available for study" but also fit our legal conception of criminal behavior.

Since prohibition days syndicated crime has become the fashion in America. Here a well-known figure in the gambling world is sworn in to testify before the Kefauver Committee in 1951. He later told about a $20 million nation-wide bookmaking operation in which he had an interest.

The "natural history" of a delinquent repeatedly shows the same career pattern. A boy in the city's slum, neglected by his divorced mother and drunken father, falls in with "bad" companions. He begins his wayward activities at a tender age with shoplifting and burglary, and soon quits or is expelled from school. In his early teens, having already been arrested for several offenses, he is finally sent to a reform school. There he learns the "tricks of the trade" and comes to despise law and authority completely. On "graduating" from reform school, he has gained the respect of his cronies and is ready to pursue his career. By the time he has aged enough to qualify as an adult criminal, he may have returned to the reformatory for some "refresher" courses and to further enhance his prestige among his peers. Before he reaches his twenty-fifth birthday he will have become well acquainted with the state penitentiary and may either take up permanent residence there or periodically move in and out.

Grossly oversimplified, this hypothetical case portrays the cycle of experiences through which many young delinquents have passed, and numerous criminals have had strikingly similar histories of behavior problems. A flaw mars our illustration, however, since many persons whose behavior stamps them as either delinquents or criminals are never convicted of any offense.

Studies show that the convict in a penitentiary is usually a young man about twenty or twenty-two years of age. He has had a difficult time adjusting at home, in school, and in the various jobs he held prior to his conviction. Very likely he comes from a poor family in one of the city's more dilapidated residential districts. He has already served time for earlier convictions and is likely to be released either on parole or after completing his sentence. If paroled, he stands an excellent chance of being convicted again for some future offense.

From this typical case there are many variations, of course. Young women represent a distinctive type of convict. They are far outnumbered by men. Offenses for which they are convicted are less likely to be crimes of violence than of sexual misbehavior. A few convicts may be feeble-minded, but just as many can boast of superior intelligence. Some come from wealthy families and educated parents. Some have committed a single crime, perhaps under great emotional stress, and are unlikely ever to repeat their wrongdoing. It is possible to find almost every conceivable kind of human being among the convict population. We should thus not fall into the common habit of believing that criminals are a special breed of man. And since so many differ from the rest of us only by being convicted, the *real* reasons for crime are all the more elusive.

FACTORS CONDUCIVE TO CRIMINAL BEHAVIOR

Social scientists have become wary in recent years of trying to specify *the cause* of crime and delinquency. They prefer to speak of "contributing factors," conditions "conducive" to crime, or environmental "risks." This caution has come about as a consequence of a number of single-factor deterministic explanations, all of which have proved on closer study to be oversimplifica-

tions. Increasingly, the criminologist has taken the position that a combination of personal and environmental factors precipitates criminal behavior. The precise nature of this bundle of causes differs with every criminal and is difficult to fathom, but continued research should gradually broaden the horizon of our knowledge of crime. Investigators already have probed deeply among the more promising leads, including personal, family, and community factors.

PERSONAL FACTORS

Biological Characteristics. Late nineteenth-century European criminologists, led by Cesare Lombroso, an Italian, tried to explain criminal behavior on purely biological grounds. Lombroso argued that criminals possessed certain physical characteristics that distinguished them from noncriminals. Because criminals were victims of hereditary influences, Lombroso referred to them as "born criminals," distinguishable by their low slanting foreheads, swarthy complexions, and stocky build. And since criminal behavior was attributable to heredity, there could be no immediate cure. Although an English criminologist later found no significant physical differences between the criminal and noncriminal population, some authorities, mainly among European criminologists, still believe that the basis of criminal behavior is biological.

A small segment of American scientists has also taken a biological approach. Earnest Hooton, an anthropologist, once studied the physical characteristics of criminals and noncriminals and concluded that convicts really do have distinctive physical traits. He measured such things as the length and width of the head, the width of the forehead, the length of the nose, and length of the ear. Interestingly, he found fewer bald and gray-headed individuals in his convict sample than in his sample of the general male population. Many criminologists today are skeptical of Hooton's findings, partly because his sampling was unrepresentative and also because the manner in which he drew his conclusions was faulty. The relative lack of gray-haired men among convicts, for example, may be explained by their relative youthfulness in comparison with the general adult male population. The search for a biological basis of criminal behavior should not be abandoned, however, simply because results have not been highly rewarding thus far. Investigators who take this avenue eventually may discover something that will add materially to our understanding of criminal behavior.

Socio-personal Characteristics. Some authorities believe that emotional disturbance and the degree of intelligence of the criminal hold the key to the causes of criminal behavior. Various studies have shown considerable emotional disturbance among the inmates of penitentiaries. It is not clear, however, that emotional disturbances are more frequent or more severe among convicts than among people outside prison walls. Criminologists once believed that feeble-mindedness was a cause of crime, but there are no more feeble-minded convicts in many prisons than their distribution in the general population would warrant. It is true that a feeble-minded person may be more easily led into criminal ways, but it is also true that his lack of intelligence makes it difficult for him to plan or execute more intricate kinds of crimes. Feeble-mindedness, of course, exempts a person from liability of conviction if he is unable "to distinguish right from wrong." Despite this technical exemption, a number of morons or dull normals have been convicted of crime. A high level of intelligence may bear some relationship to crime, especially those types of crime where intelligence is an asset, as in forgery or embezzlement. High intelligence accompanied by emotional disturbance certainly characterizes a part of the convict group. Some sex offenders, for example, score at the genius level on intelligence tests.

A personality type known as the *psychopath* has received a great deal of attention in recent years, especially in connection with homicide and sex offenses. Psychopathic individuals are difficult to identify until they commit some offense. Often they appear very normal in most respects. Their difficulty, however, is considered a defect of character. They cannot be considered insane because they are able "to distinguish right from wrong" and have "full control" of themselves. Their trouble, authorities believe, stems from their indifference to moral standards: knowing their behavior to be wrong at times, psychopaths still do as they feel, not caring whether it is right or wrong. This is why the sexual psychopath or the psychopath with homicidal tendencies is extremely dangerous, capable of committing the most brutal rape or bloody murder without remorse. And usually he gives no forewarning of what he is about to do.

What is the connection between criminal characteristics and the city? The urban way of life can hardly be blamed for possibly inherited traits, but the speed, noise, and impersonality of city living may bring out the worst in people who have inherited predispositions to emotional weaknesses. Immoral or amoral men and women may find the city an ideal place to inhabit. The anonymity of city life, the possibility that they will not be detected, constantly encourages them to commit antisocial acts.

FAMILY FACTORS

A mass of research has centered on the family and home as contributing to crime and delinquency, and the family has become a convenient scapegoat for journalists, educators, and others who have tried to explain the origins of criminal behavior. Parents are blamed for not properly caring for their children. Delinquents are often traced to broken homes. Many delinquents come from homes in which one or both parents are alcoholics or drug addicts. Sometimes the mother is a prostitute or the father an ex-convict. Divorce and other signs of a disturbed marital life are prevalent among convicts. All in all, a tremendous amount of evidence has been accumulated connecting the family with delinquency and crime.

What these findings do not explain is the fact that many individuals who are not criminals come from broken families, have immoral or negligent parents, or otherwise possess an "undesirable" family background. Similarly, there are criminals who seem to have had the benefit of attentive, respectable, loving, and law-abiding parents. We do know that convicted criminals have come most commonly from urban lower-class environments where family life frequently lacks the middle-class moral values that are embodied so completely in our criminal codes. There may well be elements in the family situation that are conducive to delinquency and crime, but they must be identified more precisely than they have been up to now before we can safely conclude that criminals are products of their families.

NEIGHBORHOOD AND COMMUNITY FACTORS

Just as no one personal or family factor completely explains crime, so neighborhood and community factors alone will not give us a final answer. It is certainly true that many criminals do come from communities that seem to be breeding places for crime. City slums are blamed as often as the broken family. Yet, as we have mentioned already, many people who are not criminals come from blighted areas. Crime records do show that more criminals come from poor and congested neighborhoods and that crime rates decrease as the quality of the neighborhood improves. The lack of adequate recreational facilities, along with the presence of pool halls, taverns, and brothels, is frequently cited as being conducive to crime. Youthful gangs and organized hoodlums concentrate in slum districts. And inasmuch as a great deal of delinquent and criminal behavior is a group activity, the opportunity to associate with "bad companions" is relatively greater in certain neighborhoods.

Considerable evidence, then, points to personal, family, and community influences on criminal behavior. The relative importance of each factor seems to vary with the individual criminal, and all generalizations on the subject are risky. It does seem obvious that the anonymity of the urban environment, together with its slums, congestion, and "gang life," have a great deal to do with the mounting rate of juvenile crimes and their growing severity. It is our city courts and juvenile agencies that have been forced to deal with thirteen-year-old murderers, nine-year-old arsonists, and eleven-year-old rapists. And the city, too, through its concentration of wealth and opportunities for "easy money," increases the temptation to crime. What can be done? It is to the subject of correction and treatment that we must now turn.

WHAT WE DO ABOUT CRIME

Human societies have tried for centuries to devise effective ways of dealing with members who violate accepted standards of behavior. Offenders have been exiled, tortured, killed, fined, whipped, and imprisoned. Prior to the eighteenth century, convicted criminals were usually punished not by being committed to a jail or penitentiary but by being branded, having their ears clipped, being whipped, or being publicly humiliated. Virtually no attempts were made to reform the criminal, and his punishment was usually motivated by revenge. But in England and America convicts were being imprisoned by the close of the eighteenth century, and severe punishment took the form of solitary confinement or the "silent" treatment. By the middle of the nineteenth century, the Irish had introduced the notion of reforming and rehabilitating the criminal.

In the United States the idea of reforming criminals was applied at first to youthful offenders only. In very recent decades, however, support has grown for the idea that criminal offenders should be reformed so far as possible outside cells and beyond high prison walls. Although newer, more enlightened ways of treating criminals have been developed, some ancient forms of punishment still persist. The state of Delaware, for example, was still using "Red Hannah"— whipping at the post—as late as 1952.

In discussing programs for treating criminals, we are obviously talking of the convicts. White-collar criminals, syndicate leaders, and others who may be guilty but avoid conviction cannot be considered within the scope of organized treatment programs. Realizing their inability to treat guilty but unconvicted persons often discourages persons and groups who devote a great deal of time and effort to combating and trying to control crime.

PUNISHMENT VERSUS REFORM

The attempt to weave reform measures into our traditional punishment-oriented programs for treating criminals has thrown our penal system into turmoil. The age-old motive of punishment is virtually as strong today as ever. Society demands its "pound of flesh" for wrongs committed against it. The punishment doctrine is founded on the belief that man acts according to his free will. Accordingly, man is a free agent in deciding what to do. When he commits an offense against society, he must be made to pay. Under the Roman *lex taliones*, "an eye for an eye and a tooth for a tooth," punishment was meted out according to the seriousness of the crime. The more serious the offense the more severe the punishment. If a person inflicted pain on someone else, or if he deprived another person of his life, he was made to suffer an equal measure of pain. Justice was thus a matter of fitting the punishment to the crime, and American laws and prison programs have departed only slightly from this position. If everyone agreed about the desirability of punishment, the nature and objectives of our penal system would be far clearer than they now are.

The philosophy of reform poses a serious challenge to our punishment-based penal programs. Advocates of reform argue that punishment has never really deterred criminals or cut the incidence of crime. The late

Rioters are subdued after an outbreak at one of our large state prisons in 1958. Our penal policy is a curious blend of attempts to reform men such as these and at the same time to punish them.

Warden Lewis E. Lawes of Sing Sing Prison showed that homicide rates were just as high in states with capital punishment as in those without it. Reformers argue also that the criminal is frequently an unfortunate victim of social circumstance, and, since society is partly at fault, society should try to rehabilitate him. This notion also presumes that there is some good in everyone and that a proper rehabilitation program will help reform the individual and enable him to return to a law-abiding, productive life outside prison walls.

One of the principal difficulties in administering today's penal system stems from this mixture of punishment and reform. Criminal laws require that the guilty be punished. When the punishment involves serving a prison sentence, the incarcerated convict is usually subjected to a rehabilitation program. Prison administrators must thus execute both the court-dictated punishment and the program of reform. Both punisher and punishee find it difficult to reconcile this paradox. This situation does little to protect society from criminals or to make criminals into law-abiding citizens. Convicts are usually released in two or three years, and the majority are subsequently convicted of another offense and jailed again.

Although proponents of punishment maintain that the programs have never been severe enough and have been weakened by reform efforts, the reformers complain that any semblance of punishment interferes with their rehabilitation efforts. All but the most ardent reformers, however, concede that many hardened habitual criminals are beyond saving. Society must be protected from the real "toughs." Yet to treat all prisoners as if they were hardened criminals is a mistake. And it is equally foolish to turn some hardened criminal back to society simply because he has paid his debt when we know full well that he will return to his old ways the minute he steps outside the prison

Not all prisoners are behind high walls. Among the inmates of this southern California prison camp are persons who were sentenced for the worst sort of crimes. The camp has no fences or gates and guards are not armed. Only two prison officials remain on duty.

walls. If reform is to be a part of the treatment, it should be directed toward the most likely prospects.

INCARCERATION

There is considerable variety among prisons and prison programs in this country. The prisons themselves range from the maximum-security type for the most dangerous criminals, such as Alcatraz, to the minimum-security type without walls, such as the prison camps in California. Between these extremes are the medium-security prisons and the mixed-security types. In medium-security prisons most inmates are housed in outside cells, dormitories, or honor rooms surrounded by fences rather than walls. The largest prisons house upwards of five thousand men, although authorities recommend that no more than twelve hundred be con-fined in one institution. In some prisons the staff is well trained and very capable, but in many others training and skill cannot be bought for the low wages offered. Prison guards and not a few wardens have been known to beat and otherwise mistreat prisoners, either to maintain discipline or to punish their charges.

Living conditions are normally uncomfortable, as you might expect where punishment is the motive. Prison food has been notoriously bad. Educational and recreational programs are limited, although they have been improved a great deal in recent years. Social life is confined largely to fellow inmates who, of course, are of the same sex. Prisoners usually work in some prison shop or enterprise, but the choice of jobs is too limited to permit any significant vocational rehabilitation. Consequently, life in the typical prison does very little in helping prepare inmates for their return to free society and a law-abiding life.

PAROLE AND PROBATION

Parole and probation are two ways of helping the convict live a reasonably normal life *outside* prison walls. *Probation* involves supervising the criminal in the community *in lieu* of his serving a sentence in a jail or prison. A court decides whether or not a convict will be placed on probation, and if the prisoner violates his probation, he runs the risk of being sent to prison. *Parole*, on the other hand, is a means of releasing a prisoner from a penal institution before he has served his maximum time so that he may spend the remaining time of his sentence under supervision beyond prison confines. A central feature of both parole and probation is the supervision of offenders outside penal institutions. Neither of these procedures should be confused with pardon. When an offender is pardoned, he regains his complete freedom and is forgiven his crime by virtue of an executive act.

The humanitarian penal philosophy of the nineteenth century gave impetus to the idea of parole. Advocates of parole now maintain that it is not a form of leniency and that it should eventually become the means by which *all* prisoners are released. When he is paroled, the convict is placed under supervision for a certain period of time before he receives his final freedom. During this intervening period the parolee's adjustment problems are greatest—hence, the argument that well-administered parole programs protect both the convict and society in general. If this argument is sound, then the major difficulty with parole lies in its administration, for records show an extremely high rate of parole violations.

Probation, on the other hand, is a much older technique than parole. English common law set the precedent for placing offenders on probation, when, under the "benefit of clergy" rule of the Middle Ages, for example, ordained clergymen could be exempted from criminal law by being placed in the custody of ecclesiastical courts. Also, when a judge thought a sentence was too severe, the old common law allowed him to grant a judicial reprieve to the accused.

It was not until the beginning of the Second World War, however, that practically all our state governments had provided for probation systems. Today, probation is sometimes used as an alternative form of punishment in cases of relatively minor offenses where the penalty involves a fine because fines are unduly burdensome to poorer people, on whom they often fall. Probation is frequently chosen as an alternative to imprisonment for much the same reason. After all, a man in prison cannot support his family. Students of crime increasingly favor extending probation to first offenders because of the contaminating effects a term inside prison walls often has on the fledgling convict. One of the most convincing arguments in favor of probation, however, is that our prisons simply will not hold all the offenders and the cost of expanding facilities is enormous.

The success of both parole and probation systems depends largely on the way in which they are administered, and administrative success can be gauged by the number of parole and probation violations. At present the burden of proof lies with the reformers, who have to face up to a vast number of parole violators and repeater criminals. Such repetition supplies ammunition for the guns of those who still campaign for more severe forms of punishment.

OMNIPRESENT CRIME

The era of crime covers all of human history. Crime varies in its nature and frequency over a period of time and from place to place, but no society has ever been completely free from it. The prevention and control of crime, therefore, is a slow and difficult process.

Since crime is essentially an offense against society and its members, almost everyone agrees on its undesirability. But not everyone agrees what should be done about it. New laws are continually being drafted, making certain actions criminal for the first time, while old laws are becoming obsolete and unenforceable in a rapidly changing urban

society. Effective deterrents to crime have yet to be found, and crime-prevention programs have had only a sporadic success. Treatment programs based both on punishment and reform have generally failed to "cure" the criminal. Courts and the police are able to apprehend and convict but a few offenders. Therefore, criminologists still search for the real causes of crime. Crime, some observers have come to feel, is really quite normal, considering the tensions, frustrations, and divided loyalties of modern life.

SOME WORDS OF SUMMARY

It is widely agreed that crime and delinquency are serious problems in an urban society. Difficulties in defining and identifying criminal behavior create uncertainty about the extent to which crime and delinquency are actually increasing. Daily news reports, however, help maintain the impression that crime runs rampant.

In keeping with the American tradition of regarding a man innocent until proved guilty, we define criminals as persons who have been duly convicted before an "impartial tribunal." Statistics on the volume of reported crimes certainly indicate a sharp increase. Yet most of our information about crime is concerned with so-called "blue-collar" crime. Sutherland's conception of "white-collar crime" affords a new way of looking at crime and criminals. It was customary, before Sutherland introduced his notion, to speak of the average criminal as coming always from a background of poverty or from a broken family and having very little education. Blue-collar criminals continue to attract by far the most attention, but criminologists now are beginning to focus on some of the characteristics of white-collar offenders.

Personal, family, and community factors have all been singled out as causes of criminal and delinquent behavior. It now appears that different crimes result from different combinations of circumstances. Although some criminologists have stressed biological factors in the search for causes, others have concentrated on the social life of the individual, his personality, and his family and community background.

The treatment of criminals has been motivated typically by the desire to punish. Only in quite modern times has there been any serious concern with reform and rehabilitation of the offender. Today, a mixture of punishment and reform characterizes most of our penal systems. As a result of this confusion of objectives, prisons have been unable to do either job very effectively. Unwelcome in free society, ex-convicts frequently find themselves back in prison soon after they are released.

Lacking adequate knowledge of the causes of crime, its prevention, or treatment, modern urban society appears doomed to live with this problem. What consolation may be forthcoming from continuing efforts to solve the problem is offset by the rising tide of urban crime.

FURTHER ROADS TO LEARNING

GENERAL ACCOUNTS

H. Barnes and N. Teeters, *New Horizons in Criminology*, 3rd ed. (Englewood Cliffs, N. J.: Prentice-Hall, 1959). A general account of crime and how we treat it.

H. Bloch and F. Flynn, *Delinquency: The Juvenile Offender in America Today* (New York: Random House, 1956). A comprehensive analysis of young offenders.

E. Sutherland, *Principles of Criminology* (Philadelphia: Lippincott, 1947). One of the most widely accepted treatises in this much-debated field.

A. Wood and J. Waite, *Crime and Its Treatment* (New York: American Book, 1941). For those who want an emphasis on criminal law.

SPECIAL STUDIES

R. Caldwell, *Red Hannah* (Philadelphia: University of Pennsylvania Press, 1947). Whipping at the post in Delaware, and recently, too!

C. Chessman, *Cell 2455, Death Row* (Englewood Cliffs, N. J.: Prentice-Hall, 1954). Life among the condemned by a condemned man who spent more than ten years in Death Row.

M. Clinard, *Black Market* (New York: Rinehart, 1952). How the illegal "fast buck" was made during World War II.

T. Dinsdale, *Vigilantes of Montana* (Norman: University of Oklahoma Press, 1953). A frontier method of control.

J. Ellingston, *Protecting Our Children From Criminal Careers* (Englewood Cliffs, N. J.: Prentice-Hall, 1948). An analysis of the program undertaken by the California Youth Authority to deal with juvenile delinquency.

S. Glueck and E. Glueck, *Unraveling Juvenile Delinquency* (New York: Commonwealth Fund, 1950). Report of a carefully designed research project aimed at locating the causes of delinquency.

E. Kefauver, *Crime in America* (New York: Doubleday, 1951). An abridged version of the final report of the Kefauver Committee following its famous investigation into criminal activity in America.

E. Reid, *Mafia* (New York: New American Library, 1954). The infamous and internationally syndicated activities of the "Black Hand" society.

H. Rhodes, *The Criminals We Deserve* (New York: Oxford University Press, 1937). A significant analysis of modern crime.

C. Shaw and M. Moore, *The Natural History of a Delinquent Career* (Chicago: The University of Chicago Press, 1931). The story of a delinquent boy.

A. Smith, *Syndicate City* (Chicago: Regnery, 1954). What happens when crime becomes well-organized.

E. Sutherland, *White Collar Crime* (New York: Dryden, 1949). Opens the door to a fresh view of criminal behavior.

D. Taft, *Criminology*, rev. ed. (New York: Macmillan, 1950). A general text that provides a specialized cultural approach to the problem of crime.

F. Thrasher, *The Gang* (Chicago: The University of Chicago Press, 1927). A dated but still useful account of the organization and operation of "boy gangs" in the city of Chicago.

G. Wilber, "The Scientific Adequacy of Criminological Concepts," *Social Forces*, XXVIII (December, 1949), pp. 165-174. Some real problems involved in understanding the causes of criminal behavior.

FICTION AND DRAMA

M. Bodenheim, *Naked on Roller Skates* (New York: Liveright, 1931). A novel on the underworld activity in Harlem.

W. Brown, *The Big Rumble* (New York: Popular Library, 1955). Savage life of teen-agers in Spanish Harlem.

W. Burnett, *Nobody Lives Forever* (New York: Knopf, 1943). An extremely accurate presentation of the character of crooks, con-men, gangster leadership, "babes," and racketeers.

T. Dreiser, *An American Tragedy* (New York: Liveright, 1929). A famous novelist indicts society as the real criminal.

N. Hawthorne, *The Scarlet Letter* (New York: Dutton, 1907). An American classic about an adulteress in early New England.

E. Hunter, *The Blackboard Jungle* (New York: Pocket Books, 1955). The severe difficulties faced by teachers in city schools that have a large number of "problem students."

J. McIntyre, *Steps Going Down* (New York: Farrar, 1936). How a real "smoothie" managed to stay one step ahead of the police for a long time.

A. Train, *Manhattan Murder* (New York: Scribner, 1936). Organized crime in New York.

R. Traver, *Anatomy of a Murder* (New York: St. Martins, 1958). This account of a person on trial for a murder provides some rare illustrations of the inner workings of the American court system and the incomplete and somewhat unsatisfactory way in which the judicial procedures answer social problems.

W. Weiner, *Four Boys and a Gun* (New York: Dial, 1944). About the lives of four boys who were members of a neighborhood gang that killed a policeman.

FILMS

Children on Trial (British Information Services, 1946, 62 min., sound, black and white). A British film that provides excellent coverage of the entire question of juvenile delinquency. It also presents some highly successful methods of treating the delinquent.

Crime in the Streets (Allied Artists Pictures, 1956, 91 min., sound, black and white). About the rehabilitation of a juvenile gang leader.

A Criminal Is Born (Teaching Film Custodians, 1939, 20 min., sound, black and white). Three boys turn to crime and are sentenced to long stretches in the penitentiary. A fourth boy is saved from crime when his father takes him fishing.

Easy Life (Teaching Film Custodians, 1946, 20 min., sound, black and white). How a boy's desire for an easy life led to bad companions, gangsterism, and death.

The F. B. I. (March of Time, 1947, 2 reels, sound, black and white). The F. B. I. employs modern procedures in crime detection in a true espionage case.

The Face of Crime (Prudential Insurance Company of America, 1958, 60 min., sound, black and white). A truly superb film covering criminal behavior.

Les Misérables (Teaching Film Custodians, 1946, 4 reels, sound, black and white). Charles Laughton and Fredric March in Victor Hugo's powerful and moving conflict between a convict and a police inspector.

Prison with a Future (RKO-Pathe, 1951, 15 min., sound, black and white). Depicts the processes of rehabilitation of prisoners in a women's reformatory in Ohio.

Who's Delinquent? (RKO-Pathe, 1948, 17 min., sound, black and white). This film presents the point of view that society is the true delinquent because it fails to provide wholesome social conditions.

Education for an Urban and Industrial Society

These high-school juniors
are discovering that learning can be an exciting
and stimulating experience.

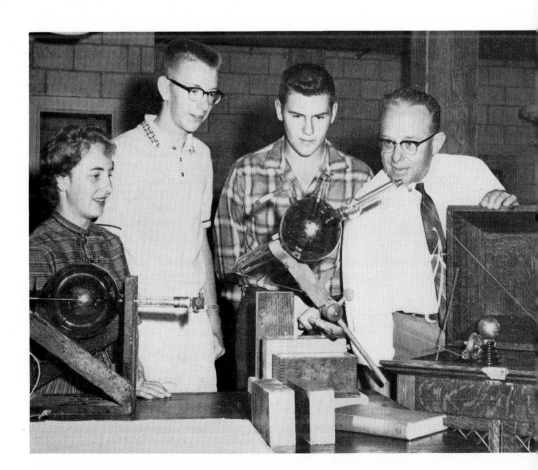

Few institutions

are more sensitive to economic and social change than education. Schools in the Western world can be expected to reflect the new industrial and urban culture that has grown up in the past few centuries. For it is the job of the schools to pass on to the coming generation the skills, knowledge, and values by which men live. Where these skills are changing, and old values and patterns of living are crumbling, a society seeks to instruct its children in the new ways of life. This process often leads to disagreement and conflict. Should education prepare the young for the life that is, or for the life that ought to be? Should it stress things that are common to children everywhere, or things that separate them one from another? Is it education's function to impart skills, or to impart knowledge? Should it teach children how to live, or how to make a living? Is the heritage of the past significant, or the needs of the present? Should schools develop young minds, or try to satisfy children's social and emotional needs? Should they experiment with new courses and methods, or cling to the anchor of tradition and customary practice?

Ever since the Industrial Revolution Western society has pondered these questions. Dependence on the machine, the great expansion of population, and the march to the cities have combined to create a crisis in educational thought. Democratic theory and the universal need for trained men in an industrial society have brought home to almost everyone the need for mass education and opportunity for the talented. But what kind of education does the average man need to live in a Western democratic nation of city-dwellers and machine-users? *

AMERICAN EDUCATION IN PERSPECTIVE

FRANKLIN'S IDEA OF "USEFUL KNOWLEDGE"

As early as 1751 Benjamin Franklin was convinced that a new approach to education was required. Existing Latin schools, with their curricula of ancient languages, philosophy, and classical studies designed to prepare young men for the ministry and for college, he thought unfit for the young of Philadelphia. The useful skills needed in an urban, commercial society should be learned in school, he believed. As to specific studies, he argued that:

... it would be well if they could be taught *every Thing* that is useful, and *every Thing* that is ornamental: But Art is long, and their Time is short. It is therefore propos'd that they learn those Things that are likely to be *most useful* and *most ornamental*. . . .

All should be taught to write a *fair Hand*, and swift, as that is useful to All. And with it may be learnt something of *Drawing*, by Imitation of Prints, and some of the first Principles of *Geometry* and *Astronomy*.

---

* We are using the term "education" in the usual American sense of "schooling." Broadly defined, of course, education would be synonymous with the whole process of socialization and include family, church, and community influences.

310

The *English* Language might be taught by Grammar.... Reading should also be taught, and pronouncing, properly, distinctly, emphatically. . . .

To form their Stile they should be put on Writing Letters to each other, making Abstracts of what they read; or writing the same Things in their own Words. . . .*

Franklin also advised that history, geography, commerce, and natural history (including gardening and planting) might be taught in the school he proposed.

If Franklin's plea for useful and practical education seems very familiar to us, it did not seem so to his contemporaries. For education in colonial America was confined largely to businessmen, ministers, lawyers, and other professional men. The colonists modeled their schools on the English secondary schools and colleges of the time, where the curriculum was likewise heavily classical. To be sure, some of the New England colonies had established compulsory instruction in reading, writing, and religion; but interest in popular education had waned nearly everywhere in the colonies at the time of the American Revolution. Indeed, most colonial leaders had a very limited faith in the capacity of the masses of men to profit from education. Almost no one believed that it was worth while to try to educate a girl. Whatever schooling the great majority of early Americans enjoyed came largely from their parents.

THE JACKSONIAN REVOLUTION

All this changed with the great democratic surge in American life that characterized the era of Andrew Jackson. His administration reflected the growing power and respect enjoyed by the common man in American affairs. Between Jackson's inauguration in 1829 and the outbreak of the Civil

---

* R. Ulich, ed., *Three Thousand Years of Educational Wisdom*, 2nd ed. (Cambridge: Harvard University Press, 1954), pp. 444-445.

War, the principle of public elementary education was firmly established in the United States. Throughout the North, and especially in New England, free public schools offering as much as six years of free education were thrown open to the children of rich and poor alike. Even a few public high schools opened their doors in these pre-Civil War years, though the Latin School and the private academy still dominated secondary education. The significance of growing free education for American democratic ideals and procedures was underscored by Ralph Waldo Emerson in one of his famous essays.

Therefore I praise New England because it is the country in the world where is the freest expenditure for education. We have already taken . . . the initial step, which for its importance might have been resisted as the most radical of revolutions, thus deciding at the start the destiny of this country,—this, namely, that the poor man, whom the law does not allow to take an ear of corn when starving, nor a pair of shoes for his freezing feet, is allowed to put his hand into the pocket of the rich, and say, You shall educate me, not as you will, but as I will: not alone in the elements, but, by further provision, in the languages, in sciences, in the useful and in elegant arts. The child shall be taken up by the State, and taught, at the public cost, the rudiments of knowledge, and at last, the ripest results of art and science.*

Here was a revolutionary step indeed! The entire community, the bachelor and the spinster included, must bear the cost of educating the children of all. How could this undertaking be justified? Champions of universal education argued that the whole community had a stake in the behavior of its children and that all should share in their support. The morals, the religion, and the politics of a city or town were intimately bound up with the degree of enlightenment of its citizens. Religion could not flourish where none could read the Bible or follow the minister's sermons; politics must suffer

---

* R. Ulich, ed., *Three Thousand Years of Educational Wisdom*, p. 578.

The George B. Emerson School in
Boston, 1850.

advantages accruing from high birth and
respectable family connections. In the South
and West, state universities were founded
in these ante-bellum years and greatly expanded the opportunities open to capable
American youngsters. More than one hundred and fifty new colleges and universities
were established in the quarter-century before the Civil War.

As yet very few persons agreed on what
kind of education should be provided in
American public schools. There was una-
nimity only in hailing the ideal of equal
educational opportunity for all. But should
the schools teach Cicero or modern history?
Latin or French? What did democracy in
education mean—equal access by all talented
pupils to the educational treasures previously
hoarded in private schools, or a whole new
curriculum designed to meet the needs of
the thousands heretofore barred from any
schooling at all? Latent in the Jacksonian
movement was the promise that schools,
like all public institutions, belonged to
the people and should serve them. It was
not a matter of the common man proving
himself worthy of the heritage of traditional
education now opened up to him, but rather
of common schools proving their worth in
preparing the average man for his future
life.

where the ignorant were shepherded by unscrupulous bosses into polling places. Workingmen's associations viewed education as a
ladder of opportunity that their own children might one day climb. Frontiersmen
believed that free schools had a leveling influence that might even out the unnatural

THE IMPACT
OF INDUSTRIALIZATION AND URBANIZATION

For three-quarters of a century this
question lay unresolved. Each change in the
curriculum spawned resistance, debate, and
controversy. Were modern languages a legitimate part of a modern education? No!
argued the retreating champions of classical
education. Compared with Greek and Latin,
which opened up two thousand five hundred
years of some of the human mind's ripest re-
flections on philosophy, drama, law, and poli-

tics, what did it matter if someone could
chatter with a waiter in French? Then what
of natural science, of biology, or physics, or
chemistry? Surely Darwin's sensational work
had proved the value of scientific study to all.
Nonsense! retorted the classicists. Darwin
himself was a man of breadth of vision, of reflective temperament, with a brilliant classical style of writing, which he owed to his
classical schooling. The purpose of educa-

tion, these traditionalists argued, was not to fill the mind with grubby facts drawn from science or modern living but to encourage a critical, inquiring, judicious habit of mind that would lend perspective to a person's life work. True, not everyone was capable of profiting from this traditional education, but then not everyone was capable of being educated. To train persons to fill positions in modern industry or commerce was certainly not objectionable, but such training should not be confused with education. On these grounds the proponents of traditional education rested their case.

By the end of the nineteenth century the industrial-urban transformation of America had greatly altered the terms of debate. Now the champions of curriculum modernization were gaining the upper hand and the traditionalists were in full retreat. The Jacksonian view of the meaning of democracy in education, now reinforced by the demands of an industrial society, was well on the way to victory in the long-standing conflict. Our educational system, more and more people felt, was out of balance with American life. Something must be done to fit the nation's youth for the new complexities it had to face. Too much time had been spent in studying ancient languages and civilization, too little in learning science, technology, and the useful arts. *Living* languages, *social* studies, and *useful* knowledge were the key terms in the academic revolution that swept through American schools in the early twentieth century.

THE YARDSTICK OF USEFULNESS

Nor was the revolution confined to the lower levels of education. In the universities as well, the yardstick of usefulness was now laid against the traditional offerings of these institutions of higher education. Courses in science, social studies, engineering, and pedagogy were gradually introduced.

Colleges of agriculture and mechanical arts were made possible by the Morrill Act of 1862. The elective system, popularized by Charles W. Eliot at Harvard, had been widely adopted by 1900. Students were now permitted to choose, often indiscriminately, among the traditional and newer offerings in the university curriculum. One critic of this trend, Albert Nock, wrote:

Under the influence of vocationalism and the fetish-worship of size and numbers, they [the universities] have stuffed out the content of this popular instruction to an incredible volume. No institution could afford to be behind its neighbours in this; all alike had to have a hand in it, for such as did not would go to the wall. It is fair, I think, to say that our institutions have conducted among themselves a grand competition for numbers, on ruinous terms; first, by shifting the burden of education from the student to the instructor, and putting pressure on the instructor to let his students go through as lightly and quickly as possible; and second, by offering a choice among an immense number of subjects that are easily taught, and easily accessible to a very low order of mind.*

This was a serious charge, and Nock would not be the last to make it. But, on the other side, defenders of the New Education pointed to what had happened to America during the nineteenth century. An educational system suited to the aristocracy of a small agrarian nation in 1800, they charged, was no longer applicable to a dynamic, expanding, industrial state in 1900.

A great deal indeed had happened. Industrialization had swept across New England to the Middle States, then to the Middle West, and finally to all corners of the country. Population had shifted from East to West, and from farm to city, all the while experiencing a remarkable growth. Transportation and communication had undergone vast changes that brought states closer

---

* A. J. Nock, *The Theory of Education in the United States* (New York: Harcourt, Brace, 1932), p. 81.

together than neighboring cities had been in 1800.

How did these changes affect education? One striking result was the prolongation of school attendance. The greater the complexity of skills and training needed for a useful life, the longer the period of formal schooling required. Adolescent youth, still useful on the farm, were unemployable in the skilled industrial market. They needed first greater maturity and more training. The rising productivity of industry, furthermore, meant a rising level of living and more leisure for people to enjoy it. More schooling would provide greater opportunity for men to enjoy their leisure time and use it profitably. As the demands for education increased, even adults began seeking more schooling to further their business, industrial, and cultural opportunities. The modern adult education movement was initiated in the last quarter of the nineteenth century in response to their needs and demands.

VOCATIONAL EDUCATION

The social changes of the nineteenth century thus brought more children into city schools for a longer period of time. These events were quietly tipping the scales in favor of the Jacksonian view of public education. First of all, if youngsters were to prepare for a career in industry, they needed vocational education. What use was Latin, or even French, to a young man whose talents and economic status were certain to lead him to an unskilled job in a heavy industry? Would not training in some useful trade, coupled with the rudiments of reading, writing, and arithmetic, serve him and society better? Furthermore, the large city schools with their greater wealth and numbers were in a position to establish a variety of educational programs to serve the needs of the manually skilled as well as the college-bound. Greater numbers also permitted

grading by age and (later on) by subject matter, all of which added to the efficiency of instruction. A large city might even be able to set up a separate high school devoted to mechanical or technological training.

If this were true of the public high school, why not the public university? It was not long after the Civil War that special schools for business, technology, engineering, and education were organized within the university framework. Agricultural colleges, as we have already mentioned, had begun to develop earlier in the wake of the Morrill Act of 1862. Theoretically there were no limits to the new courses or schools that might be introduced so long as they were meeting, or thought they were meeting, a legitimate vocational or social need.

Almost no one regarded vocational instruction as the only meat in the educational diet, however. Students should also be given work in the English language and literature, natural science and mathematics, history and social studies, and other subjects that seemed to help them lead useful and happy lives. The educational debate after 1875 centered on what balance should be preserved between these "hard" disciplines and the newer courses in the vocational, commercial, and recreational areas. The old battle-line between the champions of classical studies and the exponents of modern sciences and languages began to disappear as they made common cause against the encroachment of these still newer courses of study. Even a classicist would admit that the study of French was valuable, if the alternative were elementary typing or beginners' machine shop!

THE FEMALE TEACHER

We have already noticed in Chapter 16 one important by-product of the rise of American industry, which had a profound impact on education. This was the emancipation of women. The employment of thousands of women in the textile and other industries during the nineteenth century removed some of the stigma that the working woman had borne heretofore. By comparison, employment as a teacher or a secretary seemed genteel indeed when measured against employment in a textile mill. By the hundreds, then by the thousands, American women entered the teaching profession, until the time would come when teaching, at least in the lower grades, was popularly regarded as a female profession. Teaching had always been an unstable mode of employment for men, many of whom had ambitions for greater things, and they surrendered the field without a fight. Only in recent years has there been even a mild reversal of this pattern.

JOHN DEWEY
AND CHANGES IN EDUCATIONAL THEORY

It is clear that the industrial-urban revolution of the nineteenth century profoundly influenced America's schools by broadening opportunity, strengthening vocational studies, changing the popular image of education, and bringing women into the classroom. Equally important were the changes that overtook educational theory, which by the early twentieth century was also undergoing a drastic transformation.

In this transformation no name attracted more attention than that of John Dewey. More persuasively, more logically than any other, Dewey argued the insufficiency of the classical view of education. For it he substituted a restatement of the aims of education in the light of the vast social changes that had followed the Civil War. Properly understood, education, in Dewey's view, was both a psychological and a social process. The teacher must begin with the child as she finds him, a bubbling contradiction of individual impulses and experiences. Yet she

must also introduce him to the social world and its processes, which have already begun to mold his character and his future by the time he enters school. The good teacher must recognize and seek to harmonize this relationship between individual impulse and social good. The schoolroom must become a

John Dewey—father of the "new curriculum" in twentieth-century American education.

miniature of the real world outside the classroom. The natural impulses of children must be directed into socially acceptable channels. School and society, according to Dewey, were really one.

Dewey thus rejected not only the older classical pattern of formal indoctrination but also the newer one of specific training for a specific goal in life. Vocationalism was as one-sided as classicism. He insisted instead that the task of the school was to awaken each child to his varying capacities and skills. Education must be both individual and social. Each child must be trained along the lines of his own needs and interests, and each must also be introduced to the demands and expectations of human society. Thus, training in history, citizenship, and human relations was as important as classes in machine shop, typing, or bookkeeping. It was the *whole child* in which school and society were interested. Schools should therefore be oriented around children, their interests and needs, rather than around formal subjects and disciplines. But let Dewey express his creed in his own words:

I BELIEVE THAT

All education proceeds by the participation of the individual in the social consciousness of the race. . . .

The only true education comes through the stimulation of the child's powers by the demands of the social situations in which he finds himself. . . .

The school is primarily a social institution. . . .

Education, therefore, is a process of living and not a preparation for future living. . . .

The school must represent life, life as real and vital to the child as that which he carries on in the home, in the neighborhood, or on the playground. . . .

Much of the present education fails because it neglects this fundamental principle of the school as a form of community life. It conceives the school as a place where certain information is to be given, where certain lessons are to be learned, or where certain habits are to be formed. . . .

The true center of correlation on the school subjects is not science, nor literature, nor history, nor geography, but the child's own social activities. . . .

The only way to make the child conscious of his social heritage is to enable him to perform those fundamental types of activity which make civilization what it is. . . . This gives the standard for the place of cooking, sewing, manual training, etc., in the school. . . .

It is the business of everyone interested in education to insist upon the school as the primary and most effective instrument of social progress and reform. . . .*

* R. Ulich, ed., *Three Thousand Years of Educational Wisdom,* pp. 629-638.

THE NEW CURRICULUM

The impact of these ideas on school curricula was to confirm and accelerate the trends and changes already in motion. A sound education could not be limited to intellectual development, to training the mind in reflection and judgment; nor could it be organized around subject matter. Learning, scholarship, studying man's cultural heritage—these were no longer the aims of education. At most they were means toward other ends. The aims now centered on the growth and development of the whole child, which meant that the curriculum must be revised to meet student interests and needs. In determining whether geometry should be studied by freshmen in high school, for example, the deciding factor was not whether geometry was necessary to later studies of trigonometry or calculus but whether the freshman could understand it and use it in his daily life. The same measure was made of high-school languages, science, and history. If traditional history were arid of social applications, then it could be grouped with geography and perhaps civics in a useful course of social studies for fifteen-year-olds. No rigid graduation requirements should be fixed, because individual capacities and interests varied widely. New courses should be added each year to keep step with the changing times. Any lingering distinctions between curricular and extra-curricular activities must disappear in time since the social and recreational periods of school life were as important as sessions devoted to academic lessons. The school would thus become an institution for socializing and civilizing children.

Although Professor Dewey's words sounded revolutionary to many people, they indicated the new directions in which American education was moving. It was now clear that the American people were resolving for themselves the old paradox of the meaning

For these children, the schoolroom is what John Dewey said it should be—a microcosm of the world outside the school building.

of democracy in American education. It definitely did not mean, as Jefferson supposed, throwing open to the talented the doors of the rigid, scholarly, traditional classrooms that had stressed discipline and scholastic excellence. Rather, a democratic education meant the same amount of basic education for all, regardless of scholastic talent; and if traditional studies in mathematics or history were beyond the interest or capability of some children, then they might choose from subjects closer to their own inclination. The Jacksonian dream of democratic education, reinforced by the new psychology of learning popularized by Dewey, had triumphed over the Jeffersonian view, which survived now only among the unreconstructed educators and parents.

CLOUDS ON THE HORIZON

THE NEW CURRICULUM AT BAY

And yet there were haunting doubts. Despite the great faith in American education and the great expansion of schools after 1900, there were occasional complaints, which grew more voluble as the century wore on. Were the schools attempting too much? Were academic standards keeping pace with rising costs of education? Was the American teacher becoming only a specialist in child care? Was it true that the traditional subjects were no more important than vocational or commercial offerings? Were there no standards by which quality in teaching or learning could be measured? Had John Dewey been right?

Several critics were disturbed, too, about the failure of other countries to follow the American example in education. Instead, a procession of European visitors expressed dissatisfaction with the content of the American school system and its curriculum. Typical was the reaction of the distinguished

317

English liberal and political observer Harold Laski, who wrote:

It does not appear that in any American high school the boys and girls attach importance to the possession of intellectual distinction by one of their number. The real title to importance belongs to the successful athlete; after that, it emerges in part from the impact of the extra-curricular groups, and in part also to the fact of having exceptionally wealthy parents. . . . Nobody seems to attach particular importance to excellence in the subjects which the school is there to teach. Nobody even seems to imagine that the spinal column of the high school curriculum has much to do with life. The study of Greek and Latin, of course, has almost disappeared. The character of language-teaching in the colleges is virtually built on the assumption that the first-year undergraduate begins at very nearly the beginning. The reading of great literature for its own sake is rare.*

Even more disturbing were the charges that came from many outstanding Americans, including a number of educators, especially after World War II. These critics protested that a deep and pervasive anti-intellectualism had invaded the curriculum of American schools, had disparaged traditional learning, created a cult of mediocrity, and turned teachers into baby-sitters and group-discussion leaders. These criticisms became more serious in the context of the Cold War with the Soviet Union. For the Soviets had seemingly made great strides in their educational program, especially in the sciences, under a system that looked very much like the one America had abandoned a half-century before. To be sure, many of the charges were inaccurate and sometimes misleading. In seeking to educate all her children, America had indeed found a place for the mediocre and the inferior student. Inadequate funds, particularly in rural districts, had caused some schools to slight the sciences and other basic subjects. And the

role of incentives in drawing young people into careers other than science and scholarship had been underestimated by many critics. But when all allowances were made, America still had cause to be concerned about the curriculum of her schools, and the great educational debate that began in the 1950's probably represented a wholesome re-assessment of the American educational experience.

EDUCATION FOR ALL?

It was no longer even certain that, for all the stress on equal opportunity, Americans had succeeded in building a genuinely democratic school system. A pioneering study of social classes in American schools by W. L. Warner and his associates in the 1940's showed that a typical high school reflected the class structure of the community. A student's social class influenced his choice of a curriculum, a lower-class student had to show greater ability to receive equal rewards, and the future plans of all high-school students bore a relationship to the occupation of their fathers. In fact, the public school served as a sorting and selecting agency to maintain the American class order by eliminating most of the children along the way and permitting only a few to reach the top. Of all students with intelligence quotients of 110 or above, almost six in every ten from middle and upper-class families attended college, whereas only one in ten from lower-class families ever entered these lofty portals. Even teachers reflected middle-class aspirations in their concern to reward those students who by their dress, manners, and appearance showed their kinship with the respected classes of local society. Of course, the American high school did provide opportunities for some talented children of lower-class status to climb the social ladder, thus preserving an open-class system, but it was difficult to argue that

---

* H. J. Laski, *The American Democracy* (New York: Viking, 1948), pp. 338-339.

every American boy or girl had exactly the same opportunity as every other. Certainly a great deal of undiscovered talent lay unexploited in America's public-school youngsters.

For the young people who went on to college, social class continued to play a role in their attitudes toward politics, society, education, family, business, and even religion. The college graduate in America, according to several studies, tended to hold a better job, earn more money, stay married, have a smaller family, favor free enterprise, and lean toward Republicanism in politics and Protestantism in religion. All these characteristics were also true of the middle and upper classes in general.

MORE FEDERAL AID TO EDUCATION?

What could be done to equalize educational opportunity, to make America's schools more truly democratic? By the middle of the present century, more and more people were arguing that since America's educational problems were national, the solutions to them must also be national. Only Congress, according to the partisans of this view, was in position to tax any or all of America's wealth for the benefit of America's school children wherever they were found. They also cited precedent for such action by pointing out that federal grants had been given to land-grant colleges for nearly a century and that hot-lunch programs in our primary and secondary schools were widely accepted as a legitimate type of federal aid.

Soviet advances in education and science lent a sense of crisis to the debates that echoed through the schools, newspapers, magazines, television, radio, and the halls of Congress. In 1958, by enactment of the National Defense Education Act, Congress took a long step in the direction of assuming greater responsibility for encouraging the recruitment of teachers, expanding science

and modern-language teaching, and identifying and salvaging the able students.

But was this enough? Should the national government give still more assistance? Should it appropriate funds for school construction, for example? For scholarships at all levels? For teachers' salaries? For humanities and social science programs as well as those in the physical and biological sciences? Proponents of more federal aid based their pleas on the urgency of our national emergency, the inability of American schools and colleges to meet the Soviet challenge, the shrinking supply of college instructors, and their conviction that federal aid did not mean federal control of America's school systems.

Critics of federal aid, on the other hand, argued that education should not be added to the responsibilities of an already overburdened national government. Let the state governments and local communities do for themselves what the national government could do only with funds drawn from local citizens anyway. Most important, they insisted, was the preservation of states' rights, local initiative, and educational freedom that might well be lost in a comprehensive federal program. But despite the opposition, Congress and the Executive branch have tended more and more to support the idea of federal aid.

ELECTRONIC AND MECHANICAL TEACHERS?

One of the provisions of the National Defense Education Act was the commitment of funds for research in the use of television and motion pictures in teaching. Many congressmen and senators expressed their approval of the "significant contributions" that these media were making to effective instruction in the classroom. By 1960 practically every course—grade-school, high school, and college—from beginning reading to college physics, was being taught somewhere in the United States over television. In Nebraska and Oklahoma, for example, open-circuit television was being used to bring a variety of science courses to small rural high schools that otherwise could not offer them because of a lack of qualified teachers. Over a national television network a single course in modern physics had been taught to an estimated two hundred and seventy thousand high-school teachers, school and college students, engineers, and housewives at an hour when most Americans were still in bed. By 1960, too, one hundred and twenty colleges and universities were offering television courses for academic credit, and approximately six hundred school districts in the country were making regular use of televised instruction. A report in the late 1950's by the Fund for the Advancement of Education waxed enthusiastic about the educational future of television:

If wisely and imaginatively used, television can provide educational experience far beyond what is possible in the conventional classroom. Students can be eyewitnesses to history in the making. They can have a closeup view of physical and chemical processes that cannot be duplicated in any but the most expensive laboratories. They can hear the outstanding scholars of our age. They can have access to the great museums of art, history, and nature. A whole treasure-trove of new and stimulating experiences that were beyond the reach of yesterday's students can be brought into the classroom for today's students.*

But there were also fears that educational television might not always be "wisely and imaginatively used." Some teachers and observers have been concerned with what they have called an obsession with techniques and gadgetry in the pioneer educational programs on television. Still others have been fearful of their own academic security in an electronic age when photogenic charm and dramatic talent might count more heavily than scholarly depth in choosing "TV teachers." In general, teachers and professors were less enthusiastic and more cautious in their approval of educational television than high-school or college administrators.

Many people were also concerned, perhaps more justifiably, that teaching by television might make education even more impassive and mechanical than it now is. Could the informal give-and-take, the intellectual stimulation and excitement of the interplay of

---

* Quoted by Paul Woodring in his syndicated column in the *Newark News*, Newark, N. J., July 26, 1959.

If wisely and imaginatively used, television can supplement and vastly enrich the educational experience for students.

interested minds, the love of learning found in the small classroom, conducted by an able teacher, ever be found in the impersonal world of TV? Whatever the answer, even television's strongest critics have admitted that the possibilities of educational television have scarcely been more than tapped, and that educational television may one day play a major role in broadening and enriching the education of American students at all levels.

INTEGRATION OR SEGREGATION?

Far more troublesome than questions involving TV and mechanical teachers was the one concerning the American Negro's opportunity for an education. No problem has caused more difficulty for Americans than the status of their American Negro citizens. Following the Civil War, and especially after 1900, Negroes were confined to a tightly segregated pattern of relations with whites in trains, buses, hotels, parks, restaurants, and schools. The Supreme Court had held in 1896, in the famous case of *Plessy* vs. *Ferguson*, that such segregation did not deprive Negroes of their civil rights if the facilities offered Negroes were equal to those available to whites.

For nearly sixty years this "separate but equal" doctrine was used to justify the construction and operation of separate Negro schools, playgrounds, and parks, as well as separate waiting and rest rooms in all public buildings in more than a dozen southern states. Sometimes these facilities were equal, or occasionally even superior, to those provided for whites; but quite often they were not. In the case of southern schools, there was little question that white schools were provided with better teachers, and normally better buildings, equipment, and other resources. Furthermore, separate educational facilities in such professional schools as medicine, law, and theology were beyond the reach of most states and inherently wasteful

and uneconomical. It was in these advanced fields of study that educational segregation first began to break down in the 1940's and 1950's, aided by sympathetic federal courts.

Critics of segregation had long argued, however, that segregation of schools by race was in its very nature unconstitutional and that it resulted in inequalities. Spearheaded by the National Association for the Advancement of Colored People (N.A.A.C.P.), a group that had been championing the cause of the American Negro for several decades, the drive to break through the color line in education reached a climax in 1954 when the Supreme Court of the United States handed down an epoch-making decision on segregation in the public schools. The way had been paved for this decision by a series of court decisions dating from the early 1920's when the battle of the "white primaries" was fought. The words of the Court were clear about the departure from the older "separate but equal" doctrine:

In these days, it is doubtful that any child may reasonably be expected to succeed in life if he is denied the opportunity of an education. Such an opportunity, where the state has undertaken to provide it, is a right which must be made available to all on equal terms.

We come then to the question presented: Does segregation of children in public schools solely on the basis of race, even though the physical facilities and other "tangible" factors may be equal, deprive the children of the minority group of equal educational opportunities? We believe that it does . . . in the field of public education the doctrine of "separate but equal" has no place. Separate educational facilities are inherently unequal.*

In reaching their unanimous decision, the justices had relied heavily on "changing social conditions" and testimony that Negroes in segregated schools, however elegant the facilities and buildings, suffered from feelings of inferiority and insecurity. Schools,

---

* *Brown* vs. *Board of Education of Topeka,* 347 U.S. 483 at 493 (1954).

said the Court, could not be "equal" in the confidence and feelings of acceptance they inspired so long as their basis of admission was race.

To declare segregation unconstitutional, however, was not to usher in general school integration. Hailed by the advocates of desegregation, the Court's decision was roundly condemned by its opponents. A day of infamy—Black Monday—marks the calendar of those who most strongly resent the Court's dictum. In addition to the older arguments— infringement on states' rights, inherent racial differences, and opposition to any and all forms of social mixing among Negroes and whites—segregationists condemned the court decision on legal grounds. They argued that the judges had violated a time-honored principle of legal precedent when they overthrew the doctrine of "separate but equal" and substituted "current social conditions." Even some legal authorities questioned the Court's reasoning and the manner in which the desegregation decision was reached.

Other people argued along more moderate lines. They maintained that a racial pattern centuries in the making could not and should not be overturned at one stroke. Any change, they felt, must come gradually if it were not to create more problems than it solved. Others asserted that education had been historically a state and local matter to which the protections of the Fourteenth Amendment did not apply. Changes must come from the grass roots.

Compliance with the Court's decision was slow and sporadic. The border states and a few states in the Upper South desegregated their schools under court order in scattered communities. But the states of the Lower South, together with Virginia and Arkansas, stood steadfast against any change in their school systems. Schools were closed for extended periods in several states rather than permit integration. Violence occurred at several high schools that were preparing to admit Negro students. At Little Rock, Arkansas, the Arkansas National Guard was federalized to preserve order and protect several Negro school children after the state's governor had taken steps to prevent integration. Everywhere, in the first few years after the Court's decision, there was hesitation, uncertainty, readjustment, and waiting. In the Deep South a firm stand was taken—a stand that would brook no integration whatsoever. Elsewhere, there were signs that segregation was weakening.

A less-publicized phase of the controversy involves segregation in many northern schools. Although the law does not compel segregation, many northern schools are nevertheless completely segregated as a result of residential segregation or carefully considered school districting. And just as curious is the fact that white parents have vigorously opposed integration in their schools at the same time that they have condemned the South. Americans must seem strange indeed to foreign observers.

SOME WORDS OF SUMMARY

Education, like any other institution in human society, is sensitive to social changes. Since the onset of the Industrial Revolution, Western nations have debated the proper role of education in an industrial-urban society. In America, Benjamin Franklin argued early for a useful, functional education that would serve the immediate needs of the youth of Philadelphia. But most thoughtful Americans held to the classical view that education should inspire a critical and judicious habit of mind rather than train youngsters in the practical and useful arts.

Two developments during the nineteenth century tipped the balance against the classicists. First, the Jacksonian movement in politics stressed the role of the common man in American life and emphasized that all institutions should exist to serve his needs. Later came the expansion of American industry and the drive to the cities, all of which added to the complexity of modern life and the training needed to succeed in it. The yardstick of usefulness was applied to the traditional learning process in the public schools, which were now serving more and more young people. Educational opportunities were broadened, vocational studies became more common, and women turned teaching into a feminine profession at the primary level, and to some extent at the secondary level.

The aims of education were modified in accord with these changes. John Dewey and others argued that the school should serve both individual needs and social realities. Education was not only preparation for life; it was life itself. The school-room and its problems were as real as life in the broader world outside. Children should be indoctrinated neither in the classical studies that had dominated the school curricula during the preceding century nor in the technical skills needed by pupils who were headed for careers in industry. Rather, a curriculum should be forged from all those studies that contributed to the growth and development of the individual child. Schools should be child-centered, rather than subject-centered. Democratic education, in the view of Dewey and his followers, meant the same amount of basic education for all, regardless of scholastic ability. Each child had interests, needs, and capabilities that should be satisfied and encouraged.

Though widely accepted, the Dewey philosophy of education was challenged by those who disliked the de-emphasis of scholarship and serious study and the lack of qualitative standards in judging teaching and learning. These critics charged that the newer schools encouraged anti-intellectualism and mediocrity, and made every school subject, no matter how frivolous, as important as every other. Soviet achievements in science and education following World War II lent urgency to this re-examination of the purposes and standards of American schools.

There was concern, too, that the American school system was less democratic than the nation at large generally supposed. A study in the 1940's showed that a typical high school reflected the social divisions of the entire community. This fact was important in determining a student's success in high school, as well as his chances of going on to college. At college this element of social class continued to influence his choice of a career and even his attitudes toward politics, marriage, and religion.

A final major concern over the democratic character of American schools involved segregation of Negro pupils in southern classrooms. In 1954 the United States Supreme Court ruled that such segregated schools were inherently unequal and in violation of the federal Constitution. Though there were protests and strong forces opposed integrating the schools, some schools were desegregated, especially in the border states. In the meantime there was much uncertainty, conflict, and "watchful waiting."

FURTHER ROADS TO LEARNING

GENERAL ACCOUNTS

R. Butts, A *Cultural History of Western Education*, rev. ed. (New York: McGraw-Hill, 1955). A broad, discerning survey of the educational history of Europe and America.

J. Conant, *The American High School Today* (New York: McGraw-Hill, 1959). An eagerly awaited report of the post-Sputnik survey of American high schools by a former Harvard president.

E. Cubberley, *Public Education in the United States* (Boston: Houghton Mifflin, 1919). A classic treatment by a pioneer in the field.

M. Curti, *The Social Ideas of American Educators* (New York: Scribner, 1935). An important pioneering study of the social context of American educational thought.

E. Knight, *Education in the United States*, 3rd ed. (New York: Ginn, 1951). A widely used textbook in this field.

R. Ulich, ed., *Three Thousand Years of Educational Wisdom*, 2nd ed. (Cambridge: Harvard University Press, 1954). A most useful compilation of educational thought in all the world's great cultural traditions.

SPECIAL STUDIES

A. Blaustein and C. Ferguson, Jr., *Desegregation and the Law* (New Brunswick, N. J.: Rutgers University Press, 1957). A popular account of the background, meaning, and early results of the Supreme Court's desegregation decree.

J. Brubacher, *A History of the Problems of Education* (New York: McGraw-Hill, 1947). This book places the issues of education in historical perspective.

R. Butts, *The College Charts Its Course* (New York: McGraw-Hill, 1939). Probably the best general history of higher education in the United States.

L. Cook and E. Cook, *Sociological Approach to Education* (New York: McGraw-Hill, 1950). How community attitudes and practices affect the classroom situation.

J. Dewey, *Democracy and Education* (New York: Macmillan, 1916). This is probably Dewey's best-known statement of his views on education.

————, *The School and Society* (Chicago: The University of Chicago Press, 1899). A brief but significant little book outlining some of Dewey's early ideas.

H. Ehlers and G. Lee, *Crucial Issues in Education* (New York: Holt, 1959). An anthology of the critically important problems in American education.

E. Havemann and P. West, *They Went to College* (New York: Harcourt, Brace, 1952). A revealing study of the American college graduate and his attitudes, based on an extensive survey.

B. Meltzer, H. Doby, and P. Smith, *Education in Society: Readings* (New York: Crowell, 1958). Excellent selections on the sociology of education.

A. Nock, *The Theory of Education in the United States* (New York: Harcourt, Brace, 1932). An able defense of the classical view of education.

H. Rickover, *Education and Freedom* (New York: E. P. Dutton, 1959). A controversial critic of American education assesses the American system of education and the demands placed upon it by the atomic age.

I. Scheffler, *Philosophy and Education* (Boston: Allyn and Bacon, 1958). Another anthology devoted to basic questions on the philosophy of education.

C. Scott, *et al.*, *The Great Debate* (Englewood Cliffs, N. J.: Prentice-Hall, 1959). A collection of articles that gives the pros and cons in the great controversy about American education.

I. Thut, *The Story of Education* (New York: McGraw-Hill, 1957). A philosophical study of the history of education.

W. Warner, R. Havighurst, and M. Loeb, *Who Shall be Educated?* (New York: Harper, 1944). An important study of unequal opportunities in American schools.

L. Wilson, *The Academic Man* (New York: Oxford University Press, 1942). On the ways of life of college professors.

P. Woodring, *A Fourth of a Nation* (New York: McGraw-Hill, 1957). A brilliant examination of the "liberal arts-education quarrel" over aims in education.

FICTION AND DRAMA

H. Benjamin, *Saber-Tooth Curriculum* (New York: McGraw-Hill, 1939). An entertaining and humorous skit set in Tijuana that parodies traditional educational methods.

E. Eggleston, *Hoosier Schoolmaster* (New York: Grosset, 1871, and later editions). Entertaining account of the experiences of a pioneer schoolmaster in Indiana.

T. Hughes, *Tom Brown's Schooldays* (New York: St. Martins, 1959). Popular novel of the trials and pranks of a schoolboy at Rugby.

J. Rousseau, *Émile* (New York: E. P. Dutton, 1911; and many other editions). A famous discourse on education, written in the form of a novel.

J. Salinger, *The Catcher in the Rye* (New York: New American Library, 1957). A prematurely old lad of 16 leaves his prep school and goes "underground" in New York City for three days.

FILMS

Cambridge (British Information Service, 1944, 21 min., sound, black and white). Daily life at this famous old British university, including glimpses of lectures, laboratories, libraries, and dining halls.

Clinton and the Law (McGraw-Hill, 1957, 54 min., sound, black and white). A CBS television report on the community's reaction to desegregation of the schools in Clinton, Tennessee.

Community College (Mount San Antonio College, 1952, 30 min., sound, black and white). Background, philosophy, and activity of a typical community college.

Design of American Public Education (McGraw-Hill, 1952, 16 min., sound, black and white). The organizational structure of American education.

How Do American Schools Compare with Yours? (National Educational Television, 1957, 29 min., sound, black and white). A forum of visiting high-school students from other countries on their impressions of American schools.

Princeton (Princeton University, 1949, 28 min., sound, black and white). Insight into life and activity of a two-hundred-year-old American university.

Segregation in Schools (McGraw-Hill, 1955, 28 min., sound, black and white). A number of interviews with citizens of two southern communities illustrating the varied reactions to the Supreme Court's ruling against segregation.

Segregation Question (Almanac, 1955, 15 min., sound, black and white). Debate on segregation by Senator James Eastland of Mississippi and Senator Paul Douglas of Illinois.

CHAPTER NINETEEN

Urban Growth
and Urban Government

*Modern city government—trying
to keep pace with the rapid growth
of the modern city—provides services for, and exerts controls
over, nearly every aspect of urban living.*

Since the

time of the ancients, cities have been the political centers of civilization—seats of rule and misrule. From them national and state adventures in statecraft have been launched. From them great conquests have been planned, victories won, and defeats imposed. Cities have been sites of adventure and intrigue, ambition and yearning, power and decision, success and failure. As centers of power and of human activity they have provided a firm foundation for the governing of larger political units.

Cities, in fact, provide us with our most intimate contact with government. For it is in the city that most of the mundane business of political life runs its course. Cities must provide for street construction and maintenance, garbage and sewage disposal, police and fire protection, health and welfare administration, water and electrical services, libraries and school systems, parks and recreational facilities, as well as housing and planning. The functions of a city are wide and varied, and indeed, not very romantic or exciting. These functions are so close to us and so vitally important, yet so menial, that they sometimes escape our attention.

CITIES AS SEATS OF GOVERNMENT

THE ANCIENT CITY-STATE:
AN IDEAL GOVERNMENTAL TYPE

For the Athenian his city was his state. More than that, his city was at once his country, religion, church, school, playground, and club. In fact, his city was his life. Certainly it was an ideal, an ideal so noble that he believed it the creation of the gods. It was an entire civilization, enveloping the whole of his being and providing him with goals and aspirations. So, too, political institutions in his city were the highest and most noble; politics was an art—the highest art. Citizenship was cherished; to lose it was to lose one's identity, something worse than death itself.

We do not imply that politics in the Greek city-state lacked its seamy side or that Greeks failed to see their political inadequacies. Many were as disgusted with what they saw as we often are, and Plato was one of them. Rather, the Greek saw his city as ideal in the sense that the city was the pinnacle of human association. He could imagine no kind of intimate, shared, responsible life in a community larger than a city-state. If man ever developed an ideal society, the Greek was certain it would be a city-state; the perfect government would be a government of a city-state. All else was barbarian. The Greek was to move far beyond the limits of his city, fight the Persian Empire, and deal with states beyond his immediate world, but his ideals and his goals were always shaped by the moral and political climate of his city-state. When Alexander swooped down on their cities, destroying their civilization and institutions, making them part of a vast empire, the Greeks were left rudderless, like pieces of driftwood in a mighty sea.

Beyond the Adriatic, on the seven hills,

rested the Eternal City—Rome. This small city-state was to become master of a vast empire, capital of the known world. But it was more. It was also a city-state, endowing its citizens with ancient privileges and protecting their status in a world empire. In the simple language of one authority, Rome was a "municipal corporation" that governed a world empire. Certain advantages accrued to the citizen of the city itself. Romans long regarded their system of civil law, the *Ius Civile*, as too sacred to extend to non-Romans and to the far-flung reaches of the empire. And although Rome developed another law—the *Ius Gentium*—for the entire empire, the city and its law were kept in a favored position. The majesty that was Rome's endured for centuries.

A city-state had accommodated itself to an empire. Where the Greek had been able to extend the arc of his civic authority but a few miles beyond the city, the Roman had learned to extend civic authority to points as far distant as Britain on the one side and the Near East on the other.

THE MEDIEVAL CITY:
A STRUGGLE AGAINST CHAOS

The collapse of Rome brought in its train a state of civic anarchy. To the barbarian who overran Rome, the city was a hateful thing to be destroyed. City upon city was sacked and laid waste by successive invasions. In the end the Roman municipal system and its institutions lay in complete collapse.

During the dark times that descended on Europe after the fall of Rome, the pitiful hulks of once majestic cities fell under the protection and custody of a bishop or prince, who became *lord* over the city. Many of these cities were governed by a prior, mayor, or bailiff and a burgher council. With the disappearance of centralized civil authority, the emphasis shifted to defense. The once-

spacious older cities razed their former suburbs, built walls, and restricted their limits in order to have less area to defend. The city-state was thus replaced by a magazine or depot that was crowded on the inside, resembling a very complicated castle, and was surrounded by walls, ramparts, moats, drawbridges, and traps. Cities were fortresses trying to secure themselves from marauding robber bands and feudal lords whose castles often lay within sight of the city itself.

The chaotic political conditions left the urban communities open to attack by brigands, stifled commerce, and stunted population growth. All commerce was reduced to an unbelievable minimum, and each urban community was practically self-supporting, producing its own wood and metal and woolen articles as well as its own wheat in an area close to the city walls. If large cities cannot trade, they die. Hence, in the early Middle Ages, towns and cities were more numerous than significant, and they certainly were not very populous or rich.

The medieval city therefore had very little political significance, certainly little beyond its own walls. The lord, or superior authority, was virtual master over the inhabitants, imposing dues on them, as well as arresting and judging them. With the exception of a few "free" towns (mostly in Italy), and those such as London, Lübeck, Hamburg, and Bremen that later banded together to form the Hanseatic League to protect and foster their trade, the lord's influence extended little beyond the confines of the town itself. His town usually lay within a fief or a kingdom, with fortifications of its own, and enjoyed only such rights and privileges as some distant and exalted superior might grant. Other than collecting dues, the ruler's main function was to obtain and control the raw materials and food supply, the lifeblood of the town. As Professor Ernest Lauer, who carefully studied these towns, pointed out, "The feudal lord knew the lack of food was

The medieval city was a walled, castle-like fortress facing a dangerous and chaotic world to the outside.

death to the burgher [townsman]. Therefore, to attack him here was to attack him where he was most vulnerable." Hence, the "essence of urban politics" in this age was to protect the food supply and the peasants who grew it.

THE MODERN CITY:
A NEW POWER PHENOMENON

As commerce and trade revived and cities such as Venice and Genoa became important commercial capitals, the Middle Ages began to wane, and cities began to acquire more political significance once again. Gradually, princes and other rulers sought to extend their political authority to wider and wider areas. The upshot of it all was the emergence of the modern national state as we know it. Governments with new horizons

and techniques for exercising power took up residence in bustling cities.

The most striking feature of the modern city, of course, is its sheer bulk and power. As we saw earlier, population growth, during the nineteenth century especially, was breathtaking. A huge population will in itself deliver up great power to those who govern it, particularly when it is wedded to industrial and commercial power. For all their undesirable qualities, great industrial centers are the sinews of a strong national state. True, they depend on the countryside for food and raw materials, but they are the heart of national power.

Thus, no great city should be ignored as a center of political power. By sheer weight of population and industrial might, Chicago, New York, and Detroit may exert great influence on national policy, just as do London, Birmingham, and Manchester. Few will dispute the contention that a mayor of New York or Los Angeles is in a more powerful political position than many state governors.

THE LESSONS
OF URBAN POLITICAL HISTORY

The past is often a great teacher of many important lessons that are too frequently ignored. Great historical scholars of our urban past, such as Henri Pirenne, have bequeathed a legacy that deserves our attention. They tell us that cities are the mark of civilization. The classical scholar Richard Livingstone, for example, says that the rise of great cities signals that civilization is on the move. When city-states thrived, civilization flourished; when cities declined during the Middle Ages, civilization reached an impasse and remained rather static until town life revived in the eleventh and twelfth centuries.

THE NINETEENTH-CENTURY REVOLUTION
IN URBAN GOVERNMENT

We have already spoken of the effects of the nineteenth-century revolutions in agriculture and industry and the profound influence they had on urban population growth. The effects on government were equally profound. As the number of people increased, so did the problems of social and economic controls, as well as urban services. Although Los Angeles County performed no more than 31 services in 1859, for instance, by 1935 it was performing nearly 800, including such newcomers as airport maintenance and traffic lighting. The growth was so rapid and the changes so phenomenal that it is a wonder our urban world is not a greater wilderness than it is.

THE INCREASE
IN FUNCTIONS AND SERVICES

Health and Sanitation. Insect and germ brought disease to early American cities and periodically decimated huge portions of the population. The medical profession lent its efforts to the fight, using whatever traditional methods were available. Quarantine, inspection, elimination of swamps, and the abatement of filth all helped in the drive to stamp out disease, but the growth of cities was seemingly outstripping the advances of medical science. During the late nineteenth century, rapid advances in the science of bacteriology, paced by the work of Louis Pasteur and Robert Koch, enabled cities to gain a measure of control over infectious diseases.

Wholesale control of disease, however, does not depend on the medical profession alone. It requires legislation and enforcement. It requires huge outlays of money for public health services, hospitals, laboratories, officials to enforce the regulations, and certainly a sound program for disposal of sewage and waste.

The course of public sanitation in America has been scandalous. In his typically casual and careless way, the American has chosen the easy road by dumping his raw sewage and garbage in the most convenient place— at first usually in the street or in a stream, if there was one nearby. As a result, many streams have become flowing swamps. Not until he or someone else suffers noxious effects does the American rouse himself to do much about it. Then he begins to build sewage disposal plants, treat his sewage, and construct incinerators and sanitary land-fills to receive his garbage. Most feeble of all are the American's efforts to control the dumping of industrial refuse. The industrialist has long dumped with abandon under the guise that requiring him to comply with regulations is un-American and an infringement on the rights guaranteed him by the free-enterprise system.

Yet Americans have performed amazing engineering feats in drainage and disposal when they finally decided that something had to be done. The Chicago drainage system is a monument to sanitary engineering. Slowly the American comes to recognize needs, but only slowly and with reluctance does he move. His sluggishness is testimony to what we called his "luxury of carelessness" in Chapter 9.

Crime and Delinquency. Control of crime makes one of the largest demands on our municipal budgets. As we saw in Chapter 17, few subjects get more attention than crime; almost everybody acknowledges the need to "do something about it." Yet for all his concern about the growth of crime, the American continues to view his law-enforcing officers as impediments to his freedom, attempts to bribe them, calls them "dumb flatfeet," refuses to pay them adequate salaries, and prefers to hire the untrained local boy to the professionally trained expert. The American police profession is fighting a constant uphill battle against public indifference and contempt. Most municipal police departments are plagued with local political influences as well as agents of corruption and graft; they lack sufficient equipment and manpower; training programs are miserably short and notoriously inadequate, and, in many cities under fifty thousand population, simply do not exist.

Probably no place in American life are the inconsistencies in values that we discussed in Chapter 9 so apparent as they are in our attitude toward the law and those who enforce it. We worry about crime, especially juvenile crime; we treat it as if it were in a state of constant crisis; we may juggle statistics to prove to our own satisfaction that crime is increasing by leaps and bounds.

Then we turn about, refuse to support our law-enforcement agencies, do no more than half a job in cleaning up slums and other breeding grounds of crime, and increase our law-enforcement services only grudgingly.

Water Supply. As cities develop, private wells and springs are abandoned for central supplies to guard against contamination. For there is hardly a greater menace to human life than contaminated water. Then, too, the greatly increased risk of fire in the modern city makes necessary a central water source. The problem of maintaining plentiful supplies for large urban centers is becoming more acute as time passes. Underground supplies are playing out in the center of the continent, and coastal cities strike saline beds when they drill. With our streams polluted and our underground supplies dwindling, water may become the most critical (and expensive) industrial and urban resource of the future in many inland areas.

Fire, Smoke, and Smog. Fire was one of the greatest problems with which early American cities had to contend. Its threat led to a steady increase in fire-fighting equipment and manpower, curfews, restrictive legislation, fire codes, comprehensive building regulations, and inspection systems. As early as 1740, a fire in Charles Town, Massachusetts, led to regulations requiring that all future buildings be built of brick or stone and all frame buildings be removed in five years. We have been far more alert to the dangers of fire than to our health perils.

Smoke and smog are more recent problems. They take their toll in slow death. But it is not always slow! In 1948, nineteen residents of Donora, Pennsylvania, died from smog poisoning within a span of a few days.

Housing. In housing, the first government efforts were concerned with inspection and standards for tenement houses. But again, not until the early twentieth century did we begin to attack the problem with vigor. It took another thirty years before effective action was taken against slums and blighted areas, those eyesores of poverty, crime, and disease. Slum clearance, for one thing, involved planning, which many persons considered socialistic.

Transportation and Traffic. Most Americans are acutely aware of the parking and traffic problems that plague urbanites. No one has driven through a large city during the "rush hour" without thinking about them. But few citizens appreciate the amount of organization and human effort that must be expended to furnish adequate transportation for industry, commerce, and the ordinary services provided for citizens. Street construction, traffic lighting, terminals, loading zones, traffic routing, trucking, bus

lines, subways, rails, and airlines must be coordinated. The task is staggering and requires careful and detailed consideration and planning.

Schools and Cultural Features. The maintenance and building of schools is another heavy item in municipal expenditures. In addition, libraries, museums, civic centers, parks, playgrounds, and even symphony orchestras have taken their toll at the city coffers. As one haggard municipal official put it to one of the authors, "There's just no end to what these people want!"

THE PROBLEM OF ORDERLY DEVELOPMENT

If we were slow to meet new urban needs, we were even slower in recognizing the need for orderly development and inte-

The automobile—a boon to the worker, suburbanite, and sightseer but a headache for city officials.

gration of urban functions and services. In the words of the urban historian Arthur Schlesinger, the most impressive feature of urban development was the "lack of unity, balance, planfulness." The logic of organization was sometimes amazing. Water supplies were sometimes placed under the administration of the fire department rather than a separate water agency or the health department, probably because water is used to extinguish fires.

Still very common, even in cities over 50,000 and certainly in the smaller cities, is the lack of any orderly accounting and auditing procedures. This neglect has cost the taxpayers dearly. While we have been worrying about mounting national expenditures, the total annual tribute exacted from us for running our state and local governments has passed almost unnoticed. Yet all state and local government expenditures (including cities, counties, school districts, and all such units) climbed from a little over $5 billion in 1922 to well over $30 billion in 1953, just three decades later. Two-thirds of this amount was spent by the local units alone. With billions involved, poor organization and poor accounting really count. Surprisingly, few among the general public have shown much interest, even those who pay the tax tribute. But, then, state and local affairs are often considered too dull to attract widespread attention.

The lack of planning was unquestionably a most serious impediment to the orderly development of urban areas. Unfortunately, planning was too frequently confused with a planned economy or regimentation and consequently became suspect. Even where planning was introduced, it failed to keep pace with the rushing torrent of urban growth. The results of unplanned cities are still about us in the sprawling, chaotic wilderness of bricks, mortar, and people. We are busy rectifying our neglect. But, for too long, disorder has been the order of the day.

THE CHALLENGE
TO THE DEMOCRATIC FAITH

"As people increased, so sin abounded," moaned John Winthrop just twenty years after the *Mayflower* dropped anchor. What would have been his reaction two and one-half centuries later? The plight of our urban world would very likely have sent him reeling. For sin there surely was. The amount and variety of vice, crime, and political skulduggery infecting our late nineteenth-century cities were spectacular. At no point in our history have our municipal institutions been so depraved.

With great hordes of people being dumped into our urban environs, social maladjustment and delinquency could be expected to abound. They did. Purveyors of sin and commercialized vice stood ready to ply their trades. Shady characters flocked to the city seeking refuge and anonymity from the prying eyes of the outer world. Many came to exploit the greater opportunities for criminal activity afforded by the city. And many native city-dwellers also rose to the occasion. Indeed, the great flood of immigrants and green farm boys coming to the city to seek their fortunes was easy prey for the unsavory elements waiting to receive them.

Not that crime, vice, and lamentable social conditions are any more indigenous to the city than to other types of living, but Americans of the 1880's and 90's were almost totally unprepared for what was being thrust upon them by their rapidly changing social environment. Modern means of identifying criminals, scientific crime detection, and police intercommunication systems were still unknown. Lax methods of law enforcement exacted their toll. In many instances, the immigrant was blamed for the condition, but the truth is that cities with largely native populations had no better records.

Even more serious was the political corruption that hovered over "city hall." Writing in 1891, Andrew D. White charged that "with very few exceptions, the city governments in the United States are the worst in Christendom—the most expensive, the most inefficient, and the most corrupt." Urban governments, one by one, fell into the hands of political bosses and machine politicians who were backed by armies of organized political workers. The job of the political worker (hack) was to garner votes for the machine's candidates by whatever method he could. For his efforts he was repaid by being placed on the city's payroll at the taxpayer's expense. Political hacks herded voters to the polls to vote the straight machine ticket. And when the vote was in doubt, the ballot box would be stuffed with names taken from tombstones or drawn from pure fancy.

In return for votes came favors. If a supporter found himself in jail, his bail would be arranged. Petty offenses would be overlooked. Derelicts along skid row were given bottles of cheap wine in exchange for their votes. Widows with freezing children might receive coal. The hacks arranged employment for those without work. The political machine was at once a welfare bureau, an employment agency, and bailiff. It was all things to all people.

With the assurance that the machine would keep them in office, the political leaders raided the public domain. Corruption and fraud were the order of the day. The exploits of the Tweed Ring, Tammany Hall, and Boss Croker in New York, David Brennan and Big Bill Thompson in Chicago, as well as Cox in Cincinnati and Buckley in San Francisco, are legends in our national history. The main resource of such machines was graft, which assumed a variety of forms. A New York state senator was offered $50,000 if he would vote "right," and an East St. Louis police commissioner bought a $100,000 home on a $6,000 salary. A reform mayor, Hazen Pingree of Detroit,

refused a $50,000 bribe and a trip around the world, which were to be given on the condition that he not veto certain franchises. The philosophy prevailed that every man had his price.

One of the more serious forms of skulduggery involved the letting of contracts. Shrewd and unscrupulous businessmen took advantage of every situation they could turn into a windfall. Professor Schlesinger tells of a business deal in which six well-known capitalists merged some one hundred or more street railway systems from Minneapolis to New England. In addition, they seized some eighty gas and electric franchises between Philadelphia and Minneapolis. Salesmen and large business concerns, many of them supposedly reputable, paid substantial bribes to city officials in order to sell the city their particular type of equipment. It was good business. It meant profits. The business world did not ignore the opportunity to exploit the situation.

Certainly one of the most demoralizing aspects of this urban political mess was the connection government had with crime. In 1890, New York's Tammany executive committee was composed of one murderer and another acquitted of murder, four professional gamblers, five saloon-keepers, four liquor dealers, nine who were either former liquor dealers or sons of liquor dealers, four known hoodlums, three prize fighters, six members of the Tweed gang, and seventeen office-holders. Rackets, thugs, gangs, and known criminals, as well as professional gamblers, operated openly and without fear. They paid their price. It was like paying dues to an organization, except many of these "dues" ran into five and six figures.

Although the American had little esteem for politics and regarded most politicians as "crooked," the decadence surrounding him disturbed him greatly. He was, after all, an idealist with a missionary zeal to give democracy to the world. What he saw developing in his cities was hardly an exportable item.

The American reaction was a resounding one. Out of indignation, frustration, and disgust came a barrage of protest followed by a concerted effort to remedy the situation. "Muckrakers" took to the newspapers, magazines, and bookstands, inveighing against the sin of the cities. Several of these muckrakers immortalized themselves in their works. Such books as Lincoln Steffens' *Auto-biography* and *Shame of the Cities* are read almost as widely today as when they were written. While muckrakers turned to the printed page, others, notably Theodore Roosevelt, Woodrow Wilson, Hazen Pingree, and Newton D. Baker, entered politics as a road to reform. The shame of the cities had now become a national disgrace. Americans looked about for a Moses to lead them out of Sodom and Gomorrah, back to the promised land of "democracy."

MEETING THE CHALLENGE

DOMINATION OF CITY HALL
BY THE STATE CAPITAL

The disreputable state of urban government renewed an interest in the constitutional and legal position of city, town, and village government. About the middle of the nineteenth century, following a decade (1840-50) in which the urban population doubled, Americans began giving serious attention for the first time to the position of cities and other local units in the entire system of government. For one thing, they wondered if cities were alien to the concept of democracy. Certainly the cities seemed so.

Prior to 1840, neither cities nor their position in the framework of government attracted much attention, since the country was largely rural. There had been but a handful of cities at the time the Constitution was adopted, none of them larger than forty-two thousand in population. Since they were not yet a major factor in our national life, cities, like Topsy, "just grew." But with the rapid growth in population during the 1840's, a serious question crossed the American's mind. Were cities separate and distinct governmental units with powers and lives all their own? Or were they merely minor children of the state legislatures that had created them? Did they possess any powers and functions except those given them by the state governments?

These questions have been hotly debated for a century. On the one hand, cities have contended that local self-government is a cornerstone of democracy and local citizens should be freed from the interference of higher governing authorities and permitted to solve their own problems in accordance with what they feel to be their own welfare. After all, if state governments had powers of their own, why not the cities? The local inhabitants should have the right to choose their own government, bestow powers on it, and decide their own fate on those matters that were local in character.

They further claimed that this was a part of our English heritage. It had come to America on the *Mayflower*. Moreover, they argued, local areas were better equipped to meet local problems than were state governments. Since most state legislatures met for only one hundred days or less every two years, they were ill-equipped to deal with any emergencies that might arise in urban communities.

On the other hand, opponents of these arguments contended that cities had been created by and received their powers from a higher political authority. This position had a long historical precedent stemming

A Massachusetts town meeting. In a large city it is impossible for citizens to participate as directly in matters of local government as they often do in smaller communities.

from England and the American colonial experience. With the power to incorporate and breathe life into a city went the power to grant special rights, functions, powers, and privileges. In colonial times, for example, the power to levy direct taxes could not be exercised by cities in most of the colonies without a special grant of taxing power from the colonial legislature. It was clear, too, that a number of state constitutions written before 1850 had failed to grant cities and towns local powers of their own. Yet, despite all the historical evidence against them, the partisans of "Home Rule" fought valiantly. They had a strong defender, too, in the eminent Justice Cooley of Michigan, whose decisions restricted state powers over local governments.

The whole question came to a head in 1868, when a young physician and judge of the Iowa Supreme Court, John F. Dillon, delivered a court decision that became the basis for the present legal and constitutional position of city governments. His famous statement, known as the "Dillon Rule," has been cited from thousands of court benches since.

Municipal corporations owe their origins to and derive their powers and rights wholly from the legislature. It breathes into them the breath of life, without which they cannot exist. As it creates, so it may destroy. If it may destroy, it may abridge and control. Unless there is some constitutional limitation on the right, the legislature might, by a single act, if we could suppose it capable of so great a folly and so great a wrong, sweep from existence all the municipal corporations in the state, and the *corporation* could not prevent it. We know of no limitation on this right so far as the corporations themselves are concerned. They are, so to phrase it, mere *tenants at will* of the legislature.*

These were strong words well said. Cities had no life and no powers beyond those granted them by their state legislature. They could not act unless the legislature consented. If a commissioner wanted to tear down a partition in city hall, he had best check to see if the state legislature had given him the appropriate power.

Dillon was later appointed to the Federal District Court where he continued to expound his doctrine. In 1872, he published his world-renowned, five-volume edition of *Commentaries on the Law of Municipal Corporations*, which became probably the most authoritative statement on municipal law in the United States. In it he repeated

---

* *Clinton* vs. *Cedar Rapids & Missouri Basin R.R. Co.*, 24 *Iowa* 455 at 475 (1868).

337

his famous stand. If legislatures denied cities the power to elect mayors, they could not elect mayors. Legislatures could set salaries of city officials. In fact, unless the constitution of the state prohibited legislative interference, cities were at the complete mercy of their creator.

Advocates of the self-government idea did not give up easily, however. Was not a city a corporation and given its charter by a state legislature like any private corporation, such as a railroad? If a private corporate charter could not be tampered with by a state government, did not cities have similar immunity? The court justices simply said, "No!" To their way of thinking, a city performed governmental functions and was, hence, unlike a private company, although both were chartered.

Finally, cities sought protection under the "due process" clause of the national Constitution. As corporations, they claimed that they should be treated the same way other corporations were treated—as legal "persons" with the protections given persons under the law. It was argued that they should be free of state interference and given full rights under the United States Constitution. Cities were thus turning to the national government to protect them against their own states! The argument was that the right to local self-government was like an individual's right of free speech or trial by jury. It was a right that the states, because of the due process clause of the Fourteenth Amendment, could not deny them. But case after case met defeat in the Supreme Court. In 1922, when citizens of Trenton, New Jersey, contended that they should exercise control over their water supply without state interference, the court invoked the Dillon Rule and denied the claim. Champions of home rule went home to sorrow over their dead hopes, only to return about ten years later to hear Justice Cardozo deliver the final pronouncement: A municipal corporation has "no privileges or immunities under the federal Constitution which it may invoke in opposition to the will of its creator [state legislature]." The power of state legislatures over cities was thus "absolute." The argument was ended. State capitals dominated city halls.

THE ATTEMPT TO INVOKE THE POWER OF STATE GOVERNMENT

If the state government was dominant, then why not use the strong arm of the state against the evil-doers of the city? Many Americans had already turned to their state legislatures to clean the wickedness out of their cities. The Missouri legislature, for example, withdrew the police departments from control of the local governments of St. Louis, St. Joseph, and Kansas City and placed them under a state board appointed by the governor of Missouri.

But state officials can be corrupt, too. Political machines were able to elect their own men to the state legislatures where they could protect the interests of the machine and extend its influence. Many state legislators also had their price. Machines could simply buy them off. Racketeers were just as shabby in the state capital building as they were in city hall.

THE SEARCH FOR NEW FORMS OF GOVERNMENT

Why not attempt to change the form of city government? Nothing is more typical of the American than his tendency to tinker with the mechanics of government. When he finds something is not running smoothly, his first reaction is to try to fix it. It seldom occurs to him that the type of person he puts in the government may have more to do with its weaknesses than the structure itself. The people of Kansas City, for instance, lost patience with the excesses of their political machine during the 1920's. Setting out to change matters, they adopted the city-manager form of government and promptly went back to sleep. They woke up in 1940 to find themselves the victims of one of the most vicious political organizations in the annals of American history. This time they decided that something other than a change in form was necessary.

Many of those who were disturbed about the deplorable condition of their cities set out to find new forms of city government. A tidal wave that struck Galveston, Texas, in September, 1900, gave the people of the city the opportunity to try one new form—the *commission form*. With over six thousand dead and the city virtually destroyed, Galveston was faced with chaos. The old government, consisting of a mayor and twelve aldermen, failed in the face of the crisis. The government was then turned over to an organization of businessmen, the Deepwater Committee, which both legislated and administered the departments of the city government. The huge success of this experiment soon led other cities to adopt a similar form of government.

Essentially, the commission form calls for the election of a number of commissioners, usually five, by the people. They may be elected by separate districts or by the city as a whole. All serve as a legislature (city council) to pass the city's laws and ordinances. Each commissioner manages one of the city departments. One will serve as mayor, in charge of public affairs, another will administer the street department, and others will be responsible for police and fire, finance, and public works.

It was Des Moines, Iowa, however, that advertised the system. James Berryhill, a Des Moines attorney, studied the plan while on a business trip to Texas in 1905. When he returned he induced the Iowa legislature to offer cities the option of choosing a commission form of government. The "Des Moines Plan" called for measures to overcome city corruption. First, commissioners were to be popularly elected without party designation. Each man would run for office on his own. Since political machines were ordinarily tied to some political party, sponsors of the new plan hoped it would break their power. Second, the plan gave citizens power to initiate petitions to *recall* any local official before his term had expired. If a required number of people signed a petition, the people would then vote on whether the official should be removed. Finally, the plan gave the people similar powers to pass their own laws by petition and ballot. The *initiative* permitted citizens to draft laws and present them to the voters for approval. The *referendum* gave people a like power to repeal laws passed by the commission. All these features were included in the Des Moines Plan. Its fame spread, and by 1917, over five hundred cities were being administered under the commission form of government.

The plan did not live up to expectations, however. A commissioner is susceptible to corruption, too. Commissions also can be infiltrated by machine men. Recall proved a farce. Few officials were recalled, and when they were, the people often displayed a strange tendency to re-elect them. The people also proved less able at legislating than the men they elected to do the job.

Commissions are also wasteful. The group is a "society of equals"; that is, all have equal powers. Hence, when one man wants an appropriation of money, all the others may consent because they want him to vote for their appropriations. Besides, the people who run the departments and enforce the ordinances are the same people who pass the ordinances. The commission plan proved a disappointment in many instances.

A second remedy to which ardent advocates of municipal reform pinned their hopes was the *city-manager plan*. Originating in

Staunton, Virginia, in 1907, this plan has been much more successful than the commission plan in cleaning up the shameful mess into which many cities had fallen. Yet Kansas City, Missouri, had a city-manager system that was tightly controlled by the infamous Pendergast machine.

Although the city-manager system has many variations, its fundamentals are simple. A city council (legislature) is elected by the people. This council passes the laws and ordinances for the city and also selects a trained manager to handle the city's administration and enforce the law. The manager, in turn, appoints and removes his own administrators (e.g., the police chief, fire chief, finance officer, city attorney, and other officials), enforces the law, and administers the city as long as he pleases the council. If at any time they decide his work is not satisfactory, they are free to dismiss him and hire another.

Defenders of the system emphasize the advantage of placing government in the hands of a trained expert with no political connections. They proudly maintain that it puts the city on a "business-like" basis. Opponents claim, on the other hand, that it is undemocratic to concentrate power in the hands of a single person—the manager— especially when he is not elected. They cry "dictatorship!" The defenders waste no time in retorting that an elected council can fire him at any time; that is, the manager and his department heads are still subject to the control of the elected representatives of the people. What is more, these elected representatives pass all the laws and the manager must depend on them for funds as well as for authorization to act.

The manager system has been adopted in more than one thousand American cities. No city larger than Cincinnati, however, has given the plan an extensive trial. Large cities prefer the *strong mayor-council* system, wherein a popularly elected mayor

serves for a fixed period of time, appoints and removes the department heads of the city government, enforces the law, and manages city affairs. He is also given a veto power over the laws and ordinances passed by an elected council. This system is a revision of the *weak mayor-council* system, which has been the most widely used form of city government. Here the mayor is elected but denied most of the powers usually given an executive official. He has no veto power over laws and ordinances passed by the council. Most of the members of his administration are either elected by the people or appointed by the council or himself, but he can seldom remove them without the council's consent. If an executive cannot remove his subordinates, he is powerless to direct policy. In business or government such an officer is largely a figurehead. Underlings can ignore his directives or construe them according to their own preferences. They have nothing to fear since he cannot remove them. The weak-mayor form invites corruption and usually leaves the citizen without any way of knowing who is to blame when things go wrong.

Undeniably, all the efforts to arrive at new governmental forms were helpful in overcoming some of the dilemmas in local politics. New forms alone, however, will not solve more than a few problems, and many of those will be only partially solved.

CURE THE ILLS OF DEMOCRACY WITH MORE DEMOCRACY

Many advocates of reform turned to the idea of "democracy" itself for solutions. Men like the journalist Herbert Croly were convinced that our system needed a greater dose of democracy. More control by the people themselves was the political antibiotic we should inject into our political system. These reformers would tinker with the mechanics of government in order to ensure the voter of greater control of his government.

Among their recommendations was the adoption of the *initiative, referendum,* and *recall* that we discussed earlier in this chapter. Many of these apostles of more democracy also advocated the use of a primary system for the nomination of party candidates. Let the voters select the candidates the party presents at election time. Give the political party to the people!

These recommendations were widely adopted, with a variety of results. We have already mentioned the failures of the initiative, referendum, and recall. The primary system has run afoul of voter apathy. As Professor K. H. Porter, a keen observer of the electoral system, says, "The primary is a deserted primary." Outside the South, where a single-party system turns primaries into the "real elections," most people do not vote in primaries. Consequently, party-endorsed candidates usually win rather easily because party stalwarts do make it a point to vote. The primary system has therefore not resulted in greater popular control of the party processes.

One of the most radical suggestions made by a few reformers was to have practically all officials from president of the United States to street-sweeper elected. But some ballots are already so long and so full of names that the average voter fails to recognize most of the names listed, let alone what

the candidates stand for. The long ballot, or "jungle ballot," does nothing but confuse most voters, who do not have time to run down the necessary qualifications for a hundred or more offices as well as dig up the necessary information to assess the personal qualifications of each candidate. Yet many Texas cities have gone so far as to elect police chiefs.

THE SEARCH FOR EFFICIENCY

Several Americans who studied and toured Europe during the early part of the present century were impressed by the apparent efficiency, honesty, and incorruptibility of government and administration in Germany. They came home storming. Germany, seemingly, had achieved under an unquestionably harsh authoritarian system what democratic America apparently could not. They asserted that Americans must make their system more efficient. They recommended that all legislative and policy-making functions be kept under the control of popularly elected officials while everything else be made efficient by turning the functions over to appointed officials who were trained for their specific tasks. Thus, members of city councils should be elected, but all those who enforced and administered the law should be experts, and therefore appointed. In Wisconsin, experts were soon running many phases of state and local gov-

Here, in one of thousands of polling places in America, citizens exercise their privilege of selecting government officials. The great majority of Americans, however, do not bother to vote in local elections.

ernment. Several of these champions of the "expert" soon joined hands with those who advocated adoption of the city-manager system.

REGIONALISM
AND DEMOCRATIC PLANNING

Many scholars and professional administrators have recommended that we overcome our loyalty to boundary lines and face the facts of our social and political existence. Not as any cure, but rather as an aid, they suggest better and more realistic definition of urban areas to facilitate better law enforcement and more efficient handling of services. For example, the area from Milwaukee, Wisconsin, to Michigan City, Indiana, including all of Chicago and its suburbs, is really a single urban area with common problems. Yet it is severed by two state lines and a multitude of city, town, and village boundaries. Although cooperation exists on some matters, the water system in the Chicago area for instance, the laws of three states conflict in many places, towns and cities often fight among themselves, and the tax load is distributed in such a tangled and incomprehensible fashion that it would challenge a hundred electronic computers to decipher it all.

Such areas, the argument runs, should be a single metropolitan unit. Why? For one thing, better services could be furnished at a lower rate, and certainly law enforcement could be made more uniform. Advances in this direction have been made, but only a few. Most police, when chasing criminals, are no longer required to stop at the boundary of their state or city and shoot from there. But beyond such elementary features as this one, the forest of overlapping functions and tangled jurisdiction has scarcely been penetrated.

THE PRESENT URBAN DILEMMA

THE CITY:
A STEPCHILD OF THE STATE LEGISLATURE

The Dillon Rule has left cities securely in the control of state legislatures. A few states, Missouri, for example, have granted cities some separate powers of local self-government in their state constitutions, but such states are few in number and the powers granted are restricted. Cities must still run to their state legislatures for nearly everything they need. Legislatures could, if they so decided, give cities broader powers, but the opposite has more often been true.

Most state legislatures are not representative of the actual population. Divided into districts at a time when the ratio of farmers to city-dwellers was much higher than it is now, state legislators from the farm areas have successfully resisted attempts to change the districting to conform to the growth of cities. Hence, many state legislatures are still dominated by rural interests, even though the urban population far exceeds the rural. Illinois and New York are prime examples. As a result, cities are victimized by unfair and inadequate legislation. Many rural legislators fail to understand urban needs. Certainly, rural needs are given priority. One state legislature spent almost an entire session deciding whether to legalize the sale of colored oleomargarine and neglected to empower the cities of the state to issue bonds for street improvements.

Furthermore, about three-fourths of the state legislatures meet only once every two years, and then for a limited time (thirty-six to one hundred and twenty days in many instances). Crisis after crisis can hamstring cities in the meantime, and does each year.

An average of 40 to 50 per cent of all state legislators are serving their first term each session with no previous legislative experience of any kind. And even those who have experience cannot devote much time to legislative tasks and issues because they must depend on their business or profession for their living. The plight of cities under such conditions is obvious.

INSUFFICIENT FUNDS AND TAX SOURCES

Equally serious is the constant drain on city finances. For years cities have depended on the property tax for most of their revenue, but this source grows steadily less adequate as costs rise and public demand for services increases. Property taxes have become almost unbearable in many areas, and the situation is further aggravated by inequalities in the property-tax assessments. Buildings assessed at one time may be assigned a much lower value than structures assessed at another time. Houses in one section of town may be given a valuation far below houses of similar quality and location in another part of town. Locally elected assessors are sometimes incompetent, favor their friends, and deliberately assess many properties at a low figure to obtain votes. Furthermore, many state laws and constitutions limit the amount a city may tax and the amount of indebtedness a city may accumulate. A city may reach these limitations and still find that it needs a new sewer or school.

What about new sources of taxation? Although most states have been kind enough to leave almost all the revenue from property taxes to the local units, and use other sources for state purposes, both the state and national governments have exploited the newer and more lucrative sources of taxation (e.g., personal income and sales taxes). It becomes difficult, therefore, for city officials to find new money to perform their functions. Phila-

delphia and a few other cities have an income tax; a modest number have sales taxes. But legislatures are reluctant to empower cities to use these taxes, and when they do, the cities themselves often are unwilling to use them. Some of the load, of course, has been relieved over the years by direct grants of money from the national and state governments. State governments have been unusually generous in this regard, but their ability to increase such funds to meet the mounting costs and demands on cities is fast weakening. Cities, like most people, are having trouble making ends meet.

PUBLIC APATHY

The symbols of city government, including the buildings in which we house those governments, hardly inspire confidence and pride in the citizen. Nor do the daily chores and routine affairs in city hall excite much interest; not, that is, unless there is a scandal. How many boys and girls look forward to a career as a city official? City elections, more frequently than not, are ignored by the voter. City-council meetings are generally open to the public, but about the only people who ever show up regularly are the janitor, or at most, a newspaper reporter or two. When some issue does arise, citizens are apt to feel woefully uninformed. Ask any urbanite to tick off a few of the problems currently facing his officials in city hall! "That government which is closest to the people is the best government." We are told it and we believe it. But is it? Apathy has exacted its toll.

UNPLANNED CONFUSION

The indifference and lack of attention our fathers and grandfathers gave to the orderly development of cities is now coming home to roost. The bulky sprawling mazes of men, steel, and cement that have grown up carelessly, haphazardly, and without much thought or direction must now be reorganized and redeveloped at great cost. A great deal already has been done but much more still remains. Much of the difficulty is aggravated by our own whims and fancies. We will tear down buildings and widen streets year in and year out at huge costs, but no one will place a limit on the size of an automobile. Amazingly, there are still some large cities that have no land-use plan, give little support to city planning, and have few adequate zoning ordinances on their books. City governments, moveover, are constantly subjected to pressure by groups who resist redevelopment and slum clearance out of fear of tax increases or the loss of income from lucrative rental properties in blighted areas.

RURBANIZATION

A more recent problem is the growing conflict resulting from the blending of urban and rural cultures. When a country boy or girl comes to the city, he brings with him a set of values and a way of life that often conflicts with city ways. Born in a town where everyone knew everyone else and where neighborliness and intimate contacts operated to keep him from overstepping the bounds of morality, the country boy may soon be overwhelmed by the city. Lost in a sea of humanity, he may grow wayward and soon become a social problem. The sociologist Pitirim Sorokin maintains that a great deal of the disorganization in the urban family—the startling increase in criminality, social disorders, political instability, and class strife—stems partly from the failure of migrants to adjust to new and unfamiliar urban ways of life.

REVOLUTION IN URBAN POLITICS

Quite obviously the urban-industrial revolution has precipitated a revolution in men's attitudes and beliefs. If Sorokin's

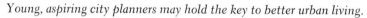
Young, aspiring city planners may hold the key to better urban living.

analysis stands up, and there is every indication to believe that it does, then we have undergone a revolution in men's minds. This has, in turn, engendered a revolution in urban politics. The typically small urban governments of a century ago were ill-fitted to meet the needs of exploding metropolitan centers. Conducted on a rather intimate and personal plane with no more than a few basic functions to perform, our earlier town and small-city governments could afford the luxury of slow change. But in a modern city where attitudes change rapidly, where the appearance of the landscape is transformed almost overnight, and where city officials do not know the vast majority of their constituents personally, unwillingness to change may be disastrous. Yet, even when we accept change willingly, the faces of our cities are altered so rapidly and so dramatically that no sooner are problems noticed and some solutions proposed than new and more serious ones have arisen. Small wonder, then, that our urban officials have been so harried and unable to meet rapidly changing conditions. Rather than condemn them, possibly we should commend them for doing as well as they have in the face of mounting difficulty. After all, theirs is a thankless and difficult task.

SOME WORDS OF SUMMARY

Flourishing cities are the mark of civilization; and conversely, the decline of the city brings a corresponding decline in civilization. The rise of the modern city has demonstrated that huge populations vested with industrial and commercial strength deliver up great political power to their rulers.

A spectacular rise in population during the nineteenth century led to a vast increase in urban government functions and services. Change and development in the fields of health, sanitation, housing, planning, and urban renewal were somewhat slow, while control of crime and delinquency lacked adequate public support. In recent years smoke and smog control, schools, traffic, and transportation have joined such matters as water supply and fire protection as urgent urban problems.

During the urban revolution America's cities grew haphazardly, without any set plan or scheme. The very idea of planning was alien to most Americans. This neglect, combined with rapid growth and a breakdown in social control, soon turned American cities into centers of vice, crime, and political corruption, which in turn prompted a political reaction in the guise of numerous reform efforts.

As early as 1850, questions about the place of urban government in the legal and constitutional framework of our federal system were being debated in the courts. Supporters of local self-government were thwarted by the Dillon Rule, a judicial interpretation which stated that cities were mere creatures of the state legislatures from which they derived all their powers. Despite their power over cities, legislatures failed to clean up the urban mess.

Many reformers turned to the popular American pastime of tinkering with the mechanics of government. While some saw great promise in new forms of city government (commission, city-manager, and strong-mayor forms), many others endorsed such measures as the initiative, referendum, recall, non-partisan elections, and direct primaries to ensure wider citizen participation and control in urban government. Travelers abroad came home impressed by the efficiency and honesty of German government and urged that the American system be reinvigorated. A more recent movement suggests that state and municipal boundary lines be ignored and that entire metropolitan areas be governed as single units.

Except for a small number of cities that have been given a modest amount of "home rule" (local self-government), most cities still remain under the thumb of state legislatures too frequently dominated by representatives from rural districts who fail to understand urban problems. Because of rising costs, dependence on the property tax, and general unavailability of new sources of revenue, the modern city is growing steadily less able to meet demands for expanded services. This condition is further aggravated by public apathy, a continued unwillingness to plan, and the problems created by rurbanization.

FURTHER ROADS TO LEARNING

GENERAL ACCOUNTS

A. de Tocqueville, *Democracy in America*. Two vols. (New York: Knopf, Vintage Books, 1954). Considered by many to be the finest analysis of American local government problems ever written.

R. Fisher, ed., *The Metropolis in Modern Life* (Garden City, N.Y.: Doubleday, 1955). An excellent series of essays on the city, some of which treat the political and legal aspects.

E. Griffith, *Current Municipal Problems* (Boston: Houghton Mifflin, 1933). An excellent discussion of city government problems by a leading authority on municipal government.

————, *History of American City Government*. Three vols. (New York: Oxford University Press, 1938). A statement of the early development of American city government written from an historical viewpoint. Also see Griffith's *The Modern Development of City Government in the United Kingdom and the United States* (London: Oxford University Press, 1927).

C. Kneier, *City Government in the United States* (New York: Harper, 1939, and later editions). A very readable, authentic text.

L. Mumford, *Culture of Cities* (New York: Harcourt, Brace, 1938). A rare contribution to the understanding of urban cultural influences.

S. Riemer, *The Modern City* (Englewood Cliffs, N.J.: Prentice-Hall, 1952). A more recent sociological assessment of modern cities.

A. Schlesinger, *The Rise of the City* (New York: Macmillan, 1933). The classic history of American cities and their emergence in the nineteenth century.

SPECIAL STUDIES

J. Addams, *The Spirit of Youth and the City Streets* (New York: Macmillan, 1912). One of the classics on the social plight of American cities at the turn of the century.

M. Cooke, *Our Cities Awake* (Garden City, N.Y.: Doubleday, Page, 1918). A statement by an avid believer in America's mission to give democracy to the world.

H. Croly, *The Promise of American Life* (New York: Macmillan, 1911). By a leading journalist who firmly believed that the ills of democracy must be cured by more democracy.

H. Farmer, *The Legislative Process in Alabama: Local and Private Legislation*, No. 16 (Tuscaloosa, Alabama: University of Alabama, 1944). One of the best analyses of the methods used by a state legislature to victimize cities.

D. Lynch, *Boss Tweed* (New York: Boni and Liveright, 1927). A comprehensive and interesting treatment of the Tweed Ring in New York City.

———, *Criminals and Politicians* (New York: Macmillan, 1932). Analysis of the connections between big-time gangsters and big-city politicians.

H. McBain, *The Law and Practice of Municipal Home Rule* (New York: Columbia University Press, 1916). Legal and historical analysis of the idea of local self-government in American cities.

R. Mott, *Home Rule for American Cities* (Chicago: American Municipal Association, 1949). A very brief and readable tract on the advantages of Home Rule.

S. Orth, *The Boss and the Machine* (New Haven: Yale University Press, 1919, and later editions). One of the best analyses of the early American political machines.

B. Pierce, *History of Chicago*. Three vols. (New York: Knopf, 1940-57). An informative and well-packed history of one of America's buzzing, growing urban centers.

H. Pirenne, *Medieval Cities* (Garden City, N.Y.: Doubleday, Anchor Books, 1956). The most thorough historical analysis of medieval cities.

J. Riis, *How the Other Half Lives* (New York: Scribner, 1903). An analysis of urban slums and poverty by a muckraker.

L. Steffens, *Shame of the Cities* (New York: Doubleday, Page, 1904); and also his *Autobiography* (New York: Harcourt, Brace, 1931). Two of the finest works on the conditions of the cities at the turn of the twentieth century.

H. Stone, *et. al.*, *City Manager Government in the United States* (Chicago: Public Administration Service, 1940). A good analysis of the first twenty-five years of city-manager systems by a sympathetic observer.

H. Zink, *City Bosses in the United States* (Durham, N.C.: Duke University Press, 1930). Another excellent analysis of "Bossism."

FICTION AND DRAMA

B. Fleming, *Colonel Effingham's Raid* (New York: Duell, Sloan and Pearce, 1943). A satire on southern politics in which a retired army officer leads a municipal reform movement.

A. Langley, *A Lion Is in the Streets* (New York: McGraw-Hill, 1945). An illiterate, but gifted, oratorical genius is politically successful through skillful skulduggery.

E. O'Connor, *The Last Hurrah* (New York: Bantam Books, 1957). An old-style boss (undoubtedly former Mayor James Curley of Boston) is pictured sympathetically in his final campaign.

R. Warren, *All the King's Men* (New York: Bantam Books, 1957). A country lawyer in the South (probably Huey Long) becomes a local dictator through demagoguery.

FILMS

Community Responsibilities (National Film Board of Canada, 1955, 11 min., sound, black and white). Where do one's community responsibilities begin and those to himself leave off?

It Happened on Yesler's Hill (Seattle Housing Authority, 1949, 20 min., silent, color). The results of a government-sponsored slum-clearance program in Seattle.

Local Government (Encyclopaedia Britannica Films, 1953, 49 frames, color). Portrays the various ways of electing local officials and illustrates their duties.

The Tiger's Tail (DuPont, 1953, 26 min., sound, black and white). The story of how Tom Nast, Harper's cartoonist, helped break the Tweed Ring and reformed New York City.

The Urban-Industrial Impact on Personality

The impersonality and aloofness of urban life
often impede the satisfaction of basic desires and create
serious personality problems for many persons.

As a center

of activity, change, and unrest, the city has become an object of great controversy, condemned for its failures and praised for its accomplishments. Those who love the city point to its many social, cultural, and commercial advantages, while critics point to the slums, congestion, noise, crime, dirt, and the hurried tempo of city living. The many changes wrought by our new urban way of life are regarded by many as a mixed blessing. Nevertheless, no matter how hard we try, we cannot escape their influence. The impact of urban change is felt in the most remote and secluded reaches of rural life. To escape it is impossible, for ours is an urban civilization.

As more and more people come under the influence of urban-industrial ways, what happens to the human personality? Are the demands of urban-industrial living worth the rewards? Will we become a nation of mental misfits because of the stresses and strains that daily city living imposes? Or, will the opportunities and advantages the city offers stimulate us to ever greater achievements and bestow on us ever richer rewards? In the highly organized urban-industrial economy are we to become "mechanical men," responding to given stimuli in an unthinking, almost automatic way? Or, will educational, recreational, and cultural opportunities be enough to nourish and protect individual initiative, freedom, and self-expression? Can highly specialized organizations and facilities provide the balance and satisfaction so essential to mental health? Or, will city folks ultimately have to flee the city to preserve their sanity?

Such are the questions with which social scientists, social workers, and psychiatrists have long been concerned. We have already traced in the preceding chapters many of the changes that have occurred within the urban-industrial setting as well as some of their implications. Our task here will be to examine ways in which the new society has affected the human personality, whether for better or worse. As we have already indicated (see Chapter 4), personality is the sum total of a person's attitudes, values, habits, mentality, and emotions. Each personality is unique because of its distinctive combination of traits, but at the same time we are alike because of our similar experiences and our common tendencies toward growth and development.

BASIC WISHES AND THE PERSONALITY

In the continual process of growth and adjustment, all people constantly strive to satisfy basic desires. Years ago a pioneer researcher in personality, W. I. Thomas, asserted that all persons seek to satisfy four kinds of fundamental wish: *for new experience, for security, for intimate response,* and *for personal recognition.* These basic types cover the realm of possible wishes about as successfully as more recent attempts at classification, and each of our specific desires and aspirations can be classified under these headings.

Authorities generally agree that satisfaction of basic wishes is essential to a "healthy" or "balanced" personality, and that the various elements of personality are in a state of equilibrium. Although balance is always relative, a balanced personality permits the individual to adapt to challenging situations and to meet the problems of daily living. Social adjustment is therefore made easier when we are able to maintain a balanced personality.

PERSONALITY AND A NEW ENVIRONMENT

Many personality needs were satisfied with relative ease in an agrarian society, where aspirations and daily social adjustments were comparatively uncomplicated. Such a society changed very slowly, and expected behavior was so standardized and clear-cut that severe and conflicting demands on the personality were rare. Close-knit family ties augmented by those of the church and local community helped satisfy basic desires for security and intimate response. New experiences were far less common than in our fast-moving society, but the desires for recognition or public acclaim were met largely by local citizens, family, and friends.

Frustration of wishes is more likely to occur in the modern industrial city, however, where people have the same fundamental needs and desires as those living in an agrarian society. Although the opportunity for new experiences may be greater in the city, a person may be so busy just "making a living" that he is unable to take advantage of them. The impersonality and aloofness of city life also frustrate our search for security and intimate response. A person may have a good job, live in a well-kept home, and enjoy the luxuries of modern labor-saving conveniences and yet feel very insecure. He can lose his job, his mortgage can be foreclosed, and the finance company can repossess his appliances. A person's desire for intimate response may be difficult to satisfy even within the family. Too often the home becomes a mere "center of operations" for members of a family, each of whom pursues a life of his own. Many families do not even eat together. Outside the home, personal recognition is frequently done up in extravagant fashion by public relations experts through news agencies and banquets "in honor of" that follow cold, impersonal lines. Impersonality thus permeates urban life, impedes the fulfillment of our basic wishes, and constantly challenges our efforts to maintain a balanced personality.

IMPERSONALITY OF MODERN LIFE

A picture in the news a few years ago showed a man carefully stepping over a prostrate human form on the steps of a subway station in New York City. Before the photo was taken, several other people had passed by, walking around or stepping over the still figure, and none had stopped to see whether the helpless man was dead or alive.

This sort of incident epitomizes the impersonality of modern urban life, where men are frequently treated as indifferently as non-human objects. No one seemed to care what happened to the crumpled figure on the subway steps. Any sense of warmth and feeling for one's fellows had apparently disappeared.

This impersonality in our relationship extends through both formal and informal associations. At school, at work, and at play, and on the streets, in stores, and in churches, the pattern of impersonality runs constant.

Very often it is concealed behind a cloak of superficial friendliness, as when a clerk in a store greets a customer, a boss speaks with his employees, or a host introduces a guest. We are not suggesting that people never display any sincere friendliness toward one another—it is just that sometimes friendliness is hard to find. This is why such expressions as "alone in the midst of millions" or "the lonely crowd" are so meaningful. Loneliness is thus one of the major consequences of this tendency toward impersonal relationships.

Impersonality in the city is rooted in the familiar zoning of residential, service, business, and industrial areas. As a rule these areas embrace fairly distinct sections of the city and are connected only in a "non-social" way. Each area and the service it provides are necessary or advantageous to the others, but none of the functions that link them together requires intimacy. Residents depend on various service establishments and retail businesses for food, travel, entertainment, and clothing. Retail stores depend on residential areas for their customers and indus-

trial areas for their commodities. Industrial areas depend on wholesale and retail houses as outlets for their produce and on residential areas for their labor force. This web of interdependence is thus vital to the welfare and even the survival of each constituent part. But relationships here are only a mutual necessity and usually lack the kind of warmth and intimacy that characterized relations between the farmer and his village storekeeper a century ago. A person's desire for intimate response is being frustrated, yet at the same time he derives a certain feeling of security from his city and from the fact that everything and everyone around him are bound together in a highly complex web of interdependent parts.

Sheer size, in fact, often affects a person's view of himself and his significance. He may be dwarfed and intimidated by the masses of people always at his elbow. On the streets, at work, at the ball game, or on a bus, he is only one among many. With so many other people around him wearing approximately the same kinds of clothes, living in similar houses, reading the same newspapers,

The big-city mission, a refuge for men "alone in the midst of millions."

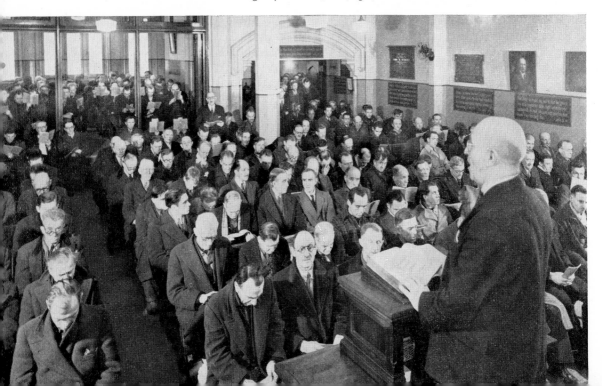

and watching the same television programs, he may feel insignificant and unimportant. Other people fail to recognize his unique qualities. Thus, our urban environment standardizes our behavior and personalities and depersonalizes our relations with others.

After all, what difference does it make which one of several thousand similar people you associate with? City living is conducive therefore to fluid relations which need not be very personal. The urbanite's personality needs, therefore, often go unsatisfied.

ROUTINES OF URBAN LIFE

ORGANIZATIONAL ROUTINES

The impersonality of our mutual relationships is reinforced by subjecting everyone in an urban-industrial environment to a considerable amount of organizational routine. In school the pupil learns the daily routine of reporting at the first bell, pausing for recess and lunch at the designated hours, and finally leaving the classroom after the last bell. In class he is expected to be quiet, respectful to his teacher, his principal, and his classmates. Throughout the day he has routine assignments to execute. He has a grade average to maintain and a diploma to win! Such conditioning experiences are an important prelude to adult work routines.

When he enters the workaday world, he becomes even more conditioned to established, even rhythmic, routines. He "punches in" each day, takes his coffee breaks and lunch period at stated intervals, and quits work when the whistle blows. He is expected to demonstrate a minimum level of skill for the job assigned, obey his superiors, uphold company rules, and cooperate with his fellow workers.

In many urban jobs the necessary routines of organizational life are multiplied by mechanization, and habitual routines are especially rhythmic on the assembly line and on automated jobs. Only policy-makers, administrators, engineers, and highly skilled workers escape the full impact of mechanized routines. As a result, the responsibility of the individual worker is reduced; there is

less need for creative talent on most jobs; the sphere of each individual's operations becomes smaller as specialization increases. Turning a switch on and off all day, either to operate an elevator or a punch press, provides little mental or emotional stimulation. Hence, mechanization increases the regularity of an already rhythmic organizational routine.

LEISURE-TIME ROUTINES

A vast assortment of activities is made available to city people to help fill their nonworking hours, some ostensibly designed to offset the humdrum effects of work routines. Why can't we just loaf in our spare time? Mainly, of course, it is because we are besieged with the middle-class philosophy of being busy, meeting social and civic obligations, improving ourselves, doing something creative. We even boast about how busy we are, so strong is the feeling that this is a virtue in urban society. Certainly there is something wrong with anyone who has nothing to do!

But the urbanite falls victim to the habit of routine as he joins or plays an active role in organization after organization during his leisure time. There are business and civic clubs, fraternal orders, labor unions, athletic clubs, veterans' groups, country clubs, church groups, and committees to rezone school districts, raise funds for a statue to place in front of the court house, change taxes, or plant a tree on main street. Many a group may be joined and most of them make it easy with their eager membership committees. Once a member, the urbanite falls into organizational routine similar to what he has done all day long. Each group has its rules and procedures; meetings are scheduled regularly, and everyone is expected to conform to the group's pattern of behavior. Many fraternal and religious groups follow rigid rituals and many civic committees abide by "parliamentary" procedures. Even square-dance clubs adopt constitutions and by-laws. So for the sake of routine, what difference does it make what group we join?

Actually a person must choose carefully if he is concerned with his social standing in the community. Prestige is attached to the "quality" of organizations a person joins as well as the number of memberships he holds. Recognition also comes from holding important offices. Belonging to volunteer "service organizations" such as the Community Chest or Red Cross usually carries greater prestige than belonging to purely recreational organizations. Moreover, by donating time—and presumably service—a person can discharge his civic duties, a most laudable undertaking by urban middle-class standards. Just like the matron from high society who gains recognition as an unpaid volunteer social worker, today's average urbanite may achieve personal recognition by participating in well-chosen leisure-time activities.

Urban-conditioned expectations about how people should spend their leisure time extend even to children. Social and extracurricular activities of high-school students, encouraged by their classmates, approved by their parents, and endorsed by educators themselves, cause students to spend countless hours rehearsing with a band or choir, practicing for a team, or preparing for a school

Even children are caught up in urban routines and expectations. Students spend countless hours rehearsing and participating in plays, sports, music groups, and other routine extra-curricular activities.

Watching and listening are favorite forms of relaxation and release among urban-dwellers. The array of such leisure-time opportunity is often bewildering.

play or dance. Then comes the event itself, a matter of great importance, and one who does not belong to something or other is considered a "failure." Though his family life and his academic work may suffer, his social life must go on.

"Watching" is another leisure-time pursuit as routine as the days of the week. Armchair participants may feel new, or at least exciting, experiences in watching a boxing match or a football game on TV and may even gain some personal recognition for their prowess in keeping abreast of the "game of the week." Regular fans can feel even greater satisfaction because they were really there. Movie-goers, concert addicts, and others follow their special customs with regularity.

What has all this to do with urban-industrial impact on personality? Just this. Established routine protects a person from the stress and strain of having to make day-by-day and minute-by-minute decisions and thereby relieves him from a great deal of uncertainty and anxiety. The rhythmic tempo of regularity, whether at home, at

school, or at work, makes for confidence and a sense of security.

But routine is a two-edged sword—although for some it brings welcome security and certainty, for others it spells loss of freedom and individuality. It can stifle individual ambition and initiative and promote a dead-level mediocrity. It may make a person feel captive, thwarted, frustrated. For most of us, in fact, there is something remarkably unappealing, unthinking, and impersonally automatic in much that we do. And a few of us try to break the spell of routine—"do-it-yourself" hobbyists, bohemian intellectuals, hoboes.

FORMALIZATION

Life in the city is as formal as it is impersonal and routine, and nothing breeds formality so much as bureaucracy. The growing world of bureaucracy, which we shall discuss in the next three chapters, is a consequence of urban-industrial development. Bureaucracies and industrial cities alike tend to formalize loyalties and dependencies among people. As a worker, a person's relationship with his employer is fairly well crystallized. It is contractual in that it may be entered freely and broken at the discretion of either party; but during the workday itself, worker and boss are tied together by a set of mutual obligations. Neither party need feel obligated for the general welfare of the other at day's end. This attitude, so typical in large business firms, stands in sharp contrast to the feelings of loyalty and obligation that exist in many smaller companies, or that used to characterize small groups of craftsmen under the old guild system. The consequences of this formal method of contracting in our way of life can be seen in the case of a worker who, when he retires, is feasted and gifted by his employer at a banquet that marks the end of all employer-employee obligations.

As a resident of a city, a person's relationship to his community is also formalized to a considerable extent. He must pay taxes and he may vote, providing he is properly registered. In return for his taxes he receives police and fire protection. Laws assure him of certain actions. If he becomes impoverished, he can receive public assistance, providing he meets community standards.

Formalities, like organizational routines, help remove uncertainties for the individual. Major decisions are either removed entirely from his province or are so remote that he need not be greatly concerned about them. Proper ways of behaving are usually spelled out in such a manner that he knows exactly what to do, the best etiquette to follow. But formalities, just like organizational and mechanical routines, may pose a threat to the well-balanced human personality. Although they help meet a person's craving for security, they fail to fulfill his need for recognition and new experiences. Routines, simply because they are routines, tend to prevent a person from trying something new, some-

thing that might be more satisfying for his personality.

VALUES AND BELIEFS

Some of us complain bitterly about the growing limitations an urban society imposes on individual choice and decision. Yet choices and decisions must be made, even in a society given over to routine, formality, and impersonal relations. Many individuals are, in fact, impressed by the number of choices afforded them in the city. The array often seems bewildering—what school to choose, what kind of house or apartment or job, how to spend leisure time. But the range of decisions is much narrower than might at first appear. Given a particular situation that demands a choice, a person's line of action is fairly well structured and routinized beforehand, as we suggested in the preceding discussion of routines and formalities. The more specialized society becomes, for example, the less opportunity for us to choose jobs outside our own specialty. The more submerged we are in routine, the less mobile we are apt to be. We may be so tied down that we cannot venture beyond the limits of the city. We may be as remote from the rest of civilization as the early pioneer in the wilderness, and our freedom of choice may be as limited as his was.

But routine and formality do not tell the whole story. For we are limited by still other factors that tend to guide human behavior in a generally similar direction and thereby restrict choice. These factors are the dominant values and beliefs of an urban-industrial world.

The American Dream. We saw in Chapter 9 that one of the leading articles in our catechism of beliefs is a firm faith in the American Dream. Put most simply, this has come to mean the right of everyone to share equally in the opportunities and bounties afforded by American life. It implies a good-paying, respectable job that enables its holder to partake of the "good things of life" and to enjoy the contentment and prestige they may afford. The cherished goal is individual success, measured in terms of conspicuous material possessions supposedly within reach of all enterprising, resourceful Americans. With success comes personal recognition, but not always a sense of security. For old personal ties may be severed and our sense of security destroyed as we struggle to climb the social ladder. The dream of success may even become a nightmare to those who never realize it.

Competence and Luck. Our firm belief that chance plays a large part in determining who will be successful comforts those who have failed and gives them hope for the future. Most of us, of course, believe just as firmly that skill and "know-how" are as essential to success as good fortune. Americans value competence and show it repeatedly by honoring and otherwise rewarding a Babe Ruth, Werner von Braun, or Sinclair Lewis. Our faith in "luck" is so strong, however, that we frequently feel our luck has failed when things go wrong. But even in failure we console ourselves by believing that our turn will come—possibly next time, if we are "lucky." Like a vast lottery, each person convinces himself, however unreasonably, that his number will turn up eventually.

Since our talents are not always recognized as quickly and completely as we think they should be, we sometimes try to influence the whims of fate. Like Indians in the Southwest, who use their "rain dance" to influence the elements, we may indulge in rituals and entertain superstitions. Maybe carrying a rabbit's foot will get us that promotion. In a more sophisticated manner, some of us believe that we can control our destiny. We may, for example, take the utilitarian tack

that "it's not what you know, but who you know that counts." After all, they say, look at Mr. So-and-So. He's a good friend of the boss. How else could he have gotten that job?

Invention. A special form of competence is displayed by the inventor, the man with the ability to contrive something new, whether it be a mousetrap, an electronic computer, or a device for firing a rocket into space. We Americans enjoy novelty for its own sake, but we value inventions highly; for in our rapidly changing urban-industrial world, material gain is all-important. Products of the inventor, therefore, may bring him glory and fame. Inventions are judged partly by standards of the American Dream, so that only those that promise to lead to better things are likely to be widely adopted. A century ago the six-shooter, barbed wire, and the steam locomotive contributed immensely to the taming and settlement of the wild and woolly western frontier. Today it is the automated factory, the air conditioner, and the helicopter that permit a step-up in living.

Tempo of Life. Speed is valued on its own merits but takes on added luster when it makes for greater efficiency in production and more punctual behavior in our daily routines. Continental Europeans are usually impressed by the pace at which Americans move. Everyone is in a hurry! Workers and bosses alike are spurred on by production schedules. Commuters must travel fast and efficiently to and from their work. Even the dentist and physician keep rigorous office schedules. This is the way Americans do things. But it is a way that stimulates and upsets and can impose cruel strains on individuals. Clock and calendar are always hounding the modern urbanite.

Increasingly more insecure, the present-day American presses onward, searching for recognition and becoming ever more sensitive to the impersonal "they." What others think of him—or what he thinks they think—may be the final and determining factor in his behavior. His desire to be accepted by others tends to overpower all other considerations. He wants to be different, but different only within the boundaries set by public opinion, which inevitably leads him in the direction of greater and greater conformity.

HOW SOCIETY LIMITS AND DIRECTS OUR BEHAVIOR

It was to this problem of conformity that the popular writer and social scientist David Riesman addressed himself. In his book *The Lonely Crowd,* he analyzed the changes wrought in our national character by the coming of industrialism and urbanism. He concluded that from a society that was rural, traditional (tradition-directed), and individualistic (inner-directed), we have become centralized, urban, and motivated by outward circumstance (other-directed or outer-directed).

Tradition-directed behavior is usually encountered in static societies, where individuals conform to rigid, clear-cut standards that have been perpetuated over many generations. A person patterns his life according to ritual, convention, and routine, which change very slowly over the centuries and are seldom questioned. He shows little tendency to innovate or to find new solutions to age-old problems such as the control of disease. Like the situation in the Chinese family we described in an earlier chapter, an individual's position and role in a static society are defined for him from birth, and he follows them without much question. In such a situation, of course, his range of choice is severely limited.

Inner-directed behavior, on the other hand, is found in more flexible and *open* societies. Here the individual is guided by standards he learned from his elders, too, but he is soon made aware of many other standards and traditions that compete with those he was taught. He is conscious of a choice.

Born to a particular status, he can within limits change it by assuming a new status and playing new roles. Baptized a Lutheran, he may later choose Catholicism or no church at all. The choice is his.

Whereas the tradition-bound person is hardly aware of his own unique individuality, the inner-directed individual harbors a capacity to be master of his own destiny. The inner-directed person has a wide choice of aims. In the United States, for example, he can aspire to money, power, possessions, fame, knowledge, and opinion leadership, to name but a few. The inner-directed are therefore inclined to be more self-reliant than the tradition-directed. And they are apt to be more flexible and adaptable to the requirements of a changing world. Traditions remain important to the inner-directed man, but a changing and highly differentiated society modifies traditions and conventions. Nineteenth-century America was largely inner-directed and individualistic.

Other-directed behavior seems most prevalent in the middle class of our large, modern cities where public opinion and the attitudes of friends define the goals and courses of action. A person does not choose his own opinions, clothes, or behavior patterns. He accepts those opinions endorsed by the majority and changes them when the majority changes theirs. He wears suits and hats that are in style and discards them for new when they go out of style. If everyone in his social circle plays bridge, so does he. "He fits the pattern," we say. He conforms rather than exercises choice. According to Riesman:

> While all people want and need to be liked by some of the people some of the time, it is only the modern other-directed types who make this their chief source of direction and chief area of sensitivity.*

Fear of being shamed keeps the tradition-directed person in line, whereas the inner-directed person is controlled by guilt feelings, or what we commonly call "conscience." But the other-directed person is more cosmopolitan, taking his behavior cues from many people in different places in a world of rapid change and conforming out of fear of what others may think. As Riesman puts it, the urban-industrial environment tends to shape our personalities along lines of shifting other-directed standards. We are consequently much less concerned with traditional ways of doing things, or with the promptings of conscience, than with how others judge us and react to us. The tradition-directed European immigrant is fast disappearing from our midst, while the nineteenth-century inner-directed individual is finding social adjustment more difficult.

EFFORTS TO STABILIZE PERSONALITY

Personality problems are not exclusively a phenomenon of the twentieth century, although opponents of the urban-industrial way of life would have us believe that they were virtually nonexistent prior to the Industrial Revolution. Problems of personality have, no doubt, plagued individuals and societies for a long time. It is more likely that they were simply not recognized so openly and generally until fairly recently when advances in psychology, psychiatry, and other related fields, as well as the development of mass communications, began to kindle greater public awareness of "mental health" problems.

A vast assault is now being directed against mental illness. Some aspects of the campaign, such as the work being done by the United States Public Health Service and by psychiatric social workers, are well organized and more or less specialized. Other phases, such as efforts to provide recreation and social outlets for those suffering from the strains and frustrations of modern living, are more diffuse and spontaneous. Still other manifestations of this search for release and peace of mind are found in the flight to suburbia, the consumption of tranquilizing drugs, and the "spectatoritis" we commented about in an earlier chapter. The whole phenomenon is indeed puzzling. Authorities and laymen alike disagree about the nature, causes, and extent of our mental health problems and what we should be doing about them. They seem to be united on one point only—that "good mental health" is desirable.

RECREATIONAL ACTIVITY

What should we be doing about personality difficulties? One answer has been expanded facilities for recreational activity, which ideally should be truly "re-creative." For most authorities believe that recreation is a "safety valve" for the individual, which permits him to release worries and frustrations that otherwise might push him to the breaking point. Whether the recreational activity is public or private, individual or group, active or vicarious, is really of little consequence so long as it serves the "safety valve" function. Though the motives for urging more recreation—especially commercialized recreation—are sometimes questionable, mental health authorities generally

---

* D. Riesman, *et al., The Lonely Crowd: A Study of the Changing American Character* (New Haven: Yale University Press, 1950), p. 38.

agree that recreation is helpful in maintaining personality balance. If all monies expended for recreational purposes are any indication, then billions of dollars represent a most enormous attempt to stabilize Americans' personalities.

CLUBS AND ORGANIZATIONS

Overlapping the purely recreational pursuits are the many clubs and organizations that help people occupy their leisure time. Informal loosely organized groups such as a neighborhood club can hardly offset all the adverse effects of urban-industrial living. Yet these same groups, for the very reason that they represent something of the friendly, intimate associations common in a preindustrial society, prove helpful in offsetting the extreme formality, routine, and impersonality of the contemporary world. This principle has been recognized by professional group workers, specialists among social workers, who concentrate on helping people organize themselves for recreational, civic, and other leisure pursuits. Fruits of their efforts may be found among such organizations as the Boy Scouts, Cub Scouts, YMCA, square-dance clubs, and organized civic groups. Partly because group workers, adult educators, and others active in community organization take their jobs too seriously, they sometimes inject too much organization or too much routine into what were originally intended to be informal and self-sustaining groups. Where this has happened, the medicine may be worse than the disease it is supposed to cure. For organizational routine is responsible for a great deal of the pressure that produced the need for social clubs in our cities in the first place.

FINANCIAL SECURITY

We live not only in a society given over to more and more organizational routine but also in a cash economy where the emphasis on financial and material success produces constant strains. A number of government programs in recent years have reduced many people's financial strains. Unemployment compensation, retirement pensions, insured bank deposits, government-backed mortgage loans, and disability benefits for workers have eased many of the gnawing insecurities that beset people a quarter-century ago. To these have been added similar programs sponsored by business and industry. Although these programs cannot guarantee individual success and prosperity, they at least assure a person of a "floor" below which he cannot fall.

Such programs, then, do afford a measure of economic security, but this does not necessarily mean that they will automatically solve a person's personality difficulties. No doubt, retired or disabled workers and crop-insured farmers do gain some sense of security. But even when a person is sheltered by security measures, he may still be frustrated. The reason for his frustration may not be related to economics at all. He may lament his ill-fortune and compare his lot unfavorably with that of others. With the image of the American Dream constantly before him, he may even blame the security measures themselves for his troubles. He may believe that the measures are inadequate and fail to meet his needs, or he may believe that they are dulling the initiative he must display to reach his goals. In other instances, a man may believe that such programs limit his opportunities or give other persons an unfair advantage.

ESCAPE FROM THE CITY

Many city-dwellers have sought a solution to urban problems by moving to the suburbs. A large number of these people desire the advantages of urban living but are unwilling to accept the routine, formality,

One of the ways to escape from the stresses and strains of city life is to forsake the city for some resort or recreational area that will provide a changed atmosphere and surroundings and the opportunity to truly "re-create" the personality.

and depersonalization of relationships that go with it. A great many suburbanites are simply unwilling to forego the advantages of their jobs in the city, despite the urge they have to get away from urban pressures.

No more than a trickle early in the century, the movement to suburbia has now reached torrential proportions. If enough people find life in the suburbs enjoyable, suburban communities should continue to grow and prosper. But already by mid-century there were clues that all was not well. Some experts noted a reverse movement of people back into cities. Wives complained of being isolated in remote commuter colonies, and husbands grumbled about the time and inconvenience of getting to work and home

again. And for some the perpetual round of bridge clubs and barbecues became a boresome routine.

Can suburban living really help compensate for some of the city's more onerous features? The answer, of course, must come from each person concerned. Riesman's threefold classification of personality differences, however, offers a clue to the general answer. Other-directed persons should gain satisfaction from the compromise between city and open-country living. Inner-directed persons may find it tolerable but trying, while tradition-directed people, so firmly set in their ways, may regard it as more distasteful than living in the heart of the city. Suburbs, then, tend to attract other-directed persons.

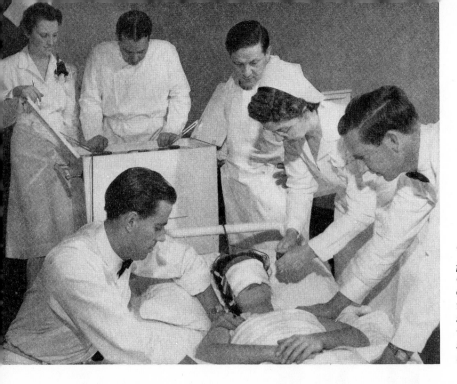

The diagnosis, care, and prevention of mental disorders are being concentrated more and more in the hands of specialists. Here a woman is being given shock treatment for a deep-seated disturbance.

PROFESSIONALIZED MENTAL HEALTH

As the general public grew increasingly aware of the inroads that urban-industrial living was making on our mental health, several deliberate steps were taken to meet the problem. Psychiatrists, psychologists, and drug firms translated the new research findings on mental illness into remedies and techniques that could be administered to patients at the clinic or their bedsides. In brief, the latest know-how in diagnosing and preventing mental disorders has been concentrated in the hands of a very few specialists.

PSYCHOLOGY AND PSYCHIATRY

Clinical psychologists and psychiatrists base their professional practice on the premise that "the individual is the patient" —not society—an approach that contrasts sharply with that of some social workers. Psychologists use batteries of tests to determine the mental ability, emotional stability, aptitudes, and interests of their cases. On the basis of their analysis, they then offer

counsel and advice. Psychiatrists, on the other hand, are medical doctors with special training in diagnosing and treating mental disorders. Surgery, psychotherapy, drugs, and other remedial techniques are all a part of a practicing psychiatrist's equipment.

The fields of clinical psychology and psychiatry have grown almost as spectacularly as our modern industrial plant. Although the causes and cures of many mental diseases still elude investigators, a simple listing of accomplishments in these two fields since 1900 would fill many pages. Actually, the growth in these areas is directly related to developments in technology. Electronic machines for scoring tests and analyzing test results, tape-recorders for interviews, one-way windows that permit specialists to observe their patients unseen, and electrodes that may be used to measure brain waves and other bodily responses are a few of the many technological developments that have contributed to the progress of psychology and psychiatry.

Psychologists and psychiatrists have both

362

had a marked degree of success in treating mental and emotional disturbances, an amazing accomplishment since they usually receive only the most severely disturbed cases. And if any credence is given the view that "society is the patient," their success is just short of miraculous. For if our urban-industrial ways are responsible for many of our personality disturbances, then treating the person without correcting his environment cannot provide a lasting cure. But, as we have noted previously in discussing problems of divorce, crime, and delinquency, effective action need not wait for scientists to determine the causes of behavior. The value of empirical methods has already been demonstrated.

MASS PRODUCTION OF DRUGS

The great demand today for headache pills and tranquilizers provides a peculiar commentary on our urban-industrial way of life. The tempo, pressures, and problems generated by modern living create the demand for medication which only a mass-production society could satisfy. Commercial drug houses have turned out millions upon millions of drugs and pills for pharmacists and physicians to dispense among distraught Americans. As advertisements constantly remind us, no one need slow down or miss anything—just take a pill or teaspoonful.

CLINICS AND HOSPITALS

Special clinics and hospitals have mushroomed over the land to care for the more aggravated cases of personality disorder. Most mental hospitals are publicly supported and usually overcrowded, with the waiting lists growing longer every day. The great increase in the number of hospital patients in recent decades, however, is in part an indication of the growing facilities that are being provided. And in part, too, it shows our mounting concern about mental health.

A GENERATION OF ROBOTS?

A foreigner who reads some of our novels or attends some of our Broadway plays might get the impression that most Americans are mentally deranged in one way or another, or at least not normal. The concept of "normality" is elusive, but normality is mainly a matter of degree. Everyone possesses some of the symptoms of mental or emotional distress at least some of the time. Authorities agree, however, that most people are normal enough to lead satisfactory lives most of the time. They are somehow able to withstand and adjust to their urban-industrial surroundings. Nevertheless, the chances are relatively good that everyone who reads this page will someday see the inside of a mental hospital either as a patient or as a visitor to some member of his family or a close friend. Not all problems of personality are serious enough to require hospitalization or treatment by a specialist, of course. Neither are all of the severe cases hospitalized. Many people must fight the daily battle of adjustment alone and with few resources.

Some pessimists have likened modern man to a robot. Robots lack emotions and are insensitive to others. Mechanical men move in response to controlled impulses that activate their mechanism. They act without an intelligence of their own and respond to routine assignments efficiently. They are "cold" in their relationships with others. Some human "robots" may be forced to follow routines uncritically, but their pent-up frustration may eventually explode in rebellion, or manifest itself in some more serious form of personality derangement or mental illness. This likelihood is one of the unique dangers confronting human robots in an urban-industrial society.

SOME WORDS OF SUMMARY

As a center of social and technological change, the modern industrial city affects the urbanite's personality profoundly. So all-pervasive is its influence that even villager and farmer feel its impact. The cold *impersonality* of the city makes it a place where "strangers" mix freely and live close to one another—where social intercourse is likely to be temporary, cold, and free of lasting obligations. Yet, this same quality of impersonality provides an outlet for persons seeking excitement, new experiences, and the protection of anonymity. Impersonality also combines with the *routine* of school, of work, and of play to provide a sense of security and certainty at the expense of feeling bored and uninspired. Classroom routine is a preview of what young folks may expect later on in the adult world of work and play. And oddly enough, the civic, social, and recreational group activities through which adults seek escape from their work routines also follow a highly rhythmic pattern. But however routine these extra-work and play activities may be, they are, nevertheless, highly rewarding for many persons desiring prestige, recognition, vicarious excitement, or participation with others. *Formality*, like impersonality and routine, also affects the city-dweller's personality. It joins with routine to enhance the certainty of events and experiences in the city. But formal and contractual relationships between persons are often distant, impersonal, and limited.

Accompanying the impersonal, formal, and routine urban patterns are the dominant values and beliefs that limit and guide behavior. Cherishing the American Dream and believing that competence will be rewarded, the urban-industrial man is spurred onward. When he falls short of his goals, he can protect his personal integrity by attributing his failure to "bad luck." Nevertheless, he is apt to feel tense and frustrated if he does not get ahead. This instability is nurtured by demands for speed, efficiency, and punctuality that tyrannize most of his waking hours.

But urban man responds to what he thinks others expect of him. He is *other-directed*. He no longer concerns himself with tried and proven traditions. Nor does his inner conscience tell him what to do. So, despite all the opportunities the city affords, urbanites are really conformists who follow urban middle-class standards.

The urban milieu has produced countless mental cases, and the widespread recognition of mental health problems has encouraged various steps to meet these problems. Truly recreational activities, social clubs and organizations, and government-sponsored programs have also been employed to relieve the strain on the urbanite. An increasingly large number of persons have tried to escape the trials and tribulations of the city by fleeing to the suburbs. For those persons who cannot adjust to or escape from the city, psychiatrists, psychologists, and hospitals have joined forces to help them in their fight against mental derangement and personality disturbance. But the problem is stubborn, and it may be that the other-directed American, depersonalized, formalized, routinized, freed from making decisions, and whose basic wishes too often go unsatisfied, is well on his way to becoming a human robot.

FURTHER ROADS TO LEARNING

GENERAL STUDIES

C. Mills, *White Collar* (New York: Oxford University Press, 1951). Provocative analysis of the relationship between urban-industrial society and the middle classes.

G. Murphy, *Personality* (New York: Harper, 1947). A broad review of studies on personality.

D. Riesman, *et al.*, *The Lonely Crowd* (New Haven: Yale University Press, 1950). A challenging treatise on the other-directedness of American character.

SPECIAL STUDIES

L. Frank, *Society as the Patient* (New Brunswick: Rutgers University Press, 1948). An analysis of role conflicts.

A. Kardiner, *The Individual and His Society* (New York: Columbia University Press, 1939). Treats the concept that a basic personality type results from cultural influences.

C. Kluckhohn, *Mirror for Man* (New York: McGraw-Hill, 1949). A good introduction to the relationship between culture and personality.

M. Komarovsky, "The Voluntary Associations of Urban Dwellers," *American Sociological Review*, XI (1946), pp. 686-698. A study of organized group affiliations of over two thousand adult New Yorkers.

R. Linton, *The Cultural Background of Personality* (New York: Appleton-Century-Crofts, 1945). A study of how personality and culture are integrated.

R. May, *The Meaning of Anxiety* (New York: Ronald, 1950). An elaboration of the theories of anxiety that discusses anxiety as a cause of many of our current problems.

W. Whyte, *Street Corner Society* (Chicago: The University of Chicago Press, 1943). Life in lower-class urban society and its influences on personality and behavior.

FICTION AND DRAMA

M. Burt, *The Interpreter's House* (New York: Scribner, 1924). A well-informed novel on shifting standards in New York society.

H. Lee, *No Measure Danced* (New York: Macmillan, 1941). How the influences and pressures of the urban business world destroy happiness for a career woman.

S. Lewis, *Dodsworth* (New York: Harcourt, Brace, 1929). An urban industrialist flees the United States to preserve his individualism.

W. Motley, *Knock on Any Door* (New York: Appleton-Century-Crofts, 1947). A boy winds up in the electric chair because of unfavorable urban influences.

FILMS

Feeling of Rejection (National Film Board of Canada, 1947, 23 min., sound, black and white). A woman fears rejection and withdraws from society.

The Nation's Mental Health (March of Time, 1951, 18 min., sound, black and white). Shows facilities for training psychiatric personnel, various methods of therapy, and the way communities can obtain help to set up mental health clinics.

Preface to Life (United States Public Health Service, 1950, 30 min., sound, black and white). This film spotlights the life of an individual to picture the impact of family and community on personality.

Our Growing World

of Bureaucracy

T H E M E

The contemporary world is a place where man's ancient loyalties have been shaken by . . . the pressures of bureaucratic organization *in almost every area of human activity upon time-honored beliefs in the central importance of the individual.*

The Fabric of Bureaucracy

*The mechanical brain, in supplementing
the human brain, has added a new dimension to bureaucracy
and reflects its growing intricacy,
complexity, and impersonality.*

Organization

seems to be a necessity in an urban-industrial society. Everywhere we turn organization envelops us. Though we chafe under its restrictions, we unquestionably need it. An industrial and urban world is, after all, an increasingly organized one. The trend toward increased organization is both profound and irresistible. It affects every aspect of our existence. The evidence is all about us: in government, foreign relations, and warfare; in commerce, industry and labor; in finance and banking; in religion and education; yes, even in art, sports, and entertainment. Not even science can escape. Today's scientist is enmeshed in governmental and industrial rules and regulations that coordinate and give purpose to many of his activities. Even the family physician has been replaced by the group clinic and specialist. Indeed, the doctor today belongs to one of the most highly organized professions in the country. Likewise the farmer, for all his individualism, has turned to organization out of sheer necessity. Everywhere we find organization intruding upon and changing traditional patterns. Few middle-class Americans are without a wallet full of organizational membership cards.

But the drive toward more and better organization is not just an American phenomenon. It is world-wide. The tendency is no less apparent in individualistic France than in industrial America and communist Russia. Germans, Frenchmen, Africans, Orientals, and Arabs are all busily organizing on a local, national, and even international plane. The businessman's Rotary Club, for example, is not American; it is international.

And the Boy Scouts, founded in 1908, was the first attempt at international organization of children. Both the League of Nations and the United Nations represent efforts at political and cultural cooperation on a world-wide plane. Within the past century we have witnessed the establishment of a procession of organizations bearing such revealing titles as the International Workers of the World, the Third International, and the International Labor Organization. Ours is a world bent on organizing.

But organization nevertheless arouses our fears. We complain of the loss of freedom and the stifling of initiative that accompany organizational routine, of inefficiency, waste, and "red tape." We grow indignant about the impersonal way in which government bureaus deal with citizens. Yet, curiously, for all our criticisms we are not really opposed to the idea of organization. Even attempts to reform impersonal and inefficient organizations usually take the form of bigger and better organization. Big business bureaucracy, for example, has been matched by big labor bureaucracy. And large farm organizations have spearheaded the drive against railroad and processing monopolies. Thus, we implicitly endorse organization even when we seek to combat it.

Organization, we might say, is an ever-expanding latticework on which the vine of civilization grows. It provides a medium for realizing an infinite variety of human goals and aspirations. As we become increasingly industrialized and urbanized, the latticework of organization becomes increasingly more complex. Indeed, organization seems inescapable in an urban and industrial world.

This trend toward more and more organization has been identified in modern literature as a bureaucratic tendency. Unfortunately, the word "bureaucracy" has acquired a rather sordid reputation in our culture. To utter it is to convey unpleasant impressions. Oddly enough, at the very time we demand more bureaucracy, we associate bureaucracy with inefficiency, unbusinesslike operations, waste, corruption, incompetence, and deceit.

Our attitudes toward bureaucracy are ambivalent, endorsing it on one side, indicting it on the other. This indictment is so strong and has been made so frequently that it has become a part of our cultural baggage. This makes it difficult to separate public usage of the term from a more precise and emotionally neutral meaning. Let us turn to a consideration of the character of bureaucracy.

THE CHARACTER OF BUREAUCRACY

BUREAUCRACY DEFINED

What then is bureaucracy? If you were asked to participate in a fund drive for the Community Chest, you would not expect to work entirely on your own. Rather, you would expect to receive some kind of direction and to have your work assignments divided up to avoid duplicating the efforts of your fellow canvassers. Generally speaking, the more persons participating in a common enterprise, the greater the need for systematizing their activities. *Organization designed to accomplish systematic coordination of large-scale tasks involving many persons is called bureaucracy.* The major objective is to ensure order and efficiency where confusion and chaos might otherwise reign. When the activities of an organization are improperly coordinated, the intent and purpose of bureaucracy have been corrupted. Where inefficiency reigns, the bureaucratic principle suffers.

Almost every phase of modern life displays some bureaucratic characteristics, not simply the military or the various branches of government. Bureaucracy is present in business, labor, education, religion, athletics, and even art. It enfolds teachers as well as policemen, office managers as well as visiting nurses. It thrives at every level of political and economic life. It may operate close to or far from the people it serves or controls. It is quiet, normally unobtrusive, and ever present.

THE HUMAN EQUATION

Bureaucracies, then, are made up of people. This may come as a shock to persons who have been exposed to the impersonal machinery of our great organizations. But bureaucracies were developed by human beings and are run by them. A bureaucracy has no personality of its own, for bureaucratic behavior is simply human behavior in macrocosm. Failure to recognize this fact causes us to attribute characteristics or actions we dislike to the sinister bureaucracy itself, rather than to the people who make up the organization. It may satisfy the soul, but it does little good to curse "bureaucracy" over some irksome rule or senseless routine. For it was some individual who made the rule or established the routine, and some person was responsible for enforcing it. "Bureaucracy," after all, is just a word that identifies a particular kind of human process, nothing more.

THE STRUCTURAL EQUATION

According to Max Weber, the renowned German sociologist, bureaucracy is an on-going process—a continuing organization composed of persons performing official functions while being bound by rules. Individuals enter and leave it, but the organization endures. Those involved at any given moment must behave according to rules. Normally, they are also subject to a systematic division of labor, wherein each has assigned functions and tasks. In a bureaucracy like the Ford Motor Company, some persons will be obligated to work on the assembly line, while others order materials, keep accounts, administer retirement programs, declare policy, or supervise production. Each has his own special tasks. The systematic division of labor in a large bureaucracy defies recounting.

A systematic division of labor is maintained through rules that define the functions and tasks that people perform. It is the task of administration to make the rules, supervise performance, and impose penalties for violations of the rules. Administrative offices are generally organized into a hierarchy wherein each lower office and its

officials are controlled and supervised by a higher office. Each office has a defined sphere of authority and control, and each office-holder is expected to possess technical qualifications and be competent in his particular area. Personnel directors, for instance, are expected to be experts in placement, recruitment, and solving labor disputes.

All actions, rules, and decisions relating to a particular function, as well as the people involved, constitute the "office." Most bureaucratic officials—occupants of the offices —are hired employees who are paid a salary and do not own the enterprise. As bureaucracy grows, more and more persons involved come to be considered (and consider themselves) as career people. Most promotions are made on the basis of seniority or achievement, though hiring is based on technical skills.

What we have just described is remarkably similar to any modern business firm,

Bureaucracies are made up of people. They were developed by human beings and are run by them.

In ancient Egypt an elaborate bureaucracy developed around "The Scribe of the Fields of the Lord," who, with his assistants and overseers, carefully measured crop yields and catalogued harvests.

government agency, or fund-raising organization. It could apply just as well in socialistic Russia as in capitalistic America. For we are talking about a product of the Industrial Revolution, something that has helped make America's high standard of living possible. But we are also talking about something that existed long before the Industrial Revolution, something that is a product of a rich historical experience.

THE HISTORICAL BASIS OF MODERN BUREAUCRACY

Bureaucracy is certainly not a new phenomenon. Like everything else, it has a history. Its roots go back two thousand years or more to ancient Babylon, Egypt, and Rome. Indeed, most of the great organizations of the past, some of which have survived into the modern era (e.g., the Catholic Church), were thoroughly bureaucratic. Many ancient societies developed large-scale bureaucracies to handle complex tasks. In Egypt under the New Empire, for example, a huge bureaucracy was developed to construct and regulate waterways. Early Persian documents show that a bureaucratic pattern of relations existed among the "water master," his subordinates, and the village heads. In other societies bureaucracies were used to control the complex movements of great armies, to codify and interpret laws, or to administer the tax system.

The classic example of bureaucracy, both ancient and modern, is found in the military. Roman legions were thoroughly bureaucratized for purposes of conquest and occupation, collection of tribute, and the administration of extensive frontiers. Max Weber attributed the success of Cromwell's "New Model" Army over the more poorly disciplined Cavaliers during the Puritan Revolution in England to the superior effectiveness of bureaucratic control. And the Prussian army, of course, offered one of the best examples of a completely bureaucratized fighting unit. Its thorough planning, careful staff work, and meticulous attention to detail made it one of the most feared fighting machines in the world and later enabled it to dominate the civil as well as the military administration in Prussia.

Despite these examples of bureaucratic development in the past, it is, nevertheless, in contemporary society that bureaucracy has found its most fertile soil. What then are some of the factors that contributed to its growth?

DEVELOPMENT
OF THE MODERN NATIONAL STATE

One factor is certainly the enormous size of the modern national state. During the Middle Ages, most political jurisdictions were very small, and even the large ones possessed no more than a weak and decentralized administration. Furthermore, beyond the government and the Church, there were but a handful of formal organizations and private associations. Today, however, national states embrace millions of subjects, vast territories, huge armies, giant corporations, and an unbelievable number of voluntary associations. In the United States alone the number of people employed by the national government has leaped from a mere eight thousand in 1820 to several million today.

This startling growth of governmental bureaucracy has been in process since the rise of absolute monarchy in Europe during the sixteenth and seventeenth centuries. In England, for instance, from the time of the Tudors, powerful governments gradually suppressed the authority and prerogatives of the old feudal nobility. As the powers of the king increased, more and more of them were taken over by the king's officials, whose functions became increasingly more technical as the affairs of government became more complex. This development necessitated a greater division of labor. Officials who had been remunerated by favors from the king were later placed on fixed salaries, and to meet the expenses of their offices and staffs, a centralized system of taxation was set up. Salaries were paid by the treasury from monies specifically appropriated for that purpose. Then when Parliament finally wrested control of the government from the king, the king's bureaucracy became Parliament's. Thus arose that huge, efficient, bureaucratic organization more politely called the British civil service. Few contested the need for it. The only question was who was to control it, Parliament or the king?

The concentration of political power in the hands of centralized national governments has produced a professionalized officialdom staffed by technically trained experts

Grey-clad German troops reoccupying the Rhineland in the 1930's —classic representatives of the classic type of bureaucratic organization—the military.

whose areas of authority and responsibility are clearly defined. The multiplication of functions and consequent division of labor make it necessary to fix duties and obligations as well as salaries. This development in turn requires a sound financing system, if the bureaucracy is to be maintained, since it is a well-known fact that officials will not stay on the job when their income is in serious jeopardy. A bureaucracy, in short, can be maintained only by an economy that can ensure an adequate and steady supply of funds for its operation.

A MONEY ECONOMY AND CAPITALISM

Many historians are convinced that a *money economy* favors bureaucratic development. To be sure, examples of bureaucracies based on favors and remuneration in kind, notably in Egypt and China, have existed. But maintenance of such a system is difficult. A money economy, on the other hand, ensures that officials will be paid and that a full-time professional staff can be maintained, which is vital to any organization in the long run. Volunteers are frequently too *independent* of the organization to submit to discipline and control. Unpaid slaves or indentured servants, at the opposite extreme, are far too *dependent* to take the initiative and assume the necessary responsibilities. Furthermore, they often lack incentive. Hence, bureaucracies seldom evolve in societies that have failed to develop a monetary system or to abolish slavery.

Some scholars contend further that a capitalistic economy, in particular, encourages the development of bureaucracy. Since capitalism requires that economic risks be calculated and investments protected from as many unpredictable forces as possible, a strong, well-organized government is necessary to ensure order and stability. Social upheaval, lawlessness, and arbitrary action in the market place must be kept to a mini-

mum. Then, of course, capitalism provides a type of money economy that permits the payment of regular salaries to hired employees. And finally, capitalism promotes bureaucratization in business, industry, and spheres of activity other than government. As business and industrial firms expand, for example, there is need for greater efficiency, a division of labor, and the expansion of administration. Despite the loud outcry concerning the threat of bureaucracy to the free-enterprise system, in other words, that system actually promotes rather than discourages bureaucracy.

THE INDUSTRIAL REVOLUTION

Another historical development that has exerted a profound influence on bureaucratic growth is the Industrial Revolution. For, as we have noted, the rise of mechanized industry brought many workers together under a single roof. This arrangement required more order, more organization—more bureaucracy. After all, the labor of many men with different jobs and different temperaments had to be coordinated and made efficient. Workers surrendered their independence to a centralized system that directed and controlled their working lives. This was especially true in mass-production industries. What better evidence is there of the need for bureaucracy? Almost every modern industry is rife with it.

EXPANDING POPULATIONS

The population increase that accompanied the Industrial Revolution also had a hand in bureaucratic growth. In fact, a rise in population anywhere will likely produce a sharper tendency toward bureaucracy. When you are alone you can follow your own discretion and whims. But the more people there are around you, the more you and they must be constrained from infringing on one another's rights. Generally, although not always, an increase in population density brings more regulation, and consequently, more administration and bureaucracy.

Certainly the surge of population to the cities has had this result. Anyone who has resided in a large city knows why. People in an industrial society move swiftly, range widely, and communicate readily. Such a society requires more controls than a nonindustrial society, and the more people there are, the more regulations are required.

THE WELFARE STATE IDEA

People in an industrial and urban society not only require more regulation, they insist on more social services. In an earlier chapter we noticed how this trend develops. Within just a few decades Americans began to reverse their traditional philosophy of government that embraced that nineteenth-century idea of the "nightwatchman state," wherein government confined its activities to maintaining order. Now government must serve as well as protect.

As a result, governments at all levels—national, state, and local—sponsor expanded programs of social welfare, public works, old-age pensions, social security, and aid to education, to name just a few. Although government has always served Americans handsomely, the present growth in functions and services and the demand for more overshadow anything that has occurred in the past. Nor has the trend been confined to America alone. Germany, for example, had social insurance before the turn of the present century; and the British now have nationalized medical services. We hardly need repeat that such increases in social services mean added personnel and administration. Bureaucracy seems almost inevitable under these conditions.

STRUCTURAL FACTORS IN THE RISE OF MODERN BUREAUCRACY

Historically, then, bureaucracies have developed in response to specific needs—the requirements of growing national states, of industrial entrepreneurs, and of expanding populations. Only the scale and the prevalence of modern bureaucracy are new.

SHEER SIZE

Most of our misgivings about modern bureaucracies, especially government bureaucracy, are prompted by their size. We denounce them as monstrosities with which the individual cannot cope. And rightly so, for the ordinary individual cannot comprehend or hope to deal with such massive and complex organization. The amount of men and material, as well as the interlocking bureaucratic relationships in a large industrial concern such as General Motors or General Electric, is difficult to conceive. And it is even more difficult to comprehend the vast amounts of money handled by the United States government.

By far the most frustrating result of bureaucratic growth and size, however, is not the individual's inability to comprehend the structure but his feeling of insignificance before it. It is the size of bureaucracy that makes him feel small and powerless by comparison. He is but an infinitesimal particle in an impersonal and on-going Goliath that shows no mercy and asks no quarter. As the organization grows he becomes increasingly more dependent on it. As a result, he is apt to find his loss of personal freedom frustrating. The individual, of course, may react in one of several ways. He may simply give up and passively accept the bureaucratic web that surrounds him; he may seek to eliminate it (which is probably futile); he may seek to control it; or he may, like most of us, just curse it. Whatever his choice, he will find, if he is perceptive, that his plight results from the power a bureaucratic organization wields. As the size of an organization increases, the power and significance of the individual person decreases.

POWER MOBILITY

Hence, for many Americans, the exercise of irresponsible power, bureaucracy, the welfare state, and the suppression of personal freedom are one and the same thing. There is a measure of truth in this popular view. For bureaucracy has a long record of restricting human freedom. A bureaucratic structure has the immense advantage over the individual of being able to command great power. Furthermore, this power can be shifted readily and easily from one part of the organization to another. Any deviation from the rules, any suspicion of insubordination, can be dealt with summarily. A recent newspaper carried the story of a government clerk who had been officially reprimanded for answering the telephone one minute after closing time. He had violated the rules.

In the situation we have just described, the individual is helpless against the system. Since power normally accompanies size, a bureaucratic organization can move more swiftly and effectively against the non-bureaucratized, the poorly organized, and the individual person. Here is the basis of the charge that bureaucracy crushes the individual, especially his initiative. "You can't fight City Hall," we say, or "You can't fight the organization." A person feels he is in the presence of overweening power, and is overcome by a sense of futility and helplessness, much as a soldier would feel who was ordered to hold off a jet bomber with a flyswatter.

To its basic meaning, then, we must add that bureaucracy *is a means of accumulating and holding power*. Whether in business, government, or the army, a bureaucracy enables its masters to control large areas of human affairs. It might be a market, an opposing political party, or the ambitions of a powerful enemy. Such control can be used for good as well as evil purposes—to raise funds to fight cancer, as well as to plan an aggressive war. Historically, bureaucratic control represents a realistic way of reaching objectives in a world growing ever more populous and complex. A lone individual cannot build or operate a national network of railways or an automotive industry. It takes bureaucracy to carry out jobs such as these!

Man's increasing physical control over nature creates a need for more and more social and political power. We now live in an atomic and space age. Moreover, as we saw in Chapter 12, the rise of industrialism has created countervailing power aggregates of labor, management, and agriculture and has hastened the growth of big government and enlarged its role as mediator among these contending groups. In short, as power accumulates in one segment of society, similar concentrations of power are apt to appear in other areas to check and balance it. Everywhere a "mad scramble" goes on to find new and more effective means of accumulating and wielding power.

Most critical of all, however, is the ability to shift power when the occasion calls for it. Power today is highly mobile. Huge organizations can mobilize their representatives and have them descend on Congress in a moment. Any organization or group that cannot marshal its power in this way is at a serious disadvantage. Industries that can re-tool rapidly to produce new products and exploit new markets or demands have a distinct advantage over competitors that cannot. As never before, armies must be bureaucratized if they are to deliver destructive power to targets thousands of miles away in a matter of minutes. Missiles will not wait for men to organize. Indeed, our world has become one in which all men, whether in industry, business, government, education, or the armed forces, must quicken to the call to man their posts. This requires organization.

EFFICIENCY, SPECIALIZATION, AND A DIVISION OF LABOR

If sheer bigness and power accumulation encourage the growth of bureaucracy, so, too, does "efficiency." One of the major reasons why we Americans expand our organizations is our belief that big operations

Most men cannot afford to remain unorganized in a world circled by menacing Sputniks.

are more efficient than small ones. And they can be, if they grow in a systematic and orderly way. Corporate consolidations and mergers are in large part attempts to improve efficiency because a large company or organization can make fuller use of time, space, manpower, and equipment. Then, too, the big company is in a better position to employ more highly specialized personnel, mobilize and shift its power with greater ease, and carry financial reserves for emergencies. Although "bigness" is certainly not always a virtue, and can be a serious hindrance, it does afford an opportunity for greater efficiency. And, as we saw in preceding chapters, Americans want things to be efficient. Indeed, we worship efficiency, too often permitting it to become the sole goal of our efforts to the exclusion of all others. Persons who value efficiency so highly and who also believe that "bigness" begets efficiency are going to spend a lot of time making their organizations larger.

The corollaries of greater efficiency are specialization and a division of labor. The objective of many small concerns is to become large enough to make maximum use of specialists through a systematic and detailed division of functions. A high degree of specialization nearly always secures special advantages for the organization that can utilize it. This fact is so widely recognized that large firms (and small ones too) are constantly competing among themselves for experts. Some even try to monopolize a particular market of top people. Following the Korean War, one firm with a handsome government contract specifically instructed its personnel section to hire as many of its competitors' specialists as possible. And after World War II, we witnessed the ruthless battle between the Russian and American governments for top German scientists whose talents represented a superior power advantage. In an industrialized world organizations must be large enough to compete for experts.

SUBSTITUTION OF THE ARTIFICIAL FOR THE INTIMATE

In many of our larger organizations individuals must cooperate in common projects without knowing one another, and often without knowing a great deal about what their associates are doing. Commercial and industrial enterprises now span great distances and include innumerable functions. Activities of persons in New York must be coordinated with duties of individuals in Los Angeles, many of which are apt to be entirely unrelated. Today, in fact, we span the entire globe at times. Standard Oil, the Aluminum Company of America, and Lloyds of London, to mention but a few, are classic examples of world-wide organizations. Our world may be growing smaller, but it is far from being any more intimate.

When direct contact and face-to-face situations are no longer possible, artificial and indirect methods must be devised. Here again, bureaucratic methods provide a ready answer. Written rules and orders replace the spoken word. Our modern communications system makes it possible to transmit directives and orders over great distances in a very short time. The bureaucratic "paper empire" establishes indirect and artificial methods of contact, identification, and control. Recording and filing systems are insituted to facilitate orderly operations and maintenance. Virtual armies of individuals may be required to accomplish these tasks. Such a system is unavoidably bureaucratic.

We constantly complain about the "paper empire," the "red tape," and all the barriers bureaucracy imposes. We view them as an ominous threat to freedom and individual initiative. Yet, we are not so psychologically constructed that we can manage large numbers of men and machines without some degree of contact and control.

THE GROWING COMPLEXITY OF ADMINISTRATION

This greater need for contact and control has produced a need for more management. As bureaucracies have increased in size and power, the number of administrators has grown by leaps and bounds. In many bureaucratic organizations, administrators sometimes outnumber producers. There are "more chiefs than Indians." Some military organizations, for example, have eight or more men behind the lines for every fighting man at the front. Whether it be the army, government, industry, education, or baseball, an increase in functions, services, or personnel will likely be accompanied by a corresponding increase in management. Increases in functions and personnel require stricter definitions of responsibilities, a greater division of labor, and more dependence on written rules, which all add up to increased bureaucracy.

PSYCHOLOGICAL FACTORS IN THE RISE OF MODERN BUREAUCRACY

Historical and structural factors tell only part of the story of bureaucratic growth. Fully as important is man himself. Bureaucracy, after all, is a human product, and every bureaucracy in existence is made up of human beings. What men have felt and believed has played a significant role in making bureaucracy what it is.

WORSHIP OF GROWTH AND BIGNESS

Organizational growth in this country, for example, cannot be attributed solely to historical and structural factors. As important as are the demands created by industrial and urban development, bureaucratic growth stems from a combination of many factors, some of which involve our attitudes and values. As we saw in an earlier chapter, Americans love bigness for its own sake. No doubt, our organizations grow partly because we want them to be *big*. For example, Americans tend to believe that the larger a college becomes, the better educational institution it will be. For some time our national pride was severly injured when we were unable to launch as large a satellite as the Russian Sputnik.

The worship of bigness extends into our organizational habitat. In America everything must grow. An American is apt to resign his position if his firm fails to increase in size. We take pride in being part of a growing and large enterprise. Moves from small to large organizations are considered promotions, even when they entail accepting lower positions in the larger firms. Our society simply attaches more prestige to positions in a large organization. Many individuals, moreover, gain a greater feeling of self-importance by being a part of vast enterprises. Some will join a larger firm at a reduced salary just to be part of something bigger.

It is frequently charged that both large and small organizations aspire to become gigantic empires. Junior colleges, for example, seek to become four-year colleges, and four-year colleges aspire to become universities. Witness the present demand by many colleges to be called universities. Empire-builders are certainly at large in our society. It is not the organizations, of course, but the people in them who have these aspirations. Students and faculties feel that they will acquire more prestige by being associated with a larger school. Such attitudes engender bureaucracy.

THE NEED FOR ORDER

And attitudes contribute in yet another way—the desire for order. We not only

desire order in our daily routine, but we insist on it. We find little security where order is lacking. Bureaucracy, once more, is a tool for bringing order out of chaos. Historically, every ruling group has used bureaucracy for this purpose. For bureaucracy provides a means whereby formal relationships can be established. In a bureaucracy the responsibilities and obligations of officials are clearly stipulated. Subordinates are usually responsible to particular superiors. An army lieutenant, for example, knows what his duties are and the superior officer to whom he is responsible. Procedures can be readily ascertained and followed. Everything proceeds according to definite and familiar rules that are not easily subject to radical or whimsical change. All this facilitates control and makes for order. Formal rules and procedures make it possible to carry out organizational policy in an orderly manner. When there is a change in policy, the proper officials can be informed through regular channels, and the rules and procedures can be adjusted in a systematic way. Without formal routine, supervision is manifestly impossible and order decays into chaos.

Certainly no one would argue that bureaucracy always functions as smoothly as we have just described it. Every bureaucratic organization has its inadequacies, and often they are serious. Nevertheless, bureaucracy does lend order to life. It permits us to determine our duties and obligations and to play our roles properly. It has the definite advantage of letting us know where we stand. And we like that!

THE SEARCH FOR SECURITY

We like, too, the security afforded by something bigger than ourselves. There is safety in numbers and there is safety in size. Bureaucracy provides both. In a bureaucracy we can settle back, perform our tasks correctly, and be somewhat secure about our future. For where relationships are formal and workers may not even know their own "boss" personally, top administrators are likely to be concerned with how we perform our tasks and nothing more. It is highly unlikely that we would be dismissed for personal reasons. Conditions such as these make us feel protected and secure. And we like that, too!

Furthermore, large organizations are apt to endure, and if they endure, so will our salaries and positions. The fabric of large bureaucracies is not easily destroyed. Inefficiencies in one part of an organization are often counterbalanced by improved efficiency in others. When functions are discontinued in one area, there will probably be expansion in others. Besides, there are all those people! The more people who surround us and the more functions all are performing, the more all of us appear indispensable. Little wonder, then, that we like to see our own organizations grow and become more bureaucratic at the same time we complain about all the other bureaucracies that threaten to envelop us.

SOME WORDS OF SUMMARY

Organization is all about us. Although our fears are aroused by it, the needs of the modern age do not permit us to escape from it. This trend toward more organization has been identified as a bureaucratic tendency. A bureaucracy is a type of human organization designed to accomplish systematic coordination of large-scale tasks involving many persons. Through it, we seek to ensure order, efficiency, and integration. As a human creation having no personality of its own, a bureaucracy is a pattern of human behavior in which individuals perform official functions in an on-going process while being bound by rules. Other dominant characteristics include a systematic division of labor, a high degree of specialization, and an administrative hierarchy.

Although bureaucracy has deep historical roots, it is in contemporary society that it has become prevalent. Some of the probable causes of its prevalence have been the rise of the modern national state, the rise of capitalism, and the Industrial Revolution. Reinforcing these factors were the phenomenal growth in population during the nineteenth century and the demand on the part of people everywhere for more public services. The growth of bureaucracy has also been aided by a simple structural factor, its sheer size. In America big bureaucracy begets big bureaucracy, if for no other reason than we must be big to compete with those who are already big. Greater size enables us to employ power more effectively and to make better and more efficient use of time, space, manpower, and equipment.

Fully as important as the historical and structural influences are our attitudes and values. The average American's belief in bigness and growth, for example, leads him to admire, even worship, vast corporate and bureaucratic enterprises. Secondly, the greater opportunity for control afforded by bureaucratic routine appeals to our desire for order. Finally, we sanction and endorse bureaucratic growth because it provides safety and security in numbers and sheer size.

It is not surprising, then, that our industrial and urban society is so bureaucratic, for the advance of industrialism relies in part on the growth of bureaucracy. For all its disadvantages, and there are many, bureaucracy has played a vital role in the spread of industrialization and in making possible our present high level of living.

FURTHER ROADS TO LEARNING

GENERAL ACCOUNTS

C. Barnard, *The Functions of the Executive* (Cambridge: Harvard University Press, 1938). An analysis of business bureaucracy.

R. Bendix, "Bureaucracy: The Problem and Its Setting," *American Sociological Review*, XII (1947), pp. 493-507; also, "Bureaucracy and the Problem of Power," *Public Administration Review*, V (1945), pp. 194-209. Two of the most discussed articles on the problem of bureaucracy, both of them by an eminent authority.

———, *Work and Authority in Industry* (New York: Wiley, 1956). This volume compares the bureaucratic structures and techniques of the United States, Great Britain, France, Germany, and Russia.

P. Blau, *Bureaucracy in Modern Society* (New York: Random House, 1956). A very readable general study that builds on Max Weber's principles.

R. Dubin, *The World of Work: Industrial Society and Human Relations* (Englewood Cliffs, N. J.: Prentice-Hall, 1958). Chapter 20 of this study deals with the causes of bureaucratic growth and examines the characteristics and functions of bureaucracy.

H. Finer, "Critics of Bureaucracy," *Political Science Quarterly*, LX (1945), pp. 100-112. A vigorous defense of bureaucracy.

R. Merton, *et al.*, *Reader in Bureaucracy* (Glencoe, Ill.: The Free Press, 1952). A superb anthology.

L. von Mises, *Bureaucracy* (New Haven: Yale University Press, 1944). Still one of the most vigorous arguments against big government by one who equates bureaucracy and socialism.

H. Simon, *Administrative Behavior* (New York: Macmillan, 1947). A good discussion of the bureaucratic decision-making processes.

M. Weber, *Essays in Sociology* (New York: Oxford University Press, 1946). A series of essays that includes the most highly regarded statement ever written on bureaucracy.

T. Whitehead, *Leadership in a Free Society* (Cambridge: Harvard University Press, 1936). A thoughtful and careful examination of bureaucratic organization.

W. F. Whyte, ed., *Industry and Society* (New York: McGraw-Hill, 1946). A collection of some of the best essays on bureaucratic administration.

SPECIAL STUDIES

C. Argyris, *Personality and Organization* (New York: Harper, 1957). Why people in human organizations act and think as they do.

P. Blau, *The Dynamics of Bureaucracy* (Chicago: The University of Chicago Press, 1955). A study of the relations among individuals in two government agencies.

M. Dalton, *Men Who Manage: Fusions of Feeling and Theory in Administration* (New York: Wiley, 1959). A comprehensive survey of the many problems confronting bureaucratic managers, especially in-group conflicts, internal power struggles, and unfriendly relations.

M. Dimock, *Administrative Vitality: The Conflict with Bureaucracy* (New York: Harper, 1959). A stimulating analysis of the reasons for bureaucratic growth.

M. Dimock and H. Hyde, *Bureaucracy and Trusteeship in Large Corporations* (T. N. E. C., Monograph No. 11, Washington, D.C.: Government Printing Office, 1940). How business bureaucrats manage to keep their positions.

A. Gouldner, *Patterns of Industrial Bureaucracy* (Glencoe, Ill.: The Free Press, 1954). A discussion of the forces that create bureaucracy.

R. Kelsall, *Higher Civil Servants in Britain* (London: Routledge and Kegan Paul, 1955). A study of the social origins of government bureaucrats.

A. Lauterbach, *Men, Motives, and Money: Psychological Frontiers of Economics* (Ithaca, New York: Cornell University Press, 1954). What makes a bureaucratic official tick?

S. Lipset, *et al., Union Democracy* (Glencoe, Ill.: The Free Press, 1956). An historical and sociological study of the bureaucratic development of the International Typographical Union.

H. Schwartz, *Russia's Soviet Economy* (Englewood Cliffs, N. J.: Prentice-Hall, 1958). An analysis of the Russian economic organization and bureaucracy.

P. Selznick, *The Organizational Weapon: A Study of Bolshevik Strategy and Tactics* (New York: McGraw-Hill, 1952). Gives a clear picture of the degree of bureaucratization in the Soviet Union.

A. Sloan, *Adventures of a White Collar Man* (New York: Doubleday, 1941). The career of an industrial bureaucrat.

H. Stein, *Public Administration and Policy Development: A Case Book* (New York: Harcourt, Brace, 1952). A series of cases that do a brilliant job of illustrating the underpinning of bureaucratic organization.

F. Taussig and C. Joslyn, *American Business Leaders* (New York: Macmillan, 1932). A pioneering study of the social origins of business bureaucrats in the United States.

FICTION AND DRAMA

C. Dickens, *Bleak House* (New York: Scribner, 1911). An early work of art by one of the great masters that clearly demonstrates that bureaucracy is not a recent phenomenon.

N. Gogol, *The Inspector-General* (New York: Knopf, 1916). A splendid satirization of bureaucracy and the corrupt officials who are sometimes found in it.

F. Kafka, *The Castle* (New York: Knopf, 1941). Few authors have surpassed this writer's ability to depict bureaucracy and the effects of it.

S. Lewis, *Gideon Planish* (New York: Random House, 1943). A satire of American organizations, especially "do-gooder" groups and charities.

FILMS

Economic and Social Council at Work (United States Army, 1952, 20 min., sound, black and white). Depicts the organization and functions of the Council and indicates the large number of agencies and commissions functioning under or cooperating with a world-wide organization.

A *Plane Is Born* (Civil Aeronautics Administration, 1949, 19 min., sound, black and white). How industrial and government bureaucracies must work together to insure the safety of aircraft.

Planning Our Foreign Policy (Encyclopaedia Britannica Films, 1955, 21 min., sound, black and white). Covers the many government agencies that are concerned with foreign policy.

Production Pioneering (Ford Motor Company, 1951, 15 min., sound, black and white). Shows the intricacies of organization necessary in mass-production industries.

Patterns
of Bureaucratic Behavior

*Few things are more indicative of a bureaucracy than
its organizational charts. We study them, revise them,
and wonder why the organization never conforms to them.*

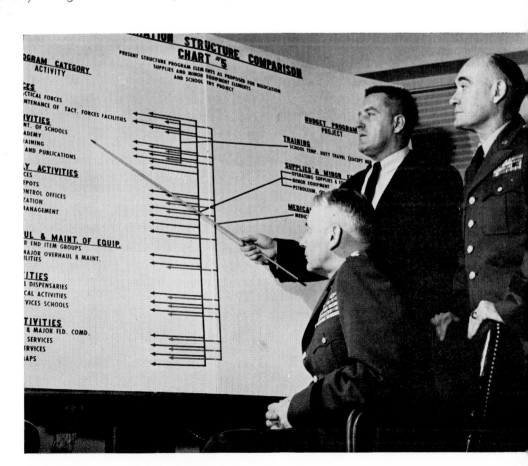

Our work

expands so as to fill the time available for its completion." This amusing commentary on the social scene is known as *Parkinson's Law*. According to its author and former member of the British War Office, Professor C. Northcote Parkinson, this "law" is basic to bureaucratic behavior. Since work habits vary so widely, the difficulty or the size of any task cannot be judged by the amount of time that is consumed in its completion. A college co-ed, for example, may consume many hours on a short class assignment, arranging her books and materials, hunting pencils she will not use, daydreaming, or going through a number of wasted motions. When finished, she will tell herself how tired she is as a result of the work. But suppose the same girl had begun the assignment a short while before an important date. Then she might have finished in less than an hour and felt no fatigue at all. Thus, work swells to fit the time, circumstances, and the person involved. "It is the busiest man who has time to spare," according to Parkinson, and most of us know this is true.

If the amount of time spent on a task provides no indication of the size of that task, then there may be no relationship between the amount of work and the size of the staff doing the work. Many persons can be kept busy doing a job that any one of them might do alone in the same space of time. It is this feature that so many bureaucratic officials exploit. Jobs and persons can be multiplied without hint of waste or unnecessary activity. If someone questions the expansion, just say, "This is a growing organization!"

ORGANIZATIONS AS DOMAINS OF VESTED INTERESTS

Each bureaucratic official tends to make work for himself, and all officials tend to make work for one another. This situation leads to expansion since more work justifies the addition of personnel and this, in turn, makes it possible for officials to increase the number of their subordinates. The more work and subordinates an official is responsible for, the more status, prestige, and income he can command, and the more indispensable he appears. He gains security in his position. Bureaucratic organization is thus a domain of vested interests for those who are a part of it.

THE NEED TO SURVIVE

The organization must continue because men's lives, security, prestige, and income depend on it. The more people involved, the greater the pressure to keep the organization going, for each member has a vested interest in the enterprise. When the purposes for which an organization was established begin to dissipate, the members will find new purposes, functions, or even new arguments for continuing their old work. Some will go so far as to stoop to deceit, camouflage, or falsification to keep themselves and their organization going. Bureaucracies resist extinction, and the larger they are, the more relentlessly they resist. Many have been able to hang on long after the reason for their being no longer existed. Several offices of the Grand Army of the Republic, for example, continued to function for some time after most Civil War veterans were dead and their organization, for all practical purposes, had become inoperative.

PROLIFERATION OF ACTIVITIES

One of the best ways to avoid extinction is to find more things for the organization to do. So bureaucrats tend to make work for each other. Many a bureaucrat hunts tirelessly for new and more things to do. He will raid other organizations to find other functions, and he will resist vigorously any attempt to deprive him of the functions he already performs. Every function and every person in his own organization is a symbol of security, prestige, and power.

The struggle for dominance in the missiles programs between the Army, Navy, and Air Force is an example of three giant bureaucratic organizations attempting to expand their activities into new realms of endeavor. Each understood that a successful missiles program would strengthen the entire organization of the branch that developed it first and would enhance its prestige with Congress and the American public. The Army, in particular, was painfully aware of this factor since air power had become such an important factor in military preparedness.

EXPANSION IN SIZE AND SCOPE OF EACH ACTIVITY

Bureaucratic organizations not only seek to increase the number of activities in which they engage but also try to expand the size and scope of everything they do. Every department wants more bureaus, and every bureau, more agencies. And no one, of course, wants to be absorbed. All organizations, big and small, look for more projects, more personnel, more work to keep them afloat. In 1940 Congress received two separate proposals for the construction of a multiple-purpose reservoir on the Kings River in California. One report was submitted by the United States Bureau of Reclamation and the other by the Army Corps of Engineers. A battle was on. The question of the feasibility of the project ran a poor second to the question of which bureaucratic empire would get the job. The public welfare waited seven years for the struggle to be resolved.

In many states the state police or highway patrols have used loopholes in the law to increase the number of speed zones and other traffic requirements within their jurisdictions in order to expand their function of traffic enforcement and even to justify the addition of personnel. There is virtually no limit to the amount of expansion and proliferation a bureaucracy will attempt if left unchecked.

PROLIFERATION OF PERSONNEL

Expansion of activity, of course, leads directly to an increase in personnel. When this expansion is combined with the operation of Parkinson's Law, even greater increases occur. For Parkinson's Law decrees that the personnel of an organization will increase even when its tasks are decreasing. Parkinson found, for example, that the British Royal Navy in 1914 had 62 capital ships with 146,000 officers and men, 3,249 dockyard officers and clerks, and 57,000 dockyard workers. Just 14 years later, though the number of capital ships had been reduced to 20, there were 100,000 officers and men, 4,558 dockyard officers and clerks, and 62,439 workers. At the same time, the number of officials in the admiralty office rose by nearly

80 per cent. "For every new foreman or electrical engineer at Portsmouth there had to be two more clerks at Charing Cross," observed Parkinson.

Growth in bureaucratic personnel, then, is not simply a matter of new functions, duties, or services. Bureaucracies multiply their numbers even in periods of decline. In any organization the addition of one official will likely bring about the addition of two more as assistants. A person surrounded by assistants enjoys both prestige and security. If the time comes when the staff must be cut, the assistants will be the first to go. Parkinson also points out that a single assistant will frequently compete against his boss, whereas two or more are more likely to compete among themselves and leave the boss relatively secure in his position. Added personnel protects vested interests. Nearly every official tends to surround himself with a ring of underlings.*

INCREASED COMPLEXITY

The complexity that accompanies bureaucratic growth also tends to serve vested interests. A secretary, for example, can make her position more secure by arranging the filing system so that only she knows where to find things. The larger the organization, the more complex management becomes, and hence, the more opportunities arise for this type of behavior. To make yourself indispensable, one of the authors was once advised, do your job in such a way that no one else can possibly figure out your system and fill your place.

In extremely complex bureaus and agencies, each unit tends to justify and reinforce the claims of the others. Professor Sydney Hook has described a situation of this sort in a 1958 article in *The Saturday Review*.

---

* For a great deal of the material in the previous paragraphs, the authors are indebted to C. Parkinson, *Parkinson's Law* (Boston: Houghton Mifflin, 1957), pp. 1-20.

During World War II the Office of War Information established radio monitoring services to intercept and analyze enemy propaganda. When the enemy radio stations in Italy fell into Allied hands, these stations were then used by the occupying forces to disseminate Allied propaganda. The OWI continued to monitor the stations, however, despite the change! When OWI executives discovered what was going on and requested an explanation, the monitoring services explained that their reports were somehow useful to those groups that were still monitoring German and Japanese stations. The latter groups quickly confirmed this reply. Undoubtedly, they were worried about losing their own jobs if Germany and Japan surrendered.

Nearly all employees identify themselves with their immediate working groups and the larger organization of which they are a part. Interlocking loyalties are often strong. Let someone from outside the organization attack some facet of the enterprise and individuals from all parts of the organization will rise to the common defense. A member of the Internal Revenue Bureau, for example, will tend to identify himself with "T" Men, the entire Treasury Department, and the United States government as a whole. Loyalty is infectious throughout a bureaucratic organization unless there are serious conflicts and disagreements over particular aims or jurisdictions.

Contrary to popular opinion, the introduction of complex labor-saving machinery can also increase rather than decrease personnel and the size of the bureaucracy. Electronic computers and other types of complex machinery require a battery of experts and assistants to operate them. Normally they will also require another battery of workers to repair and service them. Following a change, many workers are apt to be displaced. But within a short while the organization will begin to fill up with people.

CONSERVATISM, STRATIFICATION,
AND RESISTANCE TO CHANGE

All men tend to be creatures of routine and habit—bureaucrats, most people think, more so than others. Trained in a particular skill, performing it over and over, and considering his vocation a career, the bureaucrat develops a high degree of proficiency and vested professional interest that make him suspicious of change. Further, the need for rules in a bureaucracy tends to routinize his behavior. Innovation, especially of a radical sort, he distrusts because it departs from the normal way of doing things. It was difficult, for example, to get the leadership of Ford, Chrysler, or General Motors to start producing a small car even in the face of declining sales of standard models prompted in part by rising sales of small domestic and foreign cars. Political party leaders tend to resist the adoption of new platforms and creeds. The United States Post Office Department has sometimes resisted the adoption of new machinery, techniques, and changes in delivery routes. Giant businesses usually follow the same routine as long as they are earning good profits. And many churches are proud of the fact that they have changed very little over the centuries.

The social scientist Robert Park once quipped, "What a man does occupies most of his life and all of his obituary." Nearly everyone likes to keep doing something that is related to what he is now doing or has always done, especially when it comes to making a living. A bureaucrat is a job-holder. Within a given organization, each person has a certain position and status that he wants to protect against the whims of change. As time hardens and stratifies his position and relations with fellow employees, he tends toward conservatism. His entire outlook on life will revolve to some degree around the organization of which he is a part. He associates the deference he receives inside the organization with the hallowed routine of corporate life. That deference may be no more than the privilege of having his desk by a window, but to him it is vital. As he advances in salary and rank, and commands better quarters and more secretaries, he is likely to become even more conservative and doubtful about the wisdom of change. The distribution of deference, privileges, and symbols of status is a sensitive matter that often breeds resistance to change.

Another sensitive zone is work standards. Any group working on a particular program for a long time will become very defensive about its tasks. Its members will naturally

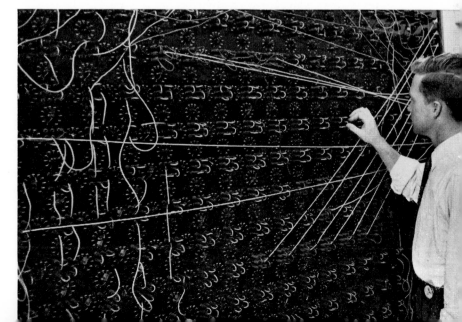

The introduction of complex labor-saving devices can add to rather than check the growth of bureaucracy. Complicated machines must be run and repaired by batteries of experts, who must be supervised by more experts, and so on.

be inclined to feel that they are experts in the area and will resist all efforts to change programs. Some groups become so self-confident that they automatically regard any suggestion that does not originate from within the group itself as unwise. Although expertness may be only an illusion, it nevertheless breeds inflexibility and resistance to innovation.

CALCULATED PROTECTION

Many times organizations protect their interests in calculated and even devious ways. Records will be falsified, output slowed to a snail's pace, or evidence "stacked" to give outsiders a particular impression of the organization's status and progress. Certainly individuals and groups tend to communicate only that information which will present them in a favorable light. Reports of college deans to their presidents and college boards, like reports of government agencies to Congress, always give the impression that the organization is doing a "bang-up" job. Failures, if they must be mentioned, are explained in a manner which demonstrates that their causes were beyond the reporting organization's control.

DOING THE JOB WELL

It would be manifestly impossible to make an accurate listing of all the ways that groups and individuals protect their stake in an organization. Vested interests are, after all, far more abundant than the number of organizations in which they are protected. And individuals are amazingly ingenious at devising methods of protecting themselves.

Probably no better method exists, however, than doing the job well and then getting the message across. The latter point is very important, for if the superiors do not know that the job is being done well, the group will not only suffer but its objectives

may be negated. Doing the job well depends heavily on a contented worker. Dissatisfaction among members of the group brings not only trouble but often disaster. Keeping the members satisfied hinges on several crucial factors. First, employees must understand the goals of the organization, and they must feel that they are contributing to them. Secondly, they must feel that their contributions are being recognized, that there is adequate opportunity for promotions, salary increases, increased prestige and status, and other rewards. Third, they must feel that rewards are being dispensed fairly and on the basis of competence. Fourth, groups and individuals in face-to-face situations need a friendly and sociable atmosphere in which to work. Fifth, the workers should share in a "we-ness" or in-group feeling, having common goals and satisfactions. Sixth, every worker needs a court of appeal to which he can carry his complaints and his problems. He must be made to believe that his superiors really care, otherwise he seethes inside, often slows up his output, and communicates his discontent to others.

The maintenance of employee morale is vital. The alternatives are high turnover and lagging production. No organization can operate at maximum efficiency if it is constantly forced to train a steady flow of new employees and help them adjust to new working conditions. Nor are men easily induced to increase output when their morale is low.

If the job is to be done well, it is also necessary to integrate functions correctly, to place responsibility properly, and to employ tolerable and adequate means of control. All segments of the organization must be properly linked by a good communication system. Poor administration, after all, simply reflects the weaknesses of those who administer. And the cure for bad administration is more effective administration rather than no administration at all.

BUREAUCRATIC POWER

With bureaucracy, as we have noticed, goes power and influence. One of the reasons for the rise of bureaucracies was the power they could deliver into a few trained hands. Bureaucratic power is one of the major vested interests that modern men seek to possess and protect. What, then, are some of the ways in which bureaucratic power can be attained?

THE ADVENT OF THE EXPERT

Few things are more essential today than the need to be specialized. This is the heyday of the expert. Today's youngster is advised to select some narrow specialty and then proceed to find out all there is to know about it. Once he has established himself, the world will beat a path to his door. He will enjoy prestige and influence, and not just in his own specialty but also in many other fields. For one of the strange characteristics of American society is the tendency to assume that skill in one field makes a person an expert in a number of others. The political views of physicians and bankers are frequently as highly regarded as their specialized professional opinions.

Employing specialization to gain power and authority is typical of bureaucracy. It is, in fact, typical of modern life everywhere. We go to the expert; he offers his advice; we do as he says. Through his advice, he wields power and influence. "It came from the horse's mouth," we quip. The expert may be our assistant, but very often we cannot argue, for we have our job, he has his, and we must depend on him to give us the correct answer in the area of his specialty. According to reports, President Franklin Roosevelt decided to undertake the atomic bomb project on the advice of Dr. Albert Einstein. In this role Dr. Einstein was exercising power seldom wielded by even the most powerful political leaders.

Expertness is used in yet another way to achieve and maintain power and control within a bureaucratic structure. Experts have specialties that lend themselves to rigorous job descriptions. When jobs are minutely described, management can easily locate those responsible for organizational successes and failures and can integrate many specific functions into a single, smoothly functioning unit.

CONTROL THROUGH HIERARCHY

What is more indicative of the presence of bureaucracy than organizational charts? We see them everywhere. Bureaucrats point to them, study them, revise them, and wonder why the organization never conforms to them. With the charts go the company manual, rule books, and stacks of daily regulations. Charts and manuals are usually associated with hierarchy, order, clear lines of command and responsibility, and the urge to violate them. The hierarchical framework outlines the fundamental structure of the organization and the basic roles and relationships of the people who carry out the policies and programs of the bureaucracy. Both managers and workers are grouped according to duties and responsibilities. Finance officers and legal advisers, for example, may be grouped into finance and legal departments, respectively. With them go their subordinates—special assistants, technicians, field representatives, "leg men," and secretaries. If the organization is large, departments will supervise and control bureaus at the next lower level, and the bureaus will control and oversee agencies.

Organizational control is impossible unless an organization is structured according to some formula and the duties and responsibilities of all employees at each level are clearly outlined. Hence, the charts, manuals, and directives. Each individual not only must know what his position is within broad limits but also must be afforded clear lines of communication and access to his superiors. Their relationship to him as well as their control over him must be defined. Every worker must know his superior, and every supervisor, his subordinates.

These are the tedious and formal traits of hierarchical organization. And their presence signifies the presence of bureaucracy. No organization ever achieves this ideal, however, because organizations are composed of human beings. Men tend to make charts into idols and rules into proverbs. And other men always have a yen to smash idols and ignore proverbs. The chart may dictate that Joe is responsible to Jim, but Jim may actually be influenced by Joe through a mutual friend. The signs on the wall may prohibit smoking, yet everyone in the organization may smoke on the job. Every bureaucratic organization, therefore, has two hierarchies—the formal one found on the charts and in the manuals, and the informal one that represents conditions as they are. At many points the two may be identical, but there are always two.

The formal hierarchy, then, is an "ideal" structure that merely shows things as they "should" be. In most cases it simply provides the broadest sort of outline. Within the outline, individual attachments and associations will form, and shortly the entire organization will be shot through with groups and cliques that are loyal to their own group as well as to the organization itself. This behavior seldom hinders effective operation unless loyalties to cliques are so strong or of such a character that they interfere with the bureaucracy's goals. A clique or group may believe that it is important to hold down production in order to avoid layoffs. If something like this happens, the over-all goals of the organization suffer. An even more serious situation may arise from rivalries between two groups. Conflict may become so severe that one group will sabotage the work of another. A third type of situation involves group standards. A group of draftsmen, for example, may develop standards of its own that differ from or are opposed to the standards of the entire enterprise.

If the informal hierarchy is permitted to displace the formal one, in a large bureaucratic concern especially, control is difficult to maintain. No one can be left completely free to do as he pleases. Since power to make decisions and to act on them must be delegated to lower officials and workers, there must be clearly defined lines of control from those who delegate power to those who exercise it. Otherwise, various segments of the organization may develop their own empires, and informal groups may become uncontrolled antagonists of the organization itself.

GOVERNMENT BY RULES

From the rulebook come guides for behavior. The rules tell us both what to do and how to do it. They are absolutely vital to a bureaucracy. For they enable the rulemaker to communicate standards to the entire organization on an impersonal and formal basis. Persons with whom the rulemaker never comes in contact can be guided and controlled through written rules. Rules are impersonal devices that can be readily substituted for face-to-face situations and direct verbal orders. Through them the employee's discretion and authority can be narrowed, and each member of the organization can be better informed about what he can and cannot do. Executives and superiors are in a far better position to control behavior throughout the entire organization. For the same rule will apply in every plant, bureau, and office throughout the country, or even the world, if the bureaucracy is that extensive. Then, too, written regulations provide an acceptable basis for punishment since penalties can be justifiably invoked when a rule has been broken.

IMPERSONALITY

Very important, however, is the impersonal character of rules that makes them into objects against which the worker can vent his wrath. He can blame "the rule" rather than the organization or his superiors. If you don't like what happens, just blame it on "red tape!" And stern executives can demand compliance by saying, "That's the rule!" It is far better for the organization and its goals if the worker finds fault with an impersonal rule rather than with the organization itself or its personnel. And bureaucratic officials are less hesitant to enforce rules when they have never met the persons to whom the rules apply. Often overlooked, too, is the increased bargaining power that rules bestow on management in its negotiations and relations with the worker. The managers are often free to let some rules go unenforced in order to win the workers' allegiance and good will.

STRATEGIC LENIENCY

Thus, there are usually rules to break as well as live by. One expert on bureaucratic organization, A. W. Gouldner, calls this "mock bureaucracy." He describes an actual situation in which a company enforced most rules rigorously, but neglected to enforce a no-smoking rule, despite the presence of large "No Smoking" signs in nearly every room and corridor of the building. The signs had been put in by the fire-insurance company, and the central office would call to warn the employees whenever the fire inspector appeared. Another authority, Peter Blau, asserts that many good foremen are able to improve morale and increase production by permitting subordinates to

violate minor rules, such as not eating or talking while working. This indulgence increases his power over his subordinates. If a foreman notices that some worker is loafing or otherwise misbehaving, he can shout, "Cut the talk! Can't you read?" A hard worker, on the other hand, will probably not be called down for talking. The "boss" is thus *strategically lenient* with him. A subordinate who understands that not every superior would do it that way will appreciate the privilege and probably work harder to keep it. According to Blau, "The mere knowledge that the rule exists, and possibly, that it is enforced elsewhere, instills a sense of obligation to liberal superiors and induces subordinates more readily to comply with their requests." Furthermore, employees appreciate the assurance that a mistake or slight deviation from the rules will not bring down the wrath of their superiors. Therefore, when supervisors are strategically lenient, workers tend to work harder, obey more willingly when asked to, and give their loyalty to the organization and its objectives.

A strategically lenient "boss" is more apt to suggest than command. He usually explains the reasons for his directives and seldom issues curt orders unless forced to. When a subordinate is in trouble with top management, he will "go to bat" for him. The power and control of a strategically lenient "boss" rest on social obligations rather than sheer force or threat of reprisal, removal, or other sanctions. His underlings feel obligated. Often they are eager to repay him for his favors, for they usually prefer such a relationship and seek to have it continued.

POWER AND SANCTION

Many of the relationships between subordinates and superiors that we have been discussing are power relationships. Too often power is considered the capacity or authority to push others around. But as we have just seen, positions of power and influence can be established through acts of leniency as well as of sternness. Kindness, cajolery, the creation of personal and social obligations, actions that evoke confidence, even knowledge and experience, are only a few of the many ways in which a power relationship can be established by one person over another. As we have seen, social and political power identifies a relationship among or between human beings. It does not refer to a special quality or personal attribute that some persons possess and others do not, although it is true, of course, that an individual's personality and training may render him better able to play power roles. Specifically, power refers to a relationship in which one or more individual persons are acting in accord with the intentions or policy of one or more other individuals. Once that relationship is established, and as long as it continues, we can say that one group occupies a position of authority over the other. But the maintenance of a position of authority depends on the compliance of those who occupy the subordinate position. In brief, if a group of workers refuses to obey the foreman, or a crew its captain, neither the foreman nor the captain has any actual power or authority, no matter what the rules, laws, charts, or manuals say. Hence, a power relationship is not established by the formal appointment of one man over another. It is something established in the course of human relationships and not something necessarily brought into being by an organizational chart, although a chart may show a power relationship that is actually followed.

Yet the hierarchy, the charts, and the rule books prescribe power relationships into which persons are supposed to fit. They define the limits of authority of each supervisor or superior official and establish the authority of superiors over their underlings. Workers must look to their supervisors for ratings, promotions, pay raises, favors, and other forms of recognition. And each superior official is expected to control his organization or group without overstepping the limits of his authority, preferably by resorting to noncoercive techniques wherever possible. Nevertheless, most officials find it necessary occasionally to resort to penalties or the threat of them. There are some people, of course, who thoroughly enjoy pushing others around. But sanctions are not formulated for that purpose. Rather, sanctions are intended only to keep authority effectively established. The foreman who commands the respect and allegiance of his men will seldom need to threaten them or offer them rewards. Actually, if he continually threatens them, he undermines his authority. His authority rests on the existence of sanctions, but if he uses them too frequently he will weaken his position. He may say, "Straighten out or I will see that you don't get a raise!" But should he keep on refusing to give the man a pay increase, he will soon have to find another sanction, for the effectiveness of his old threat will have lost a lot of its punch. Moreover, such a refusal may antagonize the worker and affect his output.

Hence, sanctions are most effective when they are not used—when the threat of their enforcement is there. Yet they are necessary, especially in large organizations where many rules must be uniform throughout the entire hierarchy. The accepted practices in a company's St. Louis plant, for example, may not be popular in its Los Angeles plant. But even the most lenient superior must invoke sanctions when his men refuse to abide by the standards that his bureaucracy's chiefs believe are absolutely vital.

ROUTINE AND FORMALISM

The modern office-worker rises at a regular hour, showers and shaves, eats his breakfast over the morning paper, and arrives at the office around a certain time every day. He puts his hat and coat on the same familiar hook, reads his morning mail, and probably calls his secretary in to take some dictation. Such a schedule is rather common. The boss can count on his being in particular places at certain hours of the day because his activities are governed by routine. All the boss must do is permit him to follow his normal routine, and few other controls will be necessary. Who has not heard the familiar statement: "I like George. You can count on him. You bet! One always knows where that fellow is"?

The routine pattern, the well-defined limits of authority, and the specific rules found in a bureaucracy all facilitate control. One of the most effective devices is the time-card each employee punches as he enters the factory's portals. In a bureaucracy everyone has a routine and ritual to follow from the time he punches in until he punches out. As he follows along in that routine and performs his daily rituals, he is controlled by them. The trip up the elevator to file his report, the session with his subordinates every Friday, and the company order forms all bind his behavior. As routine and ritual increase, the need for surveillance will likely decrease. In many instances it will almost disappear.

PROFESSIONALISM

Professional standards are also a factor in bureaucratic control. A secretary is expected to type so many words a minute, an artist to maintain standards of quality and neatness, and a draftsman to turn out a certain quantity of blueprints. Irrespective of the standards set by the organization that employs him, a professional man is bound by standards that his profession has developed, and these standards of performance and quality of workmanship may in-

deed be more influential than his employer's standards.

THE GOAL: EFFICIENCY

Years ago Max Weber pointed out that bureaucratic organization and techniques of control were really aimed at greater efficiency. All things are supposed to work together in order to increase production, lower operating costs, and eliminate wasted motion and effort. When these goals are not achieved, the real purpose of bureaucracy has failed.

Naturally, efficiency can be over-emphasized. It often is. The pressure for increased production can backfire when workers are pushed beyond the limits of their accepted

Like millions of city dwellers in other lands, residents of Tokyo, following their normal bureaucratic routine, ride great distances at regular hours to and from work over an efficiently operated and bureaucratically organized transportation system.

standards, or made to feel that efficiency and production are more important than their welfare. Bureaucratic officials must be ever watchful not to overlook the fact that they are in charge of a human organization and not just a mass of machinery.

BUREAUCRACY IN PROCESS

Most modern bureaucracies reveal many of the traits we have discussed in this chapter and the preceding one. Nevertheless, bureaucratic behavior patterns vary considerably, especially among those that are organized for different purposes. A bureaucracy organized for profit, for example, differs markedly from a voluntary type organization that has developed a bureaucratic framework. And both differ considerably from governmental bureaucracies.

BIG BUSINESS

In America big business gets bigger. Over the last fifty years or so the entire business world has experienced a wave of empire-building the like of which would have defied the imagination at the turn of the century. A constant flood of mergers, amalgamations, interlocking agreements, and consolidations, as well as just plain growth, has swept through the American business world and shows no tendency to let up. Where will it stop? We cannot say definitely, but one of the results has been the growth of bigger and bigger business bureaucracies. Government is by no means the only stronghold of bureaucracy.

Increased size brought increased specialization, and these two features created the need for a different type of business leadership than had existed in the nineteenth century. The dynamic, risk-taking, owner-managers of this earlier era were replaced by "hired" managers who transformed the modern corporation. The hallmarks of the new corporation were vastness of size, breadth of scope, separation of ownership from management, and technicality. It took administrative experts to manage it. The professional executive who took over was better educated than his predecessor had been and thus heavily oriented in the direction of planning. He also was more reliant on research, advisory staffs, and internal forms of bureaucratic control. Since he usually owned little or no stock in the enterprise, he had less incentive than the former owner-manager to take risks. He would play it safe! Although company profits continued to be an important incentive, the new-type businessman, like the government bureaucrat, steadily became more concerned about status, prestige, and security. And like government bureaucracy, too, industrial and business bureaucracy became more rigid, more dependent on hierarchical organization and control, more conservative and arbitrary.

The new business corporation leaned toward collective decision-making. Managers depended more and more on the collective opinions of experts for their decisions. Policy was set all along the hierarchical lines of responsibility. It could originate almost anywhere—in the office of field directors, sales managers, production managers, and even on the assembly line. The decision-making process was decentralized and the new-type manager became more of a coordinator than a decision-maker.

The results are now apparent. Modern corporations are typically bureaucratic. They are very often giant collectives characterized by routine, cumulative, and continuous processes. They are filled with experts. Like big government, big business is a bit "stiff at the joints," tending to be conservative and not inclined to take the big risks that so typified the methods of early American businessmen. Today's executive displays far less daring and initiative than his nineteenth-century predecessor. Throughout the business world, men are bound not only by professional standards and ethics but by those of the particular business as well. A hierarchy and its attendant charts and manuals are much in evidence, as is the "red tape."

Yet most businessmen resent being called bureaucratic. They usually deny vigorously that their business, or any other business for that matter, comes even close to being bureaucratic. So far as they are concerned, bureaucracy flourishes only in government. As a result, they often try very hard to appear non-bureaucratic. They speak enthusiastically about people in their firms who have risen to the top through their own initiative, the vast opportunities that exist for personal advancement and individual development as well as for profit. But their enthusiasm often belies a condition that, if not true of their company, at least applies to others. A person need not work hard to sell himself and others the merit of beliefs that are widely recognized as valid.

Sociologist C. Wright Mills points out that in at least one respect the modern business organization is not typical of other bureaucratic organizations. Strictly speaking, top business officials are not bureaucrats. For the top man usually does not advance by climbing from one level to the next through a hierarchy of positions. At the higher levels of the corporate world, men are neither bureaucrats nor entrepreneurs, but a composite of "speculators, men with great American fortunes, and executives in jobs with chances to make money." The bureaucrats are normally confined to the hierarchy and remain linked to the chain of command, and very few of them enter the ranks of the extremely wealthy via the "slow bureaucratic crawl." According to Benjamin Fairless,

Up, up, up goes the bureaucratic stack, floor on floor, office on office, in the world of business.

former chairman of the United States Steel Company, "Many of the executives in some of our largest corporations have spent a lifetime in the field of industrial management without ever having been able to accumulate as much as a million dollars. And I know that to be a fact, because I happen to be one of them myself." Many corporation chiefs do become millionaires, of course, but not primarily because they are skilled in industrial management. Rather, it is because of their financial skill. As Mills points out, no more than 15 per cent of professional managers had made the long bureaucratic crawl to the top as of 1950. And even these few were often aided by talents they had developed in other fields, such as law. Hence, many of the top executives are members of

397

a particular social set, which is wealthy from the start.

The major economic fact about the very rich is the fact of the accumulation of advantages: those who have great wealth are in a dozen strategic positions to make it yield further wealth. Sixty-five per cent of the very richest people in America today are involved in enterprises which their families have passed on to them or are simply living as rentiers on the huge returns from such properties.... It it not usual and never has been the dominant fact carefully to accumulate your way to the top in a slow, bureaucratic crawl. It is difficult to climb to the top, and many who try fall by the way. It is easier and much safer to be born there.*

Here Mills encapsules the facts of power relations in business. Corporate bureaucracy is the basis of continued power and privilege for those who hold the wealth and the top positions. This generally means that most bureaucrats are confined to the lower echelons and that most top executives are not bureaucrats in the same sense that their managers are.

BIG LABOR

The labor leader is another fellow who resents being called a bureaucrat. But labor leaders have taken their place alongside corporate executives and government officials in the bureaucratic camp, although they represent a somewhat different type of bureaucrat, to be sure. Since they lead and manage the affairs of a *voluntary* organization, their objectives are different from the objectives of their fellow bureaucrats in other organizations. Improved wages, hours, and working conditions are what they seek. These goals bind the membership to them and place them in a unique position. For if the goals are to be achieved, management must agree to share more of its profits with the worker.

---

* C. Mills, *The Power Elite* (New York: Oxford University Press, 1956), p. 115.

Building a union strong enough to wrest these things from powerful industrial bureaucracies is a very difficult task. Therefore, a constant objective of union officials is to strengthen their organizations, not just because their jobs depend on the union's survival but because they must be strong to fight. Growth and strength are a "must." For this reason workers will deliver great power into the hands of the leadership to get the job done.

As unions increase their influence and power, they too acquire the trappings of bureaucracy. Specialists appear, a hierarchy is imposed, and ritual, routine, and rules—the 3 R's of the school of bureaucracy—are religiously followed. Trained organizers, salaried administrators, legal specialists, mediators, and a host of experts have brought professionalism into the union movement.

"The chicken is power, and comes first; the egg is status," says Professor Mills. He calls the modern labor leaders "the new men of power." Their rise to power within labor unions has been followed by the usual bureaucratic tendencies—"stiffening at the joints" and conservatism. The organization frequently becomes an end in itself and its members seek not only to perpetuate its life but to expand its activities as far as possible. Labor bureaucracies, for example, have taken over the administration of retirement and pension programs or gone into the housing and real estate business or entered the insurance field.

Proliferation of activities and growth lend prestige to the organization and its personnel here as elsewhere. Taking over business activities in particular makes unions appear respectable in a country that is business-oriented. Many labor executives work hard at getting this message across. They proudly announce, for example, that American unionism is simply business unionism. Workers, so their argument runs, want only a greater share of the profits. In many instances, big labor joins hands with big business. The union takes over much of the company's personnel work and becomes an instrument for controlling personnel policy by joint agreement between union and company officials. The union acts as a voice of the workers, the company as a voice of the managers, and both bureaucracies begin to blend at many points. With the labor bureaucracy acting as a buffer between workers and managers, the position of the labor bureaucrat is secure. He enjoys greater prestige and status. Before long he may become very conservative and more company-oriented than union-oriented. The entire union, in fact, may grow conservative. Sometimes it even becomes the business of the union to prevent strikes and other work stoppages, as when the United Automobile Workers, under a 1945 agreement with the Ford Company, pledged to act as judge and prosecutor of any employee believed guilty of "giving leadership to an unauthorized work stoppage."

The bureaucratic trend in the union movement has had a great deal to do with making large unions more conservative, as has the separation of leadership from the union membership. Although unions are voluntary organs and are presumably democratic, since they elect their leaders, the leadership still tends to be selected from above as in other bureaucracies. In theory, of course, stockholders of a corporation elect their leadership, too. In fact, however, most stockholders have their stock voted for them by someone who holds their proxy. That "someone" is usually a "company man" who votes according to the wishes of the leadership. Likewise, labor elections, although structured so that each member can vote, usually result in the selection of men the bureaucracy favors. Voting delegates are normally instructed according to decisions reached prior to the election. These decisions are channeled down to the local leaders who obtain the necessary mandate from their members to send the *right* delegates with the *right* instructions. And the organization is large enough so that the national and state leadership will normally have sufficient voting strength in its favor to counterbalance any locals that may refuse to go along with them. A similar situation exists with respect to policy determination in unions. Consequently, the membership tends to be cut off from leadership to a considerable extent, and the bureaucracy becomes self-perpetuating and even irresponsible at times.

Big labor, then, resembles big business, big government, and other large organizations; and like them, it has its share of red tape, routine, personnel problems, and corruption. Just as banks have embezzling cashiers, so unions have their share of racketeers. In recent years a number of scandals involving major labor unions and racketeering have excited the nation's attention.

BIG GOVERNMENT

Nearly everyone agrees that modern government is bureaucratic. Bureaucracy is the hallmark of the modern national state. The American national government is one of the largest bureaucracies in the world. The distinctive feature of all government bureaucracies, of course, is their political character. As a person moves up the hierarchy from the lowest administrator to the highest executive, politics becomes an ever more significant factor.

Unlike the German bureaucracy of an earlier period, however, the managers of America's governmental machinery are not the rulers of America. For they are not the ones who make the over-all policy decisions. These are made by "outsiders" or "the executives," a group of men, many of them novices in government, who have entered government service from other professions and occupations. Professor Mills points out that most top executives and their lieutenants in the national administration do not carry the bureaucratic stamp. As of May, 1953, for example, the fifty-three top executives in the national government included only fourteen men who were either professional party politicians or former members of governmental bureaucracies. Mills' analysis of the political lieutenants revealed the following:

Among the top thirty-two deputies of the agencies, departments, and commissions, twenty-one are novices in government: many of them never held political office, nor in fact ever worked in government, before their present positions. These men usually have had fathers who were big businessmen; twelve attended Ivy League colleges; and they themselves have often been businessmen or bankers or the salaried lawyers of large corporations or members of the big law firms. Unlike professional politicians, they do not belong to the local jamboree of Elk and Legion; they are more often members of quiet social clubs and exclusive country clubs. Their origins, their careers, and their associations make them representative of the corporate rich.*

Just as in the business world, where corporate enterprise is bureaucratic but controlled by non-bureaucrats from the wealthy set, so too in government the top executives are drawn from much the same source and, strictly speaking, cannot be classed as bureaucrats. It is thus true that although a bureaucracy and its trained managers run the governmental machinery, those who play the dominant role in determining public policy are frequently from the same set as the men who establish corporate policy. This lends real irony to charges of "government bureaucracy" often voiced by the spokesmen for business interests. For men from the same group actually control both bureaucracies.

The top brass of the national government is drawn largely from the business and professional world and reflects business values. Government has taken its cue from business in matters of management, hierarchical control, job classification, staffing techniques, and programing. The American businessman insists that government be "businesslike," "efficient," and run "in the interest of business." Contrary to the deluge of opinion which creates the opposite impression, he has made it so.

The American governmental bureaucracy differs in yet another important respect from other types of bureaucratic enterprise. It depends heavily on legislative and public support. Legislatures, after all, control the public purse and authorize the establishment of offices. Not one dollar for salaries or functions can be made available without an appropriation from Congress or a state legislature. Congress, for example, can kill any national agency by simply neglecting to appropriate money for its operation. Bureaucrats are therefore kept busy cultivating the favor of Congress or a state legislature if they happen to be members of a state government bureaucracy. Many government bureaus have to lobby in various ways to influence a legislature. The American Vocational Association and its ally, the American Association of State Highway Officials, for example, have pushed many bills through Congress on behalf of highway programs never contemplated in a presidential budget. The Federal Housing Administration lobbied with state legislatures to pass statutes permitting state-chartered banks to participate in its mortgage-insurance programs for housing.

Legislative support is also obtained through exploiting prestige, sacrificing unpopular personnel and programs, staging publicity, and through outright propagandizing. Individuals with great prestige, whether inside or outside the government, are exploited. Political scientist V. O. Key cites such an example:

---

* Mills, *The Power Elite*, p. 233.

The Federal Bureau of Investigation furnishes an excellent example of this technique. Its chief, J. Edgar Hoover, has diligently cultivated public favor with after-dinner speeches, dramatic news releases, and books and articles extolling the fearless work of "G-Men." So effective has been his continuing campaign that when Mr. Hoover makes a request of Congress newspaper editors all over the land editorialize in support of his position.*

Many congressmen, and especially state legislators, can be awed rather easily by the "big shots." Hence, top executives are often chosen for their prestige, and they are judged to a considerable extent by how well they use it. The status and prestige of the "outsider" can be used when the "insiders" need it. For example, when Congress threatened to lift gasoline and tire rationing during World War II, a respected financier, Bernard Baruch, was called on to present the case for rationing. Using government personnel, data, and recommendations, he did the job. He brought very little other than prestige to the issue.

It is evident in what we have just said that legislative support depends to a great extent on public support. The popular man is frequently regarded as the best man for the job. Like the state university president who must get all that he can for his school, the departmental and bureau chiefs must get all they can for their organization. If a man is personally well-known, popular with the legislator's constituents, and has status and respect, legislators will often be forced to submit to his requests. This generally means that unpopular executives and subordinates will be sacrificed by the organization, especially if they become controversial.

Likewise, a government agency's programs need popular support. Publicizing agency activities is therefore extremely important. For if no one knows what an organization is doing, officials will go unappreciated and

* V. Key, *Politics, Parties, and Pressure Groups* (New York: Crowell, 1948), p. 711.

legislative support will not be forthcoming. But public relations activities go far beyond mere publicity. The public has to be "sold" by the "information officers" on the virtues of each agency's work. Thus, publicity shades rapidly into propaganda. This philosophy, rather crudely put, amounts to: "If you don't toot your own horn, no one will toot it for you!"

But despite their extensive use of propaganda, public relations experts have not as yet allayed the popular resentment over bureaucratic growth in government. This resentment combines distrust, hostility, and contempt with fear. The government bureaucrat we know personally, a relative or friend, usually is not identified with the bureaucrats we malign. The bureaucrat we dislike and fear is usually bureaucrat X or the one we do not know. He is the one who we think has latched onto a big desk in Washington, found a good thing living off the taxpayer's money, and won't let go!

This bureaucratic growth that worries so many people is partly a result of popular demand for more services. We may not like the bureaucrat, but we do like his services. The growth of bureaucracy is a direct result of rising population, increased complexity in human relations, and urban-industrialism. Bureaucracy in America has fed on war, crisis, and economic depression. It came into being to answer human problems and needs and is something we are not going to eliminate. As human problems and needs grow and multiply, so does government bureaucracy. We would not tolerate life without it, despite our distaste and distrust for it. The problem is to control bureaucracy, not to eliminate it.

THE BRASS HATS

Bureaucracy permeates American society. It has become so widespread and so indicative of all sorts of human activity that we sometimes overlook its continued existence and vitality in one of its oldest places of residence, the military establishment. Military organizations are the classic examples of bureaucratic organization and technique. With them bureaucracy is a tradition.

In a country whose people are preoccupied with the acquisition of wealth, the military establishment has been historically devalued. It has been regarded as at best a necessary evil and burden. It is almost unbelievable that a country the size of the United States should have had a standing army of less than a quarter-million men as late as 1939. Yet, almost paradoxically, Americans have turned to the military on many occasions for political and industrial leadership. Several generals have become presidents, and today generals are being lured into more and more executive positions in industry. In fact, since Pearl Harbor the pace of military ascendancy has quickened and military prestige has been on the upgrade. The American decision to assert world leadership has no doubt been responsible for this trend. Members of the military forces were brought into politics. Politicians depended on military experts for advice. The military budget grew and with its growth came increased prestige and power for the military expert. Few people stop to

contemplate the significance of a peacetime military budget that exceeds 50 to 60 per cent of the national budget. As politics got into the military, the military got into politics. Today, few men are treated with more respect by members of Congress than military chieftains.

Maintenance of this position and prestige makes it necessary for the military chiefs to do what the administrative bureaucracy does —namely, work hard at enlisting public support. American military organizations differ from the typical "brass hat" empires that have arisen in other countries at other times. For they are subject to civilian control, dependent on the wiles of public opinion and subservient to Congress. It is to Congress that they must look for their authority and financial support. Hence, the military has its lobbies, too. Several years ago, one observer quipped that every fourth man in the capitol building was an officer in the Army Corps of Engineers. The military is obliged to call on every source of prestige available to it, engage in programs of publicity and propaganda, and be watchful that its personnel does not offend the public. They may be Spartan, ridden with tradition, or arbitrary, but today's military bureaucrats are forced to play democratic politics.

SOME WORDS OF SUMMARY

Since it is hard to judge the difficulty or the size of any task, bureaucrats can expand their domains and protect their vested interests by making work for themselves and each other. Expansion in size, proliferation of functions, and increased amounts of "busy work" help an organization survive. Therefore, organizations frequently seek to increase the number of their activities, expand the size and scope of each activity, and add personnel.

Bureaucrats entrench themselves by mastering procedure, increasing organizational complexity, and supporting each other's activities. Vested interests are protected through habituation to routine, resistance to change, reliance on the expert, and the stratification of status, prestige, work standards, and communications. But the best way for bureaucrats to protect their interests is to do their job well. And doing the job well depends partly on keeping workers satisfied.

Among the most important features of a bureaucracy, however, is the power it gives to particular persons and groups. Specialization has given the expert untold power and facilitated hierarchical organization and control. Written rules have narrowed discretion, produced greater uniformity, and increased bargaining power. Unenforced rules have made it possible to control behavior through a policy of strategic leniency rather than strict sanctions. And sanctions are still available for use in extreme situations. Impersonality, routine, and formalism also help to regularize and control behavior, as do professional standards and group ties outside the bureaucracy. All controls are supposed to work toward one important goal—efficiency.

Of the variety of bureaucratic types, business bureaucracy shows a phenomenal capacity for growth and specialization. As the owner-manager replaced the hired manager, profit became secondary to status and security as an incentive. Although big business is conservative and filled with experts and bureaucrats, its top executives are not strictly bureaucrats since they are drawn from a particular social set rather than from the bureaucracy itself.

Labor bureaucracies are organized on a voluntary basis and seek primarily to improve wages, hours, and working conditions. Their struggle with management for a greater share of profits and company benefits has made it necessary for unions to become strong and deliver considerable power into the hands of labor leaders. A bureaucratic structure with an attendant preoccupation with status, security, and survival soon appeared. As the bureaucracy solidified, leadership became more self-perpetuating and largely autonomous of its membership.

Big government has differed from the other bureaucracies in its political character. But as in big business, its leadership has been drawn from a special social set, and many of its workers and officials have come from the business world. It consequently resembles bureaucratic business in organization and method. Government differs, however, from both business and labor in its dependence on legislative and popular support.

The military, the classic bureaucratic type, has benefited in recent years from the world political crisis. Long submerged by the American quest for economic success, it is now in the ascendant, enjoying great respect and the largest share of the national budget. But it, too, is dependent on legislative and popular support.

FURTHER ROADS TO LEARNING

GENERAL ACCOUNTS

See "Further Roads to Learning" in Chapter 21 for the works of P. Blau, R. Bendix, H. Finer, R. Merton, L. von Mises, and H. Simon.

C. Hyneman, *Bureaucracy in a Democracy* (New York: Harper, 1950). Treats power relationships in a public bureaucracy.

H. Laski, "Bureaucracy," *Encyclopedia of the Social Sciences*, III (New York: Macmillan, 1934), pp. 70-73. Builds a definition around the tendencies toward specialization and expansion.

C. Parkinson, *Parkinson's Law* (Boston: Houghton Mifflin, 1957). Full of humor and a great deal of truth about bureaucratic traits.

P. Selznick, "An Approach to a Theory of Bureaucracy," *American Sociological Review*, VIII (1943), pp. 47-54; also his "Foundations of the Theory of Organization," *American Sociological Review*, XV (1950), pp. 25-35. Two admirable attempts to mold and employ a concept of bureaucracy.

H. Simon, D. Smithburg, and V. Thompson, *Public Administration* (New York: Knopf, 1950). A superb discussion of bureaucratic behavior in government.

SPECIAL STUDIES

"Administration in the Halls of Ivy," *Public Administration Review*, XX (Winter, 1960), pp. 1-27. A symposium on bureaucracy in higher education that covers everything from presidential efficiency to the dilemmas of deanship.

P. Appleby, *Big Democracy* (New York: Knopf, 1945). This short and readable book stresses the political content of government bureaucracy.

J. Armstrong, *The Soviet Bureaucratic Elite* (New York: Praeger, 1959). One of the finest works on Soviet bureaucracy.

C. Barnard, *Organization and Management* (Cambridge: Harvard University Press, 1948). A former business executive views industrial bureaucracy.

————, *The Functions of the Executive* (Cambridge: Harvard University Press, 1938). Another work on business bureaucracy that stresses the significance of informal organization.

M. Bernstein, *The Job of the Federal Executive* (Washington, D.C.: The Brookings Institution, 1958). Here is a superb report on the functions of the national government executive. Does an able job of distinguishing between the activities of political executives and those of career men.

K. Boulding, *The Organizational Revolution: A Study of the Ethics of Economic Organization* (New York: Harper, 1953). A leading economist traces the vast changes that have overtaken modern business organizations. Be certain to read the comment by Reinhold Niebuhr.

R. Brady, *Business as a System of Power* (New York: Columbia University Press, 1943). On the power relations of big business bureaucrats.

J. Burnham, *The Managerial Revolution* (New York: Day, 1941). A controversial book on the consequences of the change from owner-managers to hired managers in the business world.

P. Drucker, *Concept of the Corporation* (New York: Day, 1946). Treats the corporation as a center of power.

R. Dubin, *Human Relations in Administration* (Englewood Cliffs, N. J.: Prentice-Hall, 1951). This volume presents a number of cases that reflect the perplexing problems attending bureaucratic organization in the business world.

B. Gardner, "The Factory as a Social System," in W. White, ed., *Industry and Society* (New York: McGraw-Hill, 1946). About the informal and social relationships in the modern industrial bureaucracy.

A. Gouldner, *Patterns of Industrial Bureaucracy* (Glencoe, Ill.: The Free Press, 1954). An excellent study of the factors that produce industrial bureaucracy as well as the results.

J. Hardaman and M. Neufield, eds., *The House of Labor: Internal Operations of Labor Unions* (Englewood Cliffs, N.J.: Prentice-Hall, 1951). All about labor's internal bureaucracy.

S. Hook, "Bureaucrats Are Human," *The Saturday Review*, XLI (May 17, 1958), pp. 12-14 ff. Professor Hook exposes Parkinson's extremist position and concludes that bureaucracy has its virtues as well as its vices.

H. Laski, *The Limitations of the Expert* (London: Fabian Tract No. 235, 1931). An enjoyable discussion of our dependence on the expert.

C. Mills, *The Power Elite* (New York: Oxford University Press, 1956). A very stimulating volume on the character and composition of the top power groups in American society.

————, *White Collar: The American Middle Classes* (New York: Oxford University Press, 1951); also, *The New Men of Power* (New York: Harcourt, Brace, 1948). Two reading "musts," the first dealing with a class that makes up the bulk of our bureaucracies, and the second dealing with the labor bureaucracy.

C. Page, "Bureaucracy's Other Face," *Social Forces*, XXV (1946), pp. 88-94. Emphasizes the unofficial and informal aspects of bureaucracy.

C. Redfield, *Communication in Management: A Guide to Administrative Communication* (Chicago: The University of Chicago Press, 1953). How to keep bureaucratic communication channels open.

W. Sayer, *The Federal Government Service: Its Character, Prestige, and Problems* (New York: The American Assembly, 1954). An excellent symposium on the national government's bureaucracy.

E. Schneider, *Industrial Sociology: The Social Relations of Industry and the Community* (New York: McGraw-Hill, 1957). Chapters 5 and 6 contain discussions of industrial bureaucracy and the role of the bureaucratic executive.

H. Speier, "The American Soldier and the Sociology of Military Organization," in R. Merton and P. Lazarsfeld, eds., *Continuities in Social Research* (Glencoe, Ill.: The Free Press, 1950). A scholarly treatment of the military bureaucracy.

F. Taylor, *Scientific Management* (New York: Harper, 1947). By the father of the scientific management movement.

W. H. Whyte, Jr., "The Corporation and the Wife," *Fortune*, XLIV (November, 1951), pp. 109-111 ff. About the important role played by wives of bureaucrats in the communication and decision-making processes.

FICTION AND DRAMA

J. Farrell, *Gas House McGinty* (New York: Vanguard, 1933). Depicts the bureaucratic routine in a large distributing house.

A. Halper, *The Chute* (New York: Vanguard, 1937). How a number of persons were enslaved by a mail-order house package chute they were feeding.

S. Spewack, *Two Blind Mice*, in *Theatre Arts*, XXXIII (December, 1949). A play satirizing red tape in the national government's bureaucracy.

L. Tolstoi, *War and Peace* (New York: Random House, Modern Library and many other editions). A truly great work of art about Napoleon's Russian expedition that presents some telling administrative problems.

FILMS

Competition and Big Business (Encyclopaedia Britannica Films, 1953, 22 min., sound, color). The roles of big business and their bearing on technological development, monopoly, and public welfare.

Maintaining Quality Standards (United States Office of Education, 1944, 10 min., sound, black and white). The function of a supervisor in maintaining quantity and quality standards.

Supervisor as a Leader, Parts I & II (United States Office of Education, 1944, 14 & 13 min., sound, black and white). A discussion of the qualities of bureaucratic leadership.

What Are the Military Services? (Coronet, 1952, 11 min., sound, black and white). By picturing a military attack, bureaucratic teamwork of specialists, clerks, crews, and engineers is shown.

Bureaucracy, Democracy, and the Individual

*In many bureaucracies we tend to lose our
identity as individuals and become mere numbers.*

The term

"bureaucracy" is one of those words that historian Crane Brinton has called the "looser" words. It is a word with many different meanings. It evokes a variety of reactions. From the standpoint of the social scientist, bureaucracy refers, as we have seen, to a specific type of human behavior and organization. Like such concepts as "personality," "group," and "power," it is used to describe and discriminate among various patterns of human behavior. Its popular meaning, however, is something quite different. It normally symbolizes something we do not like, something against which we can vent our pent-up aggressions and frustrations. To many people, "bureaucracy" is akin to a swear word. We condemn organizations we oppose by calling them "bureaucratic." Officials we dislike we brand "stupid bureaucrats." The antipathy toward bureaucracy is strong indeed.

Of the many charges leveled at modern bureaucracy, the majority fall into three categories: (1) bureaucracy is irrational, inefficient, and encourages incompetency; (2) bureaucracy is undemocratic; and (3) bureaucracy destroys individual initiative and depersonalizes the individual. These accusations are formidable and realistic. Each has substance and can be justly leveled at some organizations. But bureaucracies, like most everything else, are not all alike. To call some organization or some person "bureaucratic" does little to suggest our real objection. We must go further and specify what we are objecting to.

IRRATIONAL FACTORS IN BUREAUCRACY

That bureaucracies are sometimes inefficient or that their personnel sometimes act irrationally would be difficult to refute. For bureaucratic organizations are composed of human beings, and no one is always efficient and rational. To expect them to be so would be utopian. It is rather widely asserted, however, that certain bureaucratic features accentuate the human tendencies toward irrationality and inefficiency.

"RED TAPE"

One of these features, *red tape*, is well-known to all of us. Even a slight reference to it will likely precipitate a heated discussion on the evils of bureaucracy. Few things, in fact, generate more emotion and invective than red tape. We complain bitterly about the long lines of secretaries we must go through to reach topside. We are often distressed by the amount of time consumed in racing from one office to the next to accomplish some mission. We detest the long wait while some request or form is channeled through a number of hands to reach a single decision. A few years ago a baby died unnecessarily in the arms of its father while the latter waited helplessly in a line to have the child processed properly for entrance to a large hospital. Such mishaps feed our displeasure and antipathy toward bureaucratic red tape.

Nearly everyone is impressed by "bureau-

Many of us think of our bureaucracies as massive paper empires.

cratic paper." We are inclined to think of bureaucracies as massive "paper empires." The national government, for example, has a considerable investment in filing cabinets. Some 9 billion documents are added to the government files each year. In both government and industry, wastepaper is one of the biggest products. Indeed, the wastebasket, more affectionately called "file 13," has become a symbol of modern bureaucratic enterprise.

Without question, some of this red tape and procedure is inefficient and irrational. It is certainly inconvenient for those persons who become entwined in it. This inconvenience, together with the impersonality and the arbitrariness of the rules and procedures, the miles of paper and the long queues of people, often prompt the charge of inefficiency. But should it? Inconvenience, impersonality, and arbitrariness are hardly gauges of inefficiency. It is understandably difficult for an outsider to believe that many of the long, laborious processes he sees at work in a bureaucracy are efficient. He is

more inclined to regard them as "make-work" projects or useless procedures that cover up ineffectiveness.

Actually, the reverse is probably more often true. Bureaucratic procedures only seem inefficient. A lengthy questionnaire, for example, may contain a number of questions which seem irrelevant to the person who is answering them, but they may be important for the bureaucracy. It is far better for the bureaucracy to have people answer questions that may be irrelevant to them in most cases than to go to the expense of tracing and contacting a few persons whose specific cases demand this information. You may have to wait your turn to see someone or you may have to contact several officials to accomplish your mission. But did you ever contemplate the disorder that might result if there were no orderly routines? Think back to the last time you heard somebody complain about bureaucratic red tape. Did he carefully examine the operations within the organization? Was he in a position to judge what was inefficient? Or was he merely frustrated and finding release for his anger? Was not the source of his antagonism actually inconvenience or impersonality or ruthlessness rather than inefficiency?

THE CHARGE OF INCOMPETENCE

We frequently hear people say that bureaucracies breed and harbor incompetence. Incompetent individuals presumably find their way into the massive organizational structures, entrench themselves, and compound inefficiency and waste. Professor Parkinson humorously describes this condition as an organizational disease he calls "injelititis," which combines jealousy and incompetence. Every organization has its "injelitants" who struggle to eliminate all those who are more able than themselves. They especially resist the appointment or promotion of able persons.

He dare not say, "Mr. Asterisk is too able," so he says, "Asterisk? Clever perhaps—but is he *sound*? I incline to prefer Mr. Cypher." He dare not say, "Mr. Asterisk makes me feel small," so he says, "Mr. Cypher appears to me to have better judgment." Judgment is an interesting word which signifies in this context the opposite of intelligence; it means, in fact, doing what was done last time. So Mr. Cypher is promoted and Mr. Asterisk goes elsewhere. The central administration gradually fills up with people stupider than the chairman, director, or manager. If the head of the organization is second-rate, he will see to it that his immediate staff are all third-rate; and they will, in turn, see to it that their subordinates are fourth-rate.*

The major symptoms of the disease are "smugness," a distrust of brilliance, and low standards. These symptoms can be detected in the remarks that members of the organization make to one another. "We ought not

*C. Parkinson, *Parkinson's Law* (Boston: Houghton Mifflin, 1957), p. 81.

overextend ourselves." "We make no pretense of being top-flight." "The man who left us for Topflight Company was good but didn't really fit in here." Or, most revealing of all, "Clever people are such a dreadful nuisance."

Parkinson's humor is exceeded only by the simple truths he suggests, many of which we are eager to recognize in others, but not so quickly in ourselves. Honesty will not permit us to deny that these conditions actually exist. There is a great deal of incompetence within our bureaucratic structures, and everyone is in fact inclined to be suspicious of anyone who is more able than he. This situation does tend to result in the selection of subordinates who are inferior to the boss. But it is not a universal characteristic of bureaucracies. Nor is it indicative only of bureaucratic organization. It is found everywhere, just as is the tendency of some executives to search out the very best subordinates. It is frequently maintained that the greatest genius of both President Hoover and his successor, Franklin Roosevelt, was their willingness to make use of the ablest men they could locate.

The sheer size of modern bureaucracies, as well as their impersonality, lack of face-to-face contact, and their tendency to live by artificial rules, does protect incompetent individuals when they become entrenched. Despite this fact, however, it would be extremely difficult to prove that incompetence is any more indicative of bureaucracy than other types of human organization. Once again, when we hear the charge of incompetence leveled at bureaucrats, we ought to ask ourselves if the person making the charge is basing his claim on more than just casual observation. Very probably he is reacting on much the same basis and for much the same reasons that he may react when confronted with red tape. He is again relieving his pent-up anger over some inconvenience, some impersonal treatment, or possibly some ruthlessness.

RESISTANCE TO CHANGE

What about the charge that bureaucracy is heavy, cumbersome, slow-moving, and resistant to change? We are often told that massive size, intricate mechanics, and dependence on rules stand in the way of change and prevent progress. Do they? They do very definitely at times. Members of a smooth-functioning organization are frequently reluctant to disrupt old procedures in order to try something new. But is not this tendency true of small organizations and even individuals as well? Large organizations such as du Pont can better afford to risk changes than a small company. For the type of risks that du Pont takes might bankrupt a smaller company. Bureaucracies are not as rigid as we sometimes imagine. As we have already seen, no bureaucracy always follows all its blueprints, its charts, and its rule books. New forms and new systems are introduced when conditions and personnel change. In a large organization, just as in a small organization, the degree of change depends on the daring and initiative of the leadership as well as on the individual workers.

INDIVIDUAL AND GROUP TENSIONS

People have their own goals and some of them never converge with the aims of the organization of which they are a part. Someone's personal needs may conflict directly with the goals of the organization for which he works. A man may feel that he needs a higher position in his company in order to maintain or raise his position in society. Yet he may be of more value to his organization in his present position. In another type of circumstance an individual may feel that his job is taking him away from his family. The possibilities for individual and group conflict are legion.

These conflicts are, in turn, compounded by conflicts between group goals within the larger organization. Nearly every organization of any size is composed of many small informal groups and cliques, each of which has its own loyalties and group goals. Common aims and loyalties within informal groups are vital to the morale of the over-all organization at times. For this reason management frequently encourages the development of informal group loyalties and goals. But shared beliefs and goals can also be destructive, especially those that find expression in such phrases as: "Don't let the other outfits horn in!" "Let the other crews fend for themselves." "Don't work yourself out of a job!" "We have to pull together if we are to get what we want!" Here we have expressions of group standards that are not intended to be a part of the rational organization. They develop spontaneously among the workers themselves. They are not a part of the planning. Nor are they provided for in the organizational charts and rule books. But they exist and may conflict with the aims of other groups within the organization.

The chances of conflict among individuals, groups, and the larger organization increase directly with an increase in organizational size. Hence, it is sometimes argued that greater size and complexity nurture inefficiency if for no other reason than that increased conflict will slow down production. There is, of course, a seed of truth here. But this view sometimes neglects the fact that all organizations, big and small, are plagued with the same sort of thing. After all, every person has allegiances to all sorts of organizations and activities both within and outside his place of employment. No matter how small the organization, then, it risks the problems arising from conflicts in goals and standards.

LOYALTY TO FUNCTION
VERSUS LOYALTY TO ORGANIZATION

Very large bureaucracies (and some small ones too) often experience a problem of insularity growing out of inner-group and professional loyalties. Persons employed in a particular organization, a health office or the state highway engineer's office for example, frequently demonstrate a stronger urge to further their own projects than they do to achieve the goals of the state administration as a whole. Some offices become almost completely insulated from the rest of the administration. They may regard their goals as the only ones that are worth while. Or they may become mortal enemies of some neighboring agency or department. They are apt to struggle for a bigger slice of the budget, even recommending that funds for other agencies be cut back sharply. There are many cases on record where state health officials seemed to be more loyal to national health officials than to other state administrative agencies. When such circumstances arise, there is danger of unbalancing the state administration and seriously crippling it. Such a situation certainly lends itself to inefficient operation.

PICAYUNE RULE
VERSUS INDIVIDUAL PERSONALITY

Nearly everyone, even the newest or poorest worker, has some standard he follows. As a consequence, he regards most rules that do not conform to his own standards as an infringement on his initiative and ingenuity. One of the most pressing problems of administration, then, is to get him to impose standards of his own that are congruous with those of the organization. This is more easily said than done. Standards of workmanship vary from worker to worker, and smooth functioning depends heavily on certain minimum standards of adherence to organizational standards. Efficiency and effective performance suffer when rules are not followed or details observed. Irksome and picayune rules, on the other hand, can and do stifle incentive and enthusiasm. But when they do, it is sometimes possible to use strategic leniency effectively. A firm may be able to discard or ignore rules and details that employees resent if they serve no important purpose. And even when irksome rules cannot be discarded, there may be other ways to put them to good use. Otherwise, a firm may find itself in a slough of irrational behavior and frustration that leads to inefficiency.

THE MYTH OF SCIENTIFIC MANAGEMENT

For years now we have spoken of "scientific management," and more recently we have adopted a term called "human engineering." These two movements have represented attempts to make the management and direction of human affairs more efficient, and what some of the members of these schools regarded as scientific. The scientific management movement had its beginning in the efforts of Frederick W. Taylor, a student of business administration, who set out to find more efficient methods of industrial operation. He and his disciples made extensive studies in the area of man-hour productivity rates. They elaborated methods for planning, organizing, directing, and coordinating industrial efforts so as to maximize employee output and minimize costs and work time. Like steel or coal, human labor, Taylor believed, could be treated as a resource or commodity in the production process.

Although members of the Taylor school developed methods that raised output and contributed a great deal to the growth of industry, it is doubtful that their efforts were scientific. Their studies, moreover, took in only part of the picture. A time-and-motion study, for example, may have indicated what had to be taught to workers in order for them to perform a given task in the shortest possible time. But it did not tell employers how to get workers to accept the procedures. This weakness led to the development of motivational research, which has become so popular today. Led by Elton Mayo of the Harvard Business School, the motivational research group sought to discover the principal factors in human behavior that prompt workers to achieve maximum production. Starting with the assumption that man is basically a social being, motivational researchers tabulated and studied the social behavior and work-group patterns of workers. They attempted to define, measure, and evaluate such factors as social sentiments, in-group feeling, out-group hostility, empathy, and similarity of cultural background as well as social status.

But this approach also was inadequate. For behavior patterns, though they tell us what happened, how many times it happened, and where it happened, do not always tell why it happened. We may still be in doubt, for example, as to why a coffee break increased production in one part of an organization and not in others. Furthermore, it is difficult to establish conclusively that the coffee break increased output at all. It may have been something else. Our knowledge about human motivation is still wanting. Although many of our investigations have been very fruitful, and our methods improve almost daily, a large area of what we call human motivation remains obscure. Our information becomes more reliable as it accumulates, but a great deal still depends on what social and industrial psychologists reveal in the future. Here, as in so many other areas, information is scant.

IS BUREAUCRACY UNDEMOCRATIC?

For most Americans the potential threat of bureaucracy to democracy is probably a more serious charge than the claim of bureaucratic irrationality. Many Americans agree that bureaucracy poses a threat to democracy, but they disagree sharply over the nature of the threat. Some of this disagreement stems from a more fundamental difference over the true causes of bureaucratic growth. Of the several explanations for bureaucratic growth that we explored in Chapter 21, most Americans follow one of two lines of thought. One group attributes the bureaucratic trend to the rise of modern capitalism. Presumably, the economic advantages accruing from large-scale organization led to the rise of big business and giant industrial enterprises. This school, probably best exemplified by the well-known economist John K. Galbraith, further maintains that the growth of large-scale industry and

big business has produced a similar bureaucratic tendency in those groups that must compete with them. Large labor unions and farm organizations came into being to establish a balance or "countervailing power" to big business. The rise of bureaucracies in these sectors of the economy in turn encouraged the growth of big government that could arbitrate differences between contending factions and thus safeguard the public interest. Hence, both big government and big industrial bureaucracies are the direct result of the rise of capitalism.

On the other hand, another school of thought regards the growth of government bureaucracy as the fundamental cause of bureaucratic growth elsewhere. This group, led by another famous economist, Ludwig von Mises, asserts that government is being used more and more to regulate the national economy. This tendency, the argument runs, stimulates bureaucratic growth in the government itself and in the business world as well. Businessmen must protect themselves in the economy where government interference has disrupted the operations of the free market and given advantages to some businesses over others. The upshot is the development of business and industrial monopoly, which would never have occurred if industries had been permitted to compete freely. Both business and government bureaucracies are thus the direct result of government meddling in the free market.

Those who attribute bureaucratic growth to the rise of capitalism often fear that the power which bureaucracy delivers into a few hands gives this privileged group a distinct advantage over other persons and creates greater inequalities in a society. One large organization may balance another, but both tend to fall into fewer and fewer hands. As a result the great mass of people is left powerless. When two countervailing forces struggle with one another, the economic welfare of the public may be ignored. We have all witnessed the results of the great coal and steel strikes of recent decades. The unions and the companies fought each other for weeks and even months as the majority of citizens stood helplessly on the sidelines. In other instances entrenched leaders of competing bureaucracies may join hands in an effort to consolidate their positions. They may secretly conspire to profit at the public's expense. In such situations the interests of others in the bureaucracies as well as the public welfare may be ignored. Finally, the concentration of greater and greater bureaucratic power in fewer and fewer hands leaves the average individual without means of controlling either government or industrial bureaucracy. Most of us stand helplessly before vast power concentration, unable to influence decisions that vitally affect our interests.

Those who attribute bureaucratic growth

to government interference in the free market believe that bureaucracy leads to more government regulation, stifles individual initiative, and denies an opportunity for the individual to compete for greater wealth. Many in this school believe that bureaucracy is synonymous with socialism. Others go so far as to contend that bureaucratic growth ultimately will result in total regimentation and a totalitarian political system. For this school bureaucracy is a political monster that intrudes on the individual's economic freedom and curtails his opportunity to develop his full potentialities.

Despite the difference between the two schools, however, they do agree on one consequence of bureaucracy; namely, that bureaucracy concentrates power into fewer and fewer hands and this tendency presumably inhibits individual freedom, which both sides feel is essential to democracy. The basic difference really arises from the fact that each side defines the word "democracy" differently. One camp defines it in terms of economic and political equality; the other in terms of a capitalistic free market and the need to keep government from interfering with private initiative. What is this thing called "democracy" that both schools believe to be threatened by bureaucratic growth?

CONFUSION
OVER THE MEANING OF DEMOCRACY

"Democracy," too, is one of the looser words. There are, for example, about as many definitions for the term as there are people. For each person tends to identify what he likes with democracy and to call everything he dislikes undemocratic. Everyone agrees that "democracy" should be preserved, but ask them specifically what it is that must be preserved and invariably you get different responses. This disagreement has existed for centuries.

The Greek hero Pericles, as we saw in

Chapter 2, asserted that democracy was a condition wherein all citizens participated equally in the political processes of their society. He believed that such a condition was ideal, although another prominent Greek, Plato, felt it was anything but ideal. For Plato was convinced that democracy was rule by the lowest common denominator. It was rule by the "rabble," the uneducated, and the unqualified.

The famous philosopher John Locke identified democracy with majority rule. For Tom Paine, on the other hand, democracy was a system of government in which the people governed themselves directly or through their duly elected and appointed representatives. To the controversial and able philosopher John Dewey, democracy involved much more than a mere method of governing. "To be realized it must affect all modes of human association, the family, the school, industry, and religion," said Dewey. It was a "way of life." The political theorist T. V. Smith carried Dewey's definition a step further, calling democracy a personality trait. To him, "democratic" described "a kind of person easy to live with." At the very extreme was the famous political scientist Charles Merriam, who called democracy a "spirit, an attitude toward our fellow-men." Nearly all agree, however, that democracy involves a method of governing, whatever the division between those who believe it to be only a method of government and those who would extend the definition to a "way of life."

THE AMERICAN VIEW OF DEMOCRACY

Americans have a long historical tradition favoring limited governmental activity. Few would have disagreed with General George Marshall when he said that the cornerstone of American democracy is a government which is restricted, meaning that government can do only those things that are constitutionally permissible or not strictly forbidden by the Constitution and customary practice. Most Americans also believe that democracy guarantees to every qualified citizen a degree of opportunity to influence government decisions and actions. Succinctly stated by the political scientist Lord Lindsay of Birker, "Western democracies are constitutions based on the belief that the differences between different classes in the community can be solved by discussion; on the belief in and the capacity for compromise; on a frank recognition that the people as a whole cannot govern but that the mass of ordinary people can exercise control over the government. . . ." *

A rudimentary American definition of "democracy" begins with a constitution that guarantees all persons absolute and inalienable *civil rights*. These rights afford protection against arbitrary acts of government and must be distinguished from ordinary legal protections such as laws against slander, murder, or theft, which can be enacted and repealed by government action. Rights belong to all "persons," not just citizens. Every person, whether alien, lunatic, or infant, is entitled to counsel in a courtroom, for example. The government cannot deny such rights to anyone. If it does, the person can have the government's action set aside by the courts. The individual thus is granted an area of *freedom* into which government cannot intrude. Every governmental action must have some constitutional basis or it can be challenged by the individual person. Every public official is obliged to follow definite procedures when he goes about his business.

If individuals are to be free to influence their government and control it, they must be able "to turn the rascals out," which usually involves a *free election process* that

* For a full consideration of Lindsay's point that democracy is "government by discussion," see: A. Lindsay, *The Essentials of Democracy* (Philadelphia: University of Pennsylvania Press, 1929); and his, *The Modern Democratic State* (New York: Oxford University Press, 1947)

is open to a wide number of individuals. Free election processes depend directly on the *freedom of each individual to associate and organize* with others in an effort to take over the engines of government. *Political parties* are the agencies through which this tactic is accomplished. They are alternative or standby governments that say, "We have a program for running the country. Just elect us and we will show you." Those in power formulate policies and act on them. Those out of power offer alternative programs of policy and action.

Not every group can win an election. In a free society individuals must be able to influence policy and action by means other than elections. *Interest groups* provide just such a means. Whereas a political party is an organization of human beings with the fundamental purpose of taking over the government, *an interest group is an organization that seeks to obtain its objectives and further its interests by means other than sponsoring candidates for public office.* If individuals and interest groups are to have a hearing, channels of *public opinion* must be free and open, and the people must be willing to express opinions and tolerate disagreement. It is a tenet of the American's political creed that a free society must risk dissent and opposition to remain free. To this principle the Supreme Court of the United States has steadily dedicated its efforts. According to Justice Holmes, no society is free without a free market place for ideas.

THE BUREAUCRATIC CHALLENGE
TO DEMOCRACY

Now the question comes: To what extent does bureaucracy threaten this democratic process and our faith in it? No answer can be completely adequate since we do not know what future direction or avenues bureaucracy will take. But very few things

worry the American more than the supposed threat that bureaucracy poses.

Concentration of Power. There is little doubt that bureaucracy places more and more power into fewer and fewer hands. This condition makes for profound differences in power positions. It enables a few individuals, those in control of the bureaucratic machinery, to wield far more influence over the destiny of the organization and society itself than either members of the organization or outsiders. Those who attain these power positions entrench themselves and even pass on their power to hand-picked heirs. This inequality in power relationship persists and grows as the bureaucracy itself grows. Business corporations, for example, make a clear distinction between management and legal ownership. According to the principles of free enterprise and state laws, it is presumed that stockholders elect management. But, as we have already seen, the average stockholder has about as much choice in selecting top management as the German citizen had in electing officials under the Hitler regime. A stockholder seldom has an effective way of opposing the industrial leadership since his only choice is either to endorse the present management or not. Most large business corporations are therefore dominated by a few individuals. Only on rare occasions, such as the stockholder fight in the New York Central Railroad meeting in 1954, is any semblance of democracy revived.

In government bureaucracy, as we have seen, control over policy is frequently in the hands of individuals drawn from a particular social and economic set. Furthermore, as administrators and government functions increase in number, more and more rules are interpreted by the administration itself. An administrative agency, such as the Federal Trade Commission, investigates a rule violation, holds a hearing, and makes a decision. The hearing is not governed by strict courtroom procedures. Very few decisions are ever appealed to the courts, which means that in fact many individual rights fall within the discretion of government administrators.

Labor unions also consolidate power at the expense of democratic procedures. Opposition within unions finds it difficult to survive. For the group that gains the upper hand generally fortifies its position and sacrifices democracy in the name of unity. Minorities are suppressed on the ground that disagreement weakens the union and impedes its efforts. The objectives of higher wages, shorter hours, and better working conditions often take precedence over democracy.

Efficiency vs. Dissent. Bureaucracy differs from both democracy and autocracy in that neither the will of a majority nor the personal choice of one man takes precedence. Rather, bureaucracy is often "government by rules" according to rational and objective standards that are directed toward efficiency. It accords a special place to expert judgment. It favors efficiency in the formation, development, and operation of an organization. When problems are solved by *efficient* rather than *popular* methods, democratic values must take a secondary position at best. In many organizations dissent is frequently viewed as a threat to the goals of the organization rather than as evidence of healthy democratic opposition.

Initiative vs. Ruthlessness and "Red Tape." Disciplined obedience within a hierarchy of authority, arbitrary rules, and red tape take their toll of individual initiative. Men must conform for the good of the organization and its goals. Workers tend to settle back into the routine, enjoy the security which big

bureaucracy affords, and become watchful that they do not ruffle anyone's feathers. The sense of security itself tends to stifle initiative. Individuals who are secure are less inclined to bestir themselves to try new things than are the insecure. We ought to remember, however, that in the long run an overdose of security affords a better opportunity for increased output than does an overdose of insecurity. Too much insecurity breeds chaos.

Planning vs. Democracy. A great deal of the criticism of bureaucracy and its effects on democracy revolves around the question of planning. Efficiency, after all, is heavily dependent on planning. If plans are to be effective, they must be followed. This means considerable regimentation. Change and interruption will destroy a plan. This is as true of industry as it is of government.

Government plans that are constantly being disrupted by periodic elections can hardly be called plans. There is constant pressure therefore to put long-range plans beyond the reach of the electorate. This is the basis for the charge that government plans not only regiment individuals but threaten the democratic process. Yet, a completely unplanned government operation would be no government at all. Plans can be changed. Those that cannot be changed may become greater hindrances than assets. Blueprints are meant to serve, not to saddle and regiment! If plans are drawn with broad outlines and kept flexible within the wider bounds, there is usually plenty of opportunity for change, expression of initiative, and avoidance of regimentation.

The Threat to Free Association. A most serious accusation leveled at bureaucratization is the charge that it stifles free association. It is maintained, for example, that the members no longer govern our voluntary associations. People simply join voluntary and private groups, support them with dues and sympathy, but let the experts run them. Only a façade of democracy remains. Have you tried to change the basic policy of a national organization? You will find that members are counted but not heeded very much. Resolutions and suggestions from even a large wing of an organization are apt to get lost or be ignored. The leadership tends to select its own subordinates and successors. And it certainly dictates policy!

THE THREAT TO PUBLIC OPINION

To influence public opinion and public policy a person must be able to communicate his ideas. But in a society the size of the United States, only powerful interest groups can make themselves heard in the high places. The voice of a single person is too feeble. But when the voluntary association becomes extremely large, the individual has about as much difficulty influencing its policy as he does influencing that of the government.

THE THREAT TO FREE POLITICAL PROCESSES

Much the same condition exists in political parties and electoral processes. Parties, it is true, must appeal to voters if they are to win public offices. But winning elections requires efficient organization. For this reason political parties have tended to fall into the hands of strong political committees and machines. Platforms and candidates must appeal widely to secure victory. But the average voter lacks experience in choosing candidates and platforms that will appeal widely enough to win. Therefore, party decisions tend to remain in the hands of those who do have the experience. The leadership keeps a tight rein on party affairs. Political parties, contrary to popular belief,

do not belong to the people who support them in the elections. They belong in fact to the political managers. Voters who support the parties in an election, but take no part in deciding party policy, are similar to the fans who cheer a football team on to victory. They may believe the team is theirs, but they are not really members of the team. They call no plays. The theory of popular control over public policy thus may be more mythical than real.

AN EVALUATION

That bureaucracy endangers the democratic process in some ways cannot be doubted. Nevertheless, bureaucracy also provides new opportunities for certain kinds of freedom. Just one example will illustrate the point. It is bureaucratic organization of the automotive industry that makes it possible for nearly every American to own an automobile. We are thereby far more mobile, which means that our freedom of movement is vastly increased.

The benefits of bureaucracy are all around us. How much the average labor-union member benefits from an efficiently organized labor bureaucracy commanded by experts is not calculable. But we can safely conclude that labor would not have made the phenomenal gains it has enjoyed in recent years had there been no labor bureaucracy. And could we have produced atomic energy without bureaucratic organization? A few years ago someone estimated that each American has the equivalent of at least one hundred slaves working for him as a result of efficient bureaucratization. Because of bureaucracy man may be much freer now than ever before in history.

But what about the intrusion of the expert? It is formidable indeed. In the final analysis, however, it is still our own responsibility to accept or reject the expert's advice. A person need not be a physicist to have views on the proper uses of atomic energy. This does not imply, of course, that we always have a real choice. For those who hold the commanding positions may make commitments on atomic power that bind all of us. But then, as we saw earlier, bureaucratic decisions are not solely the result of personal whims or group choice. A bureaucracy is run according to a set of impersonal rules, and not just by the will of its officials. Rules may be arbitrary and rigid, but they are seldom as vindictive as personal decisions can be at times. For example, where employment is based on arbitrary and impersonal rules of technical qualification, a person who might otherwise be discrimi-nated against for being Chinese, an out-lander, physically unattractive, or of the "wrong" religious faith will have a much better chance of being hired.

Bureaucracy is not something we are about to be rid of. It is something we must live with and control. If bureaucracy were to disappear, we would sorely feel its loss. It will do us little good to keep on complaining about it. Raging against unfavorable decisions and red tape is worse than futile. It merely signals our impotence and does not sway an impersonal organization. A more realistic approach might be to recognize the worth of bureaucracies to human welfare and set about more realistically to control them.

BUREAUCRATIC DEPERSONALIZATION

"It's not what you know, but who you know!" "Those who run around in circles and stay close to the hub of power shall be known as wheels." Are you an organization man? Do you see no other way out but to join the crowd? Are you already repeating the cynical remarks and asking the cynical questions?

THE MAKING OF AN ORGANIZATION MAN

William H. Whyte, in his famous book, *The Organization Man*, depicts an emergent way of life that many feel is now beginning to dominate the American scene. His analysis dwells on suburbanites but is suggestive of something far broader in scope. The organization man is outgoing and other-directed. He is, in Whyte's words, "impris-oned in brotherhood." His objectives are to "join the gang" and fit the community. He adopts the standards of his neighborhood and of the work-groups at the office. He is "proper," and makes a determined effort to remain so. The organization man dresses in a style befitting his station in life, lives in a home that meets neighborhood require-ments, and owns a car that reflects his place in the bureaucracy where he works. If he advances in position, he may feel it necessary to move to a new and better neighborhood, change his mode of dress, and buy a higher-priced car, even if he cannot afford it. Con-versely, if he buys a car that is more expensive than those owned by his neighbors whose positions are similar to his, he may be very apologetic about it. The organization man regulates his life according to outer-imposed standards.

Possibly the routine of bureaucratic life, the omnipresence of rules, and the imper-sonality of the average person's contacts with his associates motivate him to seek acceptance by others when he has the oppor-tunity. When someone takes notice of him, he wants to be certain that he has created the proper impression. The "effective per-sonality" seeks to command attention by "charm." He wants to radiate self-confidence, smile, be known as a "good listener," speak in terms of the other man's interest, and be regarded as someone who "fits in easily." In the bureaucratic and corporate world, "self-hood" is sacrificed on the new personality market for favor.

THE CONSERVATIVE MOOD

Professor Russell Kirk, an analyst of the newer forms of conservatism, observes that a new mood is gripping American society, stemming from the advent of the way of life that Whyte has described. The organization man not only leads an orderly, conformist social life but he is frequently a spokesman for political conservatism. He begins to seek for and defend tradition. He demands that men conform. He denies the individual's right to control his own fate and yet, paradoxically, he extols the virtues of American individualism. Strangely enough, the new conservatism and conformity are nearly always defended in terms of individualism. Kirk maintains that the new-type individual feels overwhelmed by events. He thinks of himself as doing his best in a difficult situation. He ignores facts about the real power situation and takes refuge in the belief that society is ruled by some divine or higher intent beyond his control. The good businessman and the able politician, according to this view, are men who correctly perceive the true social forces and adjust to them. Emphasis is on proper adjustment. Traditional and customary methods, even long-established prejudices, are better guides

Standardized living in mass-produced, standardized housing—an outgrowth of a bureaucratic industrial-urban world.

to action than new and untried ideas. It is presumed that men are divided into those who perceive this higher intent and those who do not. Those who command the great bureaucracies are where they are because they properly perceive and adjust. For this reason, many assert that it is probably best to leave them there.

THE HIGHER MORALITY

The conservative mood is supported by a new code of morality. Professor Mills calls this code, which permeates the entire bureaucratic world, the "higher immorality." Its presence is indicated by the moral uneasiness of our times. Individuals are no longer able to follow the values and codes of a former era. Old codes seem hollow in the corporate era and have been replaced by new ones that sanction bureaucratic routines and practices. These newer codes of conduct approve the efforts of the organization man to win prestige, promotions, and success by being "proper" and accommodating himself to the accepted ways of the time. "Success" and "accomplishment" assume a high position in the hierarchy of values of the man who wishes to make his mark.

The new code is most lucidly revealed in the casual and innocent comments we all are inclined to make. "What's your racket?" "If you're so smart, why ain't ya rich?" "Men teach because they can't do." "Reason? There ain't no reason. It's company policy." "The smart don't get caught!" "Become an expert and make everyone beat a path to your door." "Do what it takes to succeed." We still teach youngsters that hard work and frugality are the true roads to success. We

still laud the virtues of sobriety, will power, and honesty in all matters. We call for high-mindedness and the ability to say "No!" But we forget all these lofty ideals when "success" is at stake. The morality of the past now seems a series of ponderous platitudes, full of vague and high-minded rhetoric. The principles remain with us and we profess them. But profession does not involve belief. Certainly we do not always act in accordance with them.

The organization man is under constant stress to make others believe that he is a kind of person he is not. He must embrace one code of values, including virtue, goodness, honesty, and high-mindedness, while he practices another. *The New York Times* columnist James Reston describes the modern-day official as "confounded at every turn by the hangover of old political habits and outworn institutions," while he "is no longer nourished by the ancient faith" on which they were founded. Men profess but do not believe. They know all the correct answers but do not follow them.

SUICIDE AND ULCERS

Obviously the pressures, routine, impersonality, and other features of bureaucracy, together with the conflicts in morals and loyalties that characterize our time, tend to turn our bureaucracies into ulcer factories. The pace and tempo become so fast at times that many give up the ghost entirely. Others, however, may keep their conflicts from emerging. Outwardly they are calm, proper, and in full control of themselves while inwardly they are turbulent, frustrated, and unhappy.

SOME WORDS OF SUMMARY

The word "bureaucracy" has many meanings and uses. For the social scientist it describes a particular kind of human behavior. But the average individual applies it in a variety of ways. Very often it is merely a swear word, nothing more than a whipping-boy to provide release for pent-up aggressions. Bureaucracy often seems irrational and inefficient, and people constantly complain about its red tape, impersonality, incompetence, and resistance to change. These criticisms, however, may be prompted more by our frustrations than by inefficiency and waste.

But bureaucracies do produce tension and frustration. Individual goals conflict with the aims of work-groups, while the goals of both collide with those of the overall organization. Loyalty to one's function may also conflict with loyalty to the bureaucracy. Irksome rules, too, are likely to produce resentment, destroy individual initiative, and injure both the individual and the organization. The Taylorites and the schools of scientific management and human engineering have searched for means of relieving tension and inefficiency and improving personnel practices and work-group patterns.

A wide body of opinion holds that bureaucracy threatens our democratic processes. Although most Americans agree that a threat exists, they differ over the causes and are confused about the meaning of "democracy." Definitions of democracy vary considerably, but Americans divide into two main schools—those who believe that it is a method of governing and those who believe it is an entire way of life. Most Americans agree that it involves at least a guarantee of civil rights, limited government, a wide base of free political association and of political participation. The threat of bureaucratization is believed to lie in its planning, red tape, ruthlessness, protection of incompetence, and its tendency to concentrate power. A special threat is seen in the bureaucratization of political parties and voluntary associations. Yet despite the threats it poses, bureaucracy also affords us new opportunities for freedom and development and thus is not likely to be abandoned.

But what of the effect of bureaucratization on the individual? Bureaucracy has helped to create an outgoing and outer-directed "Organization Man" who sacrifices his self-hood on the personality market for success, while he gives lip-service to older virtues of hard work, high-mindedness, and honesty. Such conflicts turn bureaucracies into ulcer factories.

FURTHER ROADS TO LEARNING

GENERAL ACCOUNTS

The reader's attention is called to the works cited in Chapters 21 and 22.

H. Finer, *The Road to Reaction* (Boston: Little, Brown, 1945). A rejoinder to Hayek (see below).

A. Gouldner, "Metaphysical Pathos and the Theory of Bureaucracy," *American Political Science Review*, XLIX (June, 1955), pp. 496-507. We are cautioned not to overemphasize the undemocratic nature of bureaucracy.

F. Hayek, *Road to Serfdom* (Chicago: The University of Chicago Press, 1944). Hayek inveighs against government interference in the economic realm.

J. Kingsley, *Representative Bureaucracy* (Yellow Springs, Ohio: Antioch, 1944). Provides some interesting insights into the democratic features of the British political bureaucracy.

L. von Mises, *Bureaucracy* (New Haven: Yale University Press, 1944). Bureaucracy is a direct result of political intervention in the free market.

SPECIAL STUDIES

J. Dewey, *The Public and Its Problems* (New York: Holt, 1927). Democracy is more than just a method of governing. It is a way of life!

J. Galbraith, *The Affluent Society* (Boston: Houghton Mifflin, 1958). Americans invest too much in material commodities and not enough in people. See his *American Capitalism* (Boston: Houghton Mifflin, 1952), Chapter 12. Capitalism breeds bureaucracy.

E. Herring, *The Politics of Democracy* (New York: Rinehart, 1940). Herring's book remains one of the very best analyses of "democratic politics" in the United States.

R. McKeon, ed., *Democracy in a World of Tensions* (Chicago: The University of Chicago Press, 1951). A series of statements on the meaning of "democracy."

A. Mason, *Bureaucracy Convicts Itself* (New York: Viking, 1941). An account of what may happen when an underling far down in the hierarchy tries to "buck" official channels.

R. Michels, *Political Parties* (Glencoe, Ill.: The Free Press, 1948). All life in a democracy depends on the delegation of power, and power delegation is always to a small group.

E. Schattschneider, *Party Government* (New York: Rinehart, 1942). Political parties are run by the managers!

P. Selznick, *TVA and the Grass Roots* (Berkeley: University of California Press, 1949). An attempt to keep a national bureaucracy—The Tennessee Valley Authority—under some local controls.

W. Whyte, *The Organization Man* (New York: Doubleday, Anchor Books, 1956). Whyte's modern classic on an emerging personality type in America.

FICTION AND DRAMA

H. Balzac, *Cousin Bette* (Boston: Roberts Brothers, 1888). The bureaucratic process infects and changes the lives of French bureaucrats and their wives.

A. Halper, *The Little People* (New York: Harper, 1942). The bureaucratic routine of a large store oppresses the employees.

F. Kafka, *The Trial* (London: Secker and Warburg, 1945). Describes the plight of a man caught in a bureaucratic web.

J. Lawrence, *The Sound of Running Feet* (Philadelphia: Stokes, 1937). A portrayal of the burdensome toils and the relationships between clerks and managers in a realty office.

FILMS

Men at Work (McGraw-Hill, 1954, 27 min., sound, black and white). Personal relationships in a washing-machine factory are disturbed by a speeded-up conveyor.

A New Supervisor Takes a Look at His Job (University of Washington, 1944, 13 min., sound, black and white). A supervisor must understand the human element.

Placing the Right Man on the Job (United States Office of Education, 1944, 13 min., sound, black and white). Why a bureaucracy must account for individual differences.

The Outer World

of Tension

and Conflict

THEME

Outside his own nation he sees further conflict *and* tension *arising from the mixture of age-old struggles between nations for environmental advantage from clashing racial strains, an explosive nationalism, an aggressive imperialism, and dangerous new political ideologies. . . .*

The Environmental Basis of Tension

In many areas of the world, agricultural practices remain quite primitive. This Vietnamese farmer still employs water-buffalo power in his rice paddy.

We are all

of us fellow-passengers on the same planet and we are all of us equally responsible for the happiness and well-being of the world in which we live." Thus spoke the popular writer Hendrik van Loon, reminding us that life is but a brief excursion on a whirling sphere called "earth." If the journey is to be enjoyable and free of unnecessary peril, then we must cooperate with our fellow-passengers in making it so. Certainly we must adapt our behavior to the nature and demands of the sphere on which we ride. We have little choice, of course, in most instances. We adapt or die. But sometimes we can cooperate with the other passengers in making the trip safer and more comfortable. We are constantly transforming this world of ours as it simultaneously works transformations on us.

History, then, can be viewed as the story of man's successes and failures in meeting the responsibility to which van Loon refers. It is more than a tale of man's relationships to his fellow men. It is also the saga of his unending struggle to conquer an indifferent natural environment and turn it to his advantage. It is not only the chronicle of man's efforts to make his sojourn on earth sweeter and longer. It includes, too, his costly missteps and the disastrous blind alleys he has encountered, his calamitous quarrels and internecine struggles. And perhaps worst of all, it records his sorry waste and continued neglect of the precious resources that nature has supplied for his journey. Like a moon-traveler viewing the desolate lunar

wastes and dreaming of the lushness of earthly vegetation, modern man may one day recall with regret the great natural inheritance he has squandered.

The history of mankind is but a great drama played on a world stage where we are actors. Geographers, as we noted in Chapter 3, are interested in both the stage and the drama played on it. They focus on more than the earth, its outer crust, atmosphere, and physical features. They also center their attention on man, his social structure, culture, and history. To the world stage, history adds the perspective of time and movement —a fourth dimension. As a distinguished geographer, Isaiah Bowman, once expressed it, "The geographical elements of the environment are fixed only in the narrow and special sense of the word. The moment we give them human associations they are as changeful as humanity itself."

Just as the world stage comes alive when seen against the changes wrought by human beings throughout history, so, too, human life and history take on significance when they are viewed in space. Indeed, our spatial pictures make a profound difference. When men believed the world was flat, their behavior differed sharply from what it was after they found it was round. Their misconceptions and understandable reluctance to journey great distances for fear of falling off the earth's edge retarded the advance of civilization. If we are to discharge the responsibility to which van Loon calls us, therefore, we must have an accurate picture of the stage on which the fascinating human drama unfolds.

THE STRUGGLE FOR THE CONTROL OF NATURE

The earth we inhabit provides us with some 196 million square miles of land and water surface. Life depends on the thin crust of land, the top layers of water, and the atmosphere surrounding them. Our food, in fact, comes from a thin skin of soil called "humus," only a few inches thick, and from mineral deposits close enough to the surface to be extracted.

SOIL FOR SUBSISTENCE

Man's reliance on the soil stems from his dependence on plant life for his food supply. The source of our food is plant life, whether we consume the plants themselves or eat the flesh of animals that feed

Few things are more fundamental than man's relationship to the soil.

on plants. Plants, in turn, receive energy from the sun, which converts the carbon dioxide and water drawn from the air, and the minerals drawn from the soil, into carbohydrates. We call this process photosynthesis.

But what about our consumption of fish and other forms of marine life? And the minerals of the sea? Are these not independent of the soil? Our answer must be, "No!" For aquatic life depends heavily for nourishment on minute forms of swimming plant and animal life called plankton. Tiny fish, and some very large fish as well, eat the plankton; and we all know that the big fish eat the little fish. A large quantity of these tiny organisms were brought originally to the sea from land, as were the minerals. Thus, fish feed on much the same elements that support land life.

Man clearly depends on soil for survival, just as he depends on the oxygen he breathes and the water he drinks. When we reflect on the rapid growth of population during the past century, and how dependent on the soil this growing population is, the prospect for the future may seem frightening. For the quantity of good soil on earth is both very limited and highly unstable. Of the 196 million square miles of the earth's surface, only about 28 per cent, or approximately 56 to 57 million square miles, is land surface. Nearly one-half of this area is unsuitable for agriculture because of cold weather and lack of rainfall. Of the remaining land, only about 3,700,000 square miles is presently under cultivation, and a sizable part of this portion is only marginally productive. Although the world also affords us another 2,000,000 square miles of pasture land, good soil capable of supporting animal and human life is very scarce.

Hard at work terracing hillsides that were once unproductive, these Chinese farmers have acquired the art of preserving precious topsoil and making the land productive for future generations.

The unstable and fragile character of the land, however, is even more serious than its scarcity. Rich topsoil, which took thousands of years to accumulate, is an extremely unstable commodity. Parts of China that were once covered with a heavy layer of fertile soil were turned into seas of yellow clay because of poor agricultural and forestation practices. Vast reaches of once-rich American acres have likewise suffered severe depletion, and in some cases, complete destruction. Why? At least one basic reason lies in the character of humus itself. Only rarely is the topsoil more than a few inches deep, while everywhere it is very loose and highly susceptible to wind and water erosion. An almost unbelievable quantity is carried out to sea each year.

A second factor, naturally enough, is man himself. His land-use practices still leave a great deal to be desired. He overcrops, fails to fertilize, and ignores proper methods of crop rotation. An Iowa farmer, for example, was once puzzled by the failure of one of his best fields to yield after planting it in corn for twenty-seven consecutive years. Ignorance thus takes its toll. But even where the best conservation practices are understood, they may not always be practiced. The demand for food or the chance for profit may lead a farmer to "mine" his land against his better judgment.

The problem is compounded by methods of deforestation. Though perhaps profitable to lumber companies, the denuding of forest lands, even extensive patch cutting, not only permits erosion and spoliation of the forest lands themselves but leads to massive destruction all along the river systems. Treeless patches on mountain or hillside permit snow to thaw rapidly and deprive the ground of a well-established root system for resisting erosion, retaining water, and protecting against drought. We are all aware of the disastrous results. The sudden release of great quantities of water, especially in springtime, produces catastrophic flooding along the water courses, destroying vast amounts of property and endangering human life. With the floods go not only the crops but huge amounts of the soil in which the crops are rooted.

These periodic crises are made even worse by outmoded habits of cultivation and use of tools. Until very recently soils were cultivated largely without regard to composition, slope, or depth. Although contour farming and terracing are now common, some farmers still have a penchant for keeping fields square and rows straight. Likewise, despite the warnings of experts, a great deal of marginally productive land is still under cultivation. Many acres in the dust bowls and semiarid regions should probably be returned to grass or native types of vegetation. Crops will also have to be better adapted to certain areas and conditions. Climate or soil conditions may make it unwise to continue growing corn in parts of

Texas and Mexico, for example, or sugar beets in Iowa. Soy beans, although a valuable legume for returning nitrogen to the soil, should not be planted on hillsides or other areas susceptible to erosion because of their fragile root system. Tools, likewise, must be adapted. It is a well-known fact, of course, that food production and soil conservation are severely impaired where implements are primitive, crude, or inefficient. Yet modern mechanization can be even more destructive if machines are employed unintelligently or are ill-adapted to the area being farmed. Mechanized power gives us an extraordinary capacity to destroy. Since machines greatly increase our productive capacity, we may emphasize efficiency, lower unit cost, and maximum output at the expense of conservation.

Machines, men, and land thus combine forces. Depending largely on the agricultural methods, the result can be increased fertility or, tragically, impoverishment of our resources. A rapid rise in population in face of a declining soil fertility has been the source of much human misery and conflict. The great migrations into Europe by hordes of drought-stricken Asiatics in the day of Genghis Khan were not just military ventures. Everybody went. An entire population does not leave its homes and familiar surroundings without good reason. Similarly, a scarcity of productive land drove the Britisher to the sea and helped turn him into an empire-builder. The need for a larger food supply was an important factor in the Japanese conquest of Manchuria. And Hitler, too, you will remember, looked eastward to the Ukraine, the breadbasket of Europe.

The prospect of rich land invigorates the conquering spirit. For many peoples rich land has always been a vision—one of their greatest dreams. To the Hebrew, the "promised land" was a land of "milk and honey." Egyptians worshiped the Nile for the fertility it brought to their soil. Few men would

envision heaven other than as a place of plenty. Examine mankind's dreams, visions, and ideals, and you have a key to human tensions and strife. Men will fight for their dreams, and land has long been one of them.

To some people, the prospects for peace and security in a world of rising population and exhausted soils seem very dim indeed. To them it seems that nature decreed that men should fight for survival or at least a larger share of nature's bounty. Hungry people who see well-fed neighbors across their boundaries are likely to become disgruntled, inflamed, and militant. Often they are easy prey for demogogues. No appeals to historic rights or international law are likely to stay the pangs of want.

Despite our wasteful practices, there is still an abundance of timber that will yield lumber and lumber products for centuries, if we employ sound cutting and reforestation practices.

Others, nonetheless, see little reason for such deep concern. They see in science and technology the key that will unlock more of nature's storehouses. They look to the day when we will be able to synthesize food from the sun's rays and mine the riches of the sea, returning to the land the mineral wealth once carried from it. New sources of power, too, may enable us to bring water to the now arid and unproductive regions of the earth. But until such possibilities become realities, the concern of the pessimists cannot be lightly dismissed.

WATER, TOO

Soil, yes, but water, too! Soils, plants, and human beings all depend on water to rotate the wheel of life. In one sense there is no shortage, for more than two-thirds of the earth's surface is covered by water. But the oceans are saline and as yet difficult to purify in quantity for human use. Fresh-water resources, on the other hand, are somewhat limited, and like good soils are unevenly dispersed over the face of the globe.

Since every living thing and so many human activities require water, it is, in a sense, our most critical resource. The phenomenal increase in human activities, as well as human population, especially during the past century, has placed a tremendous drain on our fresh-water supplies. Our traditional agricultural and forestry practices merely compound the problem.

Human Consumption. Each individual, especially if he lives in an industrialized community, uses vast quantities of water each day. In the city, for example, we wash floors, sidewalks, and streets. Baths, auto laundries, and lawns all require water. In fact, the average city-dweller consumes around three hundred gallons a day, of which only a small portion goes for the mainte-

nance of his physical well-being. Water is the lifeblood of a city. A casual glance at any map reveals that heavily populated cities are located close to what is or was once a major water supply.

Industry, of course, is largely accountable for the differences between urban and rural consumption. Whereas an unirrigated farm may use only sixty gallons of water daily, an industrial establishment, such as a cereal plant or pulp mill, consumes staggering quantities. A primary interest of an industry seeking a new location is always the available or potential water supply.

In industrialized America the results are readily apparent. The water table has been lowered to such an extent in central Illinois that many farmers are forced to haul water for miles. Los Angeles goes nearly three hundred miles for its water. Cities are continually increasing the size of their reservoirs and then worrying about how rapidly they are depleted. The revolution wrought by industry and urbanization has made water an extremely critical commodity.

Drainage. In many parts of the United States it has been necessary in the past to drain lowlands, swamps, and sloughs in order to make the land habitable. Ditches were dredged and the land was tiled to release the excess water. At times, however, we have been too eager in our efforts to reclaim swamps and marshlands. Sloughs and bogs hold back moisture, which is valuable during rainless periods. East of the Missouri River, where the bulk of such drainage takes place, we have even drained large lakes without considering the consequences for the underground water supply. Similar practices in California's San Joaquin Valley have caused the land to settle to a depth below sea level. Where land and water table have sunk, the sea has crept in, leaving many previously fertile acres saline and sterile.

Irrigation. In areas where rainfall is deficient or highly irregular, water must be led in, usually through a complicated system of irrigation ditches, aqueducts, or pipelines. Many productive acres are added to our agricultural storehouse through sound irrigation policies. Few matters have been the source of more conflict, however, than water supplies and water rights in dry regions. During the early settlement of the West, you might sooner steal a man's wife than his water. Water rights were as sacred as civil rights and often led to physical violence. Farmers who used more than their share of the water frequently found themselves in serious trouble.

Water use in dry areas is now regulated in most instances by government officials who allocate and control the supplies. But despite the many controls, we have not yet seen the end of regulation. In the Middle West, some parts of the South, and even in some areas of the arid West, water use is not sufficiently regulated to keep demands from severely depleting the supplies. This is especially true of underground water reserves. Since many of the underground deposits are the products of centuries of slow seepage, heavy pumping lowers the water table annually, thus threatening some communities with exhaustion. Actually, we need better studies of many of our underground supplies to predict the amount of pumping they can withstand.

Sewage and Waste. Populous and industrial regions are ever facing the problem of waste disposal. Mines, mills, and industry of all types cast up staggering quantities of waste that have too long been permitted to pollute and poison our fresh-water supplies. Many of our small, and even large, population centers discharge sizable quantities of sewage and waste into rivers and streams, thus threatening the water supply. Our carelessness and our search for quick profits

have helped destroy one of our most precious resources. Pollution-control measures are very expensive, but our future welfare may well depend on them.

Transportation and Travel. Rivers are highways, and so are the oceans. The high seas constitute a great broad roadway. Many national states owe a great deal of their historical development, even their appearance and national temper, to their waterways and their location in respect to the sea. It is no accident that England is a buzzing center of marine and commercial activity. Russia was first settled along her rivers from which her people fanned out to establish settlements. Until the advent of air travel, New Orleans was about as closely linked to New York by water as by land. Virtually all the large cities of America sprang up about a good harbor or were located near the banks of a navigable stream.

Despite the great strides we have made in air, rail, and highway travel during the past half-century, water remains one of the best and cheapest forms of transport. Great national states are still prone to argue and fight over water routes, seeking to control them and to gain access to them and to reap the considerable political and economic advantage that such control entails. Land-locked countries have long sought to redress their historically unfavorable positions. Russia, her northern ports frozen over most of the year, has never ceased to seek a "window to the sea." At times she has been very aggressive in her search, pushing in the direction of the Bosporus, the Persian Gulf, or Port Arthur.

National states are likewise driven to seek control of trade routes and dominance of narrows and straits that afford access to vital commercial lanes and larger bodies of water. Britain's world position during the nineteenth century was based on her dominance of the high seas and their vital trade routes. Little wonder that she took great risks to maintain her historic position against Mussolini when he sought to make the Mediterranean an Italian lake, or against Nasser when Egypt took over the Suez Canal. Control of the world's sealanes means power, and where power is involved, there is apt to be conflict.

Inland waterways, too, are a source of conflict. Rivers such as the Rhine and the Danube, and bodies of water such as the Great Lakes, are priceless possessions to the countries that utilize or control them. The irregular distribution and character of our water highways makes land-water relationships a very important factor in producing human conflict.

Water Power. Consumption, irrigation, and transportation are not the only elements involved in the struggle to control water. For with water comes a very cheap means of generating power. Cheap power invigorates industrial growth and gives people an opportunity to raise their level of living. It enables men to lead a better life, and men will fight for this opportunity when they see it within their grasp.

Recreation. Lastly, water is extremely important for recreation. Our crowded beaches and the rapid upswing in sales of small watercraft are testimony to the growing need. The problem is becoming acute in several inland urban centers. Americans have been constructing swimming pools and artificial lakes by the thousands, and the demand for them zooms upward each year.

MINERAL RESOURCES: THE VITAL LINK

The old question, "animal, vegetable, or mineral?" does not categorize as strictly as some quizmasters would have us believe, for every living thing also depends on mineral resources for its existence, and both animals and vegetables are composed of a great variety of minerals.

Without minerals, we die. As we have already seen, the land gives up a precious treasure of minerals not only to plants, man, and other animals, but also to the sea and air. The sea returns a great deal of water to the land in the form of rainfall, but it is not so generous with its minerals.

The conservation of the valuable stores of mineral resources located at various depths in the earth's surface has become critically important since the Industrial Revolution. To the world's industries, mineral resources are an absolute essential. But like good land and good water, our mineral resources are unevenly distributed, some areas being exceedingly rich, others nearly barren.

Clay, sand, stone, and gravel are found in rather large quantities throughout the earth's crust. Despite our insatiable consumption of them, scarcity is no problem here. We are not so fortunate with respect to some other mineral resources, however. Many are quite rare, especially first-grade ores. Others, although abundant, are less accessible, too costly to produce, or so much in demand that they will soon be quite scarce. The world's supply of coal, for example, should last for well over 1,500 years at the present rate of extraction. Yet one-half of this supply is of little value since it takes more power to extract it than the coal itself would produce. Natural gas and petroleum are also abundant, but their rate of consumption is so staggering that the supply will soon be exhausted unless we discover more deposits. Widespread deposits of oil-bearing shale do offer some hope of relief, especially with the satisfactory and cheap processing methods now being developed.

Iron ore is another critical mineral resource which, though abundant, is very unevenly distributed. Since processing of the ore requires large amounts of limestone and coal, it is not yet economical to exploit

A view of Pittsburgh. A plentiful supply of first-grade iron ore in Minnesota's Mesabi Range that could be transported cheaply through the Great Lakes and the accessibility of vast stores of coal for processing the ore made this city what it is today.

reserves located at great distances from these other two resources. In Brazil, for example, rises a famous mountain of nearly pure iron ore, but there is no coal nearby. Finally, a great deal of the reserve supply is low-grade ore, which is difficult to process. Depletion of the supply of first-grade ore, once believed inexhaustible, from Minnesota's Mesabi range has turned the United States into an iron-importing country.

Certain other mineral resources, although not all, are in shorter supply than iron. Yet without some of them, iron itself would be of little use. For the significance of iron to an industrial economy lies in the alloys that can be produced by combining it with other mineral resources. Nickel, for example, which is blended with iron to yield very hard alloys, exists in large quantities near the earth's center, but not in the crust. The present known supply is very short, so much so, in fact, that nickel is too precious to be used any longer for money. High-grade copper and tin, among the first metals to be used by man, are also growing short, as are some other high-grade ores. Such shortages, however, may be offset through better methods of processing low-grade ores and discovery of new deposits.

The advent of atomic power has created an increasing demand for uranium. This development may turn the Belgian Congo, one of the major sources of supply, into a bustling center of human activity. It was plentiful uranium deposits that made Czechoslovakia more important strategically in the Cold War between the United States and the Soviet Union.

TABLE **14** *CONTENT OF THE CRUST OF THE EARTH, INCLUDING THE LITHOSPHERE AND THE HYDROSPHERE, IN PERCENTAGE OF SUNDRY ELEMENTS*

Silicon	27.720	Tungsten	0.005
Aluminum	8.130	Lithium	0.004
Iron	5.010	Zinc	0.004
Calcium	3.630	Columbium	
Sodium	2.850	and	
Potassium	2.600	tantalum	0.003
Magnesium	2.090	Hafnium	0.003
Titanium	0.630	Lead	0.002
Manganese	0.100	Cobalt	0.001
Barium	0.050	Boron	0.001
Chromium	0.037	Beryllium	0.001
Zirconium	0.026	Molybdenum	0.0001
Nickel	0.020	Arsenic	0.0001
Vanadium	0.017	Tin	0.0001
Gerium		Mercury	0.00001
and		Silver	0.000001
yttrium	0.015	Selenium	0.000001
Copper	0.010	Gold	0.0000001 *

* This is equivalent to 24,500,000,000 tons of gold.
Source: E. Zimmermann, *World Resources and Industries* (New York: Harper, 1951), p. 441.

MINERAL RESOURCES AND POLITICAL TENSION

This analysis may seem pessimistic insofar as further industrial advance is concerned. Indeed, mineral shortages may appear to pose a distinct threat to civilization itself. More and more observers, in fact, do paint a woeful picture of how "have" nations struggle with each other and exploit the "have-nots." Nearly everyone presses for *more*. A great deal is lost or wasted in the struggles. Some countries, whether by war, waste, or excessive consumption, deplete their resources so rapidly that they, too, are in much the same boat as the "have-nots."

Certainly the continued well-being of industrial societies is tied directly to their supply of mineral resources, the power necessary to extract and produce them, and, very important, the location of these reserves relative to power sources. Any weakness in any of these areas is a potential source of international conflict. This applies, of course, to most scarce commodities, whether mineral, food, fiber, or otherwise. It is, for instance, unlikely that the United States would stand idly by and watch China, Russia, or another country take over the petroleum deposits of the Middle East for its own purposes only.

When an area is blessed with rich reserves of a prized or critical material, but is politically weak or immature, as in the case of Middle East countries, Indonesia, or Brazil, a power vacuum is said to exist. When strong countries begin to contend for control of such an area, a highly explosive situation may result. Conditions such as these account for the powder keg that exists in the Middle East today.

The important role that mineral resources and foodstuffs have played in international relations is a familiar story. The age-old struggle between Germany and France over control of the rich Saar Basin, for example, occupies a prominent spot in most history books. The deposits of tin in Malaya and the presence of the largest tin smelter in the world at Singapore are a constant invitation to conflict, and perhaps someday may precipitate war. As supplies of critical mineral resources grow shorter, men who are accustomed to depending on them seek further sources of power in order to extract, reclaim, and process the reserves that are more difficult and less economical to obtain and work with. Power-rich areas are therefore likely to become even more coveted than they are today. Portions of the globe that today scarcely weigh on the international scale may become "bones of contention" should they become the sources of newly discovered mineral or power reserves. Growing scarcity will make the contention more severe. As known deposits peter out, the "have-not" countries may reach outside their own boundaries to replenish their supplies. Mussolini's Italy did.

Ironically, then, higher levels of living

may lead to conflict as peoples contend for control of the resources that are vital to an affluent society. Once men have attained a certain level of living, they come to rely on it—take it for granted—and believe they have a right to it. Prospects of sinking to a lower plane stir tempers and breed envy. The physical world about us, no matter how peaceful it may appear at times, seethes with potential human conflict.

DAWN AFTER MIDNIGHT?

Thus far the picture we have painted of our planet's resources has been somewhat gloomy. Lest we become too pessimistic, we ought to reflect on a few facts. First, the picture of our planet's future would have been even darker had it been painted at a time when man knew nothing of electrical, gasoline, or atomic power; when he depended only on wind, waterwheel, and muscle. New and greater sources of power may be lying undiscovered all about us. This prospect ought to stimulate both hope and a more determined search for new sources of power.

Secondly, prophets of gloom and doom have been announcing the imminent exhaustion of our natural resources for years, only to be forced to move the date of depletion forward from time to time. Estimates vary, figures are often inaccurate, rates of consumption change, and new reserves are discovered. This in no way denies the possibility that some of our vital resources may eventually disappear, but it does throw a different light on the problem.

Furthermore, we have had a sufficient and rewarding experience with conservation to predict that resources will be used far more intelligently in the future. In some instances it is possible to expand a resource base. New methods for minimizing waste, as well as salvaging vital minerals from nearly depleted sources, are also quite likely to be developed when the pressure becomes great enough.

A very recent contribution is the concept of regional development. According to this idea, the earth is divided into well-defined regions or areas, with each region cooperating in intelligent and efficient exploitation of its resources. Benelux, an attempt at economic union between Belgium, the Netherlands, and Luxembourg, is an example on the international level. The Tennessee Valley Authority is another example within the continental limits of our own country. Although such developments offer great hope for a wiser, more efficient utilization of resources, we should remember that the costs are high in the initial stages of regional planning and development. Moreover, such efforts often are encumbered by petty jealousies that have existed between peoples for decades and centuries.

Many analysts believe that our only hope lies in limiting consumption by artificially restricting the growth of population. But there is no accurate inventory of how many people the earth's resources can support, and such a scheme would inevitably encounter widespread religious and political resistance.

Whatever happens, our future is bound up with far too many variables to permit any accurate predictions. Both gloomy prophecy and naive optimism seem unwarranted. Unbounded confidence in science's ability to solve all our problems is as misplaced as are dire predictions of impending doom. We should recognize that a great deal depends on three vital factors: namely, what happens to the world's population; our ability to calculate and control the influence of the physical environment; and, finally, our skill at living in accord with the "balance of nature."

STANDING ROOM ONLY:
THE STRUGGLE AGAINST NUMBERS

We have already said a great deal in the preceding chapters about what is commonly called a "population bomb," or that phenomenal growth in the world's population that has occurred during the industrial and urban revolutions. Improved tools, greater power resources, scientific animal- and plant-breeding, and better methods of food preservation and distribution, together with spectacular advances in modern medicine, have decreased the mortality rate, increased life expectancy, and produced a startling annual increase in the numbers of human beings on the earth. All these developments are part and parcel of the urban-industrial revolution.

PRESENT DISTRIBUTION OF PEOPLES

Overpopulation, however, is a relative matter. It must be seen against the distribution of the world's peoples, since the character of an area and its climate bear directly on the number of people it can support. The vast desolate flats of Nevada may not be able to support more than a few hundred thousand people, but a much smaller area such as Massachusetts can sustain a population of several million.

Men do gravitate toward those areas that can support large numbers of people and provide equable climates. The unevenness of population distribution reflects the result. Although mankind has always been unevenly distributed about the globe, modern technology and transportation have promoted still greater concentrations of people. Today about one half of the world's population resides in but 5 per cent of the total land area, while over 50 per cent of the world's land surface supports less than 5 per cent of its people.

Regional distribution is also uneven (see Table 15). Over half of mankind lives in Asia, including its offshore islands. About 14 per cent live in Europe, while Africa, North America, South America, and Russia (when considered separate from Asia and Europe), account for less than 10 per cent each.

TABLE **15**   *DISTRIBUTION OF WORLD POPULATION, 1957*

Areas	*Population (in millions)*
Africa	234
North America	253
South America	133
Europe and Asiatic USSR	616
Asia, excluding USSR	1,542
Australia and Oceania	15

Source: *Britannica Book of the Year, 1959.*

Quantity and distribution of population are influenced *directly* by three factors only: human fertility, mortality, and migration. If a change occurs in the level of living, the climate, or the price of rice, iron, or coal, it can affect population numbers only as it influences the reproduction rate, death rate, or net amount of migration into and out of a given area. Neglecting the factor of migration for the moment, what is important is the net gain in population resulting from recent reductions in the death rate, a phenomenon that has not been counterbalanced as yet by a corresponding decrease in the birth rate.

Mortality. Within just one hundred years, life expectancy has risen from forty to sixty-five years or more in most Western countries. Outside the West the decline in mortality rates has not been so sudden. In many instances they have remained high.

Nevertheless, non-Western countries lag behind by only a few decades, as Tables 16 and 17 make clear.

TABLE 16 CRUDE DEATH RATES * FOR SELECTED EUROPEAN AND ANGLO-AMERICAN COUNTRIES

Country	1918-22	1932	1943	1948	1954
England and Wales	13.7	12.0	13.3	10.8	11.3
France	20.0	16.0	16.4	12.4	12.0
Ireland	15.9	14.6	14.8	12.1	12.1
United States	13.5	10.9	10.9	9.9	9.2

* Deaths per thousand population.
Sources: A. Stuart, *Overpopulation: Twentieth Century Nemesis* (New York: Exposition, 1958), pp. 118-182; and *U.N. Demographic Yearbook*.

TABLE 17 CRUDE DEATH RATES * FOR SELECTED ASIAN AND LATIN-AMERICAN COUNTRIES

Country	1918-22	1932	1943	1948	1954
India	36.8	21.6	23.9	17.2	12.5
Japan	24.0	17.7	16.3	11.9	8.2
Mexico		26.1	22.4	16.8	13.1

* Deaths per thousand population.
Sources: Stuart, *Overpopulation: Twentieth Century Nemesis*, pp. 118-182; and *U.N. Demographic Yearbook*.

Fertility. In a great many countries where the decline in the death rate has been dramatic, the birth rate has likewise shown a marked though smaller decrease (see Tables 18 and 19). Birth rates, of course, are not so responsive to changing economic conditions as are death rates because of the cultural traditions involved in the former. Although some peoples stubbornly resist the introduction of modern sanitation and medicine, such resistance is far more easily overcome than opposition to birth control. Therefore, the death rate usually declines far more rapidly than the birth rate when modern industrialism and urbanization begin to develop in an area. The outcome, of course, is a phenomenal rise in population. We have come once more then to the condition that

aroused Thomas Malthus during the Industrial Revolution in England. The Malthusian doctrine, which we discussed earlier, stated simply that an unchecked population multiplies in geometric ratio, whereas the food supply increases only in arithmetic ratio. Hence, population always tends to outrun food supply, leaving most men in a rather wretched condition most of the time.

TABLE 18 CRUDE BIRTH RATES * FOR SELECTED EUROPEAN AND ANGLO-AMERICAN COUNTRIES

Country	1918-22	1932	1943	1948	1954
England and Wales	20.9	15.3	16.2	17.8	15.2
France	17.3	17.5	15.9	21.2	18.9
Ireland	20.6	19.1	21.4	22.0	21.2
United States	23.4	17.4	21.5	24.1	24.9

* Births per thousand population.
Sources: Stuart, *Overpopulation: Twentieth Century Nemesis*, pp. 118-182; and *U.N. Demographic Yearbook*.

TABLE 19 CRUDE BIRTH RATES * FOR SELECTED ASIAN AND LATIN-AMERICAN COUNTRIES

Country	1918-22	1932	1943	1948	1954
India	32.5	33.6	26.1	25.5	24.4
Japan	33.0	32.9	30.3	33.4	20.1
Mexico		43.3	45.5	44.6	46.4

* Births per thousand population.
Sources: Stuart, *Overpopulation: Twentieth Century Nemesis*, pp. 118-182; and *U.N. Demographic Yearbook*.

THE NEO-MALTHUSIAN CONTROVERSY

Critics of Malthus have charged that he did not foresee man's ability to expand his industrial and power resources and thereby multiply his means of sustenance. Men were so impressed with the increase in the food supply during the agricultural revolution that they paid little attention to the problem and proceeded to forget all about the Malthusian warning. Malthus was also criticized for making no more than a feeble gesture in the direction of encouraging birth control. The Malthusian doctrine fell quietly into disrepute and became little more than an historical curiosity in some textbooks.

But the population bomb, resulting from a falling death rate without a similar decline in the birth rate, brought Malthus back to the center of the stage. The only stable populations on earth today are found in those areas where both death and birth rates are high or where both are low. But in the interim stage from a condition where both are high to one where both are low, population grows by leaps and bounds. Thus far, only a small portion of our planet has reached the stage where both are low. Most of the world is moving rapidly into the difficult transition stage and thus experiencing a population boom.

The boom would not be so serious if it did not take so long for a country to move from the transitional stage to the stage where population levels off and becomes more stable. In India, for example, efforts to raise the level of living through increased production are frustrated by corresponding increases in the population. Each morning that India sits down to breakfast she has about twelve thousand or so more mouths to feed. Each day the number born exceeds the number who die by that figure. The daily agricultural and industrial output must increase enough to provide these twelve thousand people with their needs if India is not to slip back a notch in her level of living. Indians must run hard to stay where they are. One American observer reported that India at present needs an investment of $300 per person to sustain her population at the existing plane of living. Since the Indian population increases by 5 million annually, a billion and a half dollar increase in new capital or the gross national product is required each year just to keep the level of living where it now is. A steady increase in the number of mouths to be fed can slow a country's industrial and agricultural progress, which in turn inhibits any improvement in the living conditions of the population in general. It would seem that the Malthusian principle is not so antique after all, especially when more than two-thirds of the globe's population exists under the conditions that Malthus described.

How can the situation be improved? Would a rise in the level of living take the swell out of the population boom? Quite possibly. A lower birth rate has accompanied rising levels of living in many countries. The lower birth rate offsets the decline in the death rate and stabilizes the population. For the moment let us define the level of living as the average wealth or the total products produced divided by the population. To raise the level of living, the total produced (numerator) must rise more rapidly than the population (denominator). The American level of living has increased during the past fifty years as a result of an average annual increase of about 3 per cent in total production against an annual increase of 1.5 per cent in population. Mexico is still far from so favorable a position. She must find some means of increasing the numerator more rapidly than the denominator. The same is true in most underdeveloped areas of the world.

If the more developed countries were willing to share their substance more fully on a short-run basis to raise this numerator in other areas, the critical need might be alleviated. But few people want to share what they have already won, especially if the sums involved are large or would tend to lower their own levels of living. It is difficult for people to surrender even a fraction of those things to which they have become accustomed. In recent years, for example, there has been a loud chorus of opposition in the United States to the spending of money for foreign aid. Then, too, the underdeveloped nations may resent and even resist attempts to aid them. Or ancient customs and practices may block their advance, even when outside help is offered. The privileged and sacred cows of India, for example, have been a real hindrance to the development of that country. Furthermore, the help given is of little value unless it is used wisely. To spend money for tractors if the farmers of a country are untrained or opposed to their use is futile. Finally, in an age of rampant nationalism, strong if irrational antagonisms may further frustrate cooperation among nations.

Several years ago, agricultural scientists meeting in Texas presented convincing evidence that given the present state of fertility of the soil and agricultural technology, 2 billion human beings could be fed from what Texas alone could produce. A statement like this seems paradoxical in a world where one-half of the people are hungry and two-thirds are malnourished. Each day sees over 100,000 more people added to this planet and each year about 90 to 100 million. Over half of these new arrivals are doomed to go hungry, as do their parents. There is no automatic valve we can use to cut off population growth. Although a few countries now have more food per capita, many have less than they had fifteen or twenty years ago.

Can we keep population from overwhelming our dwindling resources? Practices that have been followed in some nonliterate societies—celibacy, infanticide, and abortion —are not at all popular in the modern world. Although practiced, both abortion and infanticide are crimes of the first rank. And, of course, society expects people to marry. Modern birth control practices have had varying acceptance and success. Frequently they run into a wall of religious opposition or contrary social taboos. Without an accurate assessment of the world's resources, furthermore, there is no way of determining the optimal population of an area and the con-

sequent degree to which birth control would aid. The Malthusian controversy proceeds.

MOBILITY AND MIGRATION

We noticed earlier that migration is the third *direct* determinant of population. As a means of adjusting numbers to a particular environment and its resources, it is very important. Historically, emigration has served as a safety valve when population pressure became very great. Industrialization and advances in transportation increased mobility and made such migrations more frequent. But the rising tide of nationalism in recent years has throttled immigration in many places and decreased its significance as a determinant of population size. America, for example, was long a haven for millions from abroad. Yet, after World War I, for a combination of reasons, many of them

In the midst of a population boom, with more than one-half the world's population facing want and starvation, the Malthusian doctrine is hardly out of date.

nationalistic, Congress shut the door on its historic "open door" policy toward foreign immigrants. Today only a few countries, such as Canada and Australia, have generous immigration policies, but even these restrict immigration to certain groups. Moreover, many of the desirable areas of the world have now been filled to capacity and others are restricted by government policies.

POPULATION PRESSURE AS A SOURCE OF TENSION

There is more to the argument for limiting the world's population than simply raising the level of living. For population pressure on resources adds to the already serious political and social tensions in the world. As we have already pointed out, population increases are often accompanied by a greater demand for land and food. Indeed, some observers believe that population pres-

sure is one fundamental cause of modern wars. It was Japan's excuse for invading China, Italy's for invading Ethiopia and Albania, and Germany's pretext for invading Poland.

The miracles of modern communication make the possibility of conflict even more likely, for news travels quickly these days and information about conditions in more advanced areas becomes widely disseminated in underdeveloped regions and feeds the fires of imagination and envy. The recent success that science has had in curbing the infant mortality rate in such underdeveloped areas as Indonesia has increased the proportion of young people in these thickly populated areas. As population pressure mounts and opportunity for youth declines, a whole country may become restive and politically volatile, even susceptible to revolutionary activity. The population bomb thus adds to our political dilemma.

THE INFLUENCE OF THE ENVIRONMENT ON MAN

The natural environment affects man in still other ways than those we have already recounted. Man-land relationships are deep and consequential. Almost everyone senses that his immediate surroundings affect his temperament, attitudes, and outlook on life. A person knows immediately when he has moved from a mountainous to a coastal community, or from an industrial to an agricultural region. Philadelphians and New Yorkers are of a different stamp from the Ohio farmer. The Tennessee merchant sees life differently from the Kansas wheatgrower. Yet, how much of the difference is attributable to the physical environment and how much to differences in education, wealth, or cultural traditions? This remains a baffling question. Strong claims are sometimes made for one or another of these factors, but evidence is scant and often unconvincing.

A good deal depends on further advance in the sciences, especially medicine and biology, as well as in the social sciences. We do know that a man's diet and habitat have a pronounced effect not only on his physical structure and well-being but also on his behavior and personality. Many social scientists have attached great importance to such factors as climate, topography, and character of the soil in shaping the outlook and the achievements of a people. A few claim, for example, that men are more restive and industrious in climates with sharp seasonal changes in temperature. Others have argued that hot sunny climes make men lazy and physically weak. For a time, the militancy of the Vikings was attributed to the north winds, their struggle with the North Sea, or the rugged terrain from which they grubbed their meager existence. Yet Norwegians and Danes are hardly militant and aggressive under the same conditions today. The truth is that many such conclusions often seem quite reasonable and a great deal of evidence can be mustered to substantiate them, but at best, they are hardly more than shrewd guesses. Opposing evidence is usually ignored or treated casually. A surprising number of educated persons have made excessive claims in behalf of certain environmental influences. Many have spent their entire adult lives in defense of their propositions.

THE MACKINDER THESIS

One of the most extravagant contentions about environmental influence was proffered by the famous German school of "geopolitics," which won favor during the dictatorship of Hitler in the Third Reich. Its premises were embedded in the earlier generalizations of a famous British scholar, Sir Halford Mackinder, who contended that "the grouping of lands and seas, and of fertility and natural pathways, is such as to lend itself to the growth of empires, and in the end of a single world empire." The connected continents of Europe, Asia, and Africa, in other words, were to him a great world-island, with the Americas and Australia as satellites. Within the world-island was a "heartland," which encompassed the territory inside a line drawn from the Baltic Sea through the lower Danube to the Black Sea, Asia Minor, Tibet, Mongolia, and back to the Baltic along the continental limits. The "heartland" he considered critical to control of all resources and men throughout the world. In Mackinder's own words:

> Who rules East Europe commands the
> Heartland
> Who rules the Heartland commands the
> World-Island
> Who rules the World-Island commands
> the World.

First stated in 1904 with an immediate purpose of urging the advantage of a British alliance with Russia, Mackinder's thesis also challenged some earlier theories that stressed the importance of naval and sea power as a determinant of political strength. For Mackinder the area under control, its resources, and its people spelled the difference in political power. Although Mackinder cannot be blamed for what others have done to his theory, in the hands of many geopoliticians the thesis has been turned into geographical determinism par excellence. The strength of a government depends on the area under control. But despite the vast claims some geopoliticians have made for the thesis, no one has as yet provided conclusive proof. Even so, Nicholas Spykman, another distinguished geographer, after studying Mackinder's theory and then rejecting it, turned around and came up with a similar interpretation of his own. Spykman's argument went something like this: "Who controls the Rimland rules Eurasia; who rules Eurasia rules the world." For Spykman it was the edge of the world-island rather than the center that counted most.

Mackinder's thesis became of more than academic interest in World War II when Karl Haushofer, father of the German school of geopolitics, used it to plan the territorial aggrandizement of Germany. Although his influence has been questioned, Haushofer certainly won fame and position for his views that Germany must conquer Eastern Europe to win hegemony over the "heartland." Thus, a form of geographic determinism brought recognition to some theorists and became part of the policy of a powerful, aggressive government, all without being substantially tested or verified.

THE TURNER THESIS

Late in the nineteenth century, Frederick Jackson Turner, a renowned historian, advanced another provocative thesis which stated that American democracy and the democratic temper of the American people were attributable to environmental influences. The return to primitive conditions along a constantly moving westward frontier had kept America equalitarian, individualistic, and democratic. Put differently, Turner held that a unique organism (the American) placed in a unique environment (the moving frontier) produced a unique condition (democratic personalities and democratic processes). Men behave as they do, said Turner, because they have mixed their personalities with a distinct type of environment. Unlike Mackinder, Turner went to great lengths to verify his proposition, as have his disciples. He did not propose any tests, however. He merely searched out the evidence that seemed to prove his point.

Like all such bold assertions, the thesis suffers from an inability to lend itself to precise testing, as well as from contrary evidence that anti-Turnerites have mercilessly exploited. And efforts to uphold Turner run head-on into a lack of knowledge about the determinants of human behavior. The Turner thesis has continued to be a challenging, if unproved, hypothesis about how America has developed. Even though the proof offered is highly questionable, Turner's thesis does provide historians with ways to explain the peculiar combination of practicality, equalitarianism, activism, and democratic idealism that characterizes the ordinary American.

MAINTENANCE OF NATURE'S BALANCE

Aside from problems of sustenance and population growth, and the need to understand man-land relations, we have a responsibility to maintain nature's balance. A world of living organisms is a world of interdependence. For nature follows balances and cycles. In an aquarium, plants, water, fish, scavengers such as snails, and filters are all interdependent. Remove any one of them and the tank may become foul. The entire earth is like that. Remove the predators from a forest and deer will become so thick that they will starve for want of food. An overpopulation of deer will destroy the range and forest undergrowth, thus harming the forest.

Where man goes he constantly threatens the balances of nature. He took rabbits to Australia where they became a national menace. He sprayed forests for budworm and found that the spray got into the streams and killed the fish. And so goes the story constantly. Luckily, the earth is large enough to permit the balance to be restored, although the process often requires years.

Nevertheless, each time the delicate balance is upset, danger threatens. As our growing technological and power potential makes it possible to upset nature's balance on a wider and wider scale, the threat looms larger. The possible effects of atomic explosions are a case in point. Our advanced technology is pregnant with latent possibilities for destruction as well as good. The great power we have harnessed and now possess ought to give us pause and remind us of our responsibility for maintaining nature's balance lest we upset it irrevocably.

GEOGRAPHY AND YOU

Man invented geography to understand and interpret the wonders of the environment around him. Yet few persons recognize the subject for what it is. We are more likely to think of geography in terms of locating towns and streams than as a valuable tool of social science. As we have already made abundantly clear in this chapter, geography is vitally important to all of us. Somehow we know this, possibly because it is such an integral part of our daily lives. Every time a farmer puts his plow in the ground he is involved in geography. Each time we give someone directions to a distant city, geography becomes important. Despite our ignorance of geography, we often worship it. We may not be able to locate the boundaries of our homeland, but we are quite prepared to defend them, with our lives if necessary. We identify ourselves with geographic objects, take them inside ourselves, and make them a part of our personalities. Boundaries, familiar terrain, the home town, or the soil we till are common objects of emotional attachment. Geography is often used to classify peoples as the scientist classifies insects. "If you live on the other side of the Rhine, you are unfit to associate with!" Coming from the "wrong side of the tracks," you may find it difficult to break into the "right" social circles. Although many such tendencies are quite unfortunate and are based on emotion rather than reason, they are remarkable demonstrations of how much geography is a part of us.

SOME WORDS OF SUMMARY

We have an ever-widening responsibility to improve the world in which we live. Fulfillment of this responsibility depends on how clearly we understand the natural and man-made environment that surrounds us.

Life is sustained by a thin and limited topsoil, mineral resource deposits, shallow waters, and the atmosphere. Some of these essential resources are becoming critically short because of poor land-use practices, heavy consumption, inadequate conservation policies, unwise drainage and sewage programs, and a general public and official apathy toward all such problems. This great drain on our resources threatens the continued existence of the human race, produces tension and strife, and makes even more valuable the dwindling resources that remain. Our somewhat dismal picture is offset by the discovery of new resources, the reduction of waste, better methods of utilizing resources, a trend toward regionalism, and population stabilization.

In the light of our scanty knowledge, neither gloom nor optimism is warranted. More information about population patterns and trends is vital. But we do know that the marked decline in mortality rates, combined with a continuing high birth rate, has produced a population boom and revived the old Malthusian fear that population will outrun the food supply. Although our present statistics reveal that population tends to stabilize with an appreciable rise in the plane of living, this condition is difficult to achieve in the underdeveloped countries because their populations increase so rapidly that any increase in the total product is normally consumed quickly. Our efforts to aid underdeveloped areas frequently run afoul of prejudice and a reluctance on the part of the "haves" to sacrifice for the "have-nots." Birth control often runs counter to religious beliefs or social customs, and migration likewise offers little in the way of solution.

A great deal of study remains to be done on the effects of environment on human beings and their behavior. The available information is very unreliable, and we still lack a sound basis for evaluating and interpreting what we already know. Those investigators who are bold enough to offer explanations find it difficult to test and verify their theories. Some, such as the geopoliticians, do not muster sufficient evidence to prove their views, while others, such as Turner, leave the testing of their suggestive theories to others. All are apt to ignore or undervalue the evidence opposing their particular theory. There are a few, such as Haushofer, who are in the game mainly for propaganda purposes.

Finally, nature tends to keep in balance, but our interdependent world is constantly open to the danger of imbalance, especially from man's interference with nature's processes. This danger increases as man's power and technology grow.

Thus geography is a fundamental bearing-wall in the house of social science.

FURTHER ROADS TO LEARNING

GENERAL ACCOUNTS

I. Bowman, *Geography in Relation to the Social Sciences* (New York: Scribner, 1934). Places geography in a social science perspective.

G. Deasy, *et al.*, *The World's Nations* (Philadelphia: Lippincott, 1958). An economic and regional geography text that contains a wealth of information.

W. East and A. Moodie, eds., *Changing World* (Yonkers, N. Y.: World Book, 1956). One of the very finest political geographies.

H. van Loon, *Van Loon's Geography* (New York: Simon & Schuster, 1932). A popular and light survey that emphasizes man's relation to his environment.

W. Woytinsky and E. Woytinsky, *World Population and Production* (New York: The Twentieth Century Fund, 1953). A complete and scholarly source book.

J. Wheeler, J. Kostbade, and R. Thoman, *Regional Geography of the World* (New York: Holt, 1955). An excellent survey with a regional perspective and economic emphasis.

SPECIAL STUDIES

G. Burch and E. Pendell, *Human Breeding and Survival* (Baltimore: Penguin Books, 1947). Develops the point that populations must be limited to avert war.

S. Chase, *Rich Land, Poor Land* (New York: McGraw-Hill, 1936). A popular analysis of the destruction of soil and its consequences.

A. Coale and E. Hoover, *Population Growth and Economic Development in Low-Income Countries: A Case Study of India's Prospects* (Princeton: Princeton University Press, 1958). A study of the basic tasks facing a country with a Malthusian problem of bringing resources into line with the growing needs of skyrocketing population.

R. Cook, *Human Fertility: The Modern Dilemma* (New York: Sloane, 1951). On the consequences of the high birth rate.

R. Francis, *The Population Ahead* (Minneapolis: University of Minnesota Press, 1958). A serious preview of future population problems.

P. Hauser, *Population and World Politics* (Glencoe, Ill.: The Free Press, 1958). This valuable volume is the work of one of the most highly respected population authorities.

J. Hertzler, *Crisis in World Population* (Lincoln: University of Nebraska Press, 1956). A leading authority examines the implications of the growth of population throughout the world.

H. Mackinder, *Democratic Ideals and Reality* (New York: Holt, 1942). Statement of the "heartland" theory.

F. Osborn, *Our Plundered Planet* (Boston: Little, Brown, 1948). A good discussion of our depleted resources and the possible results.

K. Smith, *The Malthusian Controversy* (London: Routledge and Kegan Paul, 1951). A scholarly analysis of the pros and cons of the Malthusian position.

J. Spengler and O. Duncan, *Population Theory and Policy* (Glencoe, Ill.: The Free Press, 1956). A series of readings that covers the subject comprehensively.

A. Stuart, *Overpopulation: Twentieth Century Nemesis* (New York: Exposition, 1958). The brew of a twenty-year attempt to study population trends comprehensively and objectively.

W. Thompson, *Population Problems*, 4th ed. (New York: McGraw-Hill, 1953). A comprehensive analysis of the population factor.

F. Turner, *The Frontier in American History* (New York: Holt, 1920, 1947). Turner's thesis on the influence of the frontier.

C. Walker, "Too Many People," *Harper's Magazine* (February 1948), pp. 97-104. Superb little article on the dilemma of overpopulation.

FICTION AND DRAMA

P. Buck, *The Good Earth* (New York: Modern Library, 1934). The plight of over-population and resource depletion in China.

V. Fisher, *Toilers of the Hills* (Boston: Houghton Mifflin, 1928). A novel describing the vicissitudes of benchland farmers of southeastern Idaho in their struggles against the wiles of nature.

H. Garland, *Rose of Dutcher's Coolly* (New York: Harper, 1896). How constant contact with nature and the hardships of farm life distorted and destroyed many of the more desirable aspects of life.

O. Rølvaag, *Giants in the Earth* (New York: Harper, 1927). By all odds the best novel yet written about life on the Great Plains.

M. Sandoz, *Old Jules* (Boston: Little, Brown, 1935). About a hardened and cruel immigrant in a hard and cruel environment.

D. Scarborough, *The Wind* (New York: Harper, 1925). The struggle of early Texas settlers with the wind and drought.

FILMS

Arteries of Life (Encyclopaedia Britannica Films, 1948, 10 min., sound, color). The interdependence of man, animals, forests, and water supply.

Forest Conservation (Encyclopaedia Britannica Films, 1949, 10 min., sound, color). Shows how men have devastated their forests and what can be done about it.

An Invisible Ocean, Pt. A (Scribner's, 1954, filmstrip, 30 fr., color). Analysis of the three layers of atmosphere—the troposphere, stratosphere, and ionosphere.

Our Soil Resources (Encyclopaedia Britannica Films, 1947, 11 min., sound, black and white). A clear, authentic description of the process of soil formation.

A Strand Breaks (Encyclopaedia Britannica Films, 1950, 16 min., sound, color). What happens when the balance of nature is upset.

Water (National Film Board of Canada, 1947, 10 min., sound, black and white). About the critical relationship among water, humanity, and social organization.

Water in the West (United States Bureau of Reclamation, 1951, 36 min., sound, black and white). An overview of water needs and the history of water resource development.

Race and Minority Problems around the World

Brandishing weapons as they charge
through the countryside, these South African women
protest governmental restrictions on travel
by non-whites that prevent their husbands from working in the cities.

To understand

the many tensions and conflicts that beset our twentieth-century world, we must examine the role played by the natural environment in setting men at each other's throats. This we have already done in the last chapter. We saw that geography, by dealing out unequal hands in the struggle for place and advantage between peoples, has provided an important source of international and group conflict. Likewise we have seen that history provides illustrations of the poisons that continue to plague relations between groups and nations in the twentieth century. As we shall see later, many national groups were to choose the dangerous road of hypernationalism, totalitarianism, and total war. Finally, we must consider the psychology of twentieth-century man. In this and the following chapters, we shall seek to demonstrate how the interplay of environmental, historical, and psychological forces have created tension in the world today.

Hardly a more important source of tension exists than the one between minority groups and the society around them. Both within and among the national states of the contemporary world there are tensions based on differences in race, religion, and nationality. A *minority group*, by definition, *is a collection of individuals united by its conscious position of being "different" from the larger society of which it is a part.* This difference, whether of race or religion or nationality, is frequently used to justify treatment of a particular minority as inferior. Tensions arise when minorities become conscious of their inferior status and assume an aggressive attitude about it; or, as is more often the case, when the dominant group feels that the minority poses a threat to the larger society. For the dominant group, whether in a community, region, or national state, usually moves to meet the supposed challenge. This dominant group need not be larger than the minority causing the concern. The white man, for instance, is in a majority in the United States but the Negro outnumbers him in South Africa, yet in both places the white man is a member of the dominant group.

MINORITY GROUPS AROUND THE WORLD

MINORITIES IN HISTORY

Peoples have set themselves off from their "inferiors" for centuries, but minority groups as we know them today are a more recent development. Aryans moving into India some four thousand years ago considered themselves superior to the darker-skinned natives they found there. Greeks once treated Romans as inferiors, only to be conquered by them later. Romans, likewise, spoke of the "heathen" Britons whom they encountered across the English Channel. And Britons, too, were later to turn the same contempt against "backward" Indian and African natives. Indeed, intergroup conflicts are among the most dramatic and divisive developments in history.

What makes these early relations between conqueror and conquered different from minority relations today? Although the basic patterns of domination and subordination have remained essentially the same, earlier forms of segregation and discrimination were comparatively weak in *exploitation*. It was the Industrial Revolution, hand-in-hand with modern capitalism, that brought the change. Success in industrial competition and the overseas race for empire demanded full exploitation of all available resources, including human resources. In South Africa and North America, Negroes and Indians were driven forcibly from their lands. In Latin America, soldiers and early settlers mingled and mixed with natives, only to enslave them later. Many African natives were imported to the American colonies as one of the cheapest available forms of labor. This *exploitation* of natives to an extreme and often brutal degree added a new dimension to "minority problems."

JUSTIFICATION
OF MINORITY TREATMENT

Prejudice and discrimination against minorities have always required some justification. Dominant groups need some kind of rationale to support their treatment of minorities, especially when the minorities are exploited. Such arguments are necessary to counterbalance beliefs in individual rights, equality of opportunity, or brotherly love. Over the centuries a host of arguments have made their appearance. A minority threatens the security of the majority; the white man must take up the "burden" of civilizing the underdeveloped peoples of the globe; Christianity sanctions discrimination against minorities; the minority is uneducable, lazy, or "clannish." But all arguments have in common an insistence that the minority is different and hence inferior or possibly dangerous. For the "good of all," therefore, the minority may be segregated, exploited, or otherwise discriminated against.

Racism. A century ago, a Frenchman named De Gobineau set forth the basic philosophy of racism. Stripped to its essen-

tials, his argument contained a few basic tenets that underlie most of the present-day racist positions. De Gobineau claimed that there were three major races in the world: white, yellow, and black. Of these, the white race, he said, was superior and responsible for most of man's progress. Blacks, on the other hand, were decidedly inferior, while yellow peoples ranked somewhere in between. Since these racial differences were believed to be biological, they were inherited. Under these circumstances, race mixture was unthinkable since it would dilute the high quality of superior peoples. Others have elaborated and sometimes varied De Gobineau's argument, but contemporary racists remain remarkably close to his argument in their basic attitudes and behavior.

The racist philosophy has provided a basis for action, illustrated most strikingly by Adolf Hitler's application of racist ideas to the Jews. To the dark-haired Hitler, tall blond Nordics were the superior brand of man, while Jews were the most inferior. Following a typically racist line of reasoning, these differences were held to be racial and therefore inherited. Jews accordingly must not mix with Nordics. Hitler claimed further that Jews wielded too much political and economic power. His solution was to exterminate them.

Justification in Religion. The core of Judaic-Christian beliefs contains principles of brotherly love and human equality. According to St. Paul, "There is neither Jew nor Greek, there is neither bond nor free for ye are all one in Christ Jesus," and also, "He hath made of one blood all nations of men for to dwell on the face of the earth." It is abundantly clear that the Christian movement, though not all Christians, has an anti-racist tradition. Religions of the Western World might, therefore, be expected to oppose discriminatory treatment of minorities. Generally they do. But we must make two important reservations in assessing the attitude the churches have taken toward minority problems. First, many churches themselves practice discrimination; and secondly, religion itself is sometimes used as a moral justification for discrimination.

Across the United States, in almost every community, there are churches that exclude certain minorities from attendance and membership. Such exclusion may be publicly condemned by the churches or openly insisted on by them. But the result is practically the same. Eleven o'clock on Sunday morning has been called the most segregated hour in American life. This is part of the American's moral dilemma. His churches preach brotherhood but practice discrimination.

Not all churches preach brotherhood, of course, and the Bible is often quoted in support of segregation as well as in opposition to it. Interpretations of divine scripture are numerous, and a person may easily quote passages to support a predetermined position. "Ye shall know them by their fruit"; or the words of Noah, condemning the descendants of Ham (Negroes), the Canaanites: "Cursed be Canaan, a servant of servants shall he be unto his brethren." Segregationists, thus, sometimes quote scripture to justify segregation and discrimina-

tion. Anti-segregationists on the other hand, quote other passages to help maintain their position. Thus, religion is a two-edged sword that can be used both to defend and attack discrimination.

Social Inequalities. Many minority members suffer an extremely inferior social standing. American Negroes, for instance, have below-average incomes, education, housing, and occupations. The same is true of American Indians and African natives. This condition breeds in dominant groups the conviction that social inferiority is the direct result of biological inferiority, although many students of minority-group relations view an inferior status as simply a lack of opportunity for social, political, and economic advancement. In any case, minorities occupying a lowly position are rarely afforded the educational and employment opportunities that would enable them to climb the social ladder. When they fail to improve they become subject to additional discrimination. This condition is what Gunnar Myrdal, the famous Swedish sociologist, called the "vicious circle" of discrimination. Inequality thus begets frustration in the minority and intolerance in the dominant group.

Many dominant groups impose social disabilities on minorities. Here a Negro lad points a warning finger at a white youth who acted in accordance with a traditional restriction requiring Negroes to yield the sidewalk to whites in some parts of the American South.

PATTERNS AND TECHNIQUES OF DOMINANCE

In the modern world the treatment of minorities has varied with time, place, and circumstances. The history of recent centuries is replete with examples of tolerance and intolerance, kindness and cruelty, humanitarianism and barbarism in the relations between minority groups and the dominant majority. But *domination* of minority groups is a common result, whatever the strategy. Six types are presented here to show the great range of techniques for dominating minorities: extermination, expulsion, invasion and conquest, subjugation, segregation, and conversion. Let us examine each a little more fully.

EXTERMINATION: HITLER AND THE JEWS

Adolph Hitler defined Jews as culture-destroyers. On coming to power in Germany in 1933, he launched the most vigorous and bloody campaign against the Jews the world has ever seen. Jews in Germany were dismissed from their jobs and deprived of their citizenship. Their businesses were expropriated without compensation. By 1938 Jewish stores were being demolished and thousands of Jews arrested. The reign of terror thus begun, heightened as the years sped on.

During World War II the Nazis systematically overworked, underfed, and killed Jews. Not until the Nuremberg trials after the war did the world learn the full extent of the Nazi anti-Jewish campaign. Six million Jews had been put to death before the war's end.

Almost every Jew who did not flee the Nazi wrath paid with his life. The gas chambers and crematoriums at Buchenwald, Auschwitz, and other concentration camps piled up high production records. Hitler nearly perfected the ultimate technique for majority domination of a minority. Had Germany won the war there might not be a single Jew alive today!

EXPULSION: THE WANDERING JEW

For twenty-five centuries the Jewish people have been captured, segregated, expelled, or annihilated by rulers and conquerors. Very early, the practice of expulsion or dispersal over wide areas was employed against them. In the sixth century before Christ, for example, Jews were held captive by the Babylonians. And during the first century A.D. the Roman conquerors drove them from Jerusalem and their ancient homeland in Israel.

In medieval Europe Jews were expelled successively from England (1290) and France (1306). During the fourteenth and fifteenth centuries they were driven from cities in Germany and Austria, and a number of Jewish communities in Germany were destroyed. Spain rid itself of Jews who refused to renounce their religion in 1492.

How the Jewish people have succeeded in maintaining their unity and identity in the face of repeated dispersals is an interesting question. Certainly their religion, Judaism, with its special and ancient beliefs and rituals, has been a strong and cohesive force. Confinement in separate communities and sections has helped to strengthen their sense of solidarity. So has their strong tendency to marry within their faith. Jews seldom marry non-Jews. Finally, the dispersals themselves have engendered a feeling of persecution which adds to the sense of a common history and destiny. Throughout history the Jewish people have maintained a strong feeling of unity, exclusiveness, and superiority. Without a national homeland until very recently, the Jews have still remained a unique and distinctive people.

INVASION AND CONQUEST:
EUROPEANS IN AFRICA AND AMERICA

Although extermination and expulsion will rid an area of unwanted peoples, invasion of an area and conquest of its people, on the other hand, is a means of dominating without necessarily expelling or destroying anyone. Of the many instances of this technique, two illustrations will suffice.

South Africa. In 1652, Dutch settlers first established a base at Capetown on the tip of southern Africa. Soon the Dutch were quarreling with native Hottentots over pasture lands and the theft of cattle. Gradually, however, the Hottentots began working for the Dutch colonists. Since Dutch women were scarce, the colonists intermixed with the Hottentots, breeding a group of hybrids known as Cape Coloureds.

To keep the French out, Britain occupied the Cape in 1795 and, following Napoleon's defeat at Waterloo, obtained the Cape by treaty. The Dutch (Boers) soon came to resent the British settlers and began moving northward to inland areas to avoid them.

As a result, the Boers had established two independent republics by the mid-nineteenth century. Discovery of gold and diamonds in South Africa enhanced the attractiveness of the area, and in the 1880's the English and the Boers began a series of skirmishes that led ultimately to the Boer War.

During this era of colonization and conflict the natives of South Africa were generally subdued. As the Dutch who moved northward (the Troeckboers) pushed steadily inland, some of the native tribes resisted and fought them from time to time. But in the long run it was a losing battle. Natives were unable to cope with modern European weapons. Today, therefore, the natives in South Africa are one of the most completely dominated minorities in the world, a point to which we shall return later.

America. Indians in North America had an experience quite similar to the natives of South Africa. As European settlers came in increasing numbers and the frontier moved westward, Indian tribes were either conquered or pushed from their land. Where the Indian chose to stand and fight, he was generally beaten, sometimes wiped out. Many tribes regarded the land as theirs as a matter of sacred, traditional right. Never quite understanding this concept, the white man had few qualms about driving the "savages" westward and killing those who resisted.

Tales of Indian resistance are legend. One of the most interesting cases involves the Seminole tribe of Florida. Protected by the everglade swamps, the Seminole were never conquered. Thousands of troops and thousands of dollars were expended in an effort to subjugate them, but finally, the federal government gave up and the Seminole Indians remain a "free nation" today.

European conquest and colonization were often based on the premise that "might makes right." Hence, in Africa and North America the pattern of invasion and conquest was followed in a hundred different places, accompanied by a mixture of human behavior ranging from brutality to kindness.

SUBJUGATION:
THE NEGRO SLAVE IN AMERICA

Brutality was a consistent feature of the slave trade between Africa and the Americas. African natives were enslaved to work the plantations of the white man in the New World. Cheap labor was the motive for the slave trade and a thoroughgoing subjugation of the Negro slave the result. The slave in America had virtually no rights and privileges. He was not a citizen and could not vote. He could not own property or firearms, and since no laws recognized slave marriages, children were illegitimate. To discourage insurrections, public assembly was prohibited. Slaves received no education in schools on the premise that education was dangerous to the slavery system. Those who rebelled or ran away were subject to severe punishment. Thus was the Negro slave almost completely subdued and controlled.

The manner in which the African native was captured and transported to America contributed to his subjugation. Forcibly overpowered, he frequently resisted captivity and sometimes died in efforts to escape or to stave off capture. Once on ship he was commonly crowded into dark, unsanitary quarters below deck until the ship landed on this side of the Atlantic. Importation of slaves to the United States was made illegal in 1808, but from all indications some slave traffic continued past mid-century. Slave ships, encountering government vessels on the dangerous "middle passage" from Africa to the West Indies, would sometimes throw all Negroes, chained together, overboard. The authorities could make no arrests without "evidence." On other occasions, unruly half-starved Africans would be flogged or shot. Even before debarkation time, ruthless, inhuman treatment had curbed a great deal of their rebelliousness.

Sold as a slave, the Negro faced a lifetime of servitude. On the plantations the field slave had little contact with the customs of the New World. Ignorant of the white man's ways to begin with, his adjustment was extremely difficult. Sometimes a slave family might be separated at the market place and mother, father, and children sold to different masters. Under such conditions incentive to remain on the master's plantation and to work hard was weak. As an upshot of all this, Negro slaves were dubbed "lazy, shiftless, irresponsible, and stupid," worthy only of the very limited rights they were granted.

SEGREGATION: GHETTOS AND RESERVATIONS

Still another technique of dominance practiced in the modern world is the isolation of the minority group in a limited, well-defined residential area. The dominant group thus is assured that it and the minority will have separate identities. Two of the best examples of residential segregation are to be found in the ancient ghettos of Europe and the reservations of South Africa.

Ghettos. A number of European cities by the fourteenth century contained clearly defined areas inhabited by Jews and known as ghettos. Earlier ghettos had been a mark of privilege and protection for Jews. Living together, Jews could more easily observe their religious customs and attend synagogues. In time, however, the ghetto gradually changed from a section of voluntary isolation to one of compulsory isolation. In the sixteenth century, Pope Paul IV called for the segregation of all Jews in their own quarter enclosed by a high wall. Jews, it was decreed, should not live openly among Christians, should not own real estate, and should not employ Christian servants. Whether the reason for this decree was fear that intermixing might weaken Christian faith or whether Jews were regarded as dangerous competitors in the business world is not clear. Not until the nineteenth century were Jews liberated from ghettos in Europe. In France they were made full-fledged citizens by the National Assembly in 1791. By 1870 most of the restrictions against them in Western Europe were removed, only to be clamped on again by Hitler a half-century later.

Segregation of Jews, however, has not ended. Most larger European cities still have their Jewish sections. In the United States the majority of Jews live in big cities and normally cluster in their own sections. But

A late nineteenth-century ghetto on New York's East Side. Throughout history Jews have tended to cluster in their own sections. In some instances governments have adopted policies that were deliberately designed to keep Jews confined within their ghettos.

the Jew, nevertheless, has attained legal emancipation, even though ghetto-like communities and restrictions still persist.

Reservations. Natives of South Africa and American Indians, too, have been located in special areas set aside for their residence. In Africa these areas are known as "reserves" while in the United States they are called "reservations." Conditions in both cases have been quite similar.

The Indian, pushed from the lands he originally occupied, was given special grants of land to settle, with some protection against the encroachments of the white man. Government aid and supplies, though often insufficient, usually have been forthcoming.

Generally he was free to leave the reservation, but most often he has remained with his own people. On the reservation the Indian is better able to perpetuate and enjoy his traditional ways. Off the reservation he must compete for jobs and housing in a white man's society for which he is ill-equipped and which grants him no special advantage. Lands set aside for reservations are usually poor for agricultural purposes—so poor, in fact, that it is a miracle that the Indian has survived at all. At least a few Indian tribes, however, have reaped large unanticipated benefits from timber, oil, uranium, and other resources found or developed on the reservations.

In South Africa natives are confined to

reserves of land comparable in quality to the reservations of the American Indians. Some are permitted to leave the reserves and live in cities. Generally, however, anyone leaving the reserve must have a government "pass." The pass system assures that a reservoir of native labor will be available on the reserves. Mining operators needing labor for diamond- and gold-digging have made it easy for natives to obtain the necessary permission long enough to do the necessary work. When work runs out, the native must return to the reserve. The national poll tax offers some inducement for the native to leave the reserves for at least brief periods of work each year. Farming on the reserve usually fails to bring in enough cash to enable him to pay this tax.

CONVERSION:
AMERICANIZATION OF EUROPEANS

One of the more subtle patterns of minority domination is known as conversion. When conversion of a minority occurs, the group's members take on the characteristics of the dominant group. This is the sort of pattern we have in mind when we refer to the Americanization of different cultures and nationality groups.

In reality, the history of American immigration reveals three patterns of immigrant adaptation. *The American "melting pot" has resulted from a blending and merging of diverse European cultural traits*, with immigrants giving something to the American culture and in turn absorbing a variety of new customs. *Cultural pluralism is a pattern of segregation or separateness in which the cultural traits of the "old country" are largely preserved.* The Chinatowns, Little Tokyos, Bohemias, and Italian villages are more or less pluralistic adaptations. The "old country" exists within the adopted country. Under *Americanization*, on the other hand, *immigrants lose most of their old-country traits and simply take on American attitudes, habits, and customs.*

To be truly effective, conversion requires the newcomer to change his attitudes, beliefs, and values. For many immigrants, for example, conversion would entail changing their old-country belief that churches should be supported by the government and accepting the idea of separation of church and state. Conversion is a one-way change, with the immigrant moving in the direction of becoming more like other Americans. There is some doubt, however, whether complete conversion in this sense ever actually takes place. European immigrants may learn about our national heroes, the flag, Constitution, and national anthem, but learning does not necessarily mean conversion. Moreover, in the process of interaction, some of the European ways are absorbed into the American social and cultural pattern, usually in modified form. The result, then, is more nearly a blend of European and American ways than it is a total conversion to American life.

MINORITY-GROUP REACTIONS TO DOMINANCE

SUBMISSION AND WITHDRAWAL

There are many ways in which minorities may react to the patterns of domination we have just recounted. They range from submission to open and aggressive resistance. Almost never do minority group members react in a unanimous way. Rather, their reactions are most often varied and intensely personal.

One can find various illustrations of minority submission. Some of the Japanese-Americans held in American relocation centers during World War II, for example, were extremely cooperative. They helped maintain law and order in the camps, carried out their daily assignments efficiently, and offered their services generously. Though food was below American standards, some insisted that it was perfectly all right. Among Negroes, the epithet "Uncle Tom" has been applied to congenial, deferential Negroes who show similar submission and loyalty to the white man. Two thousand years ago the Jews had their Sadducees, who wanted a Jewish nation yet were sufficiently sympathetic with the cultures of Greece and Rome to want to absorb and spread them. The above instances are examples of *submission through cooperation*. But minorities can submit in other ways—by withdrawing, for example.

A *withdrawal* generally involves some form of isolation from the surrounding society and can be carried out in several different ways. One example can be found in the religious sects that have sought preservation through withdrawal and isolation. The Puritans withdrew from England to the New World in order to escape the pattern of dominance imposed on them by the more numerous Anglicans. To Pennsylvania came the Amish, who withdrew from their new American neighbors as they had withdrawn from their former German compatriots across the ocean. Another example is the immigrant groups who establish their separate communities, intermarry within their own group, and persist in their own ways of life.

The individual, on the other hand, may seek isolation through a process of inner withdrawal. Hermits, no doubt, are a classic example. During World War II an occasional Japanese-American would withdraw and live completely apart from his fellow internees. A few suffered complete mental breakdowns and required hospitalization. The number of such mental withdrawals is difficult to determine, however, since not all cases lead to hospitalization.

From the standpoint of the dominant group, an individual or minority group that withdraws or is submissive seems less dangerous or undesirable than one that resists domination. There are, of course, many examples of minorities that do resist. Two of the more familiar patterns of resistance are *passive resistance* and *open rebellion*.

PASSIVE RESISTANCE

Although a very old technique, passive resistance has received respectful attention in the modern world through the efforts of the saintly Mohandas Gandhi in India. This austere, disciplined man taught resistance to oppression and British imperialism by nonviolent means, peaceful strikes, mass disobedience to British decrees, and noncooperation with "foreign" authorities. But he also preached against insurrection and

Mohandas Gandhi, the austere little man who won world-wide acclaim by successfully employing passive resistance to free India of British rule.

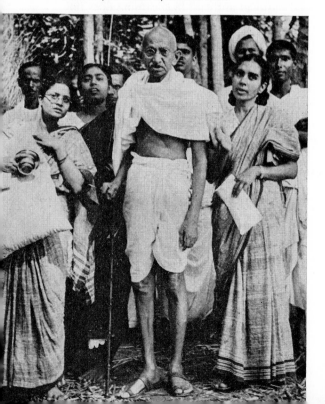

any use of violence or firearms. Against Christian and liberty-loving people such as the British, these techniques were highly effective. Indeed, their success inspired minorities in many other parts of the world.

Gandhi developed his philosophy of passive resistance while a young man visiting Africa in the 1890's. He was profoundly disturbed over the way his fellow Indians were treated in South Africa. As a result, he began to preach nonviolent resistance as the only recourse for his suffering brethren. When he returned to his native India, he directed the same techniques against the British, who controlled his homeland. He taught his Indian followers to return good for evil. Gandhi himself helped develop the Indian Red Cross, which gave aid to Indians and Britons alike, and encouraged the establishment of hospitals, schools, and charitable institutions. In short, he personified in his own life the doctrines he advocated. His was the decisive personality in forging freedom for India from British rule. Rarely has one man exerted so profound an influence on the course of world history. And even more rarely have the doctrines of one man evoked such a sympathetic response in many quarters of the globe. Gandhi and his program were indeed oddities in a world beset with hatred and violence. Little wonder, then, that he became a legend after his death.

OPEN CONFLICT

As opposed to passive resistance, open rebellion against minority status aims at forceful overthrow of the existing patterns of domination. In Kenya, for example, the secret society of the Mau Mau sought to drive the British from their land by violence and terrorism. During the late 1940's the Mau Mau terrorized and sometimes brutally murdered British residents, including women and children. British troops, reinforced by Kenya police, sought to bring the Mau Mau under control. Alleged Mau Mau leaders were imprisoned, but Britishers still dared not go unarmed even in their own homes.

An earlier example of Negro revolt against white rule occurred at the time of the French Revolution. On the island of Haiti thousands of Negroes fought for their freedom from one of the most brutal slave systems that ever existed. Great numbers of Frenchmen and Negroes died in battle, and French troops were unable to quell the rebellion until the native leader, Toussaint L'Ouverture, was captured.

Open conflict, though it occurs frequently, seldom produces a basic alteration in the minority's status. It does, however, provide a dramatic illustration of the powerful discontent of minority groups and the hopes they have for improving their situation.

MAJOR SYSTEMS OF MINORITY RELATIONS

It should be clear from our preceding remarks that there are marked differences in the patterns of domination imposed on minorities and also in the minorities' reaction to them. Throughout the world today there are innumerable tensions and conflicts associated with minority-dominant group relations. In general, three alternative patterns of relations are discernible in various parts of the world today. All three are present and no one system seems to predominate.

RACIST DOMINANCE:
THE SOUTH AFRICAN CASE

Natives in the Union of South Africa live under one of the most rigid, unrelenting, absolute systems of minority control found anywhere. As we mentioned earlier, they live on special reserves, and various means are employed to keep as many on the reserves as possible. By designating land as reserve and non-reserve, Europeans are thus protected against competition from the natives. Although laws requiring Negroes to obtain a pass before leaving the reservation were developed originally to protect white pioneers during periods of armed conflict with natives, they are now used to prevent natives from returning "prematurely" to the reserve while they are under contract to work in the mines. Laws also deter farm workers from leaving farms and city workers from moving to other cities. All such legislation aimed at curbing the movement of natives is augmented by curfew laws.

In employment and housing, the South African native is subject to severe discrimination. Natives cannot be employed in skilled jobs. Skilled work pays five to seven times as much as unskilled jobs. The government's "civilized labor policy" provides for wage subsidization to fewer than 5 per cent of the unskilled workers, the "poor whites." Housing is fully as discriminatory. On the reserves natives live in huts. At the mines they are housed in barracks, while those in cities are crowded in slums and segregated areas.

A master plan to move natives and Indians to the outskirts of cities was developed under Prime Minister Daniel Malan. It took effect first in Johannesburg in 1955 when natives involuntarily moved to a new housing-project area. The new houses were undoubtedly of higher quality than the old shacks, but Malan's main aim was to keep the central areas of cities clear for white residency, a policy continued by Malan's successors.

All public accommodations in South Africa are strictly segregated, as Gandhi found more than a half-century ago. There is virtually no exception to the rule. Parks, playgrounds, buses, trains, hotels, restaurants, and even footbridges are maintained on the basis of *apartheid*, the South African term for segregation. Nonsegregated attendance at tax-supported universities has been one of the few breaks in the pattern. Even in the

universities, however, natives have been excluded from extra-curricular activities.

A constitutional crisis developed in 1951 when Malan's administration attempted to complete segregation of the races by a legislative bill to remove the 40,000 "coloured" voters in the Cape Province from the election register. Approval was to come from a simple majority in each house of the parliament. When the highest national court ruled this act unconstitutional on the ground that such passage required a two-thirds majority of both houses of parliament sitting in joint session, Malan declared parliament the "high court." Parliament was thus given power to pass on the constitutionality of its own acts. In 1952 the parliamentary "high court" ruled the coloured voting act constitutional. The old high court then ruled the establishment of parliament as the "high court" unconstitutional. Prime Minister Johannes Strijdom, who succeeded Malan, increased the size of the Senate to give his party the necessary two-thirds vote. He also increased the membership of the high court to eleven judges by selecting five additional men of his own choice. The intricate maneuvering during this constitutional crisis demonstrates the skill, persistence, and single-mindedness of the racist leaders of South Africa. No stone is left unturned in tightening the apartheid lines.

CULTURAL PLURALISM

By contrast, the "right of a minority to be different" is respected under cultural pluralism. Here differing racial, national, or religious groups adopt a "live and let live" policy. No one group dominates the others. Indeed, a feeling persists that it is healthy to maintain and protect differences in cultural background.

The Swiss Example. Switzerland, a small country with a small population, is a society in which cultural pluralism flourishes. There is no Swiss language. German dialects predominate, followed by French and Italian. The three major languages and many dialects reflect the presence of great cultural variations in Switzerland. Protestant and Catholic churches maintain their religious differences. In addition, there are many contrasts in dress, manners, humor, attitudes, and values.

Despite these many differences, Switzerland is one of the most united of all nations. German, French, and Italian are all official languages, and government documents are translated into all three. Each subdivisional unit of government (canton) exercises considerable control over its own internal affairs. Proportional representation, initiative, and referendum protect the interests of the diverse groups. The doctrine of complete religious freedom is followed. The Swiss have learned to overcome their differences and live with them while agreeing on common loyalties. Cultural pluralism has been highly successful among the Swiss.

The American Example. In the United States a type of cultural pluralism is embedded in the "melting-pot" idea, as we noticed earlier. American society is composed of a wide variety of cultures welded into a single cultural pattern. The pattern is

In Hawaii a myriad of racial extractions live, work, and play together in harmony.

Dedicated racists gather together for initiation ceremonies into the secret order of the Ku Klux Klan.

not always clearly apparent, however. There has been considerable uncertainty and confusion in the American approach toward minorities. Immigrants have been applauded for their loyalty to old-country traditions as well as for their adaptation to the American way of life. Religious practice in America has made room for Catholic, Protestant, and Jew, yet Catholics and Jews have been the objects of discrimination in many areas.

An excellent example of American indecision toward minorities can be seen in our Indian policy. Federal policy toward the Indian has oscillated between Americanizing and Indianizing him. Late in the nineteenth century the national government took the position that the Indian should learn the white man's ways. But during the 1930's we reversed that policy by deciding to allow the Indian to perpetuate his traditional manner

of living. Nevertheless, under either policy, we actually practiced a combination of the two approaches. Should the Indians and other minorities be encouraged to abandon their native culture and become Americanized as swiftly as possible, or should they be encouraged to retain their differences in the confidence that America has room for more than one way of life? We have never really decided.

ASSIMILATION

When cultures blend slowly and to the point where original traits are indistinct, assimilation has occurred. Once this happens, tension and conflict subside since minority and majority patterns become indistinct in the new fusion of culture.

In Hawaii, however, not only cultures and

nationalities have mixed, but races as well. Hawaiians are a blend of people who came originally from the United States, Britain, Norway, Germany, Spain, Puerto Rico, Portugal, China, Japan, Korea, and the Philippines. Racially, they are Caucasoid, Mongoloid, and Negroid. Intermixture over several generations has led to an almost infinite diversity of types. For this reason Hawaii is sometimes labeled a "polyracial paradise."

Some prejudice and discrimination have existed in Hawaii, especially since World War II, when the islanders were brought into closer contact with Americans from the mainland. But a system of racial equality and intermingling still prevails. Theaters, restaurants, and hotels serve people regardless of color or nationality. Schools and residential areas are not segregated. Racial mixing is free both at work and at social gatherings. Social differentiation among Hawaiians is thus based chiefly on class, not on race or nationality.

VALUES IN CONFLICT

The primary reasons for such widespread differences in systems of minority relations lie in our social values. Assimilationism, pluralism, and racism reflect three major sets of values concerned with minority groups. The techniques of dominance, discussed earlier in the chapter, also reflect values.

The presence of different and conflicting sets of values is the most troublesome feature of minority-group relations. And this difficulty is most apparent in the United States. Many are the speeches, books, and special interest groups that press in a variety of directions. For example, Citizens' Councils vigorously advocate segregation and white supremacy while the Urban League and National Association for the Advancement of Colored People champion equality and nondiscrimination.

Equality in fact seems to be a common thread that runs through most of the arguments about minority rights in America. And as always, the question of freedom is

A ludicrous moment in American history. This Japanese - American, born in Seattle, is complying with a World War II government order by turning in several ceremonial swords that were family heirlooms. Strangely enough, native German- and Italian-Americans were not forced to endure such humiliation.

intimately bound up with it. To some, equality means that all should have similar opportunities—the unhampered or free access, for example, to schools or jobs of one's own choosing. Others feel that equalitarian standards have been met when such opportunities are "equal but separate." As long as a minority is given the opportunity to ride on a bus, their freedom to choose seats on the bus may be restricted to a particular section. Then there are those who fear equality no matter how it is defined. Extreme racists believe that certain standards of equality endanger racial purity and therefore should be avoided, or at best, restricted to certain groups.

Another area of confusion surrounds the humanitarian concept of brotherhood that has long been recognized as a pillar in the American value system. We have already pointed out that this tenet is a part of the American's rich religious heritage. It goes without saying that discrimination against people because of their race, nationality, or religion runs counter to the doctrine of brotherhood. But the doctrine can be conveniently avoided by discriminators, and frequently is, on the ground that "we are all born equal, but some of us are more equal than others." A belief in innate inferiority, of course, helps us justify our tendency to ignore the values of brotherly love and fellowship. Racial discrimination, in fact, is probably as prevalent and as strong a value as brotherhood, if we judge by the many instances of discriminatory behavior.

Gunnar Myrdal summed up our American value conflicts decisively in his book *An American Dilemma*. We speak of equality and brotherhood, he says, but we practice discrimination and segregation. We speak of democracy and opportunity, but we restrict rights of citizens. Just as we saw in Chapter 23, the great dilemma lies in the conflict and contradiction between what we profess and what we do.

SOME WORDS OF SUMMARY

Minorities have long been defined and treated as inferior by dominant groups. Although they have been the objects of prejudice and discrimination for centuries, it was not until the Europeans ventured out to colonize the world that the modern pattern of minority relations was established. For European expansion ushered in the practice of *exploiting* the native populations on a much wider basis than had hitherto prevailed.

Of the many attempts to explain the treatment of minority groups, three appear to predominate. Exploitation is one. The philosophy of racism that emerged during the last century is another. Then, too, the social inequality that separates dominant from minority groups is sometimes used to justify prejudicial and discriminatory practices.

Of the patterns that are employed to dominate minorities, Hitler's technique of extermination was one of the more extreme. At the opposite pole, conversion and absorption, if effective, will accomplish the same goal as extermination; namely, complete control of minorities. Other patterns of domination include expulsion, conquest, subjugation, and segregation.

Although minorities themselves practice discrimination, they are most often the objects of it. And their reactions to it vary widely. Many individuals submit to domination, some cooperatively, others by retreating or withdrawing. The great Indian leader, Gandhi, preferred passive resistance, a method that has since been adopted in many quarters of the world. Because his method of nonviolent opposition is especially difficult to combat, it holds great promise for many oppressed minorities. Open rebellion against the dominant group is, on the other hand, generally less effective. For, historically, few have succeeded in overthrowing their tormentors. Since minorities are generally poorly organized and ill-equipped, their prospects of ever staging a successful revolution are highly unlikely. Where they enjoy citizenship rights and legal protection, moreover, militant opposition is not apt to attract sufficient support. But even where they lack such rights, violent combat hardly improves their position.

Of the many varieties of minority-majority relations existing in the world today, three systems offer a range of conflicting choices. Non-Europeans in the Union of South Africa, for example, are subject to a severely rigid pattern of domination. Switzerland, on the other hand, illustrates a very temperate pattern of cultural pluralism, where Germans, French, and Italians live together and tolerate one another's differences. Cultural pluralism thus carries with it a respect for differences, so noticeably absent under the racist pattern in South Africa. A third pattern, called assimilation, is illustrated by Hawaii. There a number of racial minorities have mixed freely, and to the extent that the minorities have become indistinct, minority groups are nonexistent.

All these systems have their devoted followers. Assimilation seems as intolerable to the genuine racist as rascism does to the assimilationist. In the second half of the twentieth century no social issue looms larger than the problem of minority relations. The problem is world-wide in scope. Together with other sources of world tension, it provides the tinder that could set aflame an emotional and insecure mankind.

Any real and lasting solution to the problems of minority relations must be rooted in a consensus of shared values. But at the present time there is an all too obvious lack of agreement on what is most "right," as evidenced by the major systems of minority relations around the world. Even within countries such as the United States there is an incomplete sharing of values. Equality, freedom, and brotherhood are among the more confusing and conflicting values. And behavior that contradicts our professed values adds to the perplexity of value conflicts.

FURTHER ROADS TO LEARNING

GENERAL ACCOUNTS

B. Berry, *Race Relations* (Boston: Houghton Mifflin, 1951). One of the very best discussions of intergroup relations.

E. Frazier, *The Negro in the United States* (New York: Macmillan, 1949). An historical-sociological analysis of the American Negro.

R. Logan, *The Negro in the United States: A Brief History* (Princeton: Van Nostrand, Anvil Books, 1957). A concise, swift-moving report that traces the changing status of Negroes.

G. Myrdal, *An American Dilemma* (New York: Harper, 1944). A classic account of the American Negro problem by a Swedish social scientist.

G. Simpson and J. M. Yinger, *Racial and Cultural Minorities* (New York: Harper, 1953). A comprehensive discussion of prejudice, discrimination, and minorities that is especially good on anti-Semitism.

UNESCO, *The Race Question in Modern Science* (New York: Whiteside and Morrow, 1956). A survey by some of the very best authorities.

SPECIAL STUDIES

R. Adams, *Interracial Marriage in Hawaii* (New York: Macmillan, 1937). The polyracial paradise undisturbed by war and postwar developments.

G. Allport, *The Nature of Prejudice* (Garden City, N. Y.: Doubleday, Anchor Books, 1958). A thorough treatment of one of man's most perplexing tendencies.

M. Berger, *Racial Equality and the Law* (New York: Columbia University Press, a UNESCO study, 1954). A good survey of the legal restrictions that surround race relations.

B. Bettelheim, *Truants from Life* (Glencoe, Ill.: The Free Press, 1955). A study of prejudice.

R. Brandt, *Hopi Ethics* (Chicago: The University of Chicago Press, 1954). An interesting account of an isolated Indian tribe in Arizona.

L. Browne, *How Odd of God* (New York: Macmillan, 1934). How the Jews have come to be as they are.

G. Calpin, ed., *The South African Way of Life* (New York: Columbia University Press, 1954). Here is an account of the background and basis for the South African *Apartheid*.

G. Carter, *The Politics of Inequality: South Africa Since 1948* (New York: Praeger, 1958). A political study that reveals some of the strategy and techniques of racism.

H. Carter, *The Angry Scar* (New York: Doubleday, 1959). A southern moderate re-examines the Reconstruction Era following the Civil War.

J. Collier, *Indians of the Americas* (New York: Mentor Books, 1948). A penetrating report by one the world's foremost authorities.

S. Collins, *Coloured Minorities in Britain* (London: Lutterworth, 1957). How African, West Indian, and Asian immigrants to England brought a race problem with them.

C. Coon, *The Races of Europe* (New York: Macmillan, 1939). An anthropologist's classification of race differences.

O. Cox, *Caste, Class and Race* (New York: Doubleday, 1948). A provocative argument that caste systems and race relations are two different things.

T. Dobzhansky, *Evolution, Genetics and Man* (New York: Wiley, 1955). A scholarly discussion that treats human differences in a biological perspective.

E. Dvorin, *Racial Separation in South Africa: An Analysis of Apartheid Theory* (Chicago: The University of Chicago Press, 1952). This volume discusses the basic beliefs of staunch segregationists.

W. Emerson, *The Seminoles: Dwellers of the Everglades* (New York: Exposition Press, 1954). The story of the famous Indian tribe from Florida which was never subdued.

G. Foreman, *Indian Removal* (Norman: University of Oklahoma Press, 1953). How American Indians were pushed westward from their land.

G. Freyre, *The Masters and the Slaves* (New York: Knopf, 1946). An historical examination of the famous Brazilian slave system.

M. Gluckman, *Custom and Conflict in Africa* (Glencoe, Ill.: The Free Press, 1956). A discussion of a violent and changing Africa.

O. Handlin, *Race and Nationality in American Life* (New York: Doubleday, Anchor Books, 1957). Negroes became a "race" and European immigrants "nationalities" when they came to the United States.

————, *The Uprooted* (Boston: Little, Brown, 1951). A Pulitzer-Prize winner on the European immigrant.

J. C. Herold, *The Swiss Without Halos* (New York: Columbia University Press, 1948). A description of cultural pluralism in Switzerland.

R. Linton, ed., *Acculturation in Seven American Indian Tribes* (New York: Appleton-Century, 1940). What can happen when persons from several cultures are in continuous contact.

M. Montagu, *Man's Most Dangerous Myth* (New York: Columbia University Press, 1942). A discussion of the problems and evils resulting from the racial myth.

H. Patterson and E. Conrad, *Scottsboro Boy* (New York: Bantam Books, 1950). The blunt reality of a widely publicized case told by a Negro accused of rape.

A. Rose and C. Rose, *America Divided* (New York: Knopf, 1948). The economic, political, and social position of certain national, religious, and racial minorities.

UNESCO, *The Third Reich* (New York: Praeger, 1955). Chapters V, XXVI, and XXVII include probably the most thorough, short analysis of Nazi racism in existence.

FICTION AND DRAMA

N. Collins, *Black Ivory* (New York: Pocket Books, 1948). High-jacking, mutiny, and violence off the African slave coast.

L. Hobson, *Gentlemen's Agreement* (New York: Simon & Schuster, 1947). A story that exposes one of the more subtle techniques of anti-Semitism.

S. Lewis, *Kingsblood Royal* (New York: Bantam Books, 1949). Fascinating account of a white man who found he had Negro ancestry.

A. Paton, *Cry, the Beloved Country* (New York: Scribner, 1948). A penetrating description of the plight of South African Negroes.

L. Smith, *Strange Fruit* (New York: Signet Books, 1949). The agony and frustration of a white man and a Negro girl in love.

C. Sumner, *Quality* (New York: Bantam Books, 1947). A Negro girl accepted as a white returns to her colored friends.

J. Wexley, *They Shall Not Die*, in B. Mantle, ed., *The Best Plays of 1933-34* (New York: Dodd, 1934). A play depicting the events and emotions surrounding some Negro boys falsely and unjustly accused of rape.

FILMS

Americans All (McGraw-Hill, 1945, 16 min., sound, black and white). Religious and racial intergroup relations are problems confronting every American community. Moral issues need to be faced squarely.

Boundary Lines (McGraw-Hill, 1948, 10 min., sound, color). Using animation, this film analyzes the symbolism that generations of mankind have developed to give vent to their ideas. Distinctions between men based on fear, hate, and acquisitiveness can be corrected through education.

Brotherhood of Man (Brandon, 1946, 10 min., sound, color). Beginning with scientific facts, this animated color cartoon shows that racial similarities are more common than differences.

Can We Immunize Against Prejudice? (Columbia University, 1954, 7 min., sound, black and white). No conclusions are drawn in this film designed to provoke discussion on the problem of racial prejudice.

Picture in Your Mind (McGraw-Hill, 1949, 16 min., sound, color). Shows that people see themselves as superior.

The Road to Annihilation: Nationalism and Imperialism

*Having swept through Europe
and across America, nationalism and its corrosive effects
are now being felt most dramatically
in Africa and Asia, where they threaten the remaining
vestiges of colonialism,
ancient customs, and established political regimes.*

It wasn't

bloody enough!" That was the complaint of several well-dressed women a few years ago to a reporter's inquiry about their reactions to a wrestling match in Philadelphia. From the barroom to the battlefield, men (and women) fight, and many of them enjoy a good fight. Not that everyone enjoys or engages in destructive types of combat, of course. For many persons deplore conflict and shun involvement. But for everyone who runs from a fight, there is someone pursuing him who wants a battle. And even those who run may delight in watching a good tussle. So despite the loud outcry against fighting, brawls, and wars, human conflict is unusually common.

We must judge men by what they do, and just as they cooperate in some instances, so they fight in others. If all men abhorred war, there would be no wars. If human beings were not thrilled or intrigued by violence, murder, and human conflicts, our newspapers would be obliged to change their headlines. Conflict and violence are apparently more a part of us than we would care to admit. Both as individuals and in groups, men quarrel, men fight, men kill.

Causes and excuses for fighting are all around us. Whether the reasons are solid or flimsy, men take sides. When they lack reasons, they invent them. The world is thus filled with "dividers," which pit men against one another. The man on the other side of the mountain may be regarded as an enemy for no better reason than that he lives there. The natural barriers—rivers, oceans, gulfs, forests—divide the familiar from the strange. Despite their similarities,

Frenchmen on one side of the Rhine have long regarded the Germans on the other side as a threat to their security. It often takes no more than a mere boundary line to divide us. Histories of man brim with accounts of struggles over borders. There are few of us who have not read about the famous American battle cry over the Oregon boundary—"54-40 or fight!"—which nearly sent Americans to war with Great Britain in the 1840's.

As we saw earlier in this section, men are constantly contending for the riches and resources found near or at the earth's surface. It is not just the resources themselves but also access to them, the ports, trade routes, commercial outlets, and industrial sites, that become "bones of contention." In fact, there is hardly a physical feature on the earth's crust that could not at some time become a source of human rivalry. Even the Sahara is at issue today. Nature is pregnant with "dividers."

As divisive as are the earth's physical features, differences in human appearance and behavior are even more so. Skin coloring, as we saw in Chapter 25, is a common target for discrimination, rivalry, and conflict. Like color, behavioral differences invite division and strife. The black robe, skullcap, and refusal to eat pork set the Jew apart from others, making him an object of hostility and abuse. Divergent religious and marital customs soon drove the Mormons westward from Nauvoo, Illinois. Even family ties and relationships can create barriers between men. Many a member of a feuding family has found himself in the sights of an enemy rifle with no idea of how the feud started or what it was all about.

The fact that skin color, religious customs, and physical differences so often divide men doubtless stems from the ease with which they can be recognized by the least gifted and discerning individuals. Remove the outward marks of dissimilarity and division begins to blur. Jews who cast aside their tradi-

"*There are still a lot of diseases they have to find vaccines for. Ignorance, bigotry, intolerance.*"

tional garb and behavior patterns soon found life much more tolerable. Suspicion of newcomers usually subsides when they begin to react like other persons in their immediate surroundings. In short, the more evident the mark of dissimilarity, the greater the likelihood that the distinguishing factor will be employed as a basis for discrimination and hostility.

Thus far we have been concerned with obvious and simple subjects of division. But why do men seize on these divisive objects? Does it not take more than the mere exist-

ence of a boundary line to divide people? There must be a deeply rooted attachment to that boundary line and some psychological reasons for the attachment. In certain instances little more is needed than the knowledge that something valuable lies within the boundary. Yet, human attachment nearly always extends beyond mere practicalities. Men seem willing to fight for what they do not value directly, for people they will never know, for land they will never traverse, and for boundaries they cannot locate. Why? That question has plagued psychologists for a long time. Undoubtedly the answer is firmly seated in the human emotions. When men are called to act or fight for a cause, they must be emotionally identified with the cause. They must take the cause inside themselves and give it meaning. This is where the symbols that we discussed in the chapter on political loyalties perform some of their wonders. Men are busily symbolizing the life that goes on around them and taking the symbols inside themselves, giving life new perspectives, meanings, and goals. As they do so, another source of division and strife rears its head, for individuals and groups vary widely in the symbols they invent and use, and they vary even more widely in the meaning and significance that they give similar symbols. The American and Russian flags, for example, symbolize different ideals and goals, and therefore evoke considerably different responses in the two national groups.

One of the ultimate symbolic "dividers" in modern times is *nationalism*. Another is *imperialism*. And a more modern one is *colonialism*. In some ways all three present mankind with the greatest challenge in human history. The continued existence of human life on earth may in fact depend on how we meet that challenge.

The Great Wall of China, one of the wonders of the world, which stands as a reminder of our historic penchant to erect dividers between ourselves and our enemies, supposed or real.

THE EMERGENCE OF MODERN NATIONALISM

WHAT IS NATIONALISM?

In Chapter 8 we used the word "nation" to designate a group of kindred people who feel common attachments, bonds, and enthusiasm resulting from a shared historical experience, common symbols, cultural patterns, institutions, language, and often common residence in a territory. A nation is a people with a consciousness of its history and symbolic experiences. This consciousness encourages them to remain separate and independent from other peoples who do not share their common traditions and attachments.

This tendency of a people to separate and remain independent from other national groups that share different attachments and experiments is a basic characteristic of nationalism. A second and very important characteristic is the tendency of the group members to identify themselves with the national symbols. Nationalism, then, involves an "in-group" feeling that feeds on separation, exclusiveness, and monopoly. All the national group's symbols are wrapped in a single package, and the individual is expected to identify himself with them and be loyal to them. The nation is viewed as a separate entity having a life of its own—an existence apart from the persons who make it up. Individual persons come and go, but the nation goes on for centuries. The nation is idealized and becomes an object toward which men direct their undying love and loyalty. As a separate unit with a life of its own, it has a history and a destiny. All persons identified with it are expected to exalt it and to serve its destiny, with their lives if necessary. Primitives die for their totems; the devout for their gods; and the nationalists for their country.

Where men believe that their lives are tied directly to the destiny and fate of their nation, life itself has little or no meaning outside the nation. Such a condition engenders fanatical patriotism. Nations become gods that can do no wrong. "My country right or wrong!" Those persons who do not participate in the national life are regarded as threats to the national existence and to every member of the national community as well. The idealized nation has its idealized enemies. Nations with different goals and destinies become devils. A more significant "divider" of men is difficult to imagine.

To be free of these devils, nations aspire to political, economic, and cultural independence. Most of all, they desire *sovereignty,* or the *power to determine their own policies for their own group without outside interference.* The well-known historian Hans Kohn states that nationalism "presupposes the existence, in fact or as an ideal, of a centralized form of government over a distinct and large territory." The government and its subjects shall have the exclusive and monopolistic right to direct the destinies of the nation free of all foreign influence. Threats to this monopoly of power are apt to be met with hostility and war. In the

modern world the national state has become the idealized form of political association. Decisions and actions taken in its name are above question, and persons doing the deciding and acting are given vast and unquestioned powers, since their voice is presumed to be the voice of the nation. Such a condition demands an exclusive monopoly over public policy by those who identify themselves with the national symbols and total independence from those who do not. Thus do nationalism and sovereignty make common cause and march together.

The consequences are obvious. Persons desiring peace are condemned to live in a world of competing national groups where sovereignty, exclusiveness, and jealousy leave them victims of war. Although order may prevail within each national state, anarchy reigns supreme outside. We are caught up in an ugly paradox. On the one hand we depend on the deified nation and its spokesmen to maintain peace and order, and on the other hand we are committed to war and possible annihilation at the cost of defending it.

Nationalism is so much a part of us that we are inclined to believe that conditions have always been this way. It is difficult to imagine a world without national states. Yet they have not always existed in the form we now know them. And nationalism certainly is a modern phenomenon. How, then, did nationalism originate and develop?

FROM UNIVERSALISM TO NATIONALISM

If we could bring back someone who lived during the Middle Ages and ask him what he owed his country, we might find it difficult to make the gentleman understand the nature of our inquiry. Possibly he would tell us that he owed so many bushels of grain to the abbey or so much labor to the lord of the manor, but if we pressed him we might find his answers strange and somewhat unsatisfactory. During the Middle Ages people lived in a world very different from ours—a world unified under God, where national boundaries and differences in race and color were only temporary, certainly of little consequence in the eyes of God. What really mattered was a loyalty much higher than any earthly allegiance. Men passed their lives under the authority of Universal Christendom wherein emperor, prince, and administrator ruled in temporal affairs, and pope, bishop, and priest ruled in spiritual matters. "Render unto Caesar the things that are Caesar's and unto God the things that are God's." Divisions between peoples and struggles between princes were blurred by an overriding emphasis on religious goals and life after death. Men found their security in God rather than in themselves. Their future was laid up in heaven. Life was but a brief travail before the great reward, and hence earthly goals did not so readily stir the emotions. Men were identified with God, not the nation.

As Universal Christendom began to crack under the strain of increased commercial and political activity, Western Civilization began to undergo profound change. The Renaissance represented a rebirth of an interest in man himself. Men began giving more and more attention to themselves and the here and now and somewhat less to the life hereafter. The Protestant Reformation split the unity of the Christian Church and divided men's religious loyalties. Science began to develop and free itself from religious control. A rediscovery of Plato and the classics broadened the reaches of philosophical speculation. Trade routes grew and commerce extended along the coasts of Italy, Spain, and Portugal. Princes began to curb feudalism, develop stronger dynasties, and reduce the authority of the Church. In 1453 the Eastern Empire succumbed with the fall of Constantinople, and slowly the Holy Roman Empire (which was neither holy, Roman, nor an empire) began to rot and crumble.

Western Civilization was on the march, and its focus of attention was man-centered as much as it was God-centered, possibly more so. Quite naturally men were now more concerned with their security and well-being on this earth. "Life in the hereafter" was being partially obscured by a preoccupation with human problems. In the midst of this mighty current of change arose an Italian statesman, Niccolò Machiavelli, the apostle of modern nationalism. As Machiavelli saw things, man could attain security only by consolidating power and placing it in the hands of a strong ruler or government, who could defend him from a foreign yoke. It was power and the protection that went with it that paid off in a world filled with lustful, vain, and cunning men.

Princes and monarchs of the Renaissance quickly seized the opportunity to expand their influence and domains. By offering greater security to their subjects through increased political and military power, and by affording them more opportunity for justice, rulers centralized their governments and consolidated their authority over large and clearly demarcated territories. In so doing they made a bid for the allegiance of people whose loyalties were shifting from the security and symbols of religion to the available symbols and security of the temporal world. With this bid came the inauguration of nationalism.

ERA I: A COMMUNITY OF NATIONAL SOVEREIGNS *

Absolute monarchs who centralized governmental powers over vast territories were the trail-blazers of nationalism. With them the West moved into what the re-

---

* The following discussion of the three eras of nationalism is based on Carr's penetrating little volume, *Nationalism and After* (New York: Macmillan, 1945).

nowned international authority E. H. Carr called the first period of nationalism. This was a period of gradual decline in the "medieval unity of Empire and Church." It extended from the late Renaissance to the French Revolution. The distinguishing characteristic of this period, according to Carr, was "the identification of the nation with the person of the sovereign." Louis XIV loudly proclaimed that the state resided in the person of the king. It did! International relations were thus not relations among peoples, but relations among monarchs. Treaties were solemn contracts negotiated between kings or princes, matrimonial alliances were common, and international diplomacy was an instrument largely confined to royal households. Most international agreements were concluded for the purpose of enhancing the power of the monarch rather than promoting the welfare of his subjects.

Hence, civilians were not parties to international affairs, for it was the sovereign ruler and not they who was identified with the national symbols. When two monarchs went to war, subjects of both were often able to mingle freely, travel through each other's territory, and trade with one another. Most national armies were composed of paid hands (mercenary troops) rather than conscripted civilians, as is so often the case at the present time. In fact, conscription was more rare than now and was deemed a bit irregular when the monarch used it to press men into his service. Furthermore, men were relatively free to hire out as soldiers in the armies of foreign governments. Royal power reigned supreme and the average individual was free of identification with and responsibility for governmental decisions and other affairs of state.

A declining medieval unity (one world) was thus replaced by an international community of monarchs who moved in a world of their own. Within that community they spoke a common language (French); they were bound by common tradition and practice; they had a common interest in maintaining the loyalty and control of their subjects; they were obligated to one another as well as to their subjects. It was in this community that modern international law first appeared. The "law of nations" embraced rules or established standards regulating conduct and relations among sovereign monarchs. The international community of sovereign personalities had a code of conduct of its own. Enforcement of the code depended heavily on ties among its members and the allegiance of each to the common interests of the community of monarchs. Members of the community frequently rushed to aid a fellow monarch whose subjects had rebelled against him. One sovereign would aid another in extending his power and authority, providing such aid did not imperil the power or authority of the benefactor.

Allegiance to and respect for the international community of monarchs was occasionally stronger than the allegiance of any one of the sovereigns to his subjects. A French king was a monarch as well as a Frenchman, and sometimes before he was a Frenchman. The world was still *one world* politically despite the fact that power was concentrated in the hands of a small community. The modern national state and its twin, a national consciousness (nationalism), were being nurtured in the womb of an international community.

ERA II: POLITICAL INDEPENDENCE AND ECONOMIC UNITY

Then came the revolution! It was the French Revolution in this case which served as midwife at the birth of a new and militant form of nationalism. Before the nineteenth century had run its course, this innocent youngster had developed into a problem child, and by the end of the first

World War nationalism was an unmanageable monster.

As early as 1688 the world had felt the tremors and birth pangs of something new. In England, an absolute monarch, James Stuart, stole away into exile, and a people's Parliament became sovereign following a bloodless revolution. National consciousness ebbed and flowed throughout the West, reaching a new crest in 1789 when a turbulent crowd of Frenchmen stormed the Bastille and four years later lopped off the head of their king. The teeming masses of men within various national states were slowly becoming identified with power and the symbols of their sovereign nations. Napoleon disrupted the international community of monarchs and rode to power on the back of civilian armies. As the champion of an emancipated French nation he was a premature forerunner of "popular" dictators who were to appear later. Backstage loomed the ideas of the great political thinker Jean Jacques Rousseau, who had rejected the idea that the nation was identified with a sovereign person and had audaciously declared that the "will of the people" was sovereign.

Following the demise of Napoleon, a brilliant Austrian diplomat, Count Metternich, sought to restore the old order and revitalize the community of sovereigns at the Congress of Vienna. But success was only temporary. The changes wrought by the revolution, added to a surging national consciousness, were far too great to be stemmed. The people had tasted power and were not to be long denied.

Between the French Revolution and the First World War, sovereign monarchs were either deposed or forced to retreat before the growing power and influence of the "people." Monarchs who survived were soon forced to reign only and not rule. The international political community was smashed.

The masses of people, however, had not led in the French Revolution and were not yet sufficiently educated or articulate to recognize and wield the power that was becoming theirs. They needed leadership. Into the breach stepped the articulate and well-to-do merchants, tradesmen, bankers, and industrialists. Members of these groups and classes had, in fact, sponsored and led the French Revolution. Champions of the lower classes, such as Babeuf, the Frenchman, lost their heads. Property rights were soon of unparalleled importance. And possession of property was quite frequently a necessary condition for the exercise of political influence. Even Jefferson felt that a man ought to hold some property to be entitled to vote and participate in making political decisions. In short, to have a stake in the country it was necessary to own some property. The propertyless were without full membership in the nation. Only the propertied and middle classes were fully identified with the nation. Only they had a fatherland. Thus did power pass from the hands of sovereign personalities and their households into the hands of a solid and respectable middle class, and not into the hands of the masses of people as such.

International affairs were no longer dominated by the ambitions, desires, and interests of sovereign personalities, but by the ambitions, desires, and interests of middle-class groups. As a result, national wealth was no longer calculated, as in the day of the absolute sovereign, on the basis of fixed markets and the quantity of bullion stored in the king's treasury. Rather, the emphasis shifted to the production and trade carried on by the business classes. United by bonds of common interest and common ideals, a surging middle class, trained for management of both business and public affairs, forged a new economic order that emphasized the expansion of production, trade, and population as the signs of a healthy nation. With these ambitions and interests went the fortunes of international relations.

Expansion of trade, production, and population called for the opening of more trade routes, freer trade policies, colonization of empty areas, and development of industry and agriculture. These common interests gave purpose and direction to the efforts of the middle-class economic enterprisers who held the reins of power. Politically, nationalism was permitted to grow and flourish. National states remained separate, developing along distinct lines of their own. Economically, however, the common interests of the middle classes served to forge a world economic community that partially replaced the old community of sovereigns. Whereas the old order had brought a welter of nations together in a single political community of sovereign personalities, the newer one molded them into a single world economy.

The capital of this economic community was London. As a nation of merchants and traders, England had adopted a free-trade policy and opened her markets to the world. She provided a single, wide-open market for all consumable products. Contrary to present popular belief, the power that was Britain's was built as sturdily on her imports as it was on her exports. No market could challenge the one in London. As a center of trade, London soon developed into the financial capital of the world. She became the international discount market, shipping freights market, and insurance market, and soon the international money capital. As the money capital, she maintained a single international monetary standard against which various national currencies could be exchanged at fixed rates. This position, in turn, gave her the tremendous power to control the currency and exchange policies of a great many national governments through her ability to refuse to accept "unsound" currencies as

media of exchange. The Bank of England was thus the custodian of the international monetary standard. It could expand and contract the flow of money and trade, and it could influence marketing and pricing procedures all over the world. When some foreign government became obstreperous or threatened to disturb the balance of trade, the financial wizards on Lombard Street could change their policy if necessary to whip the troublesome fellows into line. Furthermore, foreign bankers and merchants were a part of the massive system. They all enjoyed its benefits and suffered no disabilities because they were foreigners. It was therefore in their interest to maintain and uphold the policies of Lombard Street. These groups, their representatives, or someone in sympathy with their interests controlled most national governments and could thereby quell or avoid threats to the balance of trade or the authority of the London counting house.

As the seat of government of the world's economy, then, London possessed great powers for maintaining world order. These powers were reinforced by the unchallenged supremacy of the British navy, as well as the might of a vast colonial empire. The laissez-faire economic philosophy that Britain championed also provided a source of support. Middle-class spokesmen worked diligently to convince the people that economic life should be free of political interference and control to prevent national political decisions from disrupting the unity and stability of the economic community. Further, the power of Lombard Street was veiled under the myth that economics wielded no influence over politics. This idea was so firmly and generally believed that even the men who wielded the power sometimes failed to recognize the extent of their influence on national affairs. Under the myth of separation of politics and economics, "economic power was a political fact." A divided political world took refuge in economic unity. This unity was not threatened until Germany finally began to use protective tariffs to challenge British domination of world trade and finance. The world was yet "one world."

ERA III: POST-WORLD WAR I AND THE BANKRUPTCY OF INTERNATIONAL UNITY

Meanwhile, throughout the nineteenth century, the masses were becoming steadily more politically conscious. More and more persons were identifying themselves with their national symbols. Andrew Jackson went to the White House surrounded by cheering masses who climbed on damask chairs in their muddy boots to identify themselves with him. Later, Lincoln would call his own actions and decisions "government of the people, by the people, and for the people." Each succeeding decade added more persons to the ranks of those who identified themselves with the government, its decisions, and the national symbols. In England and America the voting privilege was gradually extended to more and more persons. The growth of labor organizations, compulsory public education, and the democratic outlook generated by the westward movement all helped to hurry the process along.

As the masses surged forward, they demanded greater controls over national policy. Before 1910, for instance, a Wisconsin Senator, Robert LaFollette, was leading a crusade for more civilian controls over government processes. Not only should more public officials be chosen by the people, but he would have the people vote directly on legislation. Legislators would be deprived of part of their trust, and the people would make public policy themselves. His recommendation of the initiative and the referendum was adopted in many states throughout America. The masses were appropriating national symbols.

Even in the remaining monarchies such as Germany the people were on the move. German workers demanded their sickness insurance and accident compensation. Although the German citizen took little or no direct part in government, he proudly identified himself with the great German nation in all its supposed glory and honor and destiny. The Kaiser's subjects saw themselves as full participants in the nation's struggle to best the British in the great naval and arms race that developed prior to World War I. They believed it was their destiny to overthrow British commercial and naval supremacy and give Germany "a place in the sun."

In various forms and ways national symbols were becoming identified with the masses of people. Then came World War I. American doughboys marched off to war believing firmly that their war would end all wars and save the world for democracy. British Tommies were out for the same, while also admitting that they were protecting their empire, their naval supremacy, and the balance of power among nations. Germans fought to end British dominance of the sea lanes and give their nation its rightful place among the great powers. The goals of each were thus severely nationalistic and represented a sharp departure from the past.

The goal to end wars was a complete departure from the standards of international relations of the two earlier periods. War had previously been considered a legitimate step in diplomacy. Now war was apparently illegitimate, even when other diplomatic methods failed. Saving the world for democracy, or as its champion, President Woodrow Wilson, expressed it, "preserving the right of self-determination of peoples," was a new idea indeed. This doctrine proposed that each national group be given full power to determine its own type of government and direct its own policy. Each was invited to revolt, to assert itself, to follow its own course. This idea of self-determination encouraged and applauded the efforts of the masses to identify themselves with their national symbols. It delivered political power into the hands of the masses, making them a party to international affairs.

The war itself had encouraged this development. Civilians fought enemy civilians. To the American, German civilians were enemies as much as was the Kaiser. Allied propaganda pictured the German as ruthless, crude, and barbaric. He was a heartless killer, a rapist, an automaton without feelings. He was a "Hun!" Even Americans of

During World War I, propaganda did much to fan the flames of world nationalism. German soldiers, even German civilians, were depicted as barbarous murderers and marauders.

German ancestry suffered disabilities and discrimination. Their houses were painted yellow, or they were made objects of other forms of personal abuse. Sauerkraut was renamed "liberty cabbage." Civilian nationals were thus thoroughly identified with their nation. No longer was it possible for civilians to cross enemy lines and transact business as they once had. Conditions had changed from what they had been in the time of Frederick the Great. War had become a deadly serious business with no quarter offered or expected.

One of the most significant results of the war, according to Professor Carr, was the complete collapse of the old economic community. Like the community of sovereigns after the Napoleonic Wars, it lay in shambles. England had won the military struggle but failed to salvage her position as the economic capital of the world. The Germans had been partially successful in attaining their goals on that score. In the absence of a world community the people were left victims of international anarchy and rampant nationalism. Many persons who had benefited economically from the old economic community felt its loss and called for something to replace it. Moreover, the hardship, destruction, and loss of life wrought by the war brought a loud cry for some means of preventing another general war. It was President Wilson, paradoxically the advocate of the nationalistic principle of self-determination, who stepped into the breach. Under his guidance the Allied leadership hastily devised a political organization called the League of Nations, a union of sovereign national states that were to work together to keep the peace without surrendering any of their own sovereignty.

The Allied leaders provided the structure for the League's operation and then returned to their respective countries. There they found their peoples more interested in spoils and vengeance, in some cases, than in a peace of justice and reconciliation. Wilson's ideas were regarded as noble by some, but impractical by more. The United States Senate rejected both the peace treaty and the League. Wilson spent himself physically in a futile campaign to arouse the American people on behalf of the League, but the United States never did join, a fact that is commonly cited as a major reason for the League's failure.

The truth, of course, is that attitudes and conditions had changed since the nineteenth century. World communities now found the environment uncongenial. By the end of the war the masses of people had become thoroughly identified with their respective nations and national symbols. Nations were now peoples, not sovereign personalities or classes. In the democracies it was univerally acknowledged that national policy was the people's policy. Policy determination and execution were in the hands of the people's elected representatives. In many places the size of the electorate was increasing to a point where it included most of the adult population. Such things as secret diplomacy were scorned. Wilson spoke for the people in their suspicion of the secrecy and privacy of diplomatic negotiations when he asked for "open covenants openly arrived at." The people claimed not only the right to determine internal policies but demanded a voice in international affairs as well.

What many persons have failed to recognize, however, is that similar developments were taking place in the dictatorships that grew out of the First World War. Even authoritarian governments found it both wise and necessary to identify themselves with the masses of their people and to convince them that their decisions were actually decisions of the people. Adolf Hitler was a German dictator whose influence over German affairs was virtually absolute for twelve years. Yet he rested his claim to that power on the proposition that his voice was the voice of the German nation or people. When Hitler spoke, all Germans everywhere spoke. He embodied their welfare and future; in him rested the destiny of the German nation. Frederick the Great had held his subjects in contempt as uncultured Slavs, despised their customs and language, and regarded Prussia as his own personal property. But Hitler exalted all Germans and their culture as superior, identified himself and the national symbols with the German people, and gave the nation a destiny. The policies of Hitler and his henchmen were, therefore, the policies of the German people. The fact that decisions were not actually made or controlled by the people in no way prevented German civilians from identifying themselves with those decisions. Since World War I, both authoritarian and democratic countries have experienced something novel. The masses have laid claim to political power. If they do not actually exercise the power, they must be led to believe that they do. Today's national policies are founded largely on the support of the masses.

As the masses have taken over the nation and identified themselves with its policies, they have insisted that national power be used to improve their lot. The first obligation of government today is to its own subjects. It must protect and care for them first; commitments to other governments are secondary. If there is a choice between avoiding war and advancing the national interests of the people (whatever the people conceive as their interests), the national interest comes first. "Isn't this perfectly right and just?" we are apt to ask. Quite possibly. "Hasn't it always been this way?" we ask again. No! Louis XIV often felt a greater obligation to foreign sovereigns and governments than to his own people. Middle-class governments of the nineteenth century gingerly adjusted national policies to fit the needs and interests of the international economic community. The impetus that these

Governments must care for their own citizens first. General Jacob S. Coxey's army of unemployed marches on Washington during the 1894 recession to demand relief for the jobless.

economic factors lent to stability were bolstered by the power of the British navy and the art of British diplomacy, which skillfully shifted British power from side to side as other governments went for each other's throats. The nineteenth was among the most peaceful of all centuries insofar as the international scene was concerned.

Prior to 1900, then, an overriding community of international interests checked or dampened national rivalries and jealousies. After 1920, however, common interests at the international level were weak and scattered. National interests dominated while they were being shaped by the desires and needs of the people in each national state. Treaties were apt to be ignored when they conflicted with the national or popular interest. They were becoming what Hitler called them—"scraps of paper." All international commitments and obligations ran the same risk. Foreign governments refused to pay their war debts to the United States on the ground that their first obligation was to the social and economic welfare of their own people. Maintenance of order and stability in international relations was sacrificed to the welfare of the people of each national unit.

Inability to enforce international obligations spelled the demise of international law. An effective body of law requires a community of interests, a group or community of people willing to enforce it, and assurance that the members of the community will keep good faith and honor their obligations. Few if any of these conditions existed by 1930. International law was in a coma, nearly dead. It was every national state for itself—"dog eat dog." Henceforth the rules of international law would be flaunted more and more, in both war and peace. Why declare and prosecute war according to rules? This merely gave the enemy an unnecessary advantage. Japan was to attack China, and later Pearl Harbor, without warning. Total populations need have no honor, as did a personal sovereign or a special class. International law, something brought into being to serve the purposes of another age, did not fit the pattern of the times. In the absence of a community of interests, it was left without a port in which to drop anchor. Without law, there was no

481

longer a basis of any consequence for order. Where such conditions prevail, all rules of conduct disappear and the world of international relations turns back to the jungle, where Machiavelli's principles of power and cunning alone count. In such a world national policies must be dedicated to self-protection and self-advancement rather than to the maintenance of international order. International anarchy reigned supreme. The chances for success of the new international political organization called the League of Nations were remote indeed.

Nor was there much of an opportunity to establish a new economic community. America emerged from the war as the most powerful country on earth, and New York was in a position to assume the financial leadership that was once London's. But Americans were inexperienced and new at the game of international relations. Furthermore, since national policy was now founded on the support of the masses, future economic and political policy had to concentrate on improving their social and economic welfare. Governments were committed to the view that the welfare of their citizens took precedence over any foreign economic consideration. In return for their loyalty to the nation and its government, citizens demanded that the government provide them with economic security, a higher level of living, and full employment.

There were indications a half-century earlier of what was coming. In Germany Bismarck deliberately embarked on the road to a "social-service state" by granting the workers social benefits in return for their support. Nationalism was being socialized; or to put it the other way, socialism was being nationalized. The emphasis in economics shifted from the international to the national plane. In Britain and America *national* income, gross *national* products, *national* debts, and full employment became the main con-

siderations. Adolf Hitler cleverly appropriated the term "national socialism" and marched to power behind it. Following Lenin's death, the older symbols of international socialism collapsed, and Stalin emerged as the champion of "socialism in one country." Economic policy was once again completely a national matter.

With the reassertion of political power over economic policy, attention was directed toward a "balanced," "free," "planned," or some other form of national economy. The idea of a world economy was largely forgotten by all, whether radical, liberal, or conservative. In the United States, labor won its battle to close off immigration and other sources of cheap labor, industry won out in its fight for higher protective tariffs (the highest tariff in American history, the Hawley-Smoot tariff, was enacted in 1930), and the farmer won economic protection through subsidies. Political power was the instrument used in each case. In recognition of the new union of politics and economics, national income analysis and the older study of political economy were introduced into the school systems. The national government was the instrument for the betterment of the people, both rich and poor. All else was secondary.

Nationalism had acquired a social and economic conscience. But the conscience stopped at the national boundary. It was separatist and exclusive. Efforts toward social and economic adjustment beyond the borders of a national unit had to be justified in terms of the welfare of the people in the home country. Foreign aid has been sold to the American people on the basis that it is in their own interest in the long run. Otherwise they would scarcely have approved the idea. A world economic community is very difficult to visualize under such conditions.

Nationalism remains today more exclusive and more powerful than ever. No matter how much we may wish it otherwise, we live in a jungle of national units where moral force lacks a firm basis and where power alone counts a great deal. We are all nationals, all thoroughly identified with our national symbols, and all dependent on some national state for our security and welfare. On the streets of a foreign city, an American represents, yea embodies, the United States of America. No matter what he does or how he acts, he is judged by the standards foreigners call "American." We have been swallowed up in a greater whole or power—the nation.

There is real danger in a condition of this sort. Where nations represent great masses, individuals lose their identity. When they act as a mass, individuals take no responsibility for what occurs, since it is the total enterprise, not the individual persons, which presumably acts. Individuals can exploit, rob, maim, kill, and conquer in the name of the nation. It would be difficult to imagine a greater source of human conflict.

IMPERIALISM: AN ANCIENT DIVIDER

Yet, as significant a divider as nationalism is, it is hardly more important than imperialism at times. And when imperialism and nationalism join hands, the possibilities for conflict increase immensely. Imperialism, then, presents a very serious problem in the modern world, for nationalism and imperialism often go together. A great many nationalists are also imperialists or they make common cause with imperialists.

But, first, just what is imperialism? This is a question over which a good deal of controversy has raged for a long time. Most authorities agree, however, that imperialism is very old—much older than nationalism, for example. They also agree that imperialism is a type of activity in which national groups and their governments can and do engage.

Historically, the word "imperialism" has nearly always indicated a tendency toward territorial expansion. The eminent economist and student of imperialism Joseph Schumpeter has observed that imperialism was already extant in Egypt under the New Empire when the aggressive and imperialistic policies of the successors to Aahmes I carried the Egyptian domain to the Amanes and beyond the Euphrates. But even though our history books abound with examples of attempts to extend political boundaries into new and unfamiliar terrain, other authorities claim that imperialism involves a great deal more than just territorial expansion. And still others assert that its historical meaning is erroneous and misleading. Many people, for example, are convinced that economic exploitation of a foreign area and its people is usually involved. Others feel that imperialism is simply the domination of one culture by another. This latter group contends that imperialism entails the transporting of the advantages of a more advanced area to a less developed area of the world. The British, for example, took industry to India; or, as the American G. I. humorously stated it, "Americans civilized the South Sea Islanders by teaching them to drink Cokes." Then there are the Marxists, who argue that imperialism is merely the outgrowth of overripe capitalism. According to them, investment capital reaches a saturation point in the home country. Then with no further outlets for investment at home, capital goes abroad and is used to exploit underdeveloped countries.

All these contentions leave a great deal to be desired. But in most instances, *imperialism has been employed to refer to forms of extranational expansionism—political, economic, or both—in which members of a national state seek some political, economic, or cultural advantage in a foreign area.* Very often imperialism involves both domination and exploitation. Usually it occurs in the relations between an advanced and an under-developed people. Almost always it involves some advantage, real or supposed, to the imperialistic group. And seldom are the motives for imperialism philanthropic at their base.

THE MARRIAGE
OF NATIONALISM AND IMPERIALISM

Of basic importance, however, is the fact that modern imperialism has taken on a deeply nationalistic hue. Early in the post-medieval period, many of the emerging, independent, national states were soon pursuing imperialistic policies. Prior to the French Revolution, when the size of national treasuries was a prime concern of national governments, many European countries looked to the New World to fill the coffers of the Old World. This earlier imperialism took the form of a search for and the extraction of precious metals for the home treasury. Spanish freebooters exploited the immense wealth of Spanish America for the welfare of the mother country.

The English, on the other hand, settled and developed their colonial possessions. They came to stay, and with them came the nation from which they had come. They

A memorable occasion in British colonial history—the Maharajah Dhuleep Singh submits to Sir Henry Hardinge of Kanha Cushwa, India, on February 19, 1846.

conquered, assimilated, or drove out the natives and began building an economy to serve as a future market for English industries at home. These early practices became the basis of English colonial policy around the globe for several centuries. They also provided the model for American expansion once we had won our independence from Great Britain. Americans emigrated into Texas, settled down, then rebelled against the Mexican government. Likewise, American missionaries were followed by traders and pineapple-growers into Hawaii. Once again cultural clashes produced rebellion and the American flag was raised in the middle of the Pacific.

In many instances of this kind the people back home have felt no pressing urge to expand the national boundaries. They were obliged to accept what was claimed for them by those who migrated. But as we have already noticed, there is a tendency for nationalists to become imperialists, and Americans have not been exceptions to this rule. Many have welcomed expansion. As the French writer René Johannet put it, some years ago, "Patriotism, conventionally defined as love of country, turns out rather obviously to stand for love of more country."

Throughout human history in any case, nationalists have sought extranational expansion for many different reasons. Many have wanted to acquire land for some strategic or military reason. People often think that more land will afford them greater security. Others have wanted to control foreign territories that contained important raw materials, potential markets, or places for investment. Sometimes it was a matter of national pride and glory. Wider conquest, dominion, and exploitation have frequently been used to inflate the egos of those concerned. At other times nationalists have desired to transport their ideology and culture into familiar terrain. In the words of Kipling,

Take up the White Man's burden—
Send forth the best ye breed—
Go bind your sons to exile
To serve your captives' need.

The American nationalist, for instance, has felt it his mission to carry democracy to the world. His opponent in the Cold War, the Russian, has felt compelled to export the communist message to the world. Wherever the two have met, there has been danger of conflict.

THE MODERN MENACE OF IMPERIALISM

In a world of international anarchy a threat of war arises each time a citizen ventures beyond his national boundaries. For everywhere he goes he symbolizes the nation of people from which he came. If he goes into business abroad, he expects his home country to protect his business and personal interests. If he is successful, the natives are often certain that he is exploiting them. For they are nationalists, too. What is within their national boundaries should belong to them, they come to believe, and not to some foreigner. They often resent foreigners and urge their own government to do something about them. After all, their government's first obligation is to them and their welfare. This attitude can lead to serious trouble, and frequently does.

All too frequently, foreigners are regarded as intruders who are threatening the welfare of the natives. This is a major reason why foreign immigration to this country was shut off to a trickle during the 1920's. If we view a poor immigrant worker as an intruder on our job market and believe he is depriving some good American of a job, we should not be shocked when an Arab becomes alarmed about so vast a foreign enterprise as the Standard Oil Company.

These attitudes are loaded with dynamite. Situations may develop in which national governments play little or no part, and over

Deeply identified with their national symbols, thousands on thousands of Egyptians who were once British colonials throng the streets of Cairo to demonstrate against foreign imperialism.

which they have no control. All that is needed is a few foreign businessmen or foreign nationalists in an area where native nationalism is rampant. A person does not have to do any colonizing to be called a colonizer. If he comes from a highly developed country, all he has to do is to walk through an underdeveloped area. As a member of the British Foreign Office said recently, "Tragically, an Englishman anywhere in the world outside the British Isles is a colonizer by definition." Americans have likewise had their motives questioned.

THE MODERN CHARGE OF COLONIALISM

Modern nationalism has spread from Europe into Asia and Africa, and with it has gone all its corollary features. Asians want political independence (self-determination) with all its privileges. They demand freedom from foreign interference in their political and economic affairs. "Asia for the Asians" is their motto. And like all other nationalists, they expect their governments to care for them first to the exclusion of foreign commitments. They insist, too, on immediate industrialization, all the benefits of the Industrial Revolution, and a higher plane of living. And they do not expect to be a

century or even a half-century in attaining some of these aims.

Russian foreign policy has been calculated to appeal to these goals. Russians emphasize that they are Asians, too. They represent themselves as a once-exploited and colonized people who were able to industrialize rapidly once they had thrown off the "yoke" of foreign imperialism. And they continue to flay the past history of British, French, Dutch, Portuguese, and American imperialism. Finally, they make every representative of a free nation, every British pound, and every American dollar into something foreign, non-Asian, and therefore imperialistic. Every Britisher must be in Asia for a reason! What other reason could there be than to continue British colonial policies? History shows that this is what the British have always done. Ergo, this is what they are doing now. So say the Russians. Thus, to many Asian minds, every non-Asian is a colonizer and an impediment to realizing their goals. Many Asians listen attentively when the Russians advocate driving out the colonialists and adopting the Russian program of industrialization. As yet, the free world is still groping for an effective answer to this argument that will appeal to non-communist Asians.

THE STATE OF INTERNATIONAL ANARCHY

Without a community of common interests, the possibilities for avoiding war appear dim. American conservatives look back nostalgically to the nineteenth century, a peaceful and hopeful era when a community of economic interests wielded great influence. They inveigh against the social-service state and man's search for security, though they may also applaud protective tariffs and taking care of the "home folks" first. Many liberals pin their hopes on a second try at political unity through the United Nations. They are likely to eschew protective tariffs and nationalistic foreign policies. But they, too, embrace the idea that a government's first obligation is to its own people. Radicals are divided. On the one side there are the isolationists, who would adopt a unilateral foreign policy and go it alone, so to speak. They would withdraw from the United Nations unless everyone agreed with them, and they would avoid all foreign entanglements. At the opposite extreme are the radicals, who would surrender all national sovereignty to a world political organization. None of these groups has a clear notion of the consequences of its proposals. Nor would any one of them probably care to accept the full consequences of what it proposes.

We are all nationalists whether we like to be or not. We all face the consequences of what that means, including the possibility of war. Until recently, war was rather universally acknowledged as *a legitimate step in diplomacy* if all other methods failed. Most people still believe that war is legitimate in *self-defense*. Man has a right to protect himself from the onslaught of others, we say. For centuries men believed it was proper to use war as an implement of *conquest and subjugation*. But today war takes on new ramifications. Modern wars are total wars. They are wars of annihilation—wars of total victory and total defeat. We do not just defeat the enemy; we annihilate him. And it is not just a war between armies; it is everybody's war. Total populations face total populations in conflicts of obliteration. This situation raises new questions and new fears about old problems. It should result in more self-examination on the part of peoples. Certainly the effects of rampant nationalism and its corollary, imperialism, need more study and thought. To some of these effects we now turn in the next two chapters.

SOME WORDS OF SUMMARY

Men fight! And some love a fight. Since fighting involves opponents, and opponents always divide on some issue, the world has long been filled with "dividers" such as boundaries, prejudices, and symbols. Three very formidable symbolic "dividers" are *nationalism, imperialism,* and *colonialism.*

Nationalism, a condition in which the individual identifies himself with his national symbols and seeks independence for his national group, emerged from the wreckage of the medieval unity of Western Christendom. Its development has roughly corresponded to the development of the modern national state. Prior to the French Revolution national symbols were appropriated by the sovereign monarchs who were bound together in an international community of sovereigns. This community was destroyed during the French Revolution and the Napoleonic

Wars, and in its place there emerged an international economic community composed of middle-class enterprisers who manipulated political affairs from the seats of economic power. But this community, too, was utterly destroyed during World War I.

World War I thus rang down the curtain on international communities with common interests. People all over the world were now becoming thoroughly identified with their national symbols. Wilson's principle of self-determination was widely acclaimed, and nations of peoples wended their separate paths. The widespread outcry for the elimination of war and some sort of international unity impelled the Allied leadership under President Wilson to give birth to an international political organization called the League of Nations. But attitudes and conditions impeded its effective operation. With postwar national policies based on popular support, a government's first obligation was to its people and not to other governments. Inability to enforce international obligations destroyed the basis of international law and left the world without one of its most effective means for establishing international unity and cooperation.

The whole problem was compounded by the reassertion of national political control over economic policies. This development was a natural corollary of the peoples' demand for policies that would enhance their welfare. Nationalism had become socialized. It had acquired a social and economic conscience, which stopped at the nation's boundaries.

The other symbol, imperialism, is generally acknowledged to involve extranational expansion of some kind. As a corollary of nationalism, imperialism adds fuel to the fires of national ambitions and frequently results in attempts to extend national boundaries, control markets and investment opportunities, or transplant national ideologies.

In a world where international anarchy reigns supreme, imperialism is an especially troublesome force. Persons identified with national symbols are now viewed with alarm abroad. Foreigners engaged in economic activity become imperialists by definition, since natives believe that foreigners are depriving them of their rightful economic opportunities. Russian propaganda has turned these nationalistic sentiments about imperialism to the disadvantage of Western nations. The charges of colonialism have been loosed in Asia and Africa, and the Western nations appear unable as yet to meet the challenge.

A state of international anarchy darkens the prospects for peace. Some would relish a return to the nineteenth-century community of economic interests, while others place their hopes in the political union of the United Nations. Radicals divide between those who would withdraw into an isolationist shell, and those who would surrender all sovereignty to an international government. The mortal fear of modern man is not war alone but the hideous prospect of total war fought by total populations bent on total victory.

FURTHER ROADS TO LEARNING

GENERAL ACCOUNTS

E. Carr, *Nationalism and After* (New York: Macmillan, 1945). A delightful account of the historical phases of nationalism treated in this chapter.

K. Deutsch, *Nationalism and Social Communication* (Cambridge: Technology Press, 1953). This study looks into the roots of nationalism and national differences.

C. Hayes, *Essays on Nationalism* (New York: Macmillan 1926). Somewhat dated, but contains some of the best essays ever written on the subject.

————, *The Historical Evolution of Modern Nationalism* (New York: Smith, 1931). Certainly one of the very best examples of the historical approach to nationalism.

H. Kohn, *The Idea of Nationalism: A Study of Its Origins and Background* (New York: Macmillan, 1944); and *Nationalism: Its Meaning and History* (Princeton: Van Nostrand, Anvil Books, 1955). Two of the most highly regarded volumes on the subject by a scholar who views nationalism as a "state of mind"—a moving spirit in the modern world.

Royal Institute of International Affairs, *Nationalism* (London: Oxford University Press, 1939). This work, like all the Institute publications, is thorough and analytical.

J. Schumpeter, *Imperialism* (New York: Meridian Books, 1955). An eminent economist writes on the sociology of imperialism, using some of history's best-known examples.

B. Shafer, *Nationalism: Myth and Reality* (New York: Harcourt, Brace, 1955). A European historian concludes that most men have a common tendency to let nationalism become a dominant force in their lives.

L. Snyder, *The Meaning of Nationalism* (New Brunswick: Rutgers University Press, 1954). An historian of ethnic relations and theories attempts to analyze the elusive concept of nationalism.

V. Van Dyke, *International Relations* (New York: Appleton-Century-Crofts, 1957). A short, readable text that contains two excellent chapters treating nationalism and imperialism as causes of war.

F. Znaniecki, *Modern Nationalities: A Sociological Study* (Urbana: University of Illinois Press, 1952). A good sociological antidote to the many historical writings on nationalism.

SPECIAL STUDIES

W. Ball, *Nationalism and Communism in East Asia* (Melbourne: Melbourne University Press, 1952). One of the very best short treatments of Asian aims.

C. Beard, *The Idea of the National Interest* (New York: Macmillan, 1934). An early exposition of the uses of theory of the national interest from the pen of a famous American historian.

W. Buchanan and H. Cantril, *How Other Nations See Us* (Urbana: University of Illinois Press, 1953). A wonderfully clear treatise on in-group biases of nationalists.

A. Cobban, *National Self-Determination* (Chicago: The University of Chicago Press, 1944). The Wilsonian ideal in the hands of a skilled analyst.

E. Hammer, *The Struggle for Indo-China* (Stanford, California: Stanford University Press, 1954). The dismal story of the failures of European colonialism in this area.

J. Hobson, *Imperialism* (London: Allen & Unwin, 1938). A brilliant statement of the overproduction-underconsumption theory of imperialism.

W. Lippmann, *Essays in the Public Philosophy* (Boston: Little, Brown, 1955). A scathing indictment of the influence of the masses.

H. Morgenthau, *Politics Among Nations* (New York: Knopf, 1954). An unusual college text in that it has a definite thesis; namely, that the national interest is uppermost.

K. Pannikkar, *Asia and Western Dominance* (New York: Day, 1954). Simply packed with good historical material and Asian biases against America.

J. Ortega y Gasset, *Revolt of the Masses* (New York: Norton, 1932). A criticism of what happens when the masses take over.

A. Weinberg, *Manifest Destiny* (Baltimore: Johns Hopkins University Press, 1935). About American imperialism and national expansion.

FICTION AND DRAMA

E. M. Forster's novel, *A Passage to India,* and James Fenimore Cooper's *The Deer-slayer* will prove useful here. In fact, many of the familiar novels by Cooper, such as *Leatherstocking* or *The Last of the Mohicans,* help illustrate the sentimental and separatistic yearnings of early American nationalism.

The Sahib Edition of Rudyard Kipling. Ten vols. (New York: Collier, n. d.) Contains the best examples of imperialistic and nationalistic literature.

H. Rider Haggard, *King Solomon's Mines* (New York: Longmans, Green, 1926). An exciting story about an imperialistic enterprise.

FILMS

India: Asia's New Voice (McGraw-Hill, 1949, 17 min., sound, black and white). The events leading up to India's independence.

Middle East: Powder Keg on the Rim of the Communist World (March of Time, 1952, 28 min., sound, black and white). An analysis of Middle Eastern political, economic, and social conditions that demonstrates why this area is so determined to be rid of foreign influence.

Moroccan Outpost (McGraw-Hill, 1951, 18 min., sound, black and white). How demands for Moroccan independence raised problems for the West.

Nationalism (Encyclopaedia Britannica Films, 1952, 20 min., sound, black and white). Defines nationalism pictorially and treats its democratic and imperialistic manifestations.

Revolt in Hungary (Prudential Insurance Company of America, 1958, 30 min., sound, black and white). The sad story of how nationalists failed in their attempt to throw off the communist yoke.

The End of the Road:
Isms and Schisms

"Our myth is a faith; it is a passion.
And to this faith, to this grandeur, we subordinate all the rest."

The road

leading from the First World War to the Second was nationalistic and filled with barbaric totalitarians. Liberals and humanitarians found the going rough. Contrary to Woodrow Wilson's hopes, the vehicle of international justice and cooperation never left Versailles. Nor were national peoples willing to shed their provincialism and cooperate in a world organization. In the prophetic words of a French observer, Charles Maurras, nationalism was bound to breed, "the exclusive pursuit of national policies, the absolute maintenance of national integrity, and the steady increase of national power."

How dangerous the pathway of nationalism was we shall see in the next chapter. For at the end of the road lay nationalism in its ugliest and most exclusive form. In many parts of the world the "nation" would be exalted to the exclusion of all else. Humanitarians, democrats, and liberals would go on the defensive while imperialism and militarism were idealized. Domestically, too, the "nation" was to be supreme. The nation, in short, became an end in itself rather than a means to an end. Individual interests, even humanity itself, were sacrificed to the national interest. *The national ends justified the means and the nation could do no wrong.* This idea was far more dangerous than the older belief that the king could do no wrong. For it was possible for a people to rebel against their king. But now the people were the nation. It was to the nation —the people—rather than to a government that men now gave their allegiance. The

nation, in fact, demanded more than men's allegiance. It now conscripted their minds and emotions as well. "All is in the state and for the state, nothing outside the state, nothing against the state." This dictum of the Italian dictator Benito Mussolini expressed the ultimate in nationalism. *Society* and *nation* became synonyms and the *state* became an organic expression of the *nation*. This was *statism* par excellence. The state was everything!

This hypernationalism provided a fertile seedbed for radical movements, creeds, and causes. By identifying one's cause with the nation, the cause became limitless and the movement behind it knew no bounds. The total population and all national resources could be marshaled to its support. A man's noblest deed would be to die for his nation. To question the call for supreme sacrifice was to question the nation's cause and creed. Is it so surprising, then, that so many sought to make their causes national ones? The desire to do so, in fact, infected nearly every reformist and revolutionary group. Fabian Socialists, for example, sought to make the nation an instrument for the promotion of human welfare. Fascists became the most extreme nationalists of the time. And even the militantly internationalist cause of communism was guised for two decades by the statist and nationalist slogan of "socialism in one country."

Notice that all these terms are "isms." Each national state developed and nurtured its own brand of nationalism and its own causes, which it phrased in a nationalistic ideology or creed. With each national state thus pursuing its own national objectives or cause in terms of its own interests and backed by an ideology for which men were willing to die, the future became frightening indeed. For such a world, it goes without saying, is inevitably pregnant with anarchy and strife.

THE EMERGENCE OF TOTALITARIANISM

It was this kind of world that gave birth to a new brand of authoritarianism called totalitarian dictatorship. It came like "a bulletin from the battlefield laden with fateful significance," said the writer Max Lerner. More than a temporary departure from democratic practices, more than just an abnormal seizure of power, totalitarianism was assessed by Lerner as a part of the political and social fiber of the twentieth century. It was something that had been a century or more in the making.

The totalitarian seeks and exalts power. He glorifies the state and makes men willing to die for his vision of it. He appeals to the ego of his people by calling them and their way of life superior to all others. He is usually, although not always, imperialistic and expansionist, often claiming the right of his own people to dominate or eliminate others. And above all, he seeks to make the nation strong. To this end he conscripts the minds as well as the bodies of men. All men and resources, including raw materials, industry, transportation, communications, education, and even the arts, sciences, and religion, must be centrally controlled. Even if he does not glorify war (and most do), he honors the hero who dies for the motherland. His emphasis is on military preparedness and economic self-sufficiency (economic autarchy) to avoid dependence on any other nation. And he is absolutely certain that his cause is *right* and his nation can do no wrong!

Totalitarian dictatorship was obviously well adapted to the hypernationalism that swept the globe following the First World War. In one sense it should have come as no surprise. But it did. It came in fact as a startling revelation to those who believed that the world was moving rapidly in the direction of peace, plenty, and democracy. What was its true character? What made people submit to it? What sort of person is the totalitarian? What kind of system does he erect and how does it differ from other types of authoritarianism?

PORTRAIT OF AN AUTHORITARIAN

Recent investigations in personality reveal that totalitarian traits have by no means been confined to the power-hungry despot. These traits have also characterized the man in the street on whom despots depend for loyalty and support. They are found, in fact, in each and every one of us —in some more than others, of course, but in all of us nonetheless. What are these authoritarian traits?

First of all, the authoritarian personality is conformist. In our own society conformity can be recognized in loyalty to middle-class ideas, habits, and prejudices. In all societies, however, the authoritarian personality conforms to authority. Conforming is not an act involving conscious choice. Rather, it is compulsive and nearly always irrational. The individual irrationally seeks security by surrendering to some superior power or by merging with the crowd. Briefly, he is either *tradition-directed* or *other-directed* to the extreme, to recall terms we used in Chapter 20, and almost totally lacking in *inner-direction*. He is the type of person who uses "Slickum" on his hair simply because some self-appointed scalp expert says he should. Feeling compelled to surrender to something outside himself, he wants others to surrender, too. He cannot risk the chance of being different; nor can he brook differences in others. For differences appear ominous and threatening. They make him anxious and insecure.

The authoritarian person finds his refuge and security outside himself, generally in some power system or in the warmth of the "herd." He is thus power-oriented. To him life itself is a power system to which he must submit and into which he must fit. "What the world needs is more strength!" "People come in two types: strong and weak; and the strong must dominate!" Power he admires for its own sake. The authoritarian does not need to wield power so long as he knows it is close by. He is thus a good follower. In fact, power dominates the authoritarian whether he wields it or yields to it. At one moment he cowers before his superiors and the next moment he ruthlessly grinds his subordinates under his heel. We all know persons who are Casper Milquetoasts at the office and raging tyrants at home. Authoritarians follow as readily as they lead. But let power fail or let the leadership falter and the tide reverses. The authoritarian follower then shouts, "Out with them!"

Authoritarians tend to be "herd-minded" or noticeably ethnocentric, seeking refuge in their *own group* and exalting that group while rejecting and reviling other groups. For the authoritarian regards *out-groups* as ever-present threats to his own. Therefore, he pictures his own group as morally, racially, or culturally *pure*, while believing that other groups are more or less *impure*. Persons outside the authoritarian's own group are neatly classified and labeled according to hastily devised and unverifiable formulas. The world has been filled with these labels: "war mongers," "communist dupes," "dirty capitalists," "fascists," "Kikes," "Reds," "Wops," "imperialists," the "money-hungry." Though usually false, authoritarian

labels are simple and easily applied. And once applied, the authoritarian tends to see his "enemies" everywhere. He is constantly "on guard" against any trace of "enemy contamination" of himself or his group. Ever fearful, he is apprehensive, distrusting, and suspicious of those around him. Any strange action or unorthodox statement will arouse his fears.

Fear, in fact, is another important authoritarian personality trait. As we have seen, the authoritarian fears change and insecurity. He fears outsiders and those who differ from him. And he fears being alone and away from the "herd." Desiring group protection, he either hides in the crowd or gets the crowd behind him. Most of all he fears weakness. Too weak to face the world alone, he needs the strength of others or a power system in which he can submerge his individuality and find security. Many contend that this fear is actually a fear of one's own "self" and the inability of the individual to reckon with the world around him. Too weak to shoulder the responsibilities the world has thrust on him, he seeks ways of avoiding them. Minority and out-groups provide him with something to blame when things go wrong. But the power system itself affords an even better means for absolving him of his responsibilities. Honest men can cheat for the good of the company and plunder for the good of the nation.

Few traits are more apparent in the authoritarian leaders and followers than this desire to avoid responsibility. Hitler, for instance, identified himself so completely with the national symbols of the German people that his every public action was a national one. Without responsibility, he was free to act according to whim. He did not need to answer for the consequences. To the authoritarian, freedom involves no responsibility.

All these traits tend to produce a rigid and mechanical person. He can be likened to a robot reacting to a very limited number of ideas and directing all his activities into predetermined channels that he considers safe. The imagination is limited and the intelligence locked up. Not that authoritarians lack intelligence. Far from it. But their personalities restrict both their intelligence and imagination. In extreme cases the demands of the personality may shut out the imagination altogether or allow it to be directed and dominated by fear. Some persons suffer from paranoia, imagining that others are after them or have it in for them. A person who is gripped by such fears becomes very aggressive and may fanatically defend the power system that he believes vital to his security. He sees enemies behind every bush.

Some authoritarian traits are found in everyone, as we noticed earlier. Each of us is to some degree a conformist, herd-minded, and a purist. We all respond to fear, and we are also somewhat mechanical in our behavior and anxious to avoid responsibility when we can. Several years ago a group of social scientists in California tested more than two thousand persons from urban areas throughout the country and concluded that about 10 per cent of the American population was clearly authoritarian, with another 10 per cent leaning strongly in that direction. This discovery need not be alarming. But it does indicate that we are not dealing with an abnormal or momentary situation when we come to grips with twentieth-century forms of authoritarianism. The problem is as old as mankind, and it exists within each of us. Dictatorship itself is, after all, very old and has a tradition of its own, just as does democracy or kingship.

THE HALLMARKS OF TOTALITARIANISM

What of the totalitarian's world? In what kind of environment does he move and what kind of system does he erect? Answers to these questions vary according to the persons giving them. Although some observ-

ers emphasize the theory as fully as the practice of totalitarian dictatorship, others dismiss the theory as mere "frosting" or justification for what really takes place. Soldiers, diplomats, and practicing politicians who deal directly with totalitarians daily, for example, are often inclined to be more impressed by events and actual behavior than by theory or ideology. Immersed in their everyday chores and under the shadow of the huge bulk and force of totalitarianism, it is understandably difficult for these people to take totalitarian theory too seriously. Yet, even the most determined skeptics must admit that theory and ideology weigh heavily on the course of international events and cannot therefore be lightly dismissed. After all, the behavior and practices of a people are bound to reflect the ideas, beliefs, and general outlook to which the practices are anchored. This condition is as true of totalitarians as of anyone else.

The Politics of Pessimism. Irrespective of what the totalitarian claims, he is like other authoritarians in history, most of whom have been pessimistic about the potential of the average person. If not always in theory, then certainly in practice, he denies the integrity, the worth, and the rationality of the individual, and he repudiates the notion that the people can govern themselves. Looking as he does on the "dark side" of human nature and believing most men to be irrational, he ruthlessly exploits the irrational factor and reduces men to the level of animals. Many totalitarians take great pleasure in making the crowd respond on cue.

Rejection of Democratic Methods and Institutions. Having demeaned humanity, the totalitarian feels no compunction when he imposes despotic controls or employs inhumane techniques. And he is especially scornful of democracy. In fact, he seems impelled to keep democracy under constant attack. Every society, so the argument goes, is divided into the rulers and the ruled. Whether the rulers are a landed aristocracy, a cadre of government bureaucrats, a group of industrial titans, or a military junta, they constitute a political *élite* that makes the important political decisions and exercises the vital functions of government. The people merely follow. Indeed, they must follow. For the totalitarian believes that most men are congenitally incompetent and therefore incapable of governing themselves. To turn government over to the average man is to turn it over to "swine" and to expose society to the whims of the mob. To avoid chaos, the average man must be ruled. He needs someone with special abilities to care for him: a person ordained by God to rule, a born leader or "hero," a natural aristocrat, someone born to proper status, or someone who is biologically superior.

Democracy, then, is a myth or a sham. All democratic devices, such as elections and legislatures, are considered camouflages to deceive the followers into believing that they have some influence over public policy, when in fact they do not. Democratic institutions and practices may be necessary, of course, to veil power realities from the people and keep them pacified, but a small *élite* is always in control. Democracy never existed anywhere. Benito Mussolini employed this argument with gusto. He contended that political power is always held by a clique of conspiring, power-seeking individuals who conjoin force with ambition, deceit, and a "will" to dominate. Mussolini, it was said, seldom turned his back on anyone for fear of being stabbed by another power-seeker. According to him, the fascist "rises like a fox, lives like a lion, and dies like a dog." Mussolini did!

Most attacks emphasize the depravity of the average man. Most of the arguments have been employed in various forms throughout history. And most provide what the totalitarians believe to be adequate jus-

tification for strait jacketing society and employing terror to get the job done.

The Grand Design: Ideology, Cause, and Purpose. Most of us are repulsed by the strait jacket, the terror, and the effects of both on the individual and his personality. The sheer brutality of totalitarianism frequently leaves us in awesome disbelief. We may in fact be so stricken with awe that we dismiss the ideas behind them as mere window-dressing, no more than a convenient justification for the techniques employed. But the theories are more than just excuses for rationalizing brutal action and events. Contrary to what many people think, full-blown totalitarians tend to be fanatics who believe passionately in *their truth*. Passionate belief alone, however, does not establish their truth. It may take ridicule, violence, and even murder to establish it. In brief, the techniques and the action often become the weapons for fulfilling ideals and theories.

Every totalitarian system has a number of stated goals—a series of supreme purposes—which take precedence over all else. The government is seized to accomplish these purposes. For the communist, the goal has been to achieve the "classless society"; for the national socialist in Germany, it was to achieve and insure the destiny of the "master race" to dominate other peoples. According to Carl Friedrich and Zbigniew Brzezinski, two respected political scientists, every totalitarian regime has "an official ideology, consisting of an official body of doctrine covering all vital aspects of man's existence to which everyone living in that society is supposed to adhere, at least passively." * This doctrine, the authoritarian says, constitutes absolute truth. It normally envisions a final and perfect condition of mankind.

Existing conditions are therefore radically

---

* C. Friedrich and Z. Brzezinski, *Totalitarian Dictatorship and Autocracy* (Cambridge: Harvard University Press, 1956), p. 9.

rejected. All endeavor is turned toward conquering the present world in order to transform it into the one the totalitarian envisions. This purpose, or cause, *overrides* all else—whether human welfare, individual wants and needs, or personal comforts. It necessitates the subordination of all human institutions and human endeavor. All persons must have faith in the totalitarian's ideology and goals. All doubts, all questions, all hesitation must be cut away like a cancer. And all means whatsoever, whether violence, murder, ruse, treachery, or total regimentation, are justified by the goals.

The ideology, then, is a grand design, an all-inclusive and coherent body of ideas that outlines the goals, as well as the methods and techniques, for reconstructing society by force and violence. It includes also a total criticism of the existing society. As such, it is an "action-related system of ideas," which impels men to act and tells them why they must act.

The Grand Design: The Monolithic Garrison State. Since the ideology is interpreted by the leadership (totalitarian *élite*), it becomes their duty to seize the engines of government and force humanity toward their goal. Humanity's cause becomes their cause. Every pattern of behavior, every social and cultural institution, every human being will be tested by his contribution to the cause. The *élite* will do the testing; it will judge the results.

The major test is *submission* to the will of the leadership. And submission must be total. The citizen must think and act with the leadership. His mind as well as his body is put in a strait jacket. He must think no evil and do no evil. He must remain "pure" in word, deed, and thought. Submission, then, becomes the essence of loyalty and political obligation.

To obtain complete submission the totalitarian eradicates all forms of free association that are not government-approved. For freely organized groups are apt to give birth to doubt, opposition, and criticism—things totalitarians find intolerable. All human associations and institutions must be subordinated to the cause and made a part of the totalitarian web. The totalitarian is therefore not satisfied with a monopoly of political power. He seeks absolute control and direction of all phases of social and economic life. In Nazi Germany, for example, the institution of private property survived in form only, and industrialists became hardly more than paid managers of their own holdings. The totalitarian further monopolizes all technology and science. Transportation and mass communication, including press, radio, television, and cinema, are swallowed up. Churches, schools, and even art and sports are centrally controlled. The totalitarian devours and subordinates everything human. The *grand design* is smashed down on the body politic, creating a single monolithic social structure. Within the structure men are made subservient to the will of the leaders, either by subordinating or eliminating their institutions and associations. Social, cultural, and political distinctions are wiped out. What is "public" absorbs what is "private," and the sacred becomes indistinguishable from the profane. In a full-blown totalitarian system, unity and conformity would be "total" and men would be robots. There would be no issues, no questions to solve, no opposition, nothing foreign, nothing new. There would be total control for the leaders, total subordination, total submission, and total loyalty to a total state enforced by total violence. This in fact is what the term "totalitarian" signifies.

Glorification of the State. It is in the name of the state that the grand design is imposed and the totalitarian's cause carried forward. The state is made the bearer, carrier, and vehicle of human destiny and gives meaning

Nazi storm troopers—160,000 strong—listen attentively as their Führer Adolf Hitler harangues them at a party rally.

and structure to all things. Even the dictator gains his stature through identification with it. No individual, no institution has meaning outside the state. The welfare of each is equated with the welfare of the state. The state is deified, glorified, and worshiped. All must live for the state and be willing to die for it because it is all they have.

Single-party State. It is a political party that the totalitarian uses to seize the government. Like any political party, the totalitarian party seeks to control government and dispenses patronage to its loyal and faithful workers. But here the similarity with most political parties ceases. For the totalitarian party cannot brook opposition. Since the totalitarian's "cause" dictates that he and his program are infallible and beyond question, any hint of opposition must be eradicated, especially all political opposition. One of Hitler's first moves after becoming German chancellor was to stamp out free labor unions and all opposing political parties. Once established, the totalitarian one-

party system is further secured through a program of severe censorship of all communication media and all vestiges of political association.

Mass-based Party. The final move is to identify the party with the masses of people. For once the party and the people are one and the same—when every party command is considered by the people themselves to be their own command—then any opposition to the party becomes an attack against the people themselves. When successfully merged with the people and the national symbols, the party and its claims become absolute. The party leadership is then the author of morals and the final judge in all matters of human welfare.

Little wonder, then, that totalitarian dictators strive to identify themselves with the people. The modern dictator glories in his plebeian origins. Although Mussolini marched like Napoleon and talked of Caesar, he exploited the fact that he had been an army corporal and not a general. In fact, the totalitarian uses democratic mechanisms to achieve identification with the people. Elections may be rigged and ballots may contain only one candidate for each office, but Russians still go to the trouble to hold elections. A legislature, too, may be only a rubber-stamp, but it convenes, and very often the ordinary citizen is led to believe that he gives his approval to public policy through the actions of his legislature, no matter how impotent it may be.

The Spartan Bureaucracy. In a totalitarian, one-party system, the engines of government are literally owned and operated by the ruling *élite*. The party organization supplies the formula, policy, leadership, and personnel for the government. Party members move into the government bag and baggage and take command of government positions that correspond roughly with those they hold in the party. The government hierarchy is thus fitted up to resemble the party's. An analysis of party organization, behavior, and personnel, then, provides an important key to the character of the government bureaucracy.

Actually, the totalitarian party resembles an exclusive "brotherhood" or religious order. The membership constitutes a hard core of dedicated individuals, some of them fanatics, who submit readily to discipline and demonstrate an undying loyalty to duty and the leadership. Mussolini counseled his men to "Believe, Obey, Fight!" And according to Russian Communist Party rules as approved at the Eighteenth Congress in March, 1939:

The Party is a united militant organization bound together by a conscious discipline which is equally binding on all its members. The Party is strong because of its solidarity, unity of will and unity of action, which are incompatible with any deviation from its program and rules, with any violation of Party discipline, with factional groupings, or with double-

dealing. The Party purges its ranks of persons who violate its program, rules, or discipline.

. . .

A Party member is one who accepts the Program of the Party, works in one of its organizations, submits to its decisions and pays membership dues.*

Unlike most democratic parties, totalitarian parties do not recruit their membership freely. Entrance tests are severe, and expulsion is sudden and arbitrary. Within the party there is fanatical insistence on absolute obedience to the will of the leadership. The party's ideology and techniques are not to be questioned. At party meetings a great deal of time is spent on matters of duty and obligation, self-criticism, and criticism of each other. In meetings of the Russian Communist Party, members account fully for all their activities. Shortcomings, such as excessive drinking, poor performance, sexual promiscuity, or "capitalist tendencies," are aired openly. Questionable behavior may become grounds for expulsion.

It is in this environment that the totalitarian underling is "weaned, steeled and promoted." Reared in a militarized party hierarchy where their behavior and attitudes were under constant surveillance, men like Bormann in Nazi Germany and Mikoyan in Soviet Russia developed two qualities indispensable to any totalitarian bureaucrat. Both possessed superior administrative talents and both proved themselves worthy of the leader's confidence. The bureaucrat must be capable and efficient; he needs a capacity for minute detail; his loyalty must be beyond question. Without men of this stripe, the system cannot be maintained. For the political lieutenants must lead in the struggle to achieve the totalitarian goals. They are responsible for the success or failure of "five-year plans," or "the battle of the grain." But

---

* *Rules of the Communist Party of the Soviet Union,* from W. Walsh, ed., *Readings in Russian History* (Syracuse: Syracuse University Press, 1950), pp. 622-623.

even more important, it is they who keep the dictator's power from being challenged from within. It is the dictator's henchmen who implement the controls, apply the coercion, break resistance, and manipulate the terrorist apparataus. They are the real "executioners of history."

These militant Spartans who carry forward the totalitarian "mission" are organized along military lines. Both party and government bureaucracies resemble a pyramid composed of layers of officials who take orders from the layers above and channel them to the layers below. There is no democracy. Promotions are given only by the higher officials. Any decision or action, however petty, is subject to the will of the dictator (or *élite* group) at any time. In the words of Hitler's chief lieutenant, Hermann Goering, "When a decision has to be taken, none of us count more than the stones on which we are standing. It is the Führer alone who decides." Thus, the top echelon in the hierarchy occupies a position of overwhelming power seldom achieved prior to the twentieth century.

Institutionalization of Fear: The Police State. This eminence that the party *élite* enjoys distinguishes totalitarianism sharply from other types of authoritarianism. Three factors have played major roles in making this development possible. These are modern technology, more refined bureaucratic techniques, and the purge.

A casual glance will convince the observer that totalitarian dictatorships are, in part, an outgrowth of modern urban-industrialism. Modern totalitarianism would have been unthinkable in Plato's time, or even as late as Napoleon. For the technology, the methods of communication, and the modern police weapons were lacking. Indeed, George Kennan, a former ambassador to Russia, states that the use of the modern "technological component" for purposes of large-

scale control is one of the first things that impresses those who deal directly with totalitarians. Certainly the complete monopoly of the mass communication system is striking. Through control of the mass media, not only can the "party line" be disseminated and inculcated but thought control is possible. Every idea, every printed word, is subject to party scrutiny. In Communist Rumania, for example, a 1950 decree ordered every typewriter and duplicating machine brought in for registration.

Through this type of control, mass propaganda becomes a major totalitarian tool. Indeed, the Bolshevik, Fascist, and National Socialist parties were cradled in propaganda. The all-pervasiveness of totalitarian propaganda, its endless repetition, and its constant din affect every facet of society. Even the determined enemies of the regime begin to think, talk, and act in terms of the patterns styled by the regime. Propagandist catchwords such as "bourgeoisie," "vermin," "concrete achievement," and "warmongering" become a part of everyone's daily vocabulary. Russian prisoners in concentration camps, for example, mirror the thought control patterns and use value judgments imposed by the very system they abhor.

Propaganda controls are supplemented by complete domination of the educational system and the use of modern educational techniques. Like ideology, education is made an instrument for defining totalitarian "truth." Through education the child can be indoctrinated, the language doctored, and scientific theories altered to fit the "party line." For years Russian schools taught a scientifically questionable theory of environmental determinism in biology because it met the requirements of "correct Marxism." And Hitler's stormtroopers frequently threatened, and even imprisoned, university professors who refused to reject scientific evidence in favor of party doctrine.

Party controls do not end with the domination of communications and education. They extend into every nook and cranny of society. Nothing escapes. Even the home is invaded. Mothers may be told to bear more children for the fatherland. The "good citizen" is the one who indoctrinates his children. Girls and boys as young as six years may be required to belong to the party's "Youth Movement." The "Little Octobrists" of Russia and the "Hitler Youth" are cases in point.

The all-pervasiveness of totalitarian controls is indeed staggering. Artists are told what to paint; novelists what to write. Andrei Zhdanov, a former censor of Russian art, required that a painting uphold and further communist ideals. Art could be either abstract or representative, but it must also meet the ideological needs. The totalitarian believes that complete control is necessary if the existing order is to be completely destroyed. Change must be constant and total. And it does not stop with the fulfillment of a five-year plan or the "elimination of all Jews." The task is for the generations to come, and every accomplished task gives birth to another. Hitler's Reich was a "Thousand-Year Reich." For the totalitarian, the present is never good enough.

This urgency of total change begets terror. Since most persons fear sudden or complete change, they resist it. Therefore, the totalitarian employs extreme measures on a complete scale. The enemy is everywhere. To combat the enemy, the totalitarian, too, must be everywhere. And he must not shrink from employing violence. For extreme violence serves two purposes: it is a quick, decisive means of eliminating the enemy, and it terrorizes the remainder of the population. Here is where the secret police and the party's private army come in.

The machinery of terror is elaborate. First of all, it involves the type of disciplined and loyal bureaucracy we discussed earlier. Mounting terror accompanies the growth and consolidation of totalitarian bureaucracy. Stalin's rise to power, for example, was made possible by the internal growth of the communist bureaucracy, and this growth was accompanied by increased "doses" of terror as well as propaganda. Mussolini, on the other hand, failed to achieve the full potential of totalitarian strength partly because his regime was not well enough organized or fully bureaucratized.

The chief executioners of violence are the "crack corps"—the secret police. In fascist regimes, a uniformed party police force (Mussolini's blackshirts and Hitler's stormtroopers) keeps the entire society under surveillance, carries out executions and beatings for the party, breaks up gatherings, supervises concentration camps, and checks into the behavior and loyalty of party members.

Down with dictators! This Hungarian patriot showed his contempt for life in a garrison state by sending Lenin's picture up in smoke during the 1956 Hungarian revolt.

Many persons still find it difficult to believe that supposedly civilized men could commit atrocities and murder on the scale shown here. The bodies in the trailer represent a single day's killing at one of the Nazi horror camps, located at Weimar, Germany.

Its chief weapon is fear, and one of its chief means of institutionalizing fear is through an "informer system." Party members inform on one another and encourage every man, woman, and child to report any suspicious activity or conversation. No one can be certain who is an informer. It becomes dangerous to talk openly, even in one's home. For a man's own child may be an informer.

As a separate party organ, the secret police can control the civil police force, the military forces, and the party itself as effectively as they do the citizenry. Nothing escapes their attention, and few reports of suspicious activity escape their violence. In the familiar Soviet phrase, "They must protect the Soviet Union from the enemies of the people." They must find the "enemies," make them suffer, and turn them into horrible examples to frighten the rest! When there are no

enemies to use as an example, they must be invented. Totalitarian regimes must never claim the destruction of all their enemies. For doing so would constitute an admission of no further need of terror. Hence, it should not be shocking when the MVD or the Committee of State Security arrests foreign stamp collectors as suspected collaborators with the supposed "bourgeois international conspiracy."

Three major instruments of terror and control have been concentration camps, purges, and confessions. Contrary to a widely accepted viewpoint, *concentration camps* are not ordinary prisons. For the camps are actually built for the innocent. The inclusion of some common criminals is necessary to create the impression that all inmates are real criminals, but the number of real criminals is usually smaller than noncriminals. And a great many criminals are sent to camps only after finishing their regular prison term. The fact that the Russians use camps for so many regular criminals stems from a shortage of prisons and the desire to turn their whole penal system into a camp system. The camps are set up to eliminate "actual, potential, and imagined enemies of the regime, by first separating them, then humiliating, breaking, and destroying them, killing ten innocents rather than allowing one 'guilty' one to escape." This explanation of the true purpose of camps by Friedrich and Brzezinski reveals how useful camps are for eliminating persons *en masse* and for instilling fear in the rest of the population. Nazi camps were infamous. Nearly 10 million persons passed through Auschwitz alone, and some 4 million died there. Many were completely innocent, and many more had done nothing other than miss a day's work. Outside the camp, fear abounds. No one is quite sure what goes on inside. Many of those who are released from Russian camps, for example, have been sworn to secrecy under threat of being recommitted. Hence, concentration camps are surrounded by mystery. But the evidence we do obtain indicates that men are treated like animals on the inside. They are used as mere "slaves," berated, demeaned, and frequently left to suffer a slow, agonizing death.

Another technique of terror is the *purge*, a mechanism used to cleanse and strengthen the party by ridding it of its undesirable members. Purges do not indicate decay and corruption. On the contrary, they are used to consolidate and close ranks. They occur when the party is sturdy and stable, not when it is weak. The more savage and cruel the purge, the greater the evidence that the party is alert to the dangers of contamination from within. Cleansed of undesirables, the remaining members feel "purified" and steeled for the future. The purge places a premium on membership and unites the group behind the cause. Occa-

sionally, complaints have to be trumped up against innocent persons in order to justify a purge and put fire and spirit back into the organization. At other times, purges are employed to eliminate someone who is contesting the leadership's power. This was the case in Stalin's purge of Trotsky, Hitler's purge of Roehm, and Malenkov's purge of Beria. Purges, however, do not always involve mere dismissal from party ranks. Many

Andrei Vishinsky, procurator of the U.S.S.R., at the time of the purge trials, 1936.

of the purged are executed, or in the more polite term, "liquidated." Purges can be local and limited, or they may be quite general. Between 1934 and 1938, more than a million Russian party members were purged. Of these, many thousands disappeared or were executed. They were simply "vaporized!"

Another technique of terror is the *public confession* of persons purged or convicted of political crimes. It is not enough merely to kill a man. He must confess first. Russians have been especially diligent in obtaining public confessions. Their success in extracting confessions from innocent persons without employing torture has been phenomenal, although vastly overrated. For many of the accused have gone to their death or disappeared without confessing in public. The confession, of course, "proves" that the party was correct. And it gives the party an opportunity to vilify its enemies before the public. Every citizen can participate in the "hate" that is poured on the victim.

It is no doubt fitting that a portrait of totalitarianism should conclude on the note of terror. For it is through terror that the totalitarian institutionalizes and prosecutes a constant civil war against all men, enemies and friends of the system, guilty and innocent, citizen and foreigner. Through it he pulverizes not only the opposition, but everyone.

As impressive as is the reliance on terror, we should be careful not to define totalitarianism as simply government by terror and violence. Without violence, no doubt the regime would collapse. Yet, an oppressed people do not remain oppressed simply because violence is used on them. We must remember that the citizens have identified themselves with the system; they have accommodated their ways to fit the pattern. Otherwise, we would hear of more opposition and revolution. And revolutions have not been the rule in thoroughgoing totalitarian systems. Italy and Germany were overpowered from without, not from within.

THE ROOTS OF TOTALITARIANISM

What produced totalitarianism anyway? Is it just traditional authoritarianism in disguise? To this question the answer is most probably, No. Here is why.

DISTINCTIVE QUALITIES OF TOTALITARIANISM

Older and more traditional forms of authoritarianism not only lacked the distinct advantage of a highly developed technology but also governed large apathetic masses of people who had little interest in political affairs, who were often completely outside the political whirl, and who were quite illiterate in most cases, and therefore not very responsive. The propaganda and terrorist techniques of the modern dictator were thus beyond the reach of the older type authoritarian for reasons other than technology. It would have been well-nigh impossible for a dictator such as the last Roman Cola di Rienzi (1313-54), for example, to have transformed culture into propaganda and made cultural values into a salable commodity like soap. The people simply would not have listened.

Furthermore, except for the short-lived tyrannies that were ruled briefly by a strong man, most early authoritarian systems were based on a supposedly superior class, such as a landed aristocracy. Succession to power was rigorously controlled by prescribed rules of heredity or some other formula. And in most instances, although not all, tradition was something to be honored and preserved, not utterly destroyed. Furthermore, most ruling groups depended on a long-established and tradition-laden army for support. Full-blown totalitarians must establish controls over the army. Hitler's greatest threat from within came from a traditionalized army that finally made a bold attempt on his life. Ancient Greek and Roman tyrants, on the other hand, were usually given full powers to restore order when chaos threatened the society; but once order was restored, they were normally obliged to surrender those powers. Cincinnatus, it will be remembered, returned to his plow.

Finally, most traditional authoritarians, except for a few Oriental despots, were satisfied with absolute *political* power and were content to leave economic, cultural, family, and other institutional affairs alone as long as they did not impinge on political matters.

Excursions outside the political realm were the exception and not the rule. Power in traditional dictatorships was thus not total and all-pervasive. Nor was the traditional authoritarian so inclined to turn himself into a "god" as is the modern totalitarian. He might have claimed anointment by God, but he hesitated to pretend to be a god. And although ancient dictators often had popular support, as did Caesar, the identification of the masses with the regime was not so complete.

THE DECAY OF CHRISTIAN IDEALS

The womb of history has thus delivered up a new child with many of the characteristics of its forebears, yet not a mere replica by any means. Just why totalitarian dictatorships appeared when and where they did cannot be explained solely in terms of the conditions that set in following the First World War. Nor can the Industrial Revolution be held entirely accountable simply because it afforded the techniques and technology that made pervasive totalitarian controls possible. Certainly the decay of Christian values had something to do with the coming of totalitarianism. As science rose to challenge Christian dogma, the modern national state rose to challenge Christian institutions. This dual challenge, as we saw earlier, placed the whole value structure of Western Civilization in doubt. As long as social and cultural conditions remained stable, men were satisfied to live amidst a confusion of values, But once they were faced with social turbulence and economic chaos, such as beset Germany following World War I, men who questioned their own values were inclined toward desperation and seized whatever offered them security. Totalitarianism supplied a goal, a meaning for existence, and an explanation for what was wrong. It helped fill the void created by the crumbling value structure.

RISE OF ROMANTICISM
AND THE DETHRONEMENT OF REASON

As Christian values slowly disintegrated, so did Christian and non-Christian rationalism, both of which had permeated the Western outlook since the eighteenth century. Romantics like the German Richard Wagner attacked the rationalists vigorously. A "revolt against reason" followed, which took its bearings from the mysterious force called "life." Behind both nature and human life, said the German philosopher Arthur Schopenhauer, was the blind and irrational force called human "will." Reason did not control life. Just the opposite—life controlled reason. To Schopenhauer, rationality was but an illusion, for life was too difficult, too changeable, too complex to be reduced to a rational formula. To see God's purpose in our own lives, as the Christian does, is to see patterns where no patterns exist. To believe that increased rationality will order our universe and make it a better place to live, as a social reformer does, is to believe that an indifferent universe of blind forces really cares about humanity. In brief, the restless swirl of irrationality found in the blind force called "will" strives endlessly without purpose and without pattern. To give life a purpose is to be victimized by illusion. All we can do is pity the suffering. For all men are equally victims of these blind forces. All are equal in their misery. As the number of such ideas grew, rationalism began to totter.

Psychology, too, laid rationalism open to serious challenge. The American J. B. Watson, a famous behavioral psychologist, directed his attention to animal behavior in order to discover clues to human behavior. The very attempt suggested human beings were neither unique nor a special case in the universe after all. In 1908 another psychologist, William MacDougall, pointed out that men are not motivated by rational principles, but are primarily creatures of instinct (propensities) and of the external environment, which molds their personalities. In Vienna, Dr. Sigmund Freud, the father of psychoanalysis, won world attention for his studies in the "subconscious." Behavior, according to Freud, was a result of unconscious motives as well as conscious ones. In short, these men maintained that a great deal of our behavior is clearly outside the scope of any rational direction.

Psychological experimentation and research, then, cast a cloud of doubt over beliefs that had claimed men's minds for centuries. Just as the theories, discoveries, and truths of science had undermined the rationalist's castle, so, too, the findings of modern psychology were eating away at the foundations of that castle.

THE REVOLUTION OF NIHILISM:
THE EXILING OF TRADITION

"This world is a *Will to Power*—and nothing else! And even ye yourselves are this will to power—and nothing besides!" This prophetic announcement of what was coming, uttered nearly a half-century before totalitarianism put in an appearance, came not from a social or political scientist or any practical politician. Rather it came from a philosopher, Friedrich Nietzsche, whom most social scientists and politicians dismissed as interesting, but fanciful, and quite unrealistic.

"God is dead!" This was Nietzsche's observation. To him it was absurd for men to pay lip service to Christ and his teachings while rejecting them. Christ was to be admired, he thought, but not Christianity or Christian institutions. If God was dead, man's only answer was to turn to himself and become his own "God." He must become a Superman. "The Superman shall be

the meaning of the earth!" Men cannot turn to God, so they must turn to themselves—to their "will to power." Men can make their own world! Men must make their own world!

Nietzsche would not have men consign themselves to pity, as Schopenhauer had counseled. Rather, he asked them to affirm life and turn the blind forces of nature to their benefit through their will to power. A man must have courage, wrestle with fate, and become a hero. It is the will to power that counts. The great deeds of history are done by brave and unflinching heroes; they do not stem from God, nor from some mystical force.

Nietzsche himself was anti-militarist, anti-racist, and deeply respectful of many ancient values. As a Greek scholar who reasserted the values of classical Greek philosophy, he would, no doubt, have found the fascists and their program quite repugnant. Nietzsche's hero was more akin to the Greek hero than the marauding totalitarian. He hated the masses of people, for he believed they were ignorant. He hated their heroes and he would have hated any system that was based on mass support. Yet Nietzsche's philosophy smacked of nihilism. He could be used, and he was. For the nihilist thinks the world is blind force, without beginning and without end, without meaning and without purpose. All grounds for objective truth and morality he denies. All tradition, all standards, all norms of behavior he forsakes. Traditions, in fact, are holdovers from bygone ages that interfere with the effective affirmation of life. Men must have courage, become heroes, and turn the blind forces of nature to their advantage. They must not be imprisoned by the traditions and values of another age. Men must make their own values! This was Nietzsche's counsel.

EXPRESSIONS OF TOTALITARIAN DICTATORSHIP

FASCISM:

ENOUGH CHAOS TO MAKE A WORLD

The fascist did make his own values!

We have created a myth. The myth is a fact, it is a passion. It is not necessary that it shall be a reality. It is a reality by the fact that it is a goad, a faith, that it is courage.*

These words of Benito Mussolini, one of the very best fascist theorists and yet poor practitioner of fascism, demonstrate the nihilistic basis of the movement. The fascist repudiates all forms of universal, absolute, and eternal truth. *What works today is right, is truth.* If it fails to work tomorrow, it is false. According to the avowed American fascist Lawrence Dennis, "The Fascist scheme of things is an expression of human will which creates its own truths and values from day to day to suit its changing purposes." Truth is what is willed; and to the totalitarian, truth is whatever the dictator wills.

Like all totalitarians, the fascist opposes the existing order and proposes to eradicate it. There can be no compromise! For the fascist is either completely "for" or completely "against." The world is black and white. There are no shadings, no gray areas. As Hitler put it, "You are either for me or you are against me." No one must interfere or object to the fascist design to destroy the old and mold the new.

In Italy Mussolini sought to eradicate every vestige of monarchy, republicanism, socialism, democracy, and liberalism and in their stead re-establish the "glories of ancient Rome." This goal justified the use of violence (even Chicago-gangland-type murder), lies, total annihilation of all who disagreed, slave

---

* Quoted by H. Finer, *Mussolini's Italy* (New York: McGraw-Hill, 1935), p. 218.

labor, refusal to abide by international agreements, and any other means he deemed necessary.

As we shall see in the following chapter, Mussolini came to power in the wake of chaos and disillusionment. His program was intensely nationalistic, racist, imperialistic, and militaristic. "There was enough chaos to make a world." Traditional institutions were weak and unable to solve the problems. Traditional values were being questioned. To the spiritually homeless who doubted their values he gave a sense of belonging by telling them they were members of a superior nation that would rise again. He gave work to the unemployed or took them into the fascist movement. And he allayed the fears of the landowners and industrialists through an anti-labor policy directed against free unionism. Also quite important to the average Italian, the trains ran on time.

Fanatical rather than reflective, dogmatic rather than flexible, Mussolini rejected reason and rationalism. Through a rigorous propaganda campaign, he turned frustration, resentment, and insecurity into hatred and aggression. Mussolini was in full accord with the doctrine laid down in a British fascist speech of 1934, "Fascism is a real insurrection—an insurrection of feeling—a mutiny of men against the conditions of the modern world.... The Fascist ... acts, in fact instinctively, and not theoretically." This insurrection extended to every corner of Italian society except the Church, which, although feeling the impact, was able to remain much freer than other institutions. In the schools Mussolini's picture was placed in the classroom. In the economic realm he established a *corporate state.* Under it the total economy was divided into syndicates of workers, employers, and professional organizations, all of them tightly controlled by the party whose members were placed in strategic positions. Then the government established *corporations* (government administrative agencies) to control the worker and employer syndicates. Thus, the whole economic system was government-controlled.

Yet, despite Mussolini's determination and success, he failed to fulfill his goal of thoroughly regimenting society. Why? First, he was never able to subordinate the Church. In a 1929 treaty with the Vatican, the Church came off best. The Pope was permitted to appeal for peace to the outside world. This was an admission of defeat for Mussolini, for the fascist glorifies war as a test of superiority and as a "blood bath of steel" for weeding out the weak and purifying the strong. Furthermore, the mere existence of a treaty was a tacit admission that the Church was independent of his control, if only in part. The Church's goal, in fact, was still superior to his, even in the minds of his own people. Secondly, Mussolini's bureaucracy was not as well organized as it might have been. He was too suspicious of others and lacked the organizational genius that Stalin displayed. At times he was ridiculous enough to take charge of eight or nine major government departments personally. Third, the Italians never took him seriously enough. Many found him only interesting and amusing. Fourth, Italy was poor economically, despite desperate efforts that were made to overcome that condition. And she was not an industrially developed nation such as Germany. Finally, Mussolini's military establishment proved to be anything but a strong fighting force. In fact, when compared to Hitler's, it was a joke.

THE NATIONALIZATION OF SOCIALISM

The German version of fascism was undoubtedly the most successful and thoroughly totalitarian. Built on a claim

of biological superiority of Germans and Aryans as a race, Hitler set his goal to make them masters of the world. This involved exterminating the most inferior races and dominating the others. It further necessitated rooting out all vestiges of "degenerate" ideas and institutions. It was the task of the *leader* (Führer) to get the job done. He was the self-appointed "savior" who must "redeem" the race, the nation, the *Volk*, from the misery heaped on them by Jews, Bolsheviks, Slavs, and others. And he alone could protect the national and social interests of the people. According to his chief deputy, Hermann Goering, Hitler was infallible:

> ...it is axiomatic that the Leader must possess any quality attributed to him in its highest perfection. Just as the Roman Catholic considers the Pope infallible in all matters concerning religion and morals, so do we National Socialists believe with the same inner conviction that for us the Leader is in all political and other matters concerning the national and social interests of the people simply infallible.[*]

To this statement of Goering might be added the more extreme view of Dr. Engelke, leader of the German Christian movement: "God has manifested Himself not in Jesus Christ but in Adolf Hitler." [†]

Playing his role as "redeemer," Hitler smashed down his grand design on German society. He replaced the free-market system with a planned-price system, substituted state regulation for individual initiative, restricted private profits, and altered the concept of individual ownership. The government became the total possession of the National Socialist Party. The secret police were given free reign, and the entire country was placed under the severest form of censorship. No institution, no family, no person, was beyond the party's control and surveillance. Jews were herded into boxcars by

---

[*] Quoted in J. Hallowell, *Main Currents in Modern Political Thought* (New York: Holt, 1950), pp. 606-607.
[†] *Ibid.*, p. 606.

the tens of thousands and later slaughtered, while many other Germans were mustered into the army and trained to die for the fatherland. "War is the origin of all things. Let us go back to the primitive life of savages." This was Hitler's counsel. Men sleep and eat better after having knocked down an enemy, said the Nazis. The entire society was turned into a military garrison in which every individual counted for nothing beyond the contribution he could make to the total effort.

The armed forces came first. Through them Germany would prove her superiority, the enemy would be annihilated, and Germans would dominate the world. The economy was put on a permanent wartime basis. With free unionism relentlessly subdued or obliterated, employer associations, chambers of commerce, and other middle-class organizations were literally captured and united into the "Fighting Front of Industrial Middle Classes." Every business house and industry was subject to intensive government supervision and control for military considerations. Industry after industry suffered financial reverses as the government ordered changes in production to meet military needs. Agriculture was reorganized under the direction of the radical Walter Darre, who established complete dictatorship over acreage, crops, and prices. Farmers and peasants were bound to their soil. Darre's interests were as much racial as economic. Since land was the chief source of racial strength and purity (doctrine of "Blood and Soil"), farmers should be bound to their soil no matter whether they wanted to stay there or not. Under the Hereditary Farm Acts, he made it nearly impossible for farms to be mortgaged, sold, or transferred, except to the eldest son in event of a father's death. German farmers were to supply the food in event of war or blockade; farm boys were to be the source of the best soldiers; and the farm home was considered the stronghold of

German culture. They, the farmers, were the backbone of Germany. They were the *Volk*. To protect the farmers' privileged status, the Nazis fixed prices all along the line from producer to consumer.

Literature, art, drama, architecture, science, and music were dedicated to the *Volk*. Education became political education, dedicated to the advancement of the *Volk*, the *Reich*, and the *Führer*. Daring experiments were attempted in human breeding in order to purify the "race" and raise up a superior type of human being. Women were categorized according to types and mated with physically superior males in an arbitrary fashion. An all-pervasive totalitarian system —*Ein Volk, Ein Reich, Ein Führer*— bound the lives and destinies of all Germans. Inwardly, their cause was German and they were dedicated to make Germany economically self-sufficient, politically and militarily superior, and culturally dominant. Outwardly, their cause was the "world" and eventual domination of it. According to the geopolitical theory of Haushofer, which we discussed in Chapter 24, they were to conquer the "heartland" and turn Eurasia into a German world-island. From the world-island they would control the world. As hypernationalists and hyperimperialists, they demanded more space, more living room (*Lebensraum*) for all Germans. As superior peoples, they were certain that it was not only their right, but their destiny.

RUSSIAN COMMUNISM: SUFFOCATING HUMANITY IN A DEADLY EMBRACE

The communist drew his nourishment from Karl Marx and early socialist thought. His ideological cause dictated the complete annihilation of the capitalist system. The laws of history, in fact, showed that the downfall of capitalism was inevitable. It was the duty of those who saw this eventuality to turn their every effort toward

The sinews of world communism's deadly embrace. N. S. Khrushchev (right), Chairman of Ministers of the U.S.S.R., and Mao Tsetung, Chairman of the People's Republic of China.

the elimination of the profit system, the radical reorganization of the major means of production, and the establishment of collective ownership of all major productive enterprise.

With Marx as a prophet (a Moses), Lenin established himself as the tactician (a St. Paul) to spread the gospel and fulfill the mission that history dictated. From Marx, who led no revolutions, he took his cue and adopted revolution as the major method of getting the job done. To Marxism, Lenin added the mechanics of a party organization and the details for accomplishing a successful revolution. The party must lead. It must provide the brains for the masses. It must be composed of dedicated and fanatical believers in the cause who "never say die." Internally, the party was a hierarchy of committees fitted into a cellular-type structure. Members were to be trained revolutionists, adept in the arts of infiltration and illegal activity. They must know how to use front organizations, recruit spies, agents, and saboteurs. Their party activity and affiliations must be kept secret. Each must have a party name as well as a given name.

According to Lenin, the party is the leader of the proletariat—the "vanguard of the working classes." It is the maker of the

revolution, the government, the educator of the masses, the defender of the regime and the molder of the national goals, the leader in production, the source of all power, the authentic interpreter of the ideology, and the source of all values. Its major mission is "world revolution" and the radical reorganization of society. It is the "unsheathed sword of the revolution."

Lenin's major objective was to seize power and carry the revolution to the world. Stalin altered this approach a bit. He kept "world revolution" as the ultimate goal but sought the establishment and consolidation of communist power in Russia first. Russia would become the base of communist power for the ultimate conquest of the globe. With Russia as the citadel of communism, Russian foreign policy has aimed primarily at Soviet security. This egotistical aim placed an emphasis on building Soviet strength and made Russian foreign policy appear capricious, irresolute, and opportunistic to the outside world.

Internally, every effort has been made to strengthen the base. Heavy industry and heavy machine production have taken precedence over consumer production except for limited periods. The total economy has been organized, directed, and controlled centrally from the Kremlin. Once again, every person,

510

every institution, including the arts, sciences, family, and so forth, had to be so organized, dedicated, and controlled for the totalitarian cause. Propaganda, the secret police, and terrorist activity have been employed to ensure these requirements. Today nothing stands in the way of destroying the old and preparing the new. Individuals may be eliminated (vaporized), facts falsified, and historical events altered, destroyed, or even invented. Traditional institutions and methods are frequently regarded as "pests," especially religion. Churches continue to exist in Russia, but the time may come when the Kremlin will feel free to eradicate them completely. To the communist, religion is the "opiate" of the people—a menace to be eliminated. Truth is what the party declares it to be.

Thus, like other totalitarians, the communist makes his own truth, which he calls "scientific Marxism." The terrifying thing about all this is that the Russian communist, and other totalitarians, too, *can* make their own truth. For the truth of the statement that "the Moscow subway is the longest in the world" can be established if the communists can destroy all longer ones. It is a falsehood only as long as there is someone outside the Soviet orbit who has the strength to keep them from destroying longer subways!

SOME WORDS OF SUMMARY

Totalitarianism struck like lightning in a hypernationalist and imperialistic world torn by isms and schisms. It fit the patterns and responded to the needs of a nationalistic and insecure world. It was, in part, an expression of the authoritarian personality, which to some extent is found in each of us. For all of us are, to some degree, conformists, herd-minded, and purist. We all respond to fear, are quite mechanical in our behavior, and are anxious to avoid responsibility.

The hallmarks of totalitarianism are a pessimism about human nature, a contempt for the ordinary individual, and the utter rejection of all democratic methods and institutions. Totalitarian systems are characterized by well-developed ideologies covering all aspects of existence. This ideology is interpreted by a totalitarian (privileged) *élite* that imposes a garrison state on humanity, enforces complete submission to its will, eliminates all opposition and forms of free association, and demands complete control over all facets of society. The state itself is glorified, deified, and becomes the property of a single party, the members of which claim infallibility for themselves and their program. They ruthlessly eradicate all who disagree and attempt to identify their party and its cause with the masses. Mass support enlists everyone, makes the people a part of the enterprise, and gives them a feeling of "belonging."

The party supplies the formula, policy, leadership, and personnel for the government bureaucracy. A militarized brotherhood, the party is composed of dedicated and dutiful persons—steeled and efficient bureaucrats—who carry out the work of control, coercion, and terror. They defend the regime, carry out its programs, and ensure allegiance to the dictator. Organizationally, the party is a hierarchy of layers that are subject to the absolute control of the dictator. The party's major weapons are police-state techniques through which fear and terror are institutionalized. Of these techniques, propaganda, concentration camps, and the purge are the most effective.

Although rooted in older forms of authoritarianism, totalitarianism is not the same. It employs a highly developed technology and is not so encumbered as older authoritarian systems are by an apathetic citizenry, a class and status system, or tradition. In fact, totalitarians seek to overthrow tradition and attempt to subvert the traditionalized army rather than to depend on it for support. Unlike the ancient tyrannies that sought to overcome chaos, totalitarians want to make chaos a permanent condition. And totalitarian controls are more pervasive than the controls associated with traditional forms of authoritarianism.

Totalitarianism is a modern type of dictatorship that arose on the ashes of economic and social chaos following World War I. A logical extension of the urban-industrial revolution, totalitarianism took root in a world outlook that had ripened to accept it. Science and the modern national state had shaken traditional religious values, undercut rationalism, and dethroned reason. There followed a nihilistic revolt that repudiated traditional values and called on men to create their own values.

The fascists and national socialists did make their own values and used them to impose on mankind some of the most tyrannical regimes in history. The communists, on the other hand, drew their inspiration and much of their value framework from Marx. Lenin formulated Marxian ideas into an ideology and gave the ideology a party and tactics, which Stalin in turn amended. This system, too, developed into one of the most tyrannical regimes in history.

FURTHER ROADS TO LEARNING

GENERAL ACCOUNTS

H. Arendt, *The Origins of Totalitarianism* (New York: Harcourt, Brace, 1951). A strong anti-racist in a brilliant evaluation of totalitarianism.

A. Cobban, *Dictatorship* (New York: Scribner, 1939). Modern dictatorships have arisen because they promised economic improvements in return for loss of political liberties.

W. Ebenstein, *Today's Isms* (Englewood Cliffs, N. J.: Prentice-Hall, 1956). A most rewarding survey for beginners.

C. Friedrich, *Constitutional Government and Democracy* (Boston: Ginn, 1950). Excellent for comparing democracy and totalitarianism.

——— and Z. Brzezinski, *Totalitarian Dictatorship and Autocracy* (Cambridge: Harvard University Press, 1956). This book points out that totalitarianism is different from all other forms of authoritarianism.

W. Kornhauser, *The Politics of Mass Society* (Glencoe, Ill.: The Free Press, 1959). A very recent analysis of the social conditions in which mass political movements flourish.

H. Lasswell, "The Garrison State," *The American Journal of Sociology*, XLVI (January, 1941), pp. 455-468). What a completely totalitarian system would be like.

N. Machiavelli, *The Prince* (many inexpensive editions). The classic statement of authoritarian theory.

F. Neumann, *Behemoth* (New York: Oxford University Press, 1942). One of the very best studies of national socialism.

D. Spitz, *Patterns of Anti-Democratic Thought* (New York: Macmillan, 1949). A solid survey of totalitarian justifications for being.

L. Sturzo, "The Totalitarian State," *Social Research*, III (May, 1936), pp. 222-235. Good for a beginner who wants to know what is unique about totalitarianism.

SPECIAL STUDIES

T. Adorno *et al.*, *The Authoritarian Personality* (New York: Harper, 1950). What makes an authoritarian tick?

R. Crossman, ed., *The God That Failed* (New York: Harper, 1949). Why do they join the Communist party? Why do they leave?

M. Eastman, *Marxism: Science or Religion?* (New York: Norton, 1940). A claim that Marxism is unscientific.

M. Fainsod, *How Russia is Ruled* (Cambridge: Harvard University Press, 1953). A thoroughgoing survey of the Russian system.

M. Florinsky, *Fascism and National Socialism* (New York: Macmillan, 1936). All about the social and economic policies of fascist systems.

E. Fraenkel, *The Dual State* (New York: Oxford University Press, 1941). On the theory of Nazi dictatorship.

S. Hendel, *The Soviet Crucible* (Princeton: Van Nostrand, 1959). A useful collection of basic works by men who shaped Soviet Russia and by some of the most distinguished scholars of the system.

A. Hitler, *Mein Kampf* (New York: Reynal and Hitchcock, 1939). The Führer tells about his program.

G. de Huszar, *Soviet Power and Policy* (New York: Crowell, 1955). A basic survey of the entire Soviet system.

A. Kolnai, *The War Against the West* (New York: Viking, 1938). A vivid picture of the totalitarian threat to Western values and institutions.

N. Leites, *The Operational Code of the Politburo* (New York: McGraw-Hill, 1951). A short and definitive analysis of Soviet techniques.

V. Lenin, *Selected Works of V. I. Lenin* (New York: International Publishers, 1935-38). The original writings and thought of the first Soviet dictator.

M. Lerner, "The Pattern of Fascism," *The Yale Review*, XXIV (Dec., 1934), pp. 293-310. Totalitarianism fits the twentieth-century scheme of life!

K. Marx, *Capital, The Communist Manifesto, and Other Writings* (New York: Modern Library, 1932). An original source, this time from the prophet of communism.

B. Mussolini, *Fascism: Doctrine and Institutions* (Rome: Ardita, 1935). Another original source from a modern totalitarian dictator.

H. Rauschning, *The Revolution of Nihilism* (New York: Longmans, Green, 1939). A most rewarding study of national socialism by a former party member.

G. Seldes, *Sawdust Caesar* (New York: Harper, 1935). A humorous and scathing treatment of some neglected features of Italian fascism. Be certain to read the appendix.

H. Schwartz, *Russia's Soviet Economy*, 2nd ed. (Englewood Cliffs, N. J.: Prentice-Hall, 1958). A good look at one of Russia's major weapons, her economy.

FICTION AND DRAMA

F. Dostoyevski, *The Brothers Karamazov* (New York: Modern Library, 1937). A classic portrayal of a totalitarian mind and its techniques are found in the portion on "The Grand Inquisitor."

A Huxley, *Brave New World* (New York: Harper, 1932). A society dominated by science and test tubes.

A. Koestler, *Darkness at Noon* (New York: Macmillan, 1941). A penetrating analysis of how the communist mind works.

———, *The Gladiators* (New York: Macmillan, 1938). A runaway gladiator leads his fellow escapees out of Rome to build a "Sun State." He learns that freedom involves the use of coercion.

G. Orwell, *Animal Farm* (New York: Harcourt, Brace, 1946). A most entertaining parody on a communist society that was organized in a barnyard.

———, *1984* (New York: Harcourt, Brace, 1949). A preview of what a completely totalitarian system might be like.

FILMS

Camps of the Dead (Air Force Films, 1945, 20 min., sound, black and white). A shocking, authentic review of actual conditions in totalitarian prison camps.

From Kaiser to Fuehrer (Prudential Insurance Company of America, 1958, 30 min., sound, black and white). Pictorial story of the rise of national socialism.

Mussolini (Prudential Insurance Company of America, 1958, 30 min., sound, black and white). An account of the pompous Italian dictator and his regime.

The Red Sell (Prudential Insurance Company of America, Parts I, II, 1958, each part 30 min., sound, black and white). Positively the best film on Russian propaganda methods.

What Price Freedom? (Broadcasting & Film Commission, 1955, 40 min., sound, color). A story about totalitarian intrigue.

CHAPTER TWENTY-EIGHT

The Great Challenge:
Crises and Cataclysm

Frail and spent, former President Woodrow Wilson
emerges from retirement on Armistice Day, 1923, to make one of his last
public appeals for world organization and peace.

The world

went on trial in 1919. The burning hopes of millions throughout the world for democracy, peace, and plenty were about to be severely tested. The Allied victory and the collapse of the German and Austro-Hungarian empires made it appear that democracy was on the march. A demonstration of unexpected capabilities in the war by a democratic America added to this conviction. Into the center of the European peace parley stepped America's President Wilson to champion political freedom for all peoples everywhere. To many onlookers it seemed that democratic methods had proved their superiority over autocracy and despotism and were destined to sweep the world. Hopes ran high as political freedom for all peoples seemed but a short step away.

Nor did hope stop there. Economic plenty, too, seemed just around the corner. A century of industrial and material progress between the Battle of Waterloo and the Treaty of Versailles had encouraged peoples in many lands to believe that the spiral of civilization led inevitably onward and upward. Science, it was felt, would continue at an accelerated pace to harness more and more of the physical world for man's benefit. The British writer H. G. Wells spoke for millions when he confidently asserted that science would raise the level of health, wealth, and happiness for all mankind. A new age seemingly had dawned. The long night of struggle and want was over.

Foremost among human hopes was the desire for peace. A great war had been fought to end all wars. Both Lenin and Wilson offered plans for peace and plenty that had a wide appeal. Imperialism and war seemed to belong to bygone ages. Certainly the future must insure that they did! "War, even when victorious," said Norman Angell in his popular treatise, *The Great Illusion,* "can no longer achieve those aims for which people strive." War must go!

Yet, within two decades, Wilson's League of Nations was to collapse under the heel of totalitarian violence and democratic timidity; and Lenin's revolution was to blossom into one of the most powerful totalitarian regimes in history. By 1930 Europe had ten dictators to challenge democratic hopes, and by 1939 it was obvious that science was as much a tool for man's destruction as his betterment. Within a span of twenty years the passionate hopes of 1919 for peace, democracy, and general well-being were dissolving in the crucible of bitter experience.

THE TWENTY-YEAR CRISIS: 1919-1939

The period between the two great wars, or the two installments of the same war, embraced a series of never-ending crises. Even the peace conference of 1919 was far from tranquil. With the exception of Wilson and his delegation, the men who gathered in Paris were more nationalistic than internationalist, more vindictive than charitable, more anxious to dictate a selfish peace than to forge a lasting one. The French wanted German power destroyed, reparations for war damages, and dominance over the Con-

516

tinent. Britain sought to preserve her empire and world position. Italy demanded Trieste, Trentino, Fiume, and whatever else she could glean from the peace table. The defeated nations were not permitted to participate. They were simply given the terms and asked to sign.

THE UNSETTLED SETTLEMENT

The stage for future disillusionment and crises was already set ten months prior to the end of hostilities. In an address to the American Congress in January, 1918, President Wilson announced his program for peace, the famous Fourteen Points, which included: (1) a demand that covenants, treaties, diplomacy, and peace negotiations be conducted openly and in full public view; (2) freedom of the seas; (3) removal of economic barriers and establishment of equality in trade; (4) disarmament; (5) impartial adjustment of colonial claims with full consideration and participation of the populations concerned; (6) evacuation and restoration of the invaded portions of Russia, Belgium, and France; (7) adjustment of Italian boundaries according to nationality lines; (8) guarantees of independence and the territorial integrity of Poland and the Balkan states; (9) freedom for national groups in Austria-Hungary; (10) establishment of an organization of nations to guarantee political independence and territorial integrity to both large and small states. Out of the last point grew the League of Nations.

Before the armistice, world public opinion embraced Wilson's proposals as the basis for peace. In October, 1918, a provisional German government under Prince Max of Baden announced Germany's acceptance of the Fourteen Points. On November 5, the Allies agreed to the Wilson program. Yet no sooner had Wilson arrived in France with a peace plan than it became apparent that a different peace from the one he contemplated was in store. Decisions were soon being made in the traditional manner. Of the thirty or so nations that sent delegates, only France, Great Britain, and Italy participated with the United States in the important decisions. Covenants were not being reached openly, but in private. The usual diplomatic pressures, intrigue, and compromise reigned supreme.

Fateful Diplomacy. The demise of Wilson's hopes has been laid to the ascendancy of nationalism, former diplomatic commitments among the Allies, and the widespread desire of the victors to punish the vanquished. Certainly nationalism had reached a zenith. The world had become a boiling mass of national-minded peoples, each aspiring to political and economic independence. Beyond common objectives of peace, plenty, and democracy, there were few actual ties among national groups. Rarely had common interests among national states been strong enough in the past to keep them from pursuing their own selfish objectives. Now there was little question. With the nineteenth-century economic community in shambles, hopes for democracy, peace, and plenty provided but a shallow basis for common objectives.

As each national leader pursued selfish objectives, he apparently relied on democracy, science, and industrial growth to insure the future. Presumably, all that was needed was to dismember the so-called aggressors and substitute democratic for autocratic institutions in countries such as Germany. Punish the aggressor, ruin his military machine, and give him democracy! With these ends secured, each diplomat could attempt to squeeze everything he might from the peace table.

Each national leader, except possibly Wilson, pursued nationalistic objectives after making certain that public opinion in his own country supported him. The failure of

Wilson to keep the support of his own people and to convince them that his international objectives were actually in the national interest defeated the objectives he was able to salvage from the peace conference. The world was chauvinistic and divided. The people in each national group were thoroughly identified with the national symbols of their own group, and they wished to be free and independent of the influence of others.

As a result, the conference was plagued not only with claims of the victorious Allies but also with those of every national group that aspired to independence. France demanded Alsace-Lorraine and the Saar. Italy sought Trentino and Trieste. Long-overrun Poland wanted absolute independence. Before the conference ended, Czechoslovakia, Yugoslavia, Estonia, and several other new national states had been created. Throughout Europe nationalistic fervor and practical considerations resulted in some of the most sweeping and revolutionary territorial changes in history. Wilson's call for national self-determination of peoples was fanning separatism and narrow chauvinism into a white-hot heat. This tendency was almost bound to frustrate his attempts to achieve world unity.

The Policy of Vengeance. Prospects for the future were further dampened by the past commitments of the Allies and the policy of vengeance. Earlier, both Italy and Serbia had been given promises concerning the disposal of Habsburg lands along the Adriatic. There was also a great deal of argument over Allied agreements concerning boundaries in the Balkans. And France and England seemed unquestioningly committed to the dismemberment of Germany. As a result, the old Habsburg Empire of Austria-Hungary was completely cut to pieces. But far more important was the demand that the German war machine be dismantled and the German people made to suffer for the woes they had visited on the Allies. Germany, with her allies, was to pay heavy reparations to the victors for their war guilt. This requirement was to have dire consequences for the future.

The British Prime Minister, Lloyd George, came to the conference on the heels of an election that committed him to "squeeze the German orange till the pips squeak." Germans were saddled with an impossible bill for damages amounting to $5 billion a year until 1921, when they would be presented with the final statement. Germany was also required to deliver many of her merchant ships into Allied hands as well as make coal deliveries to Belgium, France, and Italy for ten years. She was stripped of her colonial empire. Her African and Pacific possessions were turned over to the control of the various Allied powers under a "mandate" system. This system was presumably designed to educate the colonial peoples in democratic methods and prepare them for national independence.

Finally, Germany had to disarm. Her army was limited to one hundred thousand men, her navy stripped to bare necessity or worse, and the Rhineland completely demilitarized. She was forbidden to possess submarines or military aircraft. The capstone of humiliation came in a treaty provision that forced her to admit full responsibility along with the other Central Powers for starting the war. Obviously, vengeance and fear of German military might outweighed the desires for a lasting peace. Or it was assumed that the way to a lasting peace was to make Germany pay for her wrongs and discourage others from starting a war. Whatever the objectives, the policy was unrealistic. A Germany weakened by war, humiliated in peace, stripped of her possessions, and saddled with an impossible demand for reparations could hardly be expected to develop the strength and economic capacity to pay the bill the

Allies demanded. Such a peace was almost bound to be a prelude to future crises.

It certainly created a crisis for German democracy. It did in fact seal the fate of one of the most democratic constitutions ever penned, the Weimar Constitution, which the Allies thrust on an unwilling and unprepared German public. It was this new democratic government of Germany that was presented with the reparations bill at the very time it lacked the means of paying it. It was democracy that was discredited for the problems Germany could not solve. Except for Wilson, democratic leaders seemed blind to the fact that Germany's failure would be interpreted as a failure of democracy.

Wilson's program for a just and lasting peace thus suffered defeat at the hands of traditional diplomacy. His plea for self-determination served to divide the world further rather than unite it. His dedication to democratic institutions led to their establishment among peoples unprepared for them. Finally, his supreme effort, the founding of a League of Nations, was destined to fall far short of achieving an international community in a world where few international ties existed. Refusal of the chief architect's own people to join the League made its success even more improbable.

A peace treaty had been written, but peace had not been secured. Relief would be temporary only. Almost immediately there was an appeal to the type of force that gave birth to totalitarianism. This antithesis of democracy spread like a prairie fire. Within a decade and a half following the war, hopes for a world of plenty were dampened by economic depression, unemployment, and want. And the yearnings for peace and unity were mocked in the same interval by military aggression, failure of disarmament proposals, and the ineffectiveness of the League of Nations. The seeds of discord planted at Versailles were already sprouting.

THE TOTALITARIAN CRISIS

An ominous note of what the world would soon be like had already sounded in war-torn Russia. In November, 1917, a disciplined band of Marxian communists overthrew the short-lived parliamentary regime that had already ousted the Czar earlier in the year. Under the firm, autocratic leadership of Nikolai Lenin, the communists bested their domestic enemies, withdrew from the war against Germany, and built the foundations for a collectivist, totalitarian regime.

The Italian Crisis. Although Russian communism would ultimately pose a greater threat to the Western democracies, the more immediate threat came from the fascists. As early as 1922, a poverty-stricken and disgruntled Italy turned to a strong man. Benito Mussolini, a disillusioned socialist turned fascist, had already organized the militant *fasci di combattimento* (groups for combat) by 1919. His following grew rapidly as salaries lagged and depression loomed, as public unrest mounted and the police wearied of suppressing disorder and reaping abuse, and as nationalist feelings surged and fear of Bolshevik revolution spread. By 1922, more than three hundred thousand Italians had joined the movement. To the idle and downtrodden, Mussolini offered something to do and causes to fight for. By making them a part of his movement and putting uniforms on their backs, he gave them status and a feeling of importance. To the middle class he offered better economic conditions and delivery from the threat of Bolshevism.

Probably the most significant factor in his success was the widespread fear of Bolshevism and communist revolution (the "Red Scare"). Even the liberal democrats in Italy shared these fears. As a result, liberal parliamentary leaders winked at fascist rioting, plunder, and murder. Army officers were encouraged to issue arms and vehicles to fascists, and police were encouraged to look the other way. Many liberals felt that the fascists were teaching the leftists an important lesson. During a reign of terror that hovered over Italy between 1920 and 1922, nearly two thousand people met death as a result of fascist violence. Offices and property of labor unions, newspapers, and leftist parties were ransacked and burned.

By 1922, what had begun as an anti-Bolshevik movement had become anti-labor and pro-industrial. It also appealed to the wealthy landowners. No longer a small, militant band, the movement had become national in scope and controlled thirty-five seats in the Italian parliament. The old government had lost control. Local police were either collaborating with the fascists or had given up fighting them. When the cabinet finally awakened to the threat and declared martial law, the king refused to sign the decree since he knew the army would not resist the fascists. The fascists marched on Rome and the king immediately (October 29, 1922) wired Mussolini to come to Rome to form a cabinet.

Within a month the new premier had obtained dictatorial powers from parliament. Contemptuously ignoring the constitution rather than rescinding it, he secured parliamentary approval of a new election law, which provided that the party winning the largest vote in a national election would receive two-thirds of the seats in parliament. Control by the fascists was thus secured. In addition, Mussolini created a fascist militia, enlarged the army, and required members of both to take an oath of allegiance to him personally.

Democracy had become a mockery. The very antithesis of constitutional democracy had been installed by constitutional means. Into a world bent on becoming more democratic and peaceful rode the "man on horseback," the opportunist who harangued

mobs from a balcony, appealed to emotions, and glorified war. For "democracy, peace, and parliamentary rule," he substituted "believe, fight, and obey." Constitutions were but scraps of paper and legislatures were "talking shops." His rise to power presented no immediate threat to the balance of world power because his country was weak. But it represented a crisis, nevertheless, for an established democracy had succumbed. The demise of Italian democracy was not just a brief halt in the forward march of democratic institutions. It was much more. It was a definite reversal of the supposed trend toward democracy all over the world. Even worse, it gave heart to anti-democrats everywhere.

The German Crisis. Stinging under the humiliation of Versailles and suffering from an illusion that neither Germany nor its army had been defeated, the German people were easy victims of fascist dogma. Since the Allies had not marched on Berlin, and since the German commander, Marshal von Hindenburg, had not signed the armistice, Germans were easily led to believe that they had been "stabbed in the back" by civilian politicians, Jews, and communists. The unreasonable Allied demands for reparations and the war-guilt clause intensified this conviction. Hating their enemies, denying their guilt, and defending their national honor, many Germans were hardly in a mood to make constitutional democracy work. Rather, they looked back nostalgically to the "glorious days" under Bismarck and the Empire. National socialism thus found a fertile seedbed in Germany.

Dedicated to force, propaganda, and German supremacy, the national socialists, like their Italian political cousins, appealed to the disgruntled, the dispossessed, and the fiercely nationalistic. Hitler, their leader, also put uniforms on the backs of the downtrodden and disillusioned, giving them status and new goals in life. He appealed to nationalist sentiments and promised reprisals for the humiliation Germany had suffered. Germany would rise again! Germany would get even! Germany would assume her rightful position of dominance over other peoples! Using the Jews and communists as scapegoats, he blamed them for the "stab in the back" and promised to rid Germany of their influence. He was vigorously anti-Semitic, calling for the liquidation of the Jewish people, branding them as a degenerate and "inferior" race.

It is now rather widely agreed that the success of Hitler's appeal stemmed from the Red scare, his opportunism, and the inability of the German republic to deal effectively with postwar disillusionment and crises. To obtain power, the national socialists needed the support of the industrialists, landowners, and upper classes. At first these groups viewed Hitler as somewhat of an hysterical maniac. But after they were convinced that Germany was in danger of going communist, they began to support him with influence and money.

The tale of the republic's ineffectiveness and national socialist opportunism begins in 1920 when an East Prussian named Kapp tried to paralyze the government and the economy by calling a general strike. Government resistance was successful, but violators escaped with light sentences. This incident was followed by a communist revolt in the Ruhr. German troops entered the demilitarized zone and aroused France, who occupied the area with troops. The German people reacted to this move by supporting reactionary and rightist candidates in the 1920 election.

Working with General Ludendorff and the "German Workers' party," Hitler emerged as party leader shortly after the Ruhr revolt. He began appealing for upper-class and industrialist support and received help from army sympathizers who fed him arms and

supplies illegally. Just as in Italy, the German fascists began a campaign of assassination and terror. Then came the terrible German inflation of 1922 and 1923. The government had failed to levy sufficient taxes to pay the expenses of the war. The German mark was soon worthless. People carried them by the sackful to buy a loaf of bread. Life savings were wiped out. As the economic crisis came to a head, the national socialists struck. Announcing a revolution in a Munich beer garden, the Nazis began a march on Berlin. But the German army resisted, the march aborted, and Hitler went to jail for a short period.

With the end of inflation the German economy stabilized, and Hitler was not given another opportunity until the impact of the 1929 depression hit Germany. Between 1930 and 1932 Nazi representation in the Reichstag (the national legislature) soared from twelve to two hundred and thirty. This time there would be no *putsch* (seizure of power), for the wily Hitler would now play politics with Chancellor Franz von Papen, a conservative nobleman and confidante of the war hero, President von Hindenburg. The Chancellor cut off Hitler's financial support from the industrialists and then began to wear him down by calling a series of elections. But Hitler waited von Papen out and eventually took advantage of a rivalry between him and the jealous opportunist, Julius Schleicher, to come to power.

When Schleicher intrigued against von Papen's reappointment to the chancellorship, Hindenburg, now angry, forced Schleicher to accept the position. Anxious for revenge, von Papen thereupon began intriguing with Hitler. He agreed to persuade the industrialists to pay Hitler's debts if Hitler would agree not to insist on the chancellorship (leaving the door open for von Papen's return to power), and Hindenburg moved to obtain Schleicher's resignation. But then Hitler shrewdly insisted on the chancellorship.

Finally, von Papen and Hindenburg foolishly consented after Hitler agreed to uphold the constitution.

January 30, 1933, was a black date for German democracy. Hitler dissolved the Reichstag almost immediately. The following election campaign was stormy and violent. On February 27, the Reichstag building was burned. Hitler blamed it on the communists. Hindenburg suspended free speech and press, but this move only made it easier for the Nazi storm troopers to use intimidation and terror. Still short of a majority in the Reichstag after the election, Hitler used his storm troopers to threaten and bully the Reichstag into conferring full dictatorial powers on him. The constitution was suspended, and it was suspended constitutionally. Soon opposing political parties were dissolved and outlawed, the Reichstag was turned into a rubber stamp, and all vestiges of constitutional government were destroyed. Democracy had again been smitten.

The disease called totalitarianism spread rapidly. By 1926 proud Poland was under the spell of Pilsudski. Later, Spain fell to General Franco, Austria to the Nazis, Hungary to Gombos, Rumania to Antonescu, Bulgaria and Yugoslavia to royal dictatorships, Japan to a military clique, and Greece to Metaxas. Meanwhile, the communist dictatorship in Russia steadily gained strength, and communists in China were making important gains. Totalitarianism rather than democracy appeared to be sweeping the world.

The Totalitarian Challenge. Democratic institutions were being severely challenged. They no longer seemed as irresistible as they once had. Certainly the presence of democratic institutions in particular countries did not ensure the people against the success of totalitarian coups. Hitler's rise to power proved rather conclusively that totalitarians could destroy democratic institutions by democratic methods, and Mussolini demon-

strated that totalitarianism could flourish under a democratic constitution. Both men jolted the democratic faith by revealing that civilized men are as susceptible to emotional and irrational appeals as to rational ones. German scientists could teach one kind of biology in a classroom and scream loudly in support of another kind at an anti-Jewish rally. Likewise, the belief that mankind was on the path toward greater humanitarianism and brotherhood was severely shaken. Violence and murder, indeed virtual gangsterism, were a part of the fascist's program. Intimidation and mistreatment were common. Worst of all, civilized human beings were capable of killing innocent Jews by the thousands. Those human incinerators consumed democratic hopes as well as the bodies of innocent victims. Nationalistic and totalitarian fanaticism overwhelmed humanitarian values and the world's hope for peace and prosperity. The prospects for peace dissipated rapidly as Hitler shouted, "War is eternal, war is universal. There is no beginning and there is no peace. War is life." Most important for Mussolini was that men know "how to die!" At the opposite end of the political spectrum, Russia's Stalin was busily steeling and consolidating his regime through the terrorist tactics of a private police force (the MVD) and a series of bloody purges. A crisis was at hand. This was not a world safe for democracy, but an extremely dangerous one.

THE SHIFT OF THE POWER CENTER

The rise of totalitarianism marked a deep gulf that separated the pessimism of the postwar years from the heady optimism of the prewar generation. For those whose lives spanned both epochs, however, there were other dramatic indications of far-reaching changes in the political and social structure of the modern world. One such change, which powerfully affected the peace and diplomacy of the years after 1919, was the shift in the world's power center. For four hundred years and more the subcontinent of Europe had been the scene of international rivalries and conflicts that had affected all parts of the globe. From Europe the lines of political power and influence radiated to North America, Asia, Africa, and the Far East. For many generations Europe had been considered a citadel of culture and the center of Western values. Europe had provided the stage for the French Revolution, and it was in Europe that the Industrial Revolution had its beginning. Europe, in brief, had been the cockpit of the globe.

During the nineteenth century Europe was unquestionably the center of world power, economically, socially, and politically. England held the balance of power not only in Europe but throughout the world. As mistress of the high seas and capital of the world economic community, England manipulated the delicate power balance in Europe and maintained a dominant position in all parts of the globe. It was another European power, the German Empire, that challenged England's position late in the nineteenth century. And Europe was the locale of the ensuing world power struggle between England and Germany. That struggle, involving an arms race and a German attempt to secure dominance in Europe as well as a vast colonial empire, culminated in a war that engulfed the entire world. But the battle lines were drawn in Europe.

Ironically, the same war doomed Europe's time-honored position in the world. A defeated Germany and a war-torn France were in no position to seize the reins. Great Britain was likewise pushed off her throne. With her economy strained by four years of war and her commercial ties weakened, England was tottering. The international economic community she had captained during the nineteenth century had been destroyed. Britain's industry was suffering and her

shipping was lagging. Under the stress of circumstances, she abandoned her balance-of-power policy in international politics. The upshot was a shift in the power center during the postwar years from Europe toward America, and soon thereafter, toward Russia also. Failure to recognize and assess the consequences of this important fact was to contribute to the crisis of the 1930's and after.

As England abdicated, a weakened France sought a stronger world position by attempting to gain greater dominance in Europe; proud Germans felt they had been betrayed and thus deprived of their rightful heritage to rule the world; Americans stood on the

One of the major reasons for the shift in the world's power center has been the phenomenal growth of Russian industry since the 1930's.

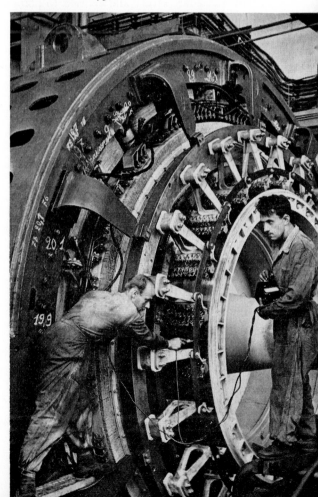

sidelines, almost completely naive about the power that had flowed into their hands. America had demonstrated her great potential when she had entered the war and quickly tipped the balance in favor of the Allies. Her economy, with its tremendous resources and industrial potential, was left practically untouched by the war. The center of international finance now shifted from London's Lombard Street to New York's Wall Street. Yet, almost tragically, few Americans were aware of what had happened, and still fewer were willing to accept the responsibilities that accompanied such a power position. Most Americans assumed that the world would soon return to its prewar state. Senator Harding won the presidency in 1920 on a platform promising a return to "normalcy." Wilson's plea for American leadership sank in a sea of isolationism. The United States Senate rejected the Versailles Treaty and refused to permit American participation in the League of Nations. To Americans the war had been a European affair in which they had become unfortunately involved. Preferring to follow George Washington's dictum of avoiding future involvement in the "sordid" affairs of Europe, they relaxed from the emotional strain of war and turned to domestic problems. The democratic world was thus deprived of leadership by the one country capable of providing it. America, the prince of power, abdicated before the crowning. What leadership there would be had to come from Britain and France. America would support in principle and practice, but she would not lead.

Despite a long experience in world affairs, British and French leadership was inadequate to counter the rise of political systems hostile to Western liberalism. Both countries simply lacked the strength. Nevertheless, they (especially Britain) took the helm. Under their leadership and without the participation of the United States, the League of Nations went into operation in 1920. It was successful in resolving two major international disputes (one between Finland and Sweden in 1920 and another between Greece and Bulgaria in 1925), and it promoted many fruitful conferences and laid the basis for a number of significant economic and social programs. Fortunately, even the United States participated in some of the League conferences on disarmament. For a while in the late 1920's it appeared that Wilson's hopes for the League might be fulfilled.

But disaster was in the offing. On the one hand, the French-British partnership was weakened by jealousy and divided aims. It was fragile at best. On the other hand, America ignored their cries for support when they did unite on issues and needed America's help. France, declining in population and impoverished from the war, supported by alliances with weaker states while posing as a great power, and mortally fearful of Germany, sought to dominate the Continent and to revenge herself on Germany. Remembering her long history of conflict with France, England suspected French aims in Europe. Furthermore, England was not so fearful as France of German recovery, and viewed a healthy German economy as a rich market for British goods. Britain, so the French thought, was doing little to secure France from future German aggression. These differences often led to a breakdown in the League of Nations, since that organ depended on British-French unity for the aggressive leadership it needed to survive.

Without the participation of the United States, it was obvious that the League would have great difficulty in meeting a bold, aggressive step by any government hostile to the liberal, democratic ideal. When the test came, a weak League led by divided and declining powers was apt to succumb. This is what happened after Japanese aggression against China in Manchuria in 1931, Hitler's

withdrawal from the League and defiant re-
arming of Germany in May of 1935, and
Mussolini's attack on Ethiopia in October of
1935. Three failures in three crises left the
League so weakened that its delegates were
forced to suffer the humiliation of being
brazenly hooted at by Italian fascists. World
democratic leadership had collapsed. It
would remain for America, preoccupied during the 1930's with a domestic depression, to
discover the threat not only to democratic
institutions but to herself late in the decade
and thus assert the leadership that had been
so urgently needed for two decades. Fortunately, when America did awaken to her
responsibilities, her economic capacity and
power potential were so vast that she was
able to swing into action almost immediately.

THE IDEOLOGICAL CRISIS

By the 1930's another source of crisis
was clear. Three conflicting ideologies were
dividing men in their struggle for control
of the world. Two of these, democracy and
communism, had already flowered before the
conclusion of the First World War. The
third, fascism, as we saw in the preceding
chapter, was a new development and came
as somewhat of a surprise.

Actually, the ideological struggle since
World War I has been between democrats
and totalitarians. But between the two wars,
the totalitarians were also divided. Both
fascists and communists developed police
states with opposed objectives and neither
would tolerate deviation from their respective goals. Both were aggressive, both were
imperialistic, and both had opposing designs

for world domination. As fascists made gains
against the democrats, communists played
the warring sides off against one another until
Germany attacked Russia. Then the communists and the democrats were joined in a
death struggle against the fascists.

For well over a century democrats had
been on the initiative. Ardent believers in
democracy had worked for a democratic and
peace-loving world, had extolled the virtues
of political liberty, and had been heartened
by the spread of popular participation in
government. Victory over authoritarianism
seemed to be within their grasp. Then, suddenly, everything changed. Russian Bolsheviks seized power and preached economic
equality at the expense of political liberty.
Fascists began teaching obedience to the
state, national solidarity, and racial superiority at the expense of both political and
economic freedom. Democrats were thrown
on the defensive, a position they were unaccustomed to handling. They were faced
with the necessity of defending their Christian and liberal ideals against two vigorous
ideologies that branded theirs as unrealistic,
sentimental, and hollow. As the totalitarian
countries grew in economic and military
strength, a crisis became imminent. That
crisis was, at best, only partially resolved by
World War II. For democrats still are confronted by the communist challenge, and
even fascism, though defeated in war, has
not yet been defeated as an idea. Fascist
regimes still exist in the world, and fascist
ideas are very much alive everywhere. Wars
are not clashes of ideas; they are clashes between men driven by ideas. Men may be
defeated in war, but these defeats do not
necessarily destroy the ideas.

THE GREAT HOLOCAUST: WORLD WAR II

An apathetic America awakened in
the late 1930's to the dangers that threatened
her. The twenty years of uncertain truce

was to end in World War II, the outcome
of which depended on the role America
played. The war had in fact already begun

in 1931 when Japan attacked Manchuria. This incident on one side of the world was followed on the other by German rearmament and occupation of the Rhineland, both actions in direct violation of the treaty of peace. Italian aggression in Ethiopia killed the League, and the Spanish Civil War in 1936 brought the great powers into direct conflict. Germans and Italians sent "volunteers" and supplies to the Spanish rebel, General Franco. Russia sent supplies to the Loyalists, and the democracies showed a pronounced sympathy for the Loyalist cause. Those countries that would soon be embroiled in World War II had already drawn their battle lines.

An emboldened Mussolini grabbed Albania, Hitler seized Austria, and both entered into the "Rome-Berlin Axis." Hitler took Czechoslovakia and Memel, concluded a nonaggression treaty with the Soviets, and divided Poland with Russia, the two latter actions violently arousing the West.

In September, 1938, Hitler had echoed Wilson by demanding self-determination for Germans in Czechoslovakia. British Prime Minister Neville Chamberlain persuaded Hitler to call a conference at Munich. There Hitler and Mussolini met Allied chiefs and won an Axis victory. The Czechs were forced to surrender their German-populated Sudeten lands to Germany in return for a promise from Hitler that he would make no further demands. Hitler never kept promises, however. In March, 1939, he took Czechoslovakia, and Poland fell that autumn. Following his truce with Russia, Hitler felt confident in facing France and England in the west. The second installment of the First World War had begun in earnest.

This, too, was a total war of total populations in total causes seeking total defeat and total victory. Germany was joined by her Axis partners, Italy and Japan. Unlike the First World War, this war would be decided in Russia, the Pacific, and North Africa, as well as in Europe. Hitler had rightly assumed that Russia was now one of the centers of world power, but he wrongly assumed that Europe was the other great center. With Western Europe on its knees and England at bay, he turned on Russia. Instead of pacifying an aroused America, already supplying Britain through lend-lease, he permitted his ally, Japan, to attack the United States.

Roosevelt and Eisenhower—two men who asserted bold leadership during World War II, and one of whom lived on to lead the Free World in the Cold War.

America proved to be far better able to prosecute a two-front war than Germany. The downfall of the Axis nations stemmed partially from Hitler's inaccurate assessment of the power shift that had taken place after World War I.

THE AFTERMATH: INNOCENT NATIONS IN A WRATHFUL WORLD

By the end of World War II, the world of 1919 seemed to have vanished. Civilization now seemed to be racing toward catastrophe rather than utopia. Prophets of gloom and doom were as numerous as prophets of hope and happiness had been in former times. Historians now foresaw a future of irrationality, less freedom, greater conformity, and less progress.

QUESTIONING OUR ASSESSMENTS

Wilson's dream of one world united under a League of Nations and Lenin's dream of one world forged by communist revolution seem premature from our vantage point today. In 1942, Wendell Willkie, a defeated presidential candidate, confidently acclaimed this to be a "one-world era" after a trip that took him around the globe. Eleven years later, another defeated candidate, Adlai Stevenson, returned from a similar tour convinced that that was not the case at all. As he saw it, the world was sharply divided. There is no doubt about the division. But need we assume that a divided world necessarily entails chaos and destruction, as quite a number of pessimists have predicted?

We are all in mortal danger of repeating the same mistake we committed between the two great wars; namely, neglecting to see that the center of power may shift. No fact is more obvious than that the United States and Russia emerged from World War II as the two great power centers. But is that power center now shifting and what does it mean if it is? As Africa and Asia go up in the world, are the United States, Russia, and Europe going down?

We are also told that because Russia and the United States possess the major implements of war, they will inevitably clash and the victor will rule the world. Yet, atomic power and intercontinental ballistic missiles may enable both Russia and the United States to destroy one another, or leave one another prostrate. Such a catastrophe might leave Asia or Africa the center of world power.

We are further told that Russia and the United States are doomed to clash because they profess opposing ideologies. Our value systems are presumably too much opposed for us to live together peacefully. Some claim that ideologies actually do the fighting. No one doubts the presence of ideological systems. But do such schisms inevitably lead to conflict? They may, sometimes do, but is it *inevitable*? As great as the power of an idea is, we must remember that there are many other components that blend into a situation which leads to physical combat. Muslims, asserts the able historian Arnold Toynbee, have long been dedicated to the destruction of Christianity, but have undertaken no "holy wars" for quite a while. Too many of the other components for conflict have been lacking. Finally, it is not the ideas that do the fighting but the men who subscribe to them. Men are frequently willing to die for an idea, and that willingness may result in war. It often does. But men do the fighting.

Others tell us that our world is divided into good and evil—democracy and Chris-

Fascist regimes continued to persist after World War II. Eva Perón, wife of the former Argentine dictator Juan Perón, attends a festival in Spain with Generalissimo Francisco Franco in 1947.

tianity *vs.* communism and atheism in this case—and good must always do battle with evil. Again, is conflict inevitable? Or need it involve bloodshed? Are there no other means for settling such matters?

A strong belief in the rightness of one's cause is a powerful incentive in persuading men to try to win the hearts and minds of others, a process that may lead to conflict. It will also charge men with a fighting spirit when they do get into a fight with the enemy. But wars are not always decided solely on the basis of who is right or wrong. Hitler lost not because he was wrong but because he was in Europe, a declining continent, and opposed by two national states with more powerful economic and military machines than his. Prior to the entry of Russia and the United States, Germany had been very successful in the war. Although a person fights harder when he believes he is right and his cause just, he is not assured of winning by that fact alone. From the American point of view, the forces representing right and justice lost in the Japanese conquest of Manchuria. Rightness of our cause does not inevitably bring victory in any battle we enter.

THE POSTWAR WORLD

What of the postwar world? Where are we? Is there any basis for assessment and prediction? The second installment of world conflagration seemingly resolved little more than the first. Problems existing prior to the war were still extant. Germany was defeated, but totalitarianism was not. The main fascist powers collapsed, but fascism still lurked on the sidelines. Nationalism, racism, and prejudice continued to flourish. And the communist movement was stronger than ever.

Like the United States in World War I, Russia proved herself in World War II. Furthermore, communism was soon to spread through Eastern Europe, China, and Southeast Asia. All Asia was on the march as a result of wartime changes, and this development posed the possibility of another major shift in world power. Finally, democrats appeared still to be as much on the defensive after the war as before. The validity of these surface appraisals, of course, must await future verification.

Because Russia and America had emerged from the war as the two main world leaders, many analysts concluded that the world had become bi-polar. In accordance with her historic objectives in foreign policy, Russia was moving before the war's end to consolidate her position and insulate her borders with friendly buffer zones, especially in Eastern Europe. To this end she used diplomatic pressures, infiltration, and outright subjugation. Poland, Czechoslovakia, and the Baltic and Balkan countries soon fell under her sway. So, too, did Yugoslavia, until Marshal Tito broke away to organize an independent communist regime.

This Russian coalition was soon opposed by a free-world coalition led by the United States. Within two years after the war, America was developing measures to aid non-communist states and prevent Russian subversion from within and aggression from without. In 1947 Secretary of State Marshall announced the famous Marshall Plan to hurry European economic recovery from the damages wrought by the war. In 1949 America brought most of the free countries of Europe and North America into a defensive alliance called the North Atlantic Treaty Organization (NATO).

A *Tri-polar World?* The world thus appeared to be divided into two camps. But was it? Was it not really tri-polar, since a large portion of the globe was uncommitted to either camp? Leaders in the United States and Russia have long since demonstrated by their actions that their struggle has been much more than a simple rivalry between two giants. Both sides have competed vigorously for the allegiance of the uncommitted peoples. Both have waged a propaganda war; both have engaged in programs of economic and technical aid; and both have staunchly championed political efforts in those areas that favored their particular goals. As the uncommitted peoples have wavered between the two great camps, they have been building a separate camp of their own. Wary of joining either side, they

hope to remain aloof from the struggle. They are especially anxious to avoid becoming involved in a war between Russia and the United States. They seek political and economic independence; they want an opportunity to develop their potentials—industrially, socially, and politically. We cannot conclude that they will necessarily accept a bid from either of the two great camps.

Decay of the Nationalistic World. Another feature of the postwar world has been a decline of nationalism outside Asia and Africa. At the end of World War I nationalism seemed to be at its zenith. But following World War II, conditions were quite different. Unqualified nationalism, in fact, seemed to be already in retreat in many places when the war began. National exaltation and enthusiasm, so apparent in 1914, were much less pronounced in 1941. National hatreds failed to run as deeply. There was no "jingoism" in England, no "hymn of hate" in Germany, and less evidence of mistreatment of persons of German ancestry in America. Before the war had ended, even the militantly nationalistic Hitler broadened his narrow "German" appeals so that they included "Aryans" and "Nordics." His armies numbered many foreigners from a dozen nationalities. These men were not recruited for the rank and file only, but for the officer corps as well, and even for his highly prized and trusted SS *élite.*

Possibly more indicative of the change is the character of the new giants on the world scene. Both the Soviet Union and the United States are made up of many nationalities, and even their names suggest no exclusiveness of national background. America has long prided herself on being a melting pot of national peoples, while the U.S.S.R. embraces the loyalties of many distinct national groups. Both appeal to multi-national symbols, and both mask their goals in internationalist trappings as well as nationalistic

In 1945 there was no question. This time America would lead in the movement toward world organization. Senator Tom Connally signs the U.N. Charter as President Truman and Secretary of State Edward Stettinius look on.

ones. Americans, for instance, are being encouraged to render more and more allegiance to the "Western" as well as to the "American" way of life. In fact, we now tend to identify the two as one.

Our postwar world is divided, but it is a new type of division. Instead of many small, independent, political units, large continental groupings seem to be emerging. The cry for self-determination can still be heard and will continue to be heard for some time. It is especially loud in Asia and Africa today. But the passage of time places a greater economic and military burden on small political units. Indications are that they will, at best, eke out but a precarious existence as independent states.

Only the future will reveal the true character of what is now forming. Even as we move toward new forms of organization, the old order is very much in evidence. The great masses of people throughout the world are still identified with national symbols. Governments remain mass-based, and mass attitudes and values continue to prevail. Total populations are still totally involved in total struggles for total victory and total

defeat. And, of course, international unity is still lacking. National hatreds continue to burn brightly and threaten what order there is in the world. The state of international anarchy, so apparent between the two great wars, has not disappeared. Nor does a new division into continental groupings promise relief from the ravages of anarchy. These large political units may be as separatist and antagonistic as smaller ones. As yet we may have merely reached the frontiers of new forms of international organization.

A More Determined Search for Collective Security. Shortly before the conclusion of the great holocaust, hopes for international organization were given new life in the United Nations. As World War II drew to a close, few questioned the need for an organization to replace the moribund League. We would try again! This time the United States showed no reluctance. Indeed, she would lead! At San Francisco in 1945 the member nations of the new organ pledged themselves to "refrain in their international relations from the threat or use of force against the territorial integrity or political independence of any state." Keeping this pledge required members to limit their struggles to such methods as the use of economic sanctions, propaganda, and fifth columns. But if it were kept, the world would have achieved a large degree of collective security.

To what extent does collective security exist today? The present missiles race between Russia and the United States, the massive armed establishments, and the intricate system of alliances belie a faith in the pledge as well as confidence in the United Nations itself. Everywhere states seek protection from the threat and use of force. The United Nations, of course, has promoted the settlement of many international disputes. Under its auspices, grave crises in such places as Palestine and Kashmir have been ameliorated. It has also been very

Heads of the two opposing camps during some of the most critical years of the Cold War—Eisenhower and Khrushchev.

successful in meeting problems of economic dislocation, hunger, and underdevelopment. It has facilitated the development of better communication, and it has provided diplomats with a meeting place and forum where countries can make their wants known. Here, too, they gain firsthand knowledge of each other's goals and methods.

Nevertheless, the machinery of the United Nations still provides no means for making unwilling parties accept settlement of a dispute. Governments must agree voluntarily. Thus, countries seeking change or protection of their interests cannot rely on the United Nations alone in achieving their goals. Collective security is, at best, only partially secured under its auspices. We only aspire to collective security; we have not realized it.

AMERICA IN A NEW ROLE

Beckoned to lead after World War I, America preferred innocence to responsibility, and declined. But World War II left us with no choice. We were literally thrust into a position of free-world leadership. Our new tasks proved difficult and frustrating. As the bulwark of the free world, we faced terrifying responsibilities, especially for a people unaccustomed to the uses and abuses of power. In our hands were placed new instruments of massive destruction. Yet their very use threatened to destroy the civilization we were committed to defend. In a world where little collective security exists, abandonment of the threat to use our great power might be suicidal. On the other hand, its use might also be suicidal. Another global holocaust, even though we were victorious, might leave us too weak to preserve the values for which we fought. This is the practical dilemma we face.

A half-century ago we were innocent of our potential might and the responsibilities it entailed. Now we are immersed in those responsibilities. We cannot renounce them in the name of virtue. We risk destruction of our own values in our defense of them. The course we follow is not altogether one of our own choosing. Paradoxically, in the hour of our greatest strength, we seem less able to do as we like than we were in our national infancy. Despite our great strength we are an innocent nation in a wrathful world.

COLD WAR AND COEXISTENCE

A major road block to the resolution of the American dilemma has been the Cold War. At the close of the second great war, the United States was far more secure and satisfied in her victory than was Russia. She sought to re-establish the balance of power disturbed by the Axis powers; she viewed herself as a powerful "have" state; and she sought to rehabilitate and repair the damages caused by the war so that everyone might get on with the business at hand. Russia, however, viewed things quite differently. Although her position was improved immensely, she sought to consolidate her strength and expand her influence through Eastern Europe into the Baltic and the Mediterranean.

Eastern Europe had been a vital factor in the outbreak of both world wars, and it was there that the Cold War began. Eastern Europe, is, after all, an ancient crossroad between Asia and Europe, Russia and the West. And Russia is vulnerable through Eastern Europe. During the war, Stalin was keenly interested in dissuading the Anglo-American alliance from attacking through the Balkans, which he had staked out for his Red Army. He was successful, too, in getting Roosevelt to agree to stop just short of Berlin at the Elbe River in Germany. General Patton was ordered not to occupy Prague, Czechoslovakia, when only a few miles from the city. The fate of the Balkans was further sealed by deciding to support the communist Tito rather than Mikhailovitch in Yugoslavia.

The war ended with the Red Army in control of Eastern Europe. Shortly after the war, coalition governments of communists and noncommunists were overthrown by communist coups. As a result, the Kremlin emerged dominant everywhere from the Baltic to Bulgaria. An iron curtain, in Churchill's historic phrase, fell across Europe. But Russia failed to obtain her objectives in the Mediterranean. Almost immediately after the war, the Kremlin began pursuing a policy aimed at controlling Greece and Turkey, the two keys to a strong Mediterranean position. But Russian attempts were thwarted by an aroused President Truman in March, 1947, when he obtained congressional approval for his Truman Doctrine, which pledged both economic and military aid to Turkey and Greece. In September, 1951, both states were invited to join the North Atlantic Treaty Organization.

With the announcement of the Truman Doctrine the lines were clearly drawn. Soon a broad chasm separated the two former allies. The Cold War had begun. Russia was on the attack, and America was committed to containing her and resisting the advance of communist ideology. Both countries fought with every available resource.

As the Cold War developed, Russia increasingly took the offensive and held it. Politically, she kept the world tense by igniting and fanning a number of "brush fires" on her periphery. The United States and her allies were kept busy answering fire alarms in Iran, Berlin, Korea, Indo-China, Suez, Quemoy, and Lebanon. Ideologically, the Kremlin waged a vigorous propaganda campaign that pictured the West as imperialistic, warlike, and decadent. In the economic sphere, Russians challenged the West to an economic race and proposed that the winner be declared victor in the Cold War. In this way the Kremlin sought to avoid a "hot war" and posed as the champion of world peace.

Russian strategy and tactics kept America and the West on pins and needles. A preventive war was unthinkable to most Americans. We sought to maintain the *status quo*. With Russia on the attack, we have usually been forced to concede the first blow in any bout. This has placed a high premium on our skill at counterpunching and retaliation. We have not always been successful. A firm defense is inevitably more difficult to maintain than an offensive posture. For the offense enjoys the advantage of surprise and sudden movement. America's role has been a trying one. We were, after all, unprepared for world leadership and largely inexperienced in the arts of diplomacy.

AMERICAN FOREIGN POLICY

Russia's challenge has seemingly produced a bipartisan American foreign policy. Democrats and Republicans, although divided on domestic issues, have endorsed a united front in the field of international diplomacy. There are important exceptions, of course, but on the critical issues, both parties have stood together. On the other hand, however, our failures and our inability to gain the offensive stimulated a vigorous controversy over the conduct of our foreign policy. One school, led by such diplomats and historians as the late John Foster Dulles and Professor Frank Tannenbaum, has maintained that the American approach to foreign affairs must be based solidly on moral and ideological foundations. There are real and vital differences in outlook and commitment to principle between East and West, this group maintains, and we cannot close our eyes to them. Our conflict with the communists is essentially ideological, rather than a simple power clash. This ideological difference deeply influences the treatment of human beings and has deep consequences for the future. Morality, moreover, is one of our strongest weapons, and if not confused with self-righteousness, may help us win the Cold War. Dexter Perkins, a most able historian, argues convincingly that men are not yet equipped to understand or assess the infinite ramifications of international power relationships. As we shall see in a later chapter, not even the experts have the necessary tools to measure all the power components. Furthermore, Perkins points out that our behavior patterns indicate rather conclusively that there is a monotonous regularity with which men turn to principles and morals. If men must have moral standards, these standards will influence foreign policy. Critics should not attack the tendency to moralize as much as how men moralize, Perkins says. Ideas and ideals are not just "frosting" or mere rationalization. They are important motivating factors. They are, according to Perkins, "mainsprings

Communist China's Premier Chou En-Lai (receiving bouquet) visits India to keep the Communist camp's bid open to India—one of the leading uncommitted nations. India's Prime Minister Nehru is at the far right.

of that courageous devotion which brings victory." No government can treat its population as if morals were nonexistent. None dares try! While not forswearing power politics completely, then, Perkins feels that we must beware of cynical bargains based on power calculations only. For example, some members of this school might say that we should not allow Red China to "shoot her way into the United Nations," however firm her grip on the Chinese mainland.

The second school, led by George Kennan, former ambassador to the Soviet Union, and the professor and scholar Hans Morgenthau, stresses the need to follow our national self-interest, irrespective of larger moral considerations. We must do those things that are necessary for our survival and the maintenance of our relative power position in the world. The diplomat must not be a moralist, these people believe, for it is the task of a diplomat to reduce frictions, find solutions to conflicts, and preserve the balance of power in a world where there is no centralized government or authority to enforce "right" and morality. We must be "realists," not "idealists," in our approach to world affairs. This means we must recognize that international law has lost much of its punch. Our policy, therefore, cannot be based on legal rules and moral restraints in situations where governments can refuse to abide by them. This school counsels us to be guided by actions and events rather than by what men say. They would consider the influence of ideology as just one more power factor to be weighed against other factors.

What has been the actual character of our policy? First of all, Americans seek to maintain the *status quo*—to keep power relationships as they are. Above all, we seek to keep the Cold War from developing into a hot one. We are more or less committed to the principle of coexistence. This means that we agree to exist alongside Russia and confine our struggles to forms of non-violent competition as long as Russia does not upset the international balance of power.

Political, economic, religious, and scientific trends have posed a profound threat to the world. Violent conflict and war seem ever to loom on the horizon. War itself has become more frightening, more destructive. Science has unleashed great power and introduced rapid change, but has not told us

"*That's what's wrong with the world. Our moral values haven't kept pace with our technical progress.*"

how to use this power. New military weapons have increased the vulnerability of populations to attack. New political methods have increased the size of armies and the effectiveness of government. New economic methods have industrialized our military establishments, and propaganda mechanisms have increased hatred and fanaticism. We are, in a sense, innocent victims of our own inventions. Modern nations are what General Omar Bradley called them, "nuclear giants and ethical infants." But need we look to the dark side? The dire predictions of today may well prove to be as erroneous as the naive optimism of yesterday.

SOME WORDS OF SUMMARY

Before the ink dried on the Treaty of Versailles, forces were at work dissolving the hopes that had heartened millions at the turn of the century. The decline of the international economic community, a retaliatory and humiliating peace, and the climax of nationalistic feelings destroyed Wilson's dreams. Communist and fascist totalitarian regimes soon challenged the march of democratic institutions throughout the world. As the center of power shifted out of Europe toward Russia and America, the democracies were left poorly protected. The United States declined leadership, refused to join the League of Nations, and left the weakened, jealous, and divided powers of Britain and France in command.

A sluggish and innocent America awoke to the danger just in time to mobilize her power for the contest. But it took a war to do it, and not until she was ruthlessly attacked did she go to work in earnest. The war itself actually began with the Japanese aggression in Manchuria, although the battle lines were clearly drawn in the Spanish Civil War when most of the major powers became involved either directly or indirectly. The climax came with the German invasion of France and the attack by Japan on Pearl Harbor.

Victory in World War II left America and Russia dominant on the international scene and the world's population in danger of mutual annihilation. Prophets of doom replaced the utopian prophets of an earlier war, and pessimism abounded as men attempted to read the signs of the future with tools no more adequate than the optimists had employed earlier in the century.

The postwar world was still divided. Two great centers of power, Russia and America, were now bidding against each other for the allegiance of a third group, the uncommitted peoples. But as the uncommitted groups wavered between the two great camps, they begin building a camp of their own and showed more hesitancy about joining either side. As this tri-polar world took shape, it appeared that unqualified nationalism was giving way to a new type of world division and organization—continental groupings.

Despite the erosive effects of rampant nationalism between the two great wars and the emergence of new power divisions after World War II, people everywhere sought collective security. In 1945, with America leading, they enthusiastically replaced the League of Nations with the United Nations. But collective security has not been realized despite the success of the United Nations in economic and political endeavors. Nation-states, therefore, still must rely on their own resources in the last analysis to protect their interests.

Most significant for Americans has been their new role of free-world leadership. Innocent of the uses of power in global terms, faced with a Cold War, inexperienced in the arts of diplomacy and leadership, Americans are confronted with a real dilemma. They must threaten to use overwhelming power while knowing that its actual use may bring about mutual devastation that threatens to destroy the very things they are sworn to preserve.

FURTHER ROADS TO LEARNING

GENERAL ACCOUNTS

R. Aron, *The Century of Total War* (Boston: Beacon, 1955). A far-reaching analysis of the world situation and what created it.

E. Carr, *The Twenty Years' Crisis* (London: Macmillan, 1946). A challenging analysis peppered with a few personal biases.

W. Churchill, *The Second World War*. Six vols. (Boston: Houghton Mifflin, 1948-1953). A rewarding series by the most literate political participant of the period.

H. Gatzke, *The Present in Perspective* (Chicago: Rand McNally, 1957). A short history of the action-packed, post-World War II years.

F. Gilbert and G. Craig, eds., *The Diplomats, 1919-1939* (Princeton: Princeton University Press, 1953). An excellent symposium covering the diplomacy of these years.

J. Ortega y Gasset, *The Revolt of the Masses* (New York: Norton, 1932). A very provocative interpretation of social values and social movements of the last half-century.

D. Perkins, *The American Approach to Foreign Policy* (Cambridge: Harvard University Press, 1952). By an eminent historian and proponent of the "idealist" approach.

A. Taylor, *The Struggle for Mastery in Europe, 1848-1918* (Oxford: Clarendon Press, 1955). Good background material on World War I.

A. Wolfers, *Britain and France Between the Two Wars* (New York: Harcourt, Brace, 1940). The best history of these two European democracies between the two wars.

SPECIAL STUDIES

G. Almond, *The Appeals of Communism* (Princeton: Princeton University Press, 1954). A thoughtful and scholarly analysis of what makes communism attractive.

T. Bailey, *A Diplomatic History of the American People*, 6th ed. (New York: Appleton-Century-Crofts, 1958). A tart, entertaining, and well-documented survey.

M. Beloff, *The Foreign Policy of Soviet Russia*. Two vols. (New York: Oxford University Press, 1952). A solid and superb survey.

P. Birdsall, *Versailles Twenty Years After* (New York: Reynal and Hitchcock, 1941). A favorable reassessment of the much maligned treaty and Wilson's role in it.

C. Bowles, *The New Dimensions of Peace* (New York: Harper, 1955). A candid appraisal of the world situation after the Second World War.

C. Cruttwell, *History of the Great War* (Oxford: Clarendon Press, 1934). The military history of World War I.

S. Fay, *The Origins of the World War*, 2nd ed. (New York: Macmillan, 1930). A detailed work on the subject.

S. Halperin, *Germany Tried Democracy* (New York: Crowell, 1946). An examination of the problems during the Weimar Republic.

G. Kennan, *Realities of American Foreign Policy* (Princeton: Princeton University Press, 1954). A short and pointed statement of the "realist" approach to foreign policy.

J. Keynes, *The Economic Consequences of the Peace* (New York: Harcourt, Brace, 1920). The classic analysis of the economic problems of the Versailles Treaty.

M. von Montgelas, *The Case for the Central Powers* (New York: Knopf, 1925). A statement of the German "revisionist" position.

H. Morgenthau, *In Defense of the National Interest* (New York: Knopf, 1951). A vigorous statement of the "realist" pattern on foreign policy.

H. Nicolson, *Peacemaking, 1919* (London: Constable, 1933). The best brief discussion of the Versailles conference.

R. Niebuhr, *The Children of Light and the Children of Darkness* (New York: Scribner, 1944), and *The Irony of American History* (New York: Scribner, 1952). Outstanding examples of postwar pessimism.

H. Seton-Watson, *Eastern Europe Between the Wars, 1918-1941* (Cambridge: Cambridge University Press, 1945). The best work on this important area during the interwar years.

J. Wheeler-Bennett, *Brest-Litovsk, The Forgotten Peace* (London: Macmillan, 1939). Crisp and brilliant treatment of the treaty of 1918 between Germany and Russia.

FICTION AND DRAMA

M. Anderson and L. Stallings, *What Price Glory?* in *Three American Plays* (New York: Harcourt, Brace, 1926). A drama of disillusionment with World War I.

J. Dos Passos, *Three Soldiers* (New York: Modern Library, 1932). A novel portraying the depth of post-war disillusionment.

E. Hemingway, *For Whom the Bell Tolls* (New York: Scribner, 1940). A novel on the Spanish Civil War, which conveys a feeling for the over-all crisis.

N. Mailer, *The Naked and the Dead* (New York: Bantam Books, 1948). Portrays the psychological effect of the Second World War on the American soldier.

E. Remarque, *All Quiet on the Western Front* (Boston: Little, Brown, 1929). A picture of the horrors of World War I.

I. Silone, *Bread and Wine* (New York: Penguin Books, 1946); and *Seed Beneath the Snow* (New York: Harper, 1942). Two novels dealing with the crisis of totalitarianism.

FILMS

Causes and Immediate Effects of the First World War (International Geographic Pictures, 1939, 23 min., sound, black and white). A film covering events from Bismarck's Triple Alliance in 1882 through the treaties of Versailles and Lausanne.

Hiroshima (Prudential Life Insurance Company of America, 1958, 30 min., sound, black and white). Dropping of the first atomic bomb.

Prelude to War (United States Government, Office of Education, 1942, 54 min., sound, black and white). The background to World War II.

Threat to Freedom (National Educational Television, 1955, 29 min., sound, black and white). A televised discussion of the rise of totalitarianism.

The World at War (Office of War Information, 1943, 44 min., sound, black and white). A world at war from the invasion of Manchuria in 1931 until Pearl Harbor.

Toward an Ideal World of Justice and Cooperation

THEME

*. . . yet man's past advances together with the recent progress he has
made in achieving social justice at home and international organization abroad, offer him some real grounds for hope that he may one
day live in an ideal world of* justice *and* cooperation.

The Quest
for Social Justice in America
Since 1900

Progressivism and its offshoot,
the New Deal, gave a new perspective to the use
of governmental powers: that they should
be used to regulate the economy and to alleviate social
and economic ills. TVA's famous Wheeler Dam
on the Tennessee River
represents the practical application of this philosophy.

Modern man

lives, as we have just seen, in a world of conflict and tension. Divided and uncertain in his personal loyalties, he looks out on a world that is similarly divided against itself. While loyalties to family, business, or community compete in his personal life, his nation vies for position in the world struggle for power and ideological dominance. Everywhere he finds conflict, tension, uncertainty, and doubt. He yearns for the old certainties, the moral simplicities of an earlier age. He searches for some foothold from which he can get a running start to attack his problems and his doubts. He wants acceptance and he craves affirmation, a positive faith to give meaning and purpose to his life. He may find this positive faith in religion, or in a primitive loyalty to self and family, or perhaps in the business world; but the faith that he shares with most other Americans and binds him to them is his faith in a future world of justice and cooperation.

Throughout their history Americans have had faith in change, in progress, and a future perfection that would set right the injustices of today. They have felt that the blessings of the future would be payment enough for sufferings undergone on behalf of reform and progress. The great democratic upsurge that occurred during the late eighteenth and nineteenth centuries had as an article of faith the belief that tomorrow's children would live more peacefully and under greater justice than their parents. The Declaration of Independence was not so much a description of things as they were as of things as they ought to be. It looked to the future. Jefferson's words found echo in the social reforms and the strivings for perfection of the Jacksonian period, and the Civil War made certain that this heritage would be transmitted undivided.

THE DEMOCRATIC HERITAGE OF AMERICA

What is this American heritage? It is, first of all, a faith. As we saw in Chapter 9, it is a faith in democratic processes both in government and in society. It signifies a government answerable and responsible to the people, where ability, not hereditary or aristocratic connections, is the sole recommendation for public office. As a way of life, democracy has usually meant a faith in the dignity of the average man, his ability to govern himself, his right to life, liberty, and happiness, and his freedom to exploit as many opportunities as he possibly can. It has come to mean equality of treatment, the absence of special privileges not granted to all, the lack of invidious distinctions between persons in dress, titles, and rights. It can mean the right to as much education as a man can absorb, that ability rather than position be the sole yardstick for selection and advancement, or the willingness to accept on equal terms all men of whatever race, belief, or economic standing. These are the ideals of that democratic faith which is our most enduring heritage from the past as well as our brightest hope for the future.

This heritage was seriously shaken by the events of the post-Civil War era. The social and political consequences of industrialism, which we have discussed in earlier chapters, posed a critical challenge to democratic ideals. Accumulation of wealth in the hands of a few deepened the gulf between rich and poor; the city worker soon outnumbered independent farmers and both suffered from the periodic crises that overtook the new industrial capitalism; politics counted for little in the life of the nation, and America's heroes were now drawn from the ranks of the *nouveaux riches*. That the tremendous capacity for good and evil inherent in the ascendancy of the new men of wealth could be subject to any form of political control was anathema to most of the business leaders of that day. "God gave me my gold," was John D. Rockefeller's reaction.

Since 1900 the quest for social justice in America has been an attempt to adjust capitalism to democratic goals, to shorten the swing of the pendulum between American ideals and American practice. Though the pendulum is still swinging, the achievement forms one of the brightest pages in our history and one that is not very clearly understood either at home or abroad. Whether it is the Kremlin denouncing the "Wall Street imperialists," a midwestern farmer complaining about eastern financiers, or other domestic critics assailing the "business tycoons running the government," their criticisms would have been more appropriate a half-century ago. Vast changes in American life have taken place in the twentieth century but none greater than the dispersion of business ownership and direction and the use of governmental power to discipline American business and industry in the public interest.

THE BIG CHANGE*

America in 1900 was in many respects a very different country from the America we know today. The population and the industrial, cultural, and recreational centers were all located in the East. The potentialities for growth in California and the Southwest were largely unforeseen. Even the city of Los Angeles, threatening to outdistance all but New York among American cities in the 1960's, was a modest community of 100,000 residents at the turn of the century. What we have witnessed in the twentieth century is a relative decline in the economic, cultural, and political power of the East. A disproportionate share of the population growth since 1900 (from 75 to 175 million in 1960) has occurred in the states west of the Mississippi River. With population growth has come political as well as eco-nomic power for westerners. Indeed, it would have been impossible in 1900 for California to claim at the same time a vice-president, a chief justice of the Supreme Court, and a majority leader of the United States Senate, as it did at one point during the 1950's. No longer is it true, either, that all the great universities, orchestras, museums, galleries, libraries, and vacation centers are found east of the Appalachian Mountains. It would not be too much to say that these vast internal shifts in population within the United States have altered the social and political patterns of the country as dramatically as the flood of immigrants who came to these shores during the early part of the same period.

Even more striking is the contrast in social and economic conditions between 1900 and 1960. By latter-day standards the gulf in incomes between the rich industrialist and the average laborer in 1900 was staggering. In the year 1900 alone Andrew Carnegie

---

* A great deal of the discussion in this section is based on Frederick Lewis Allen's instructive and entertaining book, *The Big Change* (New York: Harper, 1952).

The contrast in living conditions was severe at the turn of the present century. The art gallery in William H. Vanderbilt's palatial New York mansion was a far cry from "the dens of death" where the "other half" lived.

earned an income of $23 million while workers in his plants were averaging less than $500. The Carnegie income, furthermore, was earned in a day before an income tax was levied and when the dollar was worth several times its inflated counterpart of 1960. By comparison, the largest reported income in 1950, $600,000 earned by Charles Wilson of General Motors, seems puny indeed, especially when we remember that the Internal Revenue Service claimed about two-thirds of that amount! At the other end of the scale, the average weekly wage in 1950— $60—was six times what it had been in 1900.

The well-to-do industrialist at the beginning of the century sought to live in a style befitting his position in American life. The contrast between his way of life and the way the average American lived was highlighted by the flamboyance with which the tycoon displayed his new wealth (what Thorstein Veblen called "conspicuous consumption"). Town houses were built to resemble European palaces and summer homes were copied after English country houses or French chateaus. Frederick Lewis Allen has described the ducal palace which George W. Vanderbilt built at Asheville, North Carolina. It was, he wrote, "designed by Hunt after the manner of the great castles of the Loire. It had forty master bedrooms, a Court of

Palms, an Oak Drawing Room, a Banqueting Hall, a Print Room, a Tapestry Gallery, and a Library with 250,000 volumes. It was surrounded by an estate which gradually grew until it covered some 203 square miles, giving Vanderbilt ample scope to exercise his interest in scientific farming and forestry." The Secretary of Agriculture lamented that Vanderbilt employed more men than the Department of Agriculture and spent more money on his estate than Congress appropriated for his department!

Though some of the tycoons lived more frugally, extravagance and display were the order of the day. Great balls and parties with hundreds of invited guests were a common occurrence. Not all could afford, as could James Hazen Hyde, to transform a New York restaurant into the Grand Trianon with marble statues and entertainers imported from France for the occasion. But lack of restraint was quite common. The famous ball given by the Bradley Martins at the turn of the century cost an estimated $369,000. On another occasion the entire cast of a Broadway comedy was brought to Newport by the Cornelius Vanderbilts to entertain their guests.

The newspapers, of course, heralded these sensational social events and offered pages of detailed comment. The American people had an opportunity to read of these extravagances and for many the contrast with their own lot was shocking. At this time even such later necessities as running water and inside toilets were found only in the better homes. Bathtubs were rare and telephones a luxury. Furthermore, the decade of the 1890's had been a difficult one for the workers. A severe depression beginning in 1893 had taken a heavy toll of the health and endurance of the laborers and their families. Even in 1900 some 6½ million men were still idle during some part of the year. The American workingman during this period, moreover, faced the increasing competition of immigrant labor from southern and eastern Europe, all at a time when the closing of the frontier signified that cheap public land was no longer available to settlement in the West. The labor movement was weak and almost powerless to protect the workers' interests. Organized labor numbered only 868,000 men in 1900 as compared with 15 million in 1950, and it faced the thinly veiled hostility of business and the courts as well as public opinion.

Not only were the wages of the average worker below what trained social workers of the period called a subsistence level, but the job itself demanded more in 1900. The normal work week was still 6 days of 10 hours each, while the garment trade worked 70 hours per week. These figures were almost halved during the next half-century. Safety features in these early factories were virtually unknown, and the hazard to life and limb was correspondingly greater. On the railroads and in the mines the danger was acute. In the single year of 1901, one of every 399 railroad employees was killed and one of every 26 was injured. Nor had the employment of children ended by the turn of the century. Of boys from 10 to 15 years of age, 26 per cent were "gainfully employed," along with 10 per cent of all girls in the same age bracket. Most of these youngsters worked

on farms, but at least a quarter-million of them were working in factories and mills. The meaning of all this was summed up by Robert Hunter in 1904 in his book called *Poverty*, in which he estimated that there were at least 10 million paupers in the United States, of whom 4 million were public charges.

WHY NO GREATER PROTEST?

Why, we may ask, was there no greater protest at these shocking conditions? Why did socialism and similar doctrines have no greater appeal? For one thing, there was in America the long-standing tradition of individualism and opposition to strong social action. From colonial times Americans had been suspicious of strong government and had won their liberty in a revolt against a would-be paternalistic government. Jefferson and others had waxed eloquent on the theme that concentrated political power inevitably corrupts and that "that government governs best which governs least." When we were yet an agricultural nation of independent and self-reliant farmers, we idealized the dispersion of political power into the local communities close to the people. The doctrines of Marxism and anarchism seemed alien to most Americans at the turn of the twentieth century, and they were in fact usually preached by aliens and recent immigrants. If radical changes were needed, America had her own "tough-minded" radical tradition, which such agrarian reformers as the Populists and others were trying to revive as the century ended. Furthermore, we must remember that shocking though the condition of the underprivileged in America was, it was frequently much improved over the poverty-ridden lands from which some of our people had come. There was, too, the strong belief nourished by the popular novels of Horatio Alger that despite the growing complexity of American society the deserving man could still rise to a position of dignity and reward.

The new capitalism that remade the face of America in the last third of the nineteenth century was based on a strong faith in free competition and a conviction that government should not interfere in economic affairs. Freedom from restraint and controls in the economic field was thought to be as basic a part of American liberties as free speech and a free press. By 1900, however, the belief of the average capitalist in competition had been seriously qualified by the ruinous, cut-throat fight for markets in the early railroad, oil, steel, and other industries. In several industries competition was controlled by prior market agreements known as pools, by the organization of trusts that held the stock of a number of formerly competing companies and operated them as a unit, or later by holding companies, which were completely new corporations that bought the stock of various companies and thereby controlled their operations. The Sherman Antitrust Act of 1890 was aimed at restoring competition in major industries by prohibiting combinations that restrained trade, but owing to the attitude of the courts and the lack of governmental determination to enforce it, the law had done little by 1900 to halt the tendency toward concentration.

Critics insisted that business consolidation and concentration were leading straight to monopoly, which would leave both consumer and worker at the mercy of big business. The inflated stock of the new consolidated companies, they insisted, was unjustified and represented only the capitalization of hoped-for earnings. Defenders pointed to the advantages of integration, especially the efficiency that came from large-scale production and which would lead to lower costs to consumers. Rockefeller ascribed the success of his Standard Oil Company to the quality and cheapness of its products. The company, he wrote, "has spared no expense in utilizing the best and most efficient method of manufacture. It has sought for the best superintendents and workmen and paid the best wages. It has not hesitated to sacrifice old machinery and old plants for new and better ones."

THE "MANAGERIAL REVOLUTION"

One of the striking changes in American business during the twentieth century, as we saw in an earlier chapter, has been the shift of ownership out of a few into many hands and the rise of a new class of professional managers who direct American industry without owning it. In the type of capitalism that prevailed in 1900, the capital was put up by the men who ran the concerns and who felt a direct, proprietary interest in their operations. Carnegie, for example, owned 58 per cent of the stock of Carnegie Steel Company, while American Telegraph and Telephone Company had only 7,000 stockholders, a far cry from the more than a million who own shares in the company today. The owner-managers resented any outside interference with their companies; company records were generally not published, and even the government could not get information about them.

But since 1900 there has taken place what James Burnham called the "managerial revolution," which means that the big modern enterprise in America today is run by hired management. The manager of a corporation has become not only more professional, meaning that he holds his job because he is good at it, but like all professional men he has a responsibility to society as a whole. He must, of course, make money for the company, but even in doing this he avoids the impression of being exclusively concerned with profit and loss. As the chairman of the Standard Oil Company of New Jersey wrote, a modern manager must so conduct his business "as to maintain an equitable and working balance among the claims of the various directly interested groups—stockholders, employees, customers, and the public at large."

A CHANGING ROLE FOR GOVERNMENT

Another aspect of American business in 1900 which contrasts sharply with conditions some 60 years later was the almost complete lack of interest on the part of government in its operations. This laissez-faire attitude toward economic affairs was shared by both major political parties during the last four decades of the nineteenth century. Since there was no concern with business, there seemed to be no need for a Department of Commerce or Labor, a Federal Trade Commission, or a Federal Reserve System. As yet, the Interstate Commerce Commission, created in 1887, had but few and uncertain powers over railroad operations. Moreover, all operations of the national government in 1900 were extremely limited, and the entire national budget that year amounted only to $500 million. This figure can be contrasted with the New York State budget for 1960, which hovered around $2 billion.

WHAT CAUSED THE BIG CHANGE?

It is now clear that a veritable revolution has taken place in American social, political, and economic life in the twentieth century. But what caused it? What were the factors that converted a country of big business and weak government, new rich and underprivileged workers, into the dynamic industrial democracy of the 1960's? There was very little violence, no civil war, and no drastic changes in government or constitution.

THE MORAL REVOLUTION

What happened in this period was that Americans returned to their basic and traditional attitudes regarding fair play, equality of opportunity, and the meaning of democracy. This change was prompted in large part by the monopolistic threat implicit in big business. Frederick Lewis Allen called it a "recovery of conscience," suggesting that it was a moral rather than an economic revolt. It was summed up in the moralistic evangelism of Theodore Roosevelt, a prophet of the big change. The restless and dynamic T.R., himself no radical or have-not, preached against the "malefactors of great wealth" who had denied equality of opportunity to other Americans while clamping a stranglehold on the nation's wealth themselves. He dramatized for a whole generation of Americans the meaning of the changes that had overtaken their way of life. Men and women who knew nothing of economic theory responded to the dramatic preachments of Roosevelt and the muckraking journalists who wrote with burning indignation of the ruthless deals of a Rockefeller, the corruption of city and state politics, the frauds of the patent-medicine trust, and unsanitary conditions in the meat-packing and other food-processing industries.

REFORM WITHOUT BLUEPRINTS

The changes that took place were piecemeal and not part of an over-all program. The basic method, when some injustice or malfunctioning of the economy or government threatened, was not to overthrow the government or draw up a blueprint for a new economy but to adjust and tinker with the present system until it worked better. By these means Americans hoped to preserve the values of a free economy and a democratic government. Each problem was tackled separately on its own merits. If the gulf between incomes was growing, then the answer was an income tax. If trusts were suppressing competition and opportunity, break them up! If widespread unemployment threatened the economy, a program of public works and unemployment relief must be inaugurated. At no time, even in the midst of the New Deal, was there much over-all planning. Americans have long been wary of blueprints for the future and suspicious of theories and ideologies.

Many foreign students of American politics, as well as many Americans themselves, have asked why political parties in the United States are not organized on a clear-cut division between liberals and conservatives. Why is there no labor party as in England, so that the interests of the workers might be served? Part of the answer may lie in the fear which Americans have had of parties that are based on a frank recognition of class distinctions. It certainly is out of keeping with the fluid class structure in the American heritage and most Americans tend to view foreign class systems unfavorably. Furthermore, the two major parties, whose primary goal is to win elections and not sharpen political issues, have proved themselves flexible in responding to any widespread unrest or discontent. One cynical commentator once remarked that the Republican Party would give the American people socialism if it was convinced this was the only way to win elections!

Actually, no major American political party has ever been able to risk close ties with a single, or even a limited, number of economic, social, or class interests. Nor have major parties been able to afford the luxury of doctrinaire platforms and programs. To do so would be tantamount to party suicide. Here is why. Americans use the single-mem-

ber district system in electing their state and national officials and the winner takes all in each district. For example, in a congressional district casting 300,000 votes, a major party may garner 149,000 votes and elect no one from that district. Likewise, out of a million votes cast in a state like Minnesota, a party's presidential candidate can receive 400,000 or more votes and lose all the state's electoral votes. It is, in fact, possible for a party to obtain 30 to 35 per cent of the total vote for members of the national House of Representatives and not elect more than a handful. Our system, unlike that of many foreign countries, does not guarantee parties a number of legislative seats or electoral votes somewhat proportionate to the popular vote the party obtains. If a party is to withstand such losses and still make a strong bid for the majority of electoral votes for president, as well as a majority of the 437 seats in the House of Representatives and 100 in the Senate, it dares not alienate too many potential supporters. For a nucleus of several million voters must be kept receptive to its appeals if it is to win majorities in enough states and districts to capture control of the government. When a party appears unable to make a strong bid for power, voters fear they are wasting their votes. A major party must therefore appeal to every voter and every interest it can, from coast to coast, across sectional and state lines. It cannot become too closely identified with special or sectional interests, for that may alienate too many voters who are not closely identified with those interests. This helps explain why party platforms tend to be broad, ambiguous, and full of platitudes. It also explains why third parties featuring a doctrinaire approach to political and social questions or representing narrow or special interests have always fared poorly in American elections. Even those who are sympathetic to a third party have pragmatically refused to "throw their votes away" and preferred to support the lesser evil among those contenders who had a chance to win.

Perhaps most important in explaining why the underprivileged in America have never been attracted by ideologically based political movements is the very real expectation that they too will be given a chance to achieve a middle-class status with its opportunities for education, automobiles, homes, and leisure which workers and farmers in other lands despair of ever attaining. We need only compare the relatively class-free connotations of a word like "worker" with its German equivalent *Arbeiter*, or "farmer" with *Bauer*, to see how far America has departed from the deeply class-conscious feudal heritage of Europe. The secret of American success in dealing with the problems of a mass society has been continual, experimental, untheoretical adaptation to change so that today's dissatisfied may hope that they or their children may become the satisfied of tomorrow.

THE PROGRESSIVE MOVEMENT

What were the important steps in this quest for social justice in America during the twentieth century? The first steps came in the complex, many-sided reform movement that began early in the century and lasted until America's entry into World War I in 1917. *Progressivism*, as it was called, infected both political parties and sought to restore government to the hands of the people, where it might be used to regulate business, finance, industry, and agriculture in the interest of the many rather than the few. In Europe, where the effects of industrialism had been felt much earlier, the need for government to play a larger role in controlling business and protecting the welfare of the underprivileged had already been recognized. The Germany of Otto von Bismarck had adopted a national program of social security, including workmen's compensation,

old-age pensions, and government care of the sick in the 1880's as an answer to the radical Marxian socialists. In England there followed in the early twentieth century the New Liberalism, which resulted in national housing legislation, old-age pensions, minimum-wage laws, accident compensation, and the like.

American Progressives, as we saw in Chapter 19, sought first to bring government closer to the people through such changes in the structure of government as direct primaries, direct election of senators, and the initiative, referendum, and recall. The objective of all these measures was to give the average man a bigger voice in government and thereby loosen the stranglehold that corrupt politicians and their business allies had fastened on the national capitol, state capitols, and city halls throughout the country. On the city level the Progressives concentrated on wiping out graft and scrapping archaic political institutions. They fought, too, for slum clearance, more playgrounds, and low-cost milk for children; and they supported settlement houses, such as the famous Hull House in Chicago, where slum-dwellers were given aid and comfort as well as encouragement for the future.

The Progressives' economic program called for more control of big business. A group of writers, whom Theodore Roosevelt branded the "muckrakers," blazed the way with their sensational exposés of the evils of business monopoly and its ties to corrupt politicians. Ida Tarbell, in a series of articles that outlined the history of Rockefeller's Standard Oil Company, set the pattern by describing the way in which Rockefeller had ruined competitors and destroyed competition in the oil industry. Theodore Roosevelt revived the Sherman Antitrust Act and won a reputation as a "trust-buster" for his dramatic prosecution of a number of the larger business monopolies. On both state and national level considerable legislation was

Henry Ford proudly displaying his first automobile.

passed aimed at controlling business abuses, especially in the railroad industry, outlawing child labor, providing workmen's compensation, and regulating the hours and conditions of labor. Roosevelt's great interest in the West spurred him to make his greatest contribution—his conservation program to protect the nation's timber lands and mineral deposits.

The climax of the Progressive movement came during the first administration of Woodrow Wilson, when more reform legislation was passed than by any other administration up to that time. The banking laws were completely revised and the present system of Federal Reserve banks was established; easier credit for hard-pressed farmers was made available through a system of federal farm loan banks; and the Clayton Act defined unfair methods of business competition and exempted labor unions from the antitrust laws. A new Federal Trade Commission was also established to investigate and issue warnings to firms suspected of unfair methods of competition. Further legislation established the eight-hour day for railroad workers, improved the working conditions of seamen, and sought to outlaw

child labor nationally. The last measure, however, was later declared unconstitutional by the Supreme Court in 1918.

Sweeping changes had come to America with the Square Deal of Theodore Roosevelt and the New Freedom of Woodrow Wilson. The traditional laissez-faire attitude toward business had all but been reversed; humanitarian reforms had been carried out in the cities; a political cleansing at all levels had taken place. Perhaps most significant was the emergence of a new concept of government as an engine of social welfare that might be used to redress some of the injustices of society. The Progressive period had demonstrated, too, that progress and reform depended heavily on strong executive leadership at the national level. Congressmen, without such leadership, had often reflected only the tug of local interests and sometimes succumbed to the lure of lobbyists. Even the political parties were essentially only combinations of local machines lacking strong national cohesion. Both Theodore Roosevelt and Wilson had recognized this situation and had effectively combined the role of chief executive with that of party leader.

THE DYNAMICS OF MASS PRODUCTION

As the nation was taking its first steps toward a more just social order during the Progressive era, the economic foundations for this socio-political transformation were being laid by the system of mass production. It was Henry Ford who proved the dynamism of mass production when he produced his Model "T" in 1908. The production of a machine of interchangeable parts followed by raises in wages to the unheard-of level of $5 per day and cuts in the price of Fords demonstrated tremendous possibilities: more production meant reduced costs; higher wages meant an expanding market. The price of Fords dropped steadily from $950 to $290 in 1924. By the 1920's another important principle that stimulated lavish automobile production was introduced when Ford competitors sought to make the public style-conscious and then periodically changed the styles of their cars. But by this time Ford had proved his point. Installment buying, introduced in the 1920's, put more automobiles, as well as other durable goods, into the hands of more and more people.

During the decade of the 1920's a reform-weary people, rendered indifferent by prosperity to the great social issues of the Progressive years, reverted to the conservatism and nationalism that are so typical of postwar eras. The persuasive example of the Progressive reformers could not be altogether ignored, and Republican administrations during the 1920's continued and even expanded some of the reform and regulatory measures of the earlier era. But after the scandal-stained administration of President Harding, Calvin Coolidge caught the dominant spirit of the 1920's with his well-publicized remark, "The business of America is business." This statement summed up the laissez-faire and anti-reform philosophy that governed the administrations of the period. The national administration, in direct contrast to the Progressive years, heartily approved the consolidation of American business in fewer hands. Many of the old regulatory commissions were staffed with men identified with those very business interests they were supposed to police. Taxes were steadily reduced, especially in the corporate and higher-income brackets. Government interference with business activity was countenanced only when it was designed to aid particular industries or vested interests, as was the case with the government's tariff

Depression - spawned housing in New York City's Central Park in the 1930's.

policy, which pushed levies to new all-time highs. These policies were accepted, even applauded, by most people so long as the frenzied prosperity of the 1920's spun on; but after the stock-market crash of 1929 the public mood changed rather quickly. The ensuing depression, ugliest in American history, brought a wail of discontent from farmers, workers, small businessmen, and white-collar workers generally. Champions of reform and positive government, long silent, began to call once more for greater controls over economic activity and national programs to relieve suffering and want.

THE NEW DEAL

During the New Deal, Americans completed and extended many of the old Progressive reforms. Contrary to what many contemporaries may have thought, the domestic program of Franklin D. Roosevelt was not a revolutionary break with the past. Since the 1890's the national government had assumed an increasingly active and positive role in safeguarding human welfare. Roosevelt's New Deal was to bring government and the economy abreast again after a lag during World War I and its aftermath. Some aspects of the New Deal, such as the Tennessee Valley Authority and the social security program, did represent a sharp break with the past in the greatly expanded role of government they entailed; but most of the New Deal measures were a continuation of trends begun by the Progressives or even earlier by the Populists: aid to the farmers, controls over business, stock-market checks, banking reforms, lower tariffs, and collective bargaining for labor.

The political impact of the great depression of the 1930's was sharp and enduring. Republicans and Democrats alike have since come to accept the two cardinal principles that emerged from the despair and disillusionment it spawned: first, that the engines of government must be used, where necessary, to regulate economic life in the public interest; secondly, that government has an obligation to alleviate suffering and social injustice wherever they are known to exist. Under the New Deal the government took measures to remedy the banking crisis in several ways. A national bank holiday was declared and national inspection of banks was imposed as a condition for their reopening. Banks were barred from the investment business and deposits could be federally insured. As a result of the depression of the 1930's, government replaced Wall Street as the balance wheel of American finance. Stock-market excesses that had helped create the panic of 1929 were now carefully controlled by congressional legislation. The famous N.R.A. (National Recovery Administration) and A.A.A. (Agricultural Adjustment Administration) of the early New Deal were legislative measures designed to promote business and farm recovery. In both cases the national government cooperated with producers to limit the output of commodities in order to raise prices and thereby supposedly promote recovery.

A whole host of New Deal measures illustrated the second principle of using government as an instrument of social welfare. Roosevelt had none of Hoover's misgivings about using national government credit and monies for the relief of unemployment and distress, and soon a vast relief program was worked out in cooperation with the states. Congress provided funds to meet the special needs of young men, school children, homeowners, and farm-debtors. A huge public-works program involving professional as well as manual skills provided an alternative to the European "dole" system, so that the unemployed might maintain their self-respect through useful employment rather than receive direct handouts from the government. Among the more enduring of the Roosevelt administration's social reforms was

Along with the problem created by a disastrous depression, Roosevelt's New Deal administration had to face the crisis of the dust bowl, a vast area of the prairie states where thoughtless agricultural practices combined with drought and wind to turn the once-rich country into a barren desert of dunes of topsoil and forsaken farms.

the social security program, under which the aged, the unemployed, and the handicapped were to receive compensation from funds contributed by workers, employers, and government.

The New Deal also encouraged the organization of labor, long weakened by worker apathy, unfriendly administrations, and hostile public opinion. The economic crisis of the 1930's had created unwonted misery, even tragedy, for many industrial workers, and many now believed that organization was their only weapon against future impotence. The Roosevelt administration was unusually friendly to labor and reaped the benefits at the polls. A number of new laws assured labor's right to organize, bargain, strike, and be free of coercion and discrimination. This new freedom and encouragement, as we saw in Chapter 12, brought on a wave of labor-union recruitment and organizing activity during the 1930's and touched off a series of violent clashes as organizers moved into the hitherto unorganized heavy industries and used the sit-down strike and other tactics against resisting employers. By the end of the decade the automobile and steel industries had been almost completely unionized. Many people soon began to feel that the Roosevelt administration had perhaps gone too far in its concessions to labor and a sharp reaction followed in the late 1940's.

When the reforming zeal of the 1930's

had spent itself, an evaluation of the changes in American life wrought by the New Deal was more possible. On the debit side, there could be no question that it had vastly increased the national debt, stimulated greater class consciousness among workers and farmers, fostered government bureaucracy, and raised a serious question of how far economic controls could be extended without sacrificing traditional freedoms. On the credit side of the ledger, the Roosevelt measures had seen the American people through the most serious economic crisis they had ever encountered, yet preserved the capitalistic essence of the economy, fostered a more equitable distribution of the national wealth, and conserved many of the country's resources. Perhaps most important, it had given labor and agriculture the tools and the encouragement to maintain and promote their own interests in an increasingly complex economy, and it had given them a vision of a world of social justice where workers and farmers could live comfortably and prosperously, secure from the vicissitudes of a boom and bust economy.

By mid-century the strongly individualistic, socially indifferent businessman of 1900 had given way to the harried, sensitive executive whose business was hemmed in by government supervision and controls on the one side and strong labor unions on the other. It was scarcely a socialist order—management and ownership remained in private, conservative hands—but it was also far from the free, untrammeled enterprise of the early twentieth century. The best way to describe this new economic order is probably to call it a modified capitalism, in which a great deal has been done to right the grievances and inequalities of historic capitalism while still preserving its essential strength and vigor. It is precisely this transformation of American capitalism which few Europeans and not many Americans have understood.

THE QUICKENING TEMPO SINCE 1940

Even those who saw the meaning of these changes have not all sensed the quickening of the tempo of change since 1940. We need only contrast the mood and temper of America in 1940 with the 1950's to see the difference. In 1940 the United States was still not out of the depression, unemployment still affected several million, the population had leveled off, and the birth rate was low. Economists were speaking of a mature economy, meaning that America had reached the limits of its economic expansion, and the prevailing mood was one of caution, distrust of business, and fear of another depression. In 1955, to take the midway point of the 1950's, America experienced the most productive year of its history, unemployment was very low, and the birth rate was spiraling upward, indicating increasing confidence in the future. The economy was much sounder, most economists believed, and not based on the paper profits that had shored it up during the frenzied 1920's. The real wages of labor were up, the industrial output per man-hour was far ahead of 1940, farmers were now sharing in the prosperity, and industries undreamed of in 1940 (plas-

tics, television, frozen foods, jet aircraft, and so on) were booming. Most Americans were confident and optimistic about the future, and business had largely succeeded in erasing the suspicions with which people had regarded it during the 1930's.

Vast social changes as well have occurred since 1940. The average size of family, on the decrease throughout the first part of this century, has begun once more to mount, even among families of wealth and education, where families have always been small. The divorce rate, which skyrocketed following World War II, tapered off during the 1950's. In the area of education important changes overtook the curriculum and teacher training, and more and more young people were going on to colleges and universities. The process of Americanization was accelerated with the coming of age of the first generation of Americans which, by reason of war and immigration policy, did not contain large unassimilated groups of the foreign-born. The position of the Negro in America has been greatly improved since 1940 with the dwindling of violence and lynching, wider participation in public, professional, and economic life, and the decline or end of segregation in the armed forces, public housing, transportation, colleges, and public schools. But perhaps most significant among the social changes since 1940 is the continued democratization of American life, the advance in opportunities open to most Americans in education, business, public life, and the professions, and the further decline of unearned distinctions in position, status, or standard of living. The quest for social justice in America, while still unrealized, goes forward with steady pace as the twentieth century moves on.

SOME WORDS OF SUMMARY

Americans throughout their history have had faith in progress and the ultimate achievement of social justice based on equality of opportunity and belief in the dignity of the average man. This heritage of faith was seriously shaken by the impact of late nineteenth-century industrialism and the grave social crises it precipitated. Since 1900 a massive attempt has been made to adjust capitalism to democratic ends by narrowing the gap between rich and poor and enlarging opportunity for the great masses of people. Socialism and other radical parties or movements have had little appeal because of our long-standing traditions of individualism, fear of strong government, and the belief that opportunities in America were still greater than anywhere else in the world.

The cause of the "big change" in America since 1900 is basically a "recovery of conscience," dramatized by humanitarians, reformers, and dynamic politicians such as Theodore Roosevelt and Woodrow Wilson. A series of pragmatic adjustments to correct social evils has taken place. During the Progressive era before World War I and at the height of the New Deal of the 1930's, Americans came to accept two important modifications of traditional laissez-faire doctrine: the regulation of economic life, where necessary, in the public interest; and the obligation of government to alleviate suffering and want. The basic economic underpinning for the socio-political transformation of America was the introduction of mass-production techniques and the growing social responsibility of business under the leadership of a new managerial class. The changes in American capitalism have produced a new and modified type of business enterprise, still based on private ownership and the profit motive, but now sharing greater responsibility and decision-making power with labor unions and a greatly expanded government.

FURTHER ROADS TO LEARNING

GENERAL ACCOUNTS

F. Allen, *The Big Change* (New York: Harper, 1952). An optimistic and interestingly written book about the transformation of America, 1900-1950.

R. Davenport and the editors of *Fortune*, *U.S.A.: The Permanent Revolution* (Englewood Cliffs, N. J.: Prentice-Hall, 1951). Presents a theme very similar to Allen's, that the recent changes in American life have been more sweeping and enduring than Americans themselves have realized.

H. Faulkner, *The Quest for Social Justice, 1898-1914* (New York: Macmillan, 1931). Probably the best general treatment of the Progressive movement in its early stages.

E. Goldman, *Rendezvous with Destiny* (New York: Knopf, Vintage Books, 1956). A spirited account of American liberalism from the late 1860's to the present that is very sympathetic to the New Deal.

R. Hofstadter, *Age of Reform* (New York: Knopf, 1955). An analysis of the intellectual background of modern reform movements from Bryan to F.D.R.

A. Link, *American Epoch* (New York: Knopf, 1955). A comprehensive textbook on twentieth-century American history.

W. White, *Autobiography* (New York: Macmillan, 1946). An important source for understanding the "revolt of the American conscience" by a Kansas editor who became a national figure.

SPECIAL STUDIES

F. Abrams, "Management's Responsibilities in a Complex World," *Harvard Business Review*, XXIX (May, 1951), pp. 29-34. A commentary on the shifting roles and changing responsibilities of business enterprise in American society.

F. Allen, *Only Yesterday* (New York: Harper, 1931, and many other editions). A classic social history that deals with the "Roaring Twenties."

A. Berle, Jr., and G. Means, *The Modern Corporation and Private Property* (New York: Macmillan, 1933). The first book to outline clearly the divorce of management from control in modern American corporations.

W. Binkley, *American Political Parties: Their Natural History*, 3rd ed. (New York: Knopf, 1958). A history of political parties that stresses the continuity of their economic policies.

D. Brogan, *Politics in America* (New York: Harper, 1954). A description of the American political processes and their anomalies by a distinguished British historian who possesses a remarkable sense of humor.

J. Burnham, *The Managerial Revolution* (New York: Day, 1941). An important book on the strategic role of the manager in modern corporate life.

H. Croly, *The Promise of American Life* (New York: Macmillan, 1911). A true Progressive's faith.

M. Fainsod *et al.*, *Government and the American Economy* (New York: W. W. Norton, 1959). This book analyzes the roles and responsibilities of government in the economic realm during the present century.

E. Goldman, *The Crucial Decade: America, 1945-1955* (New York: Knopf, 1956). A competent survey of ten important years of recent history.

H. Hoover, *American Individualism* (Garden City, N. Y.: Doubleday, Page, 1922); also, Hoover's, *The Challenge to Liberty* (New York: Scribner's, 1934). Both volumes are lucid and terse statements of a political philosophy that is opposed to the philosophy of the New Deal.

M. Komarovsky, *The Unemployed Man and His Family* (New York: Dryden Press, 1940). How unemployment affects the morale of the jobless.

M. Lerner, *America as a Civilization* (New York: Simon & Schuster, 1957). A profile of the developing American society that provides a myriad of insights into the changing roles of government and business.

W. E. Leuchtenburg, *Perils of Prosperity*, 1914-1932 (Chicago: The University of Chicago Press, Phoenix Books, 1958). Covers much the same ground as Allen's *Only Yesterday* with greater perspective but less wit and style.

A. Link, *Woodrow Wilson and the Progressive Era, 1910-1917* (New York: Harper, 1954). An excellent general survey of Wilson's relationship to the currents of Progressivism.

D. Perkins, *The New Age of Franklin D. Roosevelt* (Chicago: The University of Chicago Press, Phoenix Books, 1957). A balanced, well-written introduction to the New Deal era.

H. Pringle, *Theodore Roosevelt* (New York: Harcourt, Brace, Harvest Books, 1957). Though not entirely sympathetic to Roosevelt, it is still the best available biography of this colorful leader.

A. Schlesinger, Jr., *The Crisis of the Old Order, 1919-1933* (Boston: Houghton Mifflin, 1957). In the first volume of a lengthy, projected treatment of the "Age of Roosevelt," we are given a brilliant synthesis of the ideas and events that shaped the New Deal.

D. Wecter, *The Age of the Great Depression, 1929-1941* (New York: Macmillan, 1948). A good, scholarly assessment of the social and cultural changes in American life associated with the depression of the 1930's.

FICTION AND DRAMA

E. Bellamy, *Looking Backward* (New York: Modern Library, and many other editions). A popular utopian novel purporting to view the America of 1887 from the vantage point of a perfect socialist order in the year 2000.

C. Brody, *Nobody Starves* (New York: Longmans, Green, 1932). A tragic story about the effects of the Great Depression.

J. Dos Passos, *U.S.A.* (New York: Harcourt, Brace, 1938). A trilogy that provides a panoramic view of American life during the first thirty years of this century.

E. Hemingway, *To Have and Have Not* (New York: Pocket Books, 1957). A satirical contrast of the lot of the unemployed at Key West with that of the decadent socialites who go south for the winter.

J. Herbst, *The Rope of Gold* (New York: Harcourt, Brace, 1939). An amazingly accurate and entertaining novel that depicts the economic conditions in America between 1932 and 1937.

J. Johnson, *Now in November* (New York: Simon & Schuster, 1934). An exceedingly well-written story that relates the tragic life on a run-down farmstead in Missouri during one of the worst droughts on record.

J. Steinbeck, *The Grapes of Wrath* (New York: Bantam Books, 1957). A powerful story of the survival of ideals amid poverty and degradation of the migratory farm families who moved from Oklahoma to California in the 1930's.

FILMS

Age of Reform (National Educational Television, 1956, 29 min., sound, black and white). A discussion of the book, *Age of Reform*, by Richard Hofstadter, cited above under "General Accounts."

Awakening Social Consciousness (National Educational Television, 1955, 29 min., sound, black and white). Televised discussion of the change in American economic attitudes during the early twentieth century.

Farewell to Yesterday (Films Inc., 1953, 90 min., sound, black and white). Fascinating newsreel history of the period from the Versailles Conference of 1919 to the close of the Korean War in 1953.

The Golden Twenties (McGraw-Hill, 1952, 68 min., sound, black and white). The pictorial counterpart to Frederick Lewis Allen's *Only Yesterday.*

Three R's—New Deal Version (National Educational Television, 1955, 29 min., sound, black and white). A televised discussion of Franklin D. Roosevelt's leadership in the 1930's and the legislation with which his name has become associated.

Two Decades of History (Teaching Film Custodians, 1947, 22 min., sound, black and white). A rich compilation of newsreel shots of events during the two decades from 1927 to 1947.

Woodrow Wilson: Spokesman for Tomorrow (McGraw-Hill, 1956, 27 min., sound, black and white). Through newsreel clips and reproductions of documents and cartoons, Wilson's life from 1910 to his death in 1924 is tastefully presented.

CHAPTER THIRTY

The Quest
for International Peace
and Order

The Security Council of the U.N. in session.

Our search

for social justice at home seems to be suspended in an outer world of conflict and insecurity. We needed an entire section of this book merely to sketch the background and salient features of this "time of troubles" in international relations. In the twilight of imperialism and colonialism, as we have seen, new and menacing forms of nationalism have shaken the world to its foundations. Ruthless forms of totalitarianism have arisen on the ashes of an almost forgotten peaceful, God-fearing, trade-minded world of nineteenth-century Victorians. Liberals and democrats all over the world have girded themselves for the final showdown, which they pray can somehow be averted. In their camp and in the camp of the potential enemy lie weapons more destructive and more terrifying than mankind has ever known. There is yet hope that the awful prospect of mutual annihilation will deter both sides from marching to a final Armageddon. Hope springs eternal even in hearts that have been chilled by the prospect of doom.

Although the world is still recovering from the wounds left by the second great war of this century, we have no time to lose. The tempo and violence of our times demand action. There is no escape. To this challenge Americans have addressed themselves since 1940. It has not been easy. For one thing, Americans were never schooled in world politics. Responsible action in international affairs meant not only changing our minds but our way of life as well. No longer could we go it alone; no longer could we afford the luxury of a puny military establishment. Americans did what they knew they had to do. They picked up the challenge of the totalitarians, assumed leadership of the free world, and fought a global war. After the war they put their economy at the service of their weaker allies, and they formed defensive alliances to stay the march of communism. For the first time in history they recognized that the world's struggles were their struggles.

WAR AND PEACE

THE DEMAND FOR PEACE

Yet direct entry into the world struggle in no way lessened our hopes and demands for peace. The demand for peace, in fact, is greater now than ever before. And the demand is heard throughout the world, not just in America. No doubt the Russian insistence that Americans are imperialistic warmongers and Russians a peace-loving people is a direct appeal to this widespread desire for peace.

Almost paradoxically, however, men persist in their old ways of doing and thinking, even while they demand peace. They still struggle for the world's wealth and resources, still cling to their prejudices and racial hatreds, still resort to violence at the least provocation. As badly as we may want peace, we are not goaded enough to secure it. It may be that we are unsure of what constitutes peace, or what it takes to obtain it. Are we sure that peace is a primary aim? Just what is peace?

In modern wars the entire enemy population becomes a target, and frequently civilians are caused more anguish than are soldiers. During World War II these Londoners were forced to sleep night after night in subway stations in order to escape the fury of the German blitz.

THE ANATOMY OF PEACE

Although definitions vary a great deal, *peace is usually believed to involve an absence of violence, especially armed violence.* Historically, however, the absence of violence has depended on an ability and willingness of some to use violence on others who refuse to obey the rules. A complete absence of violence has probably existed only in the imagination. For a condition of peace demands that someone be strong enough to keep the peace. Imagine for a moment a government that renounced the use of all violence. Could it remain a government? Anyone could overturn it. You will recall from Chapter 8 that governments need a monopoly of violence if they are to keep the peace and maintain order inside their own borders. Law or rules alone will not guarantee the peace. For someone must be willing to act on the law and see to it that others obey the rules. Historically, domestic peace has depended on five factors: (1) government command of sufficient military and police strength to overwhelm the physical threat of any rebel or outlaw group; (2) the existence of peaceful procedures for settling conflicts that arise in a society; (3) a system of law to provide a basis and justification for political actions; (4) general agreement on a common set of fundamental values and goals; and (5) loyalty of the people to the system.

THE ANATOMY OF WAR

Most of the time, however, we do not think of peace at the international level as the total absence of violence. Rather, we refer to the absence of a particular type of violence called war. *Generally, war refers to military combat between two or more trained military forces.* The military forces have usually represented someone other than themselves, such as a government, national state, city-state, emperor, feudal lord, religious group, or an ordinary bandit.

The above definition is hardly adequate, however. For war now, as in times past, involves more than just those who are locked in a military engagement. Throughout history ordinary citizens have often been the innocent victims of marauding armies. And today, everyone is involved in a way. The entire enemy population becomes a target. Civilians may be exposed to greater suffering than the military forces in certain instances. Japanese civilians, for example, suffered far greater damage from the atomic explosion at Hiroshima than did the Japanese military establishment.

This factor that makes war something other than just the business of men in uniform has in itself been responsible for seeking new ways of settling international conflicts. The degree to which men find war repugnant cannot be accurately measured.

Some authorities contend that war would never occur if it were completely odious to men. Others are convinced that there is a growing aversion to war. As we pointed out in Chapter 26, many people no longer accept war as a legitimate alternative for settling disputes when all other measures fail. The outcry to rid the world of war has been especially shrill since World War I. Yet the threat of war continues to be imminent. For all the protest, war remains a respectable method for unleashing aggression and fury against an official enemy.

POSSIBLE CAUSES OF WAR

Much of our inability to deal with the problem of war stems from our failure to isolate its causes successfully. Students of war have suggested a number of causes, but few of them are able to agree on the causes of any single war, to say nothing of agreeing on causes of war in general. The causes of any given war, according to Norman Hill, a longtime student of international affairs, pile up slowly, with a number of national states adding to the combustibles. Some of these combustibles we have already discussed. In the preceding chapters we have described such factors as competition for world resources, population pressure, racial and minority-group tensions, nationalism, imperialism, and totalitarianism. There are, however, several other alleged causes that deserve our attention.

*Psychological Causes.** One school of thought would begin with the individual person, with the idea that war has basic psychological origins. The Freudian school, for example, which takes its name and cue from the founder of modern psychoanalysis, Sigmund Freud, calls attention to deep-

---

* For the following materials, the authors are heavily indebted to V. Van Dyke, *International Politics* (New York: Appleton-Century-Crofts, 1957), pp. 135-152.

seated human drives of love and hate. Freud himself was convinced that men have innate drives toward aggressiveness, destruction, and cruelty. Our neighbor is not just a potential friend or helper but also someone on whom we can gratify our aggressive drives. Men are objects to exploit, humiliate, deprive of their possessions, and even to torture and kill. One psychoanalyst, Karen Horney, felt that men have an urgent need to rise above other men. Those who are disappointed with their real "selves" will imagine that they are different and develop exalted notions of superiority. For example, a man may see himself as a genius, superior leader, a supreme lover, or a better man than others. Some will see themselves as gods. Such self-glorification and neurotic ambition lead to aggression against other persons. Horney says that those possessed with these characteristics usually attempt to achieve a station and role in life befitting the image they have of themselves. They will attack, belittle, and inflict shame and defeat on others to satisfy their urges. Alfred Adler, another member of this school, claimed that man is "spurred on by his longing for superiority," while the author Erich Fromm asserts that men desire recognition and wish to avoid being powerless and insignificant. Thus, Fromm finds that men are led into conflict with each other when one person's desires for superiority conflict with another person's.

A related school of thought places a great deal of the blame for war on frustration. Almost everyone agrees that frustration tends to make men aggressive. We are apt to swear when we hit our thumb with a hammer. We will likely show some hostility toward those persons who keep us from achieving our goals. Investigations into the effects of frustration on behavior, however, are still in a tentative stage. It is difficult to determine the extent to which frustration can make an entire population aggressive. One type of frustration that results in tension stems from conflict in human desires. The political scientist Harold Lasswell contends that each individual has a hierarchy of desires around which he orders his behavior. These hierarchies differ from individual to individual, and from time to time within the same individual. One person will give higher priority to one desire than will another person, and some people cling more tenaciously to their desires than do others. These differences can lead to conflict. Two men bent on marrying the same woman may clash. College professors who want more emphasis on research in the curriculum may quarrel with their associates who desire more emphasis on classroom instruction. A government that covets more territory is likely to fight with another government that is after the same land, or with the government that already holds the territory. There is a wealth of evidence that conflicting desires make for conflicting human relations and war. But, as Lasswell points out, we cannot measure the priority that individuals assign to their desires. Nor can we measure the intensity with which they pursue them.

There is one desire that many persons believe to be central to all wars—the desire for self-preservation. The tendency of persons to cling to life, as well as to all the customs, habits, and institutions that they believe essential to life, often produces warlike behavior. Collapse of the existing structure of society, or the mere suggestion of such a collapse, will make men fearful. Many Americans, for example, believe that Europeans ought to forsake separate national independence and join a European federation, but are horrified by suggestions that Americans should do the same thing. This suggests that fear itself may be a fundamental cause of war.

Men seem always to have displayed warlike tendencies. Over the centuries they have tended to be as eager to develop destructive techniques as they have been to develop constructive ones. As early as 1816, the British navy busied itself developing rocket warfare, something most of us believe is of rather recent vintage.

Ideological Causes. Closely related to the psychological causes are the ideological. *Ideologies are value systems.* They are the *isms* that we spoke about in earlier chapters. We should now understand how nationalistic ideas and values affect political life and lead to conflict. We should also be keenly aware of the ways in which fascism, communism, and democratic liberalism clash. Many students of the question believe that this clash of ideals has been responsible for much of the strife that has plagued us during the present century.

One ideology tends to challenge others. When it does, the situation is pregnant with conflict. Just as a person who believes in the principles of the Catholic faith desires to preserve Catholic principles, so a government based on democratic principles desires to preserve them. Likewise, a communist desires to preserve communist principles and a fascist dictator will fight for fascist doctrine. Where two national states are based on similar ideological principles, the preservation of those principles becomes their common object, making the principles a basis for unity, cooperation, and friendship. But if the ideologies are antithetical, potential conflict is always a threat, particularly if one of the ideologies calls for extension of those principles to other lands and peoples. Soviet insistence on the truth of Marxist ideology and the need to extend it throughout the world appears ominous and threatening to Britishers and Americans. War is always possible in such a situation, although it is not inevitable. But ideologies that extol the virtues of conquest and war present an imminent threat to peace.

Economic Causes. Economic factors are among the most frequently cited causes of war. That men desire necessities, luxuries, and comforts cannot be doubted. Historically, as we saw in Chapter 24, men have always struggled for the bounties that nature yields. Likewise, population pressure and scarcity of resources engender tension. So do international commercial and financial activities. When American tourists and traders go abroad, the flag goes with them. They look to their government for protection. The search for profits and economic advantage has, in the past, created tensions that were in part responsible for a number of wars. Thus, as we saw earlier, imperialism, especially of an exploitative nature, is laden with potential conflict.

Trade barriers may also incite hostility. A tariff, for example, will restrict the importation and sale of foreign commodities, thus protecting the domestic industry. But it may also injure the economy of the country whose market has been cut off by the tariff. Restrictions on the importation of beef contribute to depressions in Argentina and anger the Argentines and their government. Tariffs on watches threaten the stability of the Swiss economy. Likewise, immigration quotas, the nationalization of industries, and prohibition of foreign investment are all precipitants of conflict. Japan deeply resented the American action in 1924 that excluded Japanese from immigration quotas. An Iranian move to nationalize the Anglo-Iranian Oil Company in 1951 led to serious tension with Great Britain.

Deficit spending, especially for armament, is another source of war. Governments that attempt to spend themselves out of a depression, or spend to avoid one, are often inclined to spend on arms. Normally, they try to give another reason. If there is an enemy somewhere around, then the expenditure on arms can be justified as a security measure. As the arms pile up, the enemy may become fearful. He may attack. Or his fears may lead him to pursue a policy that causes the spending country to attack.

The well-known English economist J. A. Hobson developed an overproduction-under-consumption theory of imperialism to demonstrate an economic cause of war. Where the economic system places too small a share of the income in the hands of the working class, a backlog of money and investment capital piles up in the hands of the investor and entrepreneur class. If this group saves its surplus or takes it out of circulation, the workingman and consumer are deprived of buying power to create demand. Commodities go unpurchased and surpluses build up. If the money is invested in business and industrial expansion, still greater surpluses will be created, and the results will be the same. Consequently, surplus capital will always seek investment abroad, and surplus produce will seek markets abroad. But this situation may result in imperialism. This is exactly the point Hobson made. Hobson did not, however, contend that imperialism was inevitable. Nor did he say it was desirable. He believed that imperialism was "bad business for the nation," and he felt it could be avoided through better systems of distribution.*

The highly regarded twentieth-century economist John Maynard Keynes found a seed of conflict in unemployment. Since most modern governments desire to reduce or eliminate unemployment, said Keynes, they struggle to build up an export surplus. That is, they strive to export more than they import, a policy that works to the disadvantage of other national states. To Keynes, international trade was "a desperate expedient to maintain employment at home by forcing sales on foreign markets and restricting purchases." This practice merely shifted the problem of unemployment to member nations in the international community and tended to ruffle and anger them. Keynes believed that war had many causes, but, primarily, he blamed population pressure and the struggle for markets.†

It was the Russian communist, Lenin,

however, who took the extreme position on the economic causes of war. For him, it was unquestionably the economics of the capitalist system that caused international war. Capitalism, as he saw it, concentrates the ownership of the means of production and the available money for investment into fewer and fewer hands, thus creating a virtual monopoly. As large quantities of surplus capital accumulate in fewer hands, it cannot be invested at home. For capitalism, wrote Lenin, produces a declining rate of profit under these circumstances, which makes it less and less advantageous to invest at home. Where does the money go? Why, abroad, of course! It seeks foreign markets where the profits will be higher. When money goes abroad, Lenin believed, two things occur, both of which lead to international wars. Peoples in underdeveloped countries are exploited and capitalist nations fall to struggling for markets. Although the theory is plausible, the explanation is far too simple.

As popular as economic theories of causation are, they remain highly suspect. As the renowned expert on war Quincy Wright counsels us, we are probably correct when we say that economic factors contribute to imperialism and war, but incorrect when we overemphasize their role. Wright reminds us further that all too many theories rely on unproved assumptions made about capitalist institutions and methods. He points out that "capitalist societies have been the most peaceful forms of societies yet developed. . . ." Although wars occur during eras of capitalist dominance, they have been noticeably less frequent in those areas of the world where capitalism is the most completely developed.

"Devil" Theories. Some people believe that bankers, merchants, or other businessmen bring wars on purposely. Former Senator Gerald Nye of North Dakota blamed

---

* Van Dyke, *International Politics*, pp. 103-104.
† *Ibid.*, pp. 104-105.

World War I on profiteers and munitions-makers who, he believed, had precipitated the conflict in order to reap huge profits. There are those who contend that particular men are responsible. Throughout history, of course, there have been men such as Alexander the Great, Napoleon, and Hitler, who prided themselves on being the makers of history. And they used war as a major vehicle for attaining their ends. The influence and power positions of such men are certainly vital factors, but every war has at least two sides and several causes, as well as a great backlog of historic events leading up to it. To single out one cause ignores too many other features of a situation.

War as a Principal Cause of War. As paradoxical as it sounds, war itself, or the mere expectation of it, can lead to war. Any reader who doubts this statement need only recall our earlier discussion in Chapter 28 of the events and crises that led to the Second World War. Few factors were more influential in the precipitation of the Second World War than the treaty of peace that followed the First World War. History is replete with the aftereffects of wars that have left national groups or their governments disgruntled, angry, and ready for revenge.

Furthermore, expectation of war may precipitate an early showdown. If you know someone is aching for a good fight with you, you may decide to have a showdown with him and finish the whole thing then and there. If a country is busy arming itself, even though it does not entertain the possibility of war, its neighbors may become aroused. Furthermore, governments with a power advantage that might be lost at some future date may instigate a war to assure themselves of victory. They will start a war at once to prevent a disastrous war in the future—one they might lose. This we call *preventive war.*

Whatever the causes of modern war, here is the result—a view of Nagasaki after the atomic bomb hit the city, August, 1945.

Militarism as a Cause of War. Some people, many of whom take their cue from Darwin's theory of evolution, believe that war is a normal or even necessary condition of mankind. They are convinced that it is a law of nature that men must struggle in a world where only the fittest survive. But it is the racists who are the extremists on this point. Adolf Hitler, as we saw in Chapter 27, believed that war was not only natural to man, but was physically and psychologically necessary. War invigorated the human spirit; it proved man's worth; it purified mankind. Without it, men degenerated into weaklings.

But even persons who dislike war may consider military service ennobling. Many of them view military training as a superior device for instilling loyalty, discipline, and social responsibility. Military personnel in many countries are often accorded greater status, honor, prestige, and power than civilians. Under such conditions armies are accepted as normal. And their business of prosecuting war is also likely to be accepted as normal.

Countries constantly involved in war are likewise inclined to accept war as a matter of course. They may regard war as no more than another instrument of policy. Just as some persons settle most of their differences with others by fighting, so some countries tend to settle their differences with other countries by threatening or resorting to war.

Countries with a long record of successful military exploits are inclined to accept war as a ready means to national glory and honor. They may become cocky and bellicose. An entire people sometimes prides itself on its strength and develops a haughty attitude toward others. There is also a strong tendency among men to consider conquerors "great." It makes no difference whether the military glories of the past resulted in suffering or positive good. The destruction and death wrought by successful wars are soon forgotten. Whether the country fought de-fensively or aggressively, whether the cause was good or bad, is not the question. Although thoughts of glory may not be a direct cause of war, they undoubtedly condition people to think that war is an acceptable type of human behavior.

War is sometimes used to induce unity. When things are going badly at home, a government may deliberately focus on a common enemy to draw public attention away from the domestic situation. Bismarck is said to have used foreign policy as a "lightning rod" for staving off internal threats to his government. There is an old adage that says, "Brothers will fight each other when left to themselves, but let either be attacked by another, and their differences dissolve into a unity against the tormentor."

Professor Quincy Wright has concluded that the big powers are the fighters. The possession of might apparently inclines a country toward using it. This does not mean, however, that a great power will fight simply because it possesses the means to do so. Nor does it mean that great powers which fight do so necessarily because they desire a war. After all, great powers are natural targets of other powers and therefore are more apt to be drawn into a war. Great powers are frequently feared. Other nations are jealous of them. They are easily blamed for another country's woes. A government faced with grave internal difficulties may convince its people that the real enemy is a great power that is influencing international events to their detriment.

All wars, even civil wars, tend to be international affairs. There has never been a century completely free of war. Under these circumstances we have a strong tendency to accept war as inevitable in the course of human events. The development of modern technology and the refinement of the arts of warfare, however, confront our age with the prospect of mutual annihilation. No doubt we cannot rid the world of conflict.

Very probably we would not want to, for a world without any conflict would most likely be dull and uninteresting. But do we have to risk annihilating one another simply because we disagree over certain issues? Are there no alternatives to war?

TOOLS FOR ESTABLISHING INTERNATIONAL ORDER *

To be sure, we have tools for settling international conflicts, some very highly developed ones in fact. One of the oldest and certainly the most controversial is called "balance-of-power diplomacy."

BALANCE-OF-POWER DIPLOMACY

When Rome and Carthage were at war, Syracuse offered aid to Carthage to prevent Rome from establishing a power position that would enable her "without let or hindrance, to execute every purpose and undertaking." Syracuse did not want Rome to amass enough strength to attack her, so she threw her weight on the side of Carthage. The purpose of establishing a balance-of-power relationship is to prevent any state from becoming so powerful that it can overwhelm and subject all the others. Weaker states often combine their strength to check a more powerful state that might challenge the security of any one of them.

Balance-of-power diplomacy, or a status quo policy, then, seeks to maintain the existing power relationships among states. On the other hand, a diplomatic policy that seeks to disturb the *status quo* or to change existing power relationships is aimed at improving the power position of the state pursuing it. Power balances may be simple or complex. Some have been likened to a chandelier, where several states exist in comparative equilibrium. Another type is called the "scale-type" balance in which the various powers shift partners, attaching and detaching themselves from one another to preserve a state of relative equilibrium. Graphically, this technique resembles an old-fashioned balance scale filled with weights on one side and the commodity to be weighed on the other. Ideally, if one state switches sides, the others will maneuver and shift their weight (power) to the side from which the switching state moved. Prior to World War I, for example, the Franco-Russian alliance was balanced by the Austro-German and Italian alliance. Great Britain shifted her weight from one side to the other to maintain the balance.

A balance-of-power mechanism is supposedly maintained through the use of several tools, among them intervention, compensation, and the creation of buffer zones. *Intervention* is used by a strong power in its relations with a weaker one. The strong state may intervene in the affairs of the smaller one to preserve or establish a government favorable to it. This technique the Eisenhower administration used when it sent United States Marines to Lebanon in 1958 to secure the position of a government that was already favorable to the United States. England did the same thing in 1941 when she intervened in Iraq to prevent a coup by a pro-German group.

Compensation is merely the practice whereby states within the balance system divide among themselves any spoils they may receive. When one country gains more land, for example, others are permitted to acquire relatively equal portions in order to maintain the balance.

---

* *Cf.* Van Dyke, *International Politics*, pp. 200-225, 275-278, 314-315; H. Morgenthau, *Politics among Nations* (New York: Knopf, 1954), pp. 155-245.

For several centuries strong states have found it expedient to create *buffer states* or *buffer zones* between them to guarantee each one protection from direct attack by another. Belgium, for example, has served as a buffer between Germany and France, Afghanistan as a neutral zone between Russia and British India, and Poland as a cushion between Russia and Germany.

Power balances are at best precarious. Professor Hans J. Morgenthau calls them uncertain, unrealistic, and inadequate as guides to international behavior. The great problem in maintaining a balance involves the assumption that power can be accurately weighed and balanced. Actually there are about five major assumptions involved in a balance-of-power approach. Some of these are valid, whereas others are not.

First, it is assumed that national states are determined to foster and protect their own interests, and that they will do this by any means they have available, even if it means going to war. Each state, of course, decides for itself just what its interests are—usually they are the preservation of its independence, security, form of government, territorial integrity, and way of life. States that are not so determined would presumably accept whatever demands are made of them, although this is seldom the case except in those instances where a government is so comparatively weak that it has no choice. Hence, this assumption seems rather sound.

Second, it is assumed that an even balance of power will deter a government that threatens another. In other words, governments will not attack unless they have enough strength to overwhelm their opponents. That one government may need a preponderance of power to assure itself victory in an engagement with another is obvious enough, but the belief that a balance will deter attack is not. For this belief involves the assumption that governments and

peoples are going to act rationally. There is a wealth of evidence throughout history that they do not always so act.

A much deeper implication concerning the actions of governments and peoples involves a third assumption; namely, that the existence of a power balance can be accurately determined. This assumption rests on a fourth and even more basic premise—that the elements of power can be accurately determined and weighed. Actually, however, power calculation is a complex exercise, and in some cases is well-nigh impossible. Some elements, such as geographical features, are tangible and others, such as public morale, are not.

Hans J. Morgenthau lists nine major elements of power: geography, natural resources, industrial capacity, population, military preparedness, national morale, national character, the quality of diplomacy, and the quality of government. Not all authorities agree with this list, however. Harold Sprout, another authority on the subject, erects different categories—physical resources, human resources, technology, economic development, economic organization, government organization, and so on. Irrespective of our categories, any evaluation is fraught with difficulty. Such factors as size, shape, distance of frontiers, climate, and soil fertility are tangible, important, and lend themselves to measurement. Whether a country can produce enough food to feed its own population can be assessed without too much difficulty and has a definite effect on the country's power potential. But what relative weight do we assign this economic component as compared with the size of the government's military establishment or another country's capacity to produce steel products, its military establishment, or the size of its population? Population differences are also quite easily measured. But what do they mean in terms of a power ratio? A declining population may indicate weakness but a rising population may also betray weakness in some circumstances.

In the case of intangible elements, how do we weigh in the balance such factors as the quality of diplomacy or the capabilities of one's own leadership? How do we assess the quality of another country's leadership? What is the effect of national morale? How are the effects of an ideology or an enemy's propaganda weighed? These are all elements of power. Indeed, they are very important ones. They too must be weighed. And then comes the almost impossible task of assigning relative positions of importance to them in a hierarchy of other power elements. The possibility for error is almost limitless.

To assume that we can determine when a power balance exists is at best highly questionable. To assume further that we can weigh the various elements is to be naive. Aggressive governments often assume that they possess a preponderance of power, only to be proved wrong. Others may assume that a balance exists where in fact it does not.

Finally, if the vital interests of a state are to be protected by balancing power, we clearly assume that those interests can be precisely defined and known. And that is not all. We further assume that we can determine when those interests are threatened. But can we? Is it of vital interest to the United States, for example, to keep Denmark from trading with Russia? Is it in our interest to keep France from swinging to the left? Was it a vital interest of the United States to keep Hitler from defeating Russia, or from taking Austria? Is it in our interest to keep Asian markets open for American investors? As Morgenthau says, the balance of power is clearly inadequate and uncertain as a guide to international behavior. Certainly, it is hardly an effective deterrent to war. We are probably just lucky when it works!

INTERNATIONAL LAW

There is a large body of international law in existence that has evolved over the centuries out of custom, usage, and agreement among national states. This body of law has been rather effective during certain periods of history as a means for settling international differences. It is, however, clearly encumbered with a number of drawbacks. First of all, law can be used only to settle disputes that are justiciable; that is, where both parties either consent to abide by the law or can be forced to. This point is vital. For if either one or both of the parties refuse to abide by the law, and there is no superior force to make them comply, then the law is useless.

This is precisely the problem in regard to international law today. The members of the so-called "community of nations" claim absolute sovereignty, independence, and full power to determine their own duties, rights, obligations, and interests. There is no way of forcing them to comply with law. Furthermore, international law is weak on the institutional side. There is no legislative arm at the international level to make law, and there is no executive arm to force compliance with the law. So, even though courts do exist at the international level, there is no way a country can be forced to submit its disputes to a court, and there is no known method for gaining compliance with a court's order if a country refuses. In short, under international law, the claimant must still take his right and the law into his own hands.

Every time a grave issue arises, therefore, we are apt to see the rules flagrantly disregarded. Yet a body of law does exist and it is used occasionally. It has helped settle disputes in the past, and it undoubtedly will continue to help settle them in the future. But it lacks a sufficiently large community of interests for a basis. There is no general agreement among states to abide by international law. Even the United States refuses to agree to submit *future* disputes to international tribunals, although we show willingness to submit them as they arise. Finally, there is no "long arm of the law" to make states behave according to the dictates of the law. To be effective, law must be backed by a real sense of community and a means of enforcement. International law, then, like the balance of power, does not as yet afford a realistic alternative to war.

OUTLAWING WAR

To those persons who pin their hopes on having war outlawed, all we need ask is: "Who is going to do it and how will he make his decision stick?" Present international law, after all, recognizes war and provides certain rules for its conduct. This situation could be changed, of course. International law, in fact, has been changed in the last two or three decades as a result of the war-crimes trials. But these judgments were *imposed* by victors in war! They may even set a dangerous precedent, making it possible for every victor in future wars to vent his fury on the vanquished and their leaders.

ARBITRATION

Arbitration is a word that is used far too loosely. Sometimes it refers to all sorts of methods of peaceful settlement. According to The Hague Convention of 1907, however, it refers to a method of settling disputes between states "by judges of their own choice on the basis of respect for law." It readily implies submission in "good faith" to the judgment of a special tribunal and willingness to live up to the conditions of settlement. Each party argues its own case,

and once the dispute is disposed of, the tribunal dissolves. There is then a separate tribunal for each case under arbitration.

Arbitration places us in the same bind we encountered in the analysis of adjudication under international law. The parties must submit willingly, and we must depend on their good faith to abide by the tribunal's decision. Arbitration involves a further difficulty that presents even greater complications. Suppose we are on an island where there are no law-enforcement officers present. John steals Bill's shirt. Bill, of course, knowing the shirt is his, wants it returned. John refuses. But other residents of the island bring pressure on him to do something about it. He will not return the shirt, but he does consent to arbitrate the conflict. Other residents then urge Bill to arbitrate rather than get into a fight and risk bloodshed. So Bill arbitrates. John wants one dollar to return the shirt. But Bill says the shirt was his in the first place. To get the matter settled the arbitration court agreed to by both men decides to award the shirt to Bill if he gives John fifty cents. Bill naturally feels he has been denied justice. But John, nevertheless, gets the fifty cents. By this tendency to "split the difference," arbitration can result in similar injustices in international disputes.

MEDIATION AND CONCILIATION

In certain instances a third party can be brought into a situation in an attempt to resolve differences. The third party may provide its *good offices, conciliation,* or *mediation. Good offices* refers to an attempt by a third party to get the opposing parties to arrange some sort of settlement or to negotiate. Sometimes a third party will offer its *good offices* as a medium for transmitting messages between the two opposing parties. *Conciliation* generally involves collecting the facts pertaining to a dispute and then making an impartial report of the facts, as well as proposing terms of settlement. *Mediation* is only slightly different from conciliation in that the third party here becomes an active participant in the negotiations themselves and proposes terms of settlement. In all cases, however, we are faced once again with the need for voluntary consent on the part of both sides to abide by the findings, suggestions, or terms of settlement.

DISARM!

Men have believed for centuries that disarmament would relieve international tensions. Yet there are those who place no stock in this method at all. A considerable body of opinion, for example, holds that a state which weakens itself by disarming merely invites aggression. Nevertheless, the cry for disarmament grows loud after every war and during every arms race. It is true, of course, that the states with the biggest military establishments do the most fighting. But so do the ones with the biggest industrial capacity. Yet no one dreams of asking the states to reduce their industrial output.

Disarmament, however, usually refers to the limitation and regulation of military might, not its abolition. States will disarm for many reasons. It may be imposed on them after defeat in a war. They may voluntarily disarm to achieve a propaganda advantage, to save money, to keep a neighboring state friendly, to maintain or achieve a favorable power position with other states, or to reduce the tension and likelihood of war. But disarming in hopes of reducing tension and averting war may be abortive in the long run. Why? First, disarmament agreements normally involve the reduction of arms according to a standard ratio, so that each party to a plan ends up in the same power position relative to the others as before disarmament was undertaken.

No doubt, the stockpiling of arms frightens people. But unpiling them hardly affords anything to be less frightened about. It is usually not the presence of arms that precipitates a war, although that is possible, but the men and conditions behind them.

ECONOMIC SANCTIONS *

Economic penalties also provide a means of obtaining compliance with rules or of getting another government to settle its grievances. Such penalties relate to the flow of international trade, capital, and services. By controlling these factors, a state, or a combination of states, can coerce or bring pressure to bear on other states. A government may invoke an embargo against another government's goods to express its disapproval of some action or policy of the latter. Wealthy states can grant economic aid to some states and deny it to others. They can do much the same when granting loans. They can establish controls over port facilities, shipping, and communications. They can manipulate export-import ratios. Depending on what they do and how they do it, they can help some states and injure others.

Expansion and curtailment of trade has been used frequently throughout history to enforce certain forms of behavior. A state that restricts its trade with someone else, however, often suffers itself. Actually, trade restrictions are risky. They may provoke war as easily as they deter it. Embargo and blockade are especially hazardous measures. For a government against whom such measures are invoked may react violently and precipitate a conflict. It takes, moreover, a very strong government or several cooperating governments to invoke a successful embargo. Blockades by their very nature are such warlike gestures that they are sometimes hardly

---

* *Cf.* Van Dyke, *International Politics*, pp. 346-355.

distinguishable from actual armed conflict. Frequently they involve shooting and bloodshed. Many observers believe that they constitute little more than a form of undeclared war.

The success of economic sanctions in averting war depends on a number of factors: (1) the relative strength of the two sides, (2) the extent to which the interests of the target country are affected, (3) the evaluation of these interests by the target country itself, (4) the willingness of the side invoking the sanction to risk war, and (5) the effect on the economy of the side imposing the sanction. When the League of Nations discussed the possibilities of a severe oil embargo against Italy in the 1930's, for example, Mussolini, realizing that such a measure might defeat him, threatened to attack the British fleet. His move would probably have drawn most of the League members into a war. So they decided not to take the risk. This series of events would indicate that economic sanctions are nearly worthless unless they are backed by sufficient military strength and a willingness to employ it. Economic blandishments and rewards are, however, another matter. The government that employs them gains favor with the countries it helps. But even these measures run the risk of alienating countries that do not make the privileged list.

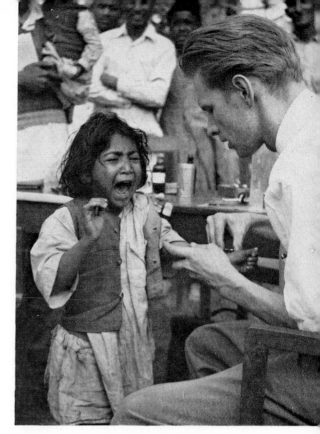

The U.N. has probably accomplished most in the areas of human welfare and aid. Dr. Erik Rollsgaard of Norway administers some of this aid here as he inoculates a Pakistani child against tuberculosis.

CONFERENCES

Conferences are rather informal and loose mechanisms. Essentially, they involve the calling of all or some of the rivals in a power struggle together, having them air their grievances, and then seeing if there is some common ground on which to build more peaceful relations. Conferences are about the least binding of all methods of settlement, among the most easily arranged, and provide the freest atmosphere for resolving differences. Amazing results are some-

times achieved through conferences. Nevertheless, they are no more of an answer to the problem of getting rid of war than are the other methods.

INTERNATIONAL ORGANIZATION

Obviously lacking in all the mechanisms we have discussed so far is a means of obtaining compliance. Are there methods short of war for making rule-breakers behave and forcing governments to live up to their commitments? Many authorities are convinced that we cannot expect to avert war until we establish an international framework for resolving disputes that contains the means for enforcing rules. Many people believe that the United Nations is slowly developing something of this sort within its framework.

The United Nations does provide an institutional framework. Using the structure of the League of Nations as a pattern, the U.N. has developed methods for dealing with the complicated relations between national states. Nearly every independent state on the globe now belongs to the U.N., and all are represented in the General Assembly, the most inclusive body within the United Nations. The General Assembly has all the appearances of a legislative body, but cannot legislate. It makes no laws. It merely recommends. And each state is free to accept or reject the recommendations as it sees fit. Each country has one vote in the General Assembly, irrespective of its size or population. The members are equal only in respect to their sovereignty. Called the "nearest equivalent to the Parliament of Man," the General Assembly is not truly representative of mankind.

The powers of the General Assembly are rather formidable, however. Most important, it controls the purse, thus determining the over-all budget of the organization. All other U.N. agencies must report to it. It appoints all non-permanent members of the Security Council, all members of the Economic and Social Council, the members of the International Court (in conjunction with the Security Council), and the Secretary General

of the United Nations. It also appoints some members of the Trusteeship Council.

It is the U.N.'s Security Council, however, that "packs the wallop." To this organization is given the primary obligation of maintaining peace and security. The Council consists of five permanent members (the United States, Soviet Russia, United Kingdom, France, and Nationalist China) and six non-permanent members who serve two-year terms. The body concerns itself with threats to the peace and with disputes that may lead to open conflict. It can request that member-states sever diplomatic relations with a state threatening the peace, and it can call for the use of armed forces as well as blockades. This is called the power of *collective security*.

When admitted to the U.N., member-states are pledged to place on call or at the disposal of the Security Council a sufficient number of armed forces and military facilities to maintain peace and security. Originally, agreements were to stipulate what each state should provide. But these agreements have never been drawn.

A far more serious matter, however, is the "veto" involved in the Security Council's voting procedure. Each of the permanent members can, on its own volition, veto any substantive decision before the Security Council. Every important decision, in other words, needs not only a vote of seven of the

Unlike its predecessor, the League of Nations, the U.N. has some "teeth." Here three members of the U.N.'s police force—Canadian, Israeli, and French— keep a sharp eye out for trouble along the Syrian-Israeli border.

eleven members of the Council, but must have the unanimous consent of the great powers, a requirement that places the great powers above the law. Unless the great powers act together, collective security hardly can be said to exist.

Custom, practice, and usage have modified this situation, however. In practice, the Council acts when a great power abstains from voting. Hence, "walkouts" or refusals to vote do not destroy the possibility for unified action. Also, the General Assembly can now by-pass the Security Council when the latter fails to exercise its primary responsibility because of a failure to act or because of a veto. The General Assembly can consider any action or threat against peace and security that has become deadlocked in the Security Council. After such

consideration, it can recommend military sanctions or the use of armed force to keep the peace.

There is, then, an institutional framework in existence that has the earmarks of a decision-making body with the power to maintain world peace and security. Although there is no legislative authority as yet, there is an embryo police power that can employ force to keep the peace. The U.N. "police force" has been used with considerable success in Korea and the Suez crisis and constitutes a long stride toward a more peaceful world. So, although the U.N. is not a government and has no jurisdiction over either individuals or states, it does provide an institutional mechanism and a means for waging peace in a far more effective way than did the League of Nations.

SOME WORDS OF SUMMARY

Mankind's quest for social justice in the present century has been paralleled by his search for international peace and order. It is anomalous that as mankind has placed a higher value on human life and happiness, there should burst on the world some of the most terrible cataclysms in man's brief sojourn on earth. No century has been so dedicated to the cause of peace, yet so decimated by the ravages of war. The demand for peace has grown steadily louder, even as the danger of the most awful cataclysm of all—a thermonuclear holocaust—has crept closer.

Just what is peace? For some persons peace is the total absence of violence, yet we know that governmental authority rests ultimately on a monopoly of force and violence. More generally, peace is thought of as an interim between wars. What then causes war? Some authorities stress population pressure, the competition for world resources, or the rise of "isms," especially nationalism, imperialism, and totalitarianism. Others are convinced that the roots of war are entwined in human psychology, in the aggressive and destructive characteristics of men, or in the soil of economic conflict over trade, capital, money, and employment. Still others suspect bankers, merchants, and munition-makers as the instigators of war, or else postulate that war itself loads the dice in favor of future wars. A few fanatics such as Adolf Hitler have regarded war as a positive good that "purifies" the race as we struggle for survival.

Historically, a most important weapon for fending off war has been balance-of-power diplomacy. This policy is aimed at keeping the peace by preserving the existing power relationships among national states through timely shifts of power to discourage would-be aggressors. Balance-of-power diplomacy is based on a number of questionable propositions, however. It assumes that all states will fight to protect their vital interests, that they know what their vital interests are, that an aggressor will be deterred by an even balance of power, and that the elements in a power equation can be weighed and computed in an accurate way.

The hopes of averting war have also rested on international law, outlawing of war, arbitration, mediation and conciliation, disarmament, economic sanctions, and international conferences. But each of these methods has proved disappointing because of our failure to enforce compliance to mutually acceptable standards of international behavior. Many modern students of the problem have concluded that our only real hope lies in establishing some effective international institutions with means of enforcing rules of acceptable conduct. One hopeful sign has been the growth in stature of the United Nations. Here, at least, are an institutional framework and the seeds of a world-wide force for peace and order in human affairs.

A FINAL WORD

It is fitting that this book should close on a note of affirmation. For despite the wars, the frustrations, and the skepticisms of this most dynamic of all centuries, men have retained their courage to hope and believe in a future more promising than the past. In his quest for social justice at home and peace abroad, twentieth-century man has affirmed his faith in life and the enduring values of human experience. He has survived conflicts of loyalties and values more serious than any faced by his ancestors. He has adapted himself to the humdrum regularity of mechanized society and the terrifying anonymity of city living. His life has become organized and bureaucratized in a way that his nineteenth-century forebear would have deemed certain to crush the human spirit. And he has lived through international slaughter and strife on a scale beyond the comprehension of his Victorian predecessor. Yet, somehow, almost incredibly, men have not only clung to life, but to such values as love, kindness, mercy, charity, and understanding. And above all, men still hope. These incomprehensible feelings continue to surge and well up in every one of us.

FURTHER ROADS TO LEARNING

GENERAL ACCOUNTS

C. Brinton, *From Many One* (Cambridge: Harvard University Press, 1948). One well-known historian's opinion on how to secure world government.

E. Carr, *Conditions of Peace* (New York: Macmillan, 1942). An able Britisher offers his views on what is needed for peace.

S. Hembelen, *Plans for World Peace Through Six Centuries* (Chicago: The University of Chicago Press, 1943). A review of some of man's abortive attempts to find international peace.

F. Northrop, *The Taming of Nations* (New York: Macmillan, 1952). This man has a recipe or two for quelling nationalism and our separatist tendencies.

F. Schuman, *The Commonwealth of Man* (New York: Knopf, 1952). A confirmed realist has a look at the possibilities for world order.

Q. Wright, *Problems of Stability and Progress in International Relations* (Berkeley: University of California Press, 1954). One of the best scholars in the business assesses some of the problems of peace.

———, *A Study of War*. Two vols. (Chicago: The University of Chicago Press, 1942). A complete historical survey of man's greatest nemesis.

V. Van Dyke, *International Politics* (New York: Appleton-Century-Crofts, 1957). Contains a thorough analysis of the causes of war and an especially trenchant criticism of the Marxian thesis of imperialism as a cause of war.

SPECIAL STUDIES

C. Burns, "Militarism," *Encyclopedia of the Social Sciences*, X (New York: Macmillan, 1934). A discussion of the various forms militarism can take.

H. Cantril, ed., *Tensions That Cause War* (Urbana: University of Illinois Press, 1950). A symposium written by experts on various topics concerning war and its causes.

A. Highley, *The First Sanctions Experiment* (Geneva: Geneva Research Center, 1938). An actual case study of economic sanctions as a tool for stopping aggression.

J. Hobson, *Imperialism* (London: Allen and Unwin, 1938). The classic statement of the "overproduction-underconsumption" theory.

S. Hook, "Violence," *Encyclopedia of the Social Sciences*, XV (New York: Macmillan, 1934). A vivid discussion of the role of violence.

E. Kingston-McCloughry, *The Direction of War* (New York: Praeger, 1955). A book that describes the changes in the conduct of war from the times of the community of sovereign monarchs to the present.

O. Klineberg, *Tensions Affecting International Understanding* (New York: Social Science Research Council, 1950). An examination of several serious sources of tension.

H. Lasswell, *World Politics and Personal Insecurity* (New York: Whittlesey House, 1935). A study of the extent to which war can be blamed on the individual, his insecurity, and expectation of war.

H. Lauterpacht, *The Function of Law in the International Community* (Oxford: Clarendon Press, 1933). An early but still highly reputed treatment of the role of international law, which provides insight into the attempts to make the world law-abiding.

M. May, *A Social Psychology of War and Peace* (New Haven: Yale University Press, 1943). On the psychological causes of war.

H. Nicolson, *Diplomacy* (New York: Harcourt, Brace, 1939). A sturdy contention that diplomacy is an art that one must play by ear as much as by power calculation and scientific evidence.

T. Pear, *Psychological Factors of War and Peace* (New York: Philosophical Library, 1950). The roots of war are in each of us.

L. Robbins, *The Economic Causes of War* (London: Jonathan Cape, 1939). Unquestionably a classic statement on this topic.

H. Sprout, *The Foundations of National Power* (Princeton: Van Nostrand, 1951). Contains Sprout's categorization of power elements.

E. Tolman, *Drives Toward War* (New York: Appleton-Century-Crofts, 1942). This book contends that human drives get us into war.

A. Vagts, *A History of Militarism* (New York: Norton, 1937). The background and history of the "brass hats."

J. Wheeler-Bennett, *The Pipe-Dream of Peace* (New York: Morrow, 1935). A scathing analysis of disarmament.

Q. Wright, *Contemporary International Law: A Balance Sheet* (Garden City, New York: Doubleday, 1955). An analysis of where we stand with respect to international law today and where international law stands, too.

FICTION AND DRAMA

W. Cather, *One of Ours* (New York: Knopf, 1922). How war was less repressive to a young man than Nebraska farm life.

S. Crane, *The Red Badge of Courage* (New York: Random House, 1942). A moving novel that portrays the psychological effects of battle.

P. Frank, *Affair of State* (Philadelphia: Lippincott, 1948). The hazards a person runs in the machinery of foreign-policy making.

J. Hasek, *The Good Soldier Schweik* (New York: Signet Books, reprint of 1930 edition). Only the insane fight and intelligent men do well to stay out of their way.

J. Thomason, *Fix Bayonets* (New York: Scribner, 1926). How war brings out the worst in us.

FILMS

Pattern for Peace (British Information Services, 1947, 15 min., sound, black and white). The structure and purpose of the U.N.

Quest for Tomorrow (Film Forum Foundation, 1948, 20 min., sound, black and white). Discusses the founding of the U.N. and the need for strengthening it.

Stalingrad (Prudential Insurance Company of America, 1958, 30 min., sound, black and white). Story of one of the bloodiest battles in history.

This Is the United Nations—Screen Magazine Nos. 1-12 (United Nations, 1950, 15 min. each, sound, black and white). A behind-the-headlines film story of the U.N.'s activities.

World Balance of Power (Encyclopaedia Britannica Films, 1952, 20 min., sound, black and white). How the balance of power works to prevent aggression and war.

Illustrations

Index

583